# The Psychology of Health, Illness, and Medical Care

.....

## AN INDIVIDUAL PERSPECTIVE

# The Psychology of Health, Illness, and Medical Care

.....

## AN INDIVIDUAL PERSPECTIVE

**M. Robin DiMatteo**

*University of California, Riverside*
*The RAND Corporation*

*Brooks/Cole Publishing Company*
*Pacific Grove, California*

**Brooks/Cole Publishing Company**
A Division of Wadsworth, Inc.

© 1991 by Wadsworth, Inc., Belmont, California 94002.
All rights reserved. No part of this book may be reproduced,
stored in a retrieval system, or transcribed, in any form or
by any means—electronic, mechanical, photocopying, recording,
or otherwise—without the prior written permission of the
publisher, Brooks/Cole Publishing Company, Pacific Grove,
California 93950, a division of Wadsworth, Inc.

Printed in the United States of America

10   9   8   7   6   5   4   3   2   1

**Library of Congress Cataloging-in-Publication Data**
DiMatteo, M. Robin.
      The psychology of health, illness, and medical care : an
individual perspective / M. Robin DiMatteo.
             p.   cm.
      Includes bibliographical references and index.
      ISBN 0-534-15048-9
      1. Health behavior. 2. Health attitudes. 3. Medical care.
4. Sick—Psychology.   I. Title
      [DNLM: 1. Attitude of Health. 2. Delivery of Health Care.
3. Disease—psychology. 4. Health Behavior. 5. Psychology,
Medical. WM 90 D582p]
RA776.9.D56   1990
155.9'16—dc20                                            90-2601
                                                            CIP

Sponsoring Editor: *Philip L. Curson, Vicki Knight*
Editorial Assistant: *Heather L. Riedl*
Production Editor: *Timothy A. Phillips*
Manuscript Editor: *Betty G. Seaver*
Permissions Editor: *Carline Haga*
Interior and Cover Design: *E. Kelly Shoemaker*
Cover Photo: *Stan Tess, The Stock Market*
Art Coordinator: *Lisa Torri*
Interior Illustration: *Lisa Torri*
Photo Coordinator: *Ruth Minerva*
Photo Researcher: *Research Plus*
Typesetting: *Weimer Typesetting Co., Inc.*
Cover Printing and Binding: *Arcata Graphics/Fairfield*

*For Michael and Gia*

# About the Author

JUDY GIBERSON

M. Robin DiMatteo is Professor of Psychology at the University of California, Riverside, where she teaches health psychology to undergraduates and graduate students in psychology and to students in the health sciences. Since receiving her Ph.D. in 1976 from Harvard University, Dr. DiMatteo's research interests have involved practitioner-patient communication, patient adherence to medical regimens, and preventive medicine. She is also Resident Consultant in the Behavioral Science Division of the RAND Corporation in Santa Monica, California, where she conducts research on social science and health policy. Dr. DiMatteo has served as a clinical research psychologist at the UCLA/San Bernardino County Medical Center. She is a licensed psychologist in the state of California, and is a consultant to health care organizations nationwide.

# Preface

*The Psychology of Health, Illness, and Medical Care: An Individual Perspective* is the story of human beings coming to terms with health and illness in their own lives and in the lives of their loved ones. The focus is on individuals and what they think, how they feel, what they do, and why. This book examines the many ways in which an individual's psychology and interpersonal relationships influence his or her responses to illness and to the possibility of avoiding illness through health-promoting practices. This individual perspective is not concerned with the role of broader social issues such as social structure, societal institutions, and systems of medical care in issues of health and illness. Instead, it concentrates on individual people and on how and why they act and interact in an attempt to achieve their goals.

This book represents an expression of my own personal and professional orientation to health and illness as very private matters. These matters are shared in the deepest sense only with loved ones, family members, and close friends. When someone is seriously ill, it is his or her loved ones whose lives are more than trivially affected. All the statistics in the world about rates of morbidity and mortality, policies for prevention, and recommendations for social change cannot begin to help us to understand the personal devastation experienced by the ill patient and those closest to him or her.

Ten years ago, I wrote my contribution to a book on health psychology that I coauthored for its first edition in 1982. Although my name is still associated with that work, I have not contributed to the more recent edition published in 1989. That book focuses more on social factors, as do several other books on health psychology on the market today.

I decided to write this book, *The Psychology of Health, Illness, and Medical Care: An Individual Perspective*, because I feel that my thinking about health, illness, and medical care has matured in a unique way. My perspective has changed to focus more on individual, intrapsychic, and privately interpersonal aspects of health psychology. I have come to see the achievement and maintenance of health, coping with illness, and attempts to seek and negotiate medical care as both determinants and expressions of the individual's deepest vision of self. Further, I have now chosen to write from what I believe is a rather unique clinical perspective on health psychology that few researchers in the field have the opportunity to acquire.

My perspective grew out of several important experiences. The least academic of them is my experience growing up "hanging around" a hospital. My mother was a member of the clinical laboratory team, and I preferred to spend my days of school vacation at the hospital with her rather than engage in what might be considered more normal pursuits like summer camp. I still don't know why, but I really liked watching what happened in hospitals. I watched people come into the emergency room worried and sometimes in severe pain. I watched the nurses and doctors spring into action to care for a trauma victim. I watched the health professionals interact with one another with hurried respect. I became very comfortable around the needles and the high-tech machines of medical care. I got accustomed to the antiseptic smell. Thanks to my mother's recognition that illness is part of life, I was able to make friends with a girl my age who had her leg amputated because of osteogenic sarcoma. She died when I was about ten years old, but she influenced me a great deal in how I have tried to come to terms with issues of illness and death.

As a graduate student in psychology at Harvard under Robert Rosenthal, I continued watching things in hospitals. This time, however, I was more systematic in my approach and what I did was called dissertation research! When I came to the University of California, I continued this research, and for 16 years I have studied the practitioner-patient relationship and variations thereof. I have also had the opportunity to gain important clinical experience. As a licensed psychologist, I have continued working directly with patients and health care providers, particularly from a perspective based on my training in family therapy. Further, as a resident consultant at the RAND Corporation, I have been fortunate to work with some inspiring physicians and social scientists who have taught me the value of fully understanding the clinical situation to which one wants to apply the theory and methods of health psychology. And because I have always had a particular interest in and exposure to the field, I have learned an unusual amount for a psychologist about clinical medicine.

Finally, for the past 14 years I have taught health psychology not only to undergraduates and graduate students in psychology but also to students in the health sciences. I developed a health psychology course for medical students in the combined UCR/UCLA Biomedical Sciences Program, and have taught students in premedical, predental, nursing, and public health programs.

I believe this book is unique because of its individual approach. The individual perspective pervades the discussions of health promotion and disease prevention, of the definition and understanding of illness, of practitioner-patient relationships, and of adjustment to acute and chronic illness and death. In doing so, a new approach to patient adherence is presented (Chapter 4). A singular interpretation emerges of the expression of psychological conflict through physical processes (Chapter 5). The subtle nuances of practitioner-patient interaction are appreciated (Chapters 7 and 8). The existential dilemmas, and sometimes despair, of ill and of dying patients are grappled with in compelling ways (Chapters 12, 13, 14).

## PEDAGOGICAL FEATURES OF THIS BOOK

I have tried to make this book interesting and accessible to advanced undergraduate and beginning graduate students of health psychology, as well as to students in the health sciences: medicine, nursing, pharmacy, occupational therapy, dentistry, public health, and the allied health professions. The material stands on its own, without requiring previous courses in psychology or in the health sciences. Technical terms are explained as they are encountered. Uniquely, this book offers a section on learning medical terminology, an essential skill for reading and working in the health professions. Attention is given throughout the book to explaining the etiology, prog-

nosis, and treatment of diseases about which the psychological implications are considered. This is done both to teach essential aspects of medicine to students in health psychology and to emphasize the importance of understanding the physiological as well as the psychological aspects of health and illness. Chapter 2 also contains a brief overview of the anatomy and physiology of the organ systems that are encountered throughout this book.

At the end of each chapter, there are detailed summaries that help the student to review what has been learned and to organize the material for study. Each chapter also has a glossary of new terms with their definitions for easy reference. And throughout the chapters are boxes that present interesting, applied issues in health psychology.

Among the most notable features of this book are the case studies. Students of health psychology and those who will enter the health sciences, as well as students who have a purely personal interest in the psychology of health and illness, will find these cases very helpful. Important clinical stories are presented in these real cases (which have been carefully altered to protect the anonymity of the individuals). These stories make the literature come alive for the student and illustrate to him or her the complexities of applying knowledge of health psychology to real people.

## ACKNOWLEDGMENTS

I would like to thank a number of reviewers who have been helpful with their comments and suggestions. They include Dr. Robert Coyle, University of Utah; Dr. Eugene R. Gilden, Linfield College, McMinnville, Oregon; Dr. Steven Hobbs, Augusta College; Dr. John Hostetler, Albion College; Dr. Wolfgang Linden, University of British Columbia; Dr. Bill Ray, Pennsylvania State University; Dr. Alan Teich, University of Pittsburgh at Johnstown; and Professor Edward Whitson, State University of New York at Geneseo.

I would like to thank a few people for their help and encouragement. They include Teresa Damush, Cindy Medley, Saba Haq, and Ariel Vitali, undergraduates extraordinaire at UCR, who assisted me with references and various details. Graduate students Nancy Dye, Linda Ogden-Niemeyer, Chris McBride, and Ralph Downey provided insightful comments and encouragement. Colleagues at the RAND Corporation, including David Kanouse, John Winkler, Robert Brook, James Kahan, Ron Hays, and Gail Zellman, gave me valuable opportunities and taught me some very important things. Carol Tomlinson-Keasey, chair of the Psychology Department at UCR, has helped to make the department an exciting and supportive place to be. The Psychology Department office staff at UCR has been extraordinarily helpful in preparing the manuscript. Finally, Michael Esnard and Nathaniel and Devers Branden have changed my thinking about some important issues and influenced me more than they probably know. Thank you all!

Finally, please note that I have changed the names and identifying information of the individuals in the case studies extensively so that the privacy of these individuals is protected. In some cases a composite was created from the circumstances of several persons in order to protect their anonymity. If the names of persons or companies in this book bear any similarity to those of actual persons or companies, the similarity is purely accidental. Also, the views presented in this book are mine and do not represent the views of the University of California or of the RAND Corporation.

*M. Robin DiMatteo*

# Brief Contents

# Contents

## 14  Terminal Illness and Bereavement   401

# 1

# Introduction

"At the very core of [bodily] complaints is a tight integration between physiological, psychological, and social meanings" (Kleinman, 1988, p. 14). In the center of every story about illness is a person whose physiological functioning is altered, who is off balance and may be pushed to the limit psychologically, and whose precious social relationships are being severely threatened.

■ ■ ■ ■ ■

Alice Alcott had diabetes virtually all of her life. Married, with two teenage children, Alice worked as a librarian in the town in which she grew up and several generations of her family had lived. With daily insulin injections and considerable self-care, Alice kept her diabetes under control. She participated fully in her family's outdoor interests of hiking and bird-watching. She had many friends and was extremely active in her community. Then she began to run up against some serious obstacles presented by the progression of her diabetes. Over the space of a few years, Alice developed severe chest pain because the disease was beginning to damage her heart. Her eyesight was threatened by diabetic retinopathy, a condition in which the retina of the eye is impaired by diabetes. And she had to have two toes and then her entire lower leg amputated because of gangrene. At one time fully functional, Alice became more and more impaired until she could no longer carry out her activities as wife, mother, friend, professional, and community member. Illness changed her entire life. Not surprisingly, Alice was quite depressed. Dr. Kleinman, a psychiatrist, met with her for the first time in the hospital after her amputation. She had refused to talk to anyone, including her family, and she was despondent and even considered suicide (Kleinman, 1988).

■ ■ ■ ■ ■

A 53-year-old man was admitted to the university hospital for severe bronchial asthma after being transferred from his hometown hospital where the usual methods for treating asthma had not worked. In the next six months, he was hospitalized six times for major medical emergencies and for severe depression.

During his depressive episodes, he voiced feelings of complete hopelessness and futility. The man's asthma stabilized when he was in the hospital, but it was noted that when he spent time at home, his condition sometimes worsened. When he spent time with his wife, he returned well, but after any contact with his mother, he developed severe wheezing and difficulty breathing. Shortly after one meeting with his mother, he was found gasping for breath and almost comatose. He died of acute bronchial asthma with markedly con-

stricted bronchial tubes in his lungs and severe damage to his heart.

The psychological history of this man revealed a very involved but conflictual relationship with his mother. She controlled many aspects of his life and predicted the failure of his first two marriages. At age 38, he married again and had become a successful businessman. His mother was involved in the business, helped him finance it, and even kept the business accounts. But when he wanted to sell the business, she told him "Do this, and something dire will happen to you." Two days later, he had his first asthma attack, although he had experienced no respiratory problems up to that point. He developed his first very serious attack when the sale of his business was complete, right after his mother told him, "Something will strike you."

When he told his mother he would reinvest the capital in another business in which she would not be involved, she told him to remember her prediction that "dire results" would occur. The man was dead within an hour (Mathis, 1964).

Here are two clear examples of the interplay of physiological, psychological, and social factors in illness. In the first case, Alice Alcott's diabetes damaged her body and also severely threatened her psychological well-being and her relationships with her family, friends, and community. Her illness had a profound effect on her feelings about herself and upon her capacity to relate to others. The ravages of her diabetes took away all hope of doing the things she loved. As a result, she was despondent and unsure that she could go on (Kleinman, 1988). In the second case, a perfectly healthy man fell victim to the threats of a not entirely kindly old mother. Although he tried to ignore her warnings, his body somehow took those warnings seriously. At the precise moment she had predicted, the cardiovascular and respiratory systems of his body, susceptible to the effects of the worst kind of psychological stress, succumbed. He was like the victims of voodoo, who must know that a curse has been placed on them in order for the curse to work (Cannon, 1942; Richter, 1957; Engel, 1971). His mind was powerful enough to put an end to his life.

In this book, we will examine the many ways in which the mind and the body are linked together in health and in illness. We will avoid the limitations of the traditional approach that emphasizes a one-to-one relationship between biological factors and bodily state, and instead we will follow the *biopsychosocial model* first introduced by psychiatrist George Engel (1977, 1980). The biopsychosocial perspective emphasizes that biological, psychological, and social factors in a person's life affect his or her state of health and illness. (We examine the biopsychosocial perspective in detail in Chapter 5.) In this book we will see that health and illness depend not only upon physiological conditions but also upon thoughts, emotions, and motivations for action. We will see that when people must contend with emotionally stressful relationships, they are sometimes left much more vulnerable than usual to ordinary illnesses. We will see that those who suffer tremendous emotional stresses, such as the death of a spouse, sometimes experience quite serious health problems shortly thereafter. We will see how the mind can affect recovery from serious illness, and how some people can regain their health against terrible odds because of their tremendous will to live, whereas others who are more passive become depressed and give up. We will see that what goes on in a person's mind can clearly affect the behaviors that influence health outcomes. For example, some people may continue to smoke cigarettes, thus endangering their health,

because they deny important facts about the dangers of smoking cigarettes. Or they may be unable to quit because cigarette smoking helps them to manage their anxiety and unhappiness. As we will see in this book, thoughts, emotions, and motivations for behavior are central to understanding health and illness.

The 20th century is probably the only period in history in which the predominant medical opinion has neglected the mind and focused attention solely on the body. During most of recorded history, illness has been attributed to all sorts of "mind" phenomena, albeit not exactly the kind to which we are referring here. The phenomena that many years ago were thought to explain illness were magical and unknowable, such as sinful thoughts, possession by evil spirits, and the will of vengeful gods. Until well into the 18th century, medicine was very, very primitive. Irrationalism was the dominant approach to illness and medical care. It's no wonder that medical people of modern time have tried to steer clear of mind issues altogether!

Let's briefly look to the past to try to understand the developing role of the mind in present day medicine.

## A BRIEF HISTORY OF MEDICINE

Western medicine had its origin in ancient Greece during the time of greatest intellectual development. Then, as throughout most of history, medicine was dominated by a focus on mysticism and superstition. Hippocrates (460–370 B.C.), the most celebrated of early Greek practitioners, tried to change that, although his was a lone voice for rationality. Hippocrates contributed a great deal to the existing medical knowledge and beliefs. He carefully noted the history of his patients' symptoms. He examined patients and recorded signs, such as temperature and respiration rate. He lis-

Hippocrates (460–370 B.C.)
SOURCE: Emilio A. Mercado/The Picture Cube

*tional medicine.* He also understood the importance of the patient's thoughts and emotions, the role played by the patient's trust in the physician, and the patient's positive expectations regarding the outcome of care. Hippocrates recognized and brought to light the psychological aspects of illness at a time when superstition and mysticism dominated explanations of illness and healing. Despite its importance, however, for the next 2000 years Hippocrates' work did not have widespread influence. Irrationalism tended to win out over science.

Claudius Galen (A.D. 131–200) is considered by many to be the greatest figure in ancient medicine because his work had a lasting influence in Europe until the Renaissance. Galen was indeed unusual for his time. He used a Hippocratic foundation to set diagnosis (the identification of disease based on the patient's signs and symptoms) on a firm base of anatomy and physiology. He based medical practice on science instead of on mystical beliefs. Still, most of "medical practice" around him emphasized the contribution of witches and demons. Throughout the next 1200 years, Galen's followers tried to promote a scientific approach to health and illness.

In the 15th century the Renaissance brought intellectualism and rationalism to the realm of medicine. Medical scientists pressed on in their attempts to focus attention on the physical aspects of illness. Of course, the introduction of firearms and the spread of the plague in the 14th century and syphilis in the 15th century overwhelmed the fledgling science. But gradually, over the next few hundred years, the foundations of medicine as we know it began to emerge.

In 1590 the microscope was invented by Van Leeuwenhoek and it became possible to view the microorganisms that were later found to play a role in disease. About that time Harvey demonstrated with painstak-

tened to patients' heartbeats with his ear on their chests. He collected data, facts about real phenomena, instead of hypothesizing about which god or demon was at work. Hippocrates believed that prognosis (the forecast of the course of a disease) was extremely important because a patient's expectations influenced his or her emotions and in turn his or her physical condition. Therefore, Hippocrates charted the course of various illnesses, making it possible for him to predict what would likely happen next. He prescribed noninvasive, supportive treatments, such as baths and massage. He also recommended dietary interventions and a few drugs from India and Egypt.

Hippocrates was unusual for his time in that he built the earliest foundation for *ra-*

The Black Plague
SOURCE: © Hulton Picture Library

ing research that certain mechanical principles applied to the human body. A short time later Sydenham further developed the careful principles of bedside observation and clinical diagnosis that were introduced by Hippocrates. Lavoisier described the nature of respiration, and in 1796 Jenner introduced the practice of vaccination and reduced the incidence of smallpox. Pasteur (c. 1857) and Koch (c. 1877) made important discoveries that contributed much to the science of bacteriology.

There was a slow but steady widening of knowledge about surgical interventions as well. In 1893 Roentgen discovered X rays. In 1846 Morton introduced anesthesia. Considering the long history of the human race, antiseptic surgery performed on an anesthetized patient is a very new phenomenon.

Around 1900 medicine began to be transformed into a clinical science. Specific treatments became available, and the physical aspects of illness and injury began to receive considerable attention. World War I brought tremendous advances in wound care and in the treatment of malaria and yellow fever.

It is the 20th century that has brought the most dramatic changes in medicine and surgery, changes unequaled in any other period in history. Humankind has gone from using leeches to suck patients' blood to procedures like plasmapheresis that mechanically filter blood of the by-products of certain diseases. We have progressed from ear-to-chest auscultation (listening for sounds within the body) to continuous electrocardiogram monitoring from remote paramedic units to faraway medical centers. Simple palpation has given way to computed tomography (as in the "CT scan") which provides computerized images of sections of organs. Today medical practitioners can probe minute structures buried deep within the human body without scratching its surface. Advances in microsurgery allow transplantation of corneas and the reattachment of tiny severed fingers. New drugs prevent tissue rejection, enabling transplantation of organs from one human being to another.

The wounded in World War I
SOURCE: Photo Researchers

## MEDICINE TODAY

Most of the great strides in medicine have taken place in quite recent time. It was not until 1943, for example, that penicillin became available for the treatment of bacterial infections. Nearly every day since that time some new physical factor has been discovered in disease or some new specific treatment intervention has been developed. The possibilities seem almost endless.

So much has changed so fast that scientific medicine seems to hold infinite promise. Yet, in the search for foolproof technology, medical professionals and laypersons alike have tended to focus so intently on physical factors in illness that they have ignored or rejected phenomena related to the mind. Efforts to avoid the nonscientific nonsense that dominated medicine throughout history have led to a single-minded focus of attention on the physical aspects of illness. In a sense, the pendulum has swung far from the old days of demons and superstition to a point at which any "mind" phenomena are considered suspicious. In many ways we have begun to act as if the scientific advances of drugs and surgeries are all that are necessary to produce better health.

## Illness and Disease

During this time of great advances in the technical aspects of medicine, it has been easy to forget the human side. The whole patient is often ignored in an effort to focus on his or her disease. In a large medical center, for example, it is commonplace for a busy doctor to refer to the "gallbladder case" in Room 302. Such a reference reflects the medical team's focus on combating disease with all the newest medical developments available. It also reflects how easy it is to forget that the patient is a person.

As we will see throughout this book, an intense focus on the technical side of medicine has prevented a clear distinction between two important phenomena: *disease* and *illness*. Disease is the collection of physical findings and symptoms that, when taken together, form a definable entity. You can look up a disease in a book like the *Professional Guide to Diseases* (Hamilton & Rose, 1982) or *Harrison's Principles of Internal Medicine* (Isselbacher, Adams, Braunwald, Petersdorf, & Wilson, 1980). There you can find a description of the condition and its clinical signs and symptoms (what the doctor sees, what the patient reports), as well as the pattern of results one might find on diagnostic tests.

Illness may involve a definable disease, but illness is something broader and something less clear. Illness may or may not involve the clinical signs and symptoms that form a known disease entity. A person can say he or she feels ill even when the most sophisticated medical tests show no organic basis for the complaints. Whether or not the patient's illness can be defined in terms of altered physiology, the illness upsets optimal functioning. Cognitions, emotions, motivations, and behaviors are clearly affected.

"Illness complaints are what patients and their families bring to the practitioner. . . . Disease, however, is what the practitioner creates in the recasting of illness in terms of theories of disorder. Disease is what practitioners have been trained to see through the theoretical lenses of their particular form of practice" (Kleinman, 1988, p. 5).

Let's consider Mary, a college student whose physical, psychological, and social functioning has been affected by illness, and for whom a disease label is finally found.

■ ■ ■ ■ ■

It is the last semester of her junior year at college and Mary feels weak and exhausted. She has trouble dragging herself out of bed, and she takes frequent naps during the day. She skips many of her classes, fails to turn in assignments, and is grumpy around her friends. She will tell you that she is ill.

According to some sociologists, Mary is ill because she says she is (Parsons, 1958). She has adopted *the sick role*. In doing so, she is legitimately excused from her day-to-day obligations. To remain in the sick role, Mary must fulfill certain societal requirements. She must seek medical help, view her illness as a negative state, and make every effort to cooperate with her doctors to get well. Mary is allowed to remain in the sick role even though she believes that she became ill because of the distress she experienced when she recently broke up with her boyfriend. She also says she's terrified about the fact that she will graduate in a little over a year and she is ambivalent about her future plans.

Mary finally makes a visit to the college health clinic. The results of her examination by the doctor and her blood test reveal that she actually has a disease, a case of infectious mononeucleosis (sometimes called mono for short). Mono is a systemic disease caused by the Epstein-Barr virus, and it can cause extreme fatigue. It can be accompanied by fever and sore throat as well. There is no treatment except rest, and it may take several weeks or even months to recover fully.

Mary is ill, and her illness involves a known disease entity. If no disease had been identified because of limitations in medical science or the idiosyncratic nature of her own mind-body interaction, *she would still be considered ill*. Further, as we will see with many patients throughout this book, Mary is not simply a body with a case of mono; she is a complex young woman with a life that affects and is affected by her disease.

In the past 50 years there has been a tremendous proliferation of knowledge about disease. Practitioners of Western medicine can now diagnose thousands of disease conditions, many of them quite rare (Hamilton & Rose, 1982). Yet, despite the availability of sophisticated medical equipment and techniques, a good portion of the time the practitioner does not know what is precisely wrong with the person who arrives at the door for help (Kleinman, 1988). A focus on disease alone misses an important aspect of the individual's unique illness process and the meaning of that illness in his or her unique life.

## Psychological Factors in Illness and Disease

Many people are surprised to find that for most medical conditions, even the easily diagnosed diseases like infectious mononucleosis, a cure does not even exist. The leading causes of death in the United States these days are heart disease and cancer. These are multifactorial in etiology (origin and cause) and in treatment (control or cure), and psychological and behavioral factors are as important as physical ones. Consider heart disease. A person's risk of having a heart attack is greatly increased by leading a sedentary lifestyle and by smoking cigarettes, two behavioral factors that have very large psychological components. As we will see in this book, an individual can significantly reduce the chances of suffering a heart attack by refraining

from smoking and by engaging in regular physical exercise. But these preventive behaviors require psychological commitment and a modification of beliefs, attitudes, and behaviors.

There is no simple, straightforward cure for heart disease. There is no single pill, no simple surgery. All treatments require participation of the whole individual. A heart attack may occasion a tremendous assault upon self-image. The patient experiences fear and panic, and often must implement a drastic change in lifestyle to enhance the likelihood of survival. A major surgical procedure called coronary bypass may be offered to the patient, but carries with it high risks and long rehabilitation. He or she must take medication, change diet, stop smoking, exercise, cut back on work pressures, and relax. The person must try to contain the fear of another heart attack. Adjustments may have to be made in sexual habits. Heart disease requires a significant degree of psychological as well as physical adaptation.

Cancer is another example of a disease whose prevention and cure affects and is affected by the whole person. As we will see in this book, unhealthy behaviors figure prominently in the etiology of cancer. For example, most cases of lung cancer and many cases of throat and bladder cancer are caused by smoking cigarettes. Cancer of the breast and cancer of the cervix may be cured only after early detection, which requires regular preventive screening measures such as mammograms and breast self-exams, as well as Pap tests. Yet inertia, fear, and other psychological barriers too often stand in the way of early detection.

The treatment of cancer may also be heavily influenced by psychological factors. Treatments may involve disfiguring surgery, pain, and discomfort from chemotherapy and radiation, as well as tremendous financial drain. The patient must work hard to maintain self-image, meaningful involvement in work, and social and family ties throughout the course of treatment. How well the patient accomplishes these psychological tasks may influence his or her physical recovery.

These are just a few of the ways in which psychological factors are important in the etiology and treatment of cancer and heart disease. Throughout this book, we will consider many others.

## THE RELATIVE IMPORTANCE OF PHYSICAL AND PSYCHOLOGICAL FACTORS

How important are psychological factors in disease? Are they more important than physical factors? Can we fully understand health and illness by considering the individual's psychology alone? Probably not.

Psychological factors do not take precedence over physical factors in understanding the etiology of a disease or in carrying out its treatment. Rather, as we will see throughout this book, psychological factors are as important as physical ones but in a different way. There is a delicate interplay between mind and body in the realm of illness.

Consider this example. Many cancer patients must undergo chemotherapy in an effort to destroy their tumor cells. In chemotherapy powerful drugs are given that destroy not only cancer cells but normal cells as well. The patient is sometimes left temporarily, but quite miserably, sick. Many patients experience severe nausea and vomiting from the powerful medications, and some quit chemotherapy as a result. Psychological interventions can help patients to minimize these reactions by assisting them in focusing their attention away from their internal sensations. Patients can also be taught to avoid tensing their muscles when faced with the chemotherapy, because tension can worsen their reactions to the drugs, thereby increasing

their distress. With such psychological help, patients are better able to follow their recommended cancer treatments. Relaxation techniques can also help cancer patients to tolerate their life stresses better and may help them to enhance their capacity to fight the disease. When psychological intervention aids the successful administration of medical treatments and cancer is successfully eradicated, it is impossible to say which intervention was the more successful, the physical or the psychological. One without the other would have been ineffective.

In this book we will see that few conditions can be understood or treated in purely physical terms. Illness involves more than disease. We will also see that it is a mistake to imagine that disease can be treated in purely psychological terms. To attempt to do so would be unproductive and perhaps even dangerous, for it would ignore the important advances of modern medical practice that are necessary to combat disease. Psychological techniques cannot replace good medicine, and technology alone is insufficient for encouraging effective health promotion and disease treatment. Together, however, psychology and medicine can elevate the treatment of illness to levels never before achieved.

# The Field of Health Psychology

Until recently, nearly all psychologists dealt fairly exclusively with "problems of the mind." In the past in the field of psychology, the word *doctor* was virtually synonymous with *psychotherapist* and the term *illness* was used to refer to a purely mental phenomenon. But in the past thirty years health psychologists have begun to recognize the potentially far-reaching implications of their work for the achievement and maintenance of physical health and well-being. They have become particularly aware of the relationship of theory, research, and practice to the prevention and treatment of disease and to understanding the meaning of illness.

In the past a select number of psychotherapists worked with medical patients in private psychotherapy practices and in teaching hospitals. The goals they pursued included evaluating the patient's mental status and attempting to control bizarre or annoying behavior. For example, a patient who responded to cancer surgery with severe depression might have been referred to a psychotherapist. This referral may have come in response to the frustration of the patient's physician and family who feared the patient would commit suicide. Or, a hospitalized patient whose hostility had become a source of great distress to the nurses might have been visited by a hospital staff psychologist in an effort to diminish this troublesome behavior and keep the hospital running smoothly.

Today information on the role of psychology in health and illness is available from research on cognitions, emotions, and behavior in the prevention and treatment of disease and the understanding of illness. Lately, a great deal of information has become available and the early work, scattered in the journals and books of many fields, has been compiled.

## THE EARLY RESEARCH LITERATURE

Throughout history a few physician educators have had opinions about the role of the patient's psychology in caring for his or her physical needs. In the fourth century B.C., for example, Hippocrates wrote about how the physician's demeanor can engender a patient's trust and encourage a patient's will to live: "The patient, though his condition is perilous, may recover his health simply through his contentment with the goodness of the physician" (Hippocrates, 1923 translation).

In 1904 Sir William Osler, a famous medical educator, lectured to medical students that they should listen to the patient because the patient's own words may reveal the diagnosis (Osler, 1904). Another famous physician, Frederick Shattuck (1907), argued that medicine is an art as well as a science.

In the 1950s articles appeared in the research literature with titles like the following: "Choosing and Changing Doctors" (Gray and Cartwright, 1953), and "Why Do People Detour to Quacks?" (Cobb, 1954). These articles, written by medical practitioners as well as by psychologists and sociologists, attempted to deal with the complex questions that surrounded the rather widespread dissatisfaction of patients toward their medical care professionals. Such papers appeared in the literature in the fields of medicine, psychiatry, nursing, psychology, sociology, pharmacy, hospital administration, medical economics, social work, and anthropology, as well as others. They pointed to the need for medical professionals to recognize and deal effectively with the psychological as well as the physical aspects of clinical care.

The psychology of physical health and illness, as a field of study, was initially limited in several ways. First, the literature was quite sparse. Few journals carried more than one or two articles a year on the psychological and social aspects of physical illness. Second, the early research was not programmatic—that is, systematically based on previous work. Researchers tended to carry out isolated studies and failed to build a fund of knowledge about a particular topic by improving on the mistakes of earlier work. Third, much of the earlier work was solely clinically based. The work of psychoanalysts on the expression of emotional illness through physical disorder is an example. Fourth, the early work was time-bound; that is, writings on health psychology issues often failed to examine general principles but instead dealt with prevailing social conditions. The fifth limitation, which will be examined in detail in the next chapter, is that the research methods used in the early days of work on the psychology of health and illness were rather unsophisticated. As a result, in many cases findings remained inconclusive and clinical applications were tentative and sometimes incorrect.

## ENTER HEALTH PSYCHOLOGY

The late 1970s saw a huge impetus to research in the study of the psychology of health, illness, and medical care. Psychologists across the country who were interested in medical issues formed an organization. Scholars, researchers, and clinicians who had once been isolated in their work on health issues found the opportunity to share ideas and encouragement. In 1978 the Division of Health Psychology (Division 38) was formed in the American Psychological Association. Currently, there are thousands of psychologists who keep in touch with one another's work through newsletters, journals, and meetings. Other organizations have also sprung up, such as the Society of Teachers of Family Medicine and the Society of Behavioral Medicine. All of these organizations have facilitated dialogue among teachers, researchers, and clinicians, and have provided outlets such as the *Journal of Behavioral Medicine* and *Health Psychology* for the publication of research. Such journals help to centralize the literature on the psychological aspects of health, illness, and medical treatment. Psychologists working in the field have begun to compile their work into edited books and texts such as this one on health psychology.

In the past ten years we have seen tremendous growth in this exciting field. With the focus of thousands of psychologists on issues of health, illness, and medical treatment, there has been a virtual explosion of information regarding both effective psychological care for ill patients and specific psychological interventions that assist in people's attempts to stay healthy. The inauguration of the field of health psychology has encouraged both the development of theory on which to build future research and systematic examinations from which to develop clinical applications.

# Being a Health Psychologist

The health psychologist has many options available for involvement in matters of health and illness. And the medical care delivery system can benefit greatly from the expertise of the psychologist.

In today's medical care arena many psychologists function as independent clinicians and as consultants to physicians. They are often indispensable in evaluating the psychological aspects of a patient's care. They work directly with patients or in consultation with the medical team to design treatments that are suited not only to the patient's physical needs but to the patient's psychological needs as well. The psychologist might work with the patient to help him or her evaluate the life-plan changes that are required to accommodate the limitations of illness and to adjust to the treatments necessary to maintain optimal functioning. The psychologist might also work with the patient's family members to assist them in coming to terms with the changes in their own lives that result from the patient's condition. The psychologist might aid their attempts to assist the patient in coping with the illness.

Some psychologists do not work directly with patients at all. Rather, they may be concerned solely with research on the various psychological issues that affect health and illness. Many researchers never provide direct patient care, yet the clinical application of their research findings might vastly improve the treatment of many thousands of patients. For instance, a researcher who discovers the connection between emotions and the functioning of the immune system may find the secret to better health for millions of people, having never left the laboratory!

Some psychologists are involved in health promotion programs in schools, in communities, and even in the mass media. Through their research these psychologists learn the most effective ways to communicate information about health promoting lifestyles. By implementing their findings, they develop media messages that have maximum impact on recipients. Many of the health messages you see today on television and elsewhere in the mass media were designed by psychologists. These include, for example, messages to quit smoking aired by the American Cancer Society. The messages implement what has been learned about how to motivate people to take action toward better health.

Of course, many health psychologists with considerable clinical training work with clients whose emotional concerns are influenced by the complications of illness. In this capacity the clinical health psychologist must be extremely knowledgeable about current research on the connection between mind and body. He or she must remain constantly up-to-date on the latest findings relevant to the connection between physical health and psychological processes.

In whatever capacity the health psychologist is working, the issues with which he or she is concerned are quite complex. A great many of the issues are critically important to the welfare of human beings, both healthy and ill. For the health psychologist, there are many opportunities for work that is meaningful and rewarding, both professionally and personally.

## The Individual Perspective

The focus of this book is on individuals and what they think, how they feel, what they do, and why they do it. With this perspective, we are concerned with cognition, emotion, motivation, and action. We will examine how these aspects of the individual's psychology influence his or her responses to illness, to the threat of illness, and to the possibility of avoiding illness through health-promoting practices. This perspective is not concerned with the role of social structure, societal institutions, or the system of medical care in issues of health and illness. Instead, we focus on individual people and on how and why they act and interact in an attempt to achieve their goals.

Consider this example. It is estimated that in the United States, roughly 390,000 people die prematurely each year because they smoked cigarettes. Cigarette smoking is the direct cause of 80% of lung cancers, and a strong contributing factor in the occurrence of heart attacks and strokes. This statistic means that every day, over 1000 people die because of cigarettes. If the same number of people died every day in airplane crashes, how many people do you think would be enthusiastic about air travel? Probably not nearly as many as currently smoke cigarettes!

If we were to take a societal perspective, we might look at this statistic and consider issues such as the following: Why aren't there laws against manufacturing and selling cigarettes? Why does the U.S.

government subsidize the tobacco industry? Why do magazines display cigarette advertisements? What can psychologists do in their communities to improve the situation? These are interesting questions, but they are the subject of politics and ethics, as well as of disciplines that take a societal perspective on health issues.

In this book we will be busy enough trying to understand the individual issues that relate to health care. For example, why would someone who knows the dangers of cigarettes continue to smoke them? We will be very busy examining the role of the individual's beliefs in his or her susceptibility to lung cancer from smoking cigarettes and his or her evaluation of the seriousness of lung cancer in threatening life. We will also examine why a person might believe that the benefits of quitting smoking do not outweigh the costs. We will consider the emotional factors that might cause a person to shut out the reality of the danger present in continued cigarette smoking. And we will look at the specific actions a person must take to overcome a habit that is both physically and psychologically addicting. In addition, we will analyze people's actions in light of their needs and desires. We will consider that people probably do the best they can at the time they must do it, even if their actions are not adaptive in the long run.

With an individual perspective, we will examine not only health behavior but illness behavior as well. We will examine when and why people come to define themselves as ill. We will examine the effect that illness has on people's lives, including the adjustments that it forces them to make in their life plans and the effect that it has on self-image. We will also see how illness affects their ability to face their lives with a sense of purpose and meaning. And finally, we will see how illness transforms their relationships with the people they care about.

# Summary

I. Health is a state that depends not only upon the workings of an individual's body but also upon many aspects of the functioning of the mind.
   A. The 20th century is probably the only period in history in which the predominant medical opinion has emphasized a focus on the body to the neglect of the mind as a factor in health.
   B. During most of recorded history, illness has been attributed to magical and unknowable phenomena, such as sinful thoughts, possession by evil spirits, and the will of vengeful gods.
II. Western medicine had its origin in ancient Greece during the time of greatest intellectual development.
   A. Hippocrates contributed a great deal to the existing medical knowledge and beliefs. Hippocrates built the earliest foundation for rational medicine.
   B. Claudius Galen is considered by many to be the greatest figure in ancient medicine.
   C. In the 15th century the Renaissance brought intellectualism and rationalism to the realm of medicine.
III. Around 1900 medicine began to be transformed into a clinical science. Most of the notable strides in medicine have taken place in even more recent years.
   A. During the time of greatest advances in the technical aspects of medicine, it has been easy to forget the human side. The whole patient may be ignored in an effort to focus on his or her disease.
   B. An intense focus on the technical side of medicine has prevented a

clear distinction between two important phenomena: disease and illness. Disease is the collection of physical findings and symptoms that, when taken together, form a definable entity. Illness may or may not involve definable disease, but illness upsets the optimal functioning of the individual and affects cognitions, emotions, motivations, and behaviors.

IV. Psychological factors are entwined with physical phenomena. This connection is manifested in many ways, some of which are discussed in the chapter.

A. Psychological factors do not take precedence over the purely physical in understanding the etiology of a disease or in carrying out its treatment. Rather, as we will see throughout this book, psychological factors are as importani as physical ones but in a different way. There is a delicate interplay between mind and body in the realm of illness.

B. Until recently, the relationship of theories, research, and practice in psychology to the understanding and treatment of physical illness has been ignored.

C. Relevant research and analytic writings have appeared in the fields of medicine, psychiatry, nursing, psychology, sociology, pharmacy, hospital administration, medical economics, social work, and anthropology, as well as others.

V. The late 1970s saw a huge impetus to research in the study of the psychology of health, illness, and medical care.

A. The inauguration of the field of health psychology has encouraged both the development of theory on which to build future research and systematic examinations on which to develop clinical applications.

B. Health psychologists have many work options available to them: as independent clinicians working with patients; as consultants to physicians and the entire medical team; as researchers; and as developers of educational programs to reach the public through the mass media, among other things.

# Glossary

**auscultation:** the process of listening for sounds within the human body.

**diabetes mellitus:** a serious condition that involves the failure of the pancreas to produce enough insulin for carbohydrate metabolism.

**diagnosis:** the identification of disease based on the patient's signs and symptoms.

**disease:** the physical findings and symptoms that, when taken together, form a definable entity.

**hypertension (high blood pressure):** a condition caused by several things: cardiac (heart) output that is too high, blood volume that is too great, or resistance in the peripheral blood vessels to the flow of blood. When the pressure that blood exerts against the blood vessel walls (blood pressure) is too high and remains untreated, there can be severe negative consequences, such as stroke and heart attack.

**illness:** a concept that is broader and less clear than disease. Illness may or may not involve clinical signs and symptoms that form a known disease entity, but illness can result in functional impairment as well as have an effect on the individual's cognitions (thoughts), emotions (feelings), and behaviors.

**infectious mononeucleosis (sometimes called mono for short):** a systemic disease caused by the Epstein-Barr virus, which can bring extreme fatigue, and is usually accompanied by fever and sore throat as well. Recovery may take several weeks or even months.

**palpation:** the application of the fingers with light pressure to the surface of the body for the purpose of determining the consistence of parts beneath in physical diagnosis.

**plasmapheresis:** a process of mechanically filtering the blood of the by-products of certain diseases.

# 2

# The Basics: Terminology, Physiology, and Methodology

This chapter will lay the basic groundwork for the study of the psychology of health, illness, and medical care. We will begin with a "crash course" in medical terminology, move to a very brief overview of anatomy and physiology and the systems of the body, and end with a more lengthy discussion of the basics of research methodology in health psychology. It is hoped that this most technical of chapters can be reviewed relatively painlessly and even enjoyed!

## The Basics of Medical Terminology

Conducting research or practice in health psychology without a working knowledge of medical terminology is like traveling in a foreign country without knowing the language. You may be able to get from one place to another, but you will not get the most out of the experience. You will have to depend upon the goodwill of others and the accuracy of their judgments to help you out. You may become quite lost and miss opportunities to do the things you desire. And you are quite likely to order something you do not necessarily want for dinner!

Problems, too, will occur for health psychologists who know little or nothing about medical terminology. They will likely fail to understand some important issues, such as the meaning and the implications of certain diseases for patients' physical, and hence psychological, health. They will not be able to communicate effectively with the "natives" of the health-care system, the medical professionals. They will always seem like outsiders in the medical setting. Their access to the relevant medical literature will be limited by their unfamiliarity with the language.

## LEARNING MEDICAL TERMINOLOGY

Medical terminology can probably be learned most effectively by learning the meaning of various word components (roots and stems) and combining these components into a medical word. The definitions of most medical terms can be arrived at by analyzing their component parts. The most important step in building a medical vocabulary is to learn categories of words that pertain to external and internal anatomical parts, body fluids, substances, and numerals, and by learning prefixes and suffixes.

Almost all medical words derive from either Greek or Latin, regardless of whether they pertain to anatomy, physiology, pathology, histology, disease, signs and symptoms of disease, or diagnostic procedures. (As we will see in more detail below, anatomy is the study of the structure of the body; physiology is the study of the normal functions and activities of the body; pathology is the study of disease; and histology is the microscopic study of the structure,

composition, and function of normal cells and tissues.)

Some interesting characteristics of medical names may be noted. For example, many anatomical names for parts of the body are derived from the shape or configuration of some object. The Greeks and Romans named some anatomical structures after familiar objects when they had no better ways to identify them.

Unlike a foreign language, the vocabulary of medicine does not remain stagnant. New words are added often to reflect the proliferation of diagnostic tests and treatments, and the identification of new diseases and disease syndromes. Except for proper names in which a disease or sign/symptom is named after the individual who first described or identified it (for example, Crohn's disease), most new medical terms will make sense within the framework already learned.

Except for the words used in anatomy, most medical terms are derived not from a single Latin or Greek word but from a combination of two or more roots, each of which has a distinct meaning. For example, *appendicitis* means inflammation (*itis*) of the appendix. Another example is *osteoarthritis* (inflammation [*itis*] of the bone [*osteo*] and joint [*arthro*]).

In the following pages of this chapter, you will be learning some very basic anatomy and physiology. Recognize that many of the stems and roots that you learn, including anatomical names, can be combined to give you a start into the world of medical terminology.

Here are several medical stems and roots of organs: *hepat* (liver); *derma* (skin); *gastr* (stomach); *nephr* (kidney); *arthr* (joint); *oste* (bone); *card* (heart); *col* (colon, large intestine); *pulm* (lung); *pleur* (lining of the lung).

As an example of building a medical word, consider: *hepat* (liver) plus *itis* (inflammation). Hepatitis is a condition of inflammation of the liver. What do you think are the meanings of *arthritis, dermatitis, nephritis,* and *pleuritis*?

The types of surgical operations and their roots are the following: *plasty* (repair); *stomy* (artificial or surgical opening); *otomy* (incision); *ectomy* (excision); *centesis* (puncture). Can you figure out *colostomy*? *gastrectomy*?

*Oma* is a suffix that refers to a tumor or neoplasm (with the exception of glaucoma). Translation of the root tells you the location of the neoplasm. For example: neuroma (on a nerve), hemangioma (on a blood vessel), lipoma (in the fatty tissue). *Osis* usually refers to a morbidly serious condition; for example, *arteriosclerosis, nephrosis.*

The six branches of science that deal with the study of the body are *anatomy* (the study of the structure of the body and relationship of its parts); *physiology* (the study of the normal functions and activities of the body; *physio* refers to relationship to nature, and *ology* means the study of); *pathology* (the study of disease); *embryology* (the study of the development of the body during the period from one week after conception to the second month of gestation); *histology* (the microscopic study of the structure, composition, and function of normal cells and tissues); and *biology* (the study of all life forms).

Here is a list of some of the most frequently encountered medical specialties:

*Pediatrics* is devoted to curing the diseases of children. (It derives from *pedia,* meaning child.)

*Gynecology* is devoted to the treatment of diseases of the female reproductive system. (*Gyneco* means female.)

*Obstetrics* is the branch of surgery that deals with pregnancy, labor, and delivery.

*Surgery* is the branch of medicine that treats diseases by operative procedures.

*Anesthesiology* is devoted to the provision of pain-killing drugs, particularly during surgery (*an,* meaning not; *esthesis* meaning feeling).

*Otolaryngology* is the branch of medicine that deals with diseases of the ear (*oto*) and the larynx, and related structures.

*Ophthalmology* (*ophthalmo,* meaning eye) is devoted to care of diseases of the eye.

*Radiology* is a branch of medicine devoted to the study of structures of the body by means of X rays, and the treatment of such diseases as cancer with X rays.

*Urology* is devoted to diseases of the urinary tract.

*Cardiology* is devoted to treatment of diseases of the heart.

*Endocrinology* is devoted to the care of the endocrine glands and their hormonal secretions.

*Dermatology* is devoted to care of diseases of the skin.

*Internal medicine* is involved in the treatment of diseases of the internal organs by a physician called an internist (who should not be confused with an intern, who is a graduate medical student receiving training in a hospital prior to licensing).

*Physical medicine (or Physiatry)* is a relatively new branch of medicine concerned with physical therapy in the treatment of disease.

*Psychiatry* (*psych,* meaning mind) is devoted to the study and treatment of diseases of the mind.

*Geriatrics* is devoted to the care of diseases of the aged, and is also a relatively new branch of medicine.

Some common prefixes used in medical terminology are the following: *a* (without, lack of), as in anemia (lack of blood); *anti* (against), as in antisepsis; *de* (away from), as in dehydrate (remove water from); *dia* (through, completely), as in diagnosis (complete knowledge); *epi* (upon, on), as in epidermis (on the skin); *hyper* (over, above, excessive), as in hypertension, or high blood pressure; *pro* (before), as in prognosis (foreknowledge); *retro* (backward, located behind), as in retrolingual (behind the tongue); and *trans* (across), as in transection (cut across).

A few important Greek and Latin derivatives used in medical terminology are the following: *algia* (pain), as in neuralgia (nerve pain); *caus* (burn), as in causalgia (burning pain); *centesis* (puncture, perforate), as in amniocentesis (puncture of amniotic sac); *dynia* (pain), as in mastodynia (breast pain); *edem* (swell), as in lymphedema (swelling of lymph nodes); *logy* (study), as in histology (study of tissues); *lysis* (breaking up, dissolving), as in glycolysis (breaking up of glucose or sugar by the body); *palpit* (flutter), as in palpitation (fluttering feeling); *phobia* (fear), as in claustrophobia (fear of close places); *plegia* (paralyze), as in paraplegia (paralysis of lower limbs); *therap* (treat, cure), as in chemotherapy (treatment with chemicals).

Whew! We have covered a lot of ground, yet we have dealt with only a small proportion of the medical terms that nurses and physicians use every day. Perhaps our analysis of some of the basics of medical terminology will help you to appreciate the complex yet elegant language of medicine, and to realize that learning medical terminology is a both valuable and achievable endeavor for a health psychologist.

# The Human Body: An Overview of Human Anatomy and Physiology

The human body is a complex structure. It consists of organs in organ systems supported by a framework of muscle and bone, enclosed in an external covering of skin.

A *cell* is the smallest unit of life. Specialized cells similar in structure and func-

tion are assembled together into a mass called *tissue*. Different kinds of tissues have varying characteristics according to their function (such as connective tissue, muscular tissue, nervous tissue, and epithelial tissue, which forms the outer surface of skin and linings of organs). Various tissues combine to form *organs* of the body, such as the heart, lungs, liver, and kidneys. Although they act as units, organs do not work independently. Several organs combine to form a *system* in order to perform a specific, complicated function. For example, the respiratory system is involved in taking oxygen into the lungs and excreting carbon dioxide, and the urinary system filters waste from the blood and eliminates it from the body. Although the systems of the body are conceptualized as distinct from each other, they are actually quite interdependent.

Let us examine several of these systems briefly. More detailed information appears in the classic textbook of anatomy and physiology by Guyton (1985) and in the text of biological principles by Nelson (1984).

## THE SKELETAL AND MUSCULAR SYSTEMS

The skeleton is the framework of the human body, made up of over 200 bones and pieces of cartilage that give the body its shape and support it (see Figure 2–1). The skeleton allows for the attachment of tendons, muscles, and ligaments, and makes body movement possible. The skeleton also affords protection to various vital organs, such as the heart and lungs.

A joint is a structure that holds separate bones together with ligaments of connective tissue. The study of bones is called *osteology*; the study of joints is called *arthrology*.

Muscle is tissue composed of long slender cells called *fibers*. These fibers are able to contract, and thus to produce movement of the body and its organs. All human activity (whether voluntary or involuntary) is

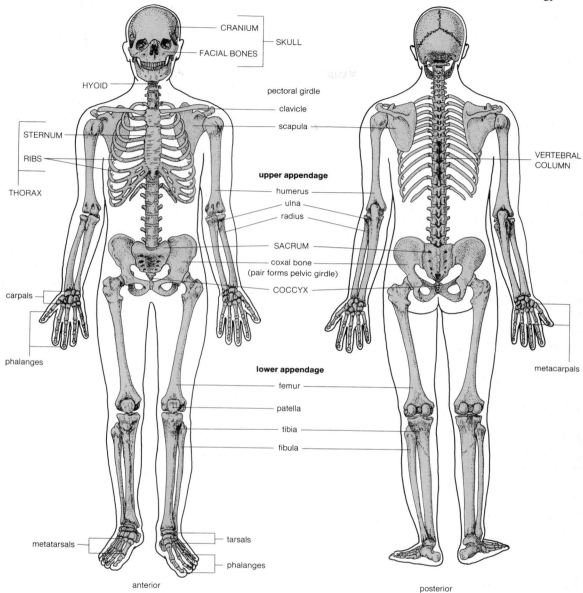

**FIGURE 2–1**   The human skeleton: anterior and posterior view.
SOURCE:  From *Human Anatomy,* by I. Fowler. Copyright © 1984 by Wadsworth, Inc. Reprinted by permission of the publisher, Wadsworth Publishing Company, 10 Davis Drive, Belmont, CA, 94002.

carried on by muscles, of which about 500 are large enough to be seen with the naked eye and thousands of others are so small that they can be seen only through a microscope. The form of a person's body is due largely to the muscles covering the bones, and an individual's posture is due to the development of certain muscles of the trunk of the body. Muscles make up many of the internal organs, such as the heart, uterus, lungs, and intestines (see Figure 2–2).

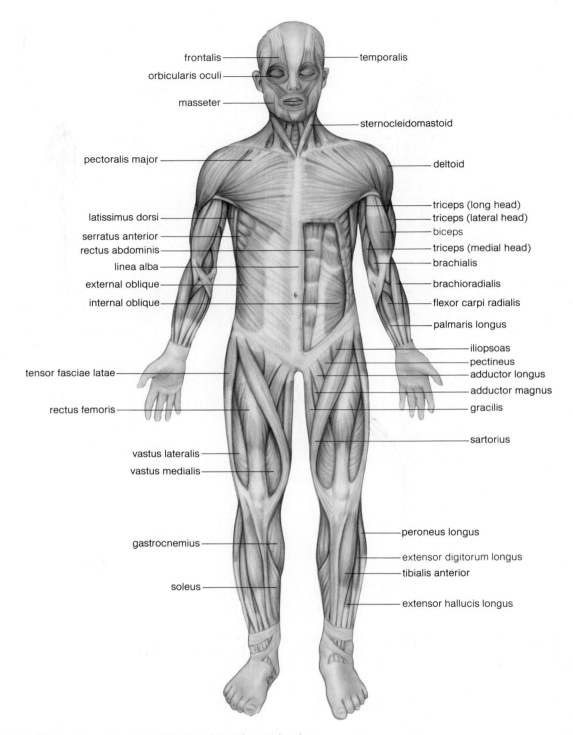

**FIGURE 2–2** The muscular system: anterior and posterior view.
SOURCE: From *Human Anatomy,* by I. Fowler. Copyright © 1984 by Wadsworth, Inc. Reprinted by permission of the publisher, Wadsworth Publishing Company, 10 Davis Drive, Belmont, CA, 94002.

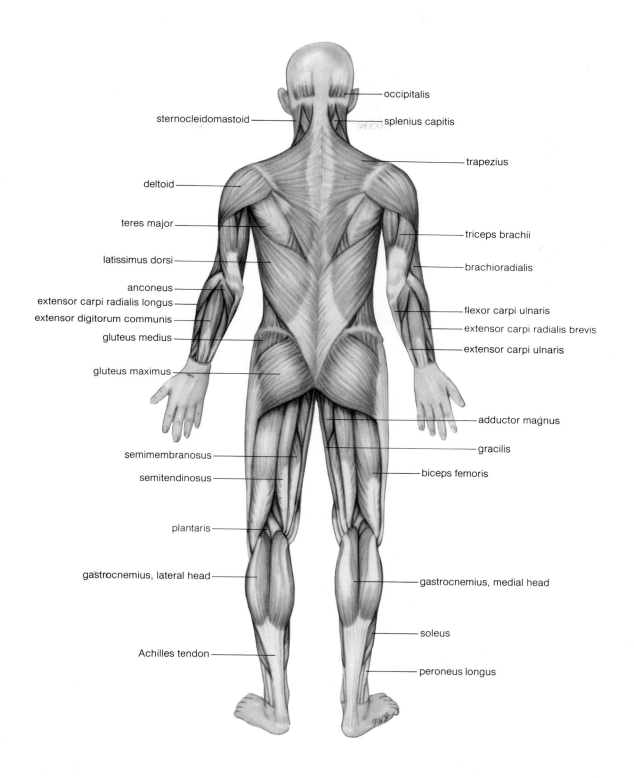

occipitalis

sternocleidomastoid

splenius capitis

trapezius

deltoid

teres major

triceps brachii

latissimus dorsi

brachioradialis

anconeus

extensor carpi radialis longus

extensor digitorum communis

flexor carpi ulnaris

extensor carpi radialis brevis

gluteus medius

extensor carpi ulnaris

gluteus maximus

semimembranosus

adductor magnus

gracilis

semitendinosus

biceps femoris

plantaris

gastrocnemius, lateral head

gastrocnemius, medial head

soleus

Achilles tendon

peroneus longus

23

Muscles are attached to bones with strong, fibrous white bands called *tendons*. *Fascia* hold together muscle bundles and *ligaments* hold together bones and keep organs in place. The motor nerve for any particular muscle causes that muscle to move.

Muscles are divided into three types: *voluntary or skeletal muscles* (striated), which compose about 40% of human body weight; *involuntary* (unstriated or smooth), such as are found in the walls of the stomach, intestines, blood vessels, glands, and eyes; and *cardiac or heart muscle*.

## THE CARDIOVASCULAR SYSTEM

The cardiovascular system consists of the heart, arteries, veins, capillaries, and blood.

The *heart*, a hollow muscular pump about the size of a clenched fist, furnishes the force to propel and circulate blood through the body. The heart is enclosed in a membranous fluid-filled sac called the *pericardium*. The middle muscular layer of the heart wall is called the *myocardium*. The heart is lined internally by the *endocardium* and externally by the *epicardium*. The heart beats over 100,000 times a day from the beginning of life until death. After leaving the heart, blood takes about one minute to make a complete circuit of the body and return.

*Arteries* carry blood from the heart to the rest of the body, and *veins* carry blood to the heart from the rest of the body. Blood traveling toward the lungs is laden with carbon dioxide, whereas blood traveling away from the lungs is oxygen rich (carbon dioxide has been expelled).

The heart is divided into four chambers. The top two are called the *right atrium* and *left atrium* and the bottom two are called the *right and left ventricles*. Carbon-dioxide-rich blood enters the heart at the right atrium and passes through a valve to the right ventricle. From the right ventri-

cle, blood is pumped to the lungs, where it is oxygenated. Then it travels to the left atrium of the heart and passes to the left ventricle, which pumps it out into the body through a large vessel called the *aorta*. The blood is pumped by means of rhythmic contractions of the myocardium (see Figure 2–3).

*Blood* is the fluid pumped by the heart through all the blood vessels in the body. Blood carries nutrients, oxygen, and water to all the cells of the body and returns carbon dioxide to the lungs for disposal. Blood carries hormones to the cells of the tissues and serves as a temperature regulator of the body. Blood also acts to protect the body against disease and infection because it contains certain complex chemical substances (such as antibodies) that are the basis of defense against injurious agents. Blood also carries away waste products that are harmful to life. The kidneys and liver, though not part of the cardiovascular system, are particularly important elements in this latter function. The kidneys receive blood and cleanse it of waste products, passing the wastes on to be eliminated in the urine. The liver receives blood both from the circulation system and from the intestinal tract. The liver cleanses the blood of bacteria and also removes and stores nutrients, such as sugars and amino acids.

*Blood pressure* is the force of the blood pushing through the body. It is also the force exerted on the artery walls as blood is pumped through the closed circulatory system. When the heart is at rest between contractions, it fills with blood. The blood pressure in this closed system measured at this rest point is called the *diastolic pressure*. When the heart pumps the blood out and through the body, the maximum force in the arteries is called the *systolic pressure*. The measurement of blood pressure is expressed as two numbers, the systolic over the diastolic. Systolic pressure is the highest because it is caused by contraction, or

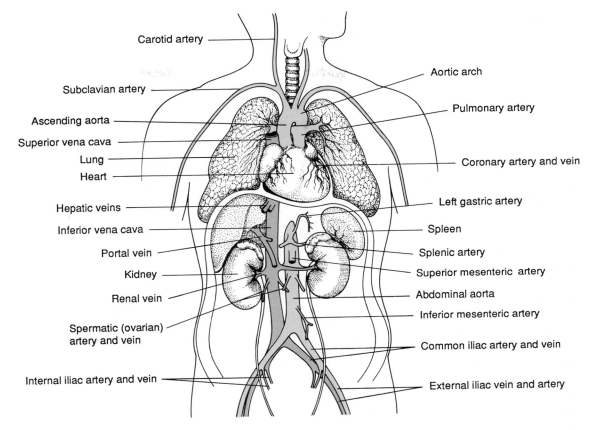

**FIGURE 2–3**    The circulatory system: the veins and arteries of the trunk.

systole, of the heart. Diastolic pressure is the lowest because it is present during relaxation, or diastole, of the heart. Normal blood pressure in a young adult is about 120 mm Hg systolic and 70 to 90 mm Hg diastolic. Hypertension is a condition in which blood pressure is elevated. Any individual whose blood pressure is over 140 mm Hg systolic and/or 90 mm Hg diastolic is considered to have high blood pressure, or *hypertension*. (Hg is the abbreviation for mercury used in the original sphygmomanometer, the instrument that measures blood pressure.)

Blood pressure is affected by several factors. Activity level tends to increase blood pressure (for example, during exercise and for a period of time thereafter).

Posture affects blood pressure so that when we go from sitting or lying down to standing, blood flow to the heart slows down, causing a drop in *cardiac output* (the volume of blood being pumped per minute through the heart). There is then a reduction in blood flow to the brain and the individual may feel dizzy. Temperature can affect blood pressure. In high temperatures blood pressure falls, making us feel sluggish and drowsy. In low temperatures blood pressure rises. Finally, emotional distress and emotional arousal (such as stress, anxiety, anger) can increase cardiac output and thereby raise both systolic and diastolic blood pressure (James, Yee, Harshfield, Blank, & Pickering, 1986). Very high systolic blood pressure (over 200 Hg.) can

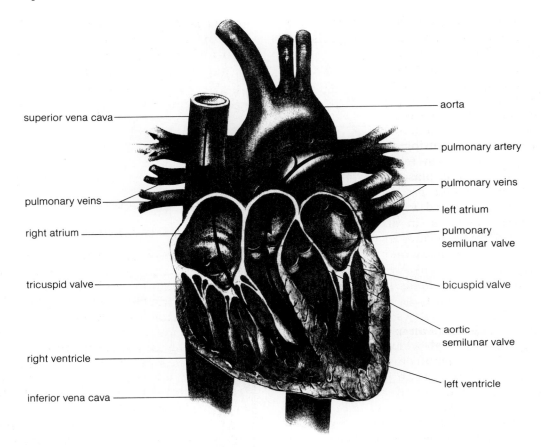

**FIGURE 2–3**  (continued)  The circulatory system: the heart.
SOURCE: From *Human Anatomy*, by I. Fowler. Copyright © 1984 by Wadsworth, Inc. Reprinted by permission of the publisher, Wadsworth Publishing Company, 10 Davis Drive, Belmont, CA, 94002.

cause constant strain on arteries and eventually may result in the rupture of a blood vessel, particularly one in the brain, causing a very serious condition called a *stroke*. Stroke can cause paralysis, loss of speech, and even death.

Blood pressure is higher among people who are overweight than among people who are of normal weight. Blood pressure also tends to be higher in males than in females, and higher in Blacks than in Whites. High blood pressure can be hereditary, but diet may also play a role in blood pressure. As we note in Chapter 3, hypertension is a

"silent killer" because many people do not know they have it. High blood pressure is an asymptomatic condition that can be very dangerous.

The composition of blood is an important issue in health. Because these days we hear a great deal about cholesterol in the blood and its effects on health, it may be helpful to examine cholesterol and other elements of the blood. Blood is composed of "formed elements" and of plasma. Formed elements of blood constitute less than 50% of it. These include *red blood cells*, which are formed in the bone marrow and contain *hemoglobin,* a protein that transports oxygen to body cells and tissue. They also include *leukocytes,* which are white blood cells that protect the body by destroying bacteria, and *platelets,* which are produced by the bone marrow and aid in the clotting of blood. Hemophilia is a disease in which platelets do not function effectively and jeopardize the clotting of blood, leaving the individual open to possibly bleeding to death. In the plasma portion of the blood are *plasma protein* (which thickens the blood) and various organic and inorganic elements. In plasma are found nutrients from digestion such as vitamins, minerals, amino acids, and fatty materials. Fatty materials make up the class of substances called *lipids.* Cholesterol is a blood lipid.

*Cholesterol* is a fatty substance that collects on the walls of an artery and narrows the opening through which blood can flow. Cholesterol is manufactured by the body, but some comes from an individual's diet. A diet high in saturated fats tends to increase the level of cholesterol in the blood. Thus, although some people may have high cholesterol levels regardless of what they eat (because of hereditary factors, for example), the amount of cholesterol in one's blood can be at least partly determined by behavioral factors, such as the kinds of food chosen.

When cholesterol builds up on the walls of an artery (in patches called *plaques*), a condition called *atherosclerosis* occurs. The walls of the artery harden because of these plaques and hardening of the arteries, or *arteriosclerosis,* results. Arteriosclerosis can cause high blood pressure. Also, when an artery becomes blocked due to atherosclerosis, blood and hence oxygen cannot get to the heart muscle and some of the heart muscle tissue can die as a result. The death of a portion of heart muscle tissue is called a *myocardial infarction,* or a heart attack.

*Angina pectoris* is a condition marked by pain and a sense of tightness in the chest. It occurs when the heart muscle is not getting enough oxygen because an artery is obstructed by plaques. As noted above, one kind of stroke (rupture of a cerebral artery) can be caused by very high blood pressure. But another kind of stroke is related to atherosclerosis. A blood clot, or *thrombosis,* becomes lodged in a cerebral blood vessel and can damage the brain by depriving it of oxygenated blood.

## THE RESPIRATORY SYSTEM

The respiratory system consists of the nose, mouth, pharynx (airway between nasal chambers, mouth, and larynx), larynx (voice box), trachea (windpipe), bronchial tubes, and lungs. The bronchial tubes divide into smaller branches called bronchioles inside the lungs and end in millions of tiny air sacs called alveoli. Each air sac consists of a thin membrane through which pass oxygen, carbon dioxide, and other gases (see Figure 2–4).

*Respiration* is the process by which the body takes in oxygen, which is required by all cells, and releases carbon dioxide as a waste product. There are three components of the cycle of respiration. The process involves inhalation (inspiration) of oxygen and exhalation (or elimination) of carbon dioxide, as well as the interval between inspiration and expiration. Oxygen is absorbed by the lungs, passed into the bloodstream, combined with hemoglobin (the oxygen carrying part of the blood), and carried to the tissues and cells of the body. Carbon dioxide is constantly formed in the body and carried by the blood back to the lungs for expiration. The respiratory center of the brain controls the rhythmic movements of respiration by way of the nerves that pass down to the chest wall and diaphragm. Chemical changes in the blood

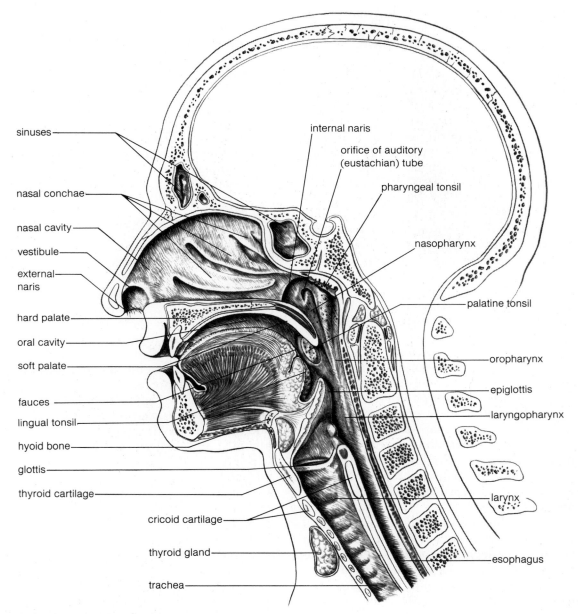

**FIGURE 2–4**  The upper respiratory system.
SOURCE: From *Human Anatomy and Physiology,* by J. Creager. Copyright © 1983 by Wadsworth, Inc. Reprinted by permission of the publisher, Wadsworth Publishing Company, 10 Davis Drive, Belmont, CA, 94002.

also stimulate the respiratory center. When excessive carbon dioxide accumulates in the blood, messages from the respiratory center in the brain cause respiration to become faster in order to rid the system of carbon dioxide. The muscles of respiration act automatically under normal circumstances. Under conditions of emotional

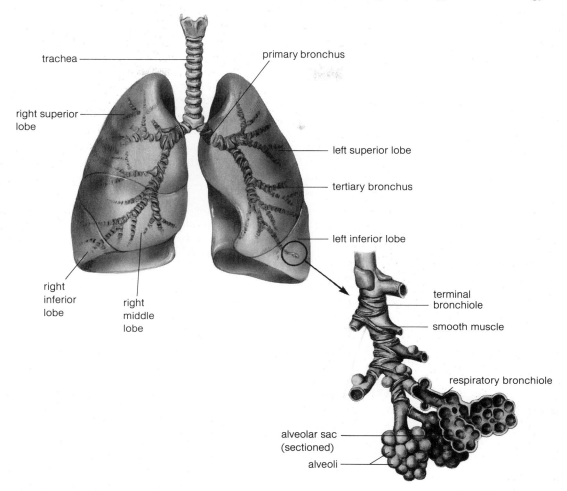

trachea

primary bronchus

right superior lobe

left superior lobe

tertiary bronchus

left inferior lobe

right inferior lobe

right middle lobe

terminal bronchiole

smooth muscle

respiratory bronchiole

alveolar sac (sectioned)

alveoli

**FIGURE 2–4** (continued)   The lungs and the bronchial tubes.
SOURCE: Courtesy of Joel Ito.

distress, respiration can be altered and shallow breathing can result.

When foreign particles and microorganisms enter the respiratory tract, protective mechanisms are put into operation. Sneezing clears irritating particles from the nasal passages, and coughing clears the lower parts of the respiratory system.

Cigarette smoking can seriously damage the respiratory system. *Emphysema*, a disease strongly linked with cigarette smoking, destroys the walls between the alveoli and decreases the surface within the lung that can be used to exchange gases. Emphysema also decreases the elasticity of lung tissue. *Chronic bronchitis*, another smoking-related disorder, is a condition in which the bronchial tubes become inflamed and produce excess mucus. *Lung cancer* is a disease characterized by the uncontrolled growth of cells in the tissues that line the bronchial tubes. Eighty percent of lung cancers are caused by cigarette smoking.

## THE GASTROINTESTINAL SYSTEM

The gastrointestinal (or digestive) system is responsible for taking in food, using nutrients, and eliminating waste products. Nutrients are absorbed from food into the bloodstream and transported to all cells of the body. Nutrients provide energy and contribute to the body's growth and repair.

The digestive system consists of the alimentary canal plus some accessory organs, such as the salivary glands, liver, pancreas, and gallbladder. The *alimentary canal* extends from the mouth through the body to the anus, and is about 30 feet long. The alimentary canal includes the esophagus, the stomach, and the small and large intestines. As food passes through the alimentary canal, the process of digestion extracts nutrients and carries waste material for elimination (see Figure 2–5).

Food is broken down by the grinding action of chewing as well as by enzymes in the mouth and stomach. *Enzymes* are substances that speed up chemical reactions. Some of the enzymes that digest different types of food are sucrase, which helps to break down sucrose or sugar, and lactase, which helps to break down the lactose in milk. Many individuals have a deficiency of lactase, particularly as they grow older, and as a result are unable effectively to digest the lactose in dairy products. They are lactose-intolerant and may experience severe gastrointestinal symptoms whenever they eat dairy products. There are enzymes in saliva that start the process of breaking down starches in the mouth. The smell and appearance of food can cause neural impulses originating in the brainstem to stimulate the release of saliva in the mouth (Nelson, 1984).

Food passes from the mouth to the *esophagus*, a tube that pushes food down to the stomach, using the action of muscle contractions called *peristalsis*. In the stomach, hydrochloric acid and pepsin break down the food into liquid that passes into the small intestine. There, further digestion, particularly of fats, takes place. Through the process of *absorption*, nutrients are absorbed through the small intestine into the bloodstream. Food material then passes into the large intestine, also called the colon, where some further absorption takes place and the material is converted through the action of bacteria into feces, which are then eliminated from the body.

As we will see in Chapter 10, emotional stress can affect the gastrointestinal system. This occurs chiefly in the formation of *ulcers*, which are sores in the lining of the stomach or intestine. These sores are believed to be caused by overproduction of acidic gastric secretions and/or decreased resistance of the mucosal lining of the stomach and duodenum (the beginning section of the small intestine) (Hamilton & Rose, 1982).

The *liver* is an essential organ that is situated in the upper right part of the abdomen. It produces bile, which converts sugar into glycogen. The liver also stores glycogen. The effective functioning of the liver can be seriously jeopardized by the two forms of *hepatitis*, a viral disease in which the liver becomes inflamed. Hepatitis A, or infectious hepatitis, is transmitted through contaminated food and water. Hepatitis B, or serum hepatitis, is transmitted through the transfusion of infected blood as well as through the sharing of needles by intravenous drug users and by vaginal or anal intercourse. Hepatitis, particularly hepatitis B, can lead to permanent liver damage.

## THE NERVOUS SYSTEM

The human body is governed by a central mechanism that serves to control and to meet all of the body's required functions: the *nervous system*.

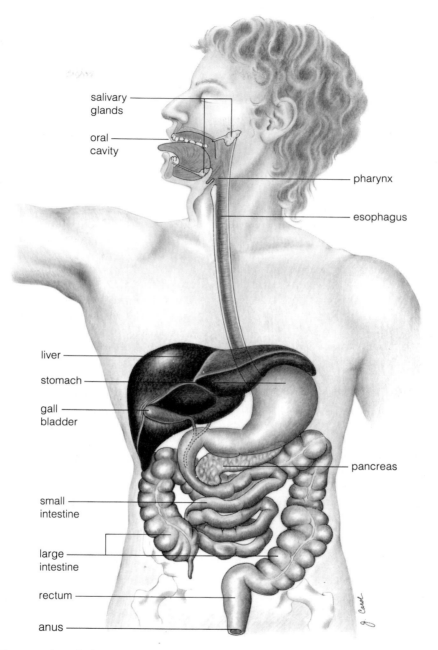

salivary glands

oral cavity

pharynx

esophagus

liver

stomach

gall bladder

pancreas

small intestine

large intestine

rectum

anus

**FIGURE 2–5**   The gastrointestinal system.

The brain relays messages to the body by way of the spinal cord through nerve fibers that radiate to every structure in the body. The cells of the nervous system are called *neurons*. They exist in the billions in an intricate network throughout the body. Neurons vary in character depending upon their function, but generally they consist of a *cell body* and branches called *dendrites*. Dendrites receive messages from adjacent neurons. These messages are passed through the neuron's long projection called the *axon*. The axon splits into branches that have small swellings—called synaptic knobs—that lie close to the dendrites of adjacent neurons. A neural message crosses the gap between neurons, called the *synapse*, to adjacent neurons. The message is electrochemical in nature. An impulse of electrical potential fires when the dendrite is stimulated. The impulse travels along the axon to the synaptic knobs, which release a kind of chemical known as a *neurotransmitter*. This chemical crosses the synapse and affects the adjacent neuronal dendrites. There are many different types of neurotransmitters, some of which excite and some of which inhibit the adjacent neurons.

Neurons are able to carry impulses rapidly for considerable distance. *Myelin*, a white fatty substance, surrounds the axons of most neurons and increases the speed of nerve impulses. As we will see in Chapter 12, the disease of *multiple sclerosis* involves a degeneration of these myelin sheaths and causes muscle weakness, loss of coordination, and spastic movements.

The nervous system can be divided into the *central nervous system* and the *peripheral nervous system*. The peripheral nervous system can be further divided into the *somatic* and the *autonomic* nervous systems. The central nervous system includes the brain and the spinal cord; the peripheral nervous system is composed of the nerves outside the brain and spinal column.

**The Central Nervous System.** The brain comprises about 98% of the central nervous system (see Figure 2–6). The brain lies within the protection of the skull and consists of three parts: the *brainstem*, the *forebrain*, and the *cerebellum*.

The *brainstem* is the lowest part of the brain and is found at the top of the spinal cord. All ascending and descending nerve tracts connect the brain with the spinal cord through the brain stem. The *midbrain* is the topmost structure of the brainstem. The midbrain relays messages from the spinal cord to the hypothalamus. Also in the brainstem is the *reticular system*, a network of neurons through the brainstem extending into the thalamus. The reticular system controls sleep as well as various stages of arousal. The *pons* is involved in facial expressions and eye movements. The *medulla* is found at the bottom of the brainstem and controls breathing, heart rate, and blood pressure. Several conditions can affect the brainstem and threaten life. The virus *poliomyelitis*, which can be virtually eradicated with effective immunization, can attack and damage the medulla and threaten life because of the central role that the medulla plays in regulating vital functions. *Epilepsy*, a condition that brings periodic convulsions and loss of consciousness, is believed to result from abnormalities in the reticular system. *Parkinson's disease* is linked to a degeneration in the midbrain. Parkinson's typically strikes older persons, and can cause motor tremors as well as tremendous stiffness and rigidity in posture.

The *spinal cord* extends down from the brainstem and lies inside the spinal column. The spinal cord conveys sensory impulses to the brain and carries motor impulses from the brain to the peripheral parts of the body. Sensory, or *afferent* neurons conduct impulses from the sense organs to the spinal cord and brain. Motor, or efferent *neurons* convey impulses from the brain and spinal cord to the muscles and glands of the body. If the spinal cord is severed in an accident, the parts of the body below the point at which the cord is severed become paralyzed.

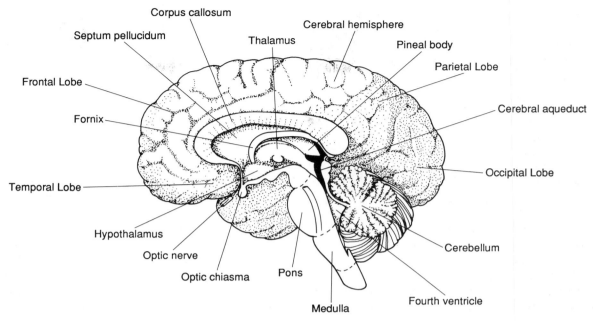

**FIGURE 2–6**    The nervous system: the brain.

*The cerebellum* at the back of the brain is a structure that maintains the body's balance and coordination by connecting to both motor and sensory centers. Injury to this part of the brain can cause jerky, uncoordinated movement called *ataxia*.

*The forebrain* is the highest part of the brain, and it consists of two parts: the *diencephalon* and the *telencephalon*.

Above the brain stem is the diencephalon consisting of the *thalamus* and the *hypothalamus*. The thalamus is a kind of relay station for sensory messages to various parts of the cerebrum in the telencephalon, as well as for motor messages to the skeletal muscles from the motor cortex of the cerebrum. The hypothalamus controls eating, drinking, and sexual activity, and maintains the temperature homeostasis of the body. The hypothalamus plays an important role in the recognition of pain, temperature, touch, and pressure, and as will be seen later in this chapter, is especially important in regulating the pituitary gland of the endocrine system.

The telencephalon consists of the *limbic system* and the *cerebrum*. The limbic system lies next to the diencephalon and plays an important role in the expression of emotions. The limbic system appears to be the seat of arousing emotions, such as anger, fear, and excitement.

The most highly developed part of the brain is the cerebrum, the surface of which is composed of billions of cells that form a gray layer called the cerebral cortex. The cerebrum is divided into motor areas that control muscular movement throughout the body, sensory areas that interpret sensory signals, and association areas that are concerned with emotional and intellectual processes. The cerebrum has two hemispheres, right and left, which are responsible for different types of processes. The motor cortex of each hemisphere controls movement on the opposite side of the body.

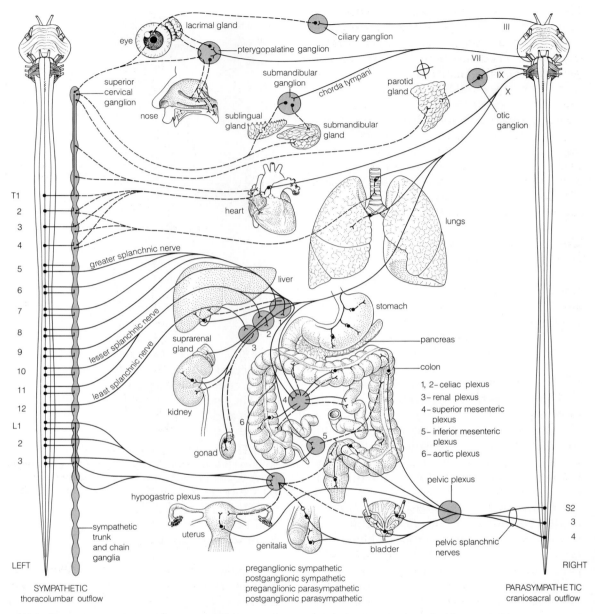

**FIGURE 2–6**  (continued)   The nervous system: the sympathetic and parasympathetic nervous systems.
SOURCE: From *Human Anatomy*, by I. Fowler. Coypright © 1984 by Wadsworth, Inc. Reprinted by permission of the publisher, Wadsworth Publishing Company, 10 Davis Drive, Belmont, CA, 94002.

The left hemisphere generally controls language processes, including speech and writing, and the right hemisphere controls visual imagery and the perception of music.

Each hemisphere has a frontal lobe, a parietal lobe, an occipital lobe, and a temporal lobe. The *frontal lobes* are involved in motor activities, as well as the association of ideas, self-awareness, speech (on the left), and emotion. Damage to the frontal lobes, such as in a frontal lobotomy, a surgery once done to reduce the symptoms of dangerous psychosis, can cause major alterations in personality and emotional reactions. The *temporal lobes* are sites of hearing and are involved in vision, memory, and speech (on the left). The *occipital lobes* contain the visual centers of the brain. Damage to them can cause blindness. The *parietal lobes* are involved in the perception of touch, as well as other bodily sensations such as pain, cold, and heat.

**The Peripheral Nervous System.** The peripheral nervous system conveys messages from the central nervous system to the muscles and glands and is divided into the somatic and the autonomic nervous systems.

The *somatic nervous system* involves *afferent neurons*, which carry messages to the spinal cord from sensory organs, and *efferent neurons*, which carry messages to skeletal muscles to initiate and sustain movement.

The *autonomic nervous system* controls internal organs, such as the glands and smooth muscles of the heart, lungs, blood vessels, lining of the stomach, and intestines. The autonomic nervous system is divided into the *sympathetic* and *parasympathetic* nervous systems. Under stress, the sympathetic nervous system dominates bodily functioning and speeds up heart rate, increases blood supply to the muscles, releases glucose, and dilates the bronchi of the lungs for increased oxygen consumption. The parasympathetic nervous system acts in opposition to the sympathetic to calm or quiet arousal responses. The parasympathetic nervous system is dominant during times of relaxation and functions to maintain the body in a condition of rest. It is also active in the digestion of food (see Figure 2–6).

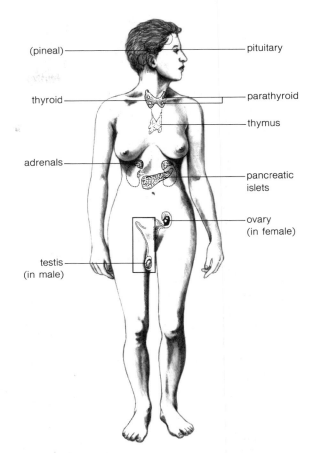

**FIGURE 2–7**  The endocrine system.
SOURCE:  From *Human Anatomy*, by I. Fowler. Copyright © 1984 by Wadsworth, Inc. Reprinted by permission of the publisher, Wadsworth Publishing Company, 10 Davis Drive, Belmont, CA, 94002.

**THE ENDOCRINE SYSTEM**

The *endocrine system* involves glands that are controlled by the autonomic nervous system. The glands in the endocrine system send messages to various parts of the body by releasing chemical substances called *hormones* directly into the bloodstream (see Figure 2–7).

The nervous and endocrine systems are linked by connections between the hypothalamus and the *pituitary gland*. The pituitary gland releases hormones into the blood that stimulate other glands to secrete their own hormones, which in turn affect physical and psychological functioning. When the sympathetic nervous system becomes aroused in response to an emergency, the hypothalamus chemically stimulates the pituitary to release ACTH (adrenocorticotropic hormone) into the blood. ACTH stimulates the release of other hormones in response to stress. The *adrenal glands*, located on top of the kidneys, are stimulated to produce *epinephrine* and *norepinephrine* (adrenalin and noradrenalin), which speed up the heart and respiration and increase the liver's output of sugar to the muscles. *Cortisol* is also released by the adrenal glands during perceived emergencies to help control swelling should injury occur. As we will see in Chapter 10, where we consider stress responses in more detail, these adrenal hormones can remain in the bloodstream long after the sympathetic nervous system response has quieted and they can be harmful to the body.

There are other glands in the endocrine system as well. These include the *thyroid* gland, which produces hormones that regulate general activity and growth. The thyroid gland is located in the neck. An excess of hormone results in *hyperthyroidism*, a condition characterized by insomnia, high activity levels, tremors, and weight loss. Hyperthyroidism is sometimes misdiagnosed as anxiety! A deficiency of thyroid hormone results in *hypothyroidism*, characterized by low levels of activity and the gaining of weight. The *thymus* gland is located in the chest and plays an important role in immunity. The thymus gland is where T-lymphocyte cells mature. Finally, the *pancreas*, located below the stomach, regulates the body's blood sugar levels. *Diabetes mellitus* is a condition in which the pancreas does not produce enough insulin. Diabetes can be controlled through diet and daily medication such as injection of insulin.

## THE IMMUNE SYSTEM

The *immune system* is the body's means of warding off foreign invaders, such as bacteria, fungi, protozoa, viruses, and carcinogenic substances. A general term for these foreign invaders is *antigens* (for "antibody generators"). Until recently, not much was known about the immune system, and most people took it for granted. With the advent of the *acquired immune deficiency syndrome*, the killer AIDS, there has been a burgeoning interest in research on how the immune system functions and what role it plays in keeping us healthy.

The *lymphatic* organs are primarily involved in immune responses. The lymphatic organs include bone marrow, the thymus gland, lymph nodes, lymph vessels, and the spleen. *Lymphocytes* are white blood cells that are critical in defending the body against antigens or foreign substances. They originate in the bone marrow, deep within the core of the bones. *Lymph nodes* are nodes of spongy tissue that are located in various parts of the body, including the neck, armpits, abdomen, and groin. Lymph nodes capture antigens and house lymphocytes and other white blood cells. The *spleen*, in the upper left side of the abdomen, filters out antigens and worn red blood cells from the blood. The spleen also houses white blood cells.

*Nonspecific immune response* involves a process called *phagocytosis* in which *phagocytes*, scavengers of the immune system, engulf and destroy antigens. The two types of phagocytes are *macrophages*, which remain attached to tissue, and *monocytes*, which freely circulate in the blood. Phagocytes are nonspecific in their action. They'll consume almost anything!

On the other hand, *specific immune responses* involve two types of immunological reactions: *humoral* and *cell-mediated* reactions. *Humoral immunity*, or antibody-mediated immunity, occurs when B-lymphocytes differentiate into plasma cells that produce antibodies to fight a foreign invader. *Antibodies* are protein molecules that attach to the surface of invading substances and help to arrange for their destruction by other elements of the immune system. They slow down an invader so that it can be destroyed by phagocytes. They also form a memory for the invader so that another like it in the future can be recognized and defended against more quickly. Finally, antibodies help to destroy the membrane of the offending microorganism. *Cell-mediated immunity* involves T-lymphocytes from the thymus gland, and is slower acting than humoral immunity. *T-cells* are infection-fighting white blood cells that have matured in the thymus gland, and their level of activity (along with lymphocyte activity) is a key element in immune system functioning. Instead of releasing antibodies into the blood, cell-mediated immunity depends directly upon T-cells. Killer T-cells directly invade tissue that is recognized as foreign, cancerous cells, and cells that have been invaded by antigens. Memory T-cells enable the body to defend itself against invaders that have been experienced in the past, by holding a memory for the invader. Helper T-cells stimulate lymphocytes to reproduce and attack invaders. And suppressor T-cells slow down or stop cell-mediated and humoral immunity when the antigen has been destroyed (Jemmott & Locke, 1984).

## Conducting Research in Health Psychology

Now let us turn to a discussion of the process of research in health psychology. In the remaining part of this chapter, we will examine issues of research design and measurement. These issues are central to the conduct of optimal research in the study of health, illness, and medical care.

A solid understanding of the details of design and measurement can serve an important purpose for the health psychologist. His or her understanding and evaluation of the existing research findings on any particular topic is always dependent upon the ability to evaluate critically the methodology used to arrive at those findings. Was the approach taken by the researchers appropriate, given what they attempted to conclude? Were the correct comparison groups employed and the right measurements utilized? Was the outcome caused by the intervention or by some entirely different phenomenon that we have yet to understand? The precise answer to each question may be less important than one's ability to answer the question.

We will learn some important general lessons about research in health psychology. First of all, findings in health psychology are typically not precise and are rarely clear-cut. When issues of health, illness, and medical care are examined, multiple factors operate. The people affected by illness (for example, the patient, the physician, and the patient's family) are embedded within such complexities of life that precision becomes impossible. The phenomena examined in health psychology research affect people in many, many ways, including physically, intellectually, emotionally, and socially.

Conducting optimal research on the psychology of health, illness, and medical care can be difficult because of the nature of the topics studied in this field. The issues are not simply and easily defined, causality is difficult to determine, and people's expectations can influence the phenomena under study.

Let's take an example. The notion that the mind influences bodily processes has turned out, in an age of self-interest and personal responsibility, to be a rather appealing notion to many people. The connection between our responses to stressful situations and our health, for instance, suggests that we may have some control over what happens to us ("mind over matter," if you will). We hope that if we have correct thoughts, we can triumph over disease. Such hopes may lead people to accept these possibilities as facts and the trends as clear causes. But the issue is not at all simple. As we will see in greater detail in Chapter 10, the idea that the character of one's thinking may play a role in one's health is supported by some current scientific findings. There is evidence that maladaptive responses to stress may have the power to make us sick. Maladaptive responses may include punishing ourselves emotionally when something goes wrong instead of figuring out what we can do to fix it, as well as feelings of self-blame for bad situations and a sense of hopelessness for the future (Seligman, 1975; Peterson & Seligman, 1984). Such thinking might, by way of complex mechanisms, lead to physical problems and emotional depression. There is some evidence, though not conclusive, that such thinking can lead to depression of the responses of the immune system (Jemmott & Locke, 1984; Peterson & Seligman, 1987; Seligman, 1975). Such preliminary evidence has prompted the popular press to display "Worrying Can Make You Sick" and other such provocative headlines. Some have touted relaxation as a means to eliminate everything from migraine headaches to cancerous tumors. These claims have been premature, however (Pelletier, 1977). Before the phenomenon can be completely understood, a great deal must be learned about the complex mechanisms involved (Kiecolt-Glaser & Glaser, 1986).

One final and very important point is that in some realms of health psychology, causality simply cannot be determined by the methods available. A true experiment might be impossible to carry out because of its prohibitive difficulty or lack of ethical justification. For example, subjects cannot be given terrible thoughts to think and the effect on their health assessed. Researchers must settle for much less direct ways of studying the complex manner in which thoughts can influence health. In general, these less direct ways leave a great deal of room for alternative explanations. Controversies arise.

## THE (CONTROVERSIAL) CANCER PERSONALITY

The notion that there is a cancer personality (a way of being that invites, or develops, cancer) illustrates what can go wrong when weaknesses in research methodology actually lead to inaccurate, though popular, conclusions. In 1956 two clinical psychologists published a review of research and theoretical literature (Le Shan & Worthington, 1956). In it they suggested that personality can play a part in the formation and development of cancer. The researchers presented what they considered to be three major threads that ran through all the studies they reviewed: people who had cancer were more likely than those without cancer (1) to be unable successfully to express hostile emotions, (2) to have more unresolved tension concerning a parental figure, and (3) to have more sexual disturbance. As one psychiatrist who wrote about the cancer personality described it, the person with cancer is ". . . driven into himself" (Evans, 1926).

Unfortunately, many people jumped to the conclusion that the inability to express hostile feelings as well as the repression of negative emotions and unresolved tensions can *cause* cancer. The popular press picked up the idea, saying that a person with a cancer personality is likely to develop malignant neoplasms. This idea worried and distressed many people. Such a conclusion was not justified, however; the research up to that point had never addressed the development of cancer.

In all the studies that had been reviewed, people who already had cancer were interviewed or subjected to a psychiatric examination. Many patients had recently received their diagnoses. They were asked about their current emotional state, their style of expressing anger, and about areas of conflict in their lives. They were interviewed by psychiatrists and psychologists who already believed in the cancer personality and who knew these people had cancer. These patients were compared with those who did not have cancer. As you may have already guessed, the fact that cancer patients had negative and even hostile feelings is not terribly surprising. They were suffering a great deal, they were in pain, and they felt very uncertain about their future survival. They may have thought "Why me?" Yet, no matter what they felt, they had to hold back their negative feelings lest they antagonize and alienate their health professionals and others around them. The psychological differences between people with cancer and those without can be easily explained by their state of mind at the time the research was done, as well as by the expectations of those who carried out the research.

Studies that avoided the serious methodological flaws of earlier research have failed to find a relationship between personality style and susceptibility to cancer (Levy, 1985b). Only one study so far has shown any promise in identifying personality factors that might play a role in the development of cancer (Dattore, Shontz, & Coyne, 1980). It employed a standardized psychological test of personality dimensions (primarily pathological ones), which was given to a large sample of people several years before any of them developed cancer. The test was the well-known Minnesota Multiphasic Personality Inventory. It was found that those who subsequently did develop cancer had scored higher on measures of repression and lower on self-

reports of depression than had those who had not developed cancer at the time of the study. More recent research published in the *Journal of the American Medical Association* (Zonderman, Costa, & McCrae, 1989) demonstrates no link between chronic feelings of depression and a person's likelihood of developing cancer. This study is held to be the first nationally representative study on the relationship between depression and the development of cancer.

Of course, despite this latest failure to find an effect, the question of whether people with certain personality traits have a greater chance than others of developing cancer remains open. It will be answered only with carefully and properly executed research.

Incorrect conclusions can be drawn from research that is not carried out properly. Research errors are usually avoidable, however. There are common tendencies that can be overcome with awareness and with considerable care in research design. It is hoped that you will learn to do this as students of health psychology.

Research need not be perfect in order to be valuable. Most research is flawed in some way, and nearly every study involves some compromises. It is critically important to know what can be logically concluded from a study as it was carried out and what cannot be concluded. A clinician who hopes to apply the findings of research to the treatment of patients needs to make distinctions between good and poor research. Those who plan to conduct research must learn to design the best possible studies to answer research questions with accuracy. The goal must be to rule out alternative explanations for the findings and to avoid logical inconsistencies in attempts to arrive at the truth.

In the next section, we will examine the major points of research design as they pertain to research in health psychology. We will examine the most common research flaws and consider how certain methodologies can lead us to correct conclusions and can form the basis for wise clinical decisions.

# Research Designs

## THE TRUE EXPERIMENT

The *true experiment*, or what in medical circles is called the *randomized clinical trial*, is a type of study from which a researcher can safely draw conclusions about causality. A statement that one phenomenon (measured by a variable) probably causes another is a *causal inference*. If a researcher is justified in drawing a causal inference about two phenomena, he or she can conclude with a high degree of certainty that Variable A causes Variable B. Thus, if there is a causal relationship between relaxation training and the control of headache pain, the implementation of relaxation through training *causes* a reduction in the severity and frequency of tension headaches. To be able to come to the point of drawing such a conclusion, the researcher would have to assign experimental subjects on a random basis to one of two treatment conditions: the *experimental group*, which receives the intended treatment, and the *control group*, which does not. *Random assignment* means that a random process (like the toss of a coin) has been used to determine whether any given subject receives the experimental treatment (in this case, the relaxation training) or the control treatment (simply some attention). After administration of the treatments, measurements would be made to determine how many tension headaches were experienced by subjects in the experimental and control groups and how severe those headaches were judged to be by the subjects. The two groups of subjects in the experiment are assumed, by virtue of their random assignment, to have been equal in headache frequency and severity before administration of the treatments. Thus, any differences between them after administration of the treatments are presumed to be the result of relaxation training.

Methodologically, this is the ideal design. The researcher has control over what happens to subjects; differences between the experimental and control groups are known to be due to the treatments administered and not to the factors that differentiated the groups before the study began (such as the desire to relax). It is known which variable is the "cause" and which is the "caused." (See Chesney & Shelton, 1976, for an actual experimental study of relaxation and biofeedback in reducing the incidence of tension headaches.)

True experiments (randomized clinical trials) are particularly useful for testing the efficacy of specific interventions or treatments. If a researcher wants to know whether a particular drug, medical procedure, or psychological intervention really works, the best bet is to conduct a true experiment. Then one can be sure that the treatment is what brought about the results.

In health psychology research, a true experiment, or randomized clinical trial, is a rather rare occurrence. The phenomena that are studied in health psychology often have far-reaching implications for subjects. It is one thing if a particular phenomenon occurs naturally in a subject's life and the researcher chooses to examine it. It is quite another, however, if the experimenter imposes the phenomenon on the subject. For example, researchers would find it virtually impossible to justify on ethical grounds the experimental administration of severe emotional stress to subjects in order to observe the effects of such stress on their health. Since many such issues are addressed by health psychologists, true experiments are relatively rare in the field.

## CORRELATION AND CAUSATION

A correlation between two variables tells nothing about their causal relationship. This is probably one of the most important facts in the methodology of psychological research, yet it is one of the most easily forgotten. A correlation refers simply to the covariation between two measures. When one measure goes up, the other goes up as well, if the correlation is positive. For example, the more stress a person experiences during a given time period, the more illness the person reports having sustained during that time period (Holmes & Masuda, 1974). If the correlation is negative, when the measure of one variable goes up, the measure of the other comes down.

It is fairly tempting, though usually incorrect, to conclude that two variables between which there is a significant correlation are indeed connected causally, that is, that one causes the other. In the realm of research linking stress and illness, this is precisely what early researchers did.

If two variables are correlated, it is just as possible for Variable A to cause Variable B as vice versa. Illness might just as easily cause stressful life events as be caused by them. For example, a male patient's undiagnosed illness might bring about tremendous fatigue, mental confusion, and a distortion in emotional reactions. Such upsets in day-to-day functioning might lead him to experience stressful life events, such as the loss of his job, divorce, and foreclosure on a mortgage. If the illness is later diagnosed, it may appear that the stressful life events caused the illness, though in fact they resulted from it. Or, there might be a third variable that caused the two measured ones. For example, his personality style may have led him to act in certain ways that brought about the problems perceived to be stressful life events. Perhaps he is very irresponsible and as a result loses his house to foreclosure and repeatedly smashes up his car. Perhaps he cannot face emotional distress, and so he translates it into real or imagined physical symptoms. Personality style could be what accounts for his disordered life *and* his poor health. Further, it is possible that an undiagnosed, slow-growing brain tumor has caused the disturbing personality characteristics, which in turn have caused both the stressful life events and illness behavior. The possibilities for explanation of a correlation are many. Thus, when two phenomena *covary*, they change in relation to one another. They are connected somehow, though not necessarily in a direct causal relationship.

Correlational studies can present problems to the researcher who wishes to draw causal connections between the variables. However, correlational studies do have some value. They can and often do provide some useful information. Sometimes, a convincing argument can be made that one variable causes another. This can be done if the researcher can trace logically the pathways by which the variables might be connected to one another. And this can also be done if the researcher can eliminate the explanations that compete with the causal one.

Figure 2–8 illustrates one way in which a correlational study done at two points in time can establish a causal relationship between stressful life events and illness. A large sample of subjects is assessed on the same measures at Time 1, and then again at Time 2, two years later. At both points in time, subjects report on the stressful life changes they have experienced over the previous two years (the measure of stress), as well as on precisely what their health

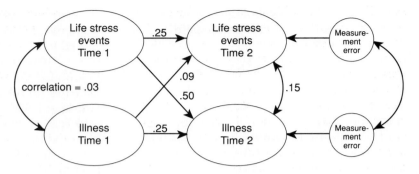

**FIGURE 2–8**  Hypothetical simple causal model linking stress and illness.

status has been during those two years (the measure of illness). In Figure 2–8 stress at Time 1 is positively correlated with illness at Time 2, and the other correlations (particularly that between illness at Time 1 and stress at Time 2) are close to zero.

The correlations in the figure show that stress and illness do not occur simultaneously. Rather, stress at Time 1 is related to illness at Time 2. This suggests that the experience of stressful life events may result in subsequent illness. Although causality cannot be determined from this correlational research, suggestions of causation can be made somewhat more confidently than if correlations between variables had been based on measurement at Time 1 alone.

## PROSPECTIVE VERSUS RETROSPECTIVE STUDIES

*Down's syndrome* (also known as mongolism or trisomy 21) is a genetic condition caused by chromosomal abnormalities that occur at conception. Down's syndrome produces mental retardation, abnormal facial features, and often serious physical abnormalities, such as heart disorders. It is obvious at birth that children with Down's syndrome are not normal. The risk of giving birth to a Down's baby is related to the age of the mother. The risk goes up significantly after the maternal age of 35.

Although it is now known that faulty division of chromosomes is responsible for Down's syndrome, it was once believed that Down's syndrome was caused by maternal anxiety (Brown, 1974). The research that concluded this involved interviewing mothers of normal babies and mothers of Down's babies soon after the birth. Mothers were asked to describe their pregnancies, particularly their feelings during pregnancy. Not surprisingly, mothers of Down's babies described their pregnancies in much more anxious terms than did mothers of healthy babies, leading the researchers to their erroneous conclusions.

This study used a method known as *retrospective* data collection. Subjects were asked to report on something in the past, and to recall what happened and how they experienced it. One major problem with retrospective studies is that the events occurring at a given time in a person's life tend to influence his or her recollection of past events. A phenomenon called *state-dependent memory* (Fischer, 1976; Fischer & Landon, 1972) partly accounts for the unreliability of retrospective reports. People tend to remember most easily the events of their past that are connected with the same emotional state they feel at the time of recall. If someone is highly anxious, he or she will recall best the instances in which the overriding emotion was anxiety. Recollections of the past are tied to the emotions experienced. Reports of facts are biased systematically by emotions.

To avoid selective recollection, a researcher must conduct studies prospectively. *Prospective research* requires that the predictor measure (in the above example, maternal anxiety) be assessed well in advance of the outcome (in this case, the child's health status). In practice, prospective research can be quite difficult to carry out. In the case noted above, one would have to design a study in which throughout the course of pregnancy, the anxiety level of the prospective mothers would be measured with questionnaires or interviews. The measures would then be saved and analyzed months later in relation to the birth outcomes of the women in the study, that is, whether or not their babies had Down's syndrome. Since the study is not a true experiment but is only correlational, we cannot know for sure whether there is a causal relationship. We can determine whether Down's syndrome and maternal anxiety covary, however. If they do, then we might undertake an attempt to determine causality. Since a true experiment would be unethical, we must use other means to close in on the truth.

## LONGITUDINAL VERSUS CROSS-SECTIONAL RESEARCH

Compared with younger ones, aged medical patients tend to be very passive in their interactions with their physicians. Older patients ask very few questions of their doctors, submit passively to medical recommendations, and rarely speak up if they are dissatisfied with their medical care. An important question is, Do meekness and lack of assertiveness increase with age?

*Cross-sectional research* on this phenomenon would involve measuring variables on different groups of people of various ages, for example, people in their 20s, 40s, 60s, and 80s. Various aspects of the subjects' interactions with physicians may be assessed along with attitudes that these people hold on the subject of asserting oneself with one's doctor. Suppose that in cross-sectional research one finds that 20- and 40-year-olds ask more questions of their doctors, interrupt their doctors more, and state more opinions on recommended treatments than do 60- and 80-year-olds. Does this mean that as people get older they become less assertive with their medical professionals? Perhaps they do, but the present study does not show this. In fact, the present study demonstrates simply that people in the older age groups are less assertive than are people in younger age groups. The difference might be due to factors other than age. Perhaps their passivity is due to their growing up at a time when few people questioned physician authority. The period of time in which they were born, or their *age cohort*, may be the most important determinant of their actions.

The only way to find out what happens to people as they age is to assess them *as they age.* This would be a *longitudinal study.* An excellent example of a prospective longitudinal study is the Framingham Heart Study, a major investigation of the risk factors for coronary disease. In Framingham, Massachusetts, 2,282 men and 2,845 women who were initially free of coronary heart disease (CHD) have been followed bienially since 1949 for the development of CHD. The researchers on this huge project have collected extensive information about each subject's life history, habits, both physical and emotional stresses, and measures of personality and psychosocial states, in addition to data from medical assessments. This research has shed considerable light on the role of many physical and psychological variables on the development of heart disease. Because of its longitudinal nature, the study is able to show the clear effect on heart disease of such factors as cigarette smoking, weight, cholesterol level, diet, exercise, the management of stress, and many other variables. (See Haynes, Levine, Scotch, Feinleib, & Kannel, 1978, for an example of one of the psychosocial studies conducted within the Framingham Heart Study.)

A researcher's choice of method can be as critical in studies of the psychology of health and illness as it is in other aspects of the medical field. Avoiding errors in the design of research and drawing appropriate conclusions from studies as they are done are difficult and have particular importance in this field. The results of such research in health psychology are often applied directly to patient care. Erroneous conclusions could lead to misunderstanding of the whole picture of a patient's illness, and when applied clinically, could do more harm than good.

# Measurement Techniques in the Study of Health, Illness, and Medical Care

Conducting sound research in health psychology involves choosing the most effective and the most accurate ways to measure both psychological and health phenomena. Because the manner in which a phenomenon has been measured determines how it can be interpreted, a researcher must be extremely careful with measurement choices.

On the following pages, we will examine some of the measurement techniques that are typically used in studies of health and illness. In doing so, we will focus on one measurement goal and see how it can be approached in several different ways.

Our goal will be to measure patient satisfaction with medical treatment. Patient-satisfaction measurements have a rather long history in health psychology and in the related fields of public health and health services research (Ware, Davies-Avery, & Stewart, 1978). In assessing patient satisfaction, we want to determine the extent to which patients of several physicians are satisfied with the treatments they have received, and to compare physicians in terms of the satisfaction felt by their patients. In utilizing various assessment techniques, we will approach the problem by defining satisfaction in several ways: in terms of patient self-reports, in terms of patient choice of preferred medical care provider, and in terms of the very subtle behaviors that occur in physician-patient interaction.

# Assessing Patient Satisfaction

The following are four methods for approaching the assessment of patient satisfaction with medical treatment. Each has its advantages and disadvantages.

## REVIEW OF DOCUMENTS

To find out something about an individual, one might try to examine where he or she has been and what he or she has been doing. The *review of documents* approach to measurement is based upon the simple theory that everyone leaves tracks (Webb, Campbell, Schwartz, Sechrest, & Grove, 1981)! To find out where people have been and what they have done, the theory goes, one should not ask them. One should look for the evidence they have left behind.

So, let's consider what kinds of evidence might give us clues to a patient's satisfaction with his or her physician's care. First, we can hypothesize that if a patient is satisfied, he or she will be more likely to continue to return to that physician. Thus, we may choose to look to physician appointment records as a source of information about patient satisfaction with medical treatment. By carefully scanning a physician's appointment records, for example, a researcher can determine how many times patients cancel appointments, whether patients have made reappointments, and how many patients went away one day, never to return. Analyzing these records can be especially enlightening because the researcher can compare two or more physicians according to retention rate for patients. Those who have a low rate of patient dropouts are presumed to be better satisfying their patients (see DiMatteo, Hays, & Prince, 1986).

One advantage of this approach is that the document measures are *nonreactive*. That is, the researcher cannot influence the phenomenon he or she is measuring by the act of measuring it. The data are there, period. All the researcher has to do is to tabulate the measures and interpret them.

Interpretation can sometimes be difficult, however, because document (or archival) measures don't always bear a straightforward relationship to what is being studied. In the present example, one must make assumptions about the meaning of a patient's failure to return to a physician. It is likely that if a patient fails to return to one doctor and goes instead to another, the cause was patient dissatisfaction with the doctor's care, but this is not necessarily the case. The patient's action might instead reflect the steep fees charged by the first doctor or the fact that the patient's health insurance will not reimburse the patient for charges from that physician. The method is not foolproof, of course, but it can provide some valuable information.

## INTERVIEWS

Perhaps the most famous example of the use of the interview technique is the work of Alfred C. Kinsey, one of the most widely known scientists of the 20th century (Pomeroy, 1972). Kinsey and his colleagues interviewed over 18,000 adults from all walks of life about the most intimate details of their sexual behavior. The interviews took place during the 1940s and 1950s, when talking about sex was an uncomfortable thing for many (maybe even most) people to do. During interviews with Kinsey and his staff, respondents gave detailed accounts of their masturbation practices, their premarital and extramarital sexual experiences, and even the more unusual aspects of their sexuality, such as their experiences having sex with animals.

Kinsey was able to elicit such information from his subjects because of his very effective interviewing style. He would never ask *whether* a respondent had engaged in a particular activity but, rather, asked *how often* he or she had done so. For example, he would ask, "How many times have you had a sexually transmitted disease?" rather than "You've never had an STD, have you?" Kinsey was able to bypass his subjects' inhibitions by careful framing and timing of questions. The face-to-face interview was, in the case of Kinsey's work, an invaluable tool for gathering some important and very sensitive information. (We examine the health interview in more detail in Chapter 7.)

To measure patient satisfaction with medical care, a researcher can interview patients directly and ask them to express their degree of satisfaction with their physician. In fact, much of the research over the past twenty years on patient reaction to medical care has employed interviews. In these studies, patients were approached by a researcher at a doctor's office or in a clinic and asked to answer a few simple questions.

This method worked well in a study of patients at an inner-city free clinic (DiMatteo, Prince, & Taranta, 1979). After their visits with the doctor in the outpatient clinic, patients were required to wait for visits with the nurse, who would give them instructions and, if necessary, their prescriptions. During this waiting time, a young researcher in a white coat requested permission for an interview "to ask a few questions about your medical care." The questions were what researchers call *provider specific*. That is, patients were asked to respond to the questions in terms of how they felt about the physician they had just seen. In other research, patients have been asked to give their impressions of physicians in general, not just of their own physicians (Ware, Davies-Avery, & Stewart, 1978; Hulka, Zyzanski, Cassel, & Thompson, 1970).

Interviews can be very valuable, partly because they have a high degree of *immediacy*. Interviewer and interviewee are involved in a brief but relatively intense interpersonal interaction with each other. There is a specific goal: to elicit information from the latter about items on the former's agenda. The immediacy allows for an intense focus on the agenda issues.

Interviewers have considerable control over the measurement situation. It is very difficult for a respondent to ignore a face-to-face encounter with an interviewer or even to avoid a particular question. Certainly, at the start of the interview respondents can refuse to participate; however, once they have agreed to start, they usually feel compelled to continue.

An advantage of the interview over other methods is that in an interview the precise nature of the information requested can be made clear to the interviewee. If the interviewee does not understand the questions being asked, he or she can ask for clarification.

Table 2–1 contains an example of the interview format that was used in some research on the determinants of patient satisfaction (DiMatteo & Taranta, 1979). The

goal of each interview was to assess the particular patient's satisfaction with the medical care delivered to him or her by a specific physician. The interviewers were bilingual.

In the example in Table 2–1 the questions asked are fairly straightforward, and a scale of response options is provided. The seven possible responses were printed in large block letters on a card shown by the interviewer to the patient. These response options were presented so that patients' answers would be limited to a specific kind of response, and so that patients' answers might be compared. This is an example of a *closed-ended question* or statement. With a closed-ended item, certain response alternatives are offered, and the respondent must choose the one that best matches how he or she feels.

The *open-ended question* leaves a subject free to respond in any way that he or she wishes. The researcher then must try to make sense of the responses and develop a scheme for coding them so that the patients' responses can be compared. Here is a very simple example. Suppose that the interviewer merely asks the patient, "In your own words, please tell me how you feel about your doctor." The researcher can set up categories for coding the responses (for example, a positive versus negative evaluation of the doctor). The researcher would then make a judgment about each response. Some statements would be very easy to code, such as "I like my doctor very much." Others may be ambiguous, such as "At least he seems to know what he's doing." There is obviously room for bias in the coding because it is based upon subjective judgment.

The possibility also exists that respondents' answers can be biased. Such bias can be the direct result of the interviewer's expectations about the results. In research on evaluations of physicians, an interviewer could have a particular bias in favor

---

**TABLE 2–1    Interview Format for Patient Satisfaction Evaluations**

[Interviewer: Determine patient's primary language. Conduct interview in Spanish if necessary.]

*Directions to be read to the patient:*   We are studying patients' satisfaction with their doctors so that we may learn more about how doctors and patients get along. We hope that this may help to improve health care for patients at all health care centers. If you will answer the following questions, you will help out the study a great deal. It should take only about two minutes of your time. Thank you for your help.

[Interviewer: Read questions, statements, and response alternatives to the patient and write the response given by the patient on this interview format.]

1.  How old are you? ____
    What language do you speak at home? _____
    Sex of patient: interviewer circle    MALE    FEMALE

2.  Is this the first visit you have had with the doctor you have just seen?  YES  NO
    (If NO): How many other visits have you had with this doctor?

    ____One other visit before this visit
    ____Two other visits before this visit
    ____More than two other visits before this visit

[Interviewer: For the next three questions, hold up card with answer format printed in large block letters. Request patient to choose one of the seven responses.]

7 ____MORE THAN ALL OTHER DOCTORS
6 ____MORE THAN MOST OTHER DOCTORS
5 ____MORE THAN SOME OTHER DOCTORS
4 ____ABOUT THE SAME AS OTHER DOCTORS
3 ____LESS THAN SOME OTHER DOCTORS
2 ____LESS THAN MOST OTHER DOCTORS
1 ____LESS THAN ALL OTHER DOCTORS

Answer format printed in large block letters and held up for patient to see.

3.  Please pick the answer that tells how much this doctor can help you compared to other doctors (answer format above).

4.  Please pick the answer that best tells how much this doctor cares about you as a person (answer format above).

5.  Please pick the answer that best tells how well this doctor can tell if you are worried (answer format above).

---

of one physician or another, perhaps as a result of personal feelings or expectations about the research outcomes. Because the interview format allows personal interac-tion between the collector and the provider of the data, the interviewer's biases can be communicated. This communication usu-ally is not verbal; that is, the interviewer does not actually tell the patient what he or she expects the patient to say. However, the interviewer typically communicates through nonverbal cues of facial expressions, body movements, and tone of voice approval or disapproval of a patient's response. Interviewer reaction may be something as subtle as the pupils of the eyes dilating, or the smile-muscles around the mouth contracting very slightly when asking, "In your own words, please tell me how you feel about your doctor." Such biases can jeopardize the objectivity of the data that are collected through the interview technique.

## QUESTIONNAIRES

Another method that researchers have employed to evaluate patient satisfaction with medical care is the written questionnaire. In a study by DiMatteo and Hays (1980), English-speaking patients were asked to fill out a 25-item questionnaire immediately after a visit with their physician. They indicated their degree of agreement with each of the various statements by marking one number of the five presented. In Table 2–2 some of the statements and the response format from this research are presented.

An obvious advantage of the questionnaire approach is that the researcher has little opportunity to bias respondents' evaluations. The patient records reactions to the various statements in accordance with level of satisfaction with the physician. Note that some of the items (3 and 4) are phrased so that agreement with the statement indicates a positive evaluation of the physician; others are phrased so that disagreement with the statement indicates a positive evaluation of the physician. The items are balanced in this way to prevent the bias that would result if a patient were to agree with most or all statements regard-

less of content. If all items were worded in the same direction (that is, with agreement indicating a positive response), it would be impossible to tell whether any patient was actually evaluating the physician positively or instead simply tending to agree with questionnaire statements (or a little of both). The ideal questionnaire has a roughly equal mixture of positively and negatively worded statements.

Of course, a patient can respond accurately only if he or she understands what is being asked. Unfortunately, one important disadvantage of the questionnaire method is that the respondent could fail to read the directions and thus not know what is expected. The respondent could follow the response format incorrectly and even misunderstand the statements to which responses are called for. If the patients are not careful in reading and writing answers, the data from the questionnaires could fail to reflect what they really feel. The researcher's presence might help to minimize these potential problems because the researcher can aid respondents to understand what they are being asked to do. Although such involvement does not guarantee quality data, it does increase the chances that patients will accurately record what they feel and believe. Questionnaires, of course, can be administered to very large groups of subjects, even thousands of them at a time.

There is no way to guarantee that patients will really respond to what is being requested of them. For example, a patient might be very upset at the way a clinic is run, at the inefficiency of the scheduling, and at the fact that there are no rest rooms near the waiting room. But because the physician's behavior is the only thing the patient is asked about, the patient expresses dissatisfaction with that. The satisfaction questionnaire gives the patient the opportunity to vent disapproval of factors unrelated to the physician's behavior.

**TABLE 2–2   Questionnaire Used in Patient Satisfaction Study**

*Directions to the patient:*   Here are some statements people sometimes make about the way their doctors treat them. Think about the doctor you have just had a visit with and rate how much you agree with each statement ABOUT THAT PARTICULAR DOCTOR. The higher the number you circle, the more you agree with the statement. The lower the number you circle, the more you disagree with the statement AS IT PERTAINS TO THE PARTICULAR DOCTOR YOU HAVE JUST SEEN. Please circle only one number for each statement.

Remember to answer about the doctor you have just seen.

| | Strongly disagree | Mildly disagree | Uncertain | Mildly agree | Strongly agree |
|---|---|---|---|---|---|
| 1. This doctor always listens to everything I have to say. | 1 | 2 | 3 | 4 | 5 |
| 2. This doctor always seems to know what he/she is doing. | 1 | 2 | 3 | 4 | 5 |
| 3. This doctor acts like I don't have any feelings. | 1 | 2 | 3 | 4 | 5 |
| 4. I feel this doctor does not spend enough time with me. | 1 | 2 | 3 | 4 | 5 |
| 5. I have a great deal of confidence in this doctor. | 1 | 2 | 3 | 4 | 5 |

## OBSERVATIONS OF BEHAVIOR

Another approach to the assessment of phenomena such as patient satisfaction is not to ask what people think but to observe what they do. Sometimes it is possible for us to infer psychological states (emotion or attitude, for example) from actions. Other times we simply make statements about the actions. In either case, observing the behaviors themselves can tell us quite a lot about what is occurring in the relationship between physician and patient.

Suppose we are interested in determining how well a particular patient gets along with a particular physician. On the basis of previous research, we would define the meaning of various nonverbal behaviors. Suppose we note ahead of time that frowns,

side-to-side shaking of the head, closed-arm position, body orientation away from the doctor, and hostile voice tone on the part of the patient indicate that the patient probably does not like the doctor or is uncomfortable or displeased with the doctor's treatment. On the other hand, the patient's smiles, head nods, open-arm positions, leaning toward the doctor, and friendly voice tone indicate that the patient probably likes the doctor and is satisfied with the doctor's care.

The researcher's goal is to videotape or somehow record the actual interaction between doctor and patient so that the incidence of the nonverbal cues listed above might be tabulated for each patient. Live observations could be made, and a coder

---

**TABLE 2–3   Coding Format for Videotaped Physician-Patient Interaction**

*Directions for coders*: Watch and listen to each videotaped segment very carefully. After each, answer the following questions. If you are not sure of your answer, play the videotape segment over again, and pay careful attention so that you can pick up the information you missed. Indicate on your coding format the number of times you played the videotaped segment.

1. What was the doctor's predominant facial expression?
   (circle one)   frowning   smiling
2. Did the doctor make eye contact with the patient?
   (circle one)   never   sometimes   often   constantly
3. Did the doctor shake hands with the patient?
   (circle one)   no   yes
4. Did the doctor orient his/her body toward or away from the patient?
   (circle one)   toward the patient   away from the patient
5. What was the doctor's tone of voice?
   (circle one on each line)   cold   warm
   friendly   businesslike
   hostile   not hostile

---

could record the nonverbal cues of concern. However, because of the practical difficulties of conducting this research properly, it would be better to record the doctor-patient interactions on videotape so that many observers can evaluate the nonverbal behaviors. Disagreements between raters can be resolved if there exists a recording that can be carefully reviewed. Table 2–3 contains an example of a format that might be used to code the behaviors of the physician in a physician-patient interaction.

Observing actual physician-patient interactions can also tell a researcher precisely how patients behave in response to what their practitioners do. Presumably, one might also be able to determine the precise effect that patient behavior has upon practitioner behavior by examining the nonverbal behaviors of physicians in response to the behaviors of their patients. In any case, the meaning of the nonverbal cues

must be known (or hypothesized) ahead of time or else determined from very careful research examination.

## RESEARCH: THE FIELD AND THE LABORATORY

One of the primary choices a health psychologist must make is whether research will be conducted in the laboratory or in the field. To consider this issue, we must begin with some definitions.

*Laboratory research* involves conditions of experimentation and/or of observation over which the researcher has a measure of control. When subjects come to the researcher's laboratory or office, for example, it is possible to control subjects' experiences as well as the manner in which their responses are measured. In a laboratory study, the researcher can minimize the extraneous factors that might inhibit correct interpretation of the research findings. Because the researcher has control over what happens in the study, the findings are usually quite clear.

In a *field study*, on the other hand, the goal is to understand events that occur naturally. Although the researcher can develop very accurate, sophisticated methods for measuring what he or she observes, he or she can exercise very little control over the variables being studied. The research takes place on the subject's "turf," in the subject's own environment. The researcher may sometimes have difficulty interpreting what he or she has observed in a field study because so little is under the researcher's control.

Let's consider, for example, research on patients' responses to physicians' *nonverbal communications* (that is, communications without words). Suppose that we are interested specifically in physicians' expressions of caring and concern to their patients. We choose to consider not what they say but rather how they say it (that is, voice tone). We also decide to examine their facial expressions and body movements in terms of specific actions that we believe signify caring.

In one approach, which would qualify as a laboratory study, the researcher might employ a physician and a patient (or actors to portray physician and patient). The researcher would design, direct, and videotape (or film) three different "scripts." In all three scripts, the verbal communications would be exactly the same, but certain nonverbal cues would change from script to script. For example, in the first script the "physician" would shake hands with the "patient" at the beginning and end of the visit. In the second script, the physician would smile often and nod. In the third, the physician would maintain a considerable amount of eye contact with the patient. Except for the specific nonverbal cues that were designed to vary among the scripts,

all other verbal and nonverbal communications from the physician would be the same in all three of the videotapes. The patient's behavior would, of course, be precisely the same in all the videotapes. Then, several people (perhaps even actual patients) would be asked to observe the three videotapes. At the end of each tape, the observers would be asked to evaluate the physician's behavior. A set of rating scales would be developed so that subjects' responses could be recorded accurately and the evaluations of the videotapes could be compared. Because of the controlled methodology, the researcher could be sure that differences in evaluation of the physician in the three videotapes were the result of the specific nonverbal behaviors enacted rather than of any other factors.

This laboratory study lacks what psychologists call *external validity*, which refers to the extent to which research findings (in this case, of the laboratory study) are applicable to the real world. If the laboratory study is conducted in a way that differs greatly from what occurs in real life (for example, respondents watch physicians on videotape rather than interact with them in person), we might doubt that we have learned much about a real phenomenon.

A different kind of approach to studying the relationship between physicians' nonverbal behaviors and patients' responses can be taken by carrying out a field study. The researcher must arrange to videotape a large number of medical visits in which physicians and patients interact, and the patients must respond to a questionnaire administered after the visits. On the questionnaire, the patient is asked to indicate how satisfied he or she is with the physician's treatment during the visit, particularly with expressions of caring and concern. Then, the researcher's task is to review the videotapes and to record which nonverbal cues were used by each physician. The researcher would record whether the physician shook hands with the patient at the beginning and/or the end of the visit, how often the physician smiled and nodded, and how much eye contact was maintained. The researcher must then correlate the tabulated nonverbal communications with the patient satisfaction ratings.

This particular field study presents a problem of causal inference because it involves correlational research: there is no way to know whether the physicians' nonverbal cues were the cause or the result of their patients' satisfaction with care. Further, the nonverbal cues were not isolated in the way that they had been in the videotapes. It is likely that many cues operated simultaneously, making it impossible to determine which did and which did not contribute to patient satisfaction.

Field research is not all correlational, of course. By definition, field research takes place in settings that are beyond the control of the researcher, and often such a situation produces correlational data. However, it is entirely possible for a researcher to manipulate conditions of a study so that it is somewhat under his or her control. Had the researcher above been able somehow to program the behaviors of the doctors and then measure patient responses, the study would have involved more control on the part of the researcher. It would also have been more like a study done in the laboratory.

It is probably most instructive to think of laboratory and field research as a continuum instead of as a dichotomy. Some studies, such as the first one described, are clearly laboratory research. Others, like the second, are almost purely field research (except for imposition of the videotape machine). The third study and others like it combine characteristics of both laboratory and field. The issue of importance is how

### BOX 2–1

### FIELD STUDY JOURNAL: THE DOCTORS

#### APRIL 17, 1975

For the past couple of weeks, I have been attempting to schedule the interns and residents to fill out the various psychological tests, as well as the measure of nonverbal communication sensitivity. This research is nothing like what I have experienced back at home, on campus. There, subjects come to me, I test them, they leave . . . simple. Here, at the hospital, I seem to be always chasing after doctors. I ask them to fill out my questionnaires and offer to pick up their X rays and run to get them coffee so they can take the time to fill out my test items. Each piece of data is obtained only with a considerable struggle.

And when I do finally corner a young doctor to participate in my study, I feel pangs of guilt at taking his or her time. Not only am I potentially interfering with patient care, I am asking for some of the very precious time they have to themselves. One resident fell asleep in the middle of testing today. He later apologized, explaining that he had been so overwhelmed with patient-care responsibilities that he had a total of about ten hours sleep in the past five days.

Some of the physicians are very kind and cooperative; they say they are happy to contribute to a research project that will help doctor-patient relationships some day. I hope my research can achieve this goal.

much control the researcher can have over the variables being studied, how they are operationalized, whether they can be manipulated, and how they can be interpreted.

Field research can be very difficult to carry out, particularly in health psychology. The settings can be inconvenient, noisy, and confusing. For example, research that takes place in a hospital clinic is an interference in the normal flow of activity there. The researcher is very often out of place.

Further, research issues in health psychology are quite complex. It can be very difficult for a researcher to know if he or she is actually tackling the issues that are of importance. When a researcher is studying physician-patient communication, for example, many aspects of the topic are relevant and need to be addressed.

Boxes 2–1 and 2–2 describe some of the difficulties encountered by a health psychologist conducting research in the medical setting. These boxes present excerpts from her field study journal. The field study for which the journal was written took place in 1975 and 1976 at a large teaching hospital on the East Coast. The researcher's

**BOX 2-2**

## FIELD STUDY JOURNAL: INTERVIEWING PATIENTS

### APRIL 18, 1975

Today was my first day in the outpatient clinic. I think I learned the first rule of conducting research in a hospital: WEAR A WHITE COAT!! Professional image is everything. Naively, I arrived wearing brown slacks and a white blouse with a colorful scarf. An older man asked me if I was the Avon lady [a door-to-door retailer of cosmetics]. Then he asked me for a date.

The clinic is incredibly busy. There is almost constant frenetic activity among the nurses and doctors. The clinic is overcrowded. Most of the patients receive their care for free or for a very slight cost. Some of them wait three or four hours to see a doctor. Many patients are very lonely, old, and poor. The younger ones are unemployed. Much of their treatment is carried out perfunctorily, with little time for anything but the barest necessities. Many are relieved to have someone to talk to.

Adhering to my interview format is very difficult. Patients want to tell me all about themselves and their medical and personal problems; they want consolation. Each three-minute interview is taking an hour. At this rate, I'll have the study completed in ten years! I must become more efficient at interviewing; I must insist that patients stick to the interview format and answer only the questions they are asked.

Yet, their needs tug at me emotionally. My goal in this research is to improve patient care, particularly the treatment of patients' psychological needs. And here is my chance to help individual people who need someone to talk to, who need information about their medical care, who need assistance in making decisions. But, if I fill the needs of the patients with whom I come in contact every day in the clinic, I will not be able to complete my research. And my research may help more patients in the long run. I am hoping that it will shed light on the complex relationship between doctors and patients and illuminate the role of the doctor's personality and communication skill in the care of patients' emotional needs.

goal was to assess several aspects of the personality and nonverbal communication skills of interns and residents in internal medicine who had completed medical school and were receiving postgraduate training. The researcher wanted to correlate these measures with the ratings made by the physicians' patients regarding satisfaction with care. Thus, the study involved giving personality tests and a videotape test of nonverbal communication to the physicians, as well as interviewing approximately ten patients of each physician after their visits in the hospital's outpatient clinic. As the field study journal demonstrates, the task of collecting these data was filled with difficulties. As in many areas of endeavor in health psychology, the research presented tremendous challenges to the researcher's patience and perseverance.

# Summary

I. Chapter 2 provided the basic groundwork for the study of the psychology of health, illness, and medical care. We began with a "crash course" in medical terminology, moved to a very brief overview of anatomy and physiology and the systems of the body, and ended with a more lengthy discussion of the basics of research methodology in health psychology.

II. Conducting research or practice in health psychology requires a working knowledge of medical terminology. The health psychologist needs such knowledge to understand some important issues, such as the meaning and the implications of certain diseases for patient health, and to communicate effectively with medical professionals.

III. Medical terminology can probably be learned most effectively by learning the meaning of various word compo-

nents (roots and stems) and combining these components into a medical word. The definitions of most medical terms can be arrived at by analyzing their component parts. The chapter examined medical terminology in the following areas: surgical operations, branches of science that deal with the study of the body; the medical specialties; common prefixes used in medical terminology; some

IV. Greek and Latin derivatives used in medical terminology.

This chapter presented a very brief overview of the following systems of the body: the skeletal system, the muscular system, the cardiovascular system, the respiratory system, the gastrointestinal system, the nervous system, the endocrine system, and the immune system.

V. The study of research methodology and measurement is extremely important for the health psychologist. Understanding and evaluation of existing research findings depend upon the ability to evaluate methodology.

A. Conducting optimal research on the psychology of health, illness, and medical care can be difficult because of the nature of the topics studied in this field. Issues are not simply and easily defined, causality is difficult to determine, and expectations can influence the phenomena under study.

B. In health psychology, causality sometimes simply cannot be determined by the methods available. A true experiment may be unethical or impossible to do.

C. The methods examined include the following:

1. The true experiment, or the randomized clinical trial, is a type of study from which a researcher can draw conclusions

about causality. In health psychology research, a true experiment is a rather infrequent occurrence. True experiments (randomized clinical trials) are particularly useful for testing the efficacy of specific interventions or treatments.

2. A correlation between two variables tells nothing about their causal relationship. A correlation refers simply to the covariation between two measures.

3. Retrospective research allows subjects to report on something in the past and to recall what happened and how they experienced it. Prospective research requires that the predictor measure be assessed well in advance of the outcome.

4. Cross-sectional research involves measuring variables on different groups of people of various ages. A longitudinal study assesses people as time passes.

VI. Methods of assessment include the following:

A. Review of documents, an approach that is nonreactive (the researcher cannot influence the phenomenon he or she is measuring by the act of measuring it).

B. Interview, an approach that provides considerable control over the measurement situation.

C. Questionnaire, which allows researchers to evaluate responses with little opportunity for bias.

D. Observation of actual situations.

VII. In laboratory studies, the experimenter controls the situation, whereas in field research, the experimenter is operating on the subject's turf.

# Glossary

**age cohort:** a group of people defined in terms of the period of time in which they were born.

**catecholamines:** the neurotransmitters, which include epinephrine and norepinephrine.

**causal inference:** a statement that one variable probably causes another. If one is justified in drawing a causal inference about two variables (for example, relaxation training and the elimination of tension headaches), one can conclude with a high degree of certainty that Variable A causes Variable B.

**closed-ended:** attribute of a question or statement that provides certain response alternatives, from which the respondent must choose the one that best matches how he or she feels.

**control group:** the group in a true experiment that does not receive the treatment.

**covariance:** the change of two phenomena in relationship to each other. When two phenomena covary, they are connected somehow, though not necessarily causally.

**cross-sectional research:** research that involves measuring different groups of people (typically of various ages) on the outcome variable and comparing them.

**experimental group:** the group in a true experiment that receives the intended treatment.

**field research:** research in which the goal is to understand events that occur naturally. The field researcher exercises very little control over the variables being studied because the research takes place in the subject's own environment.

**laboratory research:** research that involves conditions of experimentation and/or of observation over which the researcher has considerable control.

**longitudinal study:** a study that measures subjects on the dependent variables at many points in time.

**nonreactive measures:** measurements that a researcher cannot influence by the act of measuring.

**nonverbal communication:** communication without words.

**open-ended:** attribute of a question or statement that leaves the subject free to respond in any way that he or she wishes.

**prospective research:** research in which the predictor measure is assessed well in advance of the outcome.

**provider-specific measures of patient satisfaction:** measures of patient satisfaction that require the respondent to express how he or she feels about a particular provider.

**random assignment:** the assignment of subjects in an experiment to experimental or control groups based upon a random process, such as the toss of a coin.

**retrospective study:** a study in which subjects are asked to report on something in the past and to recall what happened and how they experienced it. One major problem with retrospective studies is that the events occurring at a given time in a person's life tend to influence his or her recollection of past events.

**state-dependent memory:** a phenomenon that partly accounts for the unreliability of retrospective reports. People tend to remember most easily the events of the past that are connected with the same emotional state they feel at the time of recall.

**true experiment, or randomized clinical trial:** a type of study involving an experimental and a control group from which the researcher can safely draw conclusions about causality.

# Staying Healthy

Alex McRay is 23 years old and a senior at a large West Coast university. Alex has been accepted to the business school for the fall semester and is eagerly awaiting graduation. He has planned a strategy for staying healthy and fit, and is trying to make it a routine part of his life.

Although schoolwork takes up a great deal of his day, Alex exercises at least four times a week in intense aerobic activity. Sometimes he runs five miles. Other times he takes an advanced aerobic dance class in the physical education department or swims a mile or more in the university Olympic pool. He spends at least six hours a week exercising, but Alex thinks he sleeps better at night because of exercise, and he feels better and more energetic during the day. He believes his exercise program is well worth the time it takes.

Although his friends are rarely careful about what

they eat, Alex tries hard to maintain a nutritionally sound diet. He avoids salty and processed foods. He limits his intake of fats. Alex eats lots of fresh fruits and vegetables, and whole grains. He drinks low-fat milk, and eats fish or chicken several times a week. Alex takes a multivitamin and mineral supplement every day. He practices yoga or meditation as often as he can in order to relax and manage feelings of tension. He is careful about his choice of sexual partners, and he uses condoms to prevent sexually transmitted diseases. He has his blood pressure checked at least once a year at the university health center. Alex consumes alcohol only in limited quantities (at most, an average of one beer a day). He does not smoke cigarettes, never uses illegal drugs, and always wears a safety belt when riding in a car.

Alex's health routine isn't a fad. It is based on recent scientific evidence about health promotion and disease prevention. Alex's activities constitute the basic minimum for avoiding known health risks.

■ ■ ■ ■ ■

Lois Walters is a 64-year-old widowed grandmother. Her husband died six years ago. She is in relatively good health. Five years ago, she underwent a total hysterectomy—surgery to remove her ovaries, fallopian tubes, and uterus—because of endometrial cancer. She has had no recurrence. Fortunately, Lois was conscientious about getting regular gynecology checkups. She reported abnormal bleeding to her doctor as soon as it occurred. Her cancer was detected early, and the treatment saved her life.

Lois has a routine health checkup every year. She has a sigmoidoscopy to test for colorectal cancer and a mammogram to detect breast cancer. Lois tries to eat a healthy diet, walk for exercise, and stay actively involved with her friends and family. She quit smoking fifteen years ago, but she is still overweight.

Throughout most of her life, Lois was unconcerned about her health. She smoked cigarettes, which damaged her lungs; some of the damage is reversible, of course, but Lois exposed herself to cancer risks that may never disappear completely. Her diet was high in fat, and to some extent it still is. She lived a very sedentary life and almost never exercised. So, despite her daily walks, she has little muscle tone and minimal cardiovascular strength. Her bones are becoming brittle, and now she risks fractures that could keep her bedridden for the rest of her life.

In Lois's younger days, exercise was not fashionable. There was no evidence then, as there is today, that exercise can extend one's active life span and may even contribute to greater longevity. In fact, several decades ago, people who engaged in exercise and other health habits were considered a bit eccentric. Medicine was focused on curing, and the medical-technological developments of the 1940s, 1950s, and 1960s suggested that medical science may be able to fix whatever was wrong with a person. But there turned out to be many limitations to what medicine could do.

Lois sometimes wonders whether a different style of living in the past might have led her to better health today.

Imagine life in the year 1900. If you had lived at that time in Boston, Massachusetts, you would have had access to the most sophisticated medical treatment available in the United States and probably in the world. Yet, the most likely cause of your death would have been a bacterial infection that could be cured these days with a ten-day course of antibiotics.

In the year 1900 almost 2% of the population of the United States died, many people from illnesses that we no longer consider to be very serious (Thomas, 1979). For example, in 1900 almost 12% of deaths were caused by pneumonia and influenza (the "flu")—illnesses that today are rather common and from which most people fully recover. Over 11% of deaths in 1900 were caused by tuberculosis, and over 8% were caused by dysentery (diarrhea), enteritis (bowel inflammation), and intestinal ulcer. These illnesses presented such problems because at the beginning of this century no antibiotics were available to eradicate bacterial pneumonia, tuberculosis, and intestinal infection. Further, medicine could provide little in the way of effective supportive therapy for those who had contracted severe viral infections such as influenza. Public health standards were so poor (for example, sewage systems were primitive or nonexistent, and cities were dirty) that infectious diseases spread rapidly and epidemics were common (Torrens, 1978).

Obviously, the world has changed tremendously since 1900. In the 1980s, for example, the death rate has been less than 1% of the population. The introduction of antibiotics in the 1940s completely changed the face of medicine. There was finally a means to cure bacterial infections that had plagued human beings throughout history. Means of caring for individuals with viral infections have become available, and immunizations to prevent the more problematic viruses (for example, smallpox, polio, measles, mumps, and rubella) have contributed tremendously to the health and well-being of Americans. In the 1980s, influenza and pneumonia caused less than 3% of deaths, and these deaths were usually among the elderly and among those already critically ill. Today Americans suffer from some very different health problems than in the past. Let's examine what they are.

## THE DEGENERATIVE DISEASES

In the last decade of the 20th century, people are much healthier than they were in the first decade. They also live considerably longer. Fewer people than ever before now die in their younger years from communi-

cable diseases. Deaths occur later and from different causes.

In the past decade the leading fatal diseases in the United States have been heart disease (roughly 38% of deaths), cancer (18%), and stroke (11%). Such diseases have become so prevalent partly because people now live long enough to develop them. In 1900, for example, the average person in the United States died before reaching the age at which most people now develop cancer or heart disease or have strokes (Thomas, 1979). Furthermore, it is believed by scientists today that "bad health habits" contribute to premature disability and death from these diseases (Belloc, 1973).

These three present-day killers, as well as others, such as diabetes and cirrhosis of the liver (which each account for around 2% of the death rate), are unlike communicable diseases. They are not caused by an identified pathogen, such as a bacteria or a virus. Instead, they are multifactorial in nature—that is, they stem from many factors, such as heredity and behavior (Dubos, 1959), and are referred to as the *chronic degenerative diseases*. As illustrated in Figure 3–1, failure to carry out some important health behaviors is believed to contribute to these conditions, and in some cases to cause them (Califano, 1979b).

**Heart Disease.** Consider heart disease. It is the primary cause of permanent disability in people over age 40. Most heart attacks are attributable to coronary artery disease caused by *atherosclerosis*. As we saw in Chapter 2, atherosclerosis is a condition in which fatty, fibrous plaques narrow the opening of the coronary arteries, reducing the amount of blood that can get to the heart. When these arteries become blocked, the heart muscle can be deprived of blood and hence of oxygen. This condition is a *myocardial infarction*, commonly called a heart attack, and it can cause part of the heart muscle to be damaged or destroyed. Myocardial infarction can cause a person to

| Heart Disease | Cancer | Stroke |
|---|---|---|
| • cigarette smoking<br>• emotional stress<br>• uncontrolled hypertension<br>• obesity<br>• sedentary lifestyle<br>• uncontrolled diabetes<br>• high-serum cholesterol | • cigarette smoking<br>• exposure to carcinogens in environment<br>• high-fat diet<br>• radiation exposure<br>• sunlight exposure<br>• avoidance of screening measures (for example, Pap, mammogram) | • cigarette smoking<br>• uncontrolled hypertension<br>• obesity |

FIGURE 3–1   Known behavioral risk factors for heart disease, cancer, and stroke.

become mildly to severely debilitated. It can also cause death from heart failure (Hamilton & Rose, 1982).

Atherosclerosis has been linked to many factors, only some of which can be changed or controlled: family history, hypertension, obesity, smoking, diabetes mellitus, emotional stress reactions (which we examine in Chapter 10), sedentary lifestyle, and high serum cholesterol. In fact, living an unhealthy lifestyle by smoking cigarettes, being overweight, eating a diet high in saturated fat, not exercising, and responding with hostility to stress may account for as many as 80% of heart disease deaths (Hamilton & Rose, 1982). Research has shown that several of the risk factors for heart disease can be reduced or eliminated when people change their behavior. Carefully following treatments for high blood pressure and diabetes (both predisposing factors), maintaining normal weight and a low-fat diet, avoiding smoking, engaging in regular exercise, and modifying stress reactions can help to reduce heart-disease risk. As we will see, these practices are well within the behavioral control of the person.

**Cancer.**   Cancer is not one disease but a category of conditions characterized by the growth of *neoplastic cells*. Neoplastic cells are larger and divide more quickly than do normal cells, and as far as currently known, serve no useful purpose. *Malignant* (cancerous) cells grow and spread through the body, sometimes quite rapidly. Grouped together, these cells form a tumor. A tumor can affect the normal functioning of an organ system and thereby kill the host (Hamilton & Rose, 1982).

A tremendous amount of research has been devoted to discovering the cause and cure of cancer. However, there are as yet not enough answers available. The malignant transformation of cells may result from a complex interaction of viruses, physical and chemical *carcinogens* (cancer-causing agents), genetic predisposition, compromises of the immune system, and diet. Theoretically, the human body develops cancer cells continuously, in response, for example, to carcinogens like environmental toxins, cigarettes, certain foods, and food additives. An intact, well-functioning immune system hunts out and destroys these cells, but certain factors can inhibit the immune system: aging, toxic drugs, emotional stress (see Chapter 10), radiation, and even cancer itself (Hamilton & Rose, 1982).

Scientists do not yet understand the precise mechanism by which a carcinogen renders a cell malignant or the factors that enhance or depress the immune system's ability to destroy the cancer cell. Thus, the general mechanism by which cancer comes about and the means to fight cancer are not yet known. However, there has been a great deal of empirical research on individual cancers and their particular risk factors, some of which are behavioral. This research has provided us with some important information about cancer prevention.

There are many known cancer-causing agents (such as the chemicals asbestos and benzene) in buildings and polluted waters. Obviously, preventing cancer involves avoiding these substances, a goal that may depend a great deal upon one's environment. Some drugs, such as diethylstilbestrol (DES), are carcinogenic. DES has been shown to cause reproductive organ cancers in young persons who were exposed to DES prenatally (*in utero*). And certain substances encountered day to day, such as cigarette smoke, are carcinogenic as well. Not all carcinogens can be avoided. People may be exposed to asbestos at the workplace or to medications prescribed for them long before the dangers became known. But preventing exposure to certain deadly substances such as cigarettes is within an individual's control.

Health psychologists are concerned with the behavioral risk factors in cancer, the factors in our everyday activities that contribute to cancer risk. Cigarette smoking, for example, is believed to cause at least 80% of all cases of lung cancer. Lung cancer is responsible for at least 25% of all deaths from cancer. Lung cancer is a very painful and debilitating disease, and is almost always fatal. Cigarettes have also been found to be a leading cause of cancer of the oral cavity (including the mouth and tongue) and of the upper airways, the esophagus, the pancreas, the kidneys, and the bladder. Another behavior, eating a high-fat diet, is believed to be an important factor in both colorectal cancer and the occurrence and recurrence of breast cancer (Eron, 1988). Even suntanning, exposing the skin to the sun's ultraviolet rays, can cause disfiguring skin cancers as well as a deadly form of cancer called malignant melanoma (see Box 3–1).

In the case of cancer, prevention also involves screening for early detection. Most forms of cancer have higher survival rates the earlier in the disease process the cancer is discovered (Battista & Fletcher, 1988). Thus, the primary prevention of cancer involves several important procedures for early detection. Let's examine them.

Breast cancer can have a very high survival rate following treatment if it is caught early, when the breast tumor is very small. Nearly 90% of breast lumps are initially discovered by the woman herself (Craun & Deffenbacher, 1987). Thus, regular (once-a-month) breast self-examination is critically important for a woman to perform in order to enhance her chances of stopping a cancer early in its development. Despite campaigns by the American Cancer Society and the National Cancer Institute, only about 35% of women check their breasts regularly and many do not do it correctly (National Cancer Institute, 1980). Many women fail to check their breasts for lumps because they fear what might happen if a lump were found (Trotta, 1980). Improved procedures in breast cancer treatment in recent years, however, have vastly increased the chances of cure and reduced the extent of disfigurement from surgery for breast cancer that is caught early (American Cancer Society, 1989). Cancer experts also recommend that men perform self-examinations for testicular cancer. Testicular cancer is the leading cause of death from solid tumors in men ages 15 to 34; the peak incidence is at age 32. Monthly testicular self-examination can be an effective means for detecting tumors. If caught early, chances of full recovery are very high. Finally, self-screening also

BOX
3–1

## SKIN CANCER: INFORMATION AND PREVENTION

"It's suntan turnover time," cooed the disc jockey after a half hour of pop music and acne medication commercials. "And this song is for all you lovely young ladies who are working on your deep, dark tans this weekend. . . ." The beach, as usual, was blanket-to-blanket people. Nearly all of them were lying in the hot sunshine hour after hour, hoping to turn their skin golden brown. Many, instead, would burn from overexposure and because they failed to use sunscreen properly. Some did not use it at all.

Sunbathing is a risky activity, particularly for fair-skinned people. Sun exposure vastly increases the chances of developing skin cancer. Three major types of skin cancer have been found to be related to ultraviolet radiation exposure from sunlight. These are basal cell carcinoma, squamous cell carcinoma, and malignant melanoma. Basal cell carcinoma is slow growing and almost never *metastasizes* (spreads to other parts of the body). Squamous cell carcinoma can spread to internal organs or lymph nodes, but together basal and squamous cell cancers have a high cure rate (around 90%). There are 400,000 new cases of these cancers each year. Malignant melanoma, on the other hand, can be deadly. It is the most serious form of cancer that can arise in a pigmented mole. There are about 26,000 new cases of melanoma each year, and each year about 5800 people die of melanoma. Melanoma is treatable if caught early, but if not treated promptly, it can spread throughout the body.

Skin cancers are typically treated with surgery, radiation therapy, electrical current, and freezing. Treatment may be quite disfiguring, and the patient may desire plastic surgery to restore his or her appearance. The best medicine however is prevention. Prevention involves limiting one's exposure to sunlight as well as correctly using sunscreens. It also requires regular checking of one's entire body for skin lesions or moles that look suspicious and bringing those to the attention of a doctor.

Preventive behavior in the realm of sun exposure and cancer prevention has had little study. The most extensive research in this field was done by Keesling and Friedman (1987). These researchers interviewed 120 sunbathers at California beaches to determine the factors that influenced their sun exposure as well as their use of sunscreens. Sunbathers with the darker tans who spent a good deal of time in the sun were found to have little knowledge about skin cancer. They were more relaxed, liked to take risks and were more likely to perform appearance-related actions. They were also influenced by groups of friends who valued a tan. Those who more regularly and effectively used sunscreen had higher anxiety, were more likely to know people who had skin cancer, had greater knowledge about skin cancer, and were more likely to be women. Health beliefs did not predict suntanning or sunscreen use.

Many people know they are at risk but they sunbathe anyway. By way of intervention, researchers are attempting to increase people's understanding of the severity of skin cancer by showing that it can be very disfiguring, and that malignant melanoma is one of the cancers most likely to be fatal. Health professionals are also trying to educate people about precisely how to use sunscreens for maximum protection, and how to examine their skin for cancerous or precancerous growths.

includes measures to detect skin cancers. These measures include regular checking of one's own skin surfaces for growths or for changes in moles that might signal skin cancer or malignant melanoma (Frame, 1986).

Of course, not all cancer screening can be done at home by the individual. Physician palpation for breast or testicular growths is also necessary. In addition, mammograms (X-ray studies of the breast) are recommended by physicians following guidelines from the American Cancer Society. These include mammograms every one to two years for women 40 to 50 years old and annually after age 50, with baseline X rays at age 35. Tests exist also to detect cervical cancer (the Pap test, recommended roughly every two years for all women) and cancer of the endometrial lining of the uterus (the endometrial biopsy, recommended for postmenopausal women who are at risk for endometrial cancer) (Frame, 1986).

Finally, to detect colorectal (colon and rectal) cancer, the American Cancer Society recommends that patients over 40 have an annual digital rectal examination by the physician and that patients over 50 have tests for stool occult blood yearly and sigmoidoscopy every two or three years (Frame, 1986).

The American Cancer Society recommends that every individual exercise self-responsibility and pay attention to the seven warning signs of cancer:

**C** Change in bowel or bladder habits
**A** A sore that does not heal
**U** Unusual bleeding or discharge
**T** Thickening or lump in breast or elsewhere
**I** Indigestion or difficulty in swallowing
**O** Obvious change in a wart or mole
**N** Nagging cough or hoarseness

Although cancer is more common in older individuals than in younger ones, it does occur in young adults, teenagers, and even children (American Cancer Society, 1989). Attending to the warning signs of cancer and conducting the relevant self-examinations regularly can be essential for everyone to detect cancer in its early and curable stages. The early detection of cancer requires health-promoting actions, many of which may be time consuming and even emotionally challenging to the individual (American Cancer Society, 1989). In Chapter 4, we will examine in detail the factors that contribute to an individual's decision to carry out health-promoting actions.

**Stroke.** *Stroke* (also known as a cerebrovascular accident or CVA) is a sudden impairment of circulation to the brain. A stroke usually occurs because a blood vessel has been blocked (for example, by a blood clot or a fat deposit). This blockage deprives a portion of brain tissue of oxygen and damages it permanently. CVA is the third-most-common cause of death in the United States today, striking half a million people per year. Approximately half of its victims die. Of those who do survive, about half remain permanently disabled and approximately half experience another stroke. The aftermath of a stroke can be devastating. Many individuals are left paralyzed and/or without the ability to speak, and some experience cognitive deficits such as the inability to identify certain objects with words (Krantz & Deckel, 1983).

Prevention of stroke requires lifetime control of its risk factors because most strokes occur in the aged population. One of the most important factors in preventing stroke is the control of *hypertension* or high blood pressure (Hamilton & Rose, 1982). Those who are obese, have atherosclerosis, and smoke cigarettes are most at risk. In addition, the use of oral contraceptives increases the risk of CVA, primarily among women who smoke cigarettes (U.S. Preventive Services Task Force, 1989; hereafter cited as USPSTF).

## PREVENTION IS THE KEY

The diseases and conditions described above cannot, at the present time, be eradicated. They are not amenable to treatment in the relatively simple way that bacterial infections are eliminated with antibiotics. And unlike many viruses (such as polio), the conditions of stroke, heart disease, and cancer cannot be prevented with immunizations. Some scientists, such as Lewis Thomas, believe that new discoveries in medicine and technology may someday provide a cure or immunization (Thomas, 1979), but at present, the only option available is preventive action. (See Box 3–2 for further discussion of Thomas' hypothesis.)

Above, we considered a few of the major health risks that can be controlled with appropriate health actions. In this chapter we will examine specific health actions in detail. As we do this, however, it is important to keep in mind that not all medical conditions can be prevented by simply changing one's health habits. There are likely some contributing factors that are as yet unknown, or if known are uncontrollable (for example, one's genetic predisposition). However, since some component of

**BOX 3–2**

## DISEASES OF TODAY: IS THERE HOPE FOR SIMPLE ANSWERS?

Less than 50 years ago a revolution occurred in medical practice. Sulfa drugs and penicillin were introduced into the pharmacopeia of medicine, and for the first time doctors could actually cure disease. This was astonishing, even to doctors themselves (Thomas, 1979).

It was discovered in about the mid-1800s that the greater part of medical treatment was either worthless or downright dangerous. Patients were bled, purged, starved, and administered solutions of every known plant and metal. There was no scientific basis whatever for most of what was done.

For the next 100 years, people tolerated medical practice because they were convinced of its magical powers. Others were fortunate to have chosen physicians who believed that most diseases were self-limiting and that people needed only supportive therapy, relief of anxiety, and encouragement. Diagnosis, observation, and the "art of medicine" kept physicians busy. They were able to name the disease to the patient and family, predict its course, and recommend rest and good nursing care. But doctors could do little to control or alleviate disease.

Then antibiotics came along and with them optimism and enthusiasm for all that medicine could do. Of course, antibiotic treatment was the result of ". . . many years of hard work, done by imaginative and skilled scientists, none of whom had the faintest idea that penicillin and streptomycin lay somewhere in the decades ahead. It was basic science of a very high order. . . ." (Thomas, 1979, p. 164).

The plagues of modern time are cancer, heart disease, stroke, kidney failure, arthritis, schizophrenia, diabetes, AIDS, and many others. These conditions bring tremendous costs in financial and human resources. Coronary bypass operations, restrictive diets, exercise, medications, and the avoidance of unhealthy habits are good stopgap measures and are all that is currently

risk can be reduced by taking certain preventive actions, a considerable amount of suffering, disability, and mortality may be prevented.

Let us turn now to examine *preventive health behaviors,* which are actions taken by an individual to prevent disease from developing or to forestall the negative outcomes of a disease condition. These include (low-fat) diet, exercise, the prevention of alcohol and drug abuse, quitting cigarette smoking, practicing safer sex, using automobile safety belts, and obtaining vaccinations (USPSTF, 1989). Another preventive behavior, managing and reducing stress, is critical not only for its direct but also for its indirect effect on health (by means of other behaviors, such as diet, exercise, and substance use). Stress and stress reduction are examined in detail in Chapters 10 and 11.

## Primary Prevention

*Primary prevention,* a term that has gained considerable popularity in recent years, refers to all those activities that are undertaken by apparently disease free individuals with the intent of helping them achieve maximum well-being and avoid disease (Elias & Murphy, 1986). Primary preven-

available. Such actions may control these diseases and conditions quite well but cannot alleviate them.

According to Lewis Thomas (1979), there is cause for great optimism about medicine because the necessary basic scientific research on the cardiovascular system, on the mechanisms of cancer, and on many other physical processes relevant to disease are edging closer to answers. Today's diseases are multifactorial, but that does not mean they are so complex as to be unsolvable. Wrote Thomas:

> . . . for every disease there is a single key mechanism that dominates all others. . . . The most complicated, multicell, multitissue, and multiorgan diseases I know of are tertiary syphilis, chronic tuberculosis, and pernicious anemia. In each, there are at least five major organs and tissues involved, and each appears to be affected by a variety of environmental influences. Before they came under scientific appraisal each was thought to be what we now call a "multifactorial" disease, far too complex to allow for any single causative mechanism. And yet, when all the necessary facts were in, it was clear that by simply switching off one thing—the spirochete, the tubercle bacillus, or a single vitamin deficiency—the whole array of disordered and seemingly unrelated pathologic mechanisms would be switched off, at once. (Thomas, 1979, pp. 168–169)

Although there may be many separate influences that can launch cancer, heart disease, stroke, deadly viruses, and many other of today's diseases, it is quite possible that each will be found to have a single switch at the center of things. The major diseases of human beings may be "approachable biological puzzles, ultimately solvable" (Thomas, 1979, p. 169).

Amidst this enthusiasm, however, we must remember that these puzzles may not be solved for many, many years. Therefore, despite the fact that present health protective measures and preventive health actions are not cures, they are extremely valuable because they can slow the development and spread of disease.

- Use of safety belts
- Acquiring immunizations
- Practicing safer sex
- Practicing good nutrition
- Exercising
- Avoiding obesity/
  Controlling weight
- Avoiding cigarette
  smoking
- Avoiding excessive
  alcohol use
- Limiting caffeine intake

**FIGURE 3–2**   The most effective health behaviors.

Automobile safety belts are extremely effective at preventing injury and death.
SOURCE: Bobbie Kingsley/Photo Researchers

tion thus includes both health promotion and disease prevention. Many people these days try to attain good health and vigor, and attempt to avoid the ravages of disease and forestall the declines of old age. Fortunately, such a goal is within their reach.

Let us look at some of the more important primary prevention activities that are summarized in Figure 3–2 and examine the effect they can have on life and well-being (USPSTF, 1989).

## AUTOMOBILE SAFETY BELTS

■ ■ ■ ■ ■

Susan totaled her car. It hit a pole on the side of the freeway exit ramp at a speed of 45 miles an hour. She was shaken up but escaped without a scratch. She was wearing her safety belt. Everyone who looked at the damaged car was amazed that Susan was still alive.

April's car was rammed in an intersection by a too-eager teenage driver who ran a red light. Her car was going 15 miles an hour; his was going 20. April was doing some errands close to home, and didn't think she needed her safety belt. But she couldn't hold herself back as she was thrown forward, and her jaw struck the steering wheel. The day after the accident, April felt soreness and stiffness in her neck,

shoulders, and back. The accident marked the beginning of her back problems and severe headaches. The impact had caused structural damage to her neck, back, and jaw. She had to give up dancing, and sought physical therapy. The doctors are recommending surgery to relieve her chronic pain.

Statistics about the value of automobile seat belts and shoulder harnesses (together known as safety belts) are very convincing. Safety belts vastly increase the chances of survival in automobile crashes under 60 miles an hour (Roglieri, 1980). They greatly reduce (and often wholly prevent) injury at all speeds (Campbell, 1987). A safety belt protects the individual from being thrown from the car or against the windshield, dashboard, or steering wheel. Chest injuries, for example, account for one-fourth of all trauma deaths in the United States, and most blunt chest injuries result from auto accidents in which the driver is thrown against the steering wheel. Belted drivers can better maintain control of the car. Even in cases in which a driver or passenger must get out of the car in a hurry, a safety belt allows him or her to maintain consciousness on the initial impact and then to release the safety belt and leave the car. Safety belts prevent individuals in the car from crashing into one another. Safety belts transfer the energy of a sudden stop and impact from the smaller, more vulnerable parts of a person's body, such as the head, and spread it out over stronger parts, such as the pelvis and rib cage. Studies performed in Europe, Australia, and the United States show that at *any speed* (including speeds of over 60 miles an hour), drivers and passengers using safety belts overall suffer 50% fewer serious injuries and 60% to 70% fewer fatalities in crashes than do nonusers (USPSTF, 1989; Orsay, Turnbull, Dunne, Barrett, Langenberg, & Orsay, 1988).

Safety seats for children are especially effective in preventing injury and death. Many studies have shown that even at relatively low speeds, sudden braking or impact can send a baby or small child flying out of an adult's arms and through the windshield of a car (Agran, 1981; Califano, 1979b; Christophersen, 1989; Roglieri, 1980).

Safety-belt use is surprisingly low, considering its potential benefits. In 1974, for example, when new automobiles were equipped with passive-restraint systems, only 6% of people used them. In states in which no mandatory safety belt laws exist, current use is around 10% to 15%. Use of safety belts is somewhat higher in states in which safety belt use is required by law, but unless there are mandatory fines for violations, the laws do not insure compliance.

Why do some people fail to use safety belts? Surveys show that many people feel that safety belts are too much trouble to put on, restrict their movement, and wrinkle their clothes. Some rebel against the wishes of family members. Many are not aware of the effectiveness of safety belts (Agran & Dunkle, 1982). Physicians who treat adults rarely recommend that their patients use safety belts. It is, however, becoming quite common for pediatricians to make strong recommendations to parents to protect their children with child safety seats in their cars.

## IMMUNIZATIONS

During the 1940s and 1950s in the United States, there was an *epidemic* (widely diffused and rapidly spreading occurrence) of a potentially deadly virus called poliomyelitis (often referred to as polio). Polio is an acute communicable disease that causes death in 5% to 10% of cases (Hamilton & Rose, 1982). It can also cause partial or complete paralysis. In 1955 a *vaccine* became available, developed by Dr. Jonas Salk, for *immunization* against polio. This vaccine has been called one of the wonder drugs of medicine. It stimulates the production of antibodies in the human body so that encounters with the virus do not result in infection. The Salk vaccine involves an injection; another form of the vaccine, the Sabin, named for its developer, Albert Sabin, can be taken orally.

The polio vaccine has so effectively minimized the threat of polio in the United States that today it is very difficult for many young persons to appreciate how feared the disease was. In some ways, that fear is comparable to current fears surrounding the human immunodeficiency virus (HIV), believed to cause AIDS. Polio, however, is much more easily transmitted than is HIV. The polio virus can be passed through touching, using another person's

The vaccine for immunization against polio has been called one of the wonder drugs of medicine.
SOURCE: Wide World Photos

towel or toothbrush, or licking another person's ice cream cone. Polio could spread easily among children. The death rate from polio, however, was quite a bit lower than the death rate from AIDS, which is almost surely fatal.

Outbreaks of polio occur even today, although it is easy for anyone who wants an oral vaccination to obtain it without cost in nearly every county health department in the country. In 1979, for example, there was a minor polio epidemic among the Amish of Pennsylvania, who had failed, for the most part, to immunize their children.

Why do people fail to receive immunizations against polio and other diseases? Immunization is a relatively low-cost, high-benefit preventive health measure (USPSTF, 1989). Some of the very earliest

research on health behaviors was conducted to try to determine precisely this. It concluded that people's beliefs that polio was not serious or could not harm them, or that getting vaccinated was not worth the trouble caused them not to take advantage of the free immunizations available to them (Rosenstock, 1974). We examine this research in greater detail in Chapter 4.

## SAFER SEX

Acquired immune deficiency syndrome (AIDS) is a condition that impairs its victim's immune system and hence his or her ability to fight infection. The person with AIDS is extremely susceptible to disease and typically dies of an infection, such as a serious lung condition called *Pneumocystis carinii* pneumonia, or a form of cancer called Kaposi's sarcoma, or a virus called cytomegalovirus. The AIDS victim may suffer from severe internal candidiasis (yeast infection) and even extensive herpes. Survival after the onset of AIDS is about 14 months (Lemp et al., 1990).

AIDS is believed to be caused by HIV (human immunodeficiency virus), which is transmitted from one person to another through the exchange of bodily fluids, including blood, semen, and vaginal secretions. Such exchange can occur during sexual contact or needle sharing when injecting intravenous drugs. HIV can also be transmitted by means of transfusion with infected blood and from infected mother to fetus during pregnancy. Those at highest risk for contracting AIDS are males who have had homosexual or bisexual contact (about 58% of cases through June, 1990), intravenous drug users who share needles (about 18% of cases), and those who combine such activities (6% of cases), as well as persons who received blood transfusions or hemophiliacs who received blood products before 1985 who may have been given blood contaminated with the virus (3% of cases). Others at risk are heterosexuals who are exposed to the virus during sexual contact with an infected person (5% of cases) (Centers for Disease Control, 1990). Some cases are of undetermined origin or result from a combination of risk factors. Forty-nine percent of cases among females are due to intravenous drug use and 33% result from heterosexual contact (Centers for Disease Control, 1990).

Through June 1990, 139,765 cases of AIDS have been diagnosed and reported in the United States. The Centers for Disease Control estimate that by 1992 there may be as many as 365,000 cases of AIDS and 260,000 deaths from AIDS in the United States (USPSTF, 1989). It is estimated that 1 to 1.5 million persons in the United States are infected with HIV (Centers for Disease

Control, 1988, 1990; Gail & Brookmeyer, 1990; Morgan, Curran, & Berkelman, 1990).

The *incubation period* of a disease is the time from exposure to infection to the onset of symptoms of the disease. The incubation period of HIV is estimated to be about 8 years (and may be as long as 11 years) from infection with HIV to development of the symptoms of AIDS (Lemp, et al., 1990). During this time the individual is symptom free and may pass the virus on to others through sexual contact or needle sharing when using intravenous drugs. All blood that is currently donated is subjected to a test (ELISA with Western Blot confirmation) that can identify the presence of antibodies to the HIV virus. If a test is positive, the donated blood is discarded and the donor is usually notified that he or she may have been exposed to the HIV virus. The Elisa/Western Blot is also available from private physicians and clinics for individuals who are concerned that they may have been exposed to HIV.

Since there is no cure for AIDS, prevention of HIV infection is essential (Batchelor, 1988; Brooks-Gunn, Boyer, & Hein, 1988). What can a person do to protect himself or herself from exposure to this killer? Avoiding all forms of intravenous drug use is an important health measure in general, and is particularly critical for avoidance of the HIV infection. In addition, limiting the number of sexual partners and knowing their sexual histories can help reduce risk, as can avoiding certain sexual practices that have been determined to be quite risky (such as anal intercourse, and vaginal intercourse without a condom). These practices can raise the chances of spread of the infection during sexual contact. The best method for preventing the spread of the disease through homosexual or heterosexual contact is monogamous sexual relations with an uninfected person. Beyond that, the use of condoms with spermicidal creme or jelly that contains the chemical Nonoxynol

9 is considered safer than unprotected sexual relations. Measures to prevent the spread of HIV also help to prevent the spread of other sexually transmitted diseases (STDs) such as herpes, gonorrhea, clamydia, and hepatitis B (Cates, 1987).

Recent research demonstrates that knowledge about HIV and ways to practice safer sex have changed the behaviors of homosexual men who are at high risk for infection. The majority of homosexual men in the United States have radically changed their sexual behavior in order to prevent the further spread of HIV infection (Becker & Joseph, 1988; Stall, Coates, & Hoff, 1988). The risk group currently of greatest concern in the spread of the disease is the intravenous-drug-use population (Des Jarlais & Friedman, 1988; Lemp et al., 1990).

## NUTRITION AND DIET

Think about someone you know who is described as a "meat-and-potatoes man" or as having a "sweet tooth." These labels reveal something important about how deeply ingrained eating habits can be. Anyone who has tried to alter his or her own eating habits knows that food choices and diet are difficult to change.

Yet, change may be critical to health and survival. Considerable evidence is accumulating that our dietary choices can reduce our susceptibility to disease. A diet low in fat, for example, may help to reduce the risk of breast and colon cancer as well as of heart disease (Patterson & Block, 1988). The control of dietary sodium can affect levels of blood pressure and ultimately cardiovascular disease. And while high levels of dietary *cholesterol* may lead to atherosclerosis and ultimately to coronary heart disease, certain foods can reduce serum cholesterol. The reduction of serum cholesterol through dietary interventions has been shown to lower coronary heart disease mortality (death) and morbidity

(illness) (for example, Multiple Risk Factor Intervention Trial Research Group, 1982; Grundy, 1986).

The average American diet contains 40% fat, but experts recommend reducing it to below 20%. Experts encourage eating fish and poultry rather than red meat, and broiled or baked rather than fried foods. Ice cream, butter, and other high-fat foods should be eaten rarely if at all (American Heart Association, 1984).

A diet high in insoluble fiber also helps to reduce the risk of colon cancer partly because fiber moves waste through the intestines faster than do other food products. Whole-grain breads and cereals, fruits, and vegetables are high on the list of desirable foods (American Cancer Society, 1989). In addition, there is some recent evidence that certain vitamins and minerals (specifically beta carotene, and vitamins A and C) may also have a protective effect against cancer (Menkes, Comstock, Vuilleumier, Helsing, Rider, & Brookmeyer, 1986).

A person's diet is not easily changed, however. Diet is habitual and bound by culture, environment, and preferences. The maintenance of initial dietary changes tends to be rather poor (Kasl, 1980; Leventhal, Nerenz, & Strauss, 1980). In the next chapter we will examine in detail the factors that are likely to promote many health behaviors including dietary change.

## OBESITY AND WEIGHT CONTROL

Obesity and overweight are common problems in the United States today. It is estimated that at least 14% of men and 24% of women weigh in at 20% or more above their optimal weight (Ice, 1985). (Higher estimates suggest the figure is just under 33% for men, and well over 35% for women.) Once an individual becomes obese, the condition tends to be self-perpetuating. His or her internal metabolic mechanisms readjust to maintain the higher weight. Excess girth makes it difficult to move around, and the overweight individual becomes more and more sedentary, further exacerbating the obesity (Stunkard, 1979).

Overweight contributes to many health problems. The greatest risk is of heart disease, but stroke (from high blood pressure resulting from the obesity) is also a potential outcome (MacMahon, Cutler, & Brittain, 1987). The risk of some forms of cancer is also associated with overweight, and obesity can cause adult-onset diabetes (American Diabetes Association, 1986).

Losing weight and keeping it off can be difficult, however. In one study, subjects typical of overweight individuals in general participated in a dieting program (Wilson, 1980). At the five-month point, the average participant had lost 40% of his or her target goal for weight loss. By 14 months, however, the average dieter had gained most of that weight back (about 30% of the target weight loss). Losing and regaining weight can have detrimental metabolic and health effects. Repeated cycles of weight loss and regain have been found (in research on animals) to be associated with increased metabolic efficiency, and this finding is believed to be applicable to humans as well. With such efficiency, weight is able to be maintained on fewer and fewer calories per day, and so over time it becomes more and more difficult for an individual to lose weight (Brownell, Marlatt, Lichtenstein, & Wilson, 1986). Also, it has been found in research on humans that when weight that was lost is regained, negative effects on blood pressure and cholesterol level (both risk factors for heart disease) may outweigh the positive effects of losing weight in the first place (Brownell et al., 1986).

Research shows that simple dieting alone usually does not work to get weight off and keep it off (Straw, 1983). An individual needs to consume fewer calories than he or she expends in energy, but because the metabolism has a tendency to become more efficient with dieting, eating less and cutting down one's calorie intake is not effective. The best way for an individual to lose weight and keep it off is to develop sound (low-fat) eating habits and to engage in regular physical exercise to raise the metabolic rate (Brownell & Stunkard, 1980). Several studies have shown that a low-fat diet and exercise work better than calorie reduction (though, as yet it is unclear precisely how much better) for long-term maintenance of weight loss. Low-fat diet and exercise are also more effective than pharmacological (drug) interventions (Epstein & Wing, 1980). Thus, the answer seems to lie in lifestyle change.

## EXERCISE

■ ■ ■ ■ ■

Jack is 55 years old, overweight, and has never exercised a day in his life. He drives a bus for a living. He is firmly convinced that exercise is dangerous as well as being unpleasant, and he is quick to point out the death of a famous marathon runner from heart failure. (That's the kind of news report he makes it a point to remember!) Strenuous exercise would obviously be unwise for Jack or any man his age who is sedentary and overweight. A medically supervised program of weight loss and light exercise, such as walking, is about all he can manage right now. Of course, it is possible for him to build up to a program of exercise and weight control that could lengthen his life and enhance his wellbeing. But Jack is not interested.

Jack's attitude is typical of that held by many people only a decade or so ago, but his ideas are gradually becoming outmoded. More and more Americans are coming to value exercise (USPSTF, 1989).

Undertaken regularly over the course of one's whole life, *aerobic exercise* (defined as that which dramatically increases oxygen consumption over an extended period of time—for example, walking, running, swimming, cycling) can bring some important benefits to health and well-being (Yeater & Ullrich, 1985) and reduce mortality from all causes (Blair, Kohl, Paffenbarger, Clark, Cooper, & Gibbons, 1989). Exercise helps to lower high blood pressure. Exercise contributes tremendously to weight control and raises high-density lipoprotein cholesterol, which is protective against atherosclerotic disease (arterial plaque). Exercise strengthens an individual's cardiovascular system, making the heart and lungs work more effectively and efficiently, and reducing the risk of cardiovascular disease (Leon & Blackburn, 1977; Paffenbarger, Wing, & Hyde, 1978). Weight-bearing exercise (including walking, running, aerobic dancing) prevents osteoporosis, a condition to which older women are most prone, in which bones become brittle and weak and fracture easily. Exercise reduces the aerobic requirements of day-to-day activities and makes muscles more efficient. Exercise makes everyday activities easier in terms of their stress and strain on the body. Exercise helps to delay the onset of debilitation from old age and chronic disease, and exercise increases both active-life expectancy and life expectancy itself. Exercise preserves bodily functioning and prolongs independent living in older persons (Yeater & Ullrich, 1985). Exercise also contributes to a better (subjectively rated) quality of life (Stephens, 1988). Many people report more restful sleep when they have exercised regularly, and exercisers (especially runners) list the psychological benefits of exercise nearly as often as they list the physiological benefits (Harris, 1981). Exercisers tend to report feeling lower levels of anxiety and less depression than those who are sedentary (Hughes, 1984). Runners show less depression than nonrunners (in a nonclinical population) (Tharp & Schegelmilch, 1977). Even in prospective

research, both self-selected and randomly assigned (experimental group) exercisers had lower depression than controls who did not exercise (Brown, Ramirez, & Taub, 1978; McCann & Holmes, 1984). Other studies have shown that exercise can help to reduce situational (short-term) anxiety (Long, 1984; Harper, 1978). Regular exercise also seems to be related to enhanced feelings of self-esteem (Sonstroem, 1984).

The minimum amount of activity needed to attain these benefits is 20 minutes, three times a week, in aerobic exercise at least 70% to 85% of maximum heart rate (220 minus the individual's age) (Larson & Bruce, 1987).

The value of regular exercise is acknowledged by a large number of Americans (in some surveys, over 70%) (Dishman, 1982), but only 37% actually engage in any regular physical exercise at all (Harris & Associates, 1984). And only about 50% of those who have begun an exercise program are still exercising six months later. Despite the immediate and long-term benefits, many people find exercise to be an extremely difficult endeavor. They do not enjoy exercising (or they have not found an exercise they do enjoy). They become bored with the routine, feel they cannot spare the time, or even believe that exercise is dangerous (Vertinsky & Auman, 1988). Once they lose the physical conditioning they gained, it can be unpleasant and difficult to regain it. Other statistics bear this out as well. Most adult fitness programs report success rates of only 40% to 65% in the first year, with a substantial dropoff after that time. Even when the exercise is for the purpose of rehabilitation from a cardiac problem, 30% to 50% of participants drop out during the first 12 months. Forty-five to 80% drop out within two years (Ice, 1985).

Although about 45% of Americans these days do some exercise, it is estimated that only about 10% to 15% exercise with sufficient intensity and frequency to achieve the highest levels of benefit (Stephens, Jacobs, & White, 1985). As a group, children are in particularly poor physical condition (Epstein, Wing, Valoski, & De Vos, 1988). The good news, however, is that more than ever before, Americans are making changes in their formerly sedentary habits (Ice, 1985). People are choosing to walk instead of ride, and to participate in sports rather than be spectators. And since recent research is pointing to the cardiovascular benefits of even limited physical activity, such as walking up stairs and into the workplace from distant parking spaces (USPSTF, 1989), any departure from sedentary habits can bring about some of the physical and emotional benefits of exercise.

## CIGARETTE SMOKING

There are few habits as potentially deadly as smoking cigarettes. Every year, about 390,000 people in the United States die prematurely as a direct result of smoking cigarettes (about 125,000 from cancer of the lung, trachea, and bladder; 170,000 from cardiovascular disease; and the rest from emphysema and chronic obstructive lung disease) (U.S. Department of Health and Human Services, 1989; U.S. Office on Smoking and Health, 1979). Cigarettes are responsible for a third of the deaths of men between 35 and 59 in the United States. "On the average, a 30 to 35 year old smoker who smokes 10 to 20 cigarettes per day will die about 5 years sooner than a non-smoker. A one to two pack-a-day smoker of the same age will die about 6½ years sooner" (Fisher & Rost, 1986, p. 557). Needless to say, these deaths usually come after protracted, painful, and debilitating illness.

Cigarette smoking during pregnancy may result in lower birth weights and retardation of the fetus's brain growth, as well as increased risk of malignancy in the baby, and sudden infant death syndrome (see Chapter 14) (Harrison, 1986). Furthermore, there are health risks imposed on those who breathe the smoke from the cigarettes of others (Eriksen, Le Maistre, & Newell, 1988).

Smokers are ill more often than are nonsmokers. The frequency of acute illness among male smokers is 14% higher than for male nonsmokers, and they lose 33% more workdays. For female smokers the difference is a 21% higher frequency of acute illness and the loss of 45% more workdays. Generally smokers are less healthy than nonsmokers, and they have almost twice the chance of dying in any given year (1.7 times) (Tucker, 1985).

Roughly 30% of the adults in the United States smoke cigarettes. This percentage is somewhat lower than in 1955, when 53% of the population smoked. In 1964 the first surgeon general's report on smoking (U.S. Department of Health, Education and Welfare and U.S. Public Health Service, 1964) highlighted the dangers, and an extensive publicity campaign was launched. Yet, although the percentage of male smokers in the United States decreased to 39% by 1975, the percentage of women smokers rose (from roughly 25% to 29%) (Russell & Epstein, 1988). The percentage of male and female adult smokers is now estimated to be about 33% and 28%, respectively (with a rate of 30.4% for the total population). Although the percentage has decreased since 1975, roughly 21% of female and 18% of male high school students smoke cigarettes.

The U.S. surgeon general's reports of 1964 and 1974 likely had a significant impact on smoking behavior. From 1920 to 1964, cigarette consumption had increased at a very rapid rate and peaked in 1963. But between 1964 and 1979, it is estimated that 29 million Americans quit smoking. Since the mid 1960s there has been considerable effort on the part of government agencies, the American Cancer Society, the American Lung Association, the American Heart As-

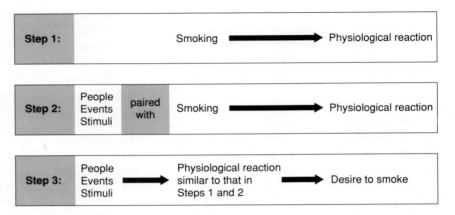

FIGURE 3–3    Steps in the classical conditioning of the desire to smoke a cigarette.

sociation, and other organizations to get out the word that smoking is dangerous.

If smoking is such an unhealthy activity, why haven't more people quit? One reason is that smoking is addictive both physically and psychologically. The nicotine in cigarettes is primarily responsible for the physical addiction (Schachter, 1980). Nicotine is a stimulant that raises blood pressure and increases heart rate. Some people are so addicted to nicotine that they can't get through a whole night without a cigarette. Some smoke a cigarette as soon as they wake up in the morning and even smoke when they are sick. But the physical addiction is not the only determinant. Psychologically, cigarettes provide a kind of crutch, something to do in tense, or uncomfortable, or boring situations. Furthermore, events, people, and places that have been paired with smoking may serve (in a manner of classical conditioning as illustrated in Figure 3–3) to trigger the desire to smoke.

Why do people start smoking in the first place? The first puffs are often accompanied by dizziness and even nausea. Yet the (usually young) individual who starts to smoke tends to respond to other cues as well. Those who persist in smoking do so typically because the reinforcement value

of smoking outweighs these negatives. For example, the peer pressure exerted on young people may be particularly strong (Evans, Smith, & Raines, 1984). There may be immediate positive consequences provided by feeling grown up, sophisticated, and accepted. The immediate negative physical feelings of smoking then eventually give way to the rewarding effects of the stimulant drug, nicotine (Ary & Biglan, 1988). See Box 3–3 for a discussion of the prevention of cigarette smoking in young people.

People probably smoke for various reasons beyond those we have discussed. For some it is simply a deeply ingrained habit, to which they may even be oblivious. Some smoke to reduce distress, anxiety, and other negative feelings. Some smoke to increase stimulation, feel relaxed, and even to gratify sensory-motor needs. There is probably no simple reason that people smoke (National Institutes of Health, 1989).

What works to help people quit? Early in research in the mid-1970s, *aversion therapy* was used with some success. The smoker was forced to take a puff every six seconds until satiated, and then to continue until smoking became aversive. It was believed that (in an operant conditioning model, such as illustrated in Figure 3–4) the negative feelings that followed taking a puff of the cigarette would serve to reduce the probability of continued smoking. Despite early fears that rapid smoking could be dangerous and precipitate heart attacks in people with latent cardiac problems (Hackett & Horan, 1978), recent work confirms that the approach is safe and effective (Hall, Sachs, Hall, & Benowitz, 1984). Other aversive techniques, such as imagining disgust-

**BOX 3-3**

## PREVENTING CIGARETTE SMOKING BY YOUNG PEOPLE

Given the difficulties of quitting smoking, the prevention of smoking by young people is obviously a worthwhile goal. Studies show that many young children have somehow (probably through the media) absorbed the message that smoking is dangerous (Evans, 1985). Their beliefs are so strong that some young children (between the ages of 4 and 11) even try to get their parents to stop smoking. By the time they reach adolescence, however, many children yield to peer pressure to smoke. They want to look sophisticated, or to be accepted by other people their age. Many follow along in the footsteps of family members who smoke. There is evidence that children as young as those in sixth or seventh grade are exposed to continual peer pressures to smoke. Some studies have shown that as many as 20% of them already do smoke at least a few cigarettes a day (Evans, 1985).

Some health psychology researchers focus on determining ways to prevent smoking before it starts (Best, Thomson, Santi, Smith, & Brown, 1988; Evans, 1985). The most effective prevention strategies seem to be those that are aimed at junior high school students (Murray, Davis-Hearn, Goldman, Pirie, & Leupker, 1988). Researchers have found that messages to these students should not be focused on arousing their fear because messages that emphasize negative health consequences far in the future tend to be ineffective. In fact, any beliefs that junior high school students may hold about the negative health effects of smoking cigarettes tend to be outweighed by three things: peer influence, parental modeling, and cigarette advertising. Evans and colleagues (Evans, 1985) developed films for junior high students to help them overcome these three kinds of pressures and to resist the temptation to begin smoking. The films contain three elements that researchers have found to be important.

First, instead of having adult narrators, the films have adolescents convey information from the researchers. Second, the films deal with the psychological and social situations that have been found to influence adolescents to smoke. The films provide particular help in resisting peer pressure. Third, the messages in the films focus on the ability of the students themselves to resist situations that might provoke them to smoke. The student narrators tell the audience: "You can decide for yourself." The films present and then refute some commonly held beliefs about smoking, such as that it's "glamorous" and that experimenting with smoking can't lead to addiction. The goal of the interventions is to help students make their own conscious decisions about smoking rather than be pressured by the momentary situation. Research on this method of prevention has demonstrated that the junior high school students who saw these films were less likely to initiate smoking than were those who did not see the films (Evans et al., 1984).

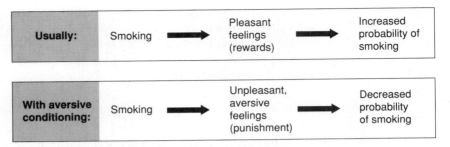

**FIGURE 3–4**  Operant conditioning of aversive therapy for smoking.

ing things associated with cigarettes, do have inital success rates (quit rates) as high as 60% to 90%, but relapse may occur if the distressing associations are forgotten over time (Leventhal & Cleary, 1980).

Exercise is one of the most promising new therapies for smoking cessation and has been found to both help people quit and prevent their returning to smoking (Brownell et al., 1986). Other therapies use operant conditioning principles such as external rewards for not smoking, self-observation, self-monitoring, cognitive interventions such as self-talk, and even self-hypnosis. (We will examine behavioral and cognitive therapies in Chapter 4 and hypnosis in Chapter 6). Probably every combination of these therapies has been tried with good initial success rates (Leventhal & Cleary, 1980). One study showed that 95% of people who quit have done so on their own (Surgeon General, 1979), and another study reported that self-quitting (with no professional help) had a success rate over 60% (with quitting maintained for over seven years) (Schachter, 1982). These findings suggest that people who attend smoking cessation clinics may be those who failed at their own personal attempts and have sought professional guidance. They may not represent the average population of smokers.

In clinical studies smoking cessation proves to be decidedly difficult to maintain. In a typical study 60% of subjects have re-

turned to smoking within only three months of quitting. After one year more than 75% have begun smoking again (Hunt, Barnett, & Branch, 1971). The failure rate of smokers to kick the habit is as high or higher than the failure rate of those who try to overcome heroin addiction (Hunt, Barnett, & Branch, 1971; Lichtenstein, 1982). Multivariate approaches to treatment appear to have the greatest success in the clinical setting (Kottke, Batista, DeFriese, & Brekke, 1988).

Why do would-be quitters have so much trouble staying away from cigarettes? The answer is multifaceted and the subject of much study. *Relapse* is particularly common in addictions (Brownell et al., 1986) and a problem that we will examine in detail in Chapter 4. *Relapse* is defined as a recurrence of symptoms of a condition after a period of improvement. In the case of smoking, *relapse* refers to returning to being a smoker after a period of having quit. Environment can play an important part in smoking relapse; that is, smoking may have become associated with many aspects of the person's social and physical environment (for example, alcohol, a cup of coffee, and friends who smoke). Some researchers have suggested that these associations actually elicit the physiological reactions that once occurred when the individual smoked. Under such circumstances, former smokers report feeling an overwhelming urge or craving (Brownell et al., 1986; Abrams & Wilson, 1986; Shumaker & Grunberg, 1986). Physiological factors cannot be ignored. Quitting smoking often brings the classic withdrawal symptoms of headache, irritability, and sleeplessness, which may last for days or weeks. Many people experience weight gain after quitting smoking. And for some people, smoking assists in dealing with emotional distress. An individual may turn back to smoking to provide a positive experience in the midst of distressful emotions, or to help eliminate those distressful feelings directly. In one study 71% of relapsed smokers had some kind of negative emotional experience immediately preceding the relapse. Most common were anxiety, anger, frustration, and depression (Shiffman, 1982). Some people go back to smoking when they no longer believe they have the ability to maintain control in avoiding cigarettes, and when they have decreased motivation to maintain the behavioral change (Shumaker & Grunberg, 1986). Social factors can be important as well. Support to refrain from smoking can be a powerful determinant of success, whereas pressure from others (for example, a spouse who smokes) to accept a cigarette can derail an attempt to stay away from cigarettes (Lichtenstein, 1982).

## ALCOHOLISM AND PROBLEM DRINKING

The excessive use of alcohol is a hazardous practice that can threaten life and health (Alden, 1980; Ashley & Rankin, 1988). It is estimated that one in every ten adult Americans is an *alcoholic*. An alcoholic is physically and psychologically addicted to alcohol and experiences health and social problems from its consumption (U.S. Department of Health and Human Services, 1981). The 10% of our population who are alcoholics drink 50% of the alcohol that is consumed in the United States (National Institute of Alcoholism and Alcohol Abuse,

1981). Alcoholics are physically addicted to alcohol, have high tolerance for it, and have little ability to control their intake. They experience severe physical symptoms of withdrawal when they attempt to stop drinking. *Problem drinkers*, on the other hand, may not evidence withdrawal symptoms but nevertheless experience social, psychological, and health problems as a result of their drinking. Alcoholics and problem drinkers usually need alcohol every day and are unable to limit the time and quantity of their intake. They continue to drink despite cognitive (for example, memory) and health impairments due to drinking (McCrady, 1988; USPSTF, 1989).

The excessive consumption of alcohol can produce some serious health problems. *Cirrhosis of the liver* is the primary cause of death among alcoholics. Cirrhosis is an accumulation of scar tissue on the liver, causing loss of functioning of this vital organ (Eckhardt et al., 1981). Heavy alcohol use can affect the constriction of the heart muscle, making it function less efficiently, and can cause nerve damage. Alcohol affects brain chemistry, and long-term heavy drinking can produce severe memory problems, disorientation, and visual disorders (Eckhardt et al., 1981).

Heavy alcohol consumption can cause infertility, and alcohol can have a direct negative effect on pregnancy and fetal development. The *fetal alcohol syndrome* affects infants of mothers who drank during pregnancy. Fetal alcohol syndrome includes mental retardation, central nervous system disorders, and growth and facial abnormalities (Pratt, 1982). Even light to moderate drinking is believed to be dangerous to the fetus, especially during the early months of pregnancy.

Problem drinkers and alcoholics put others in danger when they drive automobiles. Deaths in the United States from traffic accidents number about 55,000 a year. Approximately half of all traffic fatalities involve drunk drivers. Forty-six percent of those drunk drivers have blood alcohol levels that are close to the levels that would cause coma (Roglieri, 1980)! People who drive while intoxicated are three to 15 times more likely to have a fatal traffic accident than nondrinking drivers. Of course, drinking even moderate levels of alcohol can increase driving risk. Driving can be adversely affected by as few as three glasses of beer in a 190-pound man, and by as little as one glass of wine in a 120-pound woman (Eckhardt et al., 1981; Perrine, Waller, & Harris, 1971). Alcohol figures prominently in homicides, suicides, and accidents, the three leading causes of death in people under age 40.

Does alcohol use bring any benefits? Some research has suggested that *light* drinking (one drink a day) may provide some protection against cardiovascular disease by raising a subfraction of HDL, the "good" cholesterol that is negatively associated with heart disease (Gordon & Kannel, 1984; Gordon & Doyle, 1987; Haskell et al., 1984).

There are many theories about why people drink to excess. One classic theory is that alcohol reduces tension; it acts as a sedative and reduces anxiety, particularly in comfortable, pleasant surroundings. This simple hypothesis has not found much support, but a modified version of it has. High levels of alcohol consumption tend to decrease the strength of one's physiological response to distressing stimuli (Sher & Levenson, 1982). Rather than reducing tension, alcohol may produce tension avoidance. Furthermore, drinking can interfere with self-depreciating cognitions, making thoughts more superficial and decreasing negative ideas about oneself (Hull, 1981).

The *disease theory of alcoholism* has given rise to medically oriented treatment programs and has freed alcoholics somewhat from the stigma of their condition. While the theory is based partly on the genetic component in alcoholism, this model of alcoholism has been modified to include behavioral elements (Kamerow, Pincus, & Macdonald, 1986). Research by Marlatt and colleagues (Marlatt & Rohsenow, 1980) suggests that many of the effects of alcohol, including loss of control, may be due more to expectations and beliefs than to any pharmacological effects of alcohol. Furthermore, studies show that even severely dependent drinkers can learn to control their alcohol intake (Moos & Finney, 1983).

Current treatment programs for alcoholism and problem drinking typically use a multimodal approach—attending to biological, psychological, social, and environmental factors simultaneously (Wanburg & Horn, 1983). People learn new behaviors that are not compatible with alcohol abuse, and they learn to modify their activities and environment to eliminate the involvement with alcohol. Many programs involve a short-term, intensive, inpatient stay (for example, from ten to 60 days) with follow-up sessions. Medical detoxification may first be necessary for those with hard-core addictions to alcohol. Once the severe symptoms of detoxification have passed, therapy can begin.

One of the more successful approaches to the treatment of alcoholism is aversion therapy. Drinking alcohol is paired with an aversive event, such as nausea and vomiting (caused by a drug). Other treatment programs pair electric shock with alcohol consumption. Successful maintenance of alcohol avoidance tends, however, to require continued aversive conditioning outside therapy (Mahoney, 1974). Aversive conditioning does work in combination with other forms of therapy (U.S. Department of Health and Human Services, 1981), particularly approaches that help the individual recognize and change the factors in his or her life that contributed to the drinking. Some programs, for example, are geared to training individuals to develop the skills necessary to cope with stressful events in their lives, and to develop social skills that they can use instead of relying on alcohol (Marlatt & Gordon, 1980; Marlatt, 1982). Family therapy is also valuable in helping to identify and change the family dynamics that might rekindle and support the alcohol problem. Research suggests that the most successful programs are multimodal, and the most successful patients are those who have families to return home to, who have good job situations, and who enjoy their work (Moos & Finney, 1983).

The question of whether former alcoholics and problem drinkers can ever drink again is a subject of heated debate among many researchers. Groups such as Alcoholics Anonymous (AA) hold that a recovered alcoholic can never drink in moderation and must abstain from alcohol for the rest of his or her life. Although return to moderate drinking tends to bring about relapse to problem drinking and alcoholism in some individuals, some recovered alcoholics who fit a particular profile may be able to drink in moderation. They are those who are young and employed, and who live in supportive environments (Oxford, Oppenheimer, & Edwards, 1976). Some specific relapse prevention programs are showing promise for controlled drinking (Marlatt & Gordon, 1980).

## THE COVARIATION OF HEALTH BEHAVIORS

The various activities that we have considered in this chapter (such as maintaining normal weight, exercising, avoiding smoking) are preventive health behaviors (Kasl & Cobb, 1966). Some people, like Alex at the beginning of this chapter, carry out several actions to guard their health. Others do only one or two things. Researchers have found that, in general, preventive health behaviors tend to occur in isolation from one another. The person who maintains

normal weight and exercises, for example, may also chain-smoke cigarettes and fail to use safety belts (Baumann, 1961). (Among young adults, however, the use of various "substances" such as cigarettes, alcohol, and illegal drugs does tend to occur simultaneously [Hays, Stacy, & DiMatteo, 1984]).

Health behaviors may fail to covary precisely because they are not seen to be health behaviors at all. In fact, people tend to perceive many health-related activities to be only distantly related to health (Mechanic, 1979). For example, they may lose weight and exercise for the sake of appearance, and for the same reason refuse to wrinkle their clothing with a safety belt. They may smoke because it feels glamorous and sophisticated, and because it helps them relax in social situations. Certain actions that may seem incongruous on the dimension of health may be perfectly consistent on the dimension of appearance.

To fully understand the factors that contribute to a person's decision to engage in a particular health behavior, we must understand a great deal about his or her evaluation of that particular behavior. As we will see in the next chapter, we must be aware of precisely what a person understands, believes, feels, wants, believes other people want, intends to do, and is able to do. Only then can we understand and predict what the person *will do* to promote his or her health!

# Summary

I. In the year 1900 almost 2% of the population of the United States died. Many people died from illnesses that we no longer consider to be very serious, such as influenza and pneumonia. By 1980 the death rate had fallen to less than 1% a year and the pattern of disease had changed.

A. In the past decade the leading fatal diseases in the United States have been heart disease, cancer, and stroke. These diseases stem from many factors, such as heredity and behavior, and are referred to as the chronic degenerative diseases. These conditions are believed to be contributed to by failure to carry out some important health behaviors.

B. Heart disease is the primary cause of permanent disability in people over age 40. Most heart attacks are attributable to coronary artery disease caused by atherosclerosis. The heart muscle can be deprived of blood and hence of oxygen; this condition is a myocardial infarction, commonly called a heart attack. Research has shown that several of the risk factors for heart disease can be reduced or eliminated when people reduce serum cholesterol, control high blood pressure, quit smoking, and exercise.

C. Cancer is not one disease but a category of conditions characterized by the growth of neoplastic cells. Malignant (cancerous) cells grow and spread through the body, sometimes quite rapidly. Grouped together, they form a tumor. Various unhealthy behaviors, such as cigarette smoking, contribute to the development of cancer. Most forms of cancer have higher survival rates the earlier in the disease process the cancer is discovered, and so screening is very important.

D. Stroke (also known as a cerebrovascular accident or CVA) is a sudden impairment of circulation to the brain. A stroke usually occurs because a blood vessel has been blocked (for example, by a blood clot or a fat deposit). The blockage deprives a portion of brain tissue of oxygen, thereby damaging it permanently. Prevention of stroke requires lifetime control of hypertension. Those who are obese, have atherosclerosis, and smoke cigarettes are most at risk.

II. Preventive health behaviors are actions taken by an individual to prevent disease from developing or to forestall the negative outcomes of a disease condition.

A. Primary prevention refers to all the activities that are undertaken by apparently disease-free individuals with the intent of helping them achieve maximum well-being and avoid disease. Primary prevention includes both health promotion and disease prevention.

B. The regular use of automobile safety belts is one example of a primary prevention action.

C. Immunizations are important in disease prevention. A vaccine stimulates the production of antibodies in the human body, so that infection with a virus does not result in disease.

D. Safer sex practices are critical in preventing the spread of the human immunodeficiency virus (which causes AIDS), as well as the spread of other sexually transmitted diseases.

E. The reduction of high levels of dietary cholesterol may prevent atherosclerosis and ultimately coronary heart disease.

F. Obesity and overweight are common problems in the United States today. Once an individual becomes obese, the condition tends to be self-perpetuating.

G. Undertaken regularly over the course of one's whole life, aerobic exercise (defined as that which dramatically increases oxygen consumption over an extended period of time) can bring important benefits to health and well-being. Exercise helps to lower high blood pressure and contributes tremendously to weight control, raises high-density lipoprotein cholesterol, and strengthens the cardiovascular system.

H. Every year about 390,000 people in the United States die prematurely as a direct result of smoking cigarettes. Cigarettes can be addicting. Relapse is particularly common among cigarette smokers. Environment can play an important part in smoking relapse.

I. The excessive use of alcohol is a hazardous practice that can threaten life and health. An alcoholic is physically and psychologically addicted to alcohol and experiences health and social problems from its consumption.

# Glossary

**aerobic exercise:** exercise that dramatically increases oxygen consumption over an extended period of time, (for example, walking, running, swimming, cycling).

**alcoholic:** a person who is physically and psychologically addicted to alcohol, and who experiences health and social problems from its consumption.

**atherosclerosis:** a disease condition in which fatty, fibrous plaques narrow the opening of an artery, threatening blood flow to the heart or brain or other vital organ.

**aversion therapy:** a form of behavior modification in which punishment in the form of an aversive stimulus (for example, electric shock) is used to reduce the occurrence of a particular behavior.

**carcinogens:** cancer-causing agents.

**cholesterol:** a fatlike substance found in the blood and in organs of the body; it constitutes a large part of stones in the gallbladder and plaque on the coronary arteries.

**chronic degenerative diseases:** disease conditions that are believed to be contributed to (and in some cases caused by) failure to carry out some important health behaviors.

**cirrhosis of the liver:** a disease caused by an accumulation of scar tissue on the liver, causing loss of functioning of this vital organ.

**disease theory of alcoholism:** a theory that has given rise to medically oriented treatment programs and has freed alcoholics somewhat from the stigma of their condition.

**epidemic:** widely diffused and rapidly spreading occurrence of disease.

**fetal alcohol syndrome:** a condition caused by maternal consumption of alcohol during pregnancy. Manifestations of fetal alcohol syndrome include mental retardation, central nervous system disorders, and growth and facial abnormalities.

**hypertension:** high blood pressure.

**incubation period:** the time from exposure to infection to the onset of symptoms of the disease.

**malignant cells:** cells that grow and spread throughout the body, sometimes quite rapidly. Grouped together, they form a tumor.

**metastasis:** spread of cancer from its original site to other parts of the body.

**myocardial infarction** (commonly called a heart attack): a disease condition that can cause part of the heart muscle to be damaged or destroyed because of a lack of blood flow to the heart.

**neoplastic cells:** cells that are larger and divide more quickly than do normal cells.

**preventive health behaviors:** actions taken by an individual to prevent disease from developing or to forestall the negative outcomes of a disease condition. These include diet and exercise, the prevention of alcohol and drug abuse, stopping cigarette smoking, using automobile safety belts, and obtaining vaccinations.

**primary prevention:** a term that has gained considerable popularity in recent years and that refers to all the activities undertaken by apparently disease-free individuals with the intent of helping themselves achieve maximum well-being and avoid disease.

**problem drinkers:** persons who, although they may not evidence withdrawal symptoms, nevertheless experience social, psychological, and health problems as a result of drinking alcohol.

**relapse:** a recurrence of symptoms of a condition after a period of improvement. In the case of smoking, relapse refers to returning to being a smoker after a period of having quit.

**stroke** (also known as a cerebrovascular accident or CVA): a sudden impairment of circulation to the brain. A stroke usually occurs because a blood vessel has been blocked (for example, by a blood clot or a fat deposit).

**vaccine:** a substance that stimulates the production of antibodies in the human body, so that encounters with a pathogen (for example, virus or bacteria) do not result in infection. A vaccine is delivered during an immunization.

# Cooperating with Health Recommendations: What Determines Health-Related Behavior?

· · · · ·

Agnes Smithgard sits at her kitchen table, fiddling with the gray hair at her temples. She stares at the six pill bottles lined up in front of her. "Now, what did he say about the pink pills?" she asks herself out loud. "Before or after meals? Never with the blue ones? Oh dear, I should have asked him to write it down for me."

Agnes, age 62, has hypertension. She also has arthritis, and adult-onset diabetes. She is overweight. Her doctor has recommended that she follow a low-fat, reduced-calorie diet and that she begin a program of daily walking. Her doctor also prescribed several medications. Weight loss, exercise, and medication are expected to help reduce her blood pressure, control her diabetes, and increase the mobility of her joints, which are swollen and sore from her arthritis. There is practically no question that Agnes will feel better and be healthier if she begins her mild exercise program, but she can't seem to get around to it. The diet is a problem because sometimes Agnes feels very sad and she eats sweets to make herself feel better. And living alone as a new widow, she has some real problems remembering to take her medications.

In Chapter 3 we examined primary prevention. We considered various degenerative diseases and looked in depth at the health behaviors necessary to prevent or forestall these conditions. We examined the details of individual health behaviors, and considered some of the reasons that people fail to take these steps to promote their own health. In this chapter we examine preventive behavior in more detail, and look at the psychological factors that contribute to an individual's success or failure in efforts to adopt and maintain health actions. We look not only at primary prevention but at secondary and tertiary prevention as well (Kasl & Cobb, 1966).

## SECONDARY AND TERTIARY PREVENTION

*Secondary prevention* becomes relevant once a person has developed a condition in which he or she is at risk for further health damage. Such a condition might be hypertension (high blood pressure), which, if uncontrolled, can lead to stroke. Another condition might be arteriosclerosis (thickening of the coronary artery wall), which can lead to heart attack. Secondary prevention involves taking preventive health measures to forestall potential negative outcomes (here, of stroke and heart attack). These measures may involve medication and a special diet and exercise program, such as prescribed for Agnes Smithgard.

*Tertiary prevention* involves taking measures specifically designed to cure a disease or to control its progress. Examples of ter-

tiary prevention are the faithful taking of medication by the patient with an acute infection, or the cooperation with various aspects of treatment, such as radiation or surgery by the patient who has cancer. Tertiary prevention measures are designed to prevent further disability and handicap (Alberman, 1986; Kasl & Cobb, 1966).

Let us consider some specific examples of secondary and tertiary prevention.

**Controlling Hypertension.** Hypertension, or high blood pressure, is an unusual disorder in that it has no overt symptoms. A person can have a dangerously high blood pressure and never even suspect so because subjective feelings of blood pressure level are generally not at all accurate (Meyer, Leventhal, & Gutman, 1985). Although the name may, and often does, lead people to believe that blood pressure is elevated only when a person feels "hyper" or tense, even very relaxed people can have hypertension. Hypertension remains undetected in millions (Pennebaker & Watson, 1988).

Hypertension may be the most important risk factor for cardiovascular disease (Dawber, 1980). People with uncontrolled high blood pressure are significantly more likely to have heart attacks than are those with normal blood pressure, and the risk grows as the level of blood pressure rises. Uncontrolled high blood pressure may also result in stroke or in kidney damage.

The treatment for hypertension is multifaceted. Diligence in monitoring blood pressure regularly is necessary. Prescribed medication (usually diuretics, which reduce blood volume) are combined with a salt-restricted diet and, if necessary, weight loss, exercise, a program of relaxation, and reduced caffeine and alcohol intake (Carey, Reid, Ayers, Lynch, McLain, & Vaughan, 1976; Shapiro and Goldstein, 1982). In the first year of their lifelong regimen of self-care, however, more than 20% of hypertensives completely drop out of treatment.

Even among those who remain in treatment, less than 50% carry out their prescribed regimens to prevent further complications of their at-risk condition (DiMatteo & DiNicola, 1982).

**Controlling Diabetes.** Diabetes is a disease of metabolism. The body is unable to make or to use insulin to convert sugar and carbohydrates into energy. The failure to metabolize sugar causes an excess of glucose in the blood. Diabetes causes approximately 38,000 deaths a year, and it is estimated that, as a risk factor in heart disease and kidney failure, diabetes contributes to another 300,000 deaths per year.

Insulin-dependent diabetes (type I) develops in children, usually between 5 and 6 or between 10 and 13 years of age. Type I diabetes is managed primarily with daily injections of insulin (American Diabetes Association, 1976; Wing, Norwalk, & Guare, 1988). Type II diabetes, on the other hand, usually develops after age 40. It is not as serious as type I, and the individual produces some, though not enough, insulin. Most type II diabetics are obese (American Diabetes Association, 1976).

Diabetes can result in coma and death if it remains uncontrolled. Poor control of the disease can result in blindness and loss of extremities (for example, toes can develop gangrene from poor circulation and need to be amputated). For both type I and type II diabetes, control is complex and lifelong, requiring many behavioral changes. Diet must be restricted, sometimes severely. Eating must take place on a regular schedule. Urine or blood must be tested every day, and in the case of type I, daily self-injections of insulin must be taken (Diamond, Massey, & Covey, 1989). Safety measures, such as checking toes for sores, must be done and exercise routines followed every day. And because diabetes cannot be cured, the most any patient can hope for is preventing its terrible consequences.

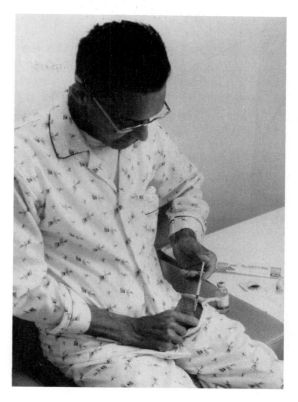

A diabetic patient self-injecting insulin.
SOURCE: Robert Goldstein/Photo Researchers

Yet, despite the serious potential outcomes of diabetes, its sufferers typically maintain very poor long-term cooperation with treatment regimens that are designed to prevent the development of further health problems. One study found that 80% of diabetics incorrectly administered their insulin; 73% did not follow their diet; 50% carried out poor foot care; 45% incorrectly tested their urine. Only 7% of the diabetes patients in the study complied with all the steps for good control (Rosenstock, 1985).

As we will see in this chapter, diabetes and hypertension are among the most difficult of conditions for physicians to treat. There are multiple reasons that people fail to regulate their own care. Not the least of these reasons is that treatment requires almost complete lifestyle change. Deeply ingrained habits must be broken and replaced with new ones. People must permanently change the daily choices they make. Finding out why they have so much difficulty can lead the way to helping patients to follow through with treatment regimens to maintain their health and prevent further disease.

## COMPLIANCE WITH MEDICAL REGIMENS

Researchers have been very actively concerned with primary, secondary, and tertiary prevention. For more than thirty years those in the fields of medicine, psychology, sociology, nursing, pharmacy, and public health have examined a phenomenon known as *patient compliance with medical regimens* (DiMatteo & DiNicola, 1982; Haynes, Taylor, & Sackett, 1979). Compliance refers to the degree of success a patient has in carrying out the prevention or medical treatment recommendations given to him or her by a health professional (a nurse or a physician, for example). *Noncompliance*, on the other hand, refers to the patient's ignoring, forgetting, or misunderstanding the regimen as directed by the medical professional and thus carrying it out incorrectly. As we noted above, secondary and tertiary prevention involve complying or cooperating with procedures for care of a diagnosed illness or condition, and primary prevention involves complying with recommendations to prevent illness from occurring in the first place.

The term *compliance* is an important one in the history of health psychology. Most research on health promotion and disease prevention can be found in the literature under the heading "patient compliance." Although many researchers now prefer to use other terms, such as *cooperation*, *adherence*, and *patient decision making*, the term *compliance* has become traditional.

BOX
4–1

## COMPLIANCE CAN MAKE YOU HEALTHY

Many people are cured of (or at least maintain control over) their diseases by following doctors' orders. Patients who cooperate with their antihypertensive regimens, for example, are more likely to have lowered blood pressure than are those who fail to comply with prescribed medications and activities (Shapiro & Goldstein, 1982). The success of a treatment recommendation is usually considered evidence that the drug or the health action prescribed was indeed effective. It's not so surprising, then, that people benefit from following effective medical treatments. What may be more surprising is that people even benefit from following recommendations that will in no way directly affect their health.

A *placebo* is a pharmacologically inert substance (such as a sugar pill) that is administered, unbeknownst to the patient, by a health professional who conveys his or her expectation that it will work. Often (and this is the best circumstance under which the placebo can be administered), the health professional also thinks that the placebo is real medication. Thus, in a *double blind* situation, both patient and practitioner think the medication is real when it is actually inert. What is important is that the health professional conveys to the patient his or her positive expectations for the medication.

One researcher conducted an extensive review of the literature on compliance with medications (Epstein, 1984). He collected only studies in which

We should keep in mind, however, that the word *compliance* suggests an attitude on the part of a health professional that his or her recommendations should be obeyed. The term presumes that the health professional's judgment is superior to that of the patient. Of course, this is not always the case. As we will see throughout this and other chapters, there are times when patients fail to follow their health professionals' recommendations precisely because they have made a different decision on their own. In fact, in the next section of this chapter, we examine the factors that determine the decisions people will make. We examine the circumstances under which people engage in or ignore potential courses of action toward primary, secondary, and tertiary prevention of health problems. The recommendations of health professionals are certainly important factors in determining health behavior, but there are many other factors as well (Rosenstock, 1988).

Box 4–1 discusses one way in which compliance may lead to positive health outcomes.

## What Determines Prevention and Treatment Behaviors?

Why might a person adopt a particular health habit, such as taking hypertension medication, using sunscreen at the beach, or exercising for cardiovascular fitness? Common sense tells us that several things are important; these might include having information, believing that the health goals are valuable, and having the ability to take the necessary steps. But commonsense analysis does not give us the whole story. To understand all of the factors that play a part in initiating and maintaining health behaviors, we must examine the various scientific models (or descriptive schemes) that psychologists use to understand health behaviors.

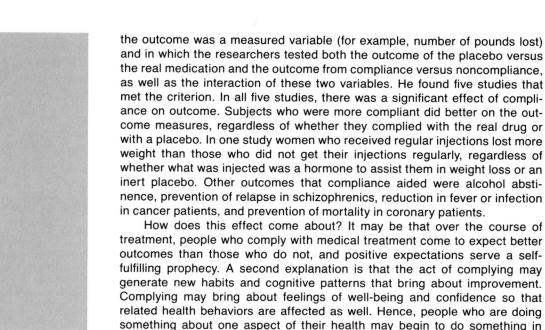

the outcome was a measured variable (for example, number of pounds lost) and in which the researchers tested both the outcome of the placebo versus the real medication and the outcome from compliance versus noncompliance, as well as the interaction of these two variables. He found five studies that met the criterion. In all five studies, there was a significant effect of compliance on outcome. Subjects who were more compliant did better on the outcome measures, regardless of whether they complied with the real drug or with a placebo. In one study women who received regular injections lost more weight than those who did not get their injections regularly, regardless of whether what was injected was a hormone to assist them in weight loss or an inert placebo. Other outcomes that compliance aided were alcohol abstinence, prevention of relapse in schizophrenics, reduction in fever or infection in cancer patients, and prevention of mortality in coronary patients.

How does this effect come about? It may be that over the course of treatment, people who comply with medical treatment come to expect better outcomes than those who do not, and positive expectations serve a self-fulfilling prophecy. A second explanation is that the act of complying may generate new habits and cognitive patterns that bring about improvement. Complying may bring about feelings of well-being and confidence so that related health behaviors are affected as well. Hence, people who are doing something about one aspect of their health may begin to do something in other areas as well, and thereby improve their outcomes.

## OVERVIEW OF A MODEL OF COMPLIANCE

What specific factors cause people to engage in the activities necessary to promote their good health, prevent illness before it occurs, and treat illness before its consequences are devastating? Throughout this chapter we will see that the following simple message comes through loud and clear: a person will not carry out a health behavior if significant barriers stand in the way, or if the steps interfere with favorite or necessary activities. Impediments such as excessive cost or impracticality must somehow be overcome. Certain sources of support (such as family enthusiasm and encouraging self-talk) can help a person to carry out the new behavior, but his or her commitment is absolutely essential. And commitment that is true and internally motivated comes only when a person believes that the health behavior will bring valued outcomes (for example, avoiding skin cancer, or achieving fitness and living longer). Real commitment comes after careful consideration of all the pros and cons of the action from many perspectives, including consideration of the wishes of family, friends, and social or cultural group. Of course, people are influenced by the content of health messages (such as how to use sunscreen, and how to engage in exercise that enhances cardiovascular fitness). They are influenced, too, by how they feel about the source of the recommendation (for example, whether they trust the health professional, or how credible they feel the media source of the information they have heard is). When commitment results from careful consideration of all these important factors, it can help the individual to overcome the many difficulties inherent in attempting health behavior change.

These are all the important factors in a very large nutshell. How will we understand what they are, and precisely how they contribute to behavior designed to promote health and prevent the ravages of illness? Systematically, of course!

# Health Information

Health information is the first necessary component and a key ingredient in any attempt to bring about health behavior. Information is a key ingredient. People will not change behaviors that they do not know are dangerous. They will not initiate behaviors they do not know are important for preserving their health. Prior to the early 1960s, for example, cigarette smoking was generally believed to be relatively safe. Then, in the 1960s, reports in the scientific literature made their way into the popular press and other media. The word was out that smoking was very dangerous to health (Surgeon General, 1964).

These days, we are learning more and more about the dangers of overexposure to the sun and the increased risk of skin cancer. We are also finding out that certain diets, high in fat and low in fiber, may increase our risk of certain other cancers as well as of heart disease. We are learning that safer sex practices, such as the use of condoms, can prevent the spread of the human immunodeficiency virus (HIV) believed to cause AIDS. Of course, this does not mean that health messages affect everyone. In a recent Harris survey (cited in Fisher & Rost, 1986), health professionals ranked "not smoking" as the number-one health protective action a person can take, but the public ranked it tenth!

### HEALTH EDUCATION FROM THE MEDIA

Health messages surround us on television, on radio, in newspapers, in magazines, and on billboards. No sooner are the studies published in scientific journals than we see reports on the evening news, in our favorite fashion magazines, and in the advertising pitches of the manufacturers who make health-promoting products.

With so many messages about health around us, it can be difficult to sort out what is worth believing and doing something about, and what is not. We are bombarded with messages about the "dangers" or risks to health "from that associated with drinking tea in styrofoam cups to the consumption of well-done hamburgers. . . . The confusion may lead some people to a fatalistic approach, thinking 'you've got to die somehow, so why worry' " (Fisher & Rost, 1986). But some risks are definitely greater than others and, after years of research, some behaviors, such as cigarette smoking, continue to be confirmed threats to health.

Unfortunately, public information campaigns often bypass the very people who are at the greatest health risk and are most in need of information (Klapper, 1960). Those with the greatest health knowledge are the most likely to attend to health messages in the first place. The relatively poor and uneducated, on the other hand, are less likely to be reached (DiMatteo & DiNicola, 1982). In general, mass media campaigns to change health behavior show fairly limited results (Hingson, Scotch, Sorenson, & Swazey, 1981). Campaigns to encourage seatbelt use, prevent unwanted pregnancies, and stop smoking show, at best, transitory, short-lived change and, at worst, no change at all (Lau, Hartman, & Ware, 1980). Many intended recipients tune out messages they do not want to hear, and are particularly oblivious to general information that focuses on abstract issues and fails to suggest specific actions that individuals must take. Mass media appeals are typically helpful only in alerting people to change health habits they may not know are dangerous (such as in the early days of alerts regarding the health risks of smoking) (Lau et al., 1980).

## HEALTH INFORMATION IN THE PHYSICIAN-PATIENT RELATIONSHIP

One potentially important source of health information is the individual's physician. The opportunity exists in the physician-patient interaction for the communication of specific information that is directly relevant to the individual. The specific behavioral steps needed to carry out the necessary health action can also be developed. Since the average American has an encounter with a physician five times a year, there are several opportunities for education (DiMatteo & DiNicola, 1982). Physicians, however, typically fail to teach their patients how to maintain their health. They devote surprisingly little time to giving information about illness prevention. A recent survey of smokers, for example, found that only 44% reported that they had ever been told to quit smoking by a physician (Anda, Remington, Sienko, & Davis, 1987). A survey of patients with AIDS showed that only 38% had ever been told by a physician how to prevent transmitting the virus to others (Valdisseri, Tama, & Ho, 1988). So, although much research demonstrates that patient compliance is enhanced when physicians give patients information and answer their questions (Hall, Roter, & Katz, 1988), this aspect of the physician's role is often neglected. (Of course, these statistics may reflect the ineffectiveness of many physicians at communicating recommendations to their patients. We examine this issue in detail in Chapter 7.) The use of nurses and health educators, as well as other auxiliary medical professionals, to convey health messages to patients has, alternatively, been quite successful (DiMatteo & DiNicola, 1982).

## SUCCESSFUL HEALTH MESSAGES

The ideal health message is one that changes a person's health behavior for the better. For example, a message about the importance of a monthly breast self-exam (BSE) would present the facts to a woman about the importance of conducting the examination and would teach her precisely how to do it properly. Then she would carry out the examination monthly, without fail. But, there's a big step from a health message to a regularly executed health behavior. In the following pages, let us trace the path.

# Beliefs and Attitudes

Our analysis of the path from health information to health behavior is built on the assumption that people act rationally on the basis of realistic and logical conclusions. We take as a given that health behavior is not driven by hidden unconscious motivations, such as the desire to be self-destructive. Rather, our model of health action is built on the assumption that if people are convinced that particular actions will take them further away from, rather than closer to, the things they value, or if they are convinced that particular actions are not in their best interests, they will rationally decide not to pursue such actions (Ajzen & Fishbein, 1977, 1980). Furthermore, if people appear at first glance to be irrational and self-destructive in their actions, we must look deeper at their thought processes. What seem to be irrational choices may, in fact, have been arrived at by using facts to which only the individuals have access or by using a reasoning process that only the individuals understand. To comprehend health decisions fully, we must analyze the process by which people evaluate health information.

First, let us define very carefully some terms that are central to understanding and predicting health-related behaviors (Stang & Wrightsman, 1981). These are

terms that most of us use every day. However, each has a specific meaning in psychology in general and in the context of models of health behavior in particular: A *belief* is a hypothetical construct that involves an assertion, often of the relationship between some object, action, or idea (for example, smoking) and some attribute (for example, is expensive, or causes cancer). While some beliefs may derive from direct experience, others may result from secondhand experience or knowledge conveyed from another person. An *attitude* is a hypothetical construct that is used to explain consistencies within people in their affective reactions to (that is, their feelings about) an object or phenomenon (for example, their dislike of brussels sprouts or final examinations) (cf. Stang & Wrightsman, 1981). Most psychological investigators agree that an attitude represents a person's emotional evaluation of an entity, and that an attitude follows from a belief (Ajzen & Fishbein, 1980). How attitudes and beliefs affect health behavior is outlined in the next section.

## THE THEORY OF REASONED ACTION

According to the *Theory of Reasoned Action* (Ajzen & Fishbein, 1980), a behavior results from an *intention* to carry out the behavior. A behavioral *intention* is an individual's commitment (to himself or herself, or to others) to carry out a behavior. An intention is brought about by two things: the individual's attitude toward the action and his or her *subjective norms* regarding it. As we will examine in more detail below, a subjective norm involves the individual's beliefs about what others (with whom he or she is motivated to cooperate) want him or her to do.

Attitudes and beliefs are related to each other in the theory in the following way. Attitudes are a function of the individual's

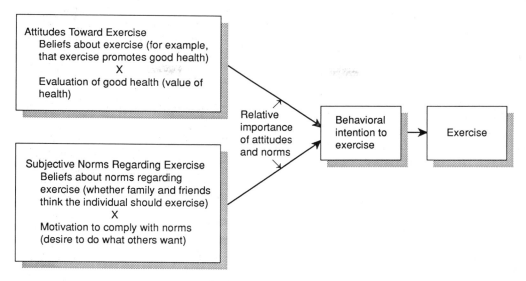

**FIGURE 4–1** Theory of Reasoned Action applied to exercise.

beliefs regarding the likely outcome of a health action and the individual's evaluation of that outcome. Thus, Karen's attitude toward quitting smoking will depend upon the extent to which she believes that quitting will lead to health *and* upon how much she values health. Furthermore, Karen's subjective norms regarding quitting (that is, what she thinks significant others want her to do) will combine with her attitude toward quitting to determine her intention to quit. Her intention is expected to be a strong determinant of whether she will actually quit.

Figure 4–1 illustrates the elements of the Theory of Reasoned Action applied to the realm of exercise. This model has considerable support from empirical research in predicting contraceptive use, weight loss, smoking cessation, and drug and alcohol use, as well as other health behaviors (Fishbein, 1980; Wallston & Wallston, 1983).

Now we turn to a detailed examination of the individual components of this model and examine research that supports its importance.

## SPECIFIC BELIEFS ABOUT HEALTH

Considerable research has been conducted on beliefs about health. These beliefs have been conceptualized in the *Health Belief Model* (Becker, 1974; Rosenstock, 1966, 1988). When the Health Belief Model was first developed, researchers expected to find that health beliefs directly caused specific health behaviors. They thought, for example, that if a person held a strong belief that immunization (against polio, for example) would protect health, he or she would always take steps to receive the immunization. The researchers discovered, however, that although beliefs do indeed affect behavior, they do not directly cause it (Rosenstock, 1974).

The Health Belief Model is quite useful, however, in that it provides us with a way to organize and understand beliefs that are relevant to health behavior. It contains components found in many models used by psychologists to explain decision making about health (Becker, 1979). To illustrate the components of the model, let's start with a case.

One day I was waiting in the lobby of a large medical office building and overheard a conversation between a young man and an older man, both smoking cigarettes. The young man said, "You know, we really should give up this habit. They say it's dangerous—can cause lung cancer."

The older man was smug. "Not a big deal," he shook his head. He gestured to the roster of physicians' names hanging on the wall. "They can always operate, you know, remove the lung. You're as good as new."

I gulped.

This man had all the answers, so he thought! His was a well-established belief that lung cancer is not very serious because it can be easily cured. Of course, he was very wrong, but we can see that his belief in the limited *severity* of the potential disease condition (lung cancer) affected his evaluation of the behavior (smoking cessation) that might help avoid the disease. Researchers have found that a belief in the severity of a disease but not the actual medical estimate of this severity affects a person's attitude toward taking steps to prevent developing the disease (DiMatteo & DiNicola, 1982; Haynes, 1979; Janz & Becker, 1984).

A second important aspect of health beliefs involves a person's assessment of his or her *susceptibility* to the disease that the health behavior is supposed to prevent. A person who holds the belief that "other people may get lung cancer, but I won't" will lack the strong belief component necessary to the commitment to stop smoking. Belief in susceptibility to the dangers of heart disease, asthma, hypertension, and obesity have been found to be important predictors

of the health actions necessary to minimize or alleviate these conditions (DiMatteo & DiNicola, 1982; Janz & Becker, 1984).

Third, research suggests that few people will initiate or maintain a behavior they don't believe will really help them preserve or regain their health. An individual must believe in the *efficacy* of an action (that is, believe it will work) in order to undertake and maintain that action. Otherwise, he or she will perceive the action as futile.

Finally, an individual must believe that the *benefits of action outweigh its costs.* Costs are not only monetary but also include things like time given up from other activities, and expected embarrassment, pain, and risk. If a person believes that following a particular course of action is more trouble than it's worth, he or she will most likely avoid the action (Ronis & Harel, 1989; Sutton & Eiser, 1990). For example, regardless of their other beliefs, people won't obtain polio vaccinations if they doubt the safety of those vaccinations. And the expectation that costs (particularly in discomfort and fear) will outweigh benefits is one explanation for the tendency of some people to avoid dental care (Kegeles, 1963).

The Health Belief Model has been valuable in developing programs to enhance patient compliance (Jones, Jones, & Katz, 1987). The components of the model are summarized in Figure 4–2.

Of course, a person might firmly believe that carrying out an action will bring a particular result. For example, Agnes, at the beginning of this chapter, may know that taking her hypertension medication will prevent premature death and disability. But if she does not particularly value the outcome, carrying out the needed action will be low on her list of priorities. The individual's evaluation of various health outcomes, then, becomes the next piece of our puzzle.

## EVALUATIONS OF HEALTH OUTCOMES AND THE VALUE OF HEALTH

The belief that certain actions will lead to a certain outcome matters only if that outcome (in this case, health) is valued. If I believe that exercise will help to make me physically strong and I value being physically strong, my attitude toward exercise will be positive. But if physical strength means nothing to me, or if I equate it with diminished femininity, I might avoid exercise altogether. Research has shown that even when people believe that certain actions will lead to health, they will carry out those actions only if they value health in the first place (Lau et al., 1986).

We might expect that everyone values health very highly, but this is not the case. Other values, such as excitement and freedom, may take priority. For example, someone who enjoys riding a motorcycle without a helmet might value the thrill of this dangerous practice above health. Research in the general population has shown that although, on average, health is the highest ranked of 18 values, between 20% and 40% of respondents do not rank health among their five highest values (Ware & Young, 1979).

The character of one's own health can affect the value placed on health in general. When people are healthy and feeling well, they tend to place a lower value on health than they do when they are facing serious illness. The value of health also varies with culture and social class. One study found that persons of lower social class were more likely to attach high value to being clean, owning a home, having insurance, and living in a good neighborhood than to good health (Larson & Sutker, 1966). Middle- and upper-class persons most valued being in good health, having a good education, being respected by people, having children,

Belief in:
- *Severity* of disease that may result from failing to take health action
- *Susceptibility* to disease that may result from failing to take health action
- *Benefits outweighing costs* (in money, time, trouble, embarrassment) of following treatment
- *Efficacy* of preventive action to be taken to prevent disease. (Belief that specific measure can be effective.)

**FIGURE 4–2**   Health Belief Model.

and having friends. Lower-social-class persons were necessarily more concerned with having their basic survival needs met than were those in the middle and upper classes, who may have taken these things for granted.

Researchers have developed a way to measure the variability in the value placed on health by using the *Value of Health Scale* (see Box 4–2). Investigations of related personality variables have also been undertaken as described in Box 4–3.

If beliefs and attitudes do not contribute positively to health behavior, can they be modified? The answer can be found in the social psychological research on belief and attitude change.

## PERSUASION: CHANGING BELIEFS AND ATTITUDES

In the last decade of this century in the United States, there is probably a greater emphasis on health promotion and disease prevention than in any previous decade in our history. As a result, we are exposed to myriad health messages intended to persuade. The American Cancer Society and the American Heart Association, for example, regularly warn us of the dangers of smoking cigarettes. We see television ad-

An effective American Lung Association anti-smoking message featuring actress Brooke Shields.
SOURCE: Courtesy of the American Lung Association

vertisements for products to increase our dietary fiber and reduce our risk of cancer. Billboard messages, at least in some of our major cities, persuade us to make sex safer. Our friends and loved ones argue that we should lose weight, exercise more, and reduce our intake of saturated fats.

As we saw earlier in this chapter, health beliefs do not arise out of nowhere. Every day, information comes our way from many sources. We accept some health messages and ignore others. What determines this difference?

Generally, people come to believe something if they are convinced it is true. This "convincing" can be carried out by an individual who engages in the process of *persuasion*. Persuasion is defined as a form of social influence in which one person uses a verbal appeal to change the beliefs and attitudes of another person (Stang & Wrights-

man, 1981). Persuasion can alter beliefs and attitudes, and thereby affect an individual's intentions to behave in a particular way.

In the field of social psychology there has been a great deal of research delineating the specific factors that influence beliefs and attitudes and cause them to change. Most relevant here are the findings of the Yale University research program on attitude change (Hovland, 1959; Hovland, Janis, & Kelley, 1953; Rosenberg & Hovland, 1960). This research has determined several important characteristics of messages that persuade successfully.

If I wish to persuade you with my message, I must convey more than just the facts. My message must put together information in ways you may never have considered, and present ideas you may never have thought of before. My message must have four characteristics: First, it must grab your attention. It must be something out of the ordinary, distinguished from the rest of the environment around you. Second, my message must be something you can understand. It must make sense to you in the context of what you already know. Third, my message must be something you can accept as worth considering, not rejecting. And fourth, my message must be retained or remembered.

Often because of time pressures, those who deliver persuasive messages present only one side of an issue, but research has found that it is better for an individual to hear both sides of an argument (for example, the advantages *and* the disadvantages of exercising with the disadvantages explicitly minimized). He or she can then decide which to believe. If the person becomes convinced by only one set of arguments, but then encounters arguments for the other point of view or experiences the disadvantages firsthand, initial beliefs may falter. When health professionals, such as patient educators, work in one-to-one interaction with a patient, their most effective strategy is to work along with the patient to examine actively arguments for and against the target health behavior.

## MESSAGES THAT AROUSE FEAR

Imagine a television advertisement that shows, in full detail, a human body without a seat belt being mangled in the front seat of a car during an accident. Or, picture a full page in a magazine that describes in detail what life is really like for a person with lung cancer. Such graphic displays of the horrible consequences of unhealthy behavior might grab your attention for a mo-

ment, but then you would probably turn the page or change the channel and deny what you saw. You might even remember it as being in poor taste.

Do scare tactics work? Usually not. Messages that arouse tremendous fear, such as pictures that show very decayed teeth, or diseased lungs, or unsightly cancerous facial growths, usually do make people upset. However, they actually may reduce the chances that a person will change his or her beliefs and behavior (Beck & Frankel, 1981). Threatening or fear-arousing messages are often unsuccessful because they increase an individual's anxiety to such a

**BOX 4–2**

## VALUE OF HEALTH SCALE

The four-item Value of Health Scale was developed by Lau, Hartman, and Ware (1986). The respondent reads each statement and then indicates his or her degree of agreement or disagreement. Two of the items are worded so that agreement indicates a high value of health (1, 4) while the other two (2, 3) are worded so that disagreement indicates a high value of health. Thus, the scoring on items 2 and 3 must be reversed before computing the total score on the scale.

| | Strongly disagree | | | Neutral | | | Strongly agree |
|---|---|---|---|---|---|---|---|
| 1. If you don't have your health you don't have anything. | 1 | 2 | 3 | 4 | 5 | 6 | 7 |
| 2. There are many things I care about more than my health. | 1 | 2 | 3 | 4 | 5 | 6 | 7 |
| 3. Good health is of only minor importance in a happy life. | 1 | 2 | 3 | 4 | 5 | 6 | 7 |
| 4. There is nothing more important than good health. | 1 | 2 | 3 | 4 | 5 | 6 | 7 |

To compute the total scale score, one must add up the four responses after first reversing the scale on items 2 and 3. Suppose a person's responses are 6, 2, 1, 6. The total score for that person is 6 + 6 + 7 + 6 = 25.

The researchers found that adults tend to place a higher value on health than do children. The average for 11-year-olds on this scale is around 12.50. For 14- to 16-year-olds, the average score is over 14. For adults the average score is almost 23. Perhaps adults no longer take good health for granted because they already have experienced health problems and limitations.

SOURCE: From "Health as a Value," by R. Lau, R. Hartman, and J. Ware, *Health Psychology*, 1986, 5(1), 25–43. Copyright © 1986 by Lawrence Erlbaum Associates, Inc. Reprinted by permission.

level that he or she denies anything is wrong and refuses to face the problem.

There are situations in which a threatening health message can work to change health behavior. The message must enhance the individual's feeling that he or she can do something to change the potential outcome and is not entirely powerless. Threatening or fear-arousing health warnings can produce change only when the warnings actually convince people that their health is in danger *and* that if they take the recommended steps they can reduce this danger. Furthermore, people must believe that they are capable of carrying out the recommended action (Beck & Frankel, 1981). To achieve change, individuals must be convinced that they can do what is necessary to avoid the terrible outcomes about which they are being warned. Therefore, a fear-arousing message should also carry specific behavioral recommendations

(Sutton & Eiser, 1990). Thus, pictures of faces ravaged by skin cancer will not work alone to get people to avoid the sun. These messages must be combined with information about how to use sunscreen and the precise steps to take to avoid overexposure (Sutton & Hallett, 1988).

## EXPOSURE TO THE MESSAGE

Research on persuasive messages has found that the more a person hears a message, the more likely he or she is to remember it and be persuaded by it (Zajonc, 1968). It is important, of course, that the message not be boring and that it be initially acceptable to the recipient. If a person is put off by a message, hearing or seeing it over and over will probably make him or her antagonistic to it and skeptical of the concept behind it.

An important phenomenon in research on persuasion is called *the sleeper effect*. The

**BOX 4–3**

## PERSONALITY AND HEALTH BEHAVIOR

What kind of people work at staying healthy? Are they people of cast-iron will who decide to commit themselves to exercise and really stick to it? Are they people with unusual self-control who modify their unhealthy dietary practices and rarely fall back into bad patterns? Who are the people who give up smoking forever because they made a decision that once and for all it's time to quit? Are they different from those who fail or don't even try? Well, it turns out that there's nothing very unusual about them. Mostly, they are people who believe they can make a difference in their lives and in their own health. They are the kind of people who believe that what they do matters.

Before we look more closely at the characteristics of those who strive to achieve health, let's examine the relative lack of success that researchers have had in studying the role of personality factors in health behavior. In early work on prevention, health promotion, and patient compliance, researchers tried to determine the extent to which people's personality characteristics determined their health actions. Mostly, personality has been a rather poor explanation for health promotion and compliance behaviors.

More than two decades ago one researcher surveyed 50 fourth-year medical students and 81 senior faculty physicians (Davis, 1966.) He asked them to state which factors they believed were general causes of patient noncompliance with medical regimens. More than 60% of each group of physicians chose "uncooperative personality" to be the primary cause

sleeper effect occurs when, a long time after exposure to a persuasive message, the recipient changes his or her belief but does not remember what influenced this change (Cook & Flay, 1978; McGuire, 1969).

For a belief to withstand external pressures, such as challenge by others, it must be stabilized (Johnson & Matross, 1975). First, the person's new belief (say, that smoking is dangerous) must be thoroughly integrated with his or her other beliefs, which may be threatened. Second, the individual must review *why* he or she holds a certain belief, and must be able to repeat the reasoning process that supports the belief. Third, the individual must innoculate himself or herself against conflicting arguments; that is, must not ignore arguments against the belief but, rather, expose himself or herself to them and learn to defend the belief. For example, he or she must learn to refute arguments that smoking is

fine because "you gotta go sometime." Finally, the belief change must come from the individual's own free choice, not from coercion by others (Johnson & Matross, 1975).

The techniques of persuasion examined above (and summarized in Table 4–1) really work. They can be used by health professionals, by organizations, by concerned friends toward the goal of promoting health beliefs, attitudes, and behaviors. These techniques increase the salience of important health information and make it more accessible to those who might potentially benefit from it.

## THE PERSUASIVE PERSON

The persuasiveness of a message is determined partly by the characteristics of the communicator. A message is more persuasive when it comes from a communicator who is liked than from one who is not. The

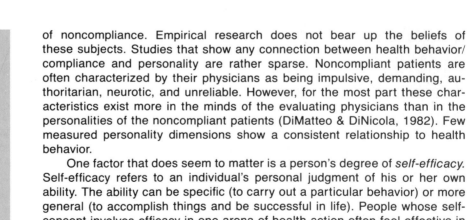

of noncompliance. Empirical research does not bear up the beliefs of these subjects. Studies that show any connection between health behavior/ compliance and personality are rather sparse. Noncompliant patients are often characterized by their physicians as being impulsive, demanding, authoritarian, neurotic, and unreliable. However, for the most part these characteristics exist more in the minds of the evaluating physicians than in the personalities of the noncompliant patients (DiMatteo & DiNicola, 1982). Few measured personality dimensions show a consistent relationship to health behavior.

One factor that does seem to matter is a person's degree of *self-efficacy*. Self-efficacy refers to an individual's personal judgment of his or her own ability. The ability can be specific (to carry out a particular behavior) or more general (to accomplish things and be successful in life). People whose self-concept involves efficacy in one arena of health action often feel effective in other areas as well. Self-efficacy is a very useful concept for understanding why some people stick to diets or stay off cigarettes for good. Several studies have found that people who believe in themselves when it comes to health behavior (who believe they can quit smoking, for example) often succeed. In one study smokers' confidence in their ability to quit was the single most important predictor of whether they even tried to do so (Eiser & van der Plight, 1986). In another, people with high self-efficacy were less likely to relapse after quitting smoking than were those with low self-efficacy (Yates & Thain, 1985).

---

**TABLE 4–1    Factors in Effective Persuasion**

*The message must*

- grab attention
- be understandable
- be something acceptable and worth considering
- be retained and remembered
- present both sides of an issue
- if a fear-arousing message, show precise steps to take to avoid dire consequences

*The person being persuaded must*

- thoroughly integrate the new message with other beliefs
- review why he or she believes what he or she does
- be innoculated against conflicting arguments

*The persuasive person must*

- be a communicator who is liked
- be enthusiastic, interested, dynamic, confident, perceived to be trustworthy, dependable, predictable, and honest

---

most effective persuader is one who is enthusiastic, interested, dynamic, and confident (Rosenberg & Hovland, 1960). Such a persuader believes the message he or she transmits and is perceived to be trustworthy, dependable, predictable, and honest, and to have motives that are in the receiver's best interest (Zimbardo, Ebbesen, & Maslach, 1977). All this can be a tall order for a health professional to fill.

Box 4–4 examines a challenge for health professionals' powers of persuasion, the patient who wishes to use unproven methods to treat cancer.

## Subjective Social Norms: What Other People Think

Beliefs and attitudes were once thought to have a very simple relationship to behavior. Psychologists once proposed that behavior follows directly from attitudes (Allport, 1935). In fact, an attitude was defined as a

state of readiness to exhibit a behavioral response. But the assumption of a direct link between attitudes and behavior was based partly on the premise that people are not at all influenced by the wishes, approval, or disapproval of others. However, many people are highly influenced by the approval or disapproval (real or imagined) of close friends and loved ones, as well as by the social and cultural group to which they belong. Such influence can provide support for health actions, making healthy behavior all the more possible to attain. Of course, the influence of others can be destructive as well, interfering with and jeopardizing the attainment of healthy action.

The term *subjective social norms* is used to refer to the expectations of others (real or imagined) for one's actions. These norms serve an important function: they give cues about what are appropriate and inappropriate actions. For example, norms for style of dress may be quite valuable for a person to know, so that the attention of others is given not to the person's attire but to what he or she says and how he or she behaves. Some norms contribute to the smooth collective functioning of a large group of people. Without certain expectations for behavior, there may be chaos (Brim & Wheeler, 1966; Rokeach, 1973).

In matters of health, certain norms become salient to an individual very early in life. These norms, usually communicated from the family of origin, may involve personal hygiene and are often concerned with specific activities, such as brushing one's teeth and avoiding using other people's towels and utensils. Other norms may arise out of the expectations of one's cultural group and involve such concerns as the best foods to eat and whether exercise and sports are valuable activities (Pratt, 1976). Usually, people are not even aware of the norms that govern their behavior until they have violated these norms and they witness the reactions of others to the deviance (Hewitt, 1979).

Of course, people vary considerably in the extent to which their intended actions

BOX 4-4

## A DIFFERENT KIND OF COMPLIANCE: USING UNPROVEN METHODS OF TREATMENT FOR CANCER

By definition, an unproven method for treating cancer is one that has not been scientifically demonstrated to be effective. For example, a major randomized clinical trial study (defined in Chapter 2) showed the drug laetrile to be worthless for prolonging the lives of cancer patients. Two randomized control trials of high-dose Vitamin C therapy in terminal cancer patients showed the vitamin to be ineffective in prolonging life (Moertel, Fleming, Creagan, Rubin, O'Connell, & Ames, 1985). Although some methods are simply unproven but benign, others are also unsafe; for example, laetrile can cause death from cyanide poisoning (Moertel, Rubin, Sarna, Young, Jones, & Fleming, 1981). Some "alternative" clinics have even infected patients with the HIV virus when providing them with purported cures derived from human-blood products (Boyd, 1985a, 1985b). At the very least, when patients turn from conventional treatments to unproven ones, they delay proper treatment until it may be too late to lengthen their survival time and even to control their pain with conventional medical treatment methods.

Five common unproven methods for cancer treatment are laetrile, Krebiozen, Hoxsey's Herbal Tonic, immunoaugmentative therapy (IAT), and Iscador. These methods are often more acceptable to patients than are conventional medical treatments because they claim to be painless and nontoxic (unlike surgery and chemotherapy). Proponents of these therapies are not cancer experts and they often attack the medical and scientific establishment. It is frequently said that the medical/scientific community is denying or hiding the effective cancer cure. Proponents espouse freedom of choice regarding cancer therapies.

Not surprisingly, the desire for unproven cancer therapies may derive from patients' difficulties in dealing with medical professionals who fail to provide them with sufficient information and emotional support. Many of those who accept unproven therapies are educated patients who place emphasis on personal responsibility and nutrition, two areas often ignored in conventional medical care.

are influenced by social expectations (Triandis, 1977; Fishbein & Ajzen, 1975). Some may act independent of relevant norms regarding their health behavior. Some may gather facts from other people but evaluate those facts independent of the opinions of others. Some may rely regularly on other people to evaluate various courses of action and to tell them what to do. The Theory of Reasoned Action takes account of differences in the salience of social norms. Note in Figure 4–1 that personal attitudes and the influence of social norms can be weighted differently by each individual.

It is important to keep in mind, of course, that not everyone is influenced by the same norms. One man might be strongly motivated to fulfill the expectations of his friends; another is affected only by what he thinks his family wants him to do. In the spirit of rebellion, a woman might even decide to do precisely the opposite of what she perceives to be the wishes of those around her. Yet another person might be influenced strongly by what he or she thinks are appropriate behaviors for a member of the cultural group, particularly if he or she has a strong sense of cultural identity (Mechanic, 1978b).

The Theory of Reasoned Action (see Figure 4–1) presents a scheme for systematically analyzing the influence of other people on an individual's commitment to a particular behavior (Ajzen & Fishbein, 1980). Let us examine how the influence of various members of an individual's social network, specific people as well as actual or imagined groups of people, can be analyzed. First, these individuals or groups must be listed: for example, parents, spouse or significant other, close friends, the people at work, heroes, and members of the cultural group. Different normative sources are likely to encourage different behaviors, and so to analyze the net effect of the influ-

ence of others, one must delineate precisely what each individual or group wants and one's motivation to comply with these desires.

Let's consider this example. Janet is trying to make a decision about whether to commit herself to an exercise program that involves weight training. She is influenced by the wishes of several people in her family, by her boyfriend, and by what she thinks are the values of her peers:

GOAL: WEIGHT TRAINING THREE TIMES
A WEEK TO DEVELOP PHYSICAL STRENGTH.

| Person or group | Value orientation toward goal | Janet's motivation to comply |
|---|---|---|
| father | positive | high |
| sister | very negative | low |
| boyfriend | very positive | very high |
| peers | negative | very high |

Note that Janet's father and boyfriend are quite positive about her proposed program. She is motivated to comply with their desires, and tends to be influenced by their appraisal of her potential actions. On the other hand, Janet's sister is very much against the whole idea of weight training; however, Janet is not eager to follow her sister's wishes anyway. The chances for the behavioral program are good, so far. One possible snag is Janet's perception of what her peers think of a young woman who lifts weights. She is particularly uncomfortable with the idea that other young women may tell her that she looks "unfeminine" with well-developed muscles. The net effect of the influence on Janet of her social norms is likely to be positive. However, the influence of norms would not be as strongly positive as it would be if she perceived other young women to be in favor of weight training or if her motivation to comply with the value orientation of her peers were quite low.

# Intentions and Commitment

In considering beliefs, attitudes, and social norms, we have been working toward an understanding of the formation of behavioral intentions. A *behavioral intention* is an individual's stated or acknowledged commitment to carry out a particular action. As we noted above, a positive attitude and supportive social norms do not necessarily change health behavior. They do, however, contribute to establishing the intention to act (see Figure 4–1). When there are no barriers standing in the way, intentions are good predictors of overt action (Triandis, 1977; Fishbein & Ajzen, 1975; Ajzen & Fishbein, 1980).

A stated intention (stated to oneself or to others) is a commitment, a pledging, or a binding to a particular course of action (Kiesler & Sakamura, 1966). Many studies have shown that if a person makes a commitment to a particular course of behavior, he or she will probably carry out that behavior. Certain troublesome factors, such as lack of money or time, might stand in the way, but because the person believes the behavior will enable reaching valued goals, and/or because the person wishes to adhere to certain social norms or please certain people, he or she will try to follow through with behavior. Commitment involves a promise to take steps to carry out the behavior. Of course, for change to occur, commitment must follow from the individual's perception that he or she is free to act otherwise.

Commitment can come in several forms: a promise to oneself, a commitment to a family member, even a written contract with a health professional. For some people, the independent decision and resulting promise to self are most effective. For others, the expectations of family members or friends might be more salient, and thus a more powerful motivating force. But some form of personal commitment is a critical step toward long-term health behaviors.

# Making Things Happen: Turning Commitment into Behavior Change

Commitment is not the final step, for even when people have made promises to themselves or to others, they can still fail. The actions they intend may be too much trouble or other priorities may capture their attention. People cannot always do what they intend because of a lack of resources, knowledge, and useful tactics. Health messages may convince, and intentions may be serious, but the typically low success rate of New Year's resolutions suggests that behavior change may be very difficult, even for the most well intentioned. Commitment does not provide an individual with the skills needed to make behavioral changes. As Figure 4–3 illustrates, good intentions do not always result in desired behavior.

People who want to be healthy, and practitioners who want to help them, need techniques to enhance the development and maintenance of health behaviors. Here are some of those techniques.

## BEHAVIOR MODIFICATION

Despite the power of their good intentions, many people find that their behaviors (good and bad) are regulated by habit. The environment and day-to-day events often seem to control the individual's health behavior. The force of habit must be tamed if an intention is to be translated into a consistent health behavior. Indeed, once an intention has been established, practice of the desired behavior is perhaps the greatest sin-

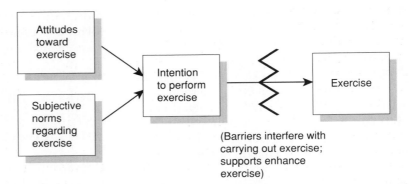

**FIGURE 4–3**  Expansion of the Theory of Reasoned Action applied to exercise.

gle factor that determines whether or not it will be acquired. The desired health behavior itself must become a powerful habit (Becker & Maiman, 1980).

Let's examine some strategies for bridging the gap between intentions and actual behavior change. These strategies are based on the fact that much of health behavior is learned and that destructive behavior patterns can be replaced with newer, healthy ones (Zifferblatt, 1975; Kasl, 1975; Rosenstock & Kirscht, 1979). The behavioral approach is among the most fruitful for establishing healthy behaviors once intentions have been stated. In fact, an entire field known as *behavioral medicine* applies the experimental analysis of behavior to the prevention or management of illness problems (Katz & Zlutnick, 1975).

The *behavioral approach* to health holds that with appropriate learning, a person can change his or her destructive behaviors and act toward the achievement of health. Once a person has come to make a commitment to the behavior change, success can be a matter of finding the right behavioral program to meet his or her needs. Using a behavioral approach, problems are defined in terms of specific behaviors and involve exactly what the person does, where, when, and with whom. Explanations that focus on

the individual's personal characteristics are avoided.

Consider Carolyn, who has a problem with binge eating. Too often Carolyn comes home from work and heads straight for the refrigerator. She has developed a habit of eating large quantities of processed, high-fat, high-calorie foods; they include ice cream, cookies, potato chips, and cola, and are clearly not nutritious for an active young woman in her 20s. Carolyn's problem, in behavioral terms, is not that she's "uncontrolled" or a "binge eater"—such labels are derogatory and unproductive. Rather, her problem behavior is that she allows herself to become exceedingly hungry by skipping lunch. She drinks coffee all afternoon, a habit that makes her feel anxious and causes her blood-sugar level to fall quite low at the end of the afternoon. In addition, she has developed a habit of eating immediately after arriving home. She uses food to reduce the tension she experiences from her work.

One solution to Carolyn's binge-eating problem would be to develop different habits. For example, she could eat balanced meals throughout the day, and after work she could take a warm bath to relax. She could also practice yoga or take an exercise class after work. Then she could prepare a nutritious dinner for herself. By focusing on specific behaviors, Carolyn could lose weight and be healthier, as well as find more effective ways to deal with her work stresses. By doing so, she would avoid self-depreciating labels that might be damaging to her self-concept.

As we noted in Chapter 3, a basic principle of the behavioral approach is that reinforcement of a particular behavior will increase the frequency with which that behavior occurs. Reinforcement is anything that increases the probability of the occurrence of a particular behavior. Rewards of various sorts can serve as reinforcements. Any behavior can be removed from the control of environmental reinforcements and brought under control of self-imposed reinforcements. In principle, all health behavior problems can be overcome by means of behavioral self-control (Goldstein & Kanfer, 1979).

## BEHAVIORAL SELF-CONTROL

The ultimate goal of the behavioral approach, as we examine it here, is for the individual to translate his or her intentions into behaviors and to maintain the performance of those behaviors. A common term for such activity is *self-control*. Although other people, such as health professionals or family members, can certainly assist the individual in carrying out health behaviors, no one else can consistently monitor his or her behavior and dispense rewards or punishments accordingly. Rather, the behavioral regimen must be based upon self-control and self-management.

The capacity for self-control involves not something that one *is* but rather something that one *does* (Thoreson & Mahoney, 1974). Self-control is a *skill* that one can acquire (Goldstein & Kanfer, 1979).

Let's review, in somewhat more detail, a few of the basic behavioral principles that

were referred to briefly in Chapter 3. Some excellent references in this field are books by Bandura (1969), Rimm and Masters (1974), Stuart and Davis (1972), and Mahoney and Thoreson (1974).

*Classical or respondent conditioning* is a process by which a behavior comes to be evoked by a once-neutral stimulus because that stimulus was paired with one that automatically evoked the behavior. As an example, imagine that I munch (popcorn, peanuts, M&M's and other delicious, enticing goodies) nearly every time I read. Pretty soon the stimulus of opening my book will evoke my desire to munch. Some smokers report that smoking is sometimes so automatically triggered by external stimuli (such as a cup of coffee, or the sight of their desk) that they find themselves half way through a cigarette with no recollection of having lit up!

Classical conditioning of unhealthy behaviors can occur readily and inadvertently. An individual who wishes to be in control of his or her behavior must be constantly aware of the stimuli in the environment and his or her response to them. Suppose that Andrea wants to limit the number of stimuli in her house that cue her to snack when she is bored. She must limit her eating to one and only one place in the house: the kitchen table. She must allow herself to eat only when sitting down with a place setting and a limited portion of food. This restriction will prevent her from eating when she is not hungry just because eating may feel like a fairly pleasurable way to keep busy. By making eating a less convenient activity, Andrea will be able to limit the amount of time she spends eating and perhaps find other diversions for herself. In this same manner, Karen can limit cigarette smoking at work to break time, and smoke only far away from her desk. In this way, she can limit the cues that trigger her desire for a cigarette. Of course, classical conditioning principles can be used not only to eliminate unhealthy behaviors but to enhance healthy behaviors as well. For example, by taking vitamins with every breakfast, John can increase the likelihood that breakfast will serve as a cue or reminder for him to take his vitamins.

*Operant conditioning* is based on the principle that behavior is shaped by the consequences that follow it. The famous psychologist B. F. Skinner (1938) persuasively demonstrated the powerful force of operant conditioning, and considerable research has been done since then on this aspect of behavior modification (Bandura, 1969; Karoly, 1980). Operant behavior that is rewarded or reinforced (by the individual himself, or by the environment) is more likely to be repeated. Reinforcement, of course, can be positive or negative. *Positive reinforcement* increases the probability that a behavior will be enacted by providing the individual with something that he or she values after enacting the target behavior. *Negative reinforcement* occurs when an individual is removed from a negatively valued (for example, uncomfortable) state as a result of enacting the behavior. Thus, alcohol abuse may be negatively reinforced (and thereby increase in probability of occurrence) if the result is a reduction in anxiety. Of course, operant behavior that is *punished* will diminish in frequency of occurrence.

Self-imposed operant conditioning occurs through the process of *self-regulation*. Self-regulation has three stages. The first, *self-monitoring*, or *self-observation*, involves deliberately and carefully attending to the precise details of one's own behavior. It may include keeping records of exactly what one eats and how often one smokes, for example. Complete details of behavior might be recorded in a diary. The exact foods eaten and their quantities, as well as the location, times, antecedent and conse-

quent events, and feelings might be listed. The individual can then analyze his or her own behavioral patterns, such as what moods trigger smoking and overeating. A great deal can be revealed that will help in behavior change.

The second stage in self-regulation is *self-evaluation*. The behaviors assessed through self-monitoring are compared against a specific criterion or ideal. For example, a person might compare the percentage of daily calories obtained from fat with the ideal, which is around 20%. Sometimes, so much is revealed to a person by self-monitoring and self-evaluation that behavior is modified without further intervention. Other times, however, behavior must be changed with some form of self-reinforcement.

The third stage of self-regulation is called *self-reinforcement*. The individual rewards or reinforces herself or himself for behavior that matches or approximates the goal. For example, a half hour of exercise might be regularly rewarded with ten minutes in the health club's steam room. Poor choices for rewards, of course, are those that actually sabotage the goal, such as having a hot fudge sundae after a week of successful dieting!

People may fail to translate their intentions into health behaviors because they lack awareness of their own current behavior and of ways to modify it. Their performance criteria may be vague (for instance they want to get in shape but really don't know how to exercise with maximum effectiveness). People may even have incorrect notions about the timing of rewards. Some may think it's fine to take the reward before performing the target behavior! This, of course, is an approach that is likely to fail miserably. Thus, patient education can contribute a great deal to assist a person in self-regulation toward the goal of healthier behaviors.

## OTHER BEHAVIORAL STRATEGIES

**Prompts and reminders.** What initially triggers health behavior that is to be reinforced? Usually the behavior is triggered by some kind of prompt or reminder, such as a note on the refrigerator door to choose fruit for a snack. As a reminder to take medication in the morning and at night, a person might place the pill bottle next to the toothbrush. Brushing one's teeth before bed and after breakfast will then serve as the stimulus, or reminder, for the necessary action. Some people use special pill packages and calendar packs, such as those that come with contraceptive medication (birth control pills), which can help to keep track of daily pill intake. Other behavioral prompts include pill containers with a special time-alarm buzzer system. Reminders from family members can be extremely helpful, as can reminder postcards and calls from health professionals, in prompting behaviors ranging from pill taking to follow-up medical and dental visits (Haynes, 1979b). Indeed, compliance with long-term regimens such as medication and lifestyle changes for the treatment of hypertension require an intensive, long-term program of initiating behaviors with consistent prompts and reminders, and then reinforcing those behaviors.

Fortunately, the longer a person has engaged successfully in a behavior, the more environmental stimuli there are to serve as prompts and reminders to carry out the behavior. After one has acquired the habit of exercising regularly, for example, many things in the environment serve as prompts to exercise (such as the shoes one uses for running or the hand weights one uses for muscle conditioning). Prompts and reminders can be used to one's advantage. Purposely keeping exercise gear nearby (in the car, for example) or interacting with people who exercise regularly can provide the necessary prompts to initiate the desired behavior.

**Shaping.** Graduated treatment implementation, or shaping, involves the application of reinforcement for successive approximations to the desired behavior. Shaping involves initially rewarding anything that vaguely resembles the target action, such as putting on running shoes and walking around outside. Over time, only progressively closer approximations to the desired behavior are reinforced. Eventually, the individual must run the entire target distance to receive reinforcement. Thus, the individual moves in a stepwise fashion to build a behavioral repertoire (Kanfer & Phillips, 1970; Matthews & Hingson, 1977).

The behavioral approach can be extremely valuable in modifying health behaviors. However, alone it may work inefficiently. Let us examine how a behavioral strategy for change can be enhanced with a strategy of cognitive modification.

# Cognitive Modification

Even after a person has established a strong behavioral intention to act, cognitive factors may continue to determine whether or not he or she is able to change successfully. Recent research suggests that the most effective methods for modifying health behaviors involve a combination of cognitive and behavioral modification techniques (Meichenbaum, 1977; Meichenbaum & Genest, 1980).

What people think can play an important role in their ability to control what they do. Assessments of and expectations for their own ability can play a decisive role in the maintenance of behavior change (Wilson, 1980).

The best behavioral regimen can be ruined by a person's use of negative self-statements. Suppose that one evening I give in to my overwhelming craving for a double hot fudge sundae (with French vanilla and chocolate fudge ice cream). I've "broken" my diet and failed at my behavioral regimen. I might then torture myself with thoughts like "See, I really have no control. I am doomed. I may as well forget the idea of ever getting into shape." Such negative self-talk can lead me to abandon my behavioral regimen altogether, and to give up my goals. This is often the outcome of one lapse by a dieter, or by a person who has quit smoking, or by a former drinker. One mistake may begin a round of self-depreciation that ends in feelings of hopelessness and in disaster for the good intentions.

A better approach for the relapsing would-be self-controller is to focus on thoughts of the intended behavior while making encouraging rather than discouraging self-statements. To really succeed at long-term maintenance and control, an individual must become aware of potentially damaging negative self-statements, and learn to use self-instructions that are compatible with success (Brownell, Marlatt, Lichtenstein, and Wilson, 1986).

Behavioral approaches work well when internal dialogues support, not interfere with, the process of behavioral self-control. When internal dialogues are negative, there is significant risk that self-regulation will be undermined.

An individual can learn to replace negative, self-depreciating self-statements with positive, encouraging ones. This can be done by applying the three self-regulation principles described above (self-monitoring, self-evaluation, and self-reinforcement) to what he or she is thinking. The individual must first become aware of the damaging self-statements by making them conscious and analyzing them. This might be accomplished by saying these thoughts as they occur out loud into a tape recorder or by writing them

down at regular intervals during the day. Then the individual needs to evaluate the statements and determine the extent to which they are encouraging or not. Finally, the discouraging, negative self-statements need to be replaced with positive ones (see Table 4–2), and the positive statements must be practiced and reinforced (Atkins, 1981).

Cognitive modification is much broader than the simple adjustment of self-statements. Vicarious learning and the modeling of the behaviors of others fall into the category of cognitive modification as well (Meichenbaum, 1977). Other forms of cognitive modification are examined in considerable detail in Chapters 6 and 11.

## PRACTICAL SUPPORTS AND BARRIERS TO BEHAVIOR CHANGE

Certain practical aspects of people's lives can either enhance their ability to carry out their intended health actions or make these actions relatively impossible to accomplish. Obviously, an individual's *access* to health services of various types (for example, immunizations) can affect whether he or she will actually use them. The longer a person is required to wait to follow through on a target health practice, such as seeing a physician or nurse to check blood pressure, the less likely he or she is to do it. Many other factors in people's lives can hinder their receiving medical care at all, such as the inability to get a baby sitter and lack of transportation (DiMatteo & DiNicola, 1982; Saunders, 1987).

The cost of medical care and of certain preventive measures is often cited as the explanation for an individual's failure to carry out intended health behaviors. Certainly, a lack of financial and other resources can constitute an impediment to the best of intentions. Many patients, for example, cite financial need as the explanation for their noncompliance with both

| TABLE 4–2 | Replacing Negative Self-Statements with Positive Ones |
|---|---|
| 1. Negative | "Exercising is uncomfortable. I wish it were over and done with." |
| Positive | "This doesn't feel too bad and when it's over, I'll feel invigorated and glad I exercised." |
| 2. Negative | "I feel stupid walking around this neighborhood. Everyone thinks I'm crazy for doing this." |
| Positive | "Probably nobody is watching me. If they are, they probably admire my dedication to my health." |
| 3. Negative | "I've only run one mile and I'm already tired. How will I ever cover another mile?" |
| Positive | "I've run one mile already. I'm half-way there. I'm into the home stretch." |
| 4. Negative | "I can't imagine taking this medication every day from now on. That's too overwhelming." |
| Positive | "I can do this one day at a time." |

therapeutic and preventive regimens. Even when treatment is free, however, many people still don't avail themselves of it (Cody & Robinson, 1977). And some health behaviors actually save people money (for example, quitting smoking, eating less). Reducing prohibitive costs works only when a person has already stated an intention to carry out the action. Once the intention has been stated, however, reducing the financial burden on the person can make the target behavior as easy as possible to carry out (DiMatteo & DiNicola, 1982).

Not surprisingly, a complex treatment regimen is more difficult to follow than is a simple one. Taking one or two pills a day, for example, can be relatively easy. The action of taking a pill can be paired with a regularly occurring activity, such as getting up in the morning, brushing one's teeth, or going to bed at night. But taking three pills is challenging and four pills more challenging still. Lunch and dinner may occur irregularly, if at all. The pill bottle may be forgotten at home as often as it is brought along to work. The pattern of regularly scheduled prompts and reminders that are

relied upon to trigger behavior may go awry, causing pills to be missed.

Special pill packages, such as those used for oral contraceptives, can help patients to remember to take their pills and to keep track of how many they have taken (Smith, 1989). Research suggests, however, that each time the number of pills per day is increased (from two to three, or from three to four) or another pill is added with its own unique schedule, failure to comply with the prescribed dosage increases dramatically (Cockburn, Gibberd, Reid, & Sanson-Fisher, 1987).

In general, it is better for an individual to tackle one behavior at a time and then *link* the successful health behaviors together. Taking on too many health resolutions at one time and making more than one change in daily lifestyle can be overwhelming and bring temptations to abandon everything out of frustration. Suppose that I want to change several of my health behaviors. I can increase my chances of success by approaching them in sequence. I might develop a behavioral regimen of self-regulation for one of my health goals, say,

Having a running partner can help support the exercise habit.
SOURCE: Michael Hayman/Stock, Boston

riding my stationary exercise bicycle four times a week. Only after this regular exercise has become a habit, reinforced perhaps with a relaxing hot shower afterward, would I begin to add on. I might decide, for example, that it is time to improve my diet. I would develop a self-regulation regimen to reduce the fat content of my diet (first to 30% and then to 20%) and cut in half my intake of simple sugars. My rewards can include purchasing some attractive, fashionable clothing and getting a facial and sports massage a few times a month to reduce the tension that once inspired my terrible diet. I might even make a point to pay for these with money I put aside every time I wanted to purchase high-fat snacks but

resisted the urge. Now the good physical feelings that accompany exercise, a hot shower, and a facial and massage, and the psychological boost that comes from looking better and wearing new clothes can become the reinforcers for a healthier diet.

## SOCIAL SUPPORT

Family and friends play a crucial role in providing encouragement for achieving health goals. Their help is the all-important ingredient called *social support*. Social support has been defined as any input that furthers the goals of the receiver of the support (Caplan, 1979). There are two major kinds of social support: *tangible support*, including physical resources that benefit the individual in some way, and *psychological support*, which provides the individual with help to develop affective or emotional states that engender well-being. Tangible social support helps the person out; psychological social support helps him or her to feel better.

Social support, particularly from a person's family and close friends, can play an important role in assisting him or her to translate intentions into health behaviors. Lack of social support, on the other hand, can be quite devastating to the health goal. Consider the example of smoking. One review found that the "best predictors of relapse following cessation among adults are the smoking habits of family and friends. . . . It is commonplace for relapsed smokers to report obtaining the cigarette with which they relapsed from a friend who may even have offered it. Those attempting to stay off cigarettes report high and troublesome levels of friends smoking in their presence" (Fisher & Rost, 1986, p. 555). On the other hand, time spent with nonsmokers as well as sustained participation in smoking cessation programs with others who have the same goal, help maintain

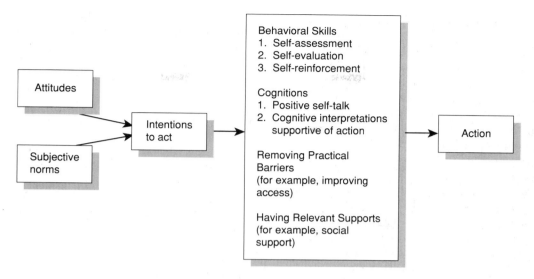

**FIGURE 4–4** Enhancing supports and removing barriers to carrying out intentions to act.

quitting (Fisher & Rost, 1986). In general, the positive presence of people who are either verbally encouraging or who themselves enact the target behavior can do much to facilitate the translation of intentions into behaviors.

Figure 4–4 summarizes the factors we have considered that can contribute to or inhibit the successful translation of behavioral intentions into health behaviors.

## Preventing Relapse

Perhaps the biggest problem facing the individual who strives to adopt healthy practices and eliminate unhealthy ones is *relapse*. As we noted in Chapter 3, relapse is defined as the recurrence of symptoms (or behaviors) after a period of improvement. The former smoker, who has abstained from cigarettes for months begins to smoke regularly. The patient who has been treated successfully for obesity begins steadily to gain weight. The diabetic, whose blood sugar levels have remained constant, loses dietary control and stops taking insulin regularly. Relapse rates are relatively high (50% to 90%) for smoking, alcohol abuse, and obesity (Hunt, Barnett, & Branch, 1971).

Not all *backsliding* (returning briefly to the past behavior) leads to relapse. Less serious is the *lapse*, described as a mistake, an error, or a slipup that involves a reemergence of the previous habit but that may or may not lead to a state of relapse. In fact, how a person looks at such a slipup or lapse can influence whether he or she remains in control, or turns a lapse into a full relapse. Research has demonstrated that to what a person attributes a lapse may determine whether or not a relapse is experienced. Those who relapsed were found to have more internal, characterological explanations for the slip than did those who did not relapse. The relapsers blamed themselves and their own personal characteristics more than they did the setting for their lapse (Brownell et al., 1986).

"The chief obstacles to maintenance of any new behavior are high-risk situations for which the individual lacks coping skills" (Rosenstock, 1985, p. 614). These situations vary from person to person but usually include negative emotional states, such as anger and frustration, interpersonal conflicts, such as arguments with a spouse or disagreements with people at work, and social pressures, such as temptations at gatherings in which other people are engaging in the behavior that the individual is trying to avoid (Brownell et al., 1986). When circumstances constitute a high-risk situation, the chances of slipup in one's established health behaviors can easily occur.

Avoiding high-risk situations is certainly a wise approach, provided doing so does not deprive the individual of experiencing other aspects of life that he or she values. Sometimes, avoidance is not possible, such as when the boss is having a cocktail party and failure to attend might put one's job in jeopardy. In fact, a high-pressure situation that cannot be avoided (such as this party) may trigger enough anxiety and negative emotion that an individual uses the forbidden behavior (smoking, drinking alcohol, overeating) as a crutch to deal with the distress. In such a case, it is still possible for the individual to stop the lapse or slipup from turning into a full relapse. He or she must recognize that the unique environmental circumstances, *not* personal shortcomings, are responsible for the initial failure, and that he or she may need to develop specific methods for coping with such circumstances in the future.

In sum, relapse can be caused by a combination of the following factors: negative emotional states, inadequate initial motivation, lack of skills to cope with the pressures to relapse, physiological factors (such as craving), lack of social support for continuing the health behavior, and environmental stimuli and contingencies that favor the unhealthy behavior (Brownell et al., 1986). Research suggests that there are three stages in the prevention of relapse (Brownell, 1986):

1. Enhancing one's motivation to continue the health behavior by providing oneself with regular rewards (such as purchasing a new outfit when weight loss is maintained) and/or by focusing on the rewarding natural consequences of the behavior (such as feeling more energetic when exercising regularly).

2. Acquiring and practicing skills to prevent and to deal with lapses, which probably will occur. For example, one might recognize the relationship between certain environmental cues (the smell of the fresh-cookie store at the mall) and relapse (eating high-fat, high calorie cookies). One might then avoid those cues if possible (by staying away from that part of the mall, particularly when one is hungry).

3. Maintaining the health behavior by continued careful monitoring, general lifestyle change, and seeking out social support.

With effort, positive health behaviors (and the avoidance of negative ones) can be maintained indefinitely. With knowledge, skill, and support, people really can change their lives and improve their health.

# A Final Word

Psychologists tell us that adopting a new health behavior and dropping a bad health habit can be quite difficult. As I write this book, I am trying to modify some of my own health behaviors. I want to add some good ones and take some bad ones away! Specifically, I want to improve my diet, a goal I have been trying to achieve for more years than I care to admit. I am trying to cut down on fat intake, and eat more complex carbohydrates including whole grains, fruits, and vegetables. I'm trying to get into a regular routine of taking vitamins, and I hope (against hope) to reduce my intake of ice cream significantly. I have very strong beliefs that these dietary goals are valuable and that they represent the path to good health. I am surrounded by supportive social norms and lots of tangible help and emotional support. Prompts and reminders greet me everywhere I turn. I have developed valuable behavioral and cognitive strategies. And they work like a charm. Mostly.

Sometimes, however, I suspend rationality and I just get tired of being good. I want ice cream, and that's all there is to it. So I give in and live a little. A week or so later, when extra pounds are becoming obvious, I reform again and hope that I have not clogged my coronary arteries too much or further increased my chances of breast cancer because of the ridiculously high fat content of my favorite brand.

At this writing, I am basically healthy. The diseases I might prevent by improving my diet would likely befall me far in the future, if they do at all. And, when I fail to eat a proper diet, I console myself with the knowledge that I exercise regularly, and I don't smoke. It is as if I bargain with some imaginary Calculator In The Sky: I can have a dish of ice cream in exchange for a half hour on the treadmill at the gym.

I wonder, though, what I might do if I were a diabetic and a slightly uncontrolled diet could put me in a coma or kill me. I wonder what would happen if I were hooked on alcohol instead of ice cream. I find I am not at all surprised at the noncompliance figures in the research literature. No wonder so much attempted health behavior results in failure. Changing can be very difficult.

I also realize, however, that if a person tries, he or she will probably make some progress. Cutting down on fat, even if there are some slipups, is much better than ignoring nutrition and subsisting on choco-

late and french fries. Walking from the dorm to classes may not be quite as good as taking Physical Education 101 four times a week, but compared to taking the campus shuttle everywhere, it is a big step toward overcoming the negative effects of a sedentary lifestyle. The psychological constructs that we have examined in this chapter (such as health beliefs, attitudes, commitment, and the techniques of self-monitoring, self-reinforcement, and shaping), whether they happen naturally or are instigated by a clinician or health psychologist, do move people along the road to better health. Probably most people have quite a long way to go to perfect health, but health psychology can help us make a good start.

## Summary

Chapter 4 examined preventive behavior in further detail and looked at the psychological factors that contribute to an individual's success or failure in efforts to adopt and continue certain health actions.

I. Secondary and tertiary prevention play essential roles in health promotion and disease prevention.
   A. Secondary prevention is necessary to forestall negative health outcomes of individuals with at-risk conditions, such as hypertension (high blood pressure) and arteriosclerosis (hardening of the arteries). Examples of secondary prevention include taking medication or following a special diet or exercise program.
   B. Tertiary prevention involves taking measures to cure or control the progress of a disease. Examples would be the use of surgery or radiation to eliminate a cancerous tumor.

C. Secondary and tertiary prevention are designed to prevent disability and handicap.

II. Patient compliance is another factor in prevention. Compliance refers to the degree of success the patient has in carrying out the prevention or treatment regimen given by a health professional.

   A. Patients can be noncompliant by ignoring, forgetting, or misunderstanding the regimen, and by carrying it out incorrectly.

   B. The term *compliance* infers an attitude on the part of the health professional that his or her recommendations should always be followed, presuming that the judgment is superior to that of the patient's. (Occasionally, this is not the case.)

III. Psychologists use scientific models, rather than just common sense, to examine and understand health behaviors.

   A. A person will not carry out a health behavior if significant barriers stand in the way, or if the steps interfere with favorite or necessary activities.

   B. A commitment to health behavior comes when a person believes the action will bring valuable outcomes, and after careful consideration of the wishes of family, friends, and social or cultural group.

   C. People are also influenced by health messages, by the sources of health recommendations, and by the credibility of the media source of information. Consideration of all factors will help the individual overcome the barriers that exist in changing health behaviors.

IV. Information about health is the first necessary component in any attempt to bring about changes in behavior.

   A. It is difficult to determine what is worth believing and what is not. The bombardment of health risks or "dangers" can lead some people to a fatalistic approach to health. But some risks *are* greater than others, and an individual's health can depend on getting the right information.

   B. Those who need health information the most, the poor and uneducated, often do not receive it. Programs can be started early in life, such as antidrug campaigns in public schools.

   C. Mass media campaigns are, in general, ineffective and short-lived because people tend to tune out messages that they do not want to hear and that are more abstract than concrete. These messages can be helpful in alerting people to change health habits they may not have known are dangerous.

   D. A physician is an important source of health information. The opportunity for education exists in the physician-patient relationship. However, physicians typically fail to teach patients how to maintain health and devote little time to teaching primary prevention.

   E. Due to their greater contact with patients, other health professionals (nurses, nurse practitioners, physician assistants, and others) may be preferable as communicators of health information.

V. The hypothetical constructs *belief* and *attitude* have specific meanings in the context of health behavior.

   A. A *belief* involves an assertion, often of the relationship between some entity or object (e.g., smoking) and an attribute of that object (e.g., causes cancer).

B. An *attitude* is used to explain consistencies within people in their affective reactions to, or feelings about, an object or phenomenon. An attitude represents an emotional evaluation of an entity.

VI. The Theory of Reasoned Action states that health behavior results from an intention to carry out a behavior. This model has empirical support in predicting many health behaviors.

   A. The intention is a strong determinant of a desired health behavior. Behavioral intentions are made up of two components: attitudes toward the action, and subjective norms regarding the action.

   B. Attitudes are a function of an individual's beliefs regarding the likely outcome of a health action and the individual's evaluation of the outcome.

VII. The Health Belief Model is useful in providing a way to organize and understand beliefs relevant to health behavior. It is used to explain health-related decision-making.

   A. A person's belief in the severity of a disease, not the medical estimate of severity, affects attitudes toward taking steps in preventing development of that disease.

   B. A person's self-perceived susceptibility to a disease is an important predictor of his or her attitude toward changing behavior related to that disease.

   C. An individual must believe in the efficacy of a treatment. In other words, he or she must believe it will work.

   D. The benefits must outweigh the costs in a person's treatment or prevention. If the person believes that following a particular course of action is more trouble than it is worth, he or she will probably avoid the action.

VIII. Though a person may believe that certain actions lead to health, he or she will carry out those actions only if he or she values health in the first place.

   A. Not everyone values health very highly, particularly when actions must be taken to preserve it.

   B. Culture and social class also have an effect on the value of health. Those in the middle and upper classes tend to value health higher than do those in the lower classes, probably because those in the latter group are concerned more than any other group with basic survival needs.

IX. In general, people come to believe something if they are convinced it is true. This is done by the process of persuasion.

   A. Persuasion is defined as a form of social influence in which one person uses a verbal appeal to change the beliefs and attitudes of another.

   B. Messages that arouse fear responses, such as showing pictures of diseased lungs, usually do not work. They may actually reduce the chances that a person will change beliefs. Fear messages may lead to denial and refusal to face the problem. These messages can produce change only when an individual is convinced he or she can take action.

   C. Hearing a message over and over again makes a person more likely to remember it and be persuaded by it. A phenomenon called the sleeper effect may account for the change of a person's beliefs without the person's knowing what influenced him or her.

   D. The persuasiveness of a message can also be determined partly by the characteristics of the communicator. Generally, a message is more persuasive if the communicator is liked. A communicator must possess enthusiasm, confidence, and dependability, among other positive traits.

X. Social norms in health become salient early in a person's life.

 A. Norms may originate from the family or from the expectations of one's cultural group. People are usually not aware that norms govern their behavior until the norms are violated in some way.

 B. People vary in the extent to which they are influenced by social norms. Some individuals act independently of most norms; others rely on what other people tell them to do, according to social expectations.

 C. The Theory of Reasoned Action suggests that the influence of personal attitudes and the influence of those in the individual's social network (for example, family or spouse) will be weighted differently by each person.

XI. Intentions and commitments may come about as a result of positive health attitudes and supportive social norms. Intentions are good predictors of overt action when there are no barriers in the way.

 A. An intention is a pledging or binding to a particular course of action.

 B. Commitment involves a promise to take steps to carry out the behavior. However, commitment must follow the individual's perception that he or she is free to act in proper fashion. A commitment can be directed to oneself or a family member, or may take the form of a contract with the health professional.

 C. For some, an independent commitment is effective; for others, expectations of family might be a more powerful motivator.

XII. Long-term changes in behavior are crucial to the development and maintenance of health behaviors.

 A. However great an intention may be, the old, destructive habit must be replaced by a newer, healthier habit.

  1. A basic principle of the behavioral approach is that reinforcement of a particular behavior will increase the frequency with which that behavior occurs.

  2. To overcome health problems, a person must have self-control, the ability to translate intentions into behaviors, and the capacity to maintain performance.

 B. Several procedures are used in behavior modification.

  1. Classical, or respondent, conditioning involves pairing of a once-neutral stimulus with a certain behavior.

  2. Operant conditioning is a powerful force that uses positive and negative reinforcement to increase the probability of a behavior. Punishment decreases its probability.

  3. Self-imposed operant conditioning involves three stages. The first, called self-monitoring or self-observation, involves deliberately and carefully attending to one's own behavior. In self-evaluation, the second stage, behaviors assessed through self-monitoring are compared against a specific criterion. An individual may then be rewarded through self-

reinforcement (the third stage) if the behaviors match the criterion.
C. Cognitive factors can determine whether or not behavior modification works. Negative self-statements can ruin a good behavioral regimen. One can learn to combat this problem by replacing the negative self-statements with positive, encouraging ones. This can be done by using the steps of self-imposed operant conditioning.
XIII. Factors in people's lives can hinder or enhance their ability to carry out intended health behaviors.
A. The cost of and limited access to medical care is often cited as the explanation for failure to carry out health behaviors, but even when the treatment is free, people do not comply.
B. The more complex a treatment regimen is, the more difficult it is for a person to follow it. If a person wants to change several behaviors, it may be better to tackle the behaviors one at a time, and link them together.
C. Family and friends can help provide encouragement for achieving health goals. This social support can come in the form of physical resources or psychological support.
D. The biggest problem in adopting new health goals is the possibility of backsliding to old behaviors.
1. Lapse involves small errors leading to a brief reemergence of the old habit. Relapse involves complete recurrence of old behaviors. Lapse can occur in high-risk situations.
2. Relapse can be caused by a combination of negative emotional states, inadequate initial motivation, lack of relapse-coping skills, physiological factors, lack of social support, and environmental stimuli favorable to the unhealthy behavior.
3. Increasing motivation and acquiring coping skills, as well as close monitoring, can help prevent relapse.

# Glossary

**attitude:** a hypothetical construct that is used to explain consistencies within a person in affective reactions to (or feelings about) an object or phenomenon (for example, dislike of brussels sprouts or final examinations). Most psychological investigators agree that an attitude represents a person's emotional evaluation of an entity and that an attitude follows from a belief. An attitude has been defined as a state of readiness to exhibit a behavioral response.
**backsliding:** returning briefly to past behavior, leading to relapse.
**behavioral approach:** an approach to the achievement of health behaviors that holds that with appropriate learning, a person can change destructive behaviors and act toward the achievement of health.
**behavioral intention:** an individual's stated or acknowledged commitment to carry out a particular action. A stated intention (stated to oneself or to others) is a commitment, a pledging, or a binding to a particular course of action.
**belief:** a hypothetical construct that involves an assertion, often of the relationship between some attitude object (for example, smoking) and some attribute of that object (for example, is expensive, or causes cancer).

**classical or respondent conditioning:** a process by which a behavior comes to be evoked by a once-neutral stimulus because that stimulus was paired with one that automatically evoked the behavior.

**compliance:** the degree of success a patient has in carrying out the prevention or medical-treatment recommendations given by a health professional.

**diabetes:** a disease of metabolism in which the body is unable to make or to use insulin to convert sugar and carbohydrates into energy. The failure to metabolize sugar causes an excess of glucose in the blood.

**double-blind situation:** both patient and physician think a medication is real when it is actually an inert placebo.

**Health Belief Model:** a model developed by researchers to determine the relationship between health beliefs and specific health behaviors.

**hypertension, or high blood pressure:** a disorder that has no overt symptoms. Hypertension may be the most important risk factor for cardiovascular disease. Uncontrolled high blood pressure may result in stroke or in kidney damage.

**insulin-dependent diabetes (type I):** a form of diabetes that develops in children between the ages of 5 and 6 or between the ages of 10 and 13. Type I diabetes is managed primarily with daily injections of insulin.

**lapse:** a less serious mistake than relapse. A lapse is a mistake, error, or slipup that is a reemergence of the previous habit but that may or may not lead to a state of relapse. In fact, how a person looks at such a slipup or lapse can influence whether he or she remains in control, or turns a lapse into a full relapse.

**negative reinforcement:** consequences that occur when an individual is removed from a negatively valued (for example,

uncomfortable) state as a result of enacting the behavior. Thus, alcohol abuse may be negatively reinforced (and thereby increase in probability of occurrence) if the result is a reduction in anxiety.

**noncompliance:** the patient's ignoring, forgetting, or misunderstanding the regimen as directed by the medical professional, and thus carrying it out incorrectly.

**operant conditioning:** conditioning based on the principle that behavior is shaped by the consequences that follow it.

**persuasion:** a form of social influence in which one person uses a verbal appeal to change the beliefs and attitudes of another person.

**placebo:** a pharmacologically inert substance (such as a sugar pill) that is administered, unbeknownst to the patient, by a health professional who conveys the expectation that it will work to improve the patient's health and/or remove his or her symptoms.

**positive reinforcement:** consequences that increase the probability that a behavior will be enacted by providing an individual with something that he or she values after enacting the target behavior.

**prompts and reminders:** the initial triggers for health behavior.

**punishment:** consequences that diminish in frequency the occurrence of an operant behavior.

**relapse:** the recurrence of symptoms (or behaviors) after a period of improvement.

**secondary prevention:** actions taken once a person has developed a condition in which he or she is at risk for further health damage. Such a condition might be hypertension (high blood pressure), which, if uncontrolled, can lead to stroke. Secondary prevention involves taking preventive health measures to forestall potential negative outcomes. These measures may involve medication and a special diet and exercise program.

**self-control:** the ultimate goal of the behavioral approach, which is for an individual to translate his or her intentions into behaviors and to maintain the performance of those behaviors.

**self-efficacy:** an individual's personal judgment of his or her own ability. The ability can be specific (to carry out a particular behavior) or more general (to accomplish things and be successful in life).

**self-evaluation:** the second stage in self-regulation, in which the individual assesses what was learned through self-monitoring and compares present behavior against a specific criterion or ideal.

**self-monitoring, or self-observation:** the first stage in self-regulation, which involves the individual's deliberately and carefully attending to his or her own behavior.

**self-regulation:** self-imposed operant conditioning that involves three stages.

**self-reinforcement:** the third stage in self-regulation, in which the individual rewards or reinforces himself or herself for behavior that matches or approximates the goal.

**shaping:** graduated treatment implementation, or shaping, involves the application of reinforcement for successive approximations to the desired behavior.

**sleeper effect:** a phenomenon in which a long time after exposure to a persuasive message, a person may change a belief and not remember what influenced him or her to do so.

**social support:** any input from other persons that furthers the goals of the receiver of the support. There are two major kinds of social support: tangible support, including physical resources that benefit the individual in some way, and psychological support, which provides the individual with help to develop affective states that engender well-being.

**subjective norms:** the individual's beliefs about what others (with whom he or she is motivated to cooperate) want him or her to do. The term *subjective social norms* is often used to refer to the expectations of others (real or imagined) for one's actions.

**tertiary prevention:** the taking of measures specifically designed to cure a disease or to control its progress. Examples of tertiary prevention are the faithful taking of medication by the patient with an acute infection, or the cooperation with various aspects of treatment such as radiation or surgery by the patient who has cancer. Tertiary prevention measures are designed to prevent further disability and handicap.

**Theory of Reasoned Action:** a social-psychological theory that posits that health behavior results from an intention to carry out a behavior. Behavioral intentions are made up of two components: attitudes toward an action, and subjective norms regarding the action.

**Type II diabetes:** a form of diabetes that usually develops after age 40. It is not as serious as type I, and the individual produces some, though not enough, insulin.

**Value of Health Scale:** a scale with which researchers have developed a way to measure the variability in the value people place on health.

# Becoming Ill

■ ■ ■ ■ ■

Wendy had felt exhausted for months. She had a great deal of trouble getting up in the morning, and she seemed to drag herself through the day. She seemed continuously to look for opportunities to take a nap, and every evening after work she fell into bed exhausted.

Wendy regularly passed up the chance to go out with her friends because she was not feeling well. The young man she had started dating stopped calling her; she was always too tired to see him. The fatigue that Wendy felt was so powerful nothing else mattered to her as much as being able to go to sleep.

Wendy felt her life was coming apart. All the things that once had mattered to her no longer made her feel enthusiastic.

Hoping that her problem could be diagnosed and cured, Wendy finally went to see her physician. She had a single complaint—fatigue—and it was a common one among the patients who presented at the office practice. The physician followed up with all the requisite blood tests, but the results were completely normal. Wendy did not have infectious mononeucleosis; she was not anemic; she had no hidden infection. So what was wrong?

Her doctor suggested a few possibilities. She might have a long-lasting virus. Perhaps she was depressed or needed a change in her job. Maybe she just needed a vacation. All these were possibilities, of course, but they didn't ring true to her. Wendy felt very sick.

After her visit with the doctor, Wendy felt worse than ever. Although she did not have any *obvious* serious disease, she wondered whether something not so obvious but quite dangerous might be wrong with her. She found it very difficult to make the decision to undergo extensive further testing. She feared she might have to look deeper into herself for a possible psychological explanation for her symptoms. She had no explanation to tell her friends, who were disappointed in her lack of companionship, or her boss, who was dissatisfied with her work. And she was beginning to doubt her own motivations and capabilities. Her self-esteem was suffering. She almost wished for a clear diagnosis, even if it were a serious one, so that she would at least have an answer.

In Chapters 3 and 4 we examined the prevention of disease and the measures that people can take to try to remain healthy. Of course, human beings do fall prey to countless external threats, such as those that are viral, bacterial, toxic, and biomechanical. Not all diseases and degenerative conditions can be prevented or even forestalled.

Becoming ill, however, is not a clear-cut event like throwing a switch or blowing a fuse. There is often no simple distinction between the healthy and the illness state. There are many gradations of each. And the label of "healthy" or "ill" that is placed on a person depends upon the integration of a multitude of factors, including test results, clinical findings, objective capabilities, self-definitions, interference with usual activities, and the nuances of diagnostic decisions.

In this chapter we will examine the phenomenon of illness from the perspectives of both patient and health professional. We will consider some important questions: How does an individual make the decision that he or she is ill? How do health professionals make that decision? What prompts a person to conclude that his or her symptoms signal illness? What brings a person to the decision to seek treatment for those symptoms? Why would a person ignore the symptoms of a heart attack or the clear signs of cancer? What does a person do when there is no clear definition of the problem—that is, no name for what is being felt? Under what circumstances will a person use illness as an excuse to take a break from the difficulties of life? What special privileges does illness bring? What would make a person accept those privileges or pass them up? How can a person overcome the limitations of illness and accomplish great things against the odds?

## Health, Illness, and Disease

To answer the questions we have posed, we need to understand the sometimes frustrating and always complex concept of *illness*. Most of us have used this word throughout our lives, believing that we know what it means. But dissect the concept and you will find more about human behavior and psychological processes than you might have imagined.

Consider this simple definition: illness is "a condition marked by the pronounced deviation from the normal healthy state" (*Dorland's Illustrated Medical Dictionary*, 1965, p. 725). When ill, an individual is unable to function normally in day-to-day activities. Further, his or her body does not feel normal; he or she may have less energy than usual, or otherwise feel not quite right.

As you can see from this definition, illness is a subjective phenomenon. It depends upon an individual's evaluation of his or her own internal state and ability to function. The definition leaves room for the effects of both physical and emotional factors. The subjectivity of illness does not make it whimsical or unreal, but it does complicate the phenomenon by making it difficult to objectify. And because people usually wait until they *feel* sick to go to a doctor, the subjective definition of his or her bodily state is what typically brings a person to seek help from a health professional.

The health professional usually looks for something called *disease*. Disease is a much more narrow concept than illness. Disease is "a definite morbid process having a characteristic train of symptoms. It may affect the whole body or any of its parts, and its etiology [theory of causation], pathology [structural or functional change in tissue caused by disease], and prognosis [forecast of the probable results of the attack of the disease] may be known or unknown" (*Dorland's Illustrated Medical Dictionary*, 1965, p. 428).

It is possible for a person to have disease but (for a time, at least) to have no outward signs, no marked deviation in functioning, and no subjective feelings of limitation or disability. In other words, un-

Sometimes it is obvious that a person is ill and also has disease (in this case, a "flu" virus).
SOURCE: © Tom Grill/Comstock

til the disease is discovered it is possible for a person to be considered not ill.

*Health* is not simply the absence of disease. A person might have no objective pathology yet not be healthy. Certainly, any deviation from a person's normal, self-defined healthy state of feeling and functioning suggests that that person is not healthy. But as more and more is learned about the critical role of specific preventive behaviors, as well as physical (and even psychological) fitness, the concept of health is broadened even further. The World Health Organization, for example, has defined health in the following manner: "Health is the state of complete physical, mental, and social well-being, and is not merely the absence of disease or infirmity" (World Health Organization, adopted 1946).

These definitions of *health, illness,* and *disease* are not altogether precise because they reflect some rather complex issues that are themselves imprecise. The definitions do, however, present guidelines to help us understand what we encounter when we consider real cases. For example, imagine a man who is "fully recovered from a myocardial infarction [heart attack, in which there is some damage to the heart muscle]. He takes no medication, observes only minimal restrictions in his diet and daily activities, appears perfectly healthy in every respect—yet he does have heart disease. Do you interrupt this man in the middle of a red-hot tennis game to tell him he's sick" (Hamilton & Rose, 1982, p. xxii)? This man has heart *disease*, yet he does not define himself as *ill*.

Illness, then, is not equivalent to the presence of disease. A person such as Wendy may have no obvious pathology yet may still be unable to function fully. Wendy is certainly experiencing deviation from her normal healthy state. She is ill. But does she have a disease? Probably only time will tell that. Either some brilliant doctor will diagnose an obscure condition, or further symptoms will develop and the diagnosis will become clear. Or some new disease syndrome will be discovered that will make sense of her constellation of symptoms. Wendy might go on for years being ill, with no diagnosis to back up her assertion. Or she might finally begin to feel like her old self again, and look back on the whole episode and be glad that it is over.

One problem with the subjectivity of illness is that we know a person is ill only if he or she says so. A man may complain that he is not feeling up to his usual level of energy or that he cannot function in his normal way. This label of "illness" must be based upon the person's notion of what is right and what is not right *for him* (Mechanic, 1968). The term *illness* applies if a marathoner suddenly cannot run more than five miles without collapsing in ex-

haustion, and if a student who usually takes six courses each quarter has barely enough energy for three. If a man cannot function at his usual activities, he is likely to define himself as ill. Likewise, if his subjective bodily feeling is one of strength, a sense of physical weakness is likely to trigger his self-definition of illness.

The subjectivity of illness and the fact that it is different from disease make the paradox of health and illness possible.

## THE PARADOX OF HEALTH AND ILLNESS

By objective standards, the health of United States citizens is quite good and has been getting better over the years. Average life expectancy rose 3.8 years from 1970 to 1984 alone. From 1950 to 1984 the average life expectancy rose 6.5 years. In 1900 life expectancy was only 47.3 years. Now it is 74.7 years. In the past thirty years age-adjusted death rates have dropped considerably for ten of the 15 most frequent causes of death, including heart disease, stroke, diabetes, and ulcers. They have remained stable only for cancer. In 1950 there were 8.4 deaths per thousand population; in 1984 that figure dropped to 5.5 deaths. In 1928 there were effective treatments available for only about 5% to 10% of the 360 most serious diseases. Now the figure is over 50% (Barsky, 1988). However,

> During the past 20 to 30 years, people's subjective sense of healthiness has not kept pace with improvements in health status; indeed, it appears to have declined. According to nationwide polls and community surveys, the proportion of Americans who are satisfied with their health and physical condition has fallen from 61 percent in the 1970's to 55 percent in the mid-1980's. . . . People report more frequent and longer-lasting episodes of serious, acute illness now than they did 60 years ago, despite the introduction of an-

tibiotics during the intervening period. (Barsky, 1988, p. 415)

In the 1920s large-scale community surveys found the average respondent reported less than one (0.82) episode a year of a serious acute disabling illness. Its average length was 16 days. In the early 1980s, on the other hand, the average respondent reported 2.12 episodes of acute disabling illness, each lasting on the average 19 days. Another aspect of the trend toward a greater incidence of illness can be found in large nationwide surveys of somatic symptoms. In these surveys respondents were asked about common somatic (bodily) complaints like dyspnea (difficult or labored breathing), heart palpitations, and pain. According to Barsky, people reported significantly more symptoms in 1976 than in 1957, and from 1976 onward there has been a decline in the proportion of respondents who reported having no symptoms at all. There has been a recent trend toward longer periods of disability, and a sharp increase in the total number of days of restricted activity, including days in bed for acute and chronic illnesses (Barsky, 1988).

Certainly, there are many possible explanations for the paradox that while objectively Americans are healthier than ever before, they say they feel worse. One explanation is that the threshold and tolerance for mild discomfort is now lower than it was in the past. People more readily seek medical help for isolated symptoms, and they are more likely than in the past to acknowledge to others that they feel ill. The standards for health have been raised so high that people today are aware of and disturbed by impairments and symptoms that once people would have ignored.

Medicine can offer more treatments than ever before for all sorts of ailments from the life threatening to the simply inconvenient. Chronic illnesses such as diabetes, rheumatoid arthritis, and heart disease cannot be cured outright, but they can be controlled. Thus, one explanation for the paradox of "doing better but feeling worse" is that today people live long enough to experience chronic illnesses that leave them with various nagging symptoms, impairments, and disabilities about which medical professionals can do little or nothing (Knowles, 1977). In addition, people seem to have raised their standards of what is healthy to a much higher level than ever before. They are willing to tolerate less and less impairment as a normal part of daily living. People have a heightened awareness of health, with most Americans now focusing some of their energies on attaining "a healthful lifestyle." The search for healthful diets and the physical fitness boom probably encourage people to expect that they can feel good much of the time and serve to focus their attention on their internal bodily feelings. Some who are quite healthy are nevertheless concerned about their health. They may even seek medical care frequently to obtain assurances that nothing is wrong. They are referred to by health professionals as the "worried well" (Barsky, 1988).

## THE PHYSICIAN'S DILEMMA

The paradox of doing-better-but-feeling-worse and the subjective character of illness itself can be sources of frustration for physicians. A patient arrives with vehement complaints of discomfort, but discussion with the physician and a careful review of systems reveal no consistent pattern of symptoms. The physical examination and diagnostic tests demonstrate no pathology. Understandably, the physician is perplexed.

Consider this real case history:

This 49-year-old woman, widowed eight years previously, lived alone and did not work. She had one daughter aged 27. HF and her husband having been fairly prosperous, her investments gave her an adequate income. With a teacher's diploma, she taught for a while before she got married, but had not since.

HF had had a hysterectomy at the age of 45 for menorrhagia [excessive menstrual bleeding]. Twelve years previously she had had a laparotomy [exploratory surgery of the abdomen] because of persistent abdominal pain. She had had mixed tension [muscle contraction] and vascular [migraine] headaches since her teens.

The patient now complained of various pains in the chest, abdomen, and lower back, headache, pressure in her chest, and dizziness. These symptoms lasted throughout most of the day. There were odd days when she felt better, but never entirely free of symptoms. Abdominal pain had started about 13 years previously, at a time when she had serious marital difficulties. She appeared to improve for a while, but her symptoms became more severe about one year after her husband died. . . . She had been convinced for about five years that she had a physical disease that none of the doctors had discovered; they had told her different diagnoses and she believed one day the true cause would be found. . . . (Kellner, 1986, pp. 300–301).

This patient presents a challenge to the physician, both to find out what's wrong with her, and to try to help improve her health and functioning. It is quite possible, of course, to accomplish the latter without accomplishing the former. To do so, however, it is necessary to dispense with the assumption that there is a one-to-one correspondence between physical tissue damage (or disease) and a patient's subjective feelings of pain or discomfort (illness). A dilemma arises only when illness is looked at in the limited traditional way: as a purely *biomedical* rather than as a *biopsychosocial* phenomenon.

# The Biomedical Versus the Biopsychosocial Model

As we examined in Chapter 2, the dominant model of disease today is biomedical. The *biomedical model* assumes that illness can be *fully* accounted for by a patient's deviations from the norm on measurable biological variables. The model holds that even the most complex illness phenomena can be reduced to certain measurable physical abnormalities. Although the means to measure all of these variables may not yet be available, such measurement is at least theoretically possible (Engel, 1977).

The biomedical model is certainly an improvement over the approach in previous centuries that emphasized demons as the cause of disease. However, the biomedical model is limited in its ability to account for many well-known health-related phenomena. For example, the presence of a biological deviation does not always result in an individual's expression of illness through behavior (Kosa & Robertson, 1975). The person with a definable abnormality may feel fine, and look and act perfectly normal. In addition, a particular physical abnormality can affect different people in vastly different ways (Robinson, 1971). Finally, it is quite clearly the case that illness can be manifested in behavior even when there are no corresponding physical parameters to point to disease. In other words, the biomedical model leads to yet another paradox. Some people with objective physical findings (such as abnormal laboratory test results) are told they are in need of treatment, when they are in fact feeling quite well. Others, like Wendy, feel astoundingly ill but are assured that they have no disease. Unfortunately, the biomedical model does not adequately describe the *reality of illness in human experience* (Kleinman, 1988).

Ice dancer Scott Gregory and his partner, Susan Semanick. Gregory competed in the 1988 Winter Olympic Games with a severe lumbar disk herniation.
SOURCE: Wide World Photos

Let's consider an example of how the biomedical model fails to account for the vast differences in human behavior that result from the very same physical phenomena. During the 1988 Winter Olympic Games, Scott Gregory, the ice-dance champion representing the United States, trained and competed with a severe herniation in a disk in the lumbar region of his spine. He adhered to a grueling schedule of training. The training required tremendous physical work, which he undertook despite severe pain and burning sensations radiating into his legs. Most people with his degree of injury would probably remain immobile and eventually become impaired by (and perhaps even quite depressed by) inactivity (Fordyce, 1976). The actual physical damage to his back was severe, yet he did something many people would consider the ultimate in physical health: he competed in the Olympic Games.

Clearly, illness is a considerably more complex phenomenon than the biomedical model allows. A much broader approach is needed.

The *biopsychosocial* model requires that psychological and social factors must be included along with the biological in any attempts to understand a person's response to symptoms and the experience of illness (Engel, 1977). Such an approach incorporates with the biological parameters various important psychological phenomena as well: (1) the meaning a person attaches to his or her condition (it is something that stops attainment of what is wanted or is something to be overcome); (2) what the person consciously or unconsciously wants (for example, to fail or to succeed; to be taken care of or to maintain independence); and (3) the person's own response style, such as whether he or she enhances or tries to minimize disabilities and discomforts. The biopsychosocial model is broad enough to incorporate the individual's cultural expectations about illness, particularly how he or she has learned from family and the culture to respond to symptoms. The biopsychosocial model takes into account psychological state, such as the extent to which the person is anxious or depressed. And it takes into account the present social context of the illness (that is, how the illness affects the individual's relationships with other people).

As we will see in detail below, there is a great deal of evidence that psychological and social factors such as these are every bit as important as tissue damage in determining people's experience of illness.

# Physical Symptoms: Interpretations and Response

A phenomenon often approached with fascination by practitioners, lay persons, and social scientists alike is the tremendous variation among people in their responses to what appear to be similar medical conditions. While one individual may hardly acknowledge a symptom, another (with perhaps an even milder form of the same

condition) will withdraw from his or her particular daily responsibilities, refrain from going to work, exhibit emotional distress, and display significant social and psychological disability. (DiMatteo & DiNicola, 1982, p. 112)

In our effort to examine how people respond to and interpret their physical symptoms, let us employ the biopsychosocial model.

## RECOGNIZING AND ATTENDING TO PHYSICAL SYMPTOMS

Some people pay a great deal of attention to the state of their bodies. They connect what they ate for lunch to the amount of energy they have in the afternoon. At any given moment they can tell you exactly how their bodies feel, where they have discomfort, twinges, muscle spasms, and feelings of heaviness and bloating. They are aware of varying degrees of fatigue, slight fluctuations in physical coordination, varying gradations of blush or pallor of their skin, and any and all limitations in their movement (Pennebaker, 1982).

Other people barely acknowledge their physical state on a conscious level. They actually seem to ignore it. Even when they feel very much out of sorts, they don't try to determine the origin of their misery. Their irritability, grumpiness, and lethargy may be the only clues that something is wrong with them. When others point out that they appear out of sorts, they require considerable time to recognize that bad feelings in their bodies are the source of the behavior. They don't even seem to have the words to describe physical distress (Pennebaker, 1982).

Several psychological factors have been found to influence people's reactions to their physical symptoms: First, people vary in the extent to which they focus their at-

| TABLE 5–1    Factors That Influence Reactions to Physical Symptoms |
|---|
| 1. Attention to threatening events |
| 2. Salience of bodily symptoms |
| 3. Scrutiny of own bodily state |
| 4. Threshold of and tolerance for symptoms, especially pain |
| 5. Childhood experiences regarding symptoms |
| 6. Cultural background |
| 7. Life circumstances at the time of experience of the physical symptoms |
| 8. Meaning attributed to the symptoms |

tention on threatening events, such as symptoms. Some people minimize the implications of these events and behave as though the events are minor. Others become vigilant, seek information, and actively confront the threat (Goldstein, 1973; Miller & Mangan, 1983).

Second, attention to bodily symptoms often depends upon their salience. People tend to focus on bodily symptoms most when issues of their health and body integrity are salient to them. When a close relative or friend has taken ill or has died of a particular condition, there is a tendency for many people to focus attention on the vulnerability of their own bodies. Many focus specifically on the organ affected in the friend or loved one (Mechanic, 1972). This phenomenon is magnified in medical students who have a high prevalence (approximately 70%) of experiencing symptoms that they attribute to some pathological process (Mechanic, 1972).

Third, some individuals chronically scrutinize their bodily state. They may have a greater than usual body awareness, vigilance, and self-consciousness (Barsky, 1988). Their increased scrutiny tends to amplify their discomfort. Barsky even suggests that some people, particularly those who depend upon modern medical "hype"

(for example, the latest diet; the latest cure-all scheme; the latest correct commercial product), may have lost faith and confidence in their own bodies. Rather than view their bodies as strong and capable, they feel weak and vulnerable, prey to the rhinoviruses on bathroom basins, and to the sudden stoppage of their hearts for no apparent reason. Interestingly, Barsky (1988) has noted that many people these days have experienced a heightened awareness of the value of health. In general, there is more of a focus on health than ever before. In 1984, for example, four of the top ten best-seller nonfiction books were about diet or fitness, whereas in 1965 none of them were.

Fourth, as we will see in more detail in Chapter 6, research has found that people differ in their threshold and tolerance for symptoms, particularly pain. The *threshold* is the level of intensity of a stimulus below which a sensation is not, and above which a sensation is, identified as pain. The *tolerance level* is the point of intensity of the stimulus at which the individual can no longer tolerate or stand the pain, and (in research at least) asks that it be stopped (Weisenberg, 1977).

Fifth, our childhood experiences contribute to our patterns of dealing with symptoms. The manner in which others have behaved toward us when ill, as well as the particular behaviors of ours that were encouraged or discouraged, tend to affect whether we ignore our bad feelings or express them to others (Mechanic, 1964, 1972).

Consider Grandma:

■ ■ ■ ■ ■

Grandma moans and holds her hand toward me. "Look," she encourages. "See what my arthritis is doing?" Her joints do look swollen. She holds her hand stiffly. "Oh, these fingers."

Then, clutching her hand over her heart, she exclaims, "Ah . . . this arthritis is gonna kill me . . . Dear God what a curse." She rolls her eyes heavenward.

I am five years old. I assume this is how everyone behaves when something hurts them.

Sixth, our cultural background tends to affect our responses to symptoms. In a New York City hospital one researcher studied the reactions of patients from tremendously varied ethnic backgrounds (Zborowski, 1952). People of Jewish and Italian ancestry responded to pain in a very emotional fashion. They talked about their pain and expressed it with gestures. People of English ancestry, on the other hand, were stoical and talked objectively about their pain, as if it were an entity separate from themselves. The Irish denied feelings of pain even when they presented to the clinic with objective symptoms.

Seventh, the circumstances of an individual's life at a given time can influence the degree of attention paid to physical symptoms. It is quite possible to be too busy to notice one's pain or discomfort, and too focused on outside activities to pay attention to the nuances of one's bodily functioning. On the other hand, a person who is

in a boring situation, or who lives alone without the company of other people, can tend to focus much more attention on his or her internal state than does someone who is actively involved in many activities (Pennebaker, 1983).

Finally, cognitive factors may strongly affect an individual's attention and reaction to symptoms. The meaning of the symptom, for example, can be quite important. Surgical patients who sustained tissue damage similar to that experienced by men wounded in war were found to react with much more distress, to express the fact that they were in pain, and to request significant amounts of pain medication (Beecher, 1959). The men wounded in battle, on the other hand, seemed to tolerate their wounds with equanimity. The tissue damage was actually interpreted as positive by the men in war, for it meant that they escaped death and would go home as heroes. Surgical patients, however, viewed their tissue damage as quite negative, as a loss of capacity, a deviation from normal, and interference in their daily lives. Other cognitive factors are also important. If one's symptoms are recognizable from the past and are believed to be unimportant or explainable, such as muscle aches after an athletic competition, they probably will be ignored. However, if the symptoms represent a new feeling that is strange and terrifying, they will likely be attended to (Safer, Tharps, Jackson, & Leventhal, 1979). Symptoms gain a person's attention if they attack a salient part of the body such as the face or eyes, or the one that is particularly salient to the individual (such as the heart for a person whose father died of heart disease) (Safer et al., 1979).

So far, we have examined the factors that prompt an individual to attend to certain feelings that arise in his or her body. Now let us turn to an examination of the actions that people take when they experience certain symptoms, particularly why and how they seek medical treatment.

## SEEKING MEDICAL HELP FOR SYMPTOMS

Research in the general population shows that at any given time, 75% to 90% of people experience symptoms that could be considered clinically relevant. However, only about a third of them seek medical help (Kellner, 1986). In one study, university students and hospital staff (who at the time were taking no medications and undergoing no medical treatments) filled out a questionnaire indicating which symptoms they had experienced in the previous 72 hours. Examples were loss of appetite, nausea, weakness, heart palpitations, dizziness on first standing up, and pain in joints and muscles. Over 80% of the respondents had experienced one or more symptoms. The median number of symptoms was two, and almost 5% of the respondents experienced six or more symptoms (Reidenberg & Lowenthal, 1968). In another study, on a 12-item symptom rating scale, over 800 of 1000 students (80%) at two universities reported at least one somatic symptom (Pennebaker, Burnam, Schaeffer, & Harper, 1977). Yet, another study found 75% of 1000 adults reported having an episode of illness in a given month, but only 25% consulted a physician about it (White, Williams, & Greenberg, 1961). Thus, many people who appear to be "healthy" and functioning in day-to-day life may be simply compensating for or ignoring their clinically important symptoms. Although some conditions are self-limiting (a backache, for example, or the cough of a cold), others may persist or grow worse. Usually, at some point, the person stops tolerating the symptoms and attempts to identify the condition and to find treatment for it. How and when the decision is made to tell others about the symptoms depends at least as heavily on an individual's psychology as it does on the objective seriousness of the symptoms.

## PSYCHOLOGICAL TRIGGERS FOR SEEKING HELP

What factors bring an individual to seek medical help for symptoms being experienced?

First, research shows that a person is likely to seek medical care for a given symptom only when the symptom becomes frightening and threat is perceived (Zola, 1973). Typically, when one's vocational and physical activity is interfered with (when one cannot work or exercise, for example), the symptom becomes a threat to one's livelihood and/or lifestyle. A person may become concerned about losing a job or about being unable to care for dependents. Eventually, the person acknowledges his or her fears openly and decides to try to solve the mystery of the illness.

Second, a person usually will attend to a symptom if he or she recalls that in the past that same symptom was a serious one (Zola, 1973). And, when the nature and quality of the symptom differs significantly from the familiar and appears to demand medical attention, the person is likely to seek expert help.

Third, people often decide to seek medical care after experiencing an interpersonal crisis. The crisis in relationships with other people might include marital difficulties or a major argument with the boss (Zola, 1973). An interpersonal crisis can raise a person's level of anxiety, making some symptoms (or uncertainty about them) intolerable. The fact that an interpersonal crisis can trigger attention to illness symptoms suggests that once a person defines himself or herself as ill, he or she may gain enough sympathy and extra attention to resolve the interpersonal crisis or at least

| TABLE 5–2    Factors That Bring People to Seek Medical Help for Symptoms |
| --- |
| 1. Symptoms are frightening, and a threat to vocational and physical activity is perceived. |
| 2. Symptoms are new and different, or familiar and serious. |
| 3. Anxiety is experienced, particularly over an interpersonal crisis. |
| 4. Symptoms threaten relationships with other people. |
| 5. There is approval or encouragement from others for seeking help. |

minimize its importance. A person might even seek to establish a warm, supportive relationship with a medical practitioner to take the place of the relationship that has been lost or threatened by the interpersonal crisis.

Fourth, when a symptom threatens the ability to relate to other people, an individual will usually seek care (Zola, 1973). Symptoms that limit social interactions, such as unsightly rashes, apparent contagiousness, and overwhelming fatigue are often dealt with readily. People don't want to be left lonely by illness.

Fifth, the decision to seek medical care is usually made when other people are supportive of it. For example, when friends suggest that a woman see her doctor, she can stop being concerned that she is overreacting to her symptoms. Approval by another person is an important trigger to seeking care (Zola, 1973).

Interestingly, recent research suggests that emotional triggers appear to be relevant only to health care seeking for adults. Emotional distress was not a relevant factor in mothers' decisions to seek care for their children's symptoms (Turk, Litt, Salovey, & Walker, 1985).

## THE LAY REFERRAL NETWORK

Very often the process of diagnosis begins much before an individual even reaches the doctor's office. The *lay referral network* con-sists of friends and family members who help the individual to attach a meaning to his or her symptoms (Freidson, 1970). Family members, friends, and co-workers typically offer advice about whether the person should seek care from a physician or instead treat the condition with a home remedy (or simply ignore it and wait for it to go away).

Regarding the last factor, it has been suggested that during the 1980s there developed a general societal sanctioning for seeking medical care. In fact, there has been a kind of "medicalization of daily life." People visit their doctors for everything from difficulty sleeping to fatigue, to a bad complexion. Although they may be living lives that are very hectic (work all day and dance all night!) or very much out of balance (all work and no play), people expect medicine to provide solutions (Barsky, 1988).

## DETERMINANTS OF MEDICAL-CARE UTILIZATION

It is important for us to note that psychological factors are not the only determinants of the use of health services. Let us briefly examine the few consistent findings available from studies of *medical care utilization* in order to get a fully rounded picture.

At various points in the life span, people are more apt than at other times to need and to utilize health services. Children and elderly people receive medical care considerably more often than do adolescents and young adults (Aday & Andersen, 1974, 1975). During adolescence and young adulthood, most people are quite healthy, but as they age, the onset of chronic diseases forces them to utilize health services. Children are usually cared for regularly by pediatricians, who treat their childhood illnesses, determine whether they are developing normally, and provide immunizations. Women use health services significantly more than do men, even for conditions that are unrelated to pregnancy and childbirth (Nathanson, 1977). It has been suggested that women are more sensitive than men to bodily dysfunctions, especially minor ones, and so are more likely to seek medical treatment (Leventhal, Nerenz, & Strauss, 1980). Of course, women may simply be more willing than are men to express pain and discomfort and seek help (Mechanic, 1964). People from lower social classes use medical care services less often than do those from upper classes, most likely because medical care is costly and their access to it is often limited (Herman, 1972). Even with the availability of free public clinics and programs like Medicare for the elderly and Medicaid (or MediCal in California) for the poor, those in the poorer social classes are less likely to have a regular physician and instead obtain care only when an emergency arises (Rundall & Wheeler, 1979).

## Delay in Seeking Treatment

Leonard, in his shirt sleeves, was just carrying in the cut-glass punch bowl of fresh eggnog, to the accompaniment of loud cheers. . . . Nell did not like the feverish wrung-out look of her husband; he did not look well, at all. But on her way to him, she was blocked by Lucy Bell and was first obliged to field her ecstatic questions. . . . [Nell later noticed him sweating profusely after he had been enlisted to beat some eggs in the hostess' kitchen.]

[Later, in the car.] "Listen, Nell," said Leonard in a constricted voice. "Did you eat any of that hot fruit salad?"

"I'm going to pull off the road," said Leonard. "I have the most terrible indigestion. It seems to be spreading all over . . ."

He angled the car toward the emergency lane. Nell looked over, saw he had passed out. . . . The next few seconds had the familiarity of a nightmare. She started to scream as the car skimmed softly from the pavement, like an airplane taking off, bounced rather gracefully down a steep grassy embankment, and began to turn over (Godwin, 1982).

A heart attack can come on suddenly, without warning. The symptoms are tightness, pressure, squeezing, or pain in the chest (sometimes radiating to the shoulders, neck, jaw, and arms) combined with shortness of breath, nausea, and/or sweating. Unfortunately, 50% to 70% of people who experience a myocardial infarction (heart attack) die before receiving any medical treatment (Gentry, 1979). Medical studies show that death can be prevented if proper action is taken within two minutes after the signals for a heart attack have begun to occur. More than half of people who die suddenly after experiencing the symptoms of a myocardial infarction do so within an hour after onset of the symptoms and prior to receiving any medical assistance (Gentry, 1979).

Nearly everywhere in the country it is possible to receive lifesaving treatment from a paramedic unit within moments of dialing 911. Thus, although it is possible to receive the necessary help to prevent death from a heart attack, most people fail to get it. Why?

Research suggests that heart attack victims fail to receive timely medical assistance because of two problems: (1) they attribute their symptoms incorrectly to conditions other than a heart attack, and (2) they delay unnecessarily even after they have decided to seek medical care (Gentry, 1979). Patients suffering from a myocardial infarction typically arrive at the hospital or into the hands of paramedical staff from less than one hour to several days after the onset of their symptoms. The median time from onset of symptoms to the initiation of medical help is between two and a half and four hours. Only about 10% of that time is used by heart attack victims for transportation. Studies show that they spend about 65% of that time trying to make the decision that the symptoms require medical treatment (Hackett & Cassem, 1969; Simon, Feinleib, & Thompson, 1972). (More often than not, as in the case of Leonard above, they wait too long.) Most patients initially attribute heart attack symptoms to such conditions as gas pains, ulcers, gallbladder disease, and a cold. Further, even after the decision has been made that medical attention should be sought, about 25% of the time between onset of symptoms and arrival at the hospital is spent doing unnecessary things such as calling the family physician (whose initial direction would be to go right to the emergency room), preparing to go to the hospital (gathering clothes and personal items), and washing up. Thus, even after they have correctly attributed the symptoms to a serious condition, such as a heart attack, people still waste considerable time before taking the necessary action to receive treatment (Gentry, 1979; Olin & Hackett, 1964).

Psychological factors thus seem to be most responsible for leading a heart attack victim to ignore the symptoms and to avoid calling paramedics or going to the hospital. Many victims of a myocardial infarction fail to seek medical help because they are afraid of looking silly if they have misinterpreted their symptoms and the problem turns out to be trivial. Many don't want to bother their doctors. Others don't want to draw attention to themselves. Another person (a spouse or a friend) usually insists on bringing the patient to the hospital emergency room, but when left alone, most heart attack victims miss the opportunity to save their own lives (Simon, Alonzo, & Feinleib, 1974).

Delay in seeking medical care for all types of problems, not just emergencies, has been a very interesting and important topic of research. In general, delay in seeking medical care is composed of three parts: (1) *appraisal time* (the time it takes the patient to appraise the symptoms as illness and to decide that the sensations mean something is wrong), (2) *illness delay* (the time from the patient's decision that he or she is ill to the decision to seek care; this gap might be caused by the patient's disbelief that the condition can be ameliorated with medical intervention), and (3) *utilization delay* (the time from the decision to seek care to the actual obtaining of medical services). The last aspect of delay involves the individual's choosing medical care that he or she feels is worth the cost, and then overcoming any barriers to utilization, such as finding a doctor and getting the money to pay for the medical visit. Total delay, from recognition of the symptom to arrival at the clinic or emergency room, is the sum of these three components (Safer et al., 1979).

In one study researchers interviewed 93 patients who were waiting to see a physician at a hospital clinic or emergency room (Safer et al., 1979). They assessed patients' reactions to their symptoms and determined when these patients first interpreted their symptoms as illness, when they decided to seek care, and when they actually did take steps to bring the problem to a medical professional. The total delay in seeking care was significantly longer among patients who had a competing life problem unrelated to health (such as a troubled marriage or a divorce), who had no pain, who had done some reading about their symptoms, who were older (over 45), who had waited for the symptoms to go away, and who believed the symptoms could not be cured.

Appraisal delay was found to be quite short when patients had obvious distressing symptoms, such as pain and bleeding. People delayed less when their symptoms were new than when their symptoms were familiar. People delayed significantly longer when they imagined the negative consequences of being sick (such as having to have surgery or various uncomfortable tests). Finally, utilization delay was highest among patients who were very concerned about the cost of receiving care; those who could not afford care delayed the longest. Again, pain was an important factor, with the least delay associated with the greatest pain. Delay was significantly higher among patients who felt that their symptoms might not be able to be cured.

It is interesting to note that strongly sensing one is quite ill tends to cause longer delay rather than immediate action (Safer et al., 1979), particularly when people feel afraid of treatment and have strong negative images of it. Under such circumstances, people tend to remain passive and simply think about their symptoms rather than do something about them.

For a disease like cancer, delay can be life threatening. The number of people whose lives are actually saved by cancer treatment is significantly lower than the number who theoretically could survive. The reason is that in practice many people delay receiving treatment for so long that their disease has progressed much too far for them to be helped by modern treatments such as surgery, chemotherapy, and radiation.

Many cancers can be completely cured if detected early. Yet, the majority of patients wait at least a month after detecting a suspicious symptom (such as a thickening or a lump, obvious change in a wart or mole, nagging cough, and so on). Between 35% and 50% of patients delay over three months. The reasons for delay involve lack of pain and incapacitation, feelings of invulnerability (feeling nothing can really hurt them) (Weinstein, 1982), and a sense of fatalism and belief that nothing can cure them (Safer et al., 1979). Others fear cancer treatments, and assume that these will be debilitating (although the treatment for cancer caught in the early stages is likely to be much less disturbing than that for more advanced cancer).

Because of fear of the disease and its treatment, many people allow their cancer to grow to the point at which more debilitating interventions are required and cure is much less certain.

A surgeon who at age 37 was diagnosed as having a malignant, non-Hodgkins lymphoma (cancer of the lymph nodes), delayed defining his symptoms as possible serious illness (cancer) even though he was trained to identify the importance of such symptoms in his patients. He eventually underwent surgery and five months of radiation treatment and survived. But he was never sure whether his cancer would return.

"... I noticed a small lump at the angle of my jaw while shaving one morning. It was with more curiosity than dread. What could happen to me? I was full of myself and invincible. Doctors as a general rule, after going through that terrible phase in medical school known as *morbid medicans*, when we think we have all the symptoms of the diseases we are studying, develop a unique ability to think of themselves as impervious to the sea of misery that we navigate through each day.

"My denial systems were activated and I ignored it. Time went by.... When it slowly enlarged I showed it to physician friends in a casual way. They said not to worry. Maybe they didn't and I didn't hear them. . . .

"Finally one night at a dinner party a psychiatrist's wife with no medical training said that the emperor has no clothes. She said, 'What is that thing under your jaw?'

"Still believing all was well, I saw a surgeon who scheduled a biopsy." (Shlain, 1979, p. 176)

# The Sick Role

Why do social and psychological factors have the power to trigger people's decisions to seek medical care? Why is it that these factors can cause a person to ignore the symptoms of disease and delay treatment?

As we noted earlier, illness depends upon self-definition. If I say I am ill, it would be unusual indeed for other people to doubt my word. My subjective account of my pain is proof enough of its existence (Kosa & Robertson, 1975). In a society such as ours that values independence, competition, and achievement, illness is considered such a negative state that no one would voluntarily adopt it for no good reason—at least in theory (Parsons, 1975).

In theory being ill involves adopting a social role known as *the sick role*. The sick role brings privileges as well as responsibilities. I may enter the sick role by declaring myself ill (and simply that). However, once I enter the sick role, I am expected to behave in the correct manner. I must view the sick role as negative. (I do not, for example, run around yelling, "Yippee! I'm sick. Now I get to stay home from work," or other such expression of satisfaction.) If I fail to view illness as negative, my motives might be somewhat suspect. In addition, I am expected to seek competent medical help (a health professional, and not a tarot-card reader, for example). I cannot maintain the self-definition of illness indefinitely without

having a doctor legitimize my claim (Parsons, 1975). Physicians are, in effect, the gatekeepers of the sick role. So, although I can complain all I wish about my illness, I am expected to back up my assertion with a visit to the doctor. And I am expected to cooperate with the doctor's recommendations.

Note that to maintain the sick role, a clear diagnosis is not required. Self-definition, combined with the fulfillment of these obligations, is all it takes to acquire the sick role and to maintain it. One can remain in the sick role even while a diagnosis eludes the physicians, as long as one is trying to get better.

Occupying the sick role can have its advantages. The sick role is guarded by the above social sanctions and comes with certain responsibilities precisely because it brings special privileges. A person who enters the sick role is exempted from working and from caring for others. He or she can expect the help of others and can also expect not to be required to fulfill promised obligations.

The sick role can bring certain *secondary gains*, the positive outcomes that balance some of the more negative aspects of being ill. Pain and illness bring increased attention from others, a chance to rest, and an opportunity to be taken care of. Pain and illness can put a stop to criticism from others. Illness can even enhance family harmony. On a deeper level the secondary gains of illness might include an excuse for why one does not succeed in life. Illness may provide a break from a job or even a style of life with which one is dissatisfied. It may provide a sense of purpose for an individual who feels that life is devoid of meaning. Illness can provide a focus for one's chronic anxiety, and a means to channel emotional distress. Finally, the secondary gains of illness can even be tangible, such as money in the form of insurance payments or worker's compensation.

Our childhood experiences can influence our expectations for the secondary gains of the sick role.
SOURCE: Michael Weisbrot/Stock, Boston

## ILLNESS AS AN EXPRESSION OF EMOTIONAL NEEDS

The fact that secondary gains can some-times make illness attractive suggests that the expression of physical distress some-times fulfills certain psychological needs. As we noted earlier in this chapter, certain aspects of one's cultural background, up-bringing, daily life circumstances, and per-sonality can make illness a natural outlet for the expression of emotional distress.

Ideally, a person would find the direct expression of emotions perfectly accept-able. A person who is in touch with his or her own emotional life might readily say so when feeling angry, anxious, or depressed. There is no smokescreen, no conscious or unconscious decision to disguise those feel-ings. For another person, however, it is safer to complain about the purely physical manifestations of distress. Instead of stat-ing "I feel very anxious," the individual will describe a pounding heart, lightheaded-ness, and difficulty breathing. Instead of ex-pressing feelings of depression, he or she will describe fatigue, lack of energy, and problems sleeping, and for these may even decide to visit a doctor.

As we noted earlier in this chapter, it is not the case that illness is a purely physical or a purely emotional phenomenon. A per-son who feels anxious typically does have tense muscles, a rapid heartbeat, and cold clammy hands. A person who is emotion-ally depressed, perhaps in reaction to the death of a loved one, is slowed down, and feels fatigued. What matters in determining whether people will adopt a psychological or a somatic interpretation is where they focus their attention, how they interpret what they are feeling, and how they explain their distress.

Most people exhibit something between the extremes of the purely physical and the purely psychological expression of distress. They may have a sense of emotional distress but be unable to find the right words to describe their psychological state. They may have been taught to repress and deny psychological interpretations of their experiences, and to hide their feelings from others (as in "Boys don't cry"). If the very things that they need, such as attention, emotional support, and practical help, become available for complaints of physical illness, the scales will likely be tipped toward the physical rather than the psychological explanation.

Usually, the decision to express physical rather than emotional distress is not made consciously. Thus, when a depressed patient presents with fatigue to the physician, a long period of time may elapse before the true source of the problem is found. Particularly if the patient is good at hiding (from both self and others) evidence of psychological distress, the physician may continue to search at length and sometimes in vain for the physical abnormality that explains the patient's subjective feelings of illness. Sometimes, in the process, such patients are subjected to needless medications, treatments, and surgeries. For example, in one study, women on a hospital neurological service who had expressed their distress in physical terms were more likely to have received a hysterectomy at some point in their lives (52%) than had women patients on a psychiatric service who had expressed their distress in primarily psychological terms (21%) (Bart, 1968).

Research suggests that expressing distress with somatic (bodily) vocabulary is not at all uncommon. In a substantial proportion of people who seek medical treatment for somatic complaints, no organic problem can be found no matter how much testing is done (Kellner, 1965). In an ear, nose, and throat clinic the number was found to be over 10% (Stoeckle, Zola, & Davidson, 1964). In cases in which the symptoms are somewhat more ambiguous than sore throat or ear pain, the estimates have been quite a bit higher. For instance, among patients with chest pain who were referred to a cardiac clinic, no organic contributing factor was found in 54% of the cases (Mayou, 1973). Most estimates of failure to find an organic component of illness range in between these extremes and are generally found to be between 10% and 30% (Kellner, 1986).

It is possible, of course, that the limitations of medicine make it impossible to find an organic factor in a patient's illness experience. Medicine does not have a diagnosis for every ailment. Some syndromes, such as chronic fatigue syndrome, are in the process of being identified, their signs and symptoms mapped out, and their incidence and prognosis identified empirically. Other ailments are not so well described, such as chest muscle tightness and spasm due to emotional tension. In fact, there are so many conditions that patients report that have no apparent cause that a commonly used medical term, *idiopathic* (arising spontaneously or from an obscure or unknown cause), is applied to them.

## SOMATIZATION AND CONVERSION

In some cases, the puzzle of symptoms cannot be solved at all by using a purely medical approach because the symptoms don't make sense physiologically. Consider *glove anesthesia*, which is the term for a condition in which only the hand, but no part of the arm, loses sensation and is unable to function. The disorder cannot be caused by an organic impairment because the neural pathways that conduct sensation to the hand also serve the rest of the arm. If any nerve damage had occurred, either part of the hand and one side of the arm would be affected, or all of the hand and all of the arm would be devoid of sensation. Sigmund Freud treated several such cases, and with Pierre Janet (1929) identified *conversion responses*, including loss of sight or speech or hearing, and various forms of muscular paralysis. Conversion responses are believed to be primitive responses to emotional conflict (cognitively primitive in the sense that they arise from very early childhood). Conversion symptoms make sense in that they tend to solve the emotional conflict facing the person who suffers from them. A man who unconsciously wishes to attack his brother may find himself unable to move his arm; a woman who is overwhelmed with guilt because of her sexual attraction to a prohibited man may find herself unable to see. These are extreme examples, of course, although they occurred with surprising frequency during Freud's time. Such disorders are not often presented to physicians in modern times. Quite common, however, are less extreme examples referred to as *somatization*, in which emotions are expressed through somatic complaints. Examples include the experience of stomach distress when one is highly anxious, and of headache when one is under tremendous pressure.

In Chapter 10 we will deal in more detail with somatization responses that result from the experience of stress. Here we consider the role of the medical professional in attempting to understand the patient's illness experience. Unfortunately, using a biomedical model, many medical professionals ascribe symptoms for which they can find no organic explanation to psychological causes, *by default*, that is, when they can find no other explanation for what ails the patient (Cassell, 1985a). Certainly, it is possible that any patient is expressing emotional distress through physical channels, as described above. But in a biopsychosocial model, diagnoses of somatization and conversion require evidence beyond the mere fact that nothing organic can be found to explain the symptoms. They require an understanding of the patient's psychological and social circumstances, as well as biomedical status.

Understandably, few patients react positively when told that their pain is "just nerves." In fact, many feel bewildered and upset. They feel rejected by the physician and sometimes quite hopeless because they believe nothing can be done to help them. Sometimes they get angry. Often they go find another doctor (Baur, 1988).

## A PATIENT WITH PSYCHOSOMATIC ILLNESS

Let's consider an example of somatization. A male patient's chest pain is appropriately attributed to anxiety because the *pattern* of chest pain is consistent with tension-related muscle spasms. Specific treatment for these spasms (muscle relaxants, physical therapy) can be prescribed to alleviate them. But when "tension" is given as the explanation, and the patient is left with no hope of specific treatment, the patient is likely to be noticeably distressed. In this example we see an excellent illustration of the phenomenon of *psychosomatic illness*, an illness condition that results from, or is exacerbated by, psychological factors. In this example illness (chest pain) develops as a consequence of anxiety and psychological stress (an issue we will examine in greater detail in Chapter 10). The patient's anxiety affects his body in a particular way. He is chronically tense and anxious, and tends to brace his back, neck and chest muscles constantly, causing a reduction in blood flow to the muscles and a buildup of lactic acid in them. The result is pain (Feldenkreis, 1981).

There is a clear connection between the psychological phenomenon and the physical findings. An astute physician will recognize this pattern in the patient and help him to find specific ways to counteract it.

The following example of a male physician talking with a male patient who has this exact problem was adapted from a real conversation that was reported verbatim, and analyzed, by Eric Cassell (1985b, pp. 158–59). The dialogue demonstrates an effective and supportive method for communicating a diagnostic conclusion of psychosomatic illness.

DOCTOR:  Well, I do think it's emotional in origin, the result of a lot of stress and tension and anxiety. But that's not a sufficient answer. We'll work on it till we get one. Now, what you've told me is that lately you've had a lot of extra problems and lots more work because your new boss won't let up. Did I hear that correctly?

PATIENT:  Yeah.

DOCTOR:  Well, I think that might cause you to brace yourself, your back, neck, and chest. It causes pain, but fortunately no lasting damage. So we have to treat the symptoms of the pain, and get at the root of what's causing your muscles to tense so much . . . what's going on in your emotions. But fortunately we don't have to deal with any damage to your body so far . . . are you with me?

PATIENT:  Yeah, I am . . .

DOCTOR:  Well, the way to see if my explanation is the right one, which I really think it is, and to try to help you with this discomfort, we need to make a dent in the process. We need to try to relax those tight muscles and see whether that changes how you feel. . . . I think it will. Of course, we also need to try to get at some of the underlying feelings that are causing you problems.

PATIENT:  Yeah. I hold in my feelings a lot.

DOCTOR:  I know that. Now it's not in my expertise to help you make lots of changes in how you feel about things and the ways in which you react emotionally. But we can find you someone who can help. What I can do is start you off changing the discomfort. I'm going to give you three days' worth of Valium, to get those muscles in your back and chest and neck to relax a little. I want you to use the steam room or hot tub at the gym and get a couple of really good massages to relax those muscles. Work on that body, okay?

The physician above is extremely reassuring. And, he is focused on solving the problem. He makes sure that the patient knows that there is no long-term damage to worry about. He tells the patient that there are several things he can do to get well. He explains how the problem likely came about in the first place. The patient is given hope that an active orientation to his pain and its underlying causes can result in his feeling better.

Psychological factors can play a significant role in physical complaints. Emotions can have a real effect on the body. As noted above, emotional distress can manifest itself, among other ways, in tight muscles that can cause pain. Chronic emotional arousal can also raise blood pressure and severely tax the cardiovascular system. In Chapter 10 we will discuss the role of psychological factors in causing actual physical damage to the human body.

## Hypochondria

The phenomenon of *hypochrondria* or *hypochondriasis* is well known even in the popular culture. People informally refer to others that they feel are overly concerned with their own health as "hypochondriacs." Although the lay public may be less discriminating in placing such a label on an individual than are health professionals, the same term is used.

Hypochondriasis is a phenomenon in which an individual displays more than just a simple propensity to pay more attention than most people to his or her bodily symptoms. "Hypochondriasis is an exaggerated and obsessive concern about the body and health, with delusion of disease or bodily dysfunction. It is often associated with a multitude of symptoms and complaints that reflect real suffering—despite the absence of organic pathology" (Hamilton & Rose, 1982, p. 83). True hypochondriacs convert personal, emotional distress into physical distress. They report symptoms that are diffuse and may change from one occasion to another. Their complaints tend to be of symptoms that occur very commonly in a large number of people and that are typically associated with stress. Yet, hypochondriacs are convinced that, for them, these symptoms indicate serious disease.

Because it is possible to use the sick role to one's advantage, hypochondria might be thought to be a form of *malingering*, which is a conscious, purposeful using of somatic complaints to achieve exemption from one's obligations. But most experts agree that hypochondriasis involves no conscious manipulation at all but, rather, the misinterpretation of vague symptoms as disease. "Hypochondria is not malingering, in which a person intentionally pretends to be sick, and it is not psychosomatic illness in which psychological stress triggers, exacerbates, or maintains a physical problem . . ." (Baur, 1988, p. 4).

A deeper analysis of the emotional experience of the hypochondriac suggests some very complex motives and needs. Being sick is one way of agreeing to be helpless. In fact, hypochondria is almost the perfect solution to this common problem, for being ill . . . the vulnerable person simultaneously obtains the protection and attention he craves, excuses his excessive dependence, binds his protector to him (who could leave someone who is seriously ill?), causes the protector a good deal of trouble which punishes him or her for being so annoyingly indispensable, and also punishes the hypochondriac for having hostile feelings toward his protector and himself. A hypochondriac thus tries to manage the confusion concerning his dependence, hostility, and guilt by confining these problems to one corner of his life—his body—and at the same time denies the primary result of his confusion, which is a pervasive lack of independence and self-esteem. (Baur, 1988, p. 5)

One form of hypochondriasis is quite common among medical students. As we noted earlier in this chapter, the "medical-student syndrome" has a high prevalence. About 70% of physicians experience it for some period of time during their medical training. The factors contributing to this temporary hypochondriasis include stress (from internal or external sources), feelings of anxiety (usually about tests or other methods of performance evaluation), and physical symptoms (common ones, such as forgetfulness, fatigue, and rapid heart rate). The medical student attaches an inordinate importance to his or her symptoms because of an incomplete knowledge of the diseases being studied, knowing enough to be worried but not enough to be reassured. The disease that the medical student is concerned about having is often something that is modeled after an anecdote heard, or a medical case studied, or a patient he or she has taken care of, or a family member who is or has been ill. Several components are necessary to promote this form of hypochondriasis in the medical student: limited information, identification with another person, definable symptoms, and anxiety or feelings of stress. Most young physicians recover quite nicely from their maladies, usually after their anxiety has passed, or they have received reassurance from a faculty member who knows more than they do, or after they have gained knowledge and sharpened their own medical judgment (Hunter, Lohrenz, & Schwartzman, 1964; Mechanic, 1972; Woods, Natterson, & Silverman, 1966).

Unlike the "worried well," patients with true, chronic hypochondriasis are typically not reassured no matter what they are told. They have a significant amount of anxiety about illness, anxiety that persists throughout their lives. The resolution of one situation gives way to a new concern. This is not to say that hypochondriacs never have disease. Certainly they do, but objective measures rarely support their subjective complaints. Their complaints may be considerably more extensive than, and even independent of, what is measurably wrong with them.

Hypochondriacs do feel real distress, much of which is emotional. Study after study has shown that patients who present physical symptoms for which no organic basis can be found are significantly more depressed than are patients for whom a diagnosis can be reached. Patients with undiagnosable ailments are not simply depressed because no one can find out what is wrong with them. Rather, many such patients have long-standing *endogenous depression* (arising from within rather than in response to the current situation) that pervades most aspects of their lives. Others are depressed in response to specific events, such as death or severe illness of a close relative. The depressions experienced by these patients precede rather than follow their symptoms (Kellner, 1986; Katon, 1982). The depression may serve, of course, to accentuate their symptoms and to reduce their involvement in outside activities, thereby increasing the focus of their

attention on the symptoms and making the symptoms even more difficult to live with. Relatedly, people who have many somatic complaints are typically more anxious than those who have few complaints. Those with definable disease entities as well as those with undiagnosed disorders report more discomfort when they are anxious than when they are not (Kellner, 1986). In fact, when antianxiety drugs are administered to anxious patients, not only is their anxiety lowered but their somatic complaints decrease as well.

Let's examine the psychological factors believed to cause hypochondriasis. First, as suggested in the case of medical students, incomplete medical information can sometimes lead people to worry about their health. Media stories frighten certain people by bringing to their attention symptoms they already have and causing them to interpret those symptoms as serious illness. Second, as we considered above, some people use chronic overconcern with disease as a mask for emotion such as depression. Illness concerns may serve as an outlet for anxiety or as an expression of intolerable internal conflict. Third, some individuals may have an overwhelming fear of disease, or a distortion in body image that causes them to experience their bodies as very vulnerable. Fourth, the physiological concomitants of emotion, such as tightness in the chest or lightheadedness, may be perceived as serious symptoms. As noted above, some people may be unable to express or describe in words the emotions they feel (psychiatrists refer to this condition as *alexithymia* [Nemiah, 1975]); instead, they can describe only their physical symptoms. Fifth, some people may present somatic symptoms in an effort to seek reassurance and support from a socially acceptable caring relationship, the one they develop with a physician or other health professional. And sixth, some people may use illness as an attention-seeking device, as a means to communicate with or manipulate others, or as a way to obtain the secondary gains of the sick role.

## PSYCHOLOGICAL FACTORS AND THE DELIVERY OF HEALTH SERVICES

It would be a gross oversimplification to conclude that emotional distress directly causes the seeking of health care. Instead, there exists a complex relationship between emotional distress and patterns of illness-related behavior.

One study attempted to examine this issue by investigating the behavior of more than 600 students at a major university (Mechanic & Volkart, 1961). The study examined the relationship between stress and illness-related behavior, and their joint effect on the use of medical facilities. Students were divided into two groups: those who had a high inclination and those who had a low inclination to use health services (as measured by several questionnaires presenting hypothetical situations). How much stress the students felt was measured by indices of their loneliness and nervousness. In the group of students who had a high inclination to use medical services, stress was a significant factor in bringing them to the physician. Seventy-three percent of those categorized as having high stress were frequent users of medical services (three or more times during the year). Among those with low stress, 46% were found to be frequent users of health services. Among those who had low stress *and* a low inclination to use medical services, only 30% were frequent users of such services. Thus, a combination of (1) the individual's general propensity to choose medical treatment as a solution to symptoms, and (2) feelings of stress that exacerbate those symptoms appears to be necessary to bring a person to seek the care of a physician.

Several studies done at the Kaiser Permanente Hospital and Health Plan in Northern California showed that patients' medical-care utilization can be changed by dealing directly with patients' psychological concerns. Researchers found that persons in emotional distress were significantly higher users of both inpatient and outpatient medical services than were those not in emotional distress (Follette & Cummings, 1967). The researchers divided patients described as emotionally distressed into two groups, and matched them on relevant variables. The experimental group was given either one free visit for psychotherapy or two to eight free psychotherapy sessions. The control group received no psychotherapy care. Patients who received one session only, with no repeat psychological visits, reduced their medical utilization by 60% over five years, with the most rapid decline in medical utilization in the second year. Utilization was reduced by 75% in those who received brief psychotherapy (two to eight sessions). There was no change in the utilization rates of the control group. And although patients appeared to benefit from the psychotherapy sessions, there was no resultant increase in demand for psychotherapy services, and patients did not overtax that aspect of the Kaiser system. The authors speculated that the results demonstrated the value of early intervention into a patient's problems. These patients were able to express their emotional concerns and to receive understanding. Therapy helped them to avoid changing emotional distress into somatic complaints and helped to reduce their use of medical services. Patients who were helped to discover and deal with their deeper-seated concerns may have even been spared the problems of some unnecessary surgeries and drug therapies, as well as the risks of multiple diagnostic tests.

In the next chapter, we turn to pain as a traditionally medical problem that can be best understood and treated using a biopsychosocial approach.

## Summary

Chapter 5 examines the phenomenon of becoming ill from the viewpoints of both patients and health professionals.

   I. There are complex and somewhat imprecise definitions of health, illness, and disease; however, they present guidelines to help understand the state of an individual.
   A. *Illness* is a subjective phenomenon, usually defined as a condition that deviates from a healthy state. It involves the subjective mental and/or physical feelings that drive an individual to seek health care.
   B. *Disease* involves a set of signs and symptoms in all or part of the body including abnormal bodily changes (pathology). The cause of disease is called its *etiology*. A forecasting of the probable results of the disease is the *prognosis*.
   C. *Health* is not the absence of disease but, rather, the complete physical, mental, and social well-being of a person.
  II. Statistics show that although the health of Americans is good and has been improving over the years, many are not satisfied with their health.
   A. More people are reporting more frequent and longer-lasting episodes of serious, acute illnesses now than they did 60 years ago, despite the change in life expectancies, death rates, and the introduction of many new drugs.
   B. One possibility for the existence of this paradox is that the threshold and tolerance for mild discomfort may be lower for Americans today than it was in the past. Also, standards of health are so high that people are more aware of their symptoms, and they may seek health care at the slightest discomfort.
   C. Another explanation would be that because people are living longer and are afflicted by chronic disorders, they may be left with various symptoms and disabilities that cannot be cured.
   D. The quest for a "health lifestyle" and the heightened awareness of health in Americans may have also made people less and less willing to tolerate impairment as a normal part of daily living.
 III. Considering that this paradox regarding health and illness exists, a physician must not assume that there is a correspondence between actual tissue damage or disease and a patient's subjective feelings of pain and discomfort. There is a dilemma when illness is viewed in a traditional biomedical sense rather than biopsychosocially.
   A. The biomedical model of disease assumes that illness can be fully accounted for by biological alterations, but a person exhibiting biological deviations may feel fine. A person can also feel ill when no physical symptoms are manifested.
   B. The biopsychosocial model includes psychological and social factors as well as biological ones when considering an individual's response to symptoms and the experience of illness.

1. The biopsychosocial model takes into consideration what a condition means to a person and how he or she responds to it.
2. One's cultural expectations can fit within the framework of the model (particularly what a patient has learned from family and culture about how to respond to symptoms).
3. A person's psychological state, such as whether he or she is anxious or depressed, is taken into account.
4. The social context of illness is also considered in the biopsychosocial approach.

IV. Several psychological factors influence the attention that people give to the symptoms they experience.
   A. The focus of attention on symptoms and their implications may vary.
   B. Attention to symptoms may depend on their salience. There is a tendency for people to focus attention on the vulnerability of their own bodies when someone close to them has died.
   C. Some may consider themselves generally weak and vulnerable, and therefore may scrutinize bodily state closely.
   D. Individuals also show differences in threshold and tolerance for symptoms, particularly pain.
   E. Experiences learned in childhood, as well as cultural experiences, will affect responses to symptoms.
   F. Circumstances in an individual's life at any given time can affect the degree of attention paid to symptoms.
   G. Cognitive factors, such as the viewing of an injury as a negative

event, can influence the attention paid to symptoms.

V. The factors that trigger the seeking of help for symptoms by an individual depend as much on his or her psychology as on the objective seriousness of the symptoms.
   A. A person is more likely to seek help if he or she perceives the symptoms as frightening and threatening; if the symptoms differ significantly from the familiar and appear to demand medical attention; or if an interpersonal crisis arises. A crisis may raise a person's anxiety level, making symptoms intolerable. Symptoms that limit one's social interaction will likely lead to seeking care. Approval or encouragement by another person will usually lead someone to seek care as well.

VI. Before a person even reaches a doctor, family members, friends, and co-workers may be conferred with about symptoms. This "lay referral network" often gives advice about and attaches meaning to symptoms.

VII. Many people delay in receiving medical treatment, usually because of faulty symptom attribution. They may also try to avoid drawing attention to themselves.
   A. Research shows that total delay in seeking care for a serious disorder, such as a myocardial infarction, is the total of appraisal time, illness delay, and utilization delay.
   B. Delays for diseases like cancer can be life-threatening. Survival rates could be higher if people would not delay in receiving treatments. Many cancers can be completely cured if detected early enough.

VIII. In our society, being ill involves adopting the sick role. With this role comes responsibilities and privileges. Self-definition is all that is needed to acquire the sick role and to maintain it.

A. There are advantages to the sick role. The person is exempted from working and from caring for others and for self. He or she can also expect help from others. Secondary gains, such as increased attention and excuses for not succeeding in life, may come about. Gains can also be tangible, such as monetary compensation.

B. Expressing emotional distress as physical symptoms is not uncommon. For example, a person who is feeling depressed may describe fatigue.

C. Idiopathic (of unknown etiology) conditions may exist. Sometimes it is impossible to find an organic cause of the patient's illness. A diagnosis does not exist for every ailment.

D. Medical professionals tend to attribute symptoms to psychological causes almost automatically if they cannot find an organic base for physical distress. Psychosomatic illnesses are caused, or aggravated, by psychological stress.

E. Hypochondria is a condition in which an individual complains often of multiple, common, stress-associated symptoms but shows no organic pathology. Despite this, the hypochondriac is convinced that something is wrong.

1. Hypochondria should not be confused with malingering, a conscious manipulation of somatic complaints to acquire the sick role. The hypochondriac's conflicts are on an unconscious level.

2. Medical students often experience a temporary form of hypochondria in which they misinterpret common symptoms as indicative of disease. This can be the result of anxiety and fatigue combined with incomplete knowledge of the disease being studied.

3. Hypochondriasis can serve to mask depression or as an outlet for anxiety. Hypochondriacs may have a fear of disease, or may unconsciously seek reassurance, attention, and support through the expression of symptoms.

# Glossary

**alexithymia:** the inability to express or describe in words emotions that are felt. An individual may be able to describe only the physical symptoms.

**biomedical model:** a model that assumes that illness can be fully accounted for by a person's deviations from the norm on measurable biological variables. The biomedical model holds that even the most complex illness phenomena can be reduced to certain measurable physical abnormalities.

**biopsychosocial model:** an approach that requires that psychological and social factors must also be included along with the biological in any attempts to understand a person's response to symptoms and the experience of illness.

**conversion responses:** symptoms such as loss of sight, speech, or hearing, and various forms of muscular paralysis. Conversion responses are believed to be primitive responses to emotional conflict. The symptoms make sense in that they tend to solve the conflict.

**delay in seeking medical care:** typically composed of three parts: (1) appraisal time (the time it takes the patient to appraise his or her symptoms as illness and to decide that the sensations mean something is wrong); (2) illness delay (the time from the patient's decision that he or she is ill to the decision to seek care); and (3) utilization delay (the time from the decision to seek care to the actual obtaining of medical services). Total delay, from recognition of the symptom to arrival at the clinic or emergency room, is the sum of these three components (Safer et al., 1979).

**disease:** (a much more narrow concept than illness) disease is ". . . a definite morbid process having a characteristic train of symptoms. It may affect the whole body or any of its parts, and its etiology (theory of causation), pathology (structural or functional change in tissue caused by disease), and prognosis (forecast of the probable results of the attack of the disease) may be known or unknown" (*Dorland's Illustrated Medical Dictionary*, 1965, p. 428).

**endogenous depression:** depression that arises from the individual's thoughts, beliefs, feelings, personality, etc., not simply in response to environmental events.

**gatekeeper:** a health professional who controls entry into the sick role, typically a physician.

**glove anesthesia:** a condition in which only the hand, but no other part of the arm, loses sensation and is unable to function. The disorder cannot be caused by an organic impairment because the neural pathways that conduct sensation to the hand also serve the rest of the arm.

**health:** "Health is the state of complete physical, mental, and social well-being, and is not merely the absence of disease or infirmity" (World Health Organization; adopted in 1946).

**hypochondriasis:** a phenomenon in which an individual displays more than just a simple propensity to pay more attention than most to his or her bodily symptoms. True hypochondriacs convert personal, emotional distress into physical distress. They report symptoms that are diffuse and may change from one occasion to another. Their complaints tend to be of symptoms that occur very commonly in a large number of people and that are typically associated with stress, yet they are convinced that these symptoms indicate serious disease.

**idiopathic:** a medical term meaning "arising spontaneously or from an obscure or unknown cause."

**illness:** a condition marked by pronounced deviation from the normal healthy state. When ill, an individual is unable to function normally in day-to-day activities, and his or her body does not feel normal.

**lay referral network:** a network of friends and family members who help an individual attach meaning to his or her symptoms. They typically offer advice about whether the person should seek care from a physician or instead treat the condition with a home remedy (or simply ignore it and wait for it to go away).

**malingering:** a conscious, purposeful using of somatic complaints to achieve exemption from one's obligations.

**medical-care utilization:** the use of health care services.

**psychosomatic illness:** illness that results from, or is exacerbated by, psychological factors.

**secondary gains:** the positive outcomes that balance some of the more negative aspects of being ill. Pain and illness bring increased attention from others, a chance to rest, and an opportunity to be taken care of.

**sick role:** a social role adopted by an individual who presents symptoms of illness. The sick role brings privileges as well as responsibilities.

**threshold:** the level of intensity of a stimulus below which a sensation is not, and above which a sensation is, identified as pain.

**tolerance level:** the point of intensity of a stimulus at which the individual can no longer stand the pain and (in research at least) asks that the stimulus be withdrawn.

# 6

# Pain

■ ■ ■ ■ ■

Helen was almost disappointed when the CT scan was perfectly normal. Some kind of growth pressing on a nerve would have explained her pain, and perhaps the pain could have been alleviated, but instead the neurologist's diagnosis was trigeminal neuralgia. Also known as *tic douloureux*, trigeminal neuralgia is an extremely painful disorder of the fifth cranial (trigeminal) nerve. Its cause is generally unknown, although sometimes it accompanies other diseases. In Helen's case, there were no explanations for what she was experiencing.

Helen's pain was destroying her life. Like other patients with the more severe form of the condition, Helen had attacks of excruciating pain on the right side of her face from the area above and in front of her ear down across her cheek to her chin. It was a sharp searing sensation that was absolutely unbearable. The pain would last roughly five minutes and occur many times a day. Each attack was typically set off by stimulation of some part of her face such as a light touching of her nose, or cheek, or gums. Helen's attacks often occurred when she was talking or drinking hot or cold beverages. Sometimes they followed a draft of air touching her cheek. To try to prevent attacks, Helen drastically restricted what she ate and drank to things of room temperature. She held her face as immobile as possible while talking. She wore a shawl to protect the right side of her face from the wind.

Certain drug treatments were tried. They helped somewhat by reducing the severity of some of her attacks, but they made her sleepy. She was beginning to consider neurosurgical intervention, which would mean resecting (cutting) parts of the nerve. Resection would prevent her from feeling any sensation in certain parts of her face and in her mouth, and would significantly interfere with her ability to move her mouth to talk and to chew. Even with surgery, a cure could not be promised. But Helen was so discouraged by her pain, she was willing to try anything. Her life had become extremely limited because of her fear of each next attack, and she felt she was hardly living at all. Understandably, Helen was very depressed.

The struggle to understand pain, what causes it, how to control it, and particularly what it *is*, is an extremely important endeavor for health psychologists. Prior to the development of recent medical and psychological advancements, pain was very poorly understood. In the past two decades, however, psychological research has prompted great strides in the field. New developments have benefited those whose lives have been touched, and sometimes devastated, by pain.

As we will see in this chapter, the mind plays an important role in the perception and interpretation of pain. To understand pain fully, we must understand the manner in which pain is linked to the mind, that is, to psychological processes. We will examine what pain is, how we know a person is in pain, and how we can assess how much pain a person is experiencing. We will examine the ways in which people differ in their perceptions of pain, and the psychological factors that affect these perceptions. We will examine how and why some people continue to strive toward their life goals when they are in pain, while others seem to give up and remain debilitated by chronic pain. We will examine the many treatments available for the management of pain and see how a patient in pain can be helped to live a happy and productive life.

## WHAT IS PAIN?

Pain is defined as "an unpleasant sensory and emotional experience associated with actual or potential tissue damage." Pain involves the "total experience of some noxious stimulus which is influenced by current context of the pain, previous experiences, learning history, and cognitive processes" (Feuerstein, Papciak, & Hoon, 1987, p. 243).

Pain has also been defined as a *psychological experience* that includes "(1) a personal, private sensation of hurt; (2) a harmful stimulus which signals current or impending tissue damage; *and* (3) a pattern of responses which operate to protect the organism from harm" (Sternbach, 1968, p. 12). "In some respects [pain] is a sensation, and in other respects it is an emotional-motivational phenomenon that leads to escape and avoidance behavior" (Weisenberg, 1977, p. 1009).

These several definitions from the psychological and the medical literature

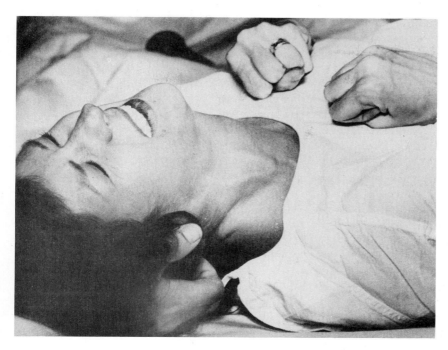

An example of pain behavior: the expression of pain during childbirth.
SOURCE: Wide World Photos

suggest that arriving at a precise understanding of pain is sometimes difficult and
confusing. Although to a person who is suffering, the experience of pain is unmistaka-
ble, researchers must strive for precision in
defining pain as a construct. Toward this
goal, Fordyce (1988) has made an important distinction between *nociception* and
*pain*. *Nociception* is defined as "mechanical,
thermal, or chemical energy impinging on
specialized nerve endings that in turn activate A-delta and C fibers, thus initiating a
signal to the central nervous system that
aversive events are occurring" (Fordyce,
1988, p. 278). Nociception can be observed
because activity in certain nerve fibers and
their synaptic connections can be observed.
Pain can result as a sensation that arises
from the stimulation of perceived nociception. It is also possible, however, for pain to
be perceived in the *absence* of nociception,

and for nociception to occur without any
perception of pain.

We can know that a person is in pain
only by assessing the effect of pain on him
or her. Observing *pain behavior* is one way.
Pain behavior is a very general term that
includes many actions that people carry
out or signals that they emit when they are
in pain. Pain behaviors include facial and
vocal expressions of distress (for example,
moaning, grimacing), distorted movements
and postures (such as moving in a guarded
fashion), expressions of negative affect
(such as being irritable), and avoidance of
activity (such as resting a great deal and
refraining from strenuous activity) (Turk,
Wack, & Kerns, 1985). These behaviors may
arise in response to nociception or for reasons other than nociception. For example,
a person may groan or grimace in response
to being ignored. Or someone may feel stab-

bing pain and give off no sign of that fact. A person can also verbally report the existence of pain but demonstrate no pain behaviors at all.

In one sense nociception can be thought of as the *input* and pain behavior as the *output*. Since this input-output system necessarily involves the brain, "prior experience, expectancies, and perceived or anticipated consequences all play a role" (Fordyce, 1988, p. 278).

## THE SIGNIFICANCE OF PAIN

Pain is an extremely salient phenomenon in human life. It is typically the symptom that is most likely to bring a person to seek medical care (Safer, Tharps, Jackson, & Leventhal, 1979). People will often tolerate the most annoying and sometimes the most apparently serious symptoms (such as lumps and abnormal bleeding) as long as they feel no pain. For many, the presence of pain is what suggests danger. When in pain, they fear for their well-being. Some seek medical care simply because they want the pain stopped (Zborowski, 1952).

There is typically little relationship, however, between the severity of a person's pain and the degree of danger that the associated condition poses to him or her. A cancerous lump, for example, may be life threatening but bring no pain at all; a serious heart attack may simply be accompanied by a feeling of annoying indigestion. Unfortunately, the lack of pain may eliminate the person's incentive to seek medical treatment (Safer, et al., 1979).

Most people fear ever having to experience terrible pain. In fact, fear of pain causes some people completely to avoid preventive medical examinations and necessary dental care (Melzack, 1973). Some avoid recommended medical treatments (such as surgery) because of a desire to avoid pain. And, what people fear most about serious illnesses, such as cancer, is the possibility of suffering *intractable pain*

(pain that cannot be relieved) (Melzak, 1973).

The anticipation of pain can itself be painful! A person may so tense muscles in anticipation of pain that painful muscle spasms may actually ensue. A person's fear of pain may well become the worst part of a medical-care experience.

I offer my own example to illustrate this point. Believe it or not, while outlining this chapter on psychological issues and pain, I was munching on some crunchy cereal, bit down, and broke a tooth. To my utter amazement, the entire lingual cusp of a second molar was sheered off, leaving a little more than half a tooth. As I explored the damage with my tongue, I waited for the excruciating pain to start. I fully anticipated being overwhelmed by pain, so I waited expectantly. The actual discomfort I experienced was minimal. Pain occurred only when I ate or drank something. Because this was not what I had expected, I called my dentist, at home, at 9:00 P.M. (He's very understanding!) I wanted to know what to do *if* my (half) tooth began to hurt *a lot*. He assured me that it was unlikely I would have any more pain than I had had up to that point, and told me to come into the office the next morning. Then, with the use of lots of novocaine, he carried out repairs. I had been spared the excruciating pain I envisioned. From my position in the dental chair, I could see a sign on the wall that was certainly meant for me: "WE CATER TO COWARDS." Through the whole experience of breaking my tooth, including the next day's dental visit for a temporary crown and the installation of the permanent crown several weeks later, the very worst part of all was my *anticipation* of pain. I was afraid that the pain would be too much for me to handle. It never was, but when my tooth was finally fixed, I was exhausted.

Of course, the point of my tale is that the experience of pain involves expectations and fears and beliefs, and all kinds of things psychological. My tooth example is a lighthearted look at these issues, and it illustrates the psychological significance of pain. People are aware that pain has the potential to overcome their ability to cope with it. When people are in pain, they can feel quite overwhelmed by it. Alleviation of their pain can become even more important to them than satisfying basic needs, such as hunger and thirst (Sternbach, 1968). Relief from pain can take precedence over maintaining a career and personal relationships. In some cases an individual's pain can become so bad that he or she cannot imagine life beyond pain. Families can be destroyed by pain. Intractable pain can even prompt some people to commit suicide. Sometimes people report that they fear intractable, uncontrolled pain even more than they fear death (Melzack, 1973).

The phenomenon of pain has tremendous economic consequences. Americans spend at least a billion dollars a year on over-the-counter remedies to reduce or alleviate pain (Fordyce, 1976; Winters, 1985). Advertisements for analgesics promise instantaneous relief from headaches, muscle aches, back pain, menstrual cramps, and other short-term ills. And close to $50 billion is spent annually on attempts to relieve chronic (long-term) pain. These costs are for medical care, prescriptions, devices, and many and varied treatments.

Let us turn now to an examination of the research findings of the past several decades that have built the foundation of our knowledge of pain and its control. We will examine efforts that have been made to understand what pain is and how it is felt. We will see that there have been several proposed theories about pain, each attempting to account for the findings of the research. We will see, too, how theorists and researchers have incorporated into their explanations of pain an understanding of psychological issues and a focus on the role of pain in the life of the person who is its victim.

## HOW IS PAIN PERCEIVED?

When a person's body is injured, signals of tissue damage follow a particular route from afferent neurons (see Chapter 2) of the peripheral nervous system to the spinal cord and then to the brain. The afferent nerve endings that respond to pain stimuli are called *nociceptors* (Chapman, 1984). When activated, these nerve endings generate impulses that travel to the central nervous system. The afferent peripheral fibers that transmit pain impulses are A-delta fibers and C fibers. A-delta fibers transmit impulses very quickly and are associated with sharp, distinct pain, whereas C fibers transmit impulses more slowly and are involved when pain is diffuse, dull, or aching (Chapman, 1984; Melzack & Wall, 1982; Mountcastle, 1980). A-delta signals send messages through the thalamus on their way to the brain's cerebral cortex and signal sharp pain, thus commanding attention. C fiber signals send pain messages to the brainstem and lower portions of the forebrain, and are believed to affect mood, general emotional state, and motivation.

Perceiving pain is not always straightforward, of course. *Referred pain* involves pain that originates in tissue in one part of the body but is perceived as coming from another part. An example is pain inside the ear from irritation in the temporomandibular joint of the jaw (Melzak & Wall, 1982). When different sensory impulses use the same pathways to the spinal cord, interpretation of the origin of the pain message is sometimes confused by the person perceiving the pain.

Sometimes pain is experienced in the absence of apparent tissue damage or noxious stimulus. *Neuralgia*, suffered by Helen earlier, is such a condition and is extremely painful. Neuralgia episodes can occur quite suddenly and pain can be provoked by minimal stimulation (such as a light wind). *Causalgia* involves severe burning pain and sometimes results after a wound has healed and damaged nerves have regenerated. Like neuralgia, causalgia can be triggered by minor stimulation. Neuralgia and causalgia are believed by some to be caused by infection (viral or bacterial) that results in nonobvious neural damage (Hare & Milano, 1985). *Phantom-limb pain* occurs when a patient who has had an amputation, or one who has a damaged peripheral nervous system, still feels pain in the missing limb or damaged part of the body. Most amputees report sensations in the amputated limb, and between 5% and 10% of amputees experience severe and progressive phantom-limb pain. Although neuralgia, causalgia, and phantom-limb pain are puzzling and often defy explanation, patients with these conditions can suffer a great deal.

# Theories of Pain

Now the news has arrived From the Valley of Vail
That a Chippendale Mupp has just bitten his tail,
Which he does every night before shutting his eyes.
Such nipping sounds silly. But, really, it's wise.
He has no alarm clock. So this is the way
He makes sure that he'll wake at the right time of day.
His tail is so long, he won't feel any pain
'Til the nip makes the trip and gets up to his brain.
In exactly eight hours, the Chippendale Mupp
Will, at last, feel the bite and yell "Ouch!" and wake up.

—SOURCE: From Dr. Seuss's Sleep Book, by Dr. Seuss. Copyright © 1962 by Theodor S. Geisel and Audrey S. Geisel. Reprinted by permission of Random House, Inc. and International Creative Management.

The perception of pain in Dr. Seuss's Chippendale Mupp seems to be quite a simple process. But, as we have seen so far in this chapter, in human beings pain is a complicated and sometimes perplexing phenomenon. Let's examine the history of theories of pain in an effort to understand more fully what pain is and how it can be controlled.

## SPECIFICITY AND PATTERN THEORIES OF PAIN

As far back as the late 19th century, medical professionals proposed that a specific bodily system is responsible for pain perception, thus formulating the *Specificity Theory of Pain*. Pain was believed to be an independent sensation like heat, cold, or touch (Mountcastle, 1974). It was thought that there existed specific receptors in the skin and that each receptor responded to a particular kind of stimulus. Further, specific routes of transmission in the central nervous system were proposed, as were special centers in the brain that registered and interpreted (only) pain (Melzack, 1983). Evidence contradicted this theory, however, because pain is not an experience separate from other sensory experiences. Rather, pain can result from excessive heat, cold, or pressure, and pain sensations do not seem to follow dedicated nervous pathways.

Another theory of pain, the *Pattern Theory*, holds that pain results from the patterning and quality of stimulation from peripheral nerve endings (Melzack, 1983). In a particular area of the body, for example, mild stimulation might result in the sensation of touch, whereas intense stimulation in the same area may result in the sensation of pain. The pattern theory also holds that sensations can summate. Nerve impulses are conducted to the spinal column and, only after reaching a certain threshold, are conducted to the brain. This summation can account for the short delay experienced between the onset of tissue damage (as in a cut or burn) and the actual experience of pain.

## THE GATE CONTROL THEORY OF PAIN

Neither of the above theories adequately explains the pain experience, yet each provides a partial explanation of what we know of the physiology of pain. Research reveals that as the Specificity Theory suggests, specific nerve fibers do conduct pain, though others can give rise to pain when they are stimulated beyond a certain threshold. Furthermore, as the Pattern Theory predicts, receptors do respond to patterned information, but there is no *direct* connection between the pain receptors in the peripheral nervous system and the brain center where pain would be perceived (Melzack & Wall, 1970).

A third theory of pain, the *Gate Control Theory*, more adequately deals with the findings of pain research than do the two earlier theories (Melzack & Wall, 1965, 1970, 1982). The Gate Control Theory acknowledges specificity in pain transmission, as well as the importance of patterning and the summation of impulses, but it also allows for the role of psychological processes in pain experience and control. It is the most valuable of the three theories in its clinical applications.

The Gate Control Theory of Pain states that certain structures in the central nervous system make possible the pain experience. The flow of pain stimulation to the brain is controlled in the dorsal horns of the spinal column. Pain sensations from the peripheral neural pathways are carried to the spinal column but are modified as they are conducted through the spinal column to the brain. As we noted earlier, pain perception involves a complex interplay of different facets of the brain and central nervous system. Nerve fibers throughout the body conduct pain sensations and project them onto various parts of the brain, including the hypothalamus, thalamus, and cerebral cortex. The involvement of the cerebral cortex is believed to be what makes cognitive judgments about the meaning of pain important in pain perception. Thus, if the higher centers of the brain interpret an event as painful, a "gating" mechanism will be open, and the sensation of pain will be transmitted to the brain. Via this central control mechanism, information from the higher centers of the nervous system is transmitted down the spinal cord to modulate the experience of pain.

It is not known precisely *how* pain messages make their way to the brain and how psychological processes affect these messages. Explanations of pain mechanisms are still without proof. But, to reiterate, according to the Gate Control Theory of Pain there are structures in the central nervous system that effect a "gating" mechanism in the spinal column. This mechanism controls pain messages to the brain (Melzack & Wall, 1982). Pain impulses do not go *directly* from nerve endings to the brain (as in the Chippendale Mupp) but are modified in the spinal cord and are influenced by downward pathways from the brain that interpret the sensations. When no painful stimuli are involved, peripheral nerves transmit sensations directly to the spinal column and up to the brain. When there are no pain sensations to transmit, the hypothesized spinal gating mechanism is closed. But when the stimulation of appropriate nerve endings is strong enough, *and* the upper centers of the brain interpret the event as painful (for example, by recognizing that the body has sustained some damage), the gate opens to allow painful sensations in.

As we noted above, stimulation of the small nerve fibers known as A-delta and C fibers open the pain gate, permitting the transmission of pain impulses. Stimulation of large fibers in the spinal cord known as A-beta fibers is believed to close the pain gate. According to this theory, certain nerve fibers *descending* in the spinal column from the brain, particularly from the higher centers such as the cortex, can inhibit transmission of pain impulses.

According to the Gate Control Theory of Pain, three factors are involved in determining how much pain is felt. First, the amount of activity in the pain fibers (A-delta and C) (determined partly by the strength of the noxious stimulation) influences the strength of the pain message that is transmitted. Second, the amount of activity in other large diameter fibers (A-beta fibers), which close the gate, inhibit the perception of pain when noxious stimulation exists. Third, messages that descend from the brain can close the gate and inhibit the transmission of pain signals.

A few implications for the control of pain are suggested. First of all, stimulation of A-beta fibers, which close the pain gate, limits the perception of pain. Pain sensations are diminished or eliminated when these fibers are affected *chemically* with medications, or stimulated *electrically* using mild transcutaneous (through the skin) electrical nerve stimulation or *physically* using counterstimulation, such as heat and massage. Second, the pain experience can be affected by such factors as an individual's thoughts or affective, emotional reactions. Pain messages can be modified or inhibited if they are not interpreted by higher centers of cognition. The gate can be closed by positive emotions, intense concentration, relaxation, and involvement in pleasurable activities. Conversely, pain is increased by conditions that open the gate, such as anxiety or worry, tension, depression, focus on the pain, boredom, and lack of involvement in life activities (Turk, Meichenbaum & Genest, 1983).

## NEUROCHEMICAL BASIS OF PAIN AND PAIN INHIBITION

Evidence in support of the Gate Control Theory of Pain demonstrates that the brain can indeed control the amount of pain an individual experiences by transmitting messages down the spinal cord to block the transmission of pain signals (Melzack & Wall, 1965, 1982). Studies showing that electrical stimulation of the brain can block the perception of pain impulses led to the discovery of a neurochemical basis of pain and the identification of *endogenous opioids*.

Endogenous opioids are opiate-like substances produced within the body that regulate pain. They appear to behave in the same way as exogenous opiods, such as the drugs heroin and morphine, in that they produce pain analgesia and feelings of well-being (Snyder, 1977; Winters, 1985). Researchers have recently identified three main groups of these endogenous opioids: beta-endorphin, proenkephalin, and prodynorphin (Akil et al., 1984).

The system of endogenous opioids and their function in the body is very complex. These substances appear to be released in response to stressful circumstances and can produce natural pain suppression. There is some evidence, for example, that intense physical exercise can trigger the release of beta-endorphin, resulting in natural, short-term pain suppression and resultant subjective feelings of physical well-being (Akil et al., 1984).

## Assessing Pain

One important thing we know about pain is what it is *not*. Pain is not a phenomenon that can be measured objectively because, as we noted earlier, pain is a wholly subjective experience. It is felt only by the person who has the pain. The tissue damage that causes the pain might be identified and examined in detail, but the pain itself cannot be perceived by the senses of anyone other than the person who has the pain. Because pain is a subjective experience, its quality may be very difficult to describe.

## THE QUALITY OF PAIN

Various highly descriptive words help to depict various types of pain experience. For example, pain may be "dull" versus "sharp," or "constant" versus "throbbing," "shooting" versus "still," "diffused" versus "focused," "stabbing" versus "pinching." The type of pain experienced will sometimes, though not always, depend upon the type of irritation or damage to the body and the part of the body that has been affected. As with other body experiences, there is probably a limit to what can be communicated with words (Schiffman, 1976).

## THE INTENSITY OF PAIN

Pain can be experienced at different levels of intensity. As with quality, communicating intensity may be very difficult. For example, a number on a 10-point scale may begin to impose some objectivity on the intensity of pain, but people will vary in their choice of numbers depending upon other factors besides the pain. One person's 4, for example, may be another person's 7. As we will see in detail below, measuring the intensity of an individual's pain is as difficult as it is important. The measurement of pain is critical to understanding and assessing the effects of clinical interventions on pain perception. One may wish to know, for example, whether a particular treatment makes a patient feel better or worse and have less or more pain.

Two concepts are central to an understanding of intensity. These are *threshold* and *tolerance*. *Threshold* refers to the point at which a person first perceives a stimulation as painful. A light touch of one's wrist with a fingernail may bring the sensation of mild pressure and even a sense of being "tickled," but if the fingernail is pushed deeper into the flesh, a sensation of considerable discomfort is eventually identified. The stimulus has crossed the pain threshold. *Tolerance* refers to the point at which the individual is not willing to accept stimulation of a higher magnitude. It is the point of saying "Uncle," "I give up," or "No more." If the stimulation increases beyond this point, the person feels that it is unbearable. Threshold appears to be determined mainly by physiological variables, whereas tolerance appears to be influenced by psychological variables, such as attitudes and motivation (Gelfand, Gelfand, & Rardin, 1965).

## ACUTE AND CHRONIC PAIN

Medical professionals make an important distinction between acute and chronic pain. *Acute pain* is temporary and lasts less than six months (Turk et al., 1983). No matter how bad it is, acute pain eventually ends. A toothache, the discomforts of childbirth, and even the pain of postoperative recovery are relatively short-lived. Acute pain can cause considerable anxiety and distress, which usually subside when the condition resolves (Fordyce & Steger, 1979). But sometimes pain lingers on. Once it has lasted longer than six months, pain is considered to be *chronic*. Chronic pain can be intermittent or constant, mild or severe. Any condition that is expected to bring only acute pain but continues for longer than six months without resolution results in chronic pain. Chronic pain can vary a great deal depending upon its type. *Chronic recurrent pain* does not become progressively worse and is characterized by intense episodes of pain followed by relief (as in the case of Helen at the beginning of this chapter) (Turk et al., 1983). *Chronic intractable benign pain* is present all the time but is not related to a progressive condition. Chronic low back pain is an example. And *chronic progressive pain* involves continuous discomfort that gradually intensifies as the condition worsens, such as the pain of cancer and advancing arthritis.

Psychologically, there is a tremendous difference between acute and chronic pain. When a patient has an acute condition, he or she can predict the likely course of the pain. The pain associated with a particular medical procedure, for example, is expected to be over sometime after the procedure ends. The pain of a broken limb is expected to subside gradually as the limb heals. But when pain endures for months or even years despite measures to relieve it, the chronic pain patient can become very discouraged. Such pain can lead to depression and to a sense of hopelessness (Melzack & Wall, 1982).

Chronic pain, such as chronic back pain or headache, can completely change a person's life. Like Helen at the beginning of this chapter, someone in pain might drastically restrict movements to those that do not trigger painful episodes and may be forced to give up favorite activities. The fatigue and debilitation that result from constant pain can restrict a person's ability to work and may severely tax interpersonal relationships. People in chronic pain can become preoccupied with *somatic* (bodily) concerns, feel a heightened sense of dependency, and experience a heightened incidence of depression (Ogden-Niemeyer & Jacobs, 1989).

Acute and chronic pain are very different entities, even though they may arise from the same source. They can produce very different reactions in their victims, and as we will see later in this chapter, they demand different courses of treatment.

## WAYS TO MEASURE PAIN

Because of the subjective nature of the pain experience, pain can be challenging to measure. Clinicians and researchers have developed many techniques for measuring the pain felt by an individual. Each technique has certain advantages and certain limitations.

Measures of pain can be classified into three basic types: *psychophysiological measures*, such as blood pressure, heart rate, and others; *behavioral measures*, which involve observations of pain behaviors such as grimacing, moaning, and complaining; and *verbal self-report* measures, which involve the patient's written or spoken description of the character and intensity of the pain, description that is relied on quite heavily by clinicians.

## PSYCHOPHYSIOLOGICAL MEASURES

Psychophysiological measures assess pain as it is reflected in changes produced in an individual's physiological activity (Lykken, 1987). One measure is the *electromyograph*, or EMG, which measures the electrical activity in muscles, thereby assessing their level of tension. Headache patients, for example, demonstrate different EMG patterns when they are having headaches than when they are not (Blanchard & Andrasik, 1985). *Autonomic activity* such as heart rate, respiration rate, blood pressure, and skin conductance are used to assess generalized arousal (which may be the result of reactions to the pain or to other stimuli). Measures of autonomic activity are believed to be most useful in assessing the emotional components of pain (Chapman et al., 1985). The *electroencephalograph* (EEG) measures electrical changes in the brain produced by stimuli. Pain stimuli produce responses called *evoked potentials* that correlate with subjective reports of pain. EEG responses increase with the intense stimulation of pain, and decrease when subjects take analgesic (pain-reducing) medication (Chapman et al., 1985).

## ASSESSMENTS OF PAIN BEHAVIORS

When a person is in pain, he or she is likely to act in a way that allows us to recognize that fact. As noted earlier, pain behaviors involve nonverbal expressions (including facial and vocal cues), distortions in movement and posture, irritability, and restrictions of activity. Procedures have been developed for assessing specific pain behaviors in both daily activities and structured clinical situations.

In assessing day-to-day activities, researchers and clinicians might record the amount of time the person spends in bed, for example, or how many complaints he or she expresses. Does the person bend over very carefully or not at all? Individuals who live with the patient, particularly the spouse, are often the best people to make these assessments (Fordyce, 1976). The spouse might, for example, keep a pain diary for the patient and record episodes of the patient's expressions of pain. Such a diary can be a trigger for discussion between the patient, spouse, and clinician regarding the meaning of the pain to the patient and spouse, their thoughts and feelings, and the effectiveness of different interventions to control the pain. In clinical situations, procedures are available for assessing expressions of pain through behavior. The *UAB Pain Behavior Scale* (Richards, Nepomuceno, Riles, & Suer, 1982) is used by nurses during routine care of patients. The patient is required to perform several activities, and the nurse rates the patient's mobility and use of medication among other things. Research suggests that behavioral assessments can be made relatively easily and reliably, and that they correlate well with patients' self-assessments of the pain experience.

## SELF-REPORTS OF PAIN

Most clinicians, as well as people in general, rely heavily on a patient's verbal report of his or her pain. *Self-report measures,* which are not precise but can be quite reliable, depend upon the individual's verbal (or written) description of the character and intensity of the pain he or she experiences. Self-report measures can take the form of interviews, in which reports of pain are spoken descriptions; rating scales, which ask the patient to quantify his or her pain level; and questionnaires, which ask about many aspects of pain, including its emotional components.

**Interviews.**    Interviews about pain can be very informative. An interview with a patient and his or her family can tell a clinician much about the patient's pain behaviors and how they affect the other members of the household. A great many details of the patient's life and the *quality* of that life in the face of pain can be assessed from the interview process (Karoly, 1985).

**Rating Scales.**    A very direct measure of pain intensity is to have an individual rate his or her discomfort on a scale (Karoly, 1985). For example, the person might choose a number from 1 to 10, with 10 meaning "excruciating" and 1 meaning "nonexistent" pain. Or a person might choose a label for his or her pain ranging in increasing intensity from "mild" to "distressing," to "intense," to "excruciating." Rating scales are useful for pain sufferers to record their pain levels at various times of the day and to examine fluctuations in pain intensity as they relate to various activities and states of mind. Repeated ratings can also point out to the pain patient and his or her family that pain is not constant but may vary a great deal depending upon circumstances (Turk et al., 1983).

**Pain Questionnaires.**    As we noted earlier, intensity is not the only dimension of pain that is relevant. The experience of pain depends upon its character and quality, as well as how it affects a person emotionally. In an effort to characterize pain in a relatively complete manner, Melzack and

Torgerson (1971) divided 102 pain-describing terms into three classes: (1) sensory quality descriptors (for example, spreading, crushing, burning); (2) affective quality descriptors (such as exhausting, awful, nauseating), and (3) evaluative descriptors of the intensity of the experience (such as agonizing, excruciating, miserable). The *McGill Pain Questionnaire* provides a method for assessing, through self-report, a patient's subjective experience of the sensory, affective, and evaluative quality of pain (Melzack, 1983). The McGill Pain Questionnaire asks the individual to select from 20 subclasses of words the terms that best describe the pain he or she feels. Each word in each class has an assigned value based on the degree of pain it reflects. The sum of points across the 20 subclasses is called the *pain rating index*.

The McGill Pain Questionnaire is very useful in that it assesses several dimensions of pain at once. However, the questionnaire requires fine distinctions among words in English and may be very difficult for people from other cultural groups and those who have limited vocabulary.

## THE SIGNIFICANCE OF PAIN ASSESSMENT

Lacking words to describe the character of pain, an individual may be able to say only *that* something hurts. But *how* something hurts can give important clues to what is causing the pain in the first place. Consider, for example, a headache. Not all headaches are alike. In fact, they fall into several broad categories. Two that are quite different from each other are the *muscle contraction headache* and the *vascular (or migraine) headache* (Blanchard & Andrasik, 1985). Muscle contraction headaches usually produce dull, persistent aches, spots that are sore and tender on the head, neck, and jaw, and feelings of tightness around the head. Sometimes the patient describes the pain

as being like "a stake or a knife in my head." The patient often describes the pain as severe, constant, and unrelenting. Headache of a vascular nature (for example, a migraine) is caused by dilation of the cranial blood vessels. Vascular headache pain is described as unilateral or bilateral aching or throbbing pain. The vascular headache is often preceded by symptoms, which include nausea, vomiting, sensitivity to light and noise, and sensory disturbances. In the rare cases in which head pain is caused by a tumor, the patient finds the pain to be most severe when he or she awakens. And if headache is caused by bleeding inside the cranium, such as in cerebral hemorrhage, there may be accompanying neurological deficits, such as muscle weakness and perceptual disturbances.

A *detailed* description of headache pain is essential to its medical diagnosis, which in turn will determine the treatment. Such a detailed description necessarily includes the duration and location of the headache as well as its nature and characteristics, concurrent symptoms, and precipitating factors. Because the treatments for the various kinds of headaches differ a great deal, an accurate diagnosis is essential. The treatment of vascular headache includes pharmacological methods for constricting the dilated cranial blood vessels, whereas the treatment for muscle-tension headaches typically includes pharmacological, psychological, and physical means to relax the tensed muscles of the head and neck. Of course, recognition from the patient's description of a possible tumor or cerebral hemorrhage can be essential.

Diagnosis of many medical conditions requires, in addition to technological measurements of the patient's physiological status, a clear picture of the character of the patient's subjective pain experience. A *biopsychosocial* approach to the care of the patient can vastly improve the accuracy of medical diagnosis.

## THE PATIENT'S STORY OF PAIN

Despite the existence of a detailed assessment instrument, such as the McGill Pain Questionnaire, clinicians often report that one of the best ways to assess the details of a patient's pain experience in the process of diagnosis is to make the simple request: "Tell me about your pain" (Cassell, 1985a). The *story* of pain has at least two characters, the person and the person's body. The action in the story that follows involves what is happening to that body.

DOCTOR:  Please tell me about the problem that brought you here today.

PATIENT:  Sure. I got up Wednesday morning and I had a pain in my stomach . . . above my waist . . . sort of a dull aching like a stomach ache. Only it didn't really feel like a stomach ache. I had it the night before as well, with chills and sweats. I just went to bed and tried to forget about it. I thought I was getting the stomach flu. But by Wednesday morning, the pain was spreading all around my torso. It was a strange, feeling . . . like my insides were not well lubricated and were rubbing against each other causing a kind of . . . I know it sounds crazy . . . a kind of painful *friction*. The only way I could reduce the pain was to not move. But it never went away. I haven't had any vomiting or diarrhea, and it's been five days, so I guess my stomach-flu theory is out. But I can't eat or drink anything because that hurts too much. Feels like it causes my insides to move more than I can stand. Breathing is real difficult too. Hurts in my back and chest.

The patient has given an excellent description of *pleuritic pain*, a pain caused by inflammation of the pleural lining of the lungs. The pain literally resulted from her "insides" "rubbing against each other" and causing "painful friction."

A patient's hypothesis about his or her pain can be very illuminating. Many years ago the famous medical educator Sir William Osler (1899) told medical students that they must *listen to the patient, for he or she will reveal the diagnosis.* Many modern physicians, who have all the most recent technological innovations at their disposal, believe that the patient has the best perspective on his or her illness, and that the diagnosis can be revealed in the *story* that the patient tells about pain (Cassell, 1985a).

> I asked a woman with left upper quadrant abdominal pain what she thought the trouble was. (That is a useful question, because patients are frequently correct, and if not, it is a very direct way of finding out what worries them.) She said, "Well, of course, I know it's heart disease, because my whole family has heart disease. But sometimes, when I think to myself that maybe it isn't heart disease, then I think, well maybe my kidney is a big cyst and it's bumping against my ribs." Bull's-eye! That was precisely correct. (Cassell, 1985b, p. 31)

# Psychological Factors and Pain

> How a person responds to pain sensations is an area of concern just as important as the specific mechanisms transmitting and generating pain experiences. Descriptions of pain based solely on physiological or neurological factors have proven inadequate in attempting to identify and account for all aspects of pain experiences. (Pinkerton, Hughes, & Wenrich, 1982, p. 262)

The causes of pain can range from the purely organic, such as tissue damage, to the psychogenic, such as muscle tension, to the purely psychological, such as hallucinations and conversion hysteria (see Chapter 5). Thus, pain reactions convey much more than the simple signal that tissue damage is occurring. A person's reaction to pain can also signal psychological turmoil and conflict brought on by conscious or unconscious desires to be legitimately excused from responsibilities, the wish to be punished, and even the need to be looked upon as a long-suffering person. Let us examine how and why.

Pain is strongly influenced by such psychological factors as thoughts, emotions, attention, and expectations. A common example of how attention can influence pain is the ability of distraction to lessen our perceptions of pain. Turning our attention away from pain can minimize it, whereas focusing on pain and thinking about the pain and analyzing its character *particularly when we are distressed* can maximize the sensation. In the midst of a competition, for example, an athlete may not even notice an injury. His or her attention may be fully focused on something else. But when outside stimulation is minimized, such as when someone with lower back pain stays home in bed, pain sensations can be quite a bit more unpleasant (Turk et al., 1983). Although "taking your mind off" discomfort is not the entire solution for a pain problem, it can help a person to feel less distressed by pain.

The *meaning* attached to pain partly determines how it is perceived and experienced, as well as how it is reacted to (Beecher, 1959). An excellent illustration of this phenomenon is the fact that men wounded in battle during World War II rarely needed medication to control their pain. As we noted in Chapter 5, a classic study by Beecher (1956) demonstrated that actual tissue damage is less important in determining pain reactions than is the *setting* in which the tissue damage occurs and what the person *thinks* about it. Among 215 men seriously wounded in battle during World War II, only 25% wanted narcotic relief for their pain, whereas over 80% of people with similar wounds resulting from

surgery wanted such relief. The difference in reactions could be attributed, according to Beecher, to the meaning of the pain, which was different for the soldiers and the patients. For soldiers, being wounded meant leaving the front lines, and perhaps even being sent home as heroes. Surgical patients, on the other hand, were missing out on the pleasurable aspects of their lives.

*Expectations* can also significantly influence pain perceptions. For centuries physicians have known the importance of suggestibility in symptom perceptions. Clinical evidence consistently demonstrates that the power of a medication often lies in the patient's belief in its effectiveness. Throughout the history of medicine, instant pain relief could sometimes be brought about with a simple substance, such as colored water, that the doctor pretended was a potent medicine. The term for any such inert substance is *placebo*, from the Latin meaning "I will please" (Shapiro, 1960). Practitioners' expectations for the good (or the bad) sequelae of a treatment have been found to be transmitted quite effectively to patients and to produce, on average, a 35% more positive (or negative) outcome (Beecher, 1959; Shapiro, 1960).

In years prior to the latter half of the 20th century, physicians had no effective remedies for most diseases; therefore, placebos were essential. Some writers have even suggested that the history of medical treatment is, in fact, the history of the placebo effect (Shapiro, 1960). As scientific medical knowledge grew, however, physicians sometimes found the placebo effect to be a nuisance. In the early stages of clinical use of a new drug, enthusiasm about it would often cause the drug to work superbly. It was not until the "magic" wore off that doctors could tell how well the drug would work clinically in the long run. Today's research on new drugs requires a *placebo control group*, in addition to an experimental group, to test a new drug or therapy. This way researchers can tell whether (and how well) the actual drug can perform up to the expectations held for it. Practitioners can communicate their positive (or negative) expectations to patients and actually affect (positively or negatively) patients' individual perceptions of pain (Melzack & Wall, 1982).

## INDIVIDUAL DIFFERENCES IN REACTIONS TO PAIN

Reactions to pain vary widely from one person to another. Faced with a painful back spasm, one person will continue to go to work and to fulfill family obligations while another will take to bed on "painkillers" and do little but watch television and sleep. One person might tolerate pain for weeks or months before seeking medical help; another goes to see a doctor at the first twinge of discomfort.

Research demonstrates that individuals' reactions to pain vary significantly depending upon several different factors. These include age, sex, social and cultural background, and personality type. Knowledge of how these factors covary with pain perceptions and pain reactions can be very useful to researchers who try to understand the nature of pain and to clinicians who try to help patients to deal with their pain experiences. Let us examine these factors in further detail.

Several studies have examined sex differences in threshold and tolerance for pain. Most studies have failed to find any sex difference at all, although a few report that women have somewhat lower threshold and tolerance than do men for certain forms of experimentally induced pain (Weisenberg, 1977). There is evidence that among postoperative patients, females obtain more prolonged pain relief from a dosage of analgesic medication (and thus require less medication) than do males (Loan & Morrison, 1967).

Research on age differences and pain shows that the threshold for pain seems to increase steadily with age (Sternbach, 1968). Of course, this increase in the pain threshold may be due to a diminished sensitivity to all stimuli that appears to occur with aging. However, the threshold change might result instead from an increasing reluctance among older persons to label noxious stimuli as painful. Understanding of the increase in pain threshold across the life span may be particularly important in pediatric medical and dental care because children tend to present certain behavioral problems in response to pain (for example, screaming and pulling away from the practitioner). Such behavioral difficulties probably reflect their somewhat higher sensitivity to pain than that of the adults who treat them. It may be incorrect to conclude that a child's report of pain is exaggerated based upon our own adult perception of the same stimulus (for example, a finger prick for a blood test or an intramuscular injection for immunization). It is quite possible that a child feels more pain at a lower threshold than does an adult. Of course, it is important to keep in mind that many psychosocial factors affect children's reactions to pain, such as their parents' own pain behaviors and the reinforcements that parents provide for their childrens' pain behaviors (Bush, 1987).

Many different personality traits have been studied as they relate to pain, sometimes with confusing and conflicting results that make generalization and application difficult. Research has found, for example, that one important personality variable that seems to be related to individual reactions to painful stimuli is the personality variable that classifies people as *augmenters* or *reducers*. Those who are most tolerant of pain tend to be perceptual reducers; they see stimuli around them as part of the larger "field" in which the stimuli are embedded. Reducers tend to have a body image with definite boundaries; they are extraverted, and have low levels of anxiety (Sternbach, 1968). Reducers tend to reduce or minimize stimulation, whereas augmenters characteristically perceive stimulation as greater than average. Augmenters respond to external stimuli directly by trying to do something to deal with it. Reducers on the other hand, play down external stimulation and deny or avoid it (Goldstein, 1973).

In general, "readiness to use pain as a symptom" (Weisenberg, 1977, p. 1019) occurs most often among people who are neurotic and self-punishing, and who have had more pain experiences in their lives. Pain as a symptom appears with the highest incidence in people who have high anxiety. For certain groups of patients, pain expression can be greater than might be expected by the extent of tissue damage experienced. These are (1) patients who show high levels of hypochondriasis; (2) people who have re-

active depression; (3) people who tend to have somatic (bodily) reactions to their psychological states; and (4) people who use their pain to manipulate others (Sternbach, 1974).

See Box 6–1 for a discussion of the effect of monetary compensation on the perception of back pain.

## CULTURE AND PAIN

There are substantial cultural and social group differences in reactions to pain. These reactions are very significant, for they can affect clinical diagnosis and even the choice of treatment. Researchers have studied Italians, Irish, Jews, Yankees, Eskimos, and American Indians, and an assortment of racial and ethnic categories around the world and have found some intriguing differences (Weisenberg, 1977).

First, variations in reactions to pain may be related to tolerance rather than to

BOX
6–1

### BACK PAIN AND COMPENSATION

Can monetary compensation for pain cause it to persist longer than it otherwise might? Does the fact that a person can stay home from work and still receive income actually interfere with his or her efforts to overcome pain and return to work? Research suggests that the answer is *yes*.

Low back pain that might otherwise have been short-term can sometimes become a deeply ingrained, long-term problem when monetary compensation is available. Research shows that people who are eligible for wage-replacement funding take significantly more time off from work than do people who are not eligible (Fordyce, 1985). Unfortunately, patients who receive compensation (from private insurance or from Social Security Disability Insurance [SSDI]) may not be aware that their incentive to get well is being destroyed. They may no longer be willing to expend the effort necessary to overcome the debilitating effects of their pain and to return to a productive life.

Low back pain is an extremely common example of this problem. Research finds that 50% to 80% of people in the United States report some problems with back pain, and roughly 20% of people in the United States have been incapacitated for periods from three weeks to six months because of back pain. Four percent of people in the United States have been incapacitated with back pain for more than six months. In recent years there has been

threshold (Weisenberg, 1977). Threshold, as we noted earlier, tends to be the result of physiological factors, whereas tolerance is highly affected by psychological factors. Thus, cultural and social differences in pain tolerance appear to be caused by anxiety stemming from certain *attitudes* held about pain. These attitudes specifically involve two opposing approaches to pain. One includes the willingness to deny or to avoid dealing with pain, and the general belief that pain should be ignored whenever possible. The other approach reflects the desire to avoid or eliminate pain at all costs, wanting the doctor to get rid of the pain (if necessary, even before finding out its cause.)

These differences in cultural attitudes clearly affect an individual's psychological functioning (Tursky & Sternbach, 1967). Yankees (that is, Protestants of British descent) have been found to have a matter-of-fact orientation to pain and tend to adapt faster than any other cultural group to research-induced electric shock. Irish subjects directly inhibit their expressions of suffering, and do not show what they are feeling; they remain very stoic. Italians, on the other hand, are expressive about pain, complain loudly, and in the laboratory display the highest heart rate in reaction to pain (probably reflecting their anxiety). In clinical situations, Jewish subjects are very future-oriented and insist on finding out the significance of their pain for their health (Zborowski, 1969). As a group, they tend to have the lowest heart rate in reaction to pain.

How do cultural factors come to influence such a private experience as pain? Weisenberg (1977) has suggested that social learning and social comparison are probably responsible. Pain is a private but also a somewhat ambiguous experience. Comparison with other people helps an individual to determine what reactions are most ap-

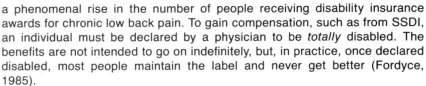

a phenomenal rise in the number of people receiving disability insurance awards for chronic low back pain. To gain compensation, such as from SSDI, an individual must be declared by a physician to be *totally* disabled. The benefits are not intended to go on indefinitely, but, in practice, once declared disabled, most people maintain the label and never get better (Fordyce, 1985).

Low back pain, in fact pain itself, does not fit well into a biomedical approach because pain is a *biopsychosocial* phenomenon. Pain can persist even without any evidence of underlying tissue, nerve, or bone damage. In fact, a person can be identified as someone in pain solely on the basis of his or her pain behaviors, such as reports of discomfort, grimacing, limitation in movement, and so on. Thus, physicians often find themselves in an awkward situation when their patients with low back pain seek pain-killing medications or certification of injury in order to receive compensation. Even when a physician cannot find anything organically wrong with the patient (which is quite common), he or she feels practically compelled to help out the individual who displays obvious signs of suffering.

There is little question, however, that psychological and behavioral factors influence the maintenance of pain and the limitations that pain places on the individual. Although initially helping the suffering person, monetary compensation might actually interfere with functional recovery (Fordyce, 1985, 1988).

propriate. Is it permissible to cry, for example, or to ask for help? Should pain be masked with analgesic medications? People learn how to express their reactions to pain by observing the reactions of others.

An individual's earliest models for appropriate behavior regarding pain are likely to have been from the members of the family and cultural group. The family is a particularly potent source of cultural norms for young children. Parental anxiety, for example, has been found to correlate with (and possibly to cause) children's difficulties in facing painful medical treatments (Bush, Melamed, Sheras, & Greenbaum, 1986; Dahlquist et al., 1986).

The social environment can influence the meaning of pain to an individual. Reactions to pain can become reinforced independent of the original physiological sensation and tissue damage. In some social and cultural groups, a person's wincing is attended to by others. (They ask, "Are you in pain? Sit down. What can we do for you?") In other groups expressions of pain are completely ignored and ultimately may become extinguished because they are not reinforced. In addition, in some environments, people learn that certain sensations are to be ignored, whereas in other environments it becomes clear that the same sensations demand the expression of great distress. Knowledge of the role of family, cultural, and social influences on pain is critical to effective pain control and therapy.

# Medical Practitioners and Pain

As we will see in Chapter 7, practitioner-patient communication is an essential component of the therapeutic relationship. Effective communication is central to patient satisfaction with treatment, to patient cooperation with care, and even to the outcome of care.

Pain can cause a significant amount of misunderstanding between medical practitioners and patients. To a physician, for example, pain is only one of the signs and symptoms that must be accounted for in formulating a diagnosis. The patient's pain understandably does not have the emotional impact on the physician that it does on the patient. Most medical practitioners are committed to minimizing or eliminating patients' discomfort whenever it is possible and safe to do so. However, medical practitioners typically see people in pain all day long and it becomes easy for them to remain unaware of the emotional aspects of their patients' pain.

A second reason that pain prompts misunderstanding between physicians and patients has to do with the timing of pain relief. Sometimes pain-relieving medications must be withheld until the source of the pain is found, such as when a patient presents with the symptoms of appendicitis. Masking such pain would preclude effective diagnosis.

Third, some patients continue to have pain despite the fact that medical professionals can find no organic basis for the pain. Clinically, the existence of pain is typically determined only by self-report. So when such patients complain about their pain and the complaints cannot be substantiated by physical evidence, medical professionals become frustrated. Patients may even be treated badly by health professionals, who believe that they are malingering or seeking secondary gains (as described in Chapter 5).

Keep in mind that the fact that pain can be affected and modified by psychological mechanisms by no means implies that pain is "all in a person's head." It also does not mean that people are always in conscious control of the psychological processes that regulate their pain. People do not have pain because they want to, and they should not be expected to simply "wish" their pain away. Psychological factors may contribute to pain but they do not completely control it.

Unfortunately, medical practitioners sometimes forget this. For example, they tend to use the placebo effect inappropriately. In one study researchers found that many medical practitioners gave placebo medications only to patients they disliked, whose pain they believed was "all in their heads." Instead of using the placebo effect as an adjunct to therapy, these practitioners used it as evidence that their patients' pain had no physiological basis (Goodwin, Goodwin & Vogel, 1979).

## The Treatment of Pain

■ ■ ■ ■ ■

When Harold got the bad news from the orthopedist, his pain seemed to grow worse. The discomfort he had been feeling in his lower back and the burning sensations in his buttocks and down the backs of his legs could now be explained. He had a "slipped" or herniated disk in the lumbar region of his spine. The soft, mucoid material in the fibrous disk between two vertebrae had been forced through the disk's torn outer rim and was impinging on spinal nerve routes, resulting in severe back pain.

Harold's back had been hurting badly ever since he tried to pick up a heavy box at work. Because of his backache, he called in sick several times a week and finally stopped going to work altogether. He lay in bed a good portion of each day, watching old movies and reading his favorite science fiction novels. The more he lay there, the more immobile he became. Harold filed for workers' compensation. That required certification by a doctor of his disability. Harold visited his family doctor and was referred to an orthopedic surgeon for tests, including a CT scan. The surgeon recommended surgery. Harold didn't argue. He wanted the pain taken away.

Harold had surgery but the pain remained. The doctors were not quite sure why, but the pain was so bad that Harold could not bear it without narcotic painkillers. He would also drink a good deal of alcohol to dull the pain. He was wholly disabled and could not work at all. He collected full compensation from his employer. Harold rarely saw his friends. He depended almost solely upon his wife for companionship. Unfortunately, her life was becoming unbearably limited.

Someone suggested that they go to the pain center at the local university hospital. Desperate, Harold and his wife contacted the staff, and he began a program of rehabilitation. Within weeks, he was off pain medications and moving around, despite his discomfort. His pain had not been taken away; rather, he was learning to manage it using relaxation techniques, biofeedback, exercise, and correct body postures. Harold also began training for a new career that he could manage with his physical limitations.

With Harold's knowledge and consent, his wife was taught to reward him with attention for ignoring his pain instead of for describing how badly he felt. She interacted with him only when he turned his own attention outward and did not dwell on his discomfort. Consequently, he became more and more involved in outside activites and stopped focusing on his pain. Harold and his wife received much support and guidance but needed to work hard to achieve their goals.

The couple accomplished the difficult task of relearning on many levels; they were both devoted to each other and to improving their lives. The pain clinic also helped Harold and his wife to achieve a happier relationship. And Harold again be-

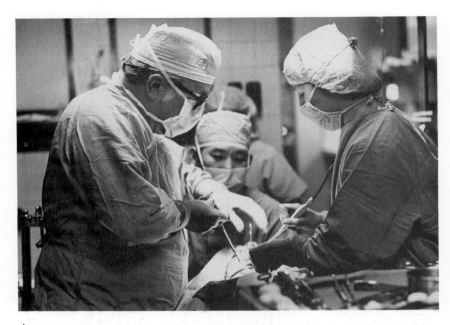

The surgical treatment of pain is a drastic intervention that may have only short-term effectiveness.
SOURCE: © Alan Carey/The Image Works

came a productive individual who was able to live a satisfying life.

During the past few decades, various physical and psychological interventions have been developed for treating both chronic and acute pain problems. Successful pain control involves two elements: (1) the elimination of pain or its reduction, and (2) increased functioning (in which the individual learns to tolerate his or her pain, and if necessary to live with it and still have a satisfying and productive life).

# Physiological Interventions for Pain

The methods of pain control that have been used most by practitioners of Western medicine following the medical model have been almost exclusively surgery and phar-

macological interventions (medications). Let's examine the advantages and disadvantages of these.

## SURGICAL TREATMENT OF PAIN

The surgical treatment of pain involves an attempt to intervene in the transmission of pain impulses to the brain. Portions of the peripheral nervous system or spinal cord are removed or disconnected in an attempt to stop pain signals from reaching the brain. Surgical methods represent a drastic intervention and can produce numbness and sometimes paralysis in the area affected by the nerves. Surgical interventions are now used less often than in the past. They can have only short-term effectiveness and some time later pain and other uncomfortable sensations return. Recent evidence suggests that the transmission of pain impulses is not as specific as was once believed and so blocked nerve pathways are eventually circumvented. After surgical intervention new pathways form, bringing pain messages to the brain by new routes (Melzack & Wall, 1982).

## DRUG TREATMENTS

Today the most common medical treatment for pain involves pain-relieving medications, of which there are several types.

*Local anesthetics* are quite familiar to anyone who has ever had a tooth repaired by a dentist. These medications, such as novocaine and lidocaine, can be applied topically but are most effective when injected into the site of the pain's origin (for example, skin that is being cut or stitched). Local anesthetics work by preventing the affected nerve cells from generating pain impulses (Hare & Milano, 1985; Winters, 1985). Local anesthetics work well to block impulses in pain fibers, but they block impulses in motor neurons as well. For this reason, a dental patient typically has little or no control over his or her mouth, tongue, lips, and cheeks for several hours after a dental procedure during which novocaine was injected.

*Sedatives* (for example, barbiturates) and *tranquilizers* (for example, diazepam; trade name, Valium) help to depress pain responses by, in a sense, depressing the individual's entire repertoire of responses. The action of sedatives and tranquilizers decreases transmission of nerve impulses throughout the central nervous system and depresses many bodily functions as well (Aronoff, Wagner, & Spangler, 1986). These drugs probably do not directly affect pain but, rather, reduce patient anxiety and help the patient to sleep (thereby escaping the pain for a while and resting so as to better tolerate the pain when awake). Related medications that tend to help patients who

are in pain are *antidepressants* (for example, doxepin), which reduce the depression that may accompany pain and are believed to affect pain-related neurotransmitters.

*Peripherally acting analgesics* are probably the best known of all pain medications. These drugs include aspirin and other over-the-counter medications, such as acetaminophen (for example, Tylenol) and ibuprofen (for example, Advil). They work by reducing inflammation at the site of tissue damage and inhibiting the synthesis in the peripheral nervous system of neurochemicals that facilitate transmission of pain impulses (Winters, 1985).

*Centrally acting analgesics* are pain-killing medications that are also called *narcotics*. Narcotics work by binding to opiate receptors in the central nervous system (Aronoff et al., 1986). They include codeine and morphine, as well as synthetic substances like heroin and methadone. Narcotics are very effective in reducing severe pain and can be taken orally or injected (the latter administration resulting in more potent action) (Winters, 1985). These drugs have tremendous potential to produce tolerance so that the person needs higher and higher doses to achieve the same effect. In addition, they can be addicting (Aronoff et al., 1986).

One drawback of some of the pain medications available (particularly sedatives and centrally acting analgesics) is that they usually dull the person's sensory perceptions, impairing the ability to walk, talk, drive a car, and make decisions. The use of pharmacologic agents in hospitalized patients or among those at home at bed rest may be quite successful, at least in the short term, but a person who must function effectively in everyday life may be impaired by taking pain medications.

It has been argued that analgesic medications work mostly by affecting the individual's predisposition to complain about pain (Beecher, 1972). Morphine, for example, is believed to reduce not so much the sensation of pain as the desire to express distress. The patient may feel the pain but remains unconcerned about it. In experimental studies in which laboratory pain is induced in subjects, pain is typically unaffected by morphine and there is no difference between reactions to morphine and to a saline solution. On the other hand, morphine can be very effective for clinical pain (caused by a clinical problem). The explanation for this phenomenon probably has to do with the anxiety associated with the disease process, accompanied by the threat of disfigurement and death. In the laboratory such anxiety is typically missing, for the subject in the pain experiment knows precisely what is causing the pain and when it will end. Reducing pain reactions in the clinical setting also requires the reduction of the individual's anxiety, which both morphine and placebos (the administration of "something") do quite well (Beecher, 1972).

## THE USE OF PAIN MEDICATIONS

Pharmaceutical interventions can be quite effective in controlling pain under certain circumstances. Narcotics are typically administered for several days after surgery to reduce or eliminate acute pain. As soon as the severe acute pain is past and tissue healing has begun to take place, the administration of narcotics is no longer necessary. For patients with progressive, debilitating, painful diseases, such as cancer, narcotic analgesics are quite appropriate, and when they are used, they can be extremely helpful for patients who are dying (Foley, 1985). Obviously, under circumstances of terminal illness, addiction issues are irrelevant and narcotics can help tremendously to improve the quality of life of those in severe pain from cancer and other diseases.

Narcotics are typically not appropriate for the treatment of chronic pain, however. They have high addiction potential, and as a patient acclimates to the dosages prescribed, higher and higher doses are needed. Non-narcotic medications are most appropriate for chronic pain (Kanner, 1986). Patients with arthritis, for example, can benefit from the use of medications that reduce local inflammation in their joints (such as the peripherally acting analgesics described above). Likewise, the use of non-narcotic medications for relatively severe chronic pain (such as back pain) can be quite effective when combined with psychological interventions such as those described below.

The control of pain has, until recently, not been well understood in medical practice. In the treatment of severe acute pain, for example, many medical professionals held to the belief that they must withhold high dosages of pain medications, such as morphine, because of the dangers of addiction (Angell, 1982). But research shows that such a fear is unfounded. Most patients do in fact successfully withdraw from their pain medications as soon as their acute pain subsides (Citron, Johnston-Early, Boyer, Krasnow, Hood, & Cohen, 1986). They do not become addicted to medications that are used for short-term, severe acute pain (Porter & Jick, 1980). (And again, for patients who are terminally ill, the issue of addiction is irrelevant.) Concerns about addiction can cause medical professionals to let their patients in acute pain suffer needlessly. Such patients can become severely depressed as a result of their pain (Angell, 1982). The opposite problem has occurred in the treatment of chronic pain. Patients are too often prescribed narcotic medications (which are, in fact, addicting) but given no opportunity to take advantage of other newly developed techniques, such as the methods described below (Reuler, Girard, & Nardone, 1980). As we will see, patients with chronic pain, such as back pain and headaches, are best treated *not* with pharmacological agents alone but rather with limited amounts of non-narcotic medication combined with psychological and behavioral interventions such as relaxation, hypnosis, and exercise.

# Cognitive and Behavioral Methods of Pain Control

What a person thinks about pain can significantly influence the impact of pain on his or her life, and even how much pain he or she feels. Typically, negative thoughts about pain focus the individual's attention on unpleasant aspects of the situation and make the pain feel worse (Turk et al., 1983; Turk & Rudy, 1986). Redefinition of the situation can help tremendously. In addition, where a person's attention is focused can affect how he or she reacts to painful stimuli, as can the images that surround perceptions of pain (Fernandez, 1986). Let's examine in detail these several aspects of cognitive strategies for the control of pain.

### ALTERING INTERPRETATIONS OF PAIN

Faulty logic can distort the reality of the pain that an individual experiences, leading to some serious negative psychological consequences and interference with the individual's ability to deal effectively with pain. Alteration of damaging cognitions, on the other hand, can facilitate an individual's ability to cope with pain and actually diminish the intensity of, and distress resulting from, pain.

Let's examine the various types of cognitive errors that tend to affect an individual's ability to deal effectively with pain. These are described more fully elsewhere (Ciccone & Grzesiak, 1984; Ogden-Niemeyer & Jacobs, 1989).

1. *Catastrophizing.* When in pain, an individual may overestimate the adverse consequences of the unfortunate event he or she has experienced (for example, having a back injury). Distress, discomfort, and inconvenience are reinterpreted as catastrophe.

2. *Overgeneralizing.* The individual in pain believes that the discomfort he or she is feeling will continue indefinitely and never end, and that suffering will endure forever. This belief is often responsible for the depression felt by patients in chronic pain.

3. *Low frustration tolerance.* The person in pain attempts to avoid present discomfort at the expense of long-range objectives. The short-term gains of disability (for example, being able to stay home from work) are accepted, while long-term gains (such as building a career or having a positive economic future) are sacrificed.

4. *External locus of control.* The patient in pain may come to believe that he or she is being operated on by forces beyond his or her control and may come to feel helpless and unwilling or unable to accept responsibility for dealing with the pain.

5. *Mislabeling somatic sensations.* Some chronic pain patients come to label all the somatic sensations they experience as "pain," thus increasing the amount of time in their lives that they feel uncomfortable.

6. *Feelings of worthlessness.* Some individuals who are in chronic pain come to experience a diminished status because they are not functioning as well as they have in the past in their jobs and in their family lives. They interpret this diminished role status as proof of personal worthlessness.

7. *Feelings of having experienced injustice.* Not surprisingly, chronic pain patients sometimes feel that they have been dealt

with by fate in a manner that is grossly unfair.

8. *Cognitive rehearsal.* Some chronic pain patients think about their pain so much that they continue over and over to reexperience it along with a high degree of anxiety. Some may even begin to feel pain *before* engaging in an activity that may have caused pain in the past.

What an individual thinks about his or her chronic pain problem can significantly affect the perception and consequences of that pain. Cognitive appraisal that emphasizes the situation as long term, hopeless, out of the patient's control, and unable to be contended with (as in "I can't stand it. It is too awful to bear.") can lead to significant distress in the form of anxiety and depression (Ciccone & Grzesiak, 1984). Interference with these negative cognitions and substitution of positive and hopeful thoughts (redefinition) can do much to help a pain patient to contend successfully with pain and to minimize its intrusiveness in his or her life (Turk et al., 1983).

## OTHER COGNITIVE STRATEGIES

Another cognitive approach to pain involves the diversion of one's attention from the pain or the source of pain onto a different stimulus (Fernandez, 1986). *Attention diversion* works best when acute pain is mild to moderate, and not severe. Thus, if a person is receiving an injection or a dental treatment, for example, he or she might deal best with the pain by attending to nonthreatening stimuli in the environment or thinking about a different issue (such as solving a math problem or remembering the words to a popular song). Even for chronic pain patients, engrossing activities (such as a movie or interesting reading) can provide some pain relief.

A more complex strategy than diversion of attention is the use of *nonpain im-*

*agery.* Discomfort is alleviated by conjuring up a mental scene that is incompatible with the pain (Fernandez, 1986). When engaging in imagery, a person might imagine a scene that is extremely pleasant, such as a beautiful valley in a mountain forest. The individual's task is to image the sight of the valley, to smell the evergreen trees, to hear the sounds of birds chirping and leaves rustling in the wind, to feel the freshness of the air, and so on. While focusing so much attention on the scene, the individual is unable to attend to the details of the pain experience. Imagery works best for mild to moderate pain, and requires considerable involvement and concentration on the part of the patient (Turk et al., 1983).

Box 6–2 presents a personal perspective on psychological methods for coping with pain.

## PROGRESSIVE RELAXATION

Relaxation is proving to be an extremely useful intervention for controlling both acute and chronic pain. Researchers have found that muscle tension builds up lactic acid in, and decreases blood flow to, muscles, and in doing so significantly increases an individual's experience of pain. Psychologists have developed various techniques of progressive muscle relaxation that work either on one muscle group or several, and that can place an individual into an overall state of low arousal (Blanchard et al., 1986; Davidson & Schwartz, 1976).

Relaxation can be accomplished by many different methods. The simplest is for an individual consciously to tense and then relax a particular set of muscles (say, the muscles in a leg) and to imagine that this particular area of the body is extremely heavy and sinking to the floor. Simultaneously, the individual might empty his or her mind of all thoughts and/or focus on one image (such as waves washing over the rocks at the seashore). An important part of the relaxation is deep breathing. In general, the individual learns to put body and mind into a state of peace.

Progressive relaxation has been used successfully to treat many different types of pain, including arthritis, headache (both migraine and tension), and low back pain (Blanchard & Andrasik, 1985; Blanchard, Andrasik, Guarnieri, Neff, & Rodichok, 1987). Relaxation is one component (and in fact may be the most important component) in bringing about the analgesic effects

**BOX 6–2**

## ON CONTROLLING PAIN WITH PSYCHOLOGY: A PERSONAL VIEW

I approached the delivery of my first child with a degree of confidence that I did not deserve. I was so sure of myself, certain that I could tolerate the "discomfort," certain I could relax when I needed to, confident that I would have presence of mind and not be afraid of childbirth. I was athletic and strong. I even studied and wrote about pain control. What could hurt me? I thought. Around the 20th hour of labor, I found out.

One of the most important lessons I learned from giving birth is that a tremendous amount of concentration is needed to affect one's pain with one's psychology. Research shows that what we think, and how we behave, can influence how much pain we feel and how terrifying that pain can be to us. But saying this is one thing, and acting on it is quite another.

As described in detail in Box 6–3, prepared childbirth is just that: *prepared*. The woman in labor must control her respiration, hold a total body relaxation throughout the powerful contractions of her uterus, and maintain a visual and cognitive focus on something other than the pain. These techniques, when done correctly, can greatly reduce the pain of childbirth. But doing them correctly was much more difficult than I had imagined. I found myself forgetting the Lamaze routine of breathing and focusing. I had not practiced enough to become fully "conditioned" (in the classical conditioning sense) to the process. I braced myself against each painful contraction despite my desire to stay relaxed. I kept forgetting to keep my visual focus on one spot. Fortunately, a very skilled labor and delivery nurse barked orders at me for the last few hours, and somehow I made it through. But each time I lost my focus and serious concentration, I lost the ability to control the pain with my own psychological processes.

Throughout this chapter I have referred to psychological methods for controlling pain perceptions and the effect that pain has on one's behavior and one's interactions with others. I want it to go on record that I truly admire the accomplishments of those who can use their minds to affect their pain. It is not an easy task. It takes a tremendous degree of mental focus and a tremendous force of will. No one can overcome pain who doubts that he or she can do it. No one can cope successfully with pain who believes, even unconsciously, that the pain might serve a purpose. No one can control pain who needs the pain even a little. No one can control pain who hesitates or holds back the effort required.

The powers of the mind are tremendous, but to release those powers one must fully engage one's mind toward its purpose. Such concentration of personal, psychological power is a huge accomplishment.

of hypnosis (considered later). Relaxation training alone has been found to reduce significantly the pain of chronic tension headaches in many patients (although about 50% of tension headaches do not yield fully to relaxation [Blanchard & Andrasik, 1985]). Regardless of the source of pain (for example, back strain, childbirth, surgery) relaxation does contribute considerably to pain reduction.

Box 6–3 examines relaxation and other techniques for the control of pain during childbirth.

### BIOFEEDBACK

Biofeedback involves a mechanical system whereby an individual is signaled by means of a light or a buzzer to bring about some particular behavior or state (usually quite

BOX
6–3

## PSYCHOLOGICAL METHODS IN PREPARATION FOR CHILDBIRTH

During the last trimester of pregnancy, a woman and her chosen labor coach learn methods of prepared childbirth. The Lamaze Method is the most widely used in the United States. Let's examine the five components of the technique (Wideman and Singer, 1984).

*Information.*    Lamaze preparation for childbirth involves the imparting of information about the development of the fetus and the process of labor and delivery. As we consider in detail elsewhere in this book, information (particularly about what will be experienced, and how it is likely to feel) is essential to enhancing an individual's sense of control in medical situations.

*Respiration techniques.*    During Lamaze training, a woman is taught to breathe properly during the various stages of labor in order to insure that she and the fetus obtain the correct amounts of oxygen and carbon dioxide. Controlled breathing is believed to play a role in reducing responsivity to stressful stimuli and thus contributing to a reduction in pain experienced. This may be because of a direct depression in autonomic nervous activity, or because controlled breathing requires concentration and thus takes the woman's attention off her pain. Correct breathing also facilitates getting oxygen to the muscles, thus preventing cramping and pain.

*Conditioned relaxation.*    Women trained with the Lamaze technique are taught to relax their muscles consciously during contractions. With neuromuscular relaxations, the woman is better able to control her response to contractions. The labor coach also provides lower back massage to help relax muscles that cause discomfort because they are tired or cramping. In fact, clinical evidence suggests that an expectant father pressing his fist over the sacrum (lower back) of his laboring partner during a uterine contraction can suppress her painful sensations from the contraction as effectively as can 50-100 mg of Demerol (a potent pain medication) (Pace, 1977).

*Cognitive techniques.*    A key component of prepared childbirth is the use of various techniques to distract the woman in labor and to focus her thoughts

subtle) in his or her body. For example, tension in the *frontalis* muscle in the forehead, the amount of blood flow to the extremities, or the temperature of the skin might be measured with electrodes attached to those parts of an individual's body. Biofeedback that measures muscle tension is called *EMG biofeedback* (EMG stands for electromyographic, meaning the measurement of electrical charge of the muscles); that which measures temperature and blood flow is referred to as *thermal biofeedback*. Biofeedback works on the principles of op-

erant conditioning, and teaches people to be aware of their bodily processes and consciously to alter them. It is a very effective treatment with some kinds of pain. For example, using thermal biofeedback, migraine headache sufferers can learn to bring blood to their hands ("hand warming") thus reducing cranial blood flow (blood flow to the head) and pain that is caused by dilated cranial blood vessels. Patients whose tension headache pain is caused by chronically tensed muscles in the head, neck, and jaw can be taught to reduce

not on pain but on other things. She learns to restructure the event cognitively (for example, interpreting the contractions not as painful assaults but instead as positive forces that operate to push the baby out). She also learns to focus on one spot, such as a spot on the ceiling, and her energy is directed to keeping her focus rather than feeling her pain.

***Social support.*** The Lamaze Method encourages social support from the coach, who is the individual who oversees practice of the techniques at home, reminds the woman to relax, provides reassurance and confidence, and whose voice is the conditioned stimulus for her specific relaxation and breathing patterns.

Lamaze is not "natural" childbirth but, rather, it is "prepared" childbirth. The Lamaze Method provides an analgesic effect through physical and psychological rather than chemical means. It is unrealistic to think that the discomfort and pain of childbirth can be completely abolished. A woman's structure, the size of the baby, and the complications of labor are important determinants of how painful the experience will be. But the goal is to alleviate the pain as much as possible, and to make childbirth a more positive and controllable experience than it is without such supports.

Prepared childbirth methods have been found to relate to some important positive outcomes of the childbirth experience. Women who have received preparation develop more positive maternal attitudes, and report a more positive birth experience. Prepared women require fewer pharmacological interventions for pain control, their pain tolerance is greater, and they experience fewer birthing complications (Wideman and Singer, 1984). We must remember, of course, that this research is correlational, not experimental, and that the dependent variables are based upon self-reports. In addition, the overwhelming majority of women who elect to learn Lamaze preparation are middle- and upper-middle-class Caucasian women, who are likely to have fewer birthing complications than poorer women. These findings are encouraging, however, and do suggest that physical and psychological preparation can contribute a great deal to the reduction of a woman's pain during childbirth and to the enhancement of her ability to cope with it.

this tension consciously, using EMG bio-feedback (Blanchard & Epstein, 1977).

Although biofeedback may be used in a very specific way to deal with a specific pain problem, the power of biofeedback can be quite general as well. Using biofeedback, people have been taught to activate their parasympathetic nervous system (which produces relaxation in response to the activation of the sympathetic nervous system during periods of fear or anxiety).

How well does biofeedback work? Is it more effective than other less complicated and less expensive techniques? Research suggests that simple relaxation techniques may work just as well as EMG biofeedback in achieving muscle relaxation (Bush, Ditto, & Feuerstein, 1985; Holroyd, Andrasik, & Westbrook, 1977; Turk, Meichenbaum & Berman, 1979). However, this issue is still debated. There is some evidence that the power of biofeedback training may be due at least partly to the placebo effect. In one study people who used biofeedback reported decreased headache pain regardless of whether they received feedback for raising, lowering, or producing no change in their forehead muscle tension (Andrasik & Holroyd, 1980). This suggests that just the fact of using the biofeedback technique, complete with its official-looking electronic instrumentation, may contribute to improvement because of the placebo effect (Blanchard et al., 1986). Furthermore, people need to be "weaned off" the electronic equipment and learn to associate the desired states with other bodily cues. And, the effects of biofeedback may be relatively short-lived (Blanchard, 1987). Relaxation techniques are, of course, much less expensive than biofeedback because they do not require the use of electronic equipment and a trained technician. Relaxation techniques can be used anywhere and are available to anyone who will practice them.

## HYPNOSIS

Hypnosis is an important psychological technique that aids in the control of (particularly acute) pain. It is a very old technique, and was used as early as the 19th century for pain control during surgery (Hilgard & Hilgard, 1975). Hypnosis is an altered state of consciousness that involves several components: (1) relaxation; (2) distraction (the diversion of attention from the pain, also referred to as narrowing of attention); and (3) suggestion (that the pain is diminishing or is replaced by a more pleasant sensation, such as warmth). Hypnosis can also include the attachment of a meaning other than threat to the pain (Barber, 1986).

For people who are susceptible to suggestion, hypnosis can be very helpful in pain relief. Researchers are not entirely sure whether hypnosis actually blocks pain or simply interferes with the reporting of it. In hypnosis for pain control, a suggestion of analgesia to the patient (that is, that he or she has an absence of sensibility to pain) tends to be a critically important ingredient. Without it, hypnotized people report as much pain as do those who are not hypnotized (Hilgard, 1978). Under hypnosis with a hypnotic suggestion of analgesia, people still show the classic physiological reactions to pain, such as changes in respiration and the increased heart rate and blood pressure that normally accompany painful stimuli (Orne, 1974, 1989). However, they tend to show no behavioral signs of pain (such as grimacing and tensing their muscles) and report verbally that they feel no discomfort (Hilgard & Hilgard, 1975). Although they may continue to recognize that they are in pain (say, by writing down their evaluation of the pain), individuals under hypnosis indicate that the pain is not affecting them or does not matter to them at all.

A patient responding to the hypnotic suggestion that her arm is very light.
SOURCE: Ken Robert Buck/The Picture Cube

Contrary to popular fears, people under hypnosis will not carry out actions they would not normally do (such as things to which they are morally opposed). But they often can do things they would like to do but did not realize were possible for them, such as remaining completely calm during a medical procedure. With hypnosis, individuals can learn to turn their attention away from their pain so that although aware of pain, they are not distressed by it (Hilgard, 1968).

Hypnosis has been used successfully on patients undergoing surgery, childbirth, and dental procedures, as well as on those receiving treatment for burns, low back pain, and headaches. There is strong evidence, much of it from laboratory and case studies and not from clinical experimentation, that hypnosis can be used very successfully in the control of pain (Barber, 1982), but precisely which people and what kinds of pain problems benefit most from hypnosis have yet to be determined. Hypnosis does *not* work for everyone. In fact, there are significant individual differences in susceptibility to hypnosis. Further, a complete understanding of the hypnotic state has not yet been achieved. Researchers such as Barber (1982) suggest that hypnosis may not be due to a trance state but, rather, to very powerful suggestions for comfort, anxiety reduction, and well-being.

## BEHAVIOR MODIFICATION
## IN CHRONIC PAIN

A patient in pain may signal the experience in a variety of ways. He or she might verbally describe the location, quality, and intensity of the pain, might sigh or moan, might limp, grimace, or massage the painful area. The behavior serves as a signal to the social environment (the people around the patient) that he or she is in pain, and the signal typically elicits some action from others (Turk et al., 1985).

Pain behavior serves many purposes. "Behavior may elicit medication from the physician, indicate to the spouse that sex is out of the question, or communicate to the boss that the person cannot perform the job effectively. Without the behavior, there would be no pain problem clinically, but only a private and personal sensation with no outward signs." (Pinkerton, Hughes, & Wenrich, 1982, p. 264).

When an individual's pain is chronic, of long duration, and unable to be cured, pain behaviors manipulate the environment in such a way as to become a disadvantage to the patient. Chronic pain is not an event but, rather, a state of existence, and the suffering patient is limited to bearing the pain and trying to live as normal a life as possible. But he or she cannot have a normal life while consistently exhibiting pain behaviors. In the presence of these behaviors, other people may pity the patient, make excuses for him or her, or expect little from him or her. Some may even suspect malingering. With vastly limited behavioral options, the individual can become hopeless and despairing. And eventually there may even come to be a distortion of self-concept or functional ability (Ogden-Niemeyer & Jacobs, 1989). The patient may lose the reality of self-appraisal and both underestimate his or her abilities and overestimate limitations. For example, the patient may state that he or she cannot sit for more than 20 minutes or cannot stand to be without pain medication, but in fact may sit and watch television for hours or go without pain medication if involved in something very interesting.

Some researchers and clinicians approach the control of chronic pain as a problem requiring operant conditioning. (Remember from earlier chapters that operant methods involve rewarding behaviors that one wishes to enhance and ignoring or punishing behaviors that one wants to eliminate or extinguish.) An operant approach to the problem of chronic pain emphasizes the role of environmental factors. Pain behaviors, although initially respondents (behaviors in response) to sensations of discomfort, can quickly become operant behaviors that trigger direct positive reinforcement (such as affection from the spouse) or negative reinforcement (such as "time out" from difficult or aversive activities). Pain behaviors can come to have very high reward value, as they bring attention, sympathy, and relief from social and work obligations. When this occurs, there is usually no reinforcement for well behaviors and the individual's entire behavioral repertoire becomes one of expressing pain (Roberts, 1986; Fordyce, 1976).

The value of behavioral methods is well illustrated by the case of a woman who had experienced constant low back pain for 20 years. She had four different surgical operations, but medical evaluation revealed no neurological damage. Normal day-to-day activities were becoming increasingly interfered with. Her treatment consisted of pain-relieving medication on a timed schedule (for example, every four hours) rather than when she experienced or complained of pain. In addition (with her consent), her family was taught to give her attention and praise for increasing her activities, and for well (nonpain) behaviors, such as walking. The family (and staff at the hospital where she was treated on an inpa-

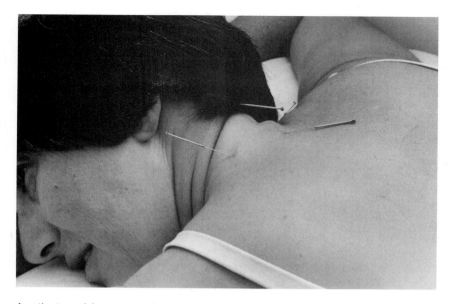

A patient receiving acupuncture.
SOURCE: © Judy S. Gelles, 1984/Stock, Boston.

tient basis) ignored such behaviors as moaning and grimacing. The patient was provided with programmed rest periods as rewards for greater involvement in physical and occupational therapy. After three weeks of inpatient and 22 weeks of outpatient treatment, the woman who had been almost totally disabled could remain physically active for up to two hours at a time without needing rest or complaining of pain. And she was able to function without pain medications. She was walking farther and faster than she had ever been able to before. In many areas of her life, she was functioning well (Pinkerton et al., 1982).

## PHYSICAL THERAPIES FOR PAIN

The principle of *counterirritation* is an important basis for the several physical therapies currently available for the treatment of pain. One form of discomfort can minimize or cancel out another (Melzack & Wall, 1982). For example, one might vigorously rub the site of an injection in an effort to override the pain caused by the needle. Counterirritation can relieve pain by diverting the individual's attention away from it. Furthermore, signals of counterirritation carried by the peripheral fibers can "close the pain gate" and inhibit the transmission of the primary pain signals to the brain.

The Gate Control Theory of pain explains the effectiveness of a pain-control technique called *transcutaneous electrical nerve stimulation* or TENS. TENS can be very effective in reducing acute pain in a large number of patients (Chapman, 1984). TENS involves the placing of electrodes on the skin near where the patient feels pain and sending a mild electrical current supplied by a portable device that looks like a small tape recorder. The electrical stimulation of the peripheral nerves interferes with the transmission of pain signals to the brain.

*Acupuncture* is an ancient Chinese pain control technique. Fine metal needles are inserted under the skin and twirled or electrically charged to create stimulation to the peripheral nerves, some of which are believed to be associated with (in some cases) distally located parts of the body (Melzack & Wall, 1982). For example, points on the foot might be associated with internal organs, such as the kidneys. Acupuncture works to provide such high levels of analgesia that in some cases people have undergone major surgery with only acupuncture for pain control. Acupuncture-induced analgesia does not occur simply as a result of distraction. Rather, it is believed that stimulation of peripheral nerve fibers serves to close the pain gate.

*Physical therapy* involves a variety of approaches to help patients who suffer from both acute and chronic pain. One example of this approach is exercise to help the arthritis patient maintain joint flexibility (Wickersham, 1984). Exercise is extremely helpful for back-pain patients who need to maintain flexibility and develop strength in key muscles to provide support for their spines. As part of an exercise program, patients are typically also taught body mechanics and proper posture to prevent further injuries.

*Deep muscle massage* and the application of heat and cold are also used quite effectively to treat chronic pain conditions such as back pain and tension headaches (Hare & Milano, 1985).

Which approach to pain control works best? The answer depends upon what the outcome of interest happens to be. In a study comparing the effectiveness of cognitive-behavioral treatments and physical therapy for pain control among patients with back pain, researchers found that their subjects in chronic pain benefited from both approaches (Heinrich, Cohen, Naliboff, Collins, & Bonnebakker, 1985). Improvements were greatest in *physical* functioning among the patients who received physical therapy. *Psychosocial adjustment* was better among patients who received the cognitive-behavioral intervention. Long-term pain reduction may require a combination of cognitive and behavioral methods (Blanchard, 1987).

## PAIN CLINICS: MULTIDIMENSIONAL TREATMENT PROGRAMS

The most effective current pain treatments involve a combination of behavioral, cognitive, physical, and analgesic approaches to pain (Ogden-Niemeyer & Jacobs, 1989). Particularly in the realm of pain control, operant learning, such as described in the behavioral treatments earlier, needs to be combined with cognitive awareness for long-term changes to take place. In addition, on a practical level exercise is incorporated in an effort to increase physical mobility and flexibility and to assist in the release of endogenous endorphins for the effective masking of pain. The judicious use of analgesics is also a part of a multifaceted approach to pain. The goals of interdisciplinary pain programs involve not only reducing the patient's experience of pain but also decreasing the use of medications, improving daily functioning, and improving psychological and social well-being.

Pain clinics can be quite effective in achieving these stated goals. Although they do vary in quality, multidisciplinary programs that incorporate the various approaches considered above tend to have the highest rates of success (Newman & Seres, 1986). Various pain clinics around the country report that as many as 75% to 90% of their chronic low back pain patients experience significant improvement in activity levels and reduction in pain medication use after participating in a multifaceted treatment program. Many go through vocational retraining programs and significantly improve their lives (Pinkerton et al., 1982; Ogden-Niemeyer & Jacobs, 1989).

The field of pain is a dynamic, fast-moving area of research. Health professionals must keep up with ever-changing treatment recommendations in order to provide their patients with the latest options for care. With the latest available treatments, people who once would have been totally debilitated by pain have the chance to live enjoyable, productive, and fulfilling lives.

# Summary

Chapter 6 examines the definition, origins, and treatment of pain.

I. Pain has been defined in several ways: (1) as an unpleasant sensory and emotional experience associated with actual or potential tissue damage, (2) as a total experience of some noxious stimulus, and (3) as a psychological experience that includes a personal, private sensation of hurt, a harmful stimulus that signals current or impending tissue damage, and a pattern of responses that operate to protect the organism from harm.

   A. Nociception is defined as mechanical, thermal, or chemical energy impinging on specialized nerve endings that activate nerve fibers and initiate a signal to the central nervous system.

   B. Nociception can be assessed because activity in certain nerve fibers and their synaptic connections can be observed.

   C. Pain can result as a sensation that arises from the stimulation of perceived nociception. Pain can occur in the absence of nociception, and nociception can occur without any perception of pain.

II. We can know that a person is in pain only by assessing the effect of pain on him or her, such as by observing pain behavior. *Pain behavior* is a very general term that includes many actions that people carry out or signals that they emit when they are in pain (such as facial and vocal expressions of distress, distorted movements and postures, expressions of negative affect, and avoidance of activity).

III. Pain is an extremely salient phenomenon in human life. It is typically the symptom that is most likely to bring a person to seek medical care. For many, the presence of pain suggests danger but there is typically little relationship between the severity of a person's pain and the degree of danger that the associated condition poses to him or her. People fear the possibility of suffering intractable pain (pain that cannot be relieved). The phenomenon of pain also has tremendous economic consequences.

IV. Pain is transmitted when stimulated nerve endings generate impulses that travel to the central nervous system. The afferent peripheral fibers that transmit pain impulses are called A-delta fibers and C fibers. A-delta fibers transmit impulses very quickly and are associated with sharp, distinct pain; C fibers transmit impulses more slowly and are involved when pain is diffuse, dull, or aching.

   A. Referred pain involves pain that originates in tissue in one part of the body but is perceived as coming from another part. Sometimes pain is experienced in the absence of apparent nociception.

   B. Several theories of pain exist. The Specificity Theory posits specific receptors in the skin that respond to a particular kind of stimulus and specific routes of transmission in the central nervous system, and special centers in the brain that register and interpret (only) pain. The Pattern Theory holds that pain results from the patterning and quality of stimulation from peripheral nerve endings. Both theories are lacking.

C. The Gate Control Theory acknowledges specificity in pain transmission, as well as the importance of patterning and the summation of impulses, but also allows for the role of psychological processes in the pain experience and its control. The Gate Control Theory holds that pain sensations from the peripheral neural pathways are carried to the spinal column but are modified as they are conducted through the spinal column to the brain. Stimulation of A-beta fibers (by chemical, electrical, or physical means) can close the pain gate and limit the perception of pain. The pain experience can be minimized if pain signals are not interpreted by higher centers of cognition. The pain gate can be closed by positive emotions, intense concentration, relaxation, and involvement in pleasurable activities. Conversely, pain is increased by conditions that open the gate, such as anxiety or worry, tension, depression, focus on the pain, boredom, and lack of involvement in life activities.

V. Pain is a subjective experience, felt only by the person who has the pain. Pain can be experienced at different levels of intensity.

A. Threshold refers to the point at which a person first perceives a stimulation as painful. Tolerance refers to the point at which the individual is not willing to accept stimulation of a higher magnitude. Threshold appears to be determined mainly by physiological variables, whereas tolerance appears to be influenced by psycho-

logical variables, such as attitudes and motivation.

B. Measures of pain can be classified into three basic types: psychophysiological measures, such as blood pressure and heart rate; behavioral measures, which involve observations of pain behaviors, such as grimacing, moaning, and complaining; and verbal self-report measures, which involve the patient's written or spoken description of the character and intensity of the pain.

C. A detailed description of pain can be essential to its medical diagnosis. Such a detailed description necessarily includes the duration and location of the pain as well as its nature and characteristics, concurrent symptoms, and precipitating factors.

D. Medical professionals make an important distinction between acute and chronic pain. Acute pain is temporary and lasts less than six months; chronic pain lasts more than six months and can be intermittent or constant, mild or severe.

VI. Psychological factors affect pain.

A. The meaning attached to pain partly determines how it is perceived and experienced, as well as how it is reacted to. Pain is also affected by the setting in which tissue damage occurs and what the person thinks about it. Expectations can also significantly influence pain.

B. The term for an inert substance that can reduce pain is *placebo*.

C. Pain perceptions depend upon age, sex, social and cultural background, and personality type of the individual. Pain tolerance appears to vary with the individual's attitudes about pain and his or her anxiety about pain. Pain reactions also vary according to the individual's cultural and social experiences. Expressions of pain are influenced by the reactions of others.

VII. There are many methods for treating pain.

A. Surgical methods represent a drastic approach. Nerve resection or removal may not be successful because, as recent evidence suggests, blocked nerve pathways are eventually circumvented to carry pain messages to the brain.

B. Today the most common medical treatment for pain involves pain-relieving medications, of which there are several types: local anesthetics, peripherally acting analgesics, centrally acting analgesics, and sedatives or tranquilizers.

C. Narcotics are typically not appropriate for the treatment of chronic pain because they have high addiction potential. They are appropriate for the treatment of short-term severe acute pain and the pain of terminal illness.

D. Cognitive methods for the treatment of pain have been found to be very successful. (1) Altering interpretations of pain can significantly affect the perception and consequences of that pain. (2) The diversion of one's attention from the pain or the source of pain onto a different stimulus can help reduce the perception of pain. (3) The use of nonpain imagery can help reduce pain.

E. Progressive relaxation is an extremely useful intervention for controlling both acute and chronic pain. Biofeedback involves a mechanical system whereby an individual is signaled by means of a light or a buzzer to bring about relaxation in a particular set of muscles. Hypnosis is an important psychological technique that aids in the control of (particularly acute) pain.

F. Behavior modification and operant conditioning to change pain behaviors are other successful approaches.

G. Physical therapies for pain are based upon the principle of counterirritation. These methods include transcutaneous electrical nerve stimulation, deep muscle massage, acupuncture, and traditional physical therapy, as well as the application of heat and cold.

H. The most effective current pain treatments involve a combination of behavioral, cognitive, physical, and analgesic approaches to pain.

# Glossary

**acupuncture:** an ancient Chinese pain-control technique in which fine metal needles are inserted under the skin to create stimulation to the peripheral nerves. Acupuncture can induce high levels of analgesia in some cases.

**acute pain:** pain that lasts less than six months and eventually ends.

**augmenters:** individuals who characteristically perceive greater environmental stimulation than does the average person. Augmenters respond to external stimuli directly by trying to do something to deal with them.

**behavioral measures of pain:** measures that involve observations of pain behaviors, such as grimacing, moaning, and complaining about pain. Most clinicians rely heavily on patients' verbal reports of their pain.

**biofeedback:** a system whereby an individual is signaled by means of a light or a buzzer to bring about some particular state of his or her body. Biofeedback works on the principles of operant conditioning and teaches people to be aware of their bodily processes and consciously to alter them.

**causalgia:** severe burning pain that sometimes results after a wound has healed and damaged nerves have regenerated.

**centrally acting analgesics:** narcotics, such as codeine and morphine, that bind to the opiate receptors in the central nervous system. Narcotics are effective in reducing pain but impair sensory and motor functioning and have high addiction potential.

**chronic intractable benign pain:** pain that is present all the time but is not related to any progressive condition.

**chronic pain:** pain that lasts longer than six months.

**chronic progressive pain:** pain that becomes progressively more intense as the condition associated with it worsens.

**chronic recurrent pain:** pain characterized by intense episodes of discomfort followed by relief.

**counterirritation:** an important basis for several physical therapies for pain. Counterirritation provides a form of discomfort to distract the individual's attention and to "close the pain gate" to transmission of the original pain signal.

**EMG biofeedback:** biofeedback that measures muscle tension, such as tension in the frontalis muscle in the head, that can cause headache.

**endogenous opioids:** opiate-like substances produced within the body that regulate pain and operate like exogenous opioids, such as the drugs heroin and morphine, by producing pain analgesia and feelings of well-being. Researchers have recently identified three main groups of these endogenous opioids: beta-endorphin, proenkephalin, and prodynorphin. These substances can produce natural pain suppression, and they appear to be released in response to stressful circumstances.

**Gate Control Theory of Pain:** a theory that more adequately deals with the findings of pain research than do the two earlier theories. It acknowledges specificity in pain transmission, as well as the importance of patterning and the summation of impulses, but also allows for the role of psychological processes in pain experience and control. Gate theory is also the most valuable of the three theories in terms of its clinical applications.

**herniated disk:** a spine condition in which the soft, mucoid material in the fibrous disk between two vertebrae has been forced through the disk's torn outer rim and impinges on spinal nerve routes, resulting in severe back pain.

**hypnosis:** an important psychological technique that aids in the control of (particularly acute) pain. Hypnosis is a very old technique, used as early as the 19th century for pain control during surgery. Hypnosis involves several components: relaxation, distraction, and suggestion.

**intractable pain:** pain that cannot be relieved.

**local anesthetics:** pain-controlling chemicals, such as novocaine or lidocaine, that when applied topically or injected under the skin prevent affected nerve cells from generating pain impulses.

**migraine headache:** headache that results from dilation of the cranial blood vessels. The headache pain is described as unilateral or bilateral aching or throbbing pain. The prodromal symptoms include nausea, vomiting, sensitivity to light and noise, and sensory disturbances.

**muscle-tension headache:** a headache that manifests in a dull, persistent ache, spots that are sore and tender on the head, neck, and jaw, and often a feeling of tightness around the head. Sometimes the patient describes the pain as being like "a stake or a knife in my head." The patient often describes the pain as severe and constant, and unrelenting.

**neuralgia:** a painful condition that is characterized by the absence of apparent tissue damage but in which pain can be provoked by minimal stimulation.

**nociception:** mechanical, thermal, or chemical energy impinging on specialized nerve endings that in turn activate A-delta and C fibers, thus initiating a signal to the central nervous system that aversive events are occurring. Nociception can be observed in the sense that activity in certain nerve fibers and their synaptic connections can be observed.

**operant methods for pain control:** methods that involve rewarding behaviors that one wishes to enhance and ignoring or punishing behaviors that one wants to eliminate or extinguish. An operant approach to the problem of chronic pain emphasizes the role of environmental factors.

**pain:** an unpleasant sensory and emotional experience associated with actual or potential tissue damage. Pain involves the total experience of some noxious stimulus that is influenced by the current context of the pain, previous experiences, learning history, and cognitive processes.

**pain behaviors:** actions that people carry out or signals that they emit when they are in pain.

**pain control:** efforts to eliminate pain or reduce it. The goal is to bring an individual to tolerate pain, and if necessary, to live with it and still have a satisfying and productive life.

**Pattern Theory of Pain:** a theory that holds that pain results from the patterning and quality of stimulation from peripheral nerve endings. In a particular area of the body, for example, mild stimulation might result in the sensation of touch, whereas intense stimulation in the same area may result in the sensation of pain. The pattern theory also holds that sensations can summate.

**peripherally acting analgesics:** pain-controlling medications taken internally that work by reducing inflammation at the site of tissue damage and inhibiting the synthesis of neurochemicals that facilitate peripheral transmission of pain impulses.

**phantom-limb pain:** pain that occurs in an amputated limb or damaged part of the peripheral nervous system.

**physical therapy:** an approach to pain control that involves a variety of measures to help the patient maintain flexibility and develop strength in key muscles and learn proper body posture and movement.

**placebo control group:** in research, the incorporation of a special control group (in addition to the experimental group) to test the success of a new drug or therapy beyond that which would be expected from a placebo.

**pleuritic pain:** pain caused by inflammation of the pleural lining of the lungs. The pain literally results from the individual's "insides" rubbing together and causing painful friction.

**psychophysiological measures of pain:** assessments of physical processes, such as blood pressure and heart rate, which typically increase in response to pain. Physiological measures can be quite objective, although it is difficult to be sure that these reactions are responses to pain and not to other stimuli.

**reducers:** individuals who tend to reduce or minimize environmental stimulation. Reducers play down or deny external stimulation.

**referred pain:** pain that originates in tissue in one part of the body but is perceived as coming from another part.

**relaxation:** an extremely useful intervention for controlling both acute and chronic pain. Psychologists have developed various techniques of relaxation that work either on one muscle or a muscle group, and that place an individual into an overall state of low arousal.

**sedatives:** medications that control pain by depressing the individual's responses, reducing the individual's anxiety, and helping him or her to sleep.

**somatic:** a term meaning bodily.

**Specificity Theory of Pain:** a theory that holds that a specific bodily system is responsible for pain perception. In this theory, pain is believed to be an independent sensation like heat, cold, or touch. It is believed that there are specific receptors in the skin that respond to specific stimuli. Further, specific routes of transmission in the central nervous system are proposed, as are special centers in the brain that register and interpret pain (and only pain).

**thermal biofeedback:** biofeedback that measures and reinforces blood flow to various parts of the body.

**threshold:** the point at which a person first perceives a stimulation as painful.

**tic douloureux:** (trigeminal neuralgia): an extremely painful disorder of the fifth cranial (trigeminal) nerve. Its cause is generally unknown, although sometimes it accompanies other diseases.

**tolerance:** the point at which an individual is not willing to accept stimulation of a higher magnitude.

**transcutaneous electrical nerve stimulation:** one of the physical therapies for pain that involves placing electrodes near where the patient feels pain and sending a mild electrical current that interferes with transmission of pain signals to the brain.

**verbal self-report measures:** measures (far from precise) that rely on an individual's verbal description of the character and intensity of pain.

# Seeking Medical Care: Medical Practitioners, Patients, and the Treatment Exchange

•••••

"Have you ever smoked?"

"If so, how much?"

"For how long?"

These were only a few of the scores of questions on the form.

Norman was sitting in the office waiting room of the internist he had selected to be his primary care physician. Norman was healthy, but when he moved to Oceanview, he went about researching the doctors in town to find the one who would be best for him. Now it was time to meet William Carey, M.D., and see if he would be a good choice. Norman wanted particularly to know how well he and Dr. Carey could communicate.

Norman thought the questionnaire was a good sign. Dr. Carey was obviously concerned about his patients' health habits and preventive care. After he finished the detailed section on parental health history, Norman was ushered into the office for his comprehensive physical examination.

■ ■ ■ ■ ■

Francine had a rash on her hands for weeks before she finally decided to go to the Immediate Care Clinic. She had noticed the place many times on her way to work, but she knew nothing about it. She had tried several home remedies given to her by her friends, but the rash kept getting worse. Francine thought it looked terrible, and the itch was very distracting, so she finally decided to see a nurse practitioner. Francine hoped the whole process would not involve tremendous time and expense. She usually avoided doctors and nurses as much as possible for just that reason. In fact, she had not gotten a medical checkup for years, and had no regular doctor. If she were ever really sick, she decided, she could just go to the local emergency room and see the doctor on call.

# Introduction: Setting the Stage

Medical practitioners and patients encounter one another under many varied circumstances. Sometimes they have known each other for years and the patient's illness can be understood readily in the context of the patient's daily life and experience. Sometimes they are complete strangers. A physician, for example, may simply provide a service, such as diagnosis and recommended treatment, a prescription, or a procedure, and the patient pays the bill.

Circumstances of care may also vary. Sometimes the patient can provide a detailed account of and considerable insight into the medical problem. Other times the

patient provides no information at all. Sometimes practitioner and patient have sufficient time to discuss the many implications of the patient's problem. Sometimes, as in some health maintenance organizations (HMO's), they have exactly five minutes.

Patients vary in their attitudes toward medical practitioners and toward the process of medical care. Some patients, like Norman above, are knowledgeable about medical matters and hold the physician to be a valuable source of information and experience (Haug and Lavin, 1983). Other patients, like Francine, know very little about their health and they care to learn even less (Krantz, Baum, & Wideman, 1980). They simply want the problem fixed. Some deny that there is anything wrong with them at all, and they believe nothing could threaten their well-being. And, as we have seen in previous chapters, some patients have high thresholds for discomfort and wait until they have seriously jeopardized their health before they "bother" their doctors. Others regularly turn to medical practitioners for comfort when anxiety overwhelms them or when they need diversion from their unhappy or boring lives (Mechanic, 1972, 1979).

Medical professionals, primarily physicians, also vary in their attitudes toward patients and toward the character of their role as healers (Mizrahi, 1984). Some physicians focus their concerns entirely on the diagnostic puzzle. They see the patient as the bodily container for disease. They view the patient's active mind as a factor that impedes rather than supports the physician's efforts. To such physicians, the best kind of patient is the one with the fascinating disease who keeps his or her mouth shut (West, 1983). Some physicians, on the other hand, prefer to focus on the patient as a person, an individual whose life affects and is affected by the disease. Such physicians try to help their patients achieve happy and productive lives whether or not a definitive diagnosis can be reached (Kleinman, 1988). Many physicians operate between these two extremes, sometimes acknowledging and attending to, sometimes forgetting, the patient's mind while treating the patient's body.

The goal of this chapter is to examine in detail what occurs when patients consult physicians and other medical professionals for the diagnosis and treatment of illness. We will examine how the medical consultation affects and is affected by several factors: the circumstances of the illness, the circumstances of the medical encounter, and the basic viewpoints (or philosophies) held by practitioner and patient about their roles with respect to each other.

In this chapter our focus will be on the relationship between medical practitioners and their patients in the health-care setting. Such a setting will be defined broadly to include everything from office or clinic visit to treatment in the emergency room. And the relationship between patients and various health professionals (physicians, nurses, orderlies, laboratory technicians, paramedics, and others) will be examined. It is important to note, however, that the research literature on the medical professional-patient relationship deals primarily with physicians. Although patients rarely interact with only physicians, it is with them that patients carry on the information exchanges that form the basis of the entire diagnostic and treatment process (Cassell, 1985a, 1985b). Of course, many of the findings of research on physician-patient communication apply to other health professionals as well.

In this and the next chapter, we will examine *communication* between medical professionals and their patients. Communication is defined as the exchange of information between individuals to arrive at a common understanding. In this chapter we will examine in detail the *verbal communi-*

*cation* that takes place between patients and practitioners in the process of diagnosis and treatment. We will analyze both subjective and objective outcomes of various kinds of communication. We will consider the points of view, or philosophies, that underlie effective and ineffective practitioner-patient communication and examine how these points of view are translated into action.

## THE FOUR PREMISES OF MEDICAL CARE

The analysis of practitioner-patient interaction in this chapter is based upon several assumptions or premises (made explicit by Eric J. Cassell, a physician whose research and theories of physician-patient communication are taught widely in medical education). The premises are as follows:

- doctors treat patients, not diseases;
- the body has the last word;
- all medical care flows through the relationship between physician and patient;
- and the spoken language is the most important tool in medicine (Cassell, 1985a, p. 1)

Most medical professionals would probably agree that, in the final analysis, what happens to the patient is what matters most. It's better to have a patient get well and never know precisely what had been wrong than to make a brilliant diagnosis of an obscure condition and have the patient die. The correctness of a diagnosis matters only insofar as it affects the prescribed treatment and the healing of the body. What really matters is that the patient recovers.

The importance of communication in the medical-care process is likely to be less clear to many medical practitioners, however. In fact, those who focus on the purely technical aspects of disease might even disagree with the last two premises. As we will see in this chapter, however, considerable research evidence supports the central role of communication in the process of medical care.

## LANGUAGE IN MEDICAL CARE: THE ROLE OF WORDS AND GESTURES

"Your tumor is malignant. I'm sorry to have to tell you that you have cancer."

Words are extremely powerful tools in medicine. They establish the reality of suffering. Because of their power, the utterance of words in the medical encounter is a very serious enterprise indeed.

Here is a poignant example of the power of words. A woman whose father had just died stood in front of his body, physically protecting him from the physician. She stated that she would not allow her father to be pronounced dead. "When saying something removes all doubt, so long as the truth remains unspoken, reality can be kept at bay" (Cassell, 1985a, pp. 57–58).

More evidence for the power of words is that practitioners and patients modify them to establish comfortable psychological distance from the illness phenomenon. A breast cancer patient, for example, refers to *"the breast,"* not *"my breast,"* and says, "If *you* have cancer, *you* have to follow these treatments." She does not focus on her own experience with treatment, or identify the cancer as her own. Her use of impersonal pronouns helps her to separate herself from her disease. In fact, a medical professional can begin to understand a patient's feelings about a condition by listening to how the patient talks about the disease process.

Of course, medical communication involves more than just words. As we will see in Chapter 8, medical professionals and patients also communicate with one another using *nonverbal cues and gestures*. In the present chapter we will examine only verbal communication; in Chapter 8 we will

see that much can be learned about patients by examining their facial expressions, body movements, and tone of voice. Likewise, medical professionals can convey a great deal to their patients with nonverbal cues, particularly when there is limited time to convey verbal messages of support and caring. Thus, Chapters 7 and 8 together present the full range of practitioner-patient communication by examining both the verbal and the nonverbal messages that are central to effective medical care (Friedman, 1982; Waitzkin, 1985).

## VIEWPOINT AND SKILL IN COMMUNICATION

Through the process of communication, practitioner and patient attempt to gain a common understanding of the patient's illness. Each gathers information from and imparts information to the other. They convey facts as well as the meaning they attach to those facts. Because of the many differences between medical practitioners and patients in knowledge, background, and perspective, communication can be extremely complex.

What happens in the communication between medical professionals and patients depends upon (1) what each party is capable of enacting (that is, his or her communication skills), and (2) what each party holds to be true about the therapeutic relationship (beliefs, viewpoints, or philosophies) (DiMatteo, 1979). These two phenomena can be interrelated, of course, if people fail to develop skills to carry out behaviors they do not value and devalue things they cannot do.

A practitioner's and/or a patient's poor communication skills can cause problems in their relationship. For example, a female nurse may value listening to patients in a supportive manner, but her skills fall short of what is needed to achieve her goals. She might consistently interrupt patients when they try to speak, and dominate all conversations with patients. She may fail to assess her own behavior and to recognize her shortcomings (Waitzkin & Stoeckle, 1976). The nurse does value listening to patients, however, and so she might be helped to develop her communication skills. Audiotaping or videotaping the medical visit has helped many medical practitioners to see and hear firsthand various aspects of their interactions with patients, including precisely how often they interrupt patients. Self-awareness has helped practitioners to correct communication patterns that are less than ideal (DiMatteo, 1985).

A female patient, for example, might also lack the skills to communicate in ways that she considers valuable. She might fervently believe that patients should have the opportunity to ask many questions of their physicians, and she might consider patient education to be a central component of the physician's role. However, this same patient becomes tongue-tied and passive during the medical visit. She is flooded with anxiety when the physician interrupts her. She never asserts her desire to ask questions.

Box 7–1 illustrates the plight of a patient who attempts to gain necessary medical information but who encounters many difficulties in asking questions.

A physician may give a patient very little opportunity to participate in his or her own care precisely because the physician believes that patient participation is not valuable and certainly not worth the trouble. This physician might be reluctant to depart from the physician's traditional role, with its high degree of power and control (West, 1984). The point is illustrated quite well by the effects of uncertainty on physician-patient communication. When a physician is unsure of a patient's diagnosis and/or prognosis, there are several choices. The patient can be told what is already known and can be kept abreast of develop-

ments and changes as test results and the reports of consulting specialists become available. Or the patient can be kept completely "in the dark" until the physician is able to give a final statement. The patient's ignorance may last weeks or months, and he or she may be quite distressed by being ill and knowing nothing about what is wrong. By witholding information, the physician maintains a position of power vis-à-vis the patient and saves the time and trouble of keeping the patient informed.

Several decades ago, it was quite common for physicians to withold relevant facts from patients until the picture of illness was quite clear. Physicians often resolved their own uncertainty long before they finally let patients know the truth. In one study from that era the parents of children who had contracted polio were waiting to hear their children's prognosis, that is, the expected course of disease (Davis, 1960). They wanted to know the likelihood that their children would remain crippled for life. For days and sometimes weeks, both physicians and nurses withheld information about prognosis from the parents and gave unclear answers to the parents' questions. These health professionals kept the parents in the dark long after the course of the disease could be predicted.

Of course, Davis's study was conducted decades ago when patients were far less assertive than they are today. A much more recent study has found that under conditions of uncertainty, some physicians actually provide their patients with *more* information than they do otherwise (Waitzkin, 1985). Still, many patients feel that their medical professionals intentionally withhold information from them (Shuy, 1976).

Certainly, some patients welcome the opportunity to be passive recipients of medical care. Their philosophy casts the physician or nurse in the role of parent or caretaker. Such a point of view has many drawbacks, of course. Patients who look to the doctor or nurse to control every aspect of their medical care may actually do little or nothing to contribute to their own well-being. They fail to voice their concerns, they ask no questions, and they allow confusions and misunderstandings to go uncorrected (Taylor, 1979).

Research suggests, however, that most patients want as much information as possible from their health professionals (Waitzkin, 1985). Patient participation in the decision-making process is dependent upon information and is critical to therapeutic effectiveness (Speedling & Rose, 1985). The provision of information increases patients' satisfaction with their health care, enhances their cooperation with treatment, and improves their ability to give accurate information to their medical practitioners (DiMatteo, 1985; DiMatteo & DiNicola, 1982; Waitzkin & Stoeckle, 1972). Information gives patients an element of psychological control when they are undergoing surgery or stressful medical treatments, and improves the outcomes of such procedures (Egbert, Battit, Turndorf, & Beecher, 1963; Egbert, Battit, Welch, & Bartlett, 1964; Johnson, 1975). As we will see in a later chapter, patients can often cope much better when they know what they are preparing for than when they do not.

Despite these positive effects, physician-patient communication typically remains rather poor. As many as 50% of patients leave a physician's office or a clinic with little or no idea what to do to care for themselves (Svarstad, 1976). They don't even have a rudimentary understanding of their medical problem. They can't describe the treatment that is prescribed for them.

**BOX 7–1**

## THE STORY OF A MEDICAL VISIT

"Doctor will be in shortly," said the nurse in a sing song voice. "Just relax."

Lucy groaned quietly as the nurse shut the examining room door and left her perched with feet dangling off the examining table. The room was cold. Lucy's fever made it difficult to sit up and her throat hurt too much to swallow without cringing.

Doctor! she thought. Why not, the doctor, or Doctor Grayson. Doctor . . . sounds like "God will be in shortly." Sure is cold in here. I wonder how long I'll be waiting.

Twenty-three minutes later, Dr. Grayson entered the room.

"Lucy. Hi, I'm Doctor Grayson. What seems to be the trouble?"

"Well, I feel really tired, and I have a fever and a terrible sore throat and . . ."

"How long?"

"Huh? What do you . . ."

"How long have you had these symptoms?"

"Uh, well, the sore throat, about a week and the fever about three days, and the fatigue . . ."

"Any nausea?"

"Uh huh . . ."

"Okay. Let me check the glands in your neck. Ever had infectious mononeucleosis?"

"I don't think so."

Yet, for a variety of reasons, patients often don't even tell the doctor of their concerns and misgivings (Roter, 1984).

## COMMUNICATION
## UNCOVERS HIDDEN PREMISES

A patient's illness problem can be dealt with fully only when his or her real concerns have been addressed. For a medical therapeutic interaction to be successful, the patient's and the practitioner's basic premises must either be shared or brought to the forefront and examined. For example, a patient who is allergic to dairy products believes that the antibiotic penicillin is made from dairy products. (It is not.) So, in an effort to avoid an allergen, the patient fails to follow the prescribed treatment regimen. To determine why this has happened, the physician must learn the premise that underlies the patient's uncooperative behav-

ior. The physician does this with effective communication (Cassell, 1985b).

The patient's premise might be deeply buried because it causes anxiety. The physician's premise might be deeply buried because it is a fact learned many, many years ago and never questioned. Let's put the two together:

■ ■ ■ ■

A female patient has a small, subcutaneous cyst (growing under the skin). The male physician's premise is that this kind of cyst is almost never cancerous and can be very easily removed. Therefore, he reasons, the patient's obvious concern must certainly be for her appearance. The physician attempts over and over to reassure the patient that the removal of the cyst will cause, at worst, a very small but barely noticeable scar. The patient knows nothing about this kind of cyst; to her any "lump" could be malignant.

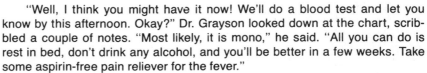

"Well, I think you might have it now! We'll do a blood test and let you know by this afternoon. Okay?" Dr. Grayson looked down at the chart, scribbled a couple of notes. "Most likely, it is mono," he said. "All you can do is rest in bed, don't drink any alcohol, and you'll be better in a few weeks. Take some aspirin-free pain reliever for the fever."

Then he turned on his heels and in another instant was opening the door. Lucy almost yelled WAIT A MINUTE, I HAVE QUESTIONS . . . but the words froze in her throat. There were lots of questions: Am I contagious to my friends? What can I take to ease the sore throat? Can I go to classes?

The lab technician came in to take the blood sample from Lucy's arm. "The doctor says maybe I have mono. What can I do to get over feeling so terrible?"

"Better ask Doctor . . . I'm not supposed to answer patients' questions."

"Great . . ." Lucy put up with the blood draw.

When she got home, Lucy rested. Later, she called the doctor's office. "Yup. You have mono," said the nurse. "Remember. Doctor said rest in bed."

"Can I do any work at all?" Lucy asked.

"Doctor said to rest. Now, you want to get better don't you, honey?"

"Sure."

"Well, then. Do what Doctor says. Bye now. Call us if you have any other questions."

"Sure won't," said Lucy after the audible click.

Then Lucy called her best friend, Margaret, who once had mono, for some advice.

She asks several times, "So, do you think it's okay, doctor?" (She does not specify that, to her, "okay" means "not malignant.") The doctor responds with an enthusiastic smile. "You won't see the scar at all. It won't be noticeable, really." After a long and unproductive interaction, the patient finally blurts out her fear: "So, uh, you . . . uh . . . you think it's probably benign?" The doctor is taken aback in complete surprise that the thought of malignancy even crossed her mind.

Such a misunderstanding is not at all unusual. In fact, in most practitioner-patient interactions the participants have differing views on various points (Waitzkin, 1985). The more basic each point is to their entire discussion, the more their attempt to understand and to communicate with one another can be undermined.

Patients tend to be more satisfied when their physicians understand and fulfill their needs for the medical visit (Like & Zyzanski, 1987). When physicians accurately recognize their patients' problems, patients are also more compliant, and they have better treatment outcomes (Starfield et al., 1981). When physicians and patients agree on what problems require follow-up, greater problem resolution can be achieved, and both physicians and patients tend to have higher expectations for improvement and perceive the outcomes of treatment to be better than when agreement is lacking. When physicians are aware of and agree with patients' concerns, patients have higher expectations for improvement (Starfield et al., 1979).

Ineffective communication can result in the physician's failing to recognize an important fact about the patient's situation and missing the entire problem:

■ ■ ■ ■ ■

A young woman comes to her female physician complaining of fatigue. The fatigue comes on in the afternoon, she relates, after classes are over, just before workout on the track team. All the tests run by the doctor show negative results. She tells the patient that there is nothing obviously wrong, provides no other information or recommendations, and sends her on her way. The patient feels that the physician has not really understood how badly she really feels, and she departs in anger to find a more satisfactory doctor.

The physician missed an important opportunity to help the patient and to win her confidence and satisfaction. What is really underlying the patient's problem is the track team. The story goes like this: The patient is a talented long-distance runner. She is on an athletic scholarship, and lately she is beginning to feel that her commitments to both schoolwork and track are overwhelming. She has no time for a normal social life. She feels that she must do well in an upcoming track meet, yet she feels conflicted about having to put so much of her energy and time into running. Her emotional response to the daily track workout is overwhelming fatigue. Thus, her problem is not physical. An astute physician would certainly run the basic tests just to be sure there was no obvious problem, but would then further explore some of the issues that the patient herself has brought up. Such a physician would certainly follow up the clue "Just before workout . . ."!

Why doesn't the patient simply come in and say, "Doctor, in two weeks I have to compete in a track event. I'm very conflicted about my athletic and academic responsibilities. Please help me deal with these emotional conflicts. Help me decide what I ought to do." Probably, the patient is not consciously aware that emotional tension is draining her energy. As we saw in Chapter 5, people can *unconsciously* translate their emotional distress into physical symptoms. A health professional can gain insight into the problem by listening carefully and actively to what the patient says.

## MACHINES AND PEOPLE: PROMOTING DIALOGUE

As modern medicine becomes dominated by technology, some medical professionals tend to give less and less attention to practitioner-patient dialogue. Despite the fact that most medical diagnoses can be made on the basis of information gathered from the patient, some medical professionals consider dialogue with the patient to be irrelevant and obtrusive (Putnam, Stiles, Jacob, & James, 1985). They find the information about illness produced by clinical tests to be more appealing than the information produced by people. Test data seem to be more direct and succinct than the patient's complex story. However, what machines can tell about patients is limited in scope and may sometimes even be inaccurate. In fact, about half of all the medical problems that patients present to family practitioners fail to show up on diagnostic tests because these problems have a strong psychological component (Marsland, Wood, & Mayo, 1976).

Faced with technological obstacles to their mutual understanding, practitioner and patient must take steps to arrive at an explicit consensus of the meaning of the medical visit, as well as of their mutual expectations. Some researchers have suggested that this be done by having the patient provide the practitioner with a list of his or her concerns and by having physician and patient together generate a list of items that they agree need follow-up (Starfield et al., 1981). Providing the patient with a tape recording of the visit has also been suggested and has been used successfully. In a study of outpatients at the Mayo Clinic, 86% of the patients who received a tape recording of their visit said that it improved their health care (Butt, 1977).

# Three Basic Models of the Physician-Patient Relationship

The character of the relationship that physician and patient develop depends, of course, upon the circumstances that surround their association and upon their beliefs about the appropriate locus of responsibility and power. This relationship can take one of three basic forms (Szasz & Hollender, 1956).

## THE ACTIVE-PASSIVE MODEL

The *Active-Passive Model* occurs when the patient is unable, because of the medical condition, to participate in his or her own care and to make decisions for his or her own welfare. The physician must take over this role. The responsibility for the patient's life is in the hands of the medical professionals who attend to the emergent condition. The patient has no say in what is done.

▪ ▪ ▪ ▪ ▪

The victim was stabbed not far from the hospital. His buddies placed him in the back seat of the car and sped down six long city blocks until they reached the emergency room of the county hospital. If they had waited to call an ambulance, he would have died. Less than a few seconds after they had arrived, the patient was on a gurney, being sped down the hospital corridor into the Trauma Center. In another few seconds his clothing was ripped off and the severed artery was found and tied. Simultaneously, other physicians and nurses worked to find a vein that had not collapsed in order to put in an intravenous line. Others were pumping oxygen into his lungs. Physicians, nurses, and technicians worked with skill and efficiency. The patient was unconscious, unable to participate in or to fight their efforts.

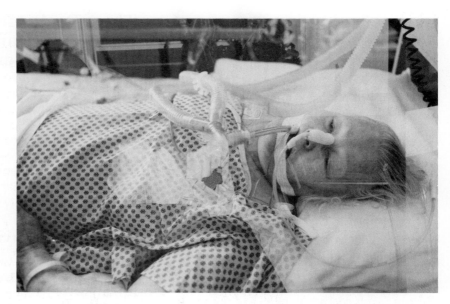

The Active-Passive Model occurs when the patient is unable to participate in the process of care and cannot make decisions.
SOURCE: Joan Tedeschi/Comstock

## THE GUIDANCE-COOPERATION MODEL

The *Guidance-Cooperation Model* occurs when the physician takes the bulk of responsibility for diagnosis and treatment. The patient answers the questions that are asked but leaves the thinking and the decisions to the physician. As we will see later in this chapter and elsewhere in this book, it is quite common for the patient who has no input into initial treatment decisions to have considerable difficulty implementing them.

■ ■ ■ ■ ■

"Do as I say, Frank, and don't ask so many questions," said the internist who was treating Frank Andersen for his hypertension. "Just take one of these little pills twice a day and you will be just fine." Frank was convinced that pushing for answers to his questions would be challenging "physician authority," so he went along, figuring the doctor knew best. He couldn't seem to remember to take the pills, however, since he didn't really have any understanding of their purpose. After all, he didn't feel sick. Why did he need pills?

## THE MUTUAL PARTICIPATION MODEL

The *Mutual Participation Model* involves physician and patient making joint decisions about every aspect of care, from the planning of diagnostic studies to the choice and implementation of treatment. There is joint input and joint responsibility. Typically, questions and concerns are aired freely. The mutual participation model represents the most effective physician-patient interchange that can occur. Physician and patient each apply expertise to the task of achieving the patient's health. They can do this only with clear and effective communication.

■ ■ ■ ■ ■

PATIENT:  I really doubt that I'll be able to eliminate dairy products from my diet immediately. They constitute a pretty large part of my diet.

DOCTOR:  Well, what do you think you can do? Can you gradually change your diet so that you eliminate dairy products more and more each day?

PATIENT:  Yes, I think I can do this gradually, but it's going to take me a while.

DOCTOR:  What can I do that might help you?

PATIENT:  Tell me again the precise purpose of the restriction. Also, can you suggest other things that I might be able to do to help my medical condition as I try to eliminate these foods?

Does this patient seem unusually assertive? Compared to most patients, he or she probably is. But assertiveness and active involvement in the care being provided are precisely what is needed for the patient to form an effective partnership with the physician. See Box 7–2 for further discussion of physician-patient partnership in co-authoring the medical record.

Let us turn now to the research on physician-patient relationships and examine the typical medical-care exchange. Research shows that it falls far short of the ideal of the Mutual Participation Model described above.

## The Medical-Care Visit

Whether medical care is delivered in a suburban doctor's office, a storefront medical clinic in a large city, or the emergency room of a famous university hospital, some basic commonalities can be found. The medical encounter follows a certain course. The medical professional, usually the physician, physician's assistant, or nurse practitioner, must talk with the patient in an effort to gather information about the patient's symptoms and the events surrounding them. The medical practitioner then performs an examination of the relevant parts of the patient's body. Finally, the practitioner makes a recommendation to the patient either to undergo further diagnostic testing or to follow a certain course of treatment. Obviously, if a patient presents with a condition such as impending childbirth or profuse bleeding, immediate treatment will be instituted. Some of the initial steps described below will be dispensed with or drastically abbreviated. Usually, however, medical care follows this logical, predetermined course.

Rarely does a patient simply walk in to a medical setting, ask to purchase a prescription or procedure, pay the bill, and leave. The usual exchange is quite a bit more complicated. The physician and the rest of the professional medical staff try to find out precisely what is wrong with the patient and to determine an appropriate treatment. Although patients can usually describe their symptoms, they rarely have the ability to diagnose. They may have stumbled upon a home remedy that temporarily alleviates their symptoms, but they usually do not have a cure. Typically, patients need medical professionals to diagnose the disease that is causing the symptoms and to recommend a specific, effective, long-term treatment.

As detailed below, the medical encounter is divided into three parts (Stiles, Putnam, Wolf, & James, 1979): *history, physical examination,* and *conclusion* (including recommendations). Each part has a particular purpose and is carried out in a particular fashion. There are no time limits for each, but there are goals. For example, during the history, the goal is to learn enough from the patient to guide the physical examination. The information that the patient gives often points the way to certain critical inquiries into the status of the patient's health. Although sometimes what is wrong with the patient is obvious, at other times the practitioner must examine the patient's entire body, hoping that some clear sign will emerge. During the final phase of the visit, the practitioner's goal is to reveal what has been found and what to do about it.

Let us use these three parts of the medical visit to organize the considerable research that has been done on practitioner-patient communication.

## THE HISTORY

The patient who presents for care possesses a wealth of information that is critical for the medical professional to collect during the *medical history* and eventually to understand. The history is that part of the medical encounter in which necessary information is elicited from the patient. This information includes such facts as what the symptoms are, when they began, what makes them improve or become worse, and how the patient has tried to overcome the problem before coming to the physician. A useful history helps to determine the tests

BOX
7–2

## COAUTHORING THE MEDICAL RECORD

Ever think you'd like to see your medical chart? Legally, in many states, you can! But could you understand it? Chances are that unless you know a great deal of medical terminology, you would not understand what you were reading. And reading the medical record might upset you.

These are the very reasons that physicians give for opposing the idea of a patient's seeing his or her own medical record. Physicians also sometimes fear that this practice would expose them to malpractice suits, or that a great deal of extra time would be required to explain the contents of their medical records to patients.

Patient-consumers disagree. They say that active patient participation in medical care can come only when patients have enough information to be self-reliant.

A fascinating study explored ways to get patients involved in their medical care by having them work with the physician to coauthor the medical record. Fischbach, Sionelo-Bayog, Needle, and DelBanco (1980) conducted this study in the ambulatory care clinic of the Harvard University-Beth Israel Hospital. Patients were asked to collaborate with their health professionals in the authorship of the medical record. Patients could thereby participate in their own health care, and practitioner and patient could forge a therapeutic alliance. The researchers felt that patients were better off as active rather than passive recipients of the information contained in the medical record. So, the researchers had patients and physicians engage in an open dialogue about what should go into the medical chart.

Patients were those with long-term chronic diseases: specifically hypertension, diabetes mellitus, and congestive heart failure. They used the Problem Oriented Medical Record (Weed, 1967) described in Box 7–4. The patient was asked to formulate a problem list, and the provider suggested modificato be carried out and eventually the diagnosis that is decided upon. The history, therefore, requires that some information be gathered about the patient's past. Has the patient had these symptoms before? What illnesses has the patient experienced? What illnesses currently exist? Have there been any hospitalizations? Are there any drug allergies? What medications are currently being taken? What illnesses have occurred in the patient's parents, siblings, and other close relatives? How does the patient feel emotionally? What impact is the illness having on the patient's day-to-day life?

During the history, the patient tells the story of the illness. Sometimes the physi-cian lets him or her do that in a free and unencumbered manner. Sometimes the story slowly manifests itself in the answers to the dozens of straightforward questions the physician asks the patient. "Do you have pain here, now?" "Did you have a fever last night?" and so on. As we see in Box 7–3, the story may unfold more or less clearly and more or less accurately, depending upon how questions are asked.

While gathering a history, the medical professional must listen actively to what the patient has to say. *Active listening* involves giving complete attention to the speaker, as well as reflecting back to him or her precisely what is understood. The medical interview also requires that the medi-

tions. Then together they coauthored the continuation notes, including records of symptoms, clinical findings, and assessment. Emphasis was placed on designing a mutually acceptable treatment plan. Patients kept notebooks with handwritten copies of the data in the medical record, including physiological measures such as blood pressure, weight, and urinary blood glucose.

Results showed that acceptance and comfort with such a procedure was not readily achieved by physician or patient. Initially, patients were particularly reluctant to express opinions and to disagree openly with their physicians. They got better at this, and eventually became active and constructive collaborators.

The joint authorship served to stimulate two-way communication. Patients found that their notebooks helped them to recall the material they had discussed with their physicians. Often patients also expected other doctors they encountered outside the clinic (specialists, for example) to coauthor the medical record in collaboration with them—much to the surprise of those physicians!

The medical professionals in this study had to adjust to a new style of writing and speaking; that is, they could not use medical terminology that their patients did not understand. They had to translate all medical terminology into language that was acceptable to their patients. In addition, the physicians sometimes had to share and deal with issues that might ordinarily be kept from the patients, at least for a while. Because patients were participating so fully and had to approve what went into the medical record, physicians had to reveal things like disturbing test results or a suspected psychosocial problem. These requirements did increase interaction time. It was found, however, that the sharing of medical information engendered patient trust and confidence, which is a first step toward physicians and patients working together.

cal professional provide the patient with privacy, including, of course, the assurance of confidentiality. There must be freedom from interruption and a high degree of interest and concern on the part of the health professional (Bernstein & Bernstein, 1980).

It is also very important for the medical professional *to establish the interview structure,* to explain the purpose of what is being done, and to tell the patient what to expect from the interview process (Cormier, Cormier, & Weisser, 1984). The physician might establish the necessary framework in the following way: "Now, Mr. Smith, I need to ask you a few questions about the pain you have been experiencing. Then, I would like to examine you so that we can determine what this pain is all about."

This step is important because sometimes physicians are unclear about what they are asking. For example, if the interviewer intersperses friendly personal questions with medical ones, a patient might become confused. The doctor asks a man, "How's your family?" and then, soon after, "Have you eaten out lately?" in an attempt to rule out hepatitis or some other communicable disease. The patient does not know the purpose of the question, and fails to mention that he usually has lunch at the little hot-dog stand near work (identified as a hazard by the local Health Department).

**BOX
7–3**

## QUESTIONS: THEIR VARIATIONS AND EFFECTS

Health professional-patient interaction typically involves a considerable amount of question asking, at least on the part of the health professional. The goal is to gain as much information as possible from the patient in order to formulate a correct diagnosis and a treatment that the patient can carry out successfully.

Many medical professionals are accustomed to asking patients a series of questions, each requiring an answer of one or a few words. The information that is revealed in the first question necessarily leads to the formulation of a second and a third question, and so on. For example:

DOCTOR:  Do you drink alcohol?
PATIENT:  Yes.
DOCTOR:  How much?
PATIENT:  About five drinks a week.
DOCTOR:  What kind of alcohol?
PATIENT:  Beer and wine, but no hard liquor.

and on and on.

The practitioner above asks closed-ended questions. *Closed-ended questions* require answers of one or a few words. They ask for a specific fact or piece of information. Closed-ended questions are best used toward the end of an inquiry because they narrow rather than broaden the area of discussion. However, when used at the outset of the interview, they inappropriately limit the information that can be gathered. In addition, the patient is left in a more dependent, seemingly constrained position. He or she may feel that the medical practitioner has complete responsibility for the success of the interview, and may fail to explore his or her own memory and ideas. The

He mentions only the nicer restaurants in an effort to manage a particular social impression of himself prompted by the seemingly "social" question.

The goal of taking a medical history is "to find out both what is happening in this body—the pathophysiology of the illness—and who the patient is" (Cassell, 1985b, p.41). Information about both these issues must be integrated. When they are, the practitioner can determine how events in the patient's body got the patient to the particular physical and emotional state he or she is in when presenting for care.

How long the medical history takes to collect depends upon several factors. If the practitioner knows the patient well, the medical history can be brief and deal only with the present illness. On the other hand, if the practitioner is seeing the patient for the first time and will be providing regular care over the coming years, the medical history may be very lengthy. The practitioner may ask about all past illnesses as well as disease conditions in the patient's blood relatives to determine genetic predispositions.

In the emergency room the medical history might be a very rushed affair. There is usually time for collecting only the essential information for treating the emergency condition. In this case the emergency room physician might ask only about the following: what medications the patient takes,

energy and attention that goes into thinking of new questions may limit the medical practitioner's ability to listen to and to understand fully what has been said by the patient (Long, Paradise, & Long, 1981).

*Open-ended questions* invite the patient to talk. They encourage elaboration. For instance, when the doctor says to a patient, "Please tell me about your use of drugs." The patient has relatively free rein to discuss the forms and extent of his or her drug use. Open-ended questions ask for information about an area of concern, but they do not direct the patient to discuss any particular aspect of the issue being examined.

*Focused questions* are more narrow than open-ended and broader than closed-ended questions. For example, the doctor asks, "Can you describe anything that makes the pain worse?" rather than "Does lying down make the pain worse? How about sitting up?" If the practitioner needs more specific information, he or she can ask the patient a closed-ended question, such as "After how many hours of sleep do you usually awaken and are unable to go back to sleep?"

There are several things that a practitioner can do to improve the quality of the questions that are asked. These guidelines are adapted from Cormier, Cormier, & Weisser (1984, p. 134):

1. Questions should be phrased simply, without medical jargon.
2. Questions should be short—that is, phrased concisely.
3. Only one question should be asked at a time.
4. Questions should be phrased in a nonaccusatory way: "Why didn't you take your medication?" may provoke patient defensiveness.
5. Questions should avoid suggesting anything that influences the patient's answer. Such a leading question might be: "Is your chest pain in the area of your heart?" Better: "Show me where the pain is."

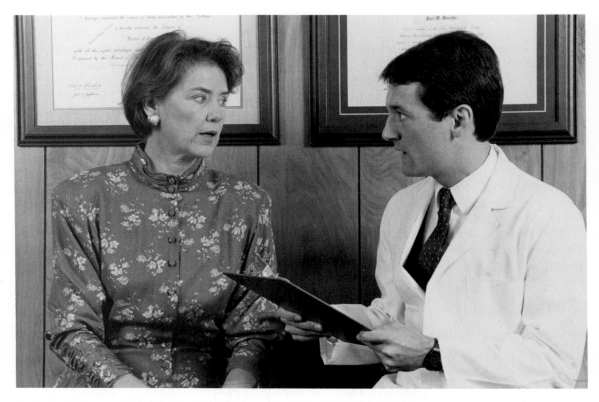

During the history portion of the medical visit, the patient tells the story of the illness.
SOURCE: © Tim Barnwell/Stock, Boston

what allergies, particularly drug allergies, the patient has, whether the patient has ever had surgery or been in the hospital, what illnesses the patient currently has, whether the patient has ever been seriously ill, and when the last time was that the patient saw a doctor for anything.

The last question helps to put a patient's problem into perspective. With it, the health professional can evaluate the patient's typical *illness behavior*, that is, how he or she usually responds to the symptoms of illness (see Chapter 5). The patient who has not seen a doctor for five years and who shows up at the emergency room with a headache is someone in need of serious attention. He or she is facing overwhelming stress, or the headache is intensely painful. Perhaps other bodily signals also tell the

patient the condition is serious. The limited medical history provides important information to the emergency room professionals. The meaning of the illness in the context of this patient's life and personality is illuminated (Cassell, 1985b). This is a patient who does not seek medical help for trivial matters. Thus, the complaint should be taken seriously and given strict and immediate attention; the patient may not have "just a headache."

**Interviewing.** The process of medical diagnosis is based on the assumption that the patient from whom the history is gathered is telling the truth. The health *interview*, the face-to-face gathering of information through the process of discussion, is relied upon by medical professionals as an important source of information about the patient. The interview is a foundation for the structuring of the patient history; it can be quite problematic, however. It is not a simple, straightforward, foolproof way to gather information from a patient about past health status. Asking people questions is not like retrieving information from a computer or a written record. People forget. Sometimes they are so anxious that they misunderstand what is being asked of them. And often they are not particularly motivated to do the work that is required for accurate recollection.

Extensive research on health interviews has shown that they can be filled with problems (Cannell, Oksenberg, & Converse, 1977; Marquis, 1970). Subjects who were healthy at the time of the interviews were asked to recall various aspects of the medical problems they had in the past. In many cases the researchers had available the respondents' medical records so that the accuracy of the responses could be checked. Subjects made the following kinds of errors. When asked specifically about past hospital visits, for example, respondents failed to report 12% to 17% of documented hospitalizations. Even when interviewed shortly after having a visit with a medical doctor, respondents failed to report 24% to 36% of these visits. Respondents also failed to mention at least 50% of chronic and acute illnesses that were documented in their medical records. Thus, there was a great deal of underreporting of very relevant information in these health interviews.

Later in this chapter we will examine ways in which medical professionals can help patients to report their conditions more accurately. Despite limitations in the accuracy of the information obtained from the medical interview, the history is the best source of information about what could be wrong with the patient. "Studies have shown that 56-85% of the diagnoses in internal medicine can be made on the basis of the history alone" (Putnam et al., 1985, p. 74). The search for ways to increase the accuracy of practitioner-patient communication is of obvious value.

Box 7–4 examines the formal medical history, how it is obtained and how the information gathered from it is synthesized by medical professionals. The manner in which the medical information is written up can determine its usefulness to other medical professionals involved in the long-term care of the patient.

## PHYSICAL EXAMINATION AND DIAGNOSTIC TESTS

As interactions between people go, the practitioner-patient interaction is a strange one. Fully clothed, the medical practitioner touches, pokes, and prods the body of the patient who is draped, at best, in a paper gown. The patient is sometimes asked to assume very uncomfortable or embarrassing positions. And this is often after answering some rather embarrassing questions.

Patients are sometimes distressed by the medical practitioner's role as it is manifested during the physical examination. There is a discrepancy of power between practitioner and patient, and here is where it shows. Granted, the power is not real, for the physician cannot force the patient to do anything he or she does not want to do, but by virtue of the circumstances in which practitioner and patient relate, the practitioner seems to have the upper hand. Thus, the physical examination is, for some patients, quite an unpleasant experience.

The first visit with a practitioner whom the patient does not know can be emotionally trying and even disorienting. This is why in many medical offices a new patient is fully clothed when he or she meets the doctor. They meet, in a sense, on equal terms socially. The history is taken in this manner, and practitioner and patient

## THE PROBLEM ORIENTED MEDICAL RECORD

In a medical interview, the physician usually asks many questions of the patient. The questions typically focus on the symptoms being experienced and how and when the symptoms developed. Questions may also be asked about many other aspects of the patient's health, past and present. Some of the questions may even seem irrelevant to the patient, but they typically are central to determining what is, and just as important, what isn't, wrong with him or her. The physician also conducts a physical examination and uses the information gathered in that part of the visit to support or refute the various hypotheses he or she has formed about what might be wrong with the patient.

What do physicians do with all the information they collect? How do they keep track of the answers that their patients give to questions? How do they integrate these answers with the results of clinical tests (like blood chemistries, urinalysis, X rays) and the recommendations they have made to patients? The answer is that all this information is entered, in an organized fashion, into the medical record.

Record keeping is a time-consuming activity for physicians, nurses, and other health professionals. Many dislike it because they see it as involving simply archival notes to be tucked away and consulted only when memory fails. But "the medical record [is] an integral part of the clinical problem solving process. In this role, the record becomes a dynamic device which closely reflects the patient's status and is important in the delivery of optimal patient care" (Enelow & Swisher, 1972, p. 66).

The medical record is one vehicle by which medical professionals communicate with one another about a patient's condition. They share their hypotheses regarding diagnosis and potential treatments, as well as their insights into what might help the patient with many aspects of the illness.

The traditional medical record that is still used in many medical centers was already well established in the 1920s at Harvard Medical School. It is not clear where it originated. This classical type of medical record includes information on the following specific topics:

1. Chief complaint (for example, patient says "I have headaches.")
2. Present illness (description of the current state)
3. Past medical history
4. Social-psychological history
5. Family history (that is, family medical history)
6. Review of systems (the patient's answers to questions about all systems of his or her body)

Items 1–6 can be completed from the interview information. Typically, a long paragraph or a whole page is written about each. The various dimensions of the individual's life are separated and isolated. Thus, physical illnesses and social-psychological problems are considered in different sections of the history even though the two are probably related. It would therefore be quite easy to fail to integrate these complementary aspects of the patient's condition.

The traditional medical record also includes:

7. Physical findings
8. Initial laboratory data

9. Formulation (or impressions about what could be wrong with the patient)
10. Diagnoses
11. Diagnostic plans (if more tests need to be done to confirm the diagnosis)
12. Therapeutic plans (if the diagnosis has been arrived at)

The drawbacks of the traditional approach are several. The chief complaint appears to suggest there is a single diagnosis that will explain the patient's illness. There may, however, be several possible conditions that interact with one another. The physician is forced to choose one of them to label the patient's problem. Psychological and social data are separated from the patient's present and past illnesses. And the historical aspects of the illness (how it developed) are separated from current physical and laboratory findings. So, the story of the illness, the process by which the condition develops and progresses, is not considered.

Lawrence Weed (1967) developed the Problem Oriented Medical Record (the POMR), which is gradually becoming widely used as an alternative to the classical medical record. The central difference in the POMR is that a well-defined list of problems covers all the difficulties the patient is experiencing at the time he or she presents to the physician. A "problem" can be a specific diagnosis (for example, hypertension) or a description of the symptoms, if the diagnosis is not clear (for example, headache). A problem can be psychosocial (for example, anxiety or depression). The POMR is compatible with the approach that is used in computer-assisted diagnostic programs.

The following is a somewhat simplified example of a Problem Oriented Medical Record. This is an abbreviated POMR for a patient who presents to the physician with a central complaint of headaches, and several related problems as well.

**PATIENT:**  Jane Doe    **PATIENT NUMBER:**  4321

*Patient complaint:*   "I have headaches all the time now, I feel exhausted, and I can't sleep."

*Patient profile:*   The patient is a 35-year-old Caucasian woman who is married and has three children. She is junior partner in a prestigious local law firm and teaches at the university law school. She sought medical care because of persistent and debilitating headaches that began three months ago and have increased in frequency and severity in the past month. She also indicates that she feels weak and is losing weight. She describes herself as feeling "nervous" and as having insomnia recently.

*Problem 1.   Headaches.*   This woman has described having severe headaches nearly every day for the past three months. At first they were relatively mild in severity, and were relieved by 1000 mg acetaminophen. In the past month, however, acetaminophen has helped very little. She reports that her vision is normal and that she has not experienced any dizziness.

*Problem 2.   Weight loss.*   In the past three months the patient has lost 20 pounds. Her normal weight is 125 pounds. She is 5 feet, 7 inches, and now weighs 105. She reports that her appetite is very much decreased in the past three months, and that she is almost never hungry.

*Problem 3.   Anxiety.*   The patient reports that she feels "nervous" most of the time, and has a great deal of difficulty relaxing. She cannot sit quietly in

*(continued)*

## THE PROBLEM ORIENTED MEDICAL RECORD *(continued)*

one place for more than a few minutes. She feels that much of her anxiety is related to her job. She was promoted to law partner three months ago, which is when her physical problems began.

***Problem 4.  Insomnia.***   Patient reports that she falls asleep exhausted at about 11:00 P.M. each night but awakens at around 3:00 A.M. and cannot get back to sleep. After 30 minutes or so without success, she gets up and does the work she has brought home. She is tired again at around 6:00 A.M., but at that time she must get ready to go back to work, and her children are getting up. So, she is exhausted all day and drinks up to six cups of coffee to stay awake at work.

***Past medical history:***   She had measles, mumps, and chicken pox as a child. Her appendix was removed at the age of 15. She has never had a head injury, and reports no problems with headaches until three months ago. Pregnancies and deliveries of all three children were normal. Patient reports generally excellent health.

***Family history:***   Patient was an only child. Both parents are living and healthy. A maternal aunt died of a cerebral hemorrhage. There is no family history of headaches, or of neurological disorders.

***Social history:***   The patient has been married for 13 years to a law school professor. She describes the marriage as stable and happy. Her children are ages 7, 5, and 3. The patient's husband and housekeeper are instrumental in helping to care for the children, but the patient reports that final decisions and ultimate responsibility for their welfare and for the household typically fall on her.

The patient describes herself as an "overachiever and a workaholic." She graduated from high school at 16, college at 19, and Harvard Law School at 23. She has worked full time as an attorney for 12 years, taking off only a few months after the birth of each child.

### REVIEW OF SYSTEMS

Only the following significant data were obtained:

Eyes: No vision changes recently. Patient wears contact lenses.
Jaw: Patient's jaw makes audible clicking noise upon opening and closing her mouth, consistent with temporomandibular joint syndrome.
Neck: Patient complains of painful spasms in neck muscles.
CNS: Patient has had headaches every day for past three months. She describes these as severe, unrelieved by acetaminophen. Headache is characterized by feeling of tightness in the back of her head and neck and in her temples. She has no visual disturbance or aura. Headaches are precipitated by fatigue and excessive work stress and family demands.
Habits: Patient does not smoke. She drinks the equivalent of two glasses of wine a week. She reports drinking as many as six cups of coffee a day. Her diet is nutritionally inadequate. Prior to being promoted to partner in her law firm, the patient exercised at least three times a week (running). She reports that in the past three months she has had no time to exercise because of additional meetings and other work demands.

Physical examination: Pulse 72 BPM; Temp. 99.0° F p.o.; BP 110/70 right arm sitting up; Ht. 67 in; Wt. 105 lbs. The patient is a tall, thin, pale woman who looks tense and exhausted. She conveys her agitation and impatience.

Skin: Normal

Head: Normal

Ear, nose, throat: Normal

Neck: Range of motion in neck is limited. Patient seems to be in pain when neck is moved or palpated.

Lymph nodes: Normal

Chest: Normal configuration. Respiration is accelerated.

Heart: Heart sounds are normal.

Peripheral vessels: Normal. Some varicose veins in legs.

Breasts: Normal, showing evidence of recent weight loss.

Abdomen: Normal

Pelvic examination: Normal

Rectal examination: Normal

Extremities: Normal

Neurological: Within normal limits

Brief mental status:

Appearance and behavior: patient appears fashionably dressed and well groomed. Behavior is agitated and worried, impatient.

Speech: Brisk and staccato; forceful, moderate-to-loud voice; clear but brief answers.

Mood: Somewhat angry, distressed, tense

Thought content: specific work and home tasks and responsibilities; concern that "things aren't getting done"

Orientation: clear

No suicidal ideas. No evidence of psychotic thought disorder.

Initial Laboratory Findings:

_____

_____

[Here the results of the blood tests, and other tests would be listed.]

## Initial Plan

### Problem 1.  Headaches

*Formulation:* The source of the headaches appears to be excessive muscle tension. Excessive caffeine intake in the form of coffee may be exacerbating headaches.

*Plan:*  diagnostic—neurological consultation
therapeutic—Valium 5mg, t.i.d. for one week only for muscle tension.
—acetaminophen 1000 mg. q.i.d. (patient declines stronger pain reliever because she feels it will interfere with her ability to work).
—relaxation training to help reduce muscle tension and eventually eliminate diazepam (Valium).

### Problem 2.  Weight Loss

*Formulation:* Patient's diet is nutritionally inadequate. It seems that she cannot relax enough to enjoy eating a meal. She has so many home and work

*(continued)*

**THE PROBLEM ORIENTED MEDICAL RECORD** *(continued)*

responsibilities that she spends virtually no time concerned with the adequacy of her diet.

*Plan:* diagnostic—have patient consult with dietician to review her precise food intake.

therapeutic—have patient work with dietician to determine ways in which she might enhance her eating habits so that she consumes more nutritionally sound calories.

—prescription of dietary supplements in the form of vitamin and mineral pills.

**Problem 3.   Anxiety**
*Formulation:* Patient seems to be highly anxious about her new position in the law firm. She notes that her work is under close scrutiny. Her increased responsibilities have taken the time she once spent on exercise, an activity that served an important tension-reducing function for her.

*Plan:* diagnostic—referral to psychologist to determine whether there are other important sources of the patient's anxiety.

therapeutic—discuss with patient the importance of returning to exercise activities, including weekly massage at the gym for control of muscle tension.

—as above, referral for training in progressive relaxation.

**Problem 4.   Insomnia**
*Formulation:* Patient's sleep appears to be disrupted because she has so much on her mind. She falls asleep easily when exhausted at night, but after one of night's normal awakenings becomes immediately aroused and concerned about the work she has to do, and is then unable to fall back to sleep.

*Plan:* diagnostic—referral to hospital sleep laboratory for evaluation.

therapeutic—prescription of .125 mg. Halcion (a short-acting benzodiazepine sleep medication)—one every other night starting in one week to help break the cycle of night awakenings and help the patient get the rest she needs to get through the day without caffeine.

—gradual withdrawal from caffeine, down to one cup of coffee in the morning only, no caffeine at all after 3:00 P.M.

—as above, relaxation training is likely to help with insomnia.

Overall: Discussion with patient should include encouragement to

1. focus more than she currently is doing on her own physical and emotional needs.
2. hire additional domestic help for the evenings (for example, to prepare lunches for the next day and clean up supper dishes) so that she can relax with her husband and children.
3. consider reordering her priorities, which might include cutting back on work, or at least putting it in better emotional perspective.
4. consider short-term psychotherapy to deal with anxiety that is based in feelings of inadequacy and low self-esteem.

discuss the factors relevant to the patient's condition. Then they go on to the examination in the usual manner. In some clinics, medical offices, and health maintenance organizations, however, this first step is omitted. The patient, wearing a paper drape, faces someone he or she has never met before and feels uncomfortable, embarrassed, and perhaps even angry.

Sue Fisher (1986) describes the situation in the following passage from her book on the treatment of women patients:

> On my initial visit [with the gynecologist] a nurse called me into an examining room, asked me to undress, gave me a paper gown to put on and told me the doctor would be with me soon. I was stunned. Was I not even to see the doctor before undressing? . . . How could I present myself as a competent, knowledgeable person sitting undressed on the examining table? But I had a potentially cancerous growth, so I did as I had been told.
>
> In a few minutes the nurse returned and said, "Lie down, the doctor is coming". Again, I complied. The doctor entered the examining room, nodded in my direction while reading my chart and proceeded to examine me without ever having spoken to me. (Fisher, 1986, p. 2)

I have learned of one patient who refused to tolerate this kind of treatment (Stahly, personal communication, March 1987). She took this situation into her own hands and simply refused to remove her clothing until after she had met the doctor. She had vowed to herself that she would never again be unclothed while meeting a physician for the first time. She stuck to her promise despite much pressure from the nurse, whose job it was to follow established office protocol. The patient met the doctor, discussed her problem, and provided the information for the history. Then she calmly removed her clothing for the physical examination.

A relationship in which one party can touch and probe the body of the other (but not vice versa), as well as ask all sorts of intimate questions, is unusual indeed. One way in which the strangeness of this relationship is dealt with is through the formality and specific decorum of the physician:

> [The physician must] bear in mind [his] manner of sitting, reserve, arrangement of dress, decisive utterance, brevity of speech, composure, bedside manners, care, replies to objections, calm self-control . . . his manner must be serious and humane; without stooping to be jocular or failing to be just, he must avoid excessive austerity; he must always be in control of himself. (Hippocrates, 1923 translation)

Besides clinical data for diagnosis of the patient's condition, the physical examination provides more information. The practitioner can learn a great deal from observing the patient's body and the patient's relationship to it. The practitioner can tell, for example, how comfortable the patient is with nakedness. This information may reveal something about the patient's attitudes toward sex. He or she may see in the patient's body something to reflect the patient's history, such as scars, malformations, and ways of moving that protect certain parts of the body.

Sir Arthur Conan Doyle, novelist and creator of the famous detective character Sherlock Holmes, was trained as a physician. He was taught the art of careful observation, such as attention to details of the patient's body and behavior, by his teacher Dr. Joseph Bell. Bell was the original model for the character Sherlock Holmes. Bell was a superb diagnostician and taught Holmes's creator the critical value of precise scrutiny, the commitment of essential details to memory, and deductive reasoning (cf. Doyle, 1984). Astute observation and excellence at deductive reasoning are no less important for the medical practitioner.

The therapeutic visit often involves diagnostic tests such as diagnostic X rays, blood tests, and urinalysis. When the history and physical examination have been completed and more information is still needed, the practitioner performs or orders diagnostic tests.

## THE RECOMMENDATION

Once the practitioner has examined the patient and has decided on a diagnosis, or to run further tests at a later time, the practitioner and patient move into the *conclusion* phase of the visit; the practitioner makes a recommendation.

Patients expect practitioners to communicate diagnostic findings and treatment plans during this phase of the medical visit (Leigh & Reiser, 1980). They expect their practitioners to provide them with information necessary to understand and to carry out their treatment (Stiles et al., 1979). Patient satisfaction with the entire medical visit can be dependent upon the explanations given by the practitioner in this third phase of the medical visit (Putnam et al., 1985).

As we will see in the next section of this chapter, however, patients are often disappointed. Practitioners typically do not provide recommendations that are clear and straightforward. They use words that are foreign to the patient. Their explanations sometimes convey secrecy and superiority (Barnlund, 1976). And when these explanations are unclear, patients fail to ask questions to clarify their confusions and misconceptions. Furthermore, patients often forget what they have been told (DiMatteo & DiNicola, 1982).

If a patient is to follow treatment recommendations, he or she must understand precisely what is to be done. Usually, the patient must know why a certain treatment regimen has been chosen and how its fulfillment will lead to eradication (or at least control) of the disease. As we examined in Chapter 4, the patient must also believe in the efficacy of the treatment regimen and

must believe that there are negative consequences of ignoring the treatment. The treatment recommendation must not conflict with the patient's family or cultural expectations. The patient must have the resources (time, money, and capacity to control behavior) to carry out the treatment regimen. Practitioners often fail to recognize when many of these factors are missing. And sometimes they make recommendations that the patient cannot possibly succeed in following (DiMatteo & DiNicola, 1982).

Box 7–5 describes one way to educate patients with patient package inserts.

**Reassurance.**  It is during the recommendation phase of the medical visit that the patient expects to receive reassurance. Reassurance consists of a hopeful attitude and of specific statements that are designed to allay patient concerns (Leigh & Reiser, 1980). These statements, of course, must be based on data or on the practitioner's experience. They must go to the source of the patient's fear; reassurance cannot be superficial. They must overturn the patient's incorrect understanding of the disease or of the procedure that is dreaded (Buchsbaum, 1986). If the truth is indeed grim, the practitioner can provide the patient with accurate information emphasizing the more positive potential outcomes.

Research suggests that patients are dissatisfied with medical treatment when they receive no reassurance from their physicians (Korsch & Negrete, 1972). Both physicians and patients have been found to rate reassurance as the most desirable type of response a physician can give to a patient (DiMatteo, Linn, Chang, & Cope, 1985; Linn & DiMatteo, 1983). Reassurance can enhance the treatment outcome, as shown in several studies of surgical patients. Patients recovered better after having received some reassurance about what they would experience (that is, that various sensations were perfectly normal) than when they received no reassurance at all (Egbert et al., 1963; Egbert et al., 1964; Langer, Janis, & Wolfer, 1975). Reassurance enhances the patient's trust in the medical practitioner (Ben-Sira, 1976, 1980; DiMatteo & DiNicola, 1982).

Reassurance, based on the truth, is particularly necessary when the patient's prog-

nosis is grave or will remain uncertain. In the 1950s and 1960s it was widely believed by physicians that telling patients "the terrible facts" was bad for them. If their diseases were incurable or forbode a terrible course, patients usually never found out. One patient with inoperable stomach cancer was told by the surgeon that some "cut-

BOX
7–5

## PATIENT PACKAGE INSERTS

These days when you open the packages of certain prescription drugs, such as antibiotics, estrogen compounds (for example, birth control pills), and ulcer medications, to name a few, you may find something called a patient package insert (PPI). Around 1980, companies that produce these medications began enclosing in their packages detailed information for patients. PPIs appeared at the request of consumers and because of certain laws requiring drug labeling. Such information allows patients to make informed decisions about their medical care.

Various studies have evaluated how well the PPIs work. Some important questions have been asked. Do people actually read the PPIs? Is the information contained in them helpful to patients or threatening to them? Do PPIs inform patients or just make trouble?

One large study was conducted in Los Angeles by the RAND Corporation (Kanouse, Berry, Hayes-Roth, Rogers, & Winkler, 1981). The findings show that PPIs are very useful to medical consumers. For example:

1. About 70% of those who receive the PPIs read them. This is true not only of well-to-do, highly educated people; in this study, the less educated were as likely to read the information as anyone else. The PPIs actually appealed most favorably to less educated and minority patients.
2. Patients used PPIs as reference documents. Around 50% of the recipients kept the PPI, and up to 32% read it more than once. This result shows that having information in hand is useful because patients can go back and refer to the information again and again.
3. PPIs lead to reliable gains in drug knowledge. This research found that people did learn from the PPI; they knew more than did those who did not receive it about how the drug worked. They knew how to use the drug, when not to use it, and how it might interact with other drugs.
4. Patients who had PPIs said it helped them to follow doctors' orders, but they were not found actually to take the drug more.
5. Almost no patients returned their medications after reading about them.
6. Although some critics suggested that patients might, through suggestion, experience more negative side effects of their medications, this did not happen. PPIs did not lead patients to report more side effects or to call their doctors to seek reassurance and information. Some critics feared that patients might call their doctors less and instead try to deal with problems themselves, but this also did not happen.

tin'" was done and the "bad stuff" was pulled out, and now "you're gonna be okay" (Cassell, 1985b, p. 148). A patient with blood chemistries that showed a pattern consistent with terminal leukemia was told that his blood was a little weak and he would feel better soon with some pills and a transfusion. Sometimes until just before they died, patients assumed they were on the road to recovery.

Since the mid-1970s, however, there has been a significant change in the attitudes of medical professionals. Most now feel that patients must have information in order to maintain their autonomy in the face of serious illness. Patients need all the facts to make their own decisions. Being truthful with patients has become a moral imperative (Bok, 1978).

Of course, telling a patient bluntly that a condition is grave or terminal and there is no hope of recovery can have devastating consequences. The manner in which the practitioner conveys the information that the illness is very serious can affect how the patient reacts. The patient may become hopeless, depressed, and despairing. Here, too, the practitioner's most important tool is reassurance. The practitioner cannot always tell the patient that he or she will get well but can reassure the patient that he or she will not be abandoned emotionally and that all possible treatments will be tried if the patient wishes. The practitioner might reassure the patient that he or she will not have to endure a lot of pain but will receive necessary pain medications.

In sum, whether the patient's condition is routine or extremely serious, reassurance can help reduce the patient's uncertainty, fear, anxiety, and emotional distress.

### RESEARCH ON PRACTITIONER-PATIENT COMMUNICATION

For several decades, the practitioner-patient relationship has been a topic of concern and analysis among social scientists (such as Parsons, 1951, 1975; Bloom, 1963) and physicians (such as Balint, 1957; Freud, 1924). This early work, however, has suffered from a major limitation. Much of the theoretical writing has dealt with what *should* occur in the physician-patient relationship, but little has examined what *does* occur. Normative statements about what *ought to be* abound in writings about medical communication. These statements often reflect the ethical position held by the writer. In the past ten years, however, more and more research has dealt with what actually occurs when practitioners and patients try to communicate with one another (Waitzkin, 1984).

Researchers have studied the practitioner-patient relationship in various ways. They have used several types of research methodologies, such as interviews and questionnaires (see Chapter 2). In other studies researchers have analyzed audiotape recordings of practitioner-patient visits. This research is extremely time consuming. Investigators may spend many hundreds of hours analyzing what is said, by whom, in what tone of voice, and with what answer. It is from this latter type of research that we have learned the most about the therapeutic relationship. Let us now turn to the results of this research as we further examine gaps in practitioner-patient communication.

## Problems and Solutions in Therapeutic Interaction

Medical practitioners and their patients do more than simply behave or act in one another's presence. They *interact*. In any interaction the two participants influence each other; one person's actions affect the other person's thoughts, feelings, and behaviors.

Each of the problematic elements of practitioner-patient communication that we consider below has the potential to (and usually does) elicit further problematic responses. For example, one person's hostile voice tone may (in fact, is likely to) elicit hostility from the other person. Or since the amount of time available for the interaction is usually limited, when one person talks a great deal, the other is able to talk only a minimal amount (Bain, 1976; Davis, 1971; Freemon, Negrete, Davis, & Korsch, 1971; Roter, 1984).

As we analyze the difficulties in practitioner-patient relationships, we must realize that assigning blame can be quite destructive. For every practitioner who failed to provide critical information there was a patient who was not assertive enough to ask for and insist upon receiving it. For every patient who did not understand what he or she was told, there was a practitioner who failed to check that things were clear to the patient in the first place. The medical interaction is (at least) a two-sided enterprise (Stiles et al., 1979; Stiles, Putnam, & Jacob, 1982).

## TIME

Time seems to be an important issue in the medical visit. Medical professionals don't have enough of it and patients usually want more.

Physicians often complain that they do not have time to spend talking with their patients. But as research suggests, the more time a physician spends with patients, the less money the physician earns (Waitzkin, 1985).

Patients cite the failure to take time with them as the cause of their decision to change doctors (DiMatteo & DiNicola, 1982). Although the *objective* amount of time that a physician spends with a patient influences how much information seeking can take place (Beisecker & Beisecker, 1990), patient satisfaction with the medical visit depends to a great extent upon the patient's *subjective* feeling that enough time was spent to meet communication needs

(DiMatteo & Hays, 1980). One survey has shown that the average visit with an internist in the United States is about 18 minutes, and with a specialist, 15 minutes (Feller, 1979). If no time is wasted in unproductive miscommunication, practitioner-patient encounters can be effective and satisfying in this brief time (Korsch et al., 1968). Yet, for full patient participation and information seeking/question asking to occur, at least 19 minutes may be essential (Beisecker & Beisecker, 1990).

Of course, miscommunication is quite common, as we will see below, and it results in patients who feel that not enough time was spent to satisfy their needs. Obviously, the recent trend toward shorter and shorter medical visits (down to five minutes in some HMO's and prepaid group medical plans) is bound to reduce the quality of practitioner-patient communication even further (Beisecker & Beisecker, 1990; Waitzkin, 1985).

## THE PATIENT'S PERSPECTIVE

Even when a medical visit is routine and there is no emergency, many patients feel quite anxious. As we will examine further in Chapter 12, the medical environment can be foreign and threatening. The patient may be in pain and frightened. Often patients anticipate being hurt or embarrassed by the medical procedures they are to experience. The anxiety of being ill can interfere with the patient's ability to communicate effectively, to say what he or she means and to hear what is being communicated (Barnlund, 1976).

Communication problems may also arise from differences in the perspectives that practitioner and patient have on illness. For example, a physician may place a higher value on health and on the healthful lifestyle required to attain it than does the patient who has many different priorities competing for attention (Larson & Sutker, 1966).

## IMPROVING THE INTERVIEW

As we examined earlier in this chapter, collecting accurate medical history data from patients through the process of interviewing can sometimes be very difficult. Many patients cannot even recall events that are quite recent. Some patients fail to provide correct information because the truth is embarrassing. Many are timid about answering questions regarding certain parts of their bodies or their sexual behavior. When asked, they may either deliberately lie or simply withhold the complete truth. Some patients may be embarrassed about their ignorance of medical issues and vocabulary (Korsch & Negrete, 1972). Their primary motivation during the medical visit may be to avoid appearing unintelligent rather than to communicate the necessary information.

Sometimes during medical interviews, those asking the questions reinforce their respondents for answering poorly, that is, for being careless and even for evading or refusing to answer the question (Marquis, 1970). These reinforcements are typically given with nonverbal cues such as head nods, smiles, and attention. Respondents are also subtly encouraged to be passive and inaccurate.

Interviewing patients can be made considerably more effective and accurate if the above problems are remedied. This can be done in several ways.

As noted earlier in this chapter, patient anxiety can be reduced by making the medical-care visit more responsive to patients' emotional needs and by providing patients with the information they wish to have. Because patient passivity and practitioner dominance often contribute to producing unreliable answers, patients who wish to be involved should be given the opportunity to become active participants in every aspect of their care (DiMatteo & DiNicola, 1982).

The accuracy of health reporting has been found to increase significantly when respondents make a commitment to provide accurate information. This commitment elicits patient effort and motivation (Cannell et al., 1977). Also, the interviewer needs to tell the patient what kind of information is wanted and the purpose of the questions. "Now, I need to ask you some questions about your chest pain . . ." or "Have you experienced any side effects from the medication? By side effects, I mean [thus and so]." The practitioner must reinforce the patient's correct efforts: "Yes, that's the kind of information I need. Tell me what else happened."

Finally, the interviewer must eliminate any possibility that the patient will be embarrassed. The medical practitioner must communicate a completely nonjudgmental attitude about issues that have the potential to embarrass a patient. Physicians who are judgmental or punitive about such issues as sexual behavior, for example, can have a lasting impact on the patient's feeling about his or her body and its functioning. Consider this example:

■ ■ ■ ■ ■

A young woman's sexuality is developing. During a routine gynecological visit, she mentions to her physician that she has not been able to experience orgasm. The physician tells her that this is because she is not married. When she is married, the physician points out, she will be able to relax. At that point, sexual fulfillment will happen naturally.

Of course, sex therapists have known for many years that lack of information is one of the primary causes of sexual difficulties. This young woman needs to learn to enhance the physical sensations she experiences during sex. This is what will help her to experience orgasm. But the physician instead passes judgment on her premarital sexual activity. The young woman is embarrassed by the physician's statement. She decides to refrain from asking any other questions about sex. Later, when she is married, she is still in need of some important information, and sex is still unsatisfying for her.

## MEDICAL JARGON

Medical professionals learn a complex language with which to communicate with one another. *Splenomegaly*, for example, is a word that conveys a great deal of information to the medical professionals who use it. The term refers to enlargement of the spleen, which is a large glandlike but ductless organ situated in the upper left side of the abdomen that breaks down red corpuscles. But *splenomegaly* means more than just spleen enlargement. The term is applied to a condition marked by hypertrophy (enlargement) of the spleen with progressive anemia (reduction below normal in the amount of hemoglobin, the volume of packed red blood cells) and no evidence of leukemia or disease of the lymph glands (*Dorland's Illustrated Medical Dictionary*, 1965, p. 1423). Of course, once the patient asks the physician for the meaning of *splenomegaly*, we can imagine him or her asking the physician to explain the explanation!

The purpose of using medical terminology is not to say big words when simple ones would suffice. Disease entities, diagnostic tests, and other medical phenomena have particular names. The terms are descriptive and precise. Yet, medical terminology serves more than efficiency. In many ways the ability to use and to understand medical terminology defines one as a member of the "in group" and as someone "in the know" (Christy, 1979). Doctors and nurses are in the know; patients are not.

A somewhat more cynical view of medical jargon was provided by the famous heart surgeon Dr. Michael DeBakey: "Most doctors don't want their patients to understand them! They prefer to keep their work a mystery. If patients don't understand what a doctor is talking about, they won't ask him questions. Then the doctor won't have to be bothered answering them." (Robinson, 1973)

"Doctor-talk" is mystifying to patients. This is the conclusion of many hundreds of patients who have been interviewed over the years in studies of patient dissatisfaction with medical care (Barnlund, 1976; DiMatteo & DiNicola, 1982; Koos, 1954). Medical practitioners talk to one another in doctor-talk. They also use doctor-talk to talk to patients. Doctor-talk is high sounding, formal, and frightening to patients (Christy, 1979). Sometimes doctor-talk is called *medical jargon*. Jargon can sometimes be impressive (Korsch et al., 1968). Some patients may take the fact that the physician has used high-sounding words as a compliment to their intelligence. Perhaps they feel that they will be "taken care" of by a physician who is obviously competent. How can they be expected to understand what the physician says?

In a series of studies on the communication between physicians-in-training and mothers of their pediatric patients, researchers found that nearly all of the physicians used words that confused and perplexed the mothers (Korsch & Negrete, 1972). These words were fairly rudimentary medical terms such as *incubation period* (which is the period of time from exposure to a disease to development of symptoms). But the words were unfamiliar and caused patients considerable anxiety. The mothers attempted to puzzle out the meaning of the words rather than ask for explanation. For example, they reasoned that incubation period sounds like incubator. Therefore, the baby is going to have to go in an incubator and be hospitalized!

Box 7–6 describes some of the interesting ways in which patients try to figure out what their practitioners are saying to them.

One reason that physicians use so much medical jargon with their patients is that they typically overestimate the amount their patients can understand. Two studies explored this issue (Samora, Saunders, & Larson, 1961; Segall & Roberts, 1980). Physicians and nurses were asked to make lists of words they felt they could use with pa-

**BOX 7-6**

## INTERNAL FLEA BITES

When you ask patients what is ailing them, you can get some pretty strange answers. Consider the patient who says he has a case of "smiling-mighty-Jesus" (spinal meningitis), or the patient with "sick-as-hell anemia" (sickle cell anemia), or the one with "fireballs" in her "Eucharist" (fibroids in her uterus). One patient even has to take the medication "peanut butter balls" (phenobarbital) for a seizure disorder.

These examples represent attempts by (perhaps creative) patients to understand Medspeak, the language of the medical profession. "Entering a hospital has now become an internment in an alien culture for most people" (Spaide, 1983, p. 5).

Patients are in foreign territory in the medical setting. They are often anxious, and the logical flow of their ideas may be impaired. Yet, patients work actively to puzzle out and make sense of what they have been told by their physicians. They are reluctant to ask questions, and may convince themselves that they will be able to reason out the meaning of their diagnosis. And they develop a language that reflects their understanding. The language is called Patientspeak (examples above).

Are the incorrect names that patients settle on simply meaningless sound-alikes or do they tell something about how patients reason about their medical problems? Probably the latter explanation is correct. The patient with sickle cell (sick-as-hell) anemia most likely does feel extremely sick. The patient who says that the ophthalmologist saw "Cadillacs" (cataracts) in his eyes probably suspects the doctor's income to be quite high, or may even be (perhaps unconsciously) distressed at how much money his eye care is costing. The patient who says she has been referred to a "groinocologist" (gynecologist) has chosen an anatomical reference to aid her understanding.

Patientspeak may not be simple linguistic misunderstanding. Consider the patient with deep-vein thrombophlebitis who reports that he has "internal flea-bites." He may have heard the suffix *itis*, which refers to inflammation of the organ whose name precedes it (as in appendicitis—inflammation of the appendix). The patient then reasons that he has a disease of thrombo-phle(pronounced "flea")-bite—some kind of flea bite disease. Because there are no apparent external bites and the pain is inside, the patient guesses that *thrombo* must mean "internal," and so guesses "internal flea bites." The patient has had to incorporate common knowledge with linguistic analysis with a kind of creative rationalization. He has worked quite hard to turn Medspeak into Patientspeak.

NOTE: I am indebted to Jim Black and Wendy Haight (personal communication, August 18, 1983) for some very interesting insights that contributed to this analysis.

tients, medical terms they believed that patients could define correctly. Yet, when these same words were presented to patients of many different backgrounds and levels of education, surprisingly few could define the terms accurately.

In Table 7–1, next to each medical term is the percentage of patients in the first study (Samora et al., 1961) who could not define the word at all. How many of these words can you define? The definitions can be found in Box 7–7.

Patients were able to define slightly more words in the second study (Segall & Roberts, 1980) than in the first. The second study took place several years after the first and involved a somewhat easier task. Patients in this study had simply to recognize rather than recall each word and they were able to complete the test at home, presumably with help and access to a medical dictionary.

| TABLE 7–1 | Fourteen Medical Terms Used by Doctors and Nurses |
|---|---|
| Medical word | Percentage of patients who could not define the word |
| Abdomen | 12.8 |
| Acute | 22.4 |
| Appendectomy | 49.6 |
| Bacteria | 27.2 |
| Cardiac | 58.4 |
| Malignant | 54.4 |
| Negative | 14.4 |
| Reaction | 12.0 |
| Respiratory | 50.4 |
| Secretions | 55.2 |
| Symptoms | 10.4 |
| Tendon | 40.8 |
| Terminal | 39.2 |
| Therapy | 44.8 |

## THE CONSEQUENCES OF IMPRECISE COMMUNICATION

A patient can become confused and terrified when he or she misunderstands a medical professional's words. Eric Cassell, M.D., tells the story of a woman patient who was extremely upset because of the imprecise words used by her former physician. The physician said, "[It] looks like your diaphragm is immobilized . . . like paralyzed," even though there was no paralysis at all and her condition was not even serious. She had a severe muscle spasm but was by no means paralyzed. Yet, she knew roughly what *paralyzed* meant, and pictured herself ending up in an *iron lung*. (An iron lung is a device into which the patient's entire body is placed and immobilized so that he or she can be helped to breathe.) The physician may not have known that the word *paralyzed* would terrify the patient so, but failed to check the patient's comprehension and understand-

ing so that certain explanations could be modified if that proved to be necessary (Cassell, 1985b, p. 181).

Medical communication is imprecise often enough to create significant problems for patients. Here is an example in which the physician asks multiple questions (from Shuy, 1976, p. 75):

DOCTOR: "Well, how do you feel? Do you have a fever?" (What should the patient answer if he does not have a fever but still feels quite sick?)

DOCTOR: "Where do you get short of breath?" (What should the patient answer?: "In my chest." or "On the stairs.")

Sometimes, the patient is unsure about his or her own concerns:

"So, is there anything you want to ask me about?" the physician asks hurriedly.

He is standing near the door of the examining room. He does not look relaxed.

Not prepared for this opportunity, the patient responds quickly. "No, it's okay . . . no, uh, questions."

"Okay. Good," says the doctor. "Bye. See you next time. Bye now."

Later the patient regrets having missed the opportunity to ask the doctor about her concerns.

## LISTENING TO PATIENTS

> "The doctor didn't listen to anything I tried to say."

Listening to the patient is a key factor in assessment and diagnosis, yet the medical practitioner's failure to listen is one of the most common complaints of patients (DiMatteo & DiNicola, 1982; Osler, 1899). Patients typically know, not necessarily consciously, a great deal of information about their conditions. They alone have the experience of the specific character and timing of their symptoms. They alone know their pain, and by describing it can give clues to the type of problem that might be causing it. To take advantage of the patient's unique perspective, the medical practitioner must allow the patient to provide valuable information.

Suppose that a patient with a severe muscle contraction (or tension) headache describes the pain in the following way: "I can't stand it. It feels like someone is sticking a sharp knife in my temple." The description tells the practitioner that the pain is localized and very sharp. It tells of the intensely distressing physical feeling under which the patient tries to function from day to day. It demonstrates how a disease entity can affect a person.

Many physicians believe that the patient has the best perspective on the illness being experienced, and that the diagnosis is

**BOX 7-7**

## CAN YOU DEFINE THESE MEDICAL TERMS?

Research has shown that medical professionals are accustomed to using words that patients do not understand. Here are the definitions of terms that patients in the study by Samora, Saunders, and Larson (1961) had difficulty defining successfully. (These definitions are taken from *Dorland's Illustrated Medical Dictionary*, 24th ed., 1965.) In the study, any answer that even vaguely resembled what the word really means was scored as correct. If a doctor or nurse used any one of these terms in speaking to you, would you know what it means?

**Abdomen:** The portion of the body that lies between the thorax and the pelvis. "When presented with the statement, 'Do you have a pain in the abdomen?' respondents identified the abdomen as the sides, buttocks, back, uterus, heart, bladder, and the entire area below the waist" (Samora et al., 1966, p. 87).

**Acute:** 1. sharp; 2. having a short and relatively severe course.

**Appendectomy:** surgical removal of the vermiform (meaning worm-shaped) appendix (in the right abdomen). ". . . some respondents . . . indicated that the term meant a cut rectum, sickness, the stomach, rupture of the appendix, a pain in the stomach, taking off an arm or leg, something contagious, something like an epidemic, something to do with the bowels" (Samora et al., 1961, p. 87).

revealed in the story that the patient tells about it. As we noted in Chapter 5, many years ago the famous medical educator Sir William Osler (1899) told medical students that they must listen to the patient because he or she will reveal the diagnosis.

Listening closely to the patient also helps the practitioner to avoid the tendency to settle too quickly on a diagnosis. Listening fully to what the patient has to say helps the practitioner to consider all the available empirical evidence and to avoid trying to fit the information collected later in the interview to a hypothesis that was formulated early on the basis of very little information. Listening also conveys respect to the patient and emphasizes that the physician is willing to establish a mutual-participation approach to the physician-patient relationship (Stone, 1979).

In practice, however, listening tends to be rather difficult for physicians to do effectively. At the very least, listening requires not talking. Yet, several major empirical studies have shown that patients don't have much of a chance to talk because physicians talk so much (Bain, 1976; Davis, 1971; Freemon et al., 1971; Stiles et al., 1979). These studies involved tape recordings of physician-patient interactions and tabulations of each person's utterances. In spite of the various settings of the studies and the various backgrounds of the patients, physicians were found to verbalize quite extensively. They spent much more time talking than did their patients. These physicians incorrectly believed, however, that their patients talked more than they did (Waitzkin & Stoeckle, 1976).

## EDUCATING PATIENTS

Physicians may talk a lot, but what they say doesn't give patients much information. In the several studies cited above, the physicians' utterances and verbalizations

**Bacteria:** pl.—a loosely used genetic name for any rod-shaped microorganism, especially intestinal bacteria.

**Cardiac:** pertaining to the heart.

**Malignant:** tending to become progressively worse. (The term usually refers to cancer.)

**Negative:** indicating a lack or absence, not positive, as in a test result.

**Reaction:** a response to stimulation or a phenomenon caused by the action of chemical agents. In psychology, a mental and/or emotional state that develops in a situation.

**Respiratory:** pertaining to respiration or the act of breathing. By patients "it was thought to mean dangerous, in the arms and legs, heart, venereal, resulting from one's work, piles, an arrested case, a sickness in which you sweat and have hot and cold flashes, tiredness, and recent." (Samora et al., 1961, p. 88).

**Secretions:** substances produced by the process of elaborating a specific product of the activity of a gland.

**Symptoms:** any functional evidence of disease or of a patient's condition; a change in the patient's condition indicative of some bodily or mental state.

**Tendon:** a fibrous cord by which a muscle is attached to bone.

**Terminal:** forming or pertaining to an end (refers to illness that is expected to lead to death).

**Therapy:** the treatment of disease, or service done to the sick.

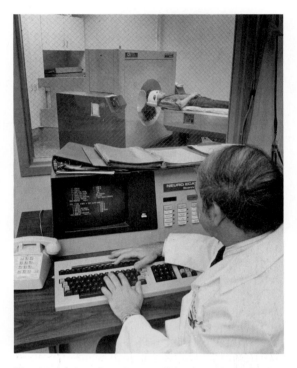

The domination of modern medicine by technology has shifted therapeutic emphasis away from practitioner-patient dialogue.
SOURCE: Spencer Grant/The Picture Cube

typically took the form of questions, acknowledgments (for example, "uh-huh"), reflections (for example, "So, your foot hurts"), clarifications (for example, "You mean you have felt at least some pain there?"), and commands (for example, "Sit back and let me examine your foot"). Very little of what was said to them was helpful in raising patients' knowledge of their illness or of the best way to care for themselves.

These studies, as well as more recent research, have found that physicians actually spend less than 10% of their interaction time with patients informing and educating them (Bain, 1976; Davis, 1971; Freemon et al., 1971; Stiles et al., 1979; Waitzkin, 1984, 1985). Waitzkin and Stoeckle (1976) found that during the medical visit, which

lasted an average of 20 minutes, physicians spent on the average less than one minute communicating information to the patient. Those same physicians estimated that they spent between 10 and 15 minutes (that is, 50% to 75% of the interaction time) giving information to their patients. In the Waitzkin (1985) study, out of an average interaction time of 16.5 minutes, physicians spent an average of 1.3 minutes giving information to their patients. When asked to estimate how much time they did spend, however, these physicians guessed an average of 8.9 minutes!

Even when physicians spend time talking with and instructing their patients, many of them are ineffective communicators. One study observed physician-patient interactions (Svarstad, 1976) and examined the manner in which physicians gave instructions to their patients regarding the medications they were to take. Of the 347 drugs prescribed to patients, 60 were never even discussed during the observed visit. In 90% of the incidents in which drugs were prescribed, the physicians gave their patients no specific verbal advice on how to use the medication (for example, to take two pills a day). Very often, the physicians made changes in patients' medication dosages or scheduling, and after once mentioning the change verbally, neither wrote down the change nor checked to see whether the patient really understood the physician's intention.

Many physicians believe that their patients have very little basic medical knowledge, and so they tend to avoid providing further explanations (Kane & Deuschle, 1967; Pratt, Seligman, & Reader, 1957). However, physicians typically underestimate patients' knowledge, and assume that little would be gained from discussing a patient's medical condition with him or her. The conclusion of a great deal of research, however, is that although patients do not understand medical terminology (jargon) they do understand simple conceptual medical explanations quite well (DiMatteo & DiNicola, 1982). But as Waitzkin (1985) found by analyzing tape recordings of 336 medical encounters in several outpatient settings, "doctors spent little time informing their patients, overestimated the time they did spend, and underestimated patients' desire for information" (p. 81). It is hoped that with insight gained from such research, health psychologists can recommend changes in the methods used by medical practitioners to provide their patients with important medical information.

## HELPING PATIENTS TO ASK QUESTIONS

Patients rarely ask for explanations, conceptual or otherwise. In fact, they ask very few questions. They do not tell their practitioners that they wish to have more information than they are getting. They rarely assert that they do not understand what their practitioners have told them (although, as we saw above, this is quite often the case). The studies cited above, which tabulated what actually occurs in physician-patient interactions, provide some insight into this phenomenon. In these studies patients spent less than 7% percent of the interaction time questionning their physicians about specific problems and treatments. They did not correct physicians' apparent misunderstandings of what they had said. They did not even politely challenge what their physicians had stated. They did not request precision when physicians were vague. Patients were typically reluctant to betray their ignorance or to appear to distrust the expertise of the physician (cf. Matthews, 1983). They conveyed complete acceptance of what was said to them. They conveyed total trust, almost to the point of indifference.

By asking questions of a practitioner, the patient gains information he or she would otherwise lack. But something else

happens as well. By asking questions, the patient signals to the practitioner that he or she wishes to be an active partner in the medical care, that the patient is the person to decide what happens to his or her own body, and that decisions must be made with the full knowledge, consent, and contribution of the patient. A patient who is passive and unassertive places full responsibility for his or her personal well-being into the hands of the practitioner. The patient relinquishes control. And because practitioners and patients sometimes have different goals in the medical-care process, the patient's relinquishing of control can have harmful consequences. Patients need to remain vigilant, inquisitive, and assertive in order to maintain their own interests.

## HELPING PATIENTS TO REMEMBER

Patients forget a great deal of the little they are told during their visits with medical practitioners. One study found that shortly after consultation with a medical practitioner, clinic outpatients forgot about one-third of what was told to them during the visit (Ley & Spelman, 1965). They forgot 56% of the instructions and 48% of the statements about treatment.

Research has shown that there are certain consistencies in what patients forget. Although patients forget much of what a doctor has told them, they tend to forget instructions and advice more than other information. The more a patient is told, the greater the proportion of information he or she forgets.

Patients remember best what they consider most important as well as what they are told first. And although there are no significant differences in recall ability by patients of different ages and levels of intelligence, patient anxiety does seem to make a difference. A moderate level of anxiety in a patient is best for recall. But if anxiety is too high or too low, a patient forgets a great deal. The more medical knowledge a patient has, the more he or she will remember what is said by the practitioner (presumably because there is a context in which to put the information). Simply writing things down doesn't help the patient a great deal; he or she must first understand what needs to be remembered (Cassata, 1978).

As you can imagine, cooperating with medical treatment can be extremely difficult when patients have little idea what it has been suggested they do. Practitioner-patient communication is certainly not the only determinant of the patient's ability to follow through with recommendations, but it is one of the most important components.

**CONCLUSION**

In the 1980s and 1990s we are entering an era in which, in many areas of the country, there is a surplus of physicians. Patients are no longer willing to choose between technical skills and communication skills in their doctors. They insist on both, as if they know intuitively what is shown in both clinical and empirical studies: good doctoring involves good talking and good listening. There is therapeutic value in avoiding the uncertainty, panic, and hopelessness that can arise in the patient when communication is poor and when secrets are kept about his or her medical condition. It is important to remember that although, as we saw earlier in the chapter, words can be powerfully devastating, they can be reassuring as well.

In the next chapter we will examine another aspect of therapeutic communication, that which takes place on a nonverbal level. We will consider the ways in which practitioners and patients affect each other with facial expressions, body movements and gestures, tones of voice, and so on. We will also examine the differences between medical practitioners and their patients in their basic orientations regarding the illness and the process of treatment. We will consider the ways in which they attempt to reconcile their differences and come to focus on one common goal: the eradication of the illness and the achievement of health in the patient.

# Summary

Chapter 7 examines in detail what occurs when patients consult physicians and other medical professionals for the diagnosis and treatment of illness.

I. We look closely at the verbal communication that takes place between patients and practitioners in the process of diagnosis and treatment. We analyze both subjective and objective outcomes of various kinds of communication. We consider the points of view, or philosophies, that underlie effective and ineffective practitioner-patient communication and review how these points of view are translated into action.

II. The proposed four premises of medical care are as follows: Doctors treat patients, not diseases. The body has the last word. All medical care flows through the relationship between physician and patient. The spoken language is the most important tool in medicine.

   A. Words are extremely powerful tools in medicine. They establish the reality of suffering. Because of their power, the utterance of words in the medical encounter is a very serious enterprise.

   B. Through the process of communication, practitioner and patient attempt to gain a common understanding of the patient's illness.

C. A practitioner's and/or a patient's poor communication skills can cause problems in their relationship.

D. A physician may give a patient very little opportunity to participate in his or her own care because the physician believes that patient participation is not valuable and not worth the trouble.

E. Communication uncovers hidden premises.

F. As modern medicine becomes dominated by technology, some medical professionals tend to give less and less attention to practitioner-patient dialogue.

III. There are three basic models of the physician-patient relationship. The Active-Passive Model occurs when the patient is unable, because of a medical condition, to participate in his or her own care and to make decisions for his or her own welfare. The Guidance-Cooperation Model occurs when the physician takes the bulk of responsibility for diagnosis and treatment. The Mutual Participation Model involves physician and patient making joint decisions about every aspect of care from the planning of diagnostic studies to the choice and implementation of treatment.

IV. The medical encounter is divided into three parts.

A. The medical history is the part of the medical encounter in which necessary information is elicited from the patient. While gathering a history, the medical professional must listen actively to what the patient has to say. The medical interview also requires that the practitioner establish the interview structure, explain the purpose of what is being done, and tell the patient what to expect from the interview process.

B. The process of medical diagnosis is based on the assumption that the patient from whom the history is gathered is telling the truth. The health interview, the face-to-face gathering of information through the process of discussion, is relied upon by medical professionals as an important source of information about the patient. The interview is a foundation for the structuring of the patient history.

C. The medical interview can be problematic.

D. Patients are sometimes distressed by the second part of the medical visit, the physical examination.

E. The third part of the medical visit is called the conclusion. The practitioner makes a recommendation. Research suggests that patients are dissatisfied with their medical treatment when they receive no reassurance from their physicians.

V. Several important problems exist in practitioner-patient interactions.

A. Physicians often complain that they do not have time to spend talking with their patients. Patients want more time with their physicians.

B. Communication problems may arise from differences in the perspective that practitioner and patient have on illness.

C. Sometimes during medical interviews, medical professionals who ask the questions reinforce their respondents for answering poorly, that is, for being careless and even for evading or refusing to answer the question. Respondents are also subtly encouraged to be passive and inaccurate. To obtain accurate answers, an interviewer must eliminate any possibility that the patient will be embarrassed.

D. "Doctor-talk" is mystifying to patients. It is high sounding, formal, and frightening to patients. Sometimes doctor-talk is called medical jargon.

E. A patient can become confused and terrified when he or she misunderstands a medical professional's words.

F. One of the most common complaints of patients is that their doctors do not listen to them.

G. Physicians typically do not give their patients much information. Physicians actually spend less than 10% of their interaction time with patients informing and educating them.

H. Even when physicians spend time talking with and instructing their patients, many of them are ineffective communicators. Physicians typically underestimate patients' knowledge and assume that little would be gained from discussing a patient's medical condition with him or her.

I. Patients forget a great deal of the little they are told during their visits with medical practitioners. One study found that shortly after consultation with a medical practitioner, clinic outpatients forgot about one-third of what was told to them during the visit.

# Glossary

**active listening:** listening that involves giving complete attention to the speaker, as well as reflecting back to

him or her precisely what is understood.

**Active-Passive Model:** a model of the practitioner-patient relationship that occurs when the patient is unable, because of a medical condition, to participate in his or her own care and to make decisions for his or her own welfare.

**closed-ended questions:** questions that require answers of one or a few words, and that ask for a specific fact or piece of information.

**communication:** a process by which information is exchanged between individuals through a common system of symbols, signs, or behaviors.

**diagnosis:** the act (or art) of identifying a disease from its signs and symptoms.

**doctor-talk:** high-sounding, formal, and frightening language used by physicians in their communication with each other and with patients.

**focused questions:** questions that are narrower than open-ended and broader than closed-ended questions.

**Guidance-Cooperation Model:** a model of the practitioner-patient relationship that occurs when the physician takes the bulk of responsibility for diagnosis and treatment. The patient answers the questions that are asked but leaves the thinking and the decisions to the physician.

**illness behavior:** how an individual usually responds to the symptoms of illness.

**incubation period:** the period of time from exposure to a disease to development of symptoms.

**interaction:** the process of mutual or reciprocal action or influence.

**interview:** the face-to-face gathering of information through the process of discussion. The interview is a foundation for the structuring of the patient history.

**malignant:** tending to become progressively worse and to result in death. A cancerous growth is considered malignant.

**medical history:** that part of the medical encounter in which necessary information is elicited from the patient. The information includes such facts as what the symptoms are, when they began, what makes them improve or become worse, and how the patient has tried to overcome the problem before coming to the physician. A useful history helps to determine the tests to be carried out and eventually the diagnosis that is decided upon.

**medical jargon:** medical terms that may not be understood by patients.

**Mutual-Participation Model:** a model of the practitioner-patient relationship in which practitioner and patient make joint decisions about every aspect of care from the planning of diagnostic studies to the choice and implementation of treatment. There is joint input and joint responsibility.

**nonverbal communication:** communication without words.

**open-ended questions:** questions that encourage elaboration and invite a patient to talk.

**physical examination:** the part of the medical visit during which the medical professional examines the patient's body to determine possible signs of disease.

**premise:** an assumption on which an argument is based.

**prognosis:** the prospect of recovery as anticipated from the usual course of disease or peculiarities of the case.

**reassurance:** emotional support consisting of a hopeful attitude and of specific statements that are designed to allay patients' fears.

**recommendation phase:** the concluding phase of the medical visit, during which the physician makes a recommendation to the patient.

**splenomegaly:** the enlargement of the spleen, a large glandlike but ductless organ situated in the upper left side of the abdomen. The spleen breaks down red corpuscles. *Splenomegaly* means more than just spleen enlargement, however. The term is applied to a condition marked by hypertrophy (enlargement) of the spleen with progressive anemia (reduction below normal in the amount of hemoglobin—the volume of packed red blood cells) and no evidence of leukemia or disease of the lymph glands.

**subcutaneous:** under the skin.

**verbal communication:** communication using words.

# Communicating Feelings in the Therapeutic Setting

At first, Art thought the doctor looked embarrassed. Her facial expression did not immediately make sense to him—at least to his conscious mind. But deep down Art knew the reason for how she looked, and precisely what she was about to tell him.

He had gone to this young dermatologist just the week before to have a mole removed from his back. The mole had begun to look a bit strange to him as he checked it in the mirror periodically. It was becoming kind of blueish-red around the edges. Besides, it was unsightly. Routinely, the tissue had been sent to the pathology lab for analysis. Not so routinely, Art was called back to the office to meet with the doctor.

And now she stood before him blinking her eyes rapidly and unnaturally as she tried to speak. Before any words came out of her mouth, Art was already gripped by panic. His heart was beating extremely fast. He began to feel faint.

Art had great difficulty focusing on the doctor's words. He did not even hear some of them. She told him that his biopsy showed evidence of malignant melanoma. There would be more testing. And then there would be several options for treatment, among them surgery and chemotherapy if necessary. He heard her say, "We'll do the best we can."

But Art barely listened. He focused on the tone of her voice, not on the carefully chosen words she spoke. Her speech was kind but halting and controlled. Her words were meant to be reassuring, but every other aspect of her communication showed anxiety and distress. Her body movements and postures were strained and uncomfortable. She looked away from Art and her eyes rarely met his. When they did, they looked terribly afraid. Art's attention was riveted on the muscles that grew tighter and tighter in her neck and throat as she spoke to him. In a mental fog, he grappled for the reason she seemed so upset.

In the past few decades, tremendous advances in medical and surgical techniques have saved countless lives and have vastly improved the quality of living for victims of illness and injury. People who, ten years ago, would have died or been severely disabled by their heart attacks today survive to lead healthy and productive lives. Victims of serious accidents are now restored to full functioning by highly trained trauma specialists using the latest advances in lifesaving technology. Patients who develop chronic illnesses are now spared devastating consequences because of newly developed medications and carefully designed medical treatment regimens.

These advances have not, however, eliminated the complications of emotional distress that typically accompany illness and injury. As we will examine in detail in Chapter 12, serious illness and bodily injury can cause severe emotional responses

that patients may be unprepared to handle. Pleasures and life-enhancing activities may be lost (Taylor, 1979). Caught in a web of pain, disappointment, threat, and confusion, most patients feel anger, profound sadness, and a host of other distressing emotions. They may vacillate between feelings of dependency and rebelliousness, between disruptive behavior and withdrawal (Moos & Tsu, 1977).

Fears may surface among some patients when they are undergoing medical care that is quite routine. Patients typically react to simple medical and surgical problems with some degree of emotional upset. Routine care for well-controlled hypertension or a simple yearly physical examination, for example, can unearth a patient's fear that a serious condition will be discovered. The medical setting triggers in many people feelings of threat to their body image, and emphasizes their sense of physical vulnerability. Fear and anxiety can overwhelm a patient who dreads pain and disfigurement. These feelings may significantly strain emotional controls. Like Art, above, he or she may feel confused and disoriented, as if "going to pieces."

■ ■ ■ ■ ■

The heart attack patient in room 507 was beginning to annoy the nurses. They complained about his aggressive behavior and his continual disregard of the medical recommendations to avoid strenuous exercise. They found him doing push-ups on the floor of his hospital room the day after his heart attack. They complained that he would pat or pinch them as they passed by him, and that he harassed them with sexual innuendos and invitations.

Diane Lowell, R.N., was not looking forward to meeting him. Yet, when she entered his room, the first thing she saw was the face of a very sad and very frightened man. He tried his usual antics with her at first, but she was not put off. She continued to look into his eyes. While she gave him his medications and checked his vital signs, she maintained a quiet, intense focus on the person in the bed before her.

He began to talk to her about what he felt. He was devastated by the recognition of his own mortality, fearful of the loss of his sexual potency, and terrified of being an invalid. Diane was not afraid of his feelings. She knew that by being there, by understanding him and not pulling away, she could reduce some of the tremendous loneliness he felt. And she would gain something critically important as well. She would experience the chance to face some of her own fears of death and disability, to connect briefly to another human being, and to feel that she made a difference in someone's life.

In this chapter we will examine the interpersonal aspects of patient care. We will see considerable evidence that medical professionals can have a tremendous impact on the ability of patients to withstand the emotional devastation of illness. As in Chapter 7, we include among others the following as medical professionals: physicians, medical psychologists, nurses, respiratory therapists, physicians' assistants, nurse practitioners, nurse midwives, phlebotomists, physical therapists and medical social workers. We will see that through their interpersonal behavior, medical professionals can make a significant difference in their patients' satisfaction with medical treatment and in their patients' willingness and ability to comply with medical regimens. In the first part of this chapter we examine the practitioner-patient relationship, particularly the role of the medical professional in helping patients to deal with the emotional aspects of illness. In the second part of the chapter we examine how that understanding is conveyed through nonverbal communication. Then in the next chapter we will examine

the effects of treating illness on the emotions of medical professionals. As we will see, medical professionals do not remain unaffected by their closeness to patients' experiences. They often feel their own emotional distress in response to what their patients are experiencing.

## EMOTIONAL REGRESSION

Illness and injury cause many patients to regress. *Regression* is a term used by psychologists and psychiatrists to indicate that a person has reverted to aspects of a child-like, dependent role characteristic of an earlier stage of his or her development (Nemiah, 1961; Lederer, 1952). Patients often remember details of being ill or injured as children and may react as they did then, when they had few emotional resources with which to adjust to being ill. Because many medical-care professionals tend to infantilize patients when they are caring for them, it is not surprising that many patients regress, sometimes to states of childishness and helplessness (Lorber, 1975).

Medical professionals witness patients' pain, fear, anger, sadness, depression, anxiety, and terror of death. They are with patients when patients' emotions are taxed to the greatest degree. Medical professionals witness patients' failures and triumphs as they struggle to contend physically and emotionally with sometimes overwhelming difficulties. Because of patients' struggles, there is inherent in the medical professional-patient relationship an opportunity for intense closeness and emotional intimacy (Cousins, 1976, 1983).

## Bedside Manner

Most people know what they mean when they talk about a doctor's *bedside manner*. Bedside manner is a broad and informal

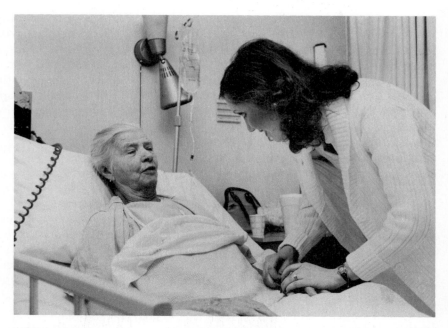

Bedside manner involves relating to the patient as someone whose feelings are worth understanding.
SOURCE: Danbury Hospital/Russ Kinne/Comstock

term used to refer to a medical practitioner's behavior toward patients. It typically refers to the provider's ability to instill trust and to respond to patients' emotional needs.

Throughout the history of medicine, medical professionals have learned bedside manner through example. Kindly mentors taught their students to be sensitive and understanding to patients. When medical educators emphasize bedside manner, somehow their students learn it (Seeman & Evans, 1961a, 1961b), and when educators consider bedside manner unimportant, that fact becomes quite clear to everyone around them. Insensitive, callous teachers turn out insensitive, callous apprentices (Klass, 1987a).

Bedside manner is, to some, a secret, like a "special edge" or a "certain something" or even "the right chemistry." Many people believe bedside manner is mysterious and elusive, making it easy to think of it as a gift.

The famous ancient Greek physician, Hippocrates, wrote in the fourth century B.C. of the enormous power of bedside manner: "The patient, though conscious that his condition is perilous, may recover his health simply through his contentment with the goodness of the physician" Hippocrates (Fourth century B.C./1923). Hippocrates, however, did not spell out precisely what this goodness involves or how to get it.

Fortunately, a few of the more current researchers in the field of health psychology have begun to dissect the phenomenon of bedside manner and to examine how it relates to patient care. Many of these researchers have worked in conjunction with medical professionals to define precisely what bedside manner consists of and how it can be achieved. They have developed methods for effectively teaching bedside manner to physicians. Let's examine some of that research now.

Bedside manner certainly involves being polite, although too often in medical interactions politeness is dispensed with (Mayerson, 1976). Many medical professionals fail to exhibit the most rudimentary polite behaviors, such as introducing themselves, exchanging pleasant words, and looking at patients as they talk to them (DiMatteo & DiNicola, 1982).

As we examined in Chapter 7, one important research method for studying medical practitioner-patient interactions involves the recording (video or audio) of the behaviors that actually occur in the medical interaction, the careful analysis of these behaviors, and the assessment of their effects on patient satisfaction with care. A recent review of the many studies using this approach has examined various aspects of bedside manner and their effects on patient satisfaction and patient compliance with medical regimens (Hall, Roter, & Katz, 1988). Some studies show that patient satisfaction with medical care is higher when physicians provide more social conversation, more positive talk, and less negative talk. As we will see below, the most important aspect of bedside manner seems to be the nonverbal cues of the medical professional.

Of course, at the very basis of the practitioner's bedside manner is his or her recognition of the importance of psychosocial as well as biological issues in treating a patient. The medical practitioner must overcome the purely biomedical view of the patient as a sack of chemicals needing an adjustment, and approach the patient as someone whose feelings are worth understanding.

# Empathy

Understanding what patients are feeling is the first step in helping them to cope emotionally with illness. But to understand fully every aspect of what a patient feels about being ill, a medical professional would have to experience precisely what the patient has gone through. The medical professional would have to face the same physical pain, emotional distress, and uncertainty that the patient faces. This is impossible, of course, because each patient faces a unique situation with a unique set of personal circumstances. Thus, the medical professional attempts to grasp the full meaning of the patient's experience through the process of empathy.

*Empathy* is a central concept in the fields of psychology, psychotherapy, and medical communication (Cormier, Cormier, & Weisser, 1984; Goldstein, 1980; Northouse & Northouse, 1985). The pioneering work of the psychologist Carl Rogers (1951, 1957) best describes the meaning of the concept of empathy. Although he examined empathy primarily in terms of the psychotherapeutic relationship, Rogers conceptualized empathy in a way that can apply easily to the medical professional-patient relationship. According to Rogers, empathy is a process that involves being sensitive to another individual's changing feelings and "connecting" emotionally to that other person. Empathy involves a process of "living for a time in the other person's life," entering his or her private perceptual world, and seeing events through his or her eyes. Empathy involves avoiding judgments about what the other is feeling and instead trying to understand fully those feelings from the person's perspective.

Health professionals witness countless cues to a patient's emotional experience.

These cues are found in what the patient says and how he or she says it, as well as in the patient's actions and expressions (Friedman, 1979). In Chapter 7 we examined the importance of words and how they express what a patient feels. The words chosen by the health professional likewise carry a great deal of information. Empathy also involves correctly perceiving what a patient is expressing through nonverbal cues and responding in a manner that conveys understanding. As we will see later in this chapter, a practitioner's accurate reading of the emotion displayed on the patient's face or expressed in the patient's voice, body movements, and other nonverbal cues is central to grasping what the individual is feeling, and hence to empathizing with the patient (DiMatteo & Taranta, 1979).

Empathy necessarily involves letting a patient know that he or she is understood (Kalish, 1971; Rogers, 1957). Such communication goes far beyond simply saying, "I understand how you feel," or nodding knowingly. Rather, empathy requires, first, the *accurate* perception of the patient's emotional experience and then the communication back to the patient in words or in gestures precisely what is understood. As we will see later in this chapter, nonverbal cues play an important role in this communication.

Empathy is not sympathy. Sympathy is the concern, sorrow, or pity that one person may feel or show for another. But "empathy is an attempt to feel *with* another person, to understand the other's feelings from the *other's* point of view. Empathy is the sharing of another's feelings and not the expression of one's own feelings" (Northouse & Northouse, 1985, p. 31). Thus, in empathy, the focus is on the client with the problem, and not on the listener. "Empathy is not denial, avoidance, false optimism, obfuscation of the issues by clever professional jargon, nor inappropriate cheering. An empathic therapeutic bond, on the contrary, requires contact, an accurate description and sharing of knowledge, . . . and the creation of a safe environment to share inner doubts" (Bertman & Krant, 1977, p. 643).

The necessity of focusing solely on the experience of the patient requires subverting the experience and feelings of the health professional. In the therapeutic interaction, only one individual's emotional needs can be dealt with at a given time. The goal of the medical practitioner-patient relationship is for the former to care for the latter, not vice versa. In the most effective of therapeutic interactions, the health professional's feelings can be expressed only if doing so is in the best interest of the patient.

## DEVELOPING EMPATHY

As we will see later in this chapter, people vary widely in their skills of understanding and expressing nonverbal cues, as well as in their sensitivity to the feelings of other people. Medical practitioners whose skills are lacking can develop their capacity for empathic communication with patients. This development requires effort and discipline on three important dimensions (Bertman & Krant, 1977):

The *cognitive* component of empathy requires the professional to observe patient behavior carefully and to know the meaning of what is observed. Empathy depends upon knowing (intellectually, at least) what constitutes the physical experience of a particular illness or injury and what its psychological effects might be on the patient. Important facts (such as in Chapter 12) about the psychological realities of illness are available from the field of health psychology. These include the effects on patients' thoughts, emotions, and behaviors when they are faced with the crisis of illness.

The *affective* component of empathy involves, as described above, being sensitive to the patient's feelings and listening to what the patient is saying about those feelings in words, in gestures, and in actions. The affective component of empathy involves the health professional's relating what he or she perceives to be the patient's emotions to his or her own emotional experience.

Finally, the *communicative* component of empathy focuses on communicating to the patient that he or she is understood, that the health professional knows the facts about what the patient is experiencing and perceives accurately what the patient is currently feeling. Empathy requires that somehow it be communicated back to the patient that he or she is understood.

Box 8–1 describes practitioner-patient negotiation, a related element of therapeutic communication.

## THE OUTCOMES OF EMPATHY

A medical practitioner's empathy for a patient's emotional state can have some important implications for the care and treatment of the patient. First, the accuracy of diagnosis can sometimes be enhanced when the medical practitioner is aware of and understands the emotional as well as the physical state of the patient. For example, a patient who experiences symptoms of anxiety, such as rapid pulse and breathing, sweating, and general agitation might be experiencing severe anxiety or panic, or may have hyperthyroidism (an overactive thyroid gland) or a prolapse of the mitral valve of the heart. The practitioner who is aware of the true (rather than just the apparent) emotional state of the patient would be able to distinguish between a physical and an emotional explanation for the presenting problem. At least he or she would know which possibility to pursue. The accuracy of diagnosis will be significantly enhanced by taking into account the patient's true feelings.

Second, empathy can enhance the process of medical treatment. Consider the patient who has had a heart attack. Panic and feelings of terror can be extremely dangerous for that patient. Research has demonstrated that frightening, upsetting, or negative emotional situations can have a very disturbing effect on cardiac rhythms and the electrical impulses of the hearts of cardiac patients (Lynch, Thomas, Mills, Malinow, Katcher, 1974). Yet, typical emergency care from home to hospital room attends very little to calming the patient and helping him or her to feel secure and emotionally at ease. Instead, practitioners hurry about and treat the patient impersonally, as if he or she is not able to function as a thinking human being. The patient is not in control of what is being done to him or her (Cousins, 1983). Obviously, it is good medicine for medical practitioners to attend to the patient's emotions as well as physical condition. Calming the patient with sensitivity and understanding may actually save his or her life.

Third, when patients feel understood by their medical practitioners, they are also more likely to follow treatment recommendations (Alpert, 1964; Hurtado, Greenlick, & Columbo, 1973; Squier, 1990). When given the opportunity to express their emotional needs and concerns, patients feel they can trust their practitioners to operate in their best interest. They feel that their real concerns have been addressed and that they have contributed to the decisions made about their care. In fact, a medical practitioner's ability to empathize with patients and to understand their concerns is a strong determinant of patients' satisfaction with care and their willingness to return to the practitioner in the future (Doyle & Ware, 1977; Aday & Anderson, 1975). On the other hand, studies show that patients who are not satisfied with the interpersonal

## HOW PRACTITIONER AND PATIENT INFLUENCE
## EACH OTHER: PRACTITIONER-PATIENT NEGOTIATION

Patients and practitioners have different perspectives on illness and injury. The most severe and terrifying threats to patients' well-being are common occurrences to medical practitioners. In one sense, pain and tragedy are just part of the job.

Practitioners and patients tend to differ in their perspective on a medical problem, their beliefs about its cause, and their goals for treatment (Leigh & Reiser, 1980). Patients are the consumers of medical care, and although they may not say so explicitly, patients do make the final decisions about what they will and will not do. Continuation of a therapeutic regimen depends upon the patient's initiative and perseverance.

As we saw in Chapter 7, patients possess information that is critically important to diagnosis and treatment. For example, they alone can describe their physical sensations, the complete history of the illness, and the manner in which the illness affects their lives. Patients must give their informed consent for procedures that are offered to them. Thus, patients usually have a firm basis for negotiation with their medical practitioners.

Because of their different perspectives, the relationship between medical practitioner and patient usually involves some conflict (Freidson, 1970; Balint, 1957). This conflict is typically best resolved through *negotiation.* Negotiation is the action or process of arriving at the settlement of some matter through discussion and compromise. Sometimes patients and medical practitioners negotiate over the treatment (such as whether painkilling medications will be given). Sometimes they negotiate over how the illness will be viewed (as potentially dangerous and needing hospitalization, or as something that can be treated at home). Sometimes they negotiate about whether unpleasant treatments are needed, and how they will be taken.

Negotiation is desirable in the practitioner-patient relationship. When communication is open between the two parties, there is an opportunity to resolve disparate perspectives that have the same ultimate goal: the health of the patient. When conflicts between practitioners and patients are not resolved, the alternatives are coercion, sabotage, rejection, and pseudo-mutuality (where both pretend to be getting along but are really very angry at each other). With a negotiated resolution, both parties can achieve satisfaction of their own individual needs and perspectives.

The most successful medical practitioners are those who can successfully negotiate with patients: ". . . They sense the patient's worries, misconceptions about the illness, and hesitations about treatment. They create an atmosphere which encourages patients to present their perspective, on one hand, and encourages them to hear the clinician's perspective, on the other hand" (Lazare, Eisenthal, & Stoeckle, 1978, p. 129). Lazare and colleagues, working at the Massachusetts General Hospital in Boston, found that physicians who were the most successful in their treatment of patients were sensitive to patients' feelings, and were warm, empathic, and understanding. They were best able to negotiate with patients to find effective solutions to the illness problem.

aspects of the care they receive from their practitioners engage in doctor shopping until they find a doctor they feel cares about them (Kasteler, Kane, Olsen, & Thetford, 1976; DiMatteo & DiNicola, 1982). Of course, an additional incentive to the medical practitioner in these days of oversupply and increasing competition among medical professionals is that greater patient satisfaction often translates into greater popularity among patients, more referrals, and a more successful practice.

Finally, when patients are satisfied with the emotional care provided by their medical professionals, they are less likely to bring malpractice suits when they are dissatisfied with the outcome of their treatment. A medical professional who has empathy for a patient is able to explore the patient's feelings of disappointment at a poor outcome and work with the patient to find a solution that is mutually acceptable to them both. Research shows that patients often become angry as a result of a failed treatment, even when they have known ahead of time the risks that accompanied it. If their medical professionals are cold and rejecting toward them, patients tend to express their anger through a third party, the malpractice attorney (Blum, 1960; Vaccarino, 1977). This is not to suggest that *malpractice*, the negligent practice of medicine, does not occur or is only in the mind of an emotionally distressed patient. Things do sometimes go wrong, and medical professionals do make mistakes. But research shows that medical professionals who are sued by their patients tend to be those who are unwilling to communicate openly and to work out a mutually satisfactory solution. Instead, they tend to be emotionally, or even physically, "unavailable," and to send their bill as usual (Vaccarino, 1977). On the other hand, medical practitioners who have empathy for their patients' feelings are willing and able to work constructively with them to

rectify what went wrong and to compensate them for their losses while avoiding litigation.

## EMPATHY AND PRACTITIONER-PATIENT RAPPORT

A term that is used in several places in this chapter and throughout this book, *rapport*, is central to understanding the medical practitioner-patient relationship. The term *rapport* describes a relationship characterized by mutual trust and emotional affinity (or liking) (Snipe, 1979). The word *mutual* suggests that both practitioner and patient respect each other and meet on the common ground of their goal of achieving the patient's health.

There has been a limited amount of research on rapport to date, and what has been done reveals that health psychologists use the term *rapport* somewhat loosely. In one study, for example, researchers had ten female psychiatric social workers evaluate the interpersonal style of nine family practice residents during videotaped interactions with their patients (Harrigan, Oxman, & Rosenthal, 1985). They rated the physicians' behavior so that those who were rated as most accepting, open, active, pleasant, and highest on closeness, positivity, leniency, calmness, and friendliness were identified as the "high-rapport" physicians. Other researchers have identified as high in rapport with their patients those physicians who received high scores on measures of patient satisfaction (DiMatteo & Taranta, 1979).

## MAINTAINING OPTIMISM AND THE WILL TO LIVE

Another important aspect of a practitioner's bedside manner involves fostering patients' optimism and the will to live (Cousins, 1976). A heart attack victim, for example, is likely to be strongly influenced

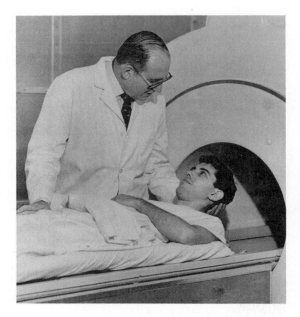

Bedside manner involves fostering the patient's optimism and the will to live.
SOURCE: Yoav Levy/Phototake NYC

by the expectations of medical practitioners for recovery (Cousins, 1983). A woman who has had a *mastectomy* (surgical removal of the breast because of cancer) may be initially tremendously affected by the response of various health professionals to her appearance after her surgery (Berger & Bostwick, 1984). Feelings of hope or despair can be fostered in patients by the behavior of their medical professionals.

Medical professionals can strongly affect patients' expectations partly because patients typically have little experience with the illness conditions they are facing. They may not know the statistics for survival; they may be unaware of different possibilities for recovery. They turn to their medical professionals for clues about what to expect. The clues come in various forms but almost always have an impact. Practitioners' expectations can operate in the manner of self-fulfilling prophecies

(see Rosenthal, 1969). Although positive expectations can spur patients on to work toward recovery, poor expectations can bring about poor outcomes. And patients can be led by pronouncements of doom from their physicians to give up hope for their recovery.

The potential for medical practitioners to influence the psychological, and in turn the physical, state of patients has been demonstrated in research. One study found a significant increase in the sudden deaths of heart attack patients in the hospital during or immediately after *ward rounds* conducted by the medical staff (Jarvinen, 1955). Ward rounds are formal procedures in which patients are presented as cases before many doctors and other health professionals. The cases are discussed while patients are present, but they are typically unable to participate. Patients are examined while members of the health care team look on. Sudden death may have been precipitated in cardiac patients by ward rounds because the emotional distress experienced by patients had a dangerous, negative effect on their cardiac rhythms (Lynch, et al., 1974).

Many patients, particularly those in busy hospitals, desperately desire information about their medical conditions and treatments but cannot get it. Some try to gather clues even from irrelevant sources. For example, a patient may try to "read" clues about his or her condition from the facial expressions of the medical professionals who stand at the bedside. Or he or she may conclude that there is some significance in how fast the physicians write things down on the medical chart. Very often, patients misinterpret ambiguous statements or responses. For example, a physician might mention that the patient has *malignant hypertension*, which is high blood pressure that is progressively getting worse. The patient may assume that this term has something to do with cancer (which it does not), and experience hopelessness and depression as a result.

Expectations can, on the other hand, contribute positively to the patient's condition. Medical professionals can tap patients' hidden emotional and intellectual resources, and help to harness these to contribute to healing. Perhaps the best known general phenomenon of this sort is the placebo effect (which we considered in detail in earlier chapters). Recall that a placebo is an inert substance that may have a physiological as well as a psychological effect upon a person (Beecher, 1955). The medical practitioner's expectations for a good outcome can be transmitted to the patient and can serve to better the patient's physical state.

Practitioners who are confident and reassuring and who have rapport with their patients and empathy for patients' feelings, can bring about positive therapeutic effects. The practitioner's faith in the treatment and in the patient's response to it may foster more positive health outcomes in the patient.

The strength of positive expectations has been one of the primary forces motivating the success of medicine throughout its entire history. In the early days of medicine, patients were given dangerous substances, such as arsenic tonics, and were subjected to treatments, such as blood letting and having holes drilled in their heads (Shapiro, 1960). Despite these barbaric treatments, patients often regained their health primarily because of the strength of positive expectations and the therapeutic effect of the practitioner-patient relationship (Eisenberg, 1977). Likewise, in today's medicine, with its emphasis on high technology, the therapeutic effect of positive expectations is still of central importance to effective patient care.

See Box 8–2 for a discussion of the conflict that sometimes exists between the technical and the interpersonal aspects of medical care.

# Nonverbal Communication and Patient-Practitioner Relationships

■ ■ ■ ■ ■

"So, how are things going, Frank?" asked Dr. Flynn. "Are you able to take your medications twice a day? Or are there some difficulties we need to work out?" Dr. Flynn had just finished taking Frank's blood pressure. He held Frank's arm firmly as he removed the blood pressure cuff, and then checked Frank's wrist pulse.

"Oh, I guess I'm, uh, doing okay . . ." Frank said, looking away.

Dr. Flynn recognized Frank's discomfort in his halting speech and averted glance. Something was not right. Dr. Flynn decided to pursue the issue. He let go of Frank's wrist. "Are the medications themselves giving you any problems? You know, a few people run into some difficulties with these medications. There are alternatives."

Frank began hesitatingly, "Uh, well, I don't know if it's the medications or what, but I started having some problems with, you know, with my wife, uh, soon after I started them. . . ." He looked down at the floor tiles.

"Sexual problems?" Dr. Flynn asked gently.

"Uh, yeah . . ." Frank hesitated.

"Impotence?"

"Uh-huh," answered Frank without looking up. "So I, uh, I stopped taking them for a while."

"I can understand that." said Dr. Flynn. "Sometimes this type of medication can bring impotence as a side effect. Let's look into changing your medications and clear up this problem right away, okay?"

In this example, Dr. Flynn recognized Frank's embarrassment and its relation to his difficulties in following the treatment regimen. Dr. Flynn was sensitive to Frank's initial reluctance to discuss things, and he met Frank's disclosures with understanding and warmth.

Of course, the fact that Dr. Flynn did these things may be obvious. *How* he did them needs some analysis.

Note, for example, that Dr. Flynn first established some legitimate physical con-

tact with his patient by checking his wrist pulse and taking his blood pressure. He could have had the nurse do this before he arrived in the examining room, but he chose to do it himself. Dr. Flynn also paid attention when Frank looked away as he answered the first question. Frank was clearly uncomfortable about something. Dr. Flynn paid attention to the patient's halting speech and his use of "uh" several times in a few sentences. Dr. Flynn noticed that his patient looked embarrassed. By continuing to be warm and accepting, Dr. Flynn provided a safe environment in which the patient could disclose his distress. Dr.

BOX
8–2

## TECHNICAL OR TENDER LOVING CARE: SHOULD PATIENTS BE FORCED TO CHOOSE?

A common stereotype of medical professionals is that they fall into two camps: the "technical wizards" and the "nice guys." According to the stereotype, the former are not very nice and the latter are not very good at what they do. The gruff, brusk, nasty surgeon with virtuoso finger tips who saves ten lives a day is a case in point. Is this stereotype accurate? Must patients choose between technically good care and tender loving care but never be able to have both? This question has been addressed in several ways, but the answer is not yet clear.

Numerous studies of patient satisfaction with medical care have been done by giving questionnaires to patients who are asked to rate their doctors (Ware, Davies-Avery, & Stewart, 1978). On these questionnaire surveys, patients are asked to indicate their evaluation of the *technical* quality of the care delivered to them by their doctors, as well as their evaluation of the *socio-emotional* aspects of care. Statements indicating technical proficiency are concerned with whether the patient thinks the doctor is competent and knowledgeable and knows what he or she is doing. Statements about the socio-emotional dimension of care are concerned with whether the patient feels cared for, and whether the health professional expresses concern for the patient's feelings.

Results of this research show that patients make very little distinction between the technical and the socioemotional aspects of their care. If they rate a medical professional high on one of these dimensions, they tend to rate him or her high on the other dimension as well. One researcher has noted that this finding can be explained by the fact that patients are simply poor judges of physician competence (Ben-Sira, 1980). In fact, some critics of the validity and usefulness of patient satisfaction measures argue that patients cannot possibly distinguish between the dimensions because they cannot judge the technical quality of their care.

Flynn attended to his patient's *meta-communication*.

## METACOMMUNICATION

Messages of warmth, empathy, understanding, and the essence of bedside manner are not always communicated directly through words. In fact, particularly in the medical setting, such messages are conveyed instead through *metacommunication*. *Metacommunication* is defined as communication about communication (Watzlawick, Beavin, & Jackson, 1967).

Consider the following example. With a smile on his face, looking directly at his male patient, the physician says in a kind, jovial voice, "Now, get out of here. I don't want to see you for at least two months." What conclusion do you draw? Is the physician angry, or rejecting? Despite his words, he probably is not. Rather, he may be joking or, even more likely, encouraging. He may be happily telling the patient that he is getting healthy again and does not need to keep coming back for further treatments.

Suppose, on the other hand, a physician answers an inquisitive patient with the following response: "Sure, Mrs. Jones, we'll talk about it." While saying this, however, the physician looks away from Mrs. Jones,

One study provides some intriguing evidence that may discount this last explanation (DiMatteo & DiNicola, 1981). This research examined physician performance as rated not only by patients but by peer physicians and faculty teachers as well. The results showed surprising similarity to the data from the patient satisfaction studies. Not only did patients fail to make the technical-socioemotional distinction but physicians failed to make the distinction as well. Physicians who were quite capable of judging the technical abilities of their associates did not judge technical proficiency to be at odds with socio-emotional care. In other words, the physicians who were technically proficient were also good at providing TLC!

An explanation for this finding is not entirely clear. Perhaps physicians who are technically competent are comfortable enough with what they are doing to provide good psychosocial care as well. On the other hand, those whose technical skills are lacking may be too insecure and defensive to deal with patients' feelings. Or it is possible that physicians' care of their patients' socioemotional needs actually improves the physical outcomes of patient care, thus reflecting on their technical abilities.

A different approach to the question has been taken by Hall, Roter, & Katz (1988). These researchers analyzed the audiotapes and transcripts of physician-patient interactions. Speech characteristics, verbal communications, and voice tone of the physicians were examined. The results showed that physicians tended to adopt a style characterized by information giving and proficiency *or* a social orientation (involving social conversation and positive reinforcement). Those who spent more time involved in technical aspects of the medical encounter spent relatively little time in social conversation and positive reinforcement. However, physicians who provided more information had a less bored voice quality than did those who failed to offer much information. This study suggests that physicians tend to engage in one or the other (that is, technical or socioemotional) orientation but not both. This important question needs further research in order to clarify the details of physician style in caring for patients.

stands up with his body oriented away from the patient, and places his hand on the knob of the door leading out of Mrs. Jones's room. Do you have much faith that Mrs. Jones will get her questions answered? Clearly, metamessages tell a great deal more than do simple words.

Suppose that a nurse tells her patient that changing the dressings on a very sore wound may be painful. While explaining what must be done, the nurse places one hand firmly on the patient's shoulder, makes eye contact with the patient, and speaks in a kind and comforting voice. The total message is that the treatment is necessary, that it may be somewhat painful, and that the nurse will provide as much comfort as the patient needs. The nurse clearly is empathizing with the patient's distress.

Metamessages can be complex, such as the ones above, or they can be quite simple. In the absence of any other cues, a smile will probably convey goodwill of some sort, but the intensity and the intention of that goodwill are unclear. A more complex message might combine a smile with five seconds of eye contact. (Try it—that's a surprisingly long time!) The communication is becoming more immediate and more intense. Then pair this message with the verbal statement "I think you're going to be okay." This complex message gives a fortunate patient good reason for optimism and hope.

Metamessages are not all intentional (Watzlawick & Weakland, 1977). Suppose that a patient is being prepared for minor surgery. Lying on the operating table, she exhibits tremendous muscular tension. She fails to respond quickly to several of the physician's verbal commands, such as to turn her head. She asks the same question three times because she cannot remember the answer she has been given. The sensitive nurse recognizes these metamessages as cues to anxiety. She says to the patient,

"You're doing very well. This will be all done before you know it," and she asks the patient what she can do to make her more comfortable. The patient, who initially felt distress and concern, now relaxes and feels that her concerns are understood.

Metamessages are not always clear and straightforward (Weakland, 1976). A patient may wish to hide the fact that he has been inconsistent in taking his prescribed medication. The physician asks whether he has followed the medication regimen as prescribed and the patient answers, "Of course, why wouldn't I?" But the patient looks away, despite the physician's attempt to maintain eye contact. The metacommunication says that something is amiss, although precisely what that is may be quite unclear. The patient's failure to maintain eye contact with the physician is a comment on the words, a communication about the communication. There is no way to know for sure precisely what the metamessage means, however. It is a comment on the message, but that is all. In the case above, the patient may be unintentionally indicating that his words are not true. On the other hand, he may be conveying that such an issue is none of the doctor's business. Or he may be reacting negatively to the doctor's question because his wife also nags him about taking his medication and he is tired of it.

Metamessages can be of various sorts. Metacommunication can consist of actions. For example, a patient may say that she is satisfied with her physician's treatment but she refuses to pay, or even work out terms to pay, her bill. One message communicates satisfaction while another conveys just the opposite. Many metamessages are conveyed through nonverbal cues, but they are not limited to the nonverbal channel of communication.

Finally, while the meanings of words can be checked in the dictionary and people can be held to the precise meaning of what they say, there is no exact metacommunication lexicon. Although some people may claim that they know the exact meaning of various nonverbal cues, such claims are not supported by research. There are some consistencies in meaning, as we will see below, but these are by no means simple. Other types of metacommunications, actions for example, can also be complex. Not paying a bill or not returning to a particular physician may indicate anger and disappointment—or something completely different. The existence of metacommunication cues admonish the receiver of the message to explore the precise meaning of the whole picture that is communicated from the patient.

# Nonverbal Communication Research

Health psychologists working with medical professionals have learned a great deal about the role of one major type of metacommunication in medical settings: nonverbal communication. Recognition of the role of empathy and the importance of the physician's affective (emotional) behavior with the patient has spurred the study of nonverbal communication between patients and medical practitioners (Harrigan et al., 1985). Let us take a look at an example of how nonverbal messages operate in patient care.

■ ■ ■ ■ ■

The young intern was ebullient. After only one month on the service, he made a definitive diagnosis that had eluded his colleagues and even his teachers. He burst into the patient's room just in time for the beginning of morning rounds. It was 8:00 A.M.

He began to describe the case to his residents and attending physician: "Mr. Anglin is a 45-year-old man who entered the hospital seven days ago with a chief complaint

of severe headaches." In his intensity and excitement, he did not acknowledge Mr. Anglin, who lay in the bed before him. The intern described several of the findings from the physical examinations and tests and then he summed up, "On the basis of new data from the bronchoscopy and biopsy, I suggest the diagnosis of a right lung primary with brain metastasis."

"Brilliant, Doctor," responded the attending physician, a stern old man who rarely gave anyone a compliment. "Excellent work." The intern was beaming; his resident smiled with pride. The intern had been the one to suggest the workup to rule out lung cancer, but it could not be ruled out. And it had spread to the patient's brain.

A look of happiness and excitement appeared on the faces of the young physicians on the medical team. They were proud to be experiencing firsthand the diagnostic capabilities of modern medicine. They had been intensely frustrated for an entire week, trying to diagnose the patient's headaches. They were puzzled by what looked like tumors on the patient's brain. Mr. Anglin looked up at them, and for a moment, caught their exuberance. He smiled.

And then Mr. Anglin watched the faces of the physicians metamorphose into a kind of horror. A couple of the faces twitched with tension. A few eyes widened. Some jaws were clenched. And in two seconds the whole display was over. He saw the faces harden one by one into sternness, and thought, and purpose.

The patient was unable to put into words what he was perceiving. He did not know the meaning of the medical terms these doctors were using. He did not know what was wrong with him. But some part of his consciousness recognized the truth precisely and without hesitation. His heart began to race; he felt faint. Yet he could not articulate anything. It all seemed remote and unreal.

Mr. Anglin's eyes, huge and pleading, met the intern's. The intern looked away, as if the facts they now shared were too painful to acknowledge. Then the doctors walked out of the room one by one to continue their morning rounds and the busy routine of diagnosis.

As we see here, patients are extremely sensitive to the metacommunications of their medical professionals. The verbal messages that patients typically encounter in medical settings are likely to be confusing. Oftentimes, medical professionals simply withhold information from their patients. They may not have the time or the inclination to explain things to them. However, as we saw in Chapter 7, patients do not exist comfortably in an information vacuum. They try to find out, for example, how serious their conditions really are and what the likely prognoses might be. For many reasons, including their own peace of mind and their desire to take control of their own lives, patients search for the answers they need.

Because illness often forces patients into a dependent state, many seek the approval of their health professionals. They look for cues that they are liked or favored by those who care for them (Friedman, 1982).

By means of their nonverbal cues, medical practitioners signal to their patients the extent to which they are willing and able to let down their own emotional defenses and really listen to their patients' expressions of pain, frustration, confusion, and sadness. "One might ask how often physicians signal that they cannot endure their patients' pain, putting a stop to sharing even before it gets started" (Bertman & Krant, 1977, p. 643).

Patients often try to judge whether things are going well in their treatment by looking to their practitioners' nonverbal cues (Friedman, 1982). Potential problems can arise, of course, when patients interpret nonverbal cues in ways that were not intended. For example, a facial expression brought about by the practitioner's fatigue, confusion, or distress about an entirely different matter may be interpreted by a patient as evidence that the practitioner is trying to conceal the patient's grave condition. Finally, many patients know little about the technical aspects of their medical care and may attempt to judge its quality on the basis of their practitioners' interpersonal behavior (DiMatteo & DiNicola, 1982).

Several major studies have shown that practitioners who are able to control their nonverbal cues and convey precisely what they want to their patients elicit greater satisfaction and cooperation than do those without such skill (DiMatteo, Taranta, Friedman, & Prince, 1980; DiMatteo, Hays, & Prince, 1986).

## READING PATIENTS' NONVERBAL CUES

As we saw earlier in this chapter, patients experience a wide range of complex emotions during the process of their medical treatment. Yet, there may be very few opportunities for patients to express their feelings verbally. Patients are often too intimidated by the treatment situation and by the behavior of their health professionals to say what they feel. Most patients, for example, are reluctant to say that they are distressed or confused or angry about a prescribed treatment regimen. Instead, they look uncomfortable and anxious. Further, when patients are asked in the perfunctory manner typical of modern medical care: "Any questions?" they say no with their words but often something else with their bodies and their faces. Patients' metacommunications can convey that no is not the complete truth (Cormier et al., 1984).

Typically, patients have little experience hiding or controlling their expressions of emotion in the medical setting. Patients' nonverbal cues provide a valuable window to their feelings (Friedman, 1982). The medical practitioner who can recognize a patient's confusion and tension, and pick up cues to other emotions is able to gather much needed information to care for the patient. If the practitioner can recognize cues of dissatisfaction, negative affect, and distress, he or she can deal with the problems from which these emotions arise before the patient terminates the therapeutic relationship, aborts the treatment, or retaliates with malpractice litigation. Likewise, the practitioner may recognize signs of a patient's enthusiasm and optimism, and harness these positive emotions in support of the patient's recovery.

The nonverbal communication skills of many physicians have been studied in research using various measurement or assessment instruments. These instruments measure both *sensitivity to patients' nonverbal cues* (that is, the ability to understand what patients are communicating with their nonverbal expressions) and the ability to control *emotional expressions by means of nonverbal cues.*

In several studies researchers assessed the ability of physicians to understand the emotion conveyed in others' facial expressions, body movements, and tone of voice. They also asked the physicians to try to express emotion intentionally through their facial, body, and voice tone nonverbal cues. In addition, several of each physician's patients were interviewed about their satisfaction with the physician's bedside manner. In one of the studies, patients' cooperation in returning for scheduled medical visits in the clinic was also examined. It was found that the physicians who scored high on the tests of nonverbal communication skill received significantly higher evaluations and greater cooperation from their patients than did those who scored low (DiMatteo et al., 1980; DiMatteo et al., 1986).

## DISSECTING NONVERBAL CUES

Considerable research has been conducted on nonverbal communication in medical as well as other settings. The findings have some important implications for patient care.

**Touch.**   Possibly more than any other component of nonverbal communication, touch is believed to serve the goal of practitioner-patient rapport. Touch can be extremely soothing to ill patients. Touch can communicate reassurance, comfort, and caring (Montagu, 1978; Blondis & Jackson, 1977). But touch can communicate some other not-so-helpful messages as well.

As with all metacommunication, the abstract meaning of a touch cannot be known. Its meaning depends upon the context (particularly the emotional context) in which the touch takes place. Suppose that a patient is on his way to surgery. His kind, empathic surgeon with whom he has rapport stands next to him as he is about to be wheeled into the operating room. The surgeon puts her hand on the patient's arm, squeezes it firmly, and says, "Are you ready to lick this together? I'm ready if you are." The therapeutic alliance is forged. Another patient, however, meets with her doctor and tries to express concern that she does not understand some things about her intended surgery. That physician interrupts her statements of concern, puts his hand on her arm and squeezes it gently, saying, "My dear, my dear. Why do you ask so many questions? You don't need to bother yourself about these things. I'm the doctor." This latter touch occurs in a very different (verbal) context than the former.

Touch can be a powerful indicator of caring, concern, and solidarity. Or it can simply be an indicator of power (Henley, 1977). Health professionals touch patients, but patients typically do not touch health professionals. In fact, were you to reach out and touch your doctor first, before he or she touched you, you might experience an awkward interpersonal moment. The meaning of the touch would not be as clear as if the physician initiated it.

Thus, the assumption that touching patients is always good is a wrong one. Like all nonverbal cues, touch depends upon context. One study, for example, analyzed videotapes of 34 first-time visits between a patient and a family physician (Larsen & Smith, 1981). Only the initial interview portion of the visit was studied. The videotapes were scored by trained judges who recorded, among other things, whether or not, and how much, the physician touched the patient. After the visit each patient filled out a questionnaire regarding his or her satisfaction with the visit. The surprising finding was that the more patients were touched by their physicians, the *less* satisfied they were with the visit. The authors suggest that because these were initial interviews, touching may have been interpreted by patients not as supportive but rather as aggressive and as an indication of power. It seems that it was necessary for the physicians to have established rapport with their patients before touching them. A further finding was that patients who were touched more were found to understand less of what their physicians told them, perhaps because being touched during the initial medical visit was distracting or disconcerting to them. (Of course, all of our interpretations must be made with caution because of the correlational nature of the data.)

**Eye Contact.** Eye contact can be a very powerful nonverbal cue that can intensify the emotion present in a given situation (Ellsworth, 1975). A pleasant interaction in which the health professional is warm and understanding with a patient is likely to be experienced as even more positive when accompanied by eye contact (La Crosse, 1975). An upsetting or threatening situation, on the other hand, will be experienced as even more negative when accompanied by eye contact (Ellsworth, Friedman, Perlick, & Hoyt, 1978). If a patient is having a hostile interchange with a medical professional, chances are good that things will be worse if the health professional stares the patient straight in the eye than if the health professional fails to make eye contact. Of course, excessive, almost constant staring at a patient can have a very negative interpersonal effect no matter what the context (Friedman, 1982; Larsen & Smith, 1981). In fact, in one study, physicians judged to have a high degree of rapport with their patients were found to engage in only moderate eye contact, less than that exhibited by physicians rated as having low rapport with their patients (Harrigan et al., 1985).

Excessive staring is not usually the problem in medical interactions, however. Typically, health professionals fail to maintain enough eye contact. They look at the chart or at the patient's body more than at the patient's face. They tend to avoid the intimacy and immediacy that eye contact represents (Harrigan et al., 1985).

How much eye contact is just right is not precisely clear. Health professionals must gauge the effects of their behavior on patients in an effort to determine what contributes to and what detracts from good bedside manner. One thing is clear, however. Eye contact is a very powerful means of metacommunication. Used wisely, eye contact can significantly enhance the positive emotional impact of the therapeutic relationship and thus aid in promoting the well-being of the patient.

**Facial Expression.** The face can tell a great deal about a person, particularly his or her physical and emotional state (Izard, 1977). Fatigue may appear as a long-lasting expression, distrust as a fleeting one. But what makes facial expressions intriguing and sometimes difficult to pin down is that more than any other nonverbal cue they can be controlled (Ekman & Friesen, 1974).

Research demonstrates that when physicians can control their facial expressions of emotion and convey what they intend, their patients are quite satisfied with the medical care they receive. Further, medical professionals who can understand the meaning of their patients' facial expressions of emotion have been found in research to be able to elicit greater satisfaction and cooperation with treatment (DiMatteo et al., 1980; DiMatteo et al., 1986).

**Tone of Voice.** How something is said by a physician or a patient is as important as what is said. Variations in the pitch, loudness, emphasis, and pacing of speech, as well as stutters and pauses, convey information about emotional states. These are called *extralinguistic cues*—cues outside the spoken language. Although we cannot always identify the precise extralinguistic cues we have heard, we rarely miss the emotional impact of these cues when we are spoken to. We know, for example, when we have heard an angry, hostile communication, although we might not identify it as faster and louder than a kind, relaxed communication. We probably would not notice that the hostile message is the one having more vocal emphasis on the verbs.

Patients may be unable to identify precisely what cues they have heard, but they are influenced by the voice tone and the specific vocal quality of their medical practitioners. One study found that the anger judged to be in a physician's voice when he was talking *about* alcoholics could be used

to predict accurately his rate of failure at getting alcoholic patients to enter a treatment program (Milmoe, Rosenthal, Blane, Chafetz, & Wolf, 1967). In another study the degree of hostility judged to be in the voices of both physicians and patients reflected the discomfort and interpersonal difficulties that resulted when patients attempted to ask questions (Hall, Roter, & Rand, 1981). Thus, medical professionals can convey a great deal, good and bad, to their patients through their voice tone. They can also learn a lot about their patients' emotions by listening carefully to what is conveyed in their patients' voices.

**Body Language.** Body movements and postures can convey a considerable amount of information about an individual's emotional state. This is particularly true because body cues are typically the least controlled of nonverbal messages. People may monitor their facial expressions, but typically do not (or cannot) monitor their body movements. Emotional expressions have been found in research to "leak" unintentionally through the body-movement channel. Thus, a patient's anxiety, depression, and distress, or conversely energy and positivity, may best be learned by watching how he or she walks, moves about, changes position, and so on. A person's stride may tell about self-confidence and hopefulness regarding his or her condition. Fidgeting and self-touching (such as pulling on earlobes, or playing with hair) may signify anxiety and the individual's unsureness about what he or she is stating verbally, and may even signal efforts to deceive (Riggio & Friedman, 1983; Friedman, Hall, & Harris, 1985).

Despite the fact that we do not know precisely what every nonverbal cue means, certain body movements and postures do convey certain important messages. Particular gestures of the health professional tend to be perceived positively by patients. For

Examples of facial expression and body movement cues from the research on nonverbal sensitivity by Rosenthal et al., 1979.
SOURCE: Courtesy of Professor Robert Rosenthal

example, while closed-arm positions tend to communicate coldness and rejection, open-arm positions convey warmth and immediacy (Spiegel & Machotka, 1974). Physicians judged to have a high degree of rapport with their patients were found in one study to exhibit more open-arm and -leg positions, greater forward lean, and more orientation of their bodies toward the patient than physicians judged to have a low degree of rapport. High-rapport physicians also sat closer to their patients (Harrigan et al., 1985). Patients have been found to be most satisfied with a physician who orients his or her body in the patient's direction and who leans forward toward the patient instead of backward and away from the patient (Larsen & Smith, 1981). Similarly, in research on psychotherapists, head nods, hand gestures, and a slight forward lean when talking with clients has been found to increase clients' perceptions of the warmth and friendliness of their therapists (La Crosse, 1975; Smith-Hanen, 1977).

Are some nonverbal cues more important than others in the medical therapeutic setting? One study examined the combined impact of many nonverbal cues of medical professionals in order to determine which were the most important in conveying an overall positive impression in interaction with a patient (Harrigan et al., 1985). In this study, nine family practice residents were each videotaped during the interview portion of medical visits with two of their patients. The initial minute of the interview and a minute chosen randomly from the midportion of the interview were selected from each of the two interviews. The physicians were evaluated by independent judges (psychiatric nurses) on a global measure of their rapport with the patient. Several nonverbal cues were found to affect judgments of rapport differentially. Cues of bodily alignment (particularly body orientation and arm and leg position) tended to be more important in influencing the ratings than did specific nonverbal actions such as smiles, gestures, and nods, although the latter were still important. Body orientation toward the patient, and open-arm and -leg positions tended to have a very strong effect on ratings of rapport. These conveyed immediacy and a strong emotional connection (Mehrabian, 1972) particularly when coupled with forward lean and mutual gaze.

## THE COMMUNICATION OF EMOTION

In the medical-care setting both practitioners and patients often have strong feelings. Sometimes they feel happy and proud and hopeful. Unfortunately, they often feel sad, angry, confused, powerless, and exhausted. Whether they like it or not, and whether they will acknowledge it or not, practitioners and patients have such feelings. And whether it is their intention or not, patients' and practitioners' feelings influence the messages they convey to one another through their nonverbal cues.

As we saw above, nonverbal cues may operate alone to convey an emotion or they may add subtle information to a verbal message. Nonverbal cues can show how each person feels about what he or she is saying. And such a message may or may not be under the person's conscious control.

Nonverbal messages can be extremely powerful. For example, entire medical interactions may be regulated by the nonverbal cues of one or more of the interactants. A practitioner may completely determine, with his or her own nonverbal cues, just how much information the patient is able to convey and the number and quality of questions the patient is able to ask. These messages may include the avoidance of eye contact, a frowning facial expression, and the orientation of his or her head away from the patient, focusing totally on the chart. The practitioner might also interrupt the patient and dominate the interaction with amplitude (loudness) of voice. Of course, a practitioner can also convey some important supportive messages with nonverbal cues, as we noted earlier.

Understanding patients' nonverbal communications can give a medical practitioner an important advantage in caring for patients. By recognizing cues of dissatisfaction and negative affect in the body language of a patient, a practitioner can become aware of problems that the patient is unable to articulate. These can be dealt with and remedied before the patient leaves the relationship or fails to cooperate with treatment or retaliates with malpractice litigation.

There is growing evidence, then, that a practitioner's bedside manner consists partly of his or her ability to understand patients' metamessages and to convey metamessages that are supportive and beneficial to patients. (See Box 8–3 and Box 8–4 for further discussion of the role of interpersonal behavior in patient care.)

## CONCLUSION

Earlier in this chapter we examined briefly the typical frustrations and difficulties that patients face when they are ill. (These are examined in further detail in Chapter 12.) We also examined the practitioner-patient relationship, particularly the role of the medical professional in helping patients to deal with the emotional aspects of illness. We saw how important such help can be to a patient's emotional well-being. In the second part of the chapter we examined how that understanding is conveyed through nonverbal cues and other aspects of metacommunication.

In the next chapter we will examine the frustrations and difficulties of being a medical practitioner. We will see how the stresses and pressures of delivering medical care can sometimes motivate practitioners to be less than supportive in their treatment of patients. As we will see, medical professionals do not remain unaffected by their closeness to patients' experiences. They often feel their own emotional distress in response to what their patients are feeling. We will see how some health professionals become damaged by their own failed expectations and by a system of training that can be quite unresponsive to their needs as human beings.

## Summary

Chapter 8 discusses the role that medical professionals can play to help patients to withstand the emotional devastation of illness. It also discusses patient satisfaction with medical treatment.

I. Illness and injury can cause a patient to regress; that is, a person reverts to aspects of a childlike, dependent role. Patients often react like children to professionals' tendencies to infantilize their patients.

II. Bedside manner is important in a patient-professional relationship. Medical professionals often learn bedside

BOX
8–3

**TRANSITION TO PARENTHOOD:
HOW MEDICAL PROFESSIONALS CAN HELP**

Becoming parents for the first time can be a "crisis" for a couple. Their established family structure disintegrates and a new constellation must form. The transition can require a great deal of emotional energy, and the many changes that the couple faces can bring considerable emotional distress.

Pregnancy, labor, and delivery may be perceived by the couple as dangerous and painful. The financial pressures of new parenthood may be excessive. The couple may experience a great deal of anxiety about the process on which they are about to embark, as well as about the health of their baby and their own ability to meet the demands of parenthood.

Emotional support from medical professionals can do a great deal to help a couple make a smoother transition to parenthood, and simultaneously to develop as individuals and as partners. First, during the prenatal months, physicians, nurses, and other medical professionals can provide information and reassurances about the normal process of pregnancy. Involvement of the father in prenatal care can do a great deal to encourage the couple to approach the pregnancy as a joint venture, and to support each other emotionally. Childbirth preparation classes can help the couple to enhance their own sense of efficacy in dealing with the process of labor and delivery. When both spouses attend childbirth classes, they have the opportunity to get to know other couples who are having similar experiences and to provide and derive emotional support.

Direct support provided to the couple by the birth attendants (typically nurses and doctors) during the process of labor and delivery can have an important impact on the quality of the couple's experience of the birth and, as is believed by some, on their feelings toward the newborn infant. Fathers who participate in the process of labor and delivery and who spend more time with their infants following delivery report more feelings of attachment to their infants. Of course, attendance at childbirth is not enough to ensure a positive outcome; the father needs to feel involved and useful, and to be supported in that involvement by the medical staff (Herzberger & Potts, 1982).

manner by example. Some learn to be polite and considerate; others learn to be rude and insensitive. Bedside manner needs to be analyzed further to be understood.

A. Empathy is a process that involves being sensitive to another person's changing feelings and "connecting" emotionally to that person. By empathizing with the patient, a professional can make an effective diagnosis, enhance treatment, and make the patient more likely to follow a treatment regimen. The patient will also be satisfied that he or she has received proper care.

B. Fostering patients' optimism and

BOX
8–4

## DOES THE GENDER OF THE PHYSICIAN AFFECT THE DOCTOR-PATIENT RELATIONSHIP?

These days there are increasing opportunities for patients to choose among various potential physicians. One important dimension on which patients can choose is the gender of the doctor. But which should they select? Should a patient choose a male or a female physician?

The answer to this question is not simple, and it is only in recent years that researchers have been able to study the effects of physician gender on the therapeutic relationship. Until recently, few women practiced medicine in the primary adult-patient care specialties of family practice, internal medicine, and obstetrics and gynecology.

As we have seen in this and the previous chapters, patient satisfaction, cooperation, and even health status are affected by several aspects of physician behavior. This is particularly true of the communication of information and the affective tone of the relationship. These factors are influenced by the gender of the medical practitioner. In the realm of attitudes, research shows that female physicians and medical students are, on the average, more highly oriented than are males toward interpersonal relations in medical practice. Men, on the other hand, are more science-oriented and more reserved interpersonally, on the average. In the realm of behavior, research shows that female physicians spend more time in face-to-face contact with each patient than do male physicians. Women have been found to be more comfortable than men with patients' questions and with patient assertiveness. Women are also more likely to consider psychological issues in patient care (see Weisman & Teitelbaum, 1985, for a review).

Several studies have found either no differences in patients' preferences for male or female doctors, or a higher demand for women physicians. In general, the research shows that same-sex physician-patient interactions are characterized by more effective communication and by stronger rapport than are opposite-sex dyads (Weisman & Teitelbaum, 1985). Gender congruence (when physician and patient are of the same sex) may be a key factor in promoting communication, establishing rapport, and facilitating negotiation, particularly when patients discuss material of a highly personal or sensitive nature. When a long-term relationship is required, such as when the patient must make a major lifestyle change, a physician of the same sex may be just what the patient needs.

their will to live is another important aspect of effective care. Optimism and the will to live can influence a patient's condition, both physically and emotionally.

C. Nonverbal messages can be extremely powerful. Understanding patients' nonverbal messages can give a medical practitioner important advantages in caring for patients.

1. Metacommunication, communication about communication, is a complex, and occasionally unclear, process. In patient care, metacommunication can involve actions and subtle nonverbal signals about a patient's condition.

2. Practitioners who are able to recognize a patient's nonverbal cues can usually gather much needed medical information to care for the patient.

3. Touch can be a powerful indicator of reassurance, comfort, and caring. However, touching out of context can be detrimental to patient-practitioner rapport.

4. Eye contact can intensify the emotion of a given situation. Typically, health professionals fail to maintain proper eye contact with patients.

5. Facial expressions can reveal a person's emotional and physical state in great detail.

6. Variation in pitch, loudness, emphasis, and the pacing of speech reveal information about emotional states.

7. Body movements and postures are the least controlled of nonverbal messages. By observing how a patient walks, moves about, and so on, the practitioner can perceive anxiety, depression, and positivity among other things.

# Glossary

**affective component of empathy:** the component of empathy that involves being sensitive to the patient's feelings and listening to what the patient is saying about those feelings in words, in gestures, and in actions.

**bedside manner:** a broad and informal term used to refer to a medical practitioner's behavior toward patients. It typically refers to the physician's ability to instill trust and to respond to patients' emotional needs.

**body movements:** nonverbal cues that involve body movements and positions and convey emotion.

**cognitive component of empathy:** the component that requires a health professional to observe patient behavior carefully and to know the meaning of what is observed.

**communicative component of empathy:** the component of empathy that involves communicating back to a person that he or she is understood.

**emotional expressiveness:** the ability to convey emotion through nonverbal cues.

**empathy:** a central concept in the fields of psychology and medical communication. Empathy is the process that involves being sensitive to another individual's changing feelings and "connecting" emotionally to that person. Empathy involves a process of "living for a time in the other person's life" and entering his or her private perceptual world.

**extralinguistic cues:** cues apart from the spoken language, including pauses, stutters, sighs.

**eye contact:** a potentially very powerful nonverbal cue that can intensify the emotion present in a given interpersonal situation.

**malpractice:** the negligent practice of medicine.

**mastectomy:** surgical removal of the breast because of cancer.

**medical professionals:** physicians, medical psychologists, nurses, respiratory therapists, physicians' assistants, nurse practitioners, nurse midwives, phlebotomists, physical therapists, medical social workers, and other professionals who tend to the care of patients.

**metacommunication:** communication about communication.

**negotiation:** the action or process of arriving at the settlement of some matter through discussion and compromise.

**rapport:** a relationship characterized by mutual trust and emotional affinity.

**regression:** a term used by psychologists and psychiatrists to indicate that a person has reverted to aspects of a child-like, dependent role characteristic of an earlier stage of development.

**sensitivity to patients' nonverbal cues:** the ability to understand what patients are communicating with their nonverbal expressions.

**socioemotional aspects of medical care:** components of treatment that deal with patients' emotions and with the social contexts of their illnesses.

**technical quality of medical care:** the technical expertise of the medical practitioner in the realms of diagnosis and treatment.

**touch:** a nonverbal cue that is believed to be very important in the practitioner-patient relationship. Touch can convey reassurance, comfort, and caring.

**voice tone:** character and emphasis of the voice in the communication of emotion.

**ward rounds:** formal procedures in which patients are displayed before many physicians and other health professionals. Their cases are discussed with the patients present but unable to participate. Patients are often examined as members of the health care team look on.

# Medical Professionals in Training and Practice

▪ ▪ ▪ ▪ ▪

It was Karen Harding's fourth year in medical school. On the first day of her new rotation in the pediatrics department, she entered her patient's room prepared to examine him. She was not at all prepared for what she saw.

A little boy with a bald head and pale gray skin was sitting in his mother's lap. There were huge, dark circles around his eyes, which were sunken in their sockets. His mother was trying to interest him in a book about kittens, but he didn't have the energy to focus on what she was saying. He flopped like a rag doll back against her body, listless and uninterested. Karen looked at him, thinking that he resembled a little old man, but she knew he was only 3 years old and most likely he would not live to the age of 4.

The little boy had a congential ne-phroblastoma, a cancerous tumor of the kidneys that occurs primarily in children. It had been there every moment of his short life, having grown along with all his healthy cells from the time he was a fetus. But now the cancer had metastasized to his brain, causing neurological impairment. The pediatric cancer team tried to stop the disease with surgery, radiation treatments, and chemotherapy, but the metastases were spreading.

The radiation treatments and chemo-therapy weakened him severely. His hair fell out, and he had severe nausea and vom-iting. His neurological status was getting worse every day. Sometimes he couldn't hold onto his toys.

His mother seemed to be in another world. She was numb with emotional pain. She sat in her son's room day after day, watching him die. She was overwhelmed with ambivalence and could barely func-tion. She had to make a decision that was impossible for her to make. Several of the doctors had suggested transferring him to a hospice, a special hospital for terminally ill patients, where the entire family could be helped to deal with the little boy's death. At the hospice he could be made consider-ably more comfortable, but some of the other physicians wanted to continue searching for a way to prolong his life. They ordered more and more tests and subjected the child to painful procedures. They ar-gued that if there was any chance at all to cure him, it should be tried. The mother agreed in theory because she could not bear to give up all hope for her son's survival. But when it came time to carry out any medical procedures, she could not contain her distress at watching her baby suffer.

Her husband was overwhelmed with pressure and with grief. He came to the hos-pital less and less often as he tried to create a fairly normal life for their 7-year-old daughter. He worked hard at his job so that he could pay the medical bills. The close and happy relationship of the couple was being strained tremendously. Immersed in their individual grief, the parents of this once-beautiful, bright little boy suffered alone. The young father was trying to keep the family going financially and care for their little girl while his wife stayed to comfort their son. That is how Karen found her.

"I have to draw some blood," she said to the mother as gently as she could.

"No. No more. He's had enough" was her reply. She held the child tighter.

Karen felt annoyed. Her intern would be very upset if she failed to collect the blood samples he ordered, but she was pre-pared to argue with him. The mother's wishes had to be respected, and plenty of other people on the medical team would back her up. If that were her child, she felt, she would do the same thing.

But then, unexpectedly, Karen's eyes began to burn and fill with tears. She worked hard to hold them back. She re-membered when her own baby sister died before reaching the age of 3. Karen had been only 6 at the time. She couldn't re-member the baby much, but she remem-bered her mother's bottomless grief, the incredible sadness that engulfed their fam-ily for what seemed like an endless time, her father's emotional withdrawal, and how she felt terribly alone and guilty for being the healthy one. Then Karen looked at the child's mother before her and she rec-ognized for the first time what things must have been like for her own mother 20 years before.

Karen went over and sat next to the young woman. In a soft voice she said, "It's very hard for you, isn't it?" and the moth-er's face contorted as she pulled her child closer to her. She fell slightly forward with her head hanging down and wept softly.

Karen put her arm around the young mother and cried with her.

In the process of providing patient care, medical professionals experience unusual and sometimes overwhelming pressures. They are expected to have a large fund of knowledge and well-developed skills at their disposal, and to be able to call upon these under the most extreme circumstances. The work that medical professionals do can have serious consequences. A mistake can be much more than inconven-

ient. A mistake can kill. And as they deal with some of the most difficult of human experiences, they are expected to maintain the highest levels of emotional control and to comfort and care for their patients.

In this chapter we will examine both the physical and the psychological pressures inherent in the role of a medical professional. We will look closely at the process of medical and nursing training (below and in Boxes 9–1 and 9–2) and consider how such training can affect those who undergo it. We will examine the many

BOX
9–1

### THE FACTS ABOUT MEDICAL TRAINING

Training to be a physician is a long and arduous process. Almost from the first day of college the future physician must put virtually all of his or her energies into preparing for medical school. The competition for acceptance is very intense, with more than 60% of applicants rejected. The student must earn a high grade-point average, particularly in science courses. The application and interview procedures can be strenuous.

Once in medical school, students spend the first two years learning the basic sciences that form the foundation of medical practice. Among these are biochemistry, physiology, and anatomy. Medical students are faced with an overwhelming amount of material to memorize, and sometimes they have difficulty seeing the relevance of it to their clinical work with patients. At this point they begin to face the first sign of their limitations.

It is during the third and fourth years of medical school, however, that actual contact with patients begins. During these *clinical years,* the medical student serves as a *clinical clerk* on a *service* such as surgery, internal medicine, obstetrics, or pediatrics. The medical student occupies the lowest position on the team, and is required to carry out a considerable amount of patient-care activity under the direction of a supervising (or attending) physician and several residents and interns. At this stage of their training medical students are referred to as "doctor" in front of patients and must assume the professional role even if they do not really know what they are doing. Fortunately, this is a time for them to learn, and medical students are supervised closely.

After graduation from medical school comes the *internship,* which is perhaps the most difficult year of all. An intern may spend as much as every third night in the hospital working all night. The other days may be filled with work, from 7:00 A.M. to 7:00 P.M. or later. The maintenance of life outside the hospital can be taxing, or impossible. The next several years of training, the *residency* years, bring somewhat shorter hours but increasing responsibility for the final decisions regarding patient care.

and sometimes serious consequences of the physical and emotional exhaustion of medical practitioners. These consequences include callousness toward patients and their own personal physical and emotional impairment. Finally, we will probe the process of decision making by medical practitioners, and discuss how such decisions can sometimes become biased and inaccurate.

## The Physical Pressures

Medical professionals are required to function effectively in all sorts of physically demanding situations and often under tremendous time pressures. They experience various physical stresses, such as sleep deprivation, irregular schedules for meals, poor nutrition, and few opportunities for relaxation and exercise.

### TIME PRESSURES

From the first days of medical and nursing school and throughout their entire careers, physicians and nurses are plagued by severe time pressures. During the first two years of medical school, students are universally concerned that the amount of material they are required to learn is overwhelming and impossible to cover in

**BOX 9–2**

**NURSING: THE SEARCH FOR AUTONOMY**

Until they are hospitalized, few people recognize what a major role nurses play in patient care. Nurses regularly observe their hospitalized patients and are responsible for solving problems that arise, often without the consultation of a physician. Nurses dress wounds, administer intravenous medications, assess patients' vital signs. They talk to patients and listen to them, and they are usually instrumental in recognizing the role that patients' emotions play in their illnesses. They deal with patients' psychosocial problems. Nurses provide patients with the important information they need but may not get from their physicians (Heron, 1987; Stein, Watts, & Howell, 1990).

There have been times in history when nurses provided most of what medical care existed (Lindeman, 1984). Before the advent of male-dominated, scientific medicine, care consisted of supporting the patient's physical and emotional needs while his or her body healed itself. Nurses fulfilled this role well, but as medicine changed, the nursing profession was forced to take a back seat. One example of this shift is the longtime attempt by physicians to prevent nurse-midwives from delivering babies both in and out of the hospital. In many cases nurses have been forced into the role of helpers to physicians. This may be due, of course, to the fact that over 90% of nurses in the United States are women. And medicine is still a male-dominated profession.

In some medical environments nurses' roles are limited and involve little intellectual challenge. In such environments many nurses become highly dissatisfied with the discrepancy between what they have been taught in school about taking care of patients and what they are able to do in practice (Kramer, 1974). Many nurses are now seeking work environments that allow them more autonomy in caring for patients (Stein et al., 1990). In private-practice medicine, for example, nurses are given an ever-increasing role in the care of patients. In many teaching hospitals, nurses function as critically important and equal contributors to the medical-care team.

the time available (Lloyd & Gartrell, 1983; Murphy, Nadelson, & Notman, 1984). Many medical and nursing students complain that they are "lectured to death," that their curriculum is poorly organized, and that they are given an overwhelming amount of unintegrated technical information (Awbrey, 1985; Parkes, 1985). In the face of difficulties accessing and integrating the information they need, most of these students feel tremendous pressure to succeed academically (Lloyd & Gartrell, 1983).

During the clinical years of medical school and during the internship and residency, a physician in training is likely to spend more than 80 hours a week in patient care. This time is very often characterized by rushing from one patient-care activity or one charting activity to another. Interruptions are frequent, and concentrated, focused thought and effort sometimes impossible (McCue, 1985; Lurie, Rank, Parenti, Woolley, & Snoke, 1989). Time pressures and continuous interruptions also characterize the clinical aspects of nursing training (Heron, 1987; Parkes, 1982).

Time pressure is also one of the most distressing aspects of medical practice (Mawardi, 1979). A dedicated physician in full-time practice tends to work between 50 and 60 hours a week, and much of his or her "off" time at home (including supper time, weekends, and middle of the night) is interrupted by work-related telephone calls and pages (Linn, Yager, Cope, & Leake, 1985). Among the medical specialties, neonatologists (who care for sick newborns and premature neonates) report particularly high levels of time pressure from caring for a typically large number of very sick patients (Clarke et al., 1984). While practicing nurses, nurses in training, and technicians usually work closer to 40 hours a week, their work is strenuous and demanding, and time shifts are often out of synchrony with the rest of the working world (say, 3:00

P.M. to 11:00 P.M., or 11:00 P.M. to 7:00 A.M.), adding additional pressures to the course of everyday living (Parkes, 1982, 1985).

## SLEEP DEPRIVATION

It is not unusual for medical professionals, particularly physicians, to function with four or fewer hours of sleep in a 24-hour period. The few hours that they are able to sleep are often spent uncomfortably, on a cot in an "on-call room." They are interrupted and oftentimes have considerable difficulty sleeping effectively, even when there is an opportunity to do so. One study of how interns and residents spend their nights on call in the hospital showed that the greatest total amount of time any of the physicians got to sleep in any night was a little over four hours. However, even this was not continuous sleep. Length of uninterrupted sleep ranged from only 40 to 86 minutes. It seems that no physician got to sleep longer than an hour and 26 minutes at a stretch (Lurie et al., 1989). Several other studies have documented the punishing deprivation of sleep that occurs during clinical medical training (McCue, 1985; Sheehan, Sheehan, White, Leibowitz, & Baldwin, 1990).

Although research has found that interns and residents (also called "house officers") can function after only a few hours of sleep, such functioning occurs at a relatively rudimentary level. They can walk and talk and perform physical tasks that they know how to do very well. But sleep deprivation can cause significant deficits in higher-order cognitive abilities, such as basic rote memory, language, numeric skills, and tasks requiring intellective abilities and judgment, such as decision making (Hawkins, Vichick, Silsby, Kruzich, & Butler, 1985). As we will see below, sleep deprivation also contributes to emotional impairment, such as depression (McCue, 1985).

An exhausted physician-in-training.
SOURCE: © Ed Eckstein/Phototake NYC

During medical and nursing training (both undergraduate and postgraduate education) medical professionals experience additional physical strains as well. Unable to obtain regular, nutritious meals, particularly after normal business hours in the hospital cafeteria, many subsist on a diet consisting of snacks, candy, soft drinks, and coffee from the hospital vending machines. Research has found that a "junk-food diet" also contributes to a substantial decrement in house officers' cognitive and intellectual functioning, and in their psychomotor performance (Hawkins et al., 1985). For example, a sleepy, poorly nourished physician may be more likely to misplace a decimal point while writing a prescription order and to misread an X ray of an unfamiliar type than one who is rested and well nourished (Hawkins et al., 1985).

Other physical pressures occur as well. Much has been written lately about the phenomenon of "medical student abuse" (Silver, 1982; Rosenberg & Silver, 1984). Recent research is uncovering examples of pervasive physical and emotional abuse of medical students by their faculty and house officer superiors. The maltreatment consists of physical abuse as well as verbal insults, public criticism, and humiliation in response to a mistake. A poll of U.S. medical school deans suggested that they found the idea of medical student abuse almost ridiculous and believed that abuse never occurred in their schools (Rosenberg & Silver, 1984), but surveys of present and former medical students paint an entirely different picture. In one study 85% of a class of third-year medical students reported being "yelled at or shouted at" at least once in their medical training, and 73% reported being cursed or sworn at. Being required to stand holding a retractor in surgery for six to ten hours was quite common. Forty-four percent reported being placed at unnecessary medical risk by supervising physicians and nurses (for example, risking a needle stick through inexperience while doing a venipuncture on a patient with AIDS) (Sheehan et al., 1990). In another study the entire student population of a major medical school was surveyed. Overall, 46.4% of the respondents indicated that they had been abused while enrolled in medical school, and 80.6% of the seniors reported having been abused at some point in their medical school training. Types of abuse reported included verbal attacks and humiliation, as well as physical threats and inappropriate or overtly negative physical contact. Two-thirds found the experience of major importance and very upsetting (Silver & Glicken, 1990).

Why are physicians in training expected to endure sleep deprivation and other forms of physical abuse? Do such strains provide good preparation for being a physician, or are they simply part of a hazing process? This issue is a very controversial one in medical education (Cousins, 1981a, 1981b). Three main categories of reasons are suggested to explain the punishing format of medical training (McCue, 1985). First, it is argued that the clinical years of medical school, internship, and residency serve as intensive training for the difficult events that physicians experience at all hours of day or night in practice. The physical punishment of internship and residency, it is believed, provides good preparation for being called upon in the middle of the night to perform procedures or to make a decision. Unfortunately, observations of how nights on call are spent suggests that residents carry out little patient care and receive virtually no faculty instruction during the night. They spend most of their time writing in patients' charts and responding to nurses' questions (Lurie et al., 1989). Second, the brutal schedules of medical training represent a sort of hazing in which the young physician "proves" himself or herself. Surviving residency may take on a ritualistic meaning justifying a sense of superiority and separateness from other people (Gapen, 1980). Unfortunately, as we will see later in this chapter, such a hazing process is lengthy and pervasive and as a result can cause serious emotional damage in physicians. A third explanation is that to learn a great deal about medicine, a resident needs to see as many patients as possible. But, as has been noted, the in-depth knowledge and care of fewer patients may be more valuable to the learning of the treatment of disease than is the superficial care of many patients (McCue, 1985; Kleinman, 1988). Of course, a somewhat more cynical explanation is one that notes that interns and residents provide a very inexpensive labor force for the hospital. They can work up to 80 hours a week performing procedures that are billed to public-assistance programs or to private insurance companies at high rates. The house officers themselves are paid very low salaries for the work they do, but the hospitals and senior physicians benefit.

# The Emotional Challenges

The challenges of medical training and practice, as we will see next, are heavily emotional. These challenges affect not only physicians but nurses and other medical professionals as well. Many of the difficulties are so pervasive that they can damage the health professional's coping mechanisms, affect his or her attitudes toward patients, and limit social support (McCue, 1982).

## SOCIAL ISOLATION

One of the greatest difficulties of medical training, particularly of internship and residency, is the social isolation it brings. By spending so much time working, those in clinical medical training have little or no free time (particularly quality time in which they are awake and feeling well) to relate to their loved ones and friends (Mawardi, 1979). They are usually isolated from the people who are closest to them because they spend their days and nights at the hospital.

Particularly during the training years, but also in practice, physicians tend to have severely limited time for their spouses and children. When they are home, they are often exhausted and regularly interrupted with patient-care needs. Medical marriages and family life do suffer because of this (McCue, 1985; Gerber, 1983).

Yet, to cope with all the other emotional demands of medical practice, physicians rely appropriately on social support from family and friends. In fact, research has suggested that physicians' family lives and social relations away from work, as well as their mental health status, contrib-

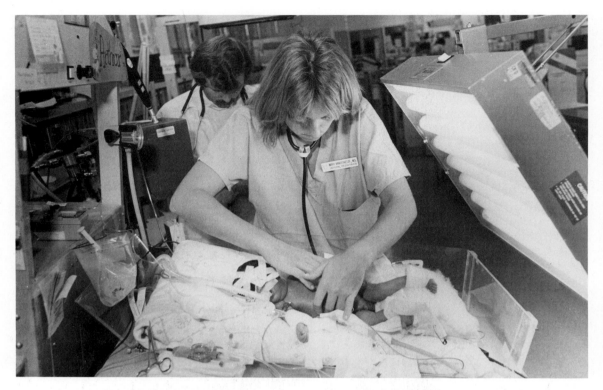

Medical professionals who care for critically ill newborns experience particularly high levels of stress.
SOURCE: © MCMLXXXV Peter Menzel/Stock, Boston

uted more to their work satisfaction than did job-related factors. Family and friends were among the greatest contributors to overall life satisfaction (Linn, Yager, Cope, & Leake, 1986).

## DEALING WITH PATIENTS

Medicine and nursing are among the few professions in which the professionals must not only deal every day with people but must also endure work that is physically demanding and involves tremendous responsibility for the lives of others. Only a few professions come close. For example, air traffic controllers often have tremendous responsibilty for people's lives. Firemen and police officers risk their own lives

in addition to having responsibility for other people. As will be discussed in Chapter 10, these jobs, just as medicine and nursing, can take a heavy physical toll on those who perform them.

Medical professionals face somewhat unique emotional challenges, however. As we saw in the case of Karen Harding above, the medical professional's connection to patients is intense and immediate. In their direct involvement in the details of patients' lives, medical professionals often experience one sad human situation after another. They witness suffering and they are expected to help alleviate it. They are reminded constantly that human life can involve tragedy, and they are reminded of their own mortality and that of their loved ones. For some physicians and nurses, the reminders occur daily (Klass, 1987a). For example, in one study of neonatologists, the greatest source of stress involved dealing every day with sick or dying patients. This stress was high enough to cause a significant number of these physicians to consider changing their specialty (Clarke et al., 1984). Further, uncertainty about many things (for example, the correctness of diagnoses, the efficacy of treatments) confronts medical practitioners with a day-to-day existence that is unsettling at best (McCue, 1982; Hay & Oken, 1972).

Many students who select medicine and nursing as careers expect to be rewarded with gratifying interactions with patients (McCue, 1982). Such relationships can be important sources of satisfaction for those in the medical professions (Linn et al., 1986; Shore & Franks, 1986; Mawardi, 1979). However, satisfying encounters with patients happen all too infrequently. Medical practitioners regularly deal with sick people who, because of the real or imagined burdens of their illnesses, are often anxious, uncomfortable, distressed, and at their worst when dealing with those who take care of them (McCue, 1982). In addition, patients sometimes expect more comfort and understanding from their medical professionals than can possibly be provided (Kleinman, 1988; McCue, 1982). But when the medical professional falls short of a patient's expectations, the patient may become angry and the medical professional may feel inadequate.

Medical professionals typically have little recourse when they are faced with patients who are unpleasant to work with, particularly those who are noncompliant, demanding, and clinging (McCue, 1982; Krakowski, 1982). Furthermore, clinical training typically does not provide medical practitioners with tools for dealing with patients' complex psychosocial problems or

for dealing with their own complicated feelings toward these patients.

Sometimes medical practitioners experience emotional conflicts because the issues they face are highly symbolic for them (that is, these issues represent other salient issues in their lives). When treating older patients, for example, medical professionals may be constantly reminded of the potential for sickness and infirmity in their own parents. Or they may feel engulfed by the dependency of their patients and fear their own feelings of dependency, of which they may be ashamed. Some medical professionals may have difficulty setting limits on what patients can demand, and thus allow patients' needs to engulf their own lives (Hellerstein, 1986).

Unresolved emotional issues and symbolic conflicts in the medical professionals' own lives are unlikely to be resolved in the stressful realm of providing medical care. Medical training and practice do not provide a protective atmosphere for a vulnerable personality (Vaillant, Sobowale, & McArthur, 1972). Even among individuals who are quite healthy emotionally, medical training and practice can be tremendously taxing. The physical stresses combine with constant responsibility for each of one's actions and with the continual experience of patients' suffering and reminders of human pain and tragedy. Taken together, these can take a heavy toll on the medical professional.

## THE LOSS OF IDEALISM

Although most people view physicians, nurses, and other medical professionals as operating in an atmosphere of idealism and altruistic service to others, research on professional training paints a different picture. As we have seen so far, the picture is one of physical and emotional brutality inflicted on those in training, and a subsequent loss of their idealistic views of patient care (Becker & Geer, 1958; Sheehan et al., 1990).

In the first two years of medical school, for example, the student's idealistic notions about learning everything there is to know in medicine are put aside in favor of a more realistic approach, particularly a more self-protective one. Students typically discover what the faculty considers important and what will be covered on the tests. During the first year, students develop what Becker and Geer (1958), two sociologists, called "student culture." Students work together and try to help one another with their studies. They support and console one another over the issue of grades. During the second year of medical school contact with patients begins. Students are taught techniques of interviewing and how to do physical examinations. During the third and fourth years of medical school, as students become involved in day-to-day patient care, cynicism tends to overtake idealism and students tend to become less concerned than they once were about their patients as human beings. Emotional abuse by supervising personnel causes as many as a third of medical students in the third year to consider dropping out of medicine, and as many as three-fourths to state that they have become more cynical about academic life and the medical profession. One-fourth report that if they had known in advance about the abuse in medical training, they would have chosen a different profession (Sheehan et al., 1990).

Several other factors contribute to the development of cynicism (Lief & Fox, 1963). Medical students often find themselves in the throes of anxiety brought about by the presence of death and suffering. There is a need to distance themselves enough from the phenomena they encounter to reduce that anxiety. They also become absorbed in the technical aspects of the cases they deal with because of what the faculty requires during their education and because of their own scientific interests. There is often not enough time to get to know their patients as people. Idealism typically increases, and cynicism subsides, when students have chosen a particular specialty that they will pursue in internship and residency (Becker & Geer, 1958). In practice, however, increasing stresses tend to be associated with a further loss of idealism and subsequently with increasing depression (May & Revicki, 1985).

Among nurses, expressions of idealism and optimism tend to vary with the work situations in which the nurses find themselves during nursing practice. Young nursing students often expect that they can influence their patients in many ways (for example, to change unhealthy habits or to cope with the distressing circumstances of their illnesses). However, the reality of caring for the psychosocial needs of patients often demonstrates that it is quite difficult to do. For example, despite what they may know about noncompliance, many nurses have been found to experience fear and confusion when confronted with a patient who has disobeyed doctor's orders (Barron-McBride, 1976).

Studies of nursing students have found that although idealism is usually high among those in the first year, optimism about how much they can help patients and contribute to their lives usually falls by the senior year. Like physicians, senior nursing students become more disease-oriented than patient-centered as time goes on, and over the course of training they spend less and less time meeting patients' nonmedical needs. Student nurses come to see themselves as more and more valuable both to the technical medical care of patients and to the physicians they assist. However, they perceive somewhat less challenge in their work, which becomes more and more routine (Aiken, 1983).

## FAILED EXPECTATIONS
## ABOUT MEDICINE

> Even though you learn individually, disease by disease, about the limitations of medicine, somehow the overall message is to cure. And during your training you have to come to terms, all by yourself, with the reality that most of what you do has little to do with curing. Sometimes you make people better. Often they get better by themselves. Sometimes you make them more comfortable while they get sicker. Sometimes you make them more miserable while they get sicker. Maybe what we need is an increased level of respect both for the patient's own ability to get better and for the power of disease. (Klass, 1987a, p. 205).

Many medical professionals once dreamed of having power over life and death. Wave a magic wand of medical science and people's miserable lives are transformed. They become happy. That's what happened on the old television shows like *Ben Casey*, *Young Dr. Kildare*, and *Marcus Welby, M.D.* But real medicine mostly isn't like that (McCue, 1982). Most patients have diseases that can be managed but not cured. Unless they are comfortable providing other kinds of help and emotional support to their patients, physicians tend to feel helpless when faced with patients who do not get better (Kleinman, 1988).

> There's a lot of hope that the hospital may be able to offer . . . hope for improved quality of life, longer life—but not cure. Get that word right out of your mind (Klass, 1987a, p. 201).

It's frustrating to want to cure, to carry with you the expectation that somehow you should be able to cure, and then not be able to cure. It can make you dislike particular diseases, and even particular patients. Doctors are notoriously bad with dying patients, those emblems of medical failure, and sometimes the patient who isn't actually dying but who's sick with some chronic and incurable disease can present the same kind of unpleasant prospect. (Klass, 1987a, p. 203)

Some argue that medical intervention clearly improves a patient's health status in only a small percentage of cases and sometimes actually renders the patient worse off than if he or she had never even sought care at all (Robin, 1984). In a large percentage of cases, medical intervention doesn't matter all that much because the condition was self-limiting, or because the symptoms stemmed from emotional factors like depression, or anxiety, or because the problem was caused by health-damaging behaviors, such as smoking, alcohol abuse, and obesity, which likely will continue to occur (DiMatteo & DiNicola, 1982). And as we noted in detail in Chapter 4, even when medical practitioners can offer patients the means to achieve better health, a large percentage of patients reject the opportunity and are noncompliant with treatment regimens (Haynes, Taylor, & Sackett, 1979).

Finally, medicine is not an exact science. (Indeed, some say it is not a science at all, but rather an art.) All the right things done correctly do not guarantee a happy, healthy patient. Sometimes patients die when there is no reason they should do so. Some of them get better against all the odds. Medical professionals cannot actually take the credit for many of the successes of medicine or blame for many of its failures. Often the best they can do is to help their patients to cope with and find meaning in the suffering (Kleinman, 1988).

## THE NEED TO CONTROL EMOTIONS

Most medical professionals eventually become accustomed to the sight of blood, to needles, human tissue, and the sounds and smells of illness. They get used to examining people, and sometimes to cutting into their bodies as well. They even get used to giving bad news. But not entirely. Many medical professionals are shaken considerably by the discovery that people they are caring for have become seriously or even terminally ill. Although most health professionals learn to cope with human suffering and tragedy, they do not become immune to these experiences. Suffering can engender strong feelings in medical professionals. They are sometimes profoundly affected by what happens to their patients (Cartwright, 1979; McCue, 1982; Parkes, 1985, 1986).

■ ■ ■ ■ ■

Janet Caron, M.D., was in her family practice office on Tuesday morning when the blood-test results arrived from the laboratory. She flipped through them quickly, intending to analyze each one in detail later in the day when she reviewed her patients' charts. One finding caught her eye. She bit her lower lip. Ann Smith's HIV test was positive. Caron's stomach tightened. She began to feel the same dull ache she had experienced over and over during medical training, whenever she knew she had some devastating news to tell a patient.

Alone in her office, she sat back in her big swivel chair and tried to brace her body against the tears that were filling her eyes. She looked at the pile of patient charts on her desk, and at the full appointment schedule in front of her. She thought of Ann, a young woman she had treated for several years and had grown to like very much. "Why can't this be just a job?," she asked herself. "Why does this always hurt so much?"

She picked up the phone and dialed. "Ann Smith, please. This is Dr. Caron calling."

One problem with having these feelings is that medical professionals are expected *not* to express what they feel: not sadness, not anger, not despair. They are expected to hide their emotions from their patients and colleagues. To do this, they must often hide these emotions from themselves (Hellerstein, 1986).

To avoid burdening a patient or undermining a patient's confidence, a medical professional must be concerned but remain detached. For example, it is usually best for a physician to keep distress about a patient's condition to himself or herself while encouraging the patient to turn his or her own energies to healing. A nurse must regularly tolerate patients' emotional expressions and, for example, not admonish a patient who is moaning in pain to quiet down because the sound is annoying. When a medical practitioner talks with a patient who is terminally ill, it is the patient's feelings that must take priority, not the practitioner's. These are clear examples in which the medical professional's own emotions must remain unexpressed, particularly to the patient.

Unfortunately, medical professionals typically do not allow the expression of emotion even amongst themselves. In fact, young physicians and nurses often idealize those who have the greatest emotional detachment (Hellerstein, 1986). They hold up as heroes the physicians who can slice into the chest of a human being and never acknowledge the tremendous significance of such an action. They admire those who can walk away from the bedside of a patient who has just died and coolly manipulate the emotions of the family to get them to agree to an autopsy. They are impressed by people who can watch an autopsy while eating their lunch. Medical professionals who want to be truly macho don't wince, not in front of one another, not even to themselves.

> Macho in medicine can mean a number of things. Everyone knows it's out there as a style. Macho can refer to your willingness to get tough with your patients. . . . It can refer to your eagerness to do invasive procedures. . . . (Klass, 1987a, p. 77)

When the disease has essentially won and the patient continues to present the challenge, the macho doctor is left with no appropriate response. He cannot sidestep the challenge by offering comfort rather than combat, because comfort is not in his repertoire. And unable to do battle against the disease to any real effect, he may feel almost ready to battle the patient. (Klass, 1987a, p. 79)

Because of their own and others' expectations, as well as the requirements of the job, many medical professionals refuse to experience and accept their own feelings. They regularly ignore their own emotional reactions, or they try to force themselves to stop feeling what they feel. They are regularly supported for "disowning" their emotions, particularly their frustration, anger, and sadness.

*Emotional disowning* is a common coping mechanism among medical professionals. Emotions and feelings that are held very strongly are presented as foreign to oneself (Branden, 1971). To some extent, medical professionals are chosen for their ability to disown their emotions. Students with a single-minded focus on science are often the most successful applicants at many medical schools. Despite the greater emphasis on caring in the nursing profession, technical skills and emotional detachment are the qualities that, particularly in critical care (emergency, intensive care), become the most highly valued (Heron, 1987).

Most important, perhaps, is the fact that medical professionals hide their emotions from one another. Although they are the very people who best understand the stresses and emotional complexities of patient care, their efforts to appear emotionally controlled with one another deprive them of a potentially valuable system of support. As we will see, their isolation and emotional disowning can have very serious consequences.

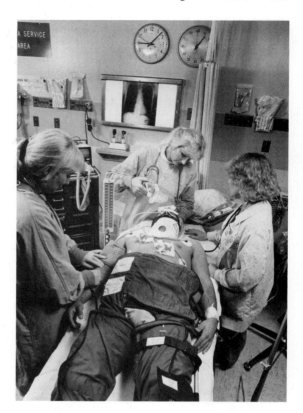

Medical professionals are expected to deal with all kinds of human tragedies yet completely control their own emotional reactions.
SOURCE: Spencer Grant/Stock, Boston

## The Consequences of the Physical and Emotional Pressures

Not every health professional is vulnerable to distress from the physical and emotional pressures of medical-care training. Each health professional's unique history, life experiences, and personality interact with the environmental pressure to affect work performance, emotional reactions, personal and family relationships, relationships with patients, and the adaptiveness of methods chosen for coping (Murphy et al., 1984). Some health professionals do very well, but for the unfortunate few who are vulnerable, the outcomes of these pressures can be serious problems and the costs of a career in medicine can be tremendous.

## ANXIETY, DEPRESSION, AND SUICIDE

During their training, medical professionals (particularly physicians) face intensely stressful experiences and assume responsibility for extremely difficult issues involving death and disability. Very mature behavior is demanded of physicians who, because of their commitments to premedical and medical education, have had to ignore their personal development and may never have had the chance to live independent adult lives. The insulated world of the teaching hospital contributes to delays in emotional maturation (Pfeiffer, 1983; Ziegler, Kanas, Strull, & Bennet, 1984).

Unfortunately, lack of maturity is not the only consequence of the physical and emotional pressures of training. By the end of medical school over half of graduates need psychotherapy, although only a very small percentage receive it (Duffy, 1970). At least a third of interns have frequent or severe emotional distress (Valko & Clayton, 1975). The stresses of medical training, particularly residency, have been found to be a major factor in the precipitation of episodes of depression (Reuben, 1985; Weinstein, 1983; Tokarz, Bremer, & Peters, 1979; May & Revicki, 1985). In the first year of residency alone at least 30% of residents experience serious depression (Reuben & Noble, 1990). And there is evidence that the emotional impairment of physicians is on the increase (Hardison, 1986; Smith, Denny, & Witzke, 1986).

Both depression and anxiety seem to be regular accompaniments of a career in medicine. In a survey of academic and clinical faculty of a major medical school, at least mild depression was reported by ap-

proximately 13% of the physicians. Four percent reported moderate to severe depression. Anxiety levels were considerably higher, with 27% reporting beyond normal anxiety, and 13% reporting moderate or severe anxiety (Linn et al., 1985). Rates of anxiety among physicians seem to be quite a bit higher than those in the general community (Linn et al., 1985).

Although practicing physicians tend to display levels of depression and hopelessness that are not significantly higher than those of the general population, such is not the case during medical training. During internship and residency, at least 25% of physicians have serious thoughts of committing suicide (suicidal ideations) (McCue, 1985; Valko & Clayton, 1975).

The leading cause of death of physicians under 40 is suicide (Blachly, Disher, & Roduner, 1968; Everson & Fraumeni, 1975; McCue, 1982). Every year an entire medical school class (average size, 130 students) must be trained to replace the physicians in the United States who have killed themselves. Overall, the suicide rate of physicians is 2 to 3 times greater than that in the general population (Ross, 1971; Rose & Rosow, 1973). Suicide among male physicians across all age groups is about 1.5 times the rate of suicide in males in the general population. The rate of suicide among women physicians is 4 times that among females in the general population (Pitts, Schuller, Rich, & Pitts, 1979; Weinstein, 1983). (Below we examine some of the special problems that women physicians face.)

## PHYSICIAN IMPAIRMENT

*Physician impairment* is defined as the inability of the physician to practice medicine adequately because of physical or mental illness, including alcoholism or drug dependence (Reuben & Noble, 1990). On the simplest level, emotional stress affects health professionals' job effectiveness. For example, in the preclinical and clinical training of medical school, unfavorable stress tends to result in poor academic performance (Murphy et al., 1984), as well as in compromised patient care (Linn & Zeppa, 1984; Spiegel, Smolen, & Hopfensperger, 1986). But impairment goes beyond the inability to do the job effectively. Impairment includes the inability to function because of serious addiction to drugs and alcohol.

Drug abuse and alcoholism are significant problems among physicians and among nurses. Physicians are prone to alcoholism at rates estimated to range from about 8% to over 12% of practicing physicians (Newsom, 1977; McCue, 1982). Although this is estimated to be the rate in the general population, underreporting of physician alcoholics is quite likely (McCue, 1982). Drug addiction is estimated to be 30 to 100 times more common among physicians than in the general population, and even higher compared to persons in socioeconomically matched control groups (Vaillant et al., 1972). The easy availability of drugs to physicians is believed to be one of the reasons for drug addiction among physicians. Physicians also have access to the most potent, pure forms of various addictive drugs, and so they become much more intensely addicted to these substances than do lay drug users. Early estimates were that at least 5% of practicing physicians regularly abuse addictive drugs (Modlin & Montes, 1964; McCue, 1982). But recent research has found at least 10% of physicians regularly using psychoactive (mood-altering drugs), particularly tranquilizers and opiates for self-treatment. Three percent admit to a history of drug dependency (McAuliffe et al., 1986). Probably because physicians are trained to look for medical solutions to all sorts of problems, many are tempted to use pharmacological agents to regulate their moods, emotions, levels of fatigue, and internal conflicts.

There is evidence that health professionals are quite aware of one another's habits of alcohol and drug use. One survey of medical students showed that 25% of the students had on at least one occasion witnessed a faculty member engage in drug or alcohol abuse. Nineteen percent had witnessed drug or alcohol abuse by nurses (Sheehan et al., 1990).

The problem of medical professional impairment is tremendous and deserves serious attention. It is estimated that each year the equivalent of seven medical school classes are lost to suicide, alcoholism, and drug dependence (Mawardi, 1979). Impairment can result in self-destructive actions and can interfere with medical practitioners' ability to carry out effective patient care. Their judgment, memory, and manual dexterity can be severely compromised. Their sensitivity to patients' emotional needs may suffer.

Medical professionals are usually not inclined to seek assistance for their impairment, a situation that makes detection and treatment quite difficult. Medical training seems to reinforce tendencies toward self-deprivation and avoidance of emotional assistance. To deal with this problem, several county and state medical and nursing societies have developed programs for identifying and helping impaired medical professionals. Physicians and nurses work with members of their own professions to help those who are impaired to recognize and confront their problems. These programs have experienced a high degree of success (Newsom, 1977; McCue, 1985).

## PERSONAL AND FAMILY RELATIONSHIPS

In response to the intellectual, physical, and emotional demands of patient care, the most common adaptation of health professionals, particularly physicians, tends to be withdrawal from loved ones and retreat from family life (Vaillant et al., 1972; Fine, 1981). Emotional separation from the family occurs progressively, and eventually the willingness and ability to share feelings is lost. Time spent with family is limited because of late office hours, interruptions of family time by telephone calls and pages, and visits to hospitalized patients even on days off. The consequences of such withdrawal can be devastating (Brent & Brent, 1978). Personal, particularly family, relationships have been found to be among the most important factors in determining physicians' life satisfaction (Linn et al., 1986). Family and peer support can be critical to physicians' and nurses' abilities to cope with stress (May & Revicki, 1986; Parkes, 1985).

Why do health professionals, particularly physicians, allow the erosion of their family lives and peer relationships to occur? Why do they jeopardize the elements of their lives that bring them the greatest satisfaction and opportunity for successful coping? There are several reasons (McCue, 1982). First, there is peer pressure. A hard-working physician who surrenders a happy personal life to the care of patients wins the respect of colleagues. Second, a physician who works all the time cannot be faulted for a poor patient outcome. After all, misfortune occurred despite having done his or her best. Working all the time tends to help a physican deal with the inevitable uncertainties of medical practice. Third, a physician may feel uncomfortable with economic prosperity and feel that only long hours and fatigue can justify it. And finally, a physician may gain greater ego gratification and sense of self-importance in the process of patient care than in normal day-to-day life. At the hospital, where the pace is fast and exciting, the physician is in charge. At home, the physician is just another spouse or parent.

## RELATIONSHIPS WITH PATIENTS

The disowning of their own emotions can cause medical professionals to numb themselves against the feelings of their patients. In denying their own emotions, it is possible for medical professionals to lose their capacity to recognize and to respond to emotions in others. They may expect patients to deny their own feelings, as the medical professionals themselves do. As a result, patients may feel they are not getting the attention they need and want, and they may feel misunderstood (Lazarus, 1985). Indeed, the personal warmth and caring necessary for an effective physician-patient relationship is likely to be missing among physicians who experience serious personal deprivations. Those who are treated badly may in turn treat their patients badly (Edwards & Zimet, 1976). Thus, when health professionals attempt to avoid acknowledging their own feelings about patient care, they ignore their patients' emotions and instead focus solely on the technical aspects of the medical care they deliver. When they do this, medical professionals fail to incorporate the critical components of emotional care of their patients. They may diminish the importance of the human side of treatment (Lazarus, 1985; Wills, 1978).

One psychologist has analyzed the problem as that of *trivializing patients' distress* (Lazarus, 1985). Some health professionals cannot face the reality of the plight of very sick patients whose prognoses are poor and whose lives are severely compromised by their physical illness. These health professionals try to avoid their patients' pain and encourage them in the most superficial manner to "put on a happy face." To empathize and to experience fully what such a patient is feeling may be extremely painful for the professional, so instead he or she creates "professional distance" between them. However, as we saw in Chapter 8, it is only by sharing the patient's perspective for a time that the health professional can give his or her patient understanding and help to reduce feelings of fear, sadness, and helplessness.

Because of their own emotional conflicts, medical professionals may even fail to recognize their patients' distress. In one study of the practice of medical internists, more than 48 out of 87 patients were seriously distressed about something (finances, work, sex) and 10% had suicidal tendencies. Yet, "except in the most obvious instances, internists repeatedly underestimated patients' distress—even after long experience with them—despite the fact that the patients were not at all reluctant to reveal such feelings when asked" (Lazarus, 1985, pp. 288–289).

Practitioners' own distress is sometimes manifested in pessimism about their patients (Wills, 1978). When practitioners feel that their patients have poor prospects for improving their lives or their health, they may refrain from presenting much information to them and withhold offers of help.

There is also a tendency for health professionals, particularly those overly burdened emotionally, to see patients' problems as the patients' fault. They may even feel that their patients would not be sick if they had not done something "wrong." Usually, the medical professionals will focus on the unhealthy behaviors that may have contributed to their patients' illnesses. The mechanism of "blaming the victim" is put into operation. *Blaming the victim* is a psychological phenomenon in which the victim of an untoward event is blamed for having brought misfortune upon himself or herself. Such a conclusion tends to stem from *belief in a just world* (Lerner, 1980). Belief in a just world involves an individual's conviction that people get what they deserve and deserve what they get. Thus, someone who is the victim

of illness is blamed for doing something that brought that illness on (Lerner, 1980). Medical professionals are as prone as other people to the natural tendency to believe that bad things happen not randomly but systematically to people who deserve them (Lazarus, 1985). Psychological equilibrium is maintained through self-deceit. Further, health professionals may come to believe that certain patients have certain problems because of their flawed personalities. Such an approach involves not only self-deception but also the inability to support patients emotionally when they need support.

## CALLOUS HUMOR

"This patient is an LOL with GOK, and at present seems to be CTD."

Spoken in front of the female patient, this sentence might confuse and alienate. But confusion would be better than what she would feel if she heard her doctors say what they really mean: "This patient is a Little Old Lady with God-Only-Knows, and at present seems to be Circling The Drain." *Circling the drain* is a medical professionals' "in-group" term that means the patient is on her way "out." In this case the patient is probably going to die and nobody knows what's wrong with her.

It is common for medical professionals to use humor to reduce the tension of their pressure-filled work. Their jokes often serve the purpose of separating them from their patients and reducing the chances of identifying too closely with them. However, the jokes might be considered by many to be in poor taste.

*Medical humor* is a well-established coping mechanism for physicians and nurses. It has been studied at length by psychologists and sociologists. Humor serves to enhance the cohesiveness of the group of medical professionals who form a team. They demonstrate their recognition of one another's professional identity, and acknowledge the stressful nature of their work (Fox, 1959; Robinson, 1977).

Humor may serve to reduce tension among medical professionals and to enhance solidarity on the patient-care team. However, some have argued that such humor also reflects a certain degree of callousness among medical professionals. Those who hear and appreciate jokes and humorous statements about the tragic conditions of their patients' lives and health are bound to be affected. They may fail to take very seriously the misery that their patients are feeling or they may learn to view their patients from an unaffected position that makes them emotionally immune to the suffering around them.

Of course, some argue that medical professionals are not laughing at patients at all but at themselves, at their own errors, their fears, their foibles. A resident in pediatrics, for example, was called upon to treat the severe chest pain of the grandfather of one of her young patients. Although she is a pediatrician and remembers almost nothing from her medical school days about the treatment of potential heart attacks, everyone turns to her because she's the doctor. As she relates this story to her fellow physicians, they laugh, *not* at the unfortunate grandfather whose life may have been in jeopardy, but at the position in which this doctor found herself, and perhaps at the dilemmas presented by the specialization of medicine today (Klass, 1987b).

## JOB DISSATISFACTION AND BURNOUT

In the past few years, the phenomenon of *burnout* has received intense interest from psychologists. Burnout is a negatively valued psychological response that is characterized by physical and emotional exhaustion, an increase in cynicism about and dehumanization of patients, a decrease in concern and respect for patients, a loss of positive feeling for others, and a tendency to blame others for distress. Burnout results commonly in quitting the job that has brought burnout, abusing drugs and alcohol, and in an increase in mental illness, as well as marital and interpersonal discord. Burnout occurs among individuals whose job it is to care for other people, particularly when the demands are seen as excessive. These individuals include human-service workers and medical professionals (Maslach, 1976, 1982). Medical practitioners who care for very ill or dying children and for psychotic patients may be particularly prone to burnout (Clarke et al., 1984).

Burnout involves the tendency of the professional to disparage the recipients of caretaking. Individuals with burnout focus on the problems they encounter rather than on the positive, healthy aspects of their jobs. The chances of developing burnout increase drastically in settings in which the probability of successful intervention is low, and workers see that their efforts make little difference in the lives of their clients. Burnout increases when staff have higher expectations for recipients of care than is warranted by the reality of the situation, and when they are unable to see a resolution of the problem (usually true in cases of chronic, degenerative illness). Burnout also increases when patients' anger is directed at caregivers.

The term *burnout* has lately come to be used very loosely, and inaccurately. Burnout is not just fatigue. The exhaustion that accompanies burnout is primarily emotional, although, of course, it may be manifested in physical fatigue as well. Some researchers have suggested that burnout among medical practitioners results from their attempts to disown the complex and sometimes disquieting emotions they feel in the course of caring for their patients. Others argue that burnout is the natural outcome of practitioners' expectations of patient gratitude, appreciation, and admiration for their selfless care. Still others argue that the primary cause of burnout is the requirement of continual face-to-face involvement with people (Edelwich & Brodsky, 1980; Jones, 1981).

Can burnout be cured? Can a health professional whose emotional well-being is severely threatened by burnout return to his or her previous level of functioning? Attempts to prevent and treat burnout involve providing medical professionals with encouragement and the opportunity for emotional expression. In some cases support groups have been helpful in reducing the stress that medical professionals feel. In other cases mental health professionals, such as psychologists and psychiatrists, work with physicians and nurses. They help them to become aware of and to understand their emotions, as well as to determine the best courses of action for them to follow in caring for their patients. The health professionals are encouraged to attend to their own needs as well as to the needs of others. They are encouraged to engage in actively reducing their stress through physical exercise and relaxation training. Medical professionals are also helped to reevaluate the meaning of their work as part of a process. They are encouraged to share their feelings with their families. And they are helped to communicate effectively with other staff members to enhance their ability to deal with the pressures of patient care (Parkes, 1985).

# Women in Medicine: The Struggle and the Ideal

More and more these days young women whose interests lie in patient care are choosing to go to medical school. Currently, approximately 30% of the medical students in the United States are women (Uhlenberg & Cooney, 1990). This statistic represents a big change from the 1960s, when the percentage was only about 6%. In the past decade a successful medical career has become more and more of a possibility for a woman. Specialties such as surgery and obstetrics and gynecology, once closed to women, are beginning to open their doors. And careers in academic medicine are being pursued successfully by women who combine a medical career with family and children (Levinson, Tolle, & Lewis, 1989).

Women who entered medicine in the 1950s, 1960s, and 1970s were trailblazers in medical education. They endured tremendous personal difficulties to become physicians. They were often insulted by male physicians ("What are you doing here? Don't you know women belong at home having babies, and not in medical school? What's the matter, don't you like being a woman?"). They were often rejected ("I refuse to share my operating room with a woman surgeon"). Although today women in medicine refuse to accept such ill-treatment and are able to turn to one another for support, obstacles continue to exist for women. Even though direct abuse seems to be no greater toward women than men in medical school (Silver & Glicken, 1990), women medical students still experience a significant degree of sexual harassment (Sheehan et al., 1990). They must fight slurs and prejudices, and challenge sexist remarks. Even today women who venture into male-dominated specialties, such as surgery, can face considerable hostility (Richman & Flaherty, 1990).

Current research on women's reactions to medical training suggests that at least in some realms women experience more stress than do men. Although women have been found to have lower stress levels and higher mental health than men during the early years of medical school (Richman & Flaherty, 1990), later clinical training tends to embody more stressors for females than males. These include distress over separa-

Research suggests that, on the average, female physicians are more sensitive than male physicians to the social and humanistic aspects of patient care.
SOURCE: © 1985 David Powers/Stock, Boston

tion from family, friends, and loved ones during clinical training. Women medical students have been found to express more concern about feelings of loneliness, being out of place, and being unable to achieve their goals than have men (Edwards & Zimet, 1976). And in one study of third-year medical students, women reported more stress-related symptoms than did men (Spiegel, Smolen, & Jonas, 1986).

Women physicians who also have spouses and children tend to face some limitations in their professional career advancement. Studies show that when women physicians marry, the majority (between 50% and 75%) choose husbands who are also physicians (Uhlenberg & Cooney, 1990). Others marry professionals, such as attorneys. In most cases the husbands are highly career-oriented and do not cut back on their own work to support their wives' careers. Instead, women physicians, particularly those who have children, tend to take salaried hospital positions or to work in health maintenance organizations. In these cases, they are able to work only about 40 hours a week, with some additional time on call. As a result, their earnings are lower than those of male physicians (Uhlenberg & Cooney, 1990). Studies show, too, that women physicians are often responsible for virtually all of the housework, shopping, cooking, child care, and money management in their homes. And while their physical juggling of all these responsibilities is difficult enough, the emotional aspects of their role conflict are even greater. If a woman physician wants to take a few years off to have and care for her children, she may lose the necessary diagnostic and/or surgical skills she has worked so hard to acquire. When she does go back to work and is caring for her patients, she may feel she is neglecting her children. When home with her children, she worries about patients who might need her (Cartwright, 1977, 1978, 1979).

In recent years there has been a recognition of the important contribution that women physicians make to the profession of medicine. First, women tend to express the personal characteristics of sensitivity and empathy for patients that we have seen are so valuable in patient care. In their attitudes they have been found to be, on average, more sensitive than male physicians to the doctor-patient relationship, more accepting of patients' feelings, and more open to the social and humanistic aspects of patient care (Kaufman-Cartwright, 1972; Maheux, Dufort, & Béland, 1988). In addition to more positive attitudes toward the psychosocial aspects of patient care, women physicians are more likely than men to engage in medical-care practices to promote the psychological and social well-being of their patients (Maheux, Dufort, Béland, Jacques, & Lévesque, 1990). Second, women physicians tend to be more concerned than males about balancing work responsibilities and family life, so that their own emotional needs and social support, as well as the welfare of their families are not sacrificed (Levinson et al., 1989). Although women physicians can help to change medicine for the better, simply admitting more women into medicine will not be enough to enhance the psychosocial care of patients and the mental health and adaptiveness of physicians (Eisenberg, 1989). Rather, "the task will be to cultivate the humane qualities in all health professionals by making career paths, and the reward structure that reinforces them, consonant with that goal" (Eisenberg, 1989, p. 1544).

How might medicine be changed to foster both the personal development of physicians and their psychosocial orientation to patients? Our examination of the many issues considered in this chapter suggests some possible solutions.

## HUMANIZING MEDICINE

As we have seen so far in this chapter, patient care can be extremely trying for medical practitioners and can severely tax their abilities to deal with the demands placed upon them. Particularly in the early years of their training, medical practititioners face tremendous challenges to their emotional control and to the integrity of their personalities. To help them face these challenges, they choose various courses of action, some that may be detrimental to patients and some that may be detrimental to the medical professionals themselves.

Although the mechanisms of defense and coping that are common to medical

professionals may be difficult to break from, it is possible for those in medicine to choose a different path (Klass, 1987a). First, the medical practitioners themselves must recognize that with regard to the difficult feelings engendered by medical practice, there is typically a conspiracy of silence (McCue, 1985). Early recognition of the complex emotional aspects of patient care and awareness and examination of these feelings are critical (Weinstein, 1983). Opportunities for peer discussion need to be available, so that medical professionals can support one another to deal with the difficulties they encounter caring for patients. Further, confidential counseling for impairment should be available and encouraged at all levels of medical training and practice (Weinstein, 1983). The mental health and social support needs of medical professionals at all levels of training need to be recognized and provided for (Awbrey, 1985).

Of course, the working conditions of medical practice are unlikely to improve unless some of the more punishing aspects of medical training and practice are eliminated. The emotional and physical abuse of medical students must not be tolerated, and improved working conditions for interns and residents must be instituted (Silver & Glicken, 1990). Time for family relationships must be guarded, and a medical professional's efforts to develop and nurture his or her family life must be valued and protected (Eisenberg, 1989).

In addition, the admissions policies of medical schools must come more into line with these goals.

> Medical-school admission is geared to the very bright, achievement-oriented students who have accumulated top grades in scientific subjects. This necessarily selects qualities of intense competitiveness, intellectual narrowness—belonging to young people who often have neglected interper-

sonal relations and have not permitted the leavening of their own sensibilities and their capacities to reach out. (Lown, 1983, p. 25)

Humanistic values must be selected for as well as nurtured in the process of medical education.

So far in this book, we have examined the emotional aspects of medical treatment, not only from the point of view of patients but from the perspective of medical practitioners as well. Now we turn to an examination of the difficulties and complexities of making medical decisions that can significantly affects patients' lives and well-being. We will examine the ways in which those decisions can be made most effectively, as well as the ways in which the decision-making process can go awry.

# Medical Practitioners and the Puzzle of Illness

In today's modern world, very high expectations are held both for the scientific field of medicine and for the members of the medical professions. Implicit in these expectations are demands that diagnostic and treatment miracles occur on a regular basis (McCue, 1982; Mizrahi, 1984). Lay persons turn to medical professionals for answers about the state of their bodies and about what they can do to achieve and maintain health. And as we saw in Chapter 5, some people express emotional pain through their bodies and expect their medical professionals to provide not only the alleviation of their physical distress but happiness and emotional fulfillment as well.

BOX
9–3

## IATROGENIC ILLNESS

Errors of judgment in patient care can be far more serious than errors of judgment in most other fields of endeavor. Drawing the wrong conclusion, making a hasty decision, or making an incorrect assumption about a missing piece of data can kill a patient or seriously jeopardize his or her well-being.

Conditions or illnesses that result from the actions of medical professionals are *iatrogenic*. Obviously, many of the medical miracles of today come with a certain degree of risk. And with a clear idea of what that risk might be, the patient and physician together may decide that the benefits of intervention outweigh the risks. But iatrogenic episodes present unplanned costs; the patient is harmed as the result of an error in diagnosis or treatment.

Iatrogenic episodes are surprisingly common. Writing of his medical training, a young physician noted: "Distressingly, much of the disease one encountered in the high-technology hospital setting was actually caused by previous treatment" (Hellerstein, 1986, p. 8). These problems are the result of (among other things) the erroneous interpretation of test results, inaccurate diagnoses, drug allergies, drug interaction effects, incorrect treatment choices, poor surgical techniques, and nosocomial infections. (*Nosocomial infections* are hospital-acquired infections, transmitted to the patient as a result of infractions in required sterile technique by hospital personnel.)

Eugene Robin, M.D., professor of medicine at Stanford University, gives many examples of iatrogenic illness (Robin, 1984). One case clearly illustrates the *cascade* effect, in which one problem leads to another, bigger problem, which leads to another, bigger problem, and so on.

In recent decades, developments in medicine have been astounding. Yet, despite all that medicine can do, the field and its practitioners have limitations. Sometimes physicians cannot figure out what is wrong with a patient. Necessary information about diagnosis and treatment may be unavailable because medical knowledge has not developed far enough or because the medical professional's capacity for processing and integrating the relevant information may be limited. Sometimes no cure or acceptable management strategy exists. Medical care can even be dangerous, such as when certain diagnostic tests and treatments bring about additional problems that themselves require treatment. There is even a name for a physician-induced medical problem. It is *iatrogenic,*

which means "resulting from the activity of physicians" (*Dorland's Illustrated Medical Dictionary*, 1965) (see Box 9–3). In the interests of patients' well-being, these limitations must be acknowledged.

## MEDICAL DIAGNOSIS

Medical professionals deal with patients under conditions of uncertainty. A medical professional almost never knows for sure the state of a patient's body, only what is probable or likely. Despite the wonders of modern medicine, caring for patients is almost always a matter of dealing with unknowns and probabilities (Allman, Steinberg, Keruly, & Dans, 1985).

Patients present their symptoms to medical professionals and are often sur-

A young man was to be operated on for an ingrown toenail. He entered the hospital and was given general anesthesia because he was apprehensive. While the anesthesia was being administered, his heart stopped. The surgeon had to open his chest, with no time for sterile technique, in order to start his heart. The patient survived but developed a serious infection of the lining of the heart. Also, while being wheeled to his hospital room after surgery, his leg was broken in an elevator accident. The young man then developed a pulmonary embolus (blood clot in his lung) as a result of his leg fracture, the further surgery on his heart to drain the infection, and the high dose of antibiotics he was given intravenously. When the young man was administered an anticlotting drug to dissolve the blood clot, he had massive bleeding from his stomach ulcer. After several months he was discharged from the hospital, although his ingrown toenail had never been fixed. Why did all these problems occur? The original error in treatment was to give the young man general anesthesia for the trivial surgical procedure required to fix his ingrown toenail.

How can a patient protect himself or herself from iatrogenic illness? Dr. Robin recommends finding a physician whose competence is high. The patient must also remain constantly vigilant and aware of decisions that are made for him or her. The patient must follow the logic of the medical reasoning done on his or her behalf, and must question decisions that do not seem to make sense. The patient must find out whether decisions about treatment will be affected by the results of diagnostic tests before submitting to the tests; if they will not, the tests should be declined. Before accepting any treatment decision, the patient must be sure to know the risks, the potential costs, and the potential benefits of the intervention, and must hope that he or she is one of the lucky ones who is helped, rather than harmed, by modern medicine.

prised to learn that medical diagnosis is not a simple one-to-one matching between the patient's bodily condition and a diagnostic label. Diagnosing illness can be like completing a puzzle. As an illustration, consider the condition of pregnancy. A standard obstetrics and gynecology textbook lists the physical signs and symptoms on which a clinical diagnosis of pregnancy is based (Benson, 1984). These findings are divided into *presumptive*, *probable*, and *positive* manifestations of pregnancy. Some of the *presumptive* manifestations of pregnancy, those that suggest a possible pregnancy, are the symptoms amenorrhea (lack of menstrual period), nausea and vomiting, mastodynia (pain or discomfort in the breasts), urinary bladder irritability, constipation, weight gain, fatigue, thinning and softening of nails, quickening (the first perception of fetal movement), chloasma (darkening of the skin on the forehead, nose, and cheeks) and other skin changes, basal body temperature elevation, increased growth of facial or body hair, breast changes (enlargement, vascular engorgement), abdominal enlargement, and changes in the pelvis and uterine cervix. Of course, any one or all of these presumptive signs and symptoms could be due to a condition other then pregnancy—which is why the signs and symptoms are called presumptive.

The signs and symptoms that are the *probable* manifestations of pregnancy are those that point to a substantial probability of, but do not confirm, pregnancy. These include, among others, uterine contractions and detection of a rushing sound when moving the uterus (indicating the presence of amniotic fluid). Most laboratory pregnancy tests have up to now been considered only probable signs of pregnancy, although in the past few years the radioimmunoassay of the hormone human chorionic gonadotropin (HCG) in the mother's blood

has become very accurate in detecting pregnancy.

The *positive* manifestations of pregnancy are objective signs that confirm beyond doubt that a pregnancy exists. No matter what appears to be the case to the doctor or the presumed mother, the only positive (sure) signs of pregnancy are the detection of fetal heartbeat and the detection of the presence of a fetus by X ray or ultrasound. But despite all the symptoms and apparent indications of pregnancy, the only way to know for sure is to have a test that directly assesses the presence of a fetus inside the woman's body. Today such tests are readily available and are easy and noninvasive.

The point of this discussion is that what is going on *inside* the human body is usually not apparent to people on the *outside* and must be deduced by examining signs and symptoms. The health professional collects these data and attempts to integrate the information in an effective manner (Pauker & Kassirer, 1987). Pregnancy is one of the easier conditions because positive tests such as ultrasound are available and noninvasive. (And if these tests were not available, the truth would eventually become apparent because at delivery a newborn baby would emerge!) Other medical conditions, however, do not offer clear-cut answers so easily. For example, the signs and symptoms of an alteration in liver functioning may or may not indicate liver cancer. Gathering information from the patient's history is the least invasive approach but may provide only presumptive signs of disease. Certain diagnostic tests (such as an X-ray liver scan) may provide probable signs. But tests that provide positive signs of liver cancer tend to be invasive methods, such as biopsy, where a portion of the presumed tumor is surgically removed and subjected to histological examination. Where to stop on this continuum in attempting to rule out the existence of liver cancer in a patient involves a subjective decision on the part of the physician (sometimes in conjunction with the patient). Greater certainty comes at increasing cost (in money, risk, pain, distress) to the patient (Allman et al., 1985).

With any condition, finding out what is going on in a person's body involves a process of *clinical reasoning*. The medical practitioner collects information from the patient during the medical visit (in a manner such as described in Chapter 7). He or she may conduct several laboratory tests as well. The process of diagnosis involves interpreting data, developing and revising hypotheses, constructing a treatment plan, and then testing and reevaluating that plan. Of course, this process is based upon likelihoods and probabilities. The practitioner sees a set of signs and symptoms that look like a particular syndrome, but each patient's case will be unique. The practitioner must decide whether the signs and symptoms displayed by the patient are indicative of a particular disease, and he or she must differentiate the patient's signs and symptoms from other possible causes. The practitioner's job during the clinical reasoning process is to show that the patient's signs and symptoms are more like those that would manifest with a particular disease entity, and are differentiated from those that would manifest with another. This process is called *differential diagnosis*.

## DECISION MAKING BY MEDICAL PROFESSIONALS

Clinical reasoning skills are fundamental to the practice of medicine. Clinical reasoning requires logical thinking, incorporation of all the data available, and avoidance of biases. Often, disagreements among "experts" regarding both diagnosis and treatment can be the result of differences in their subjective judgments and the clinical reasoning process (Eddy, 1982; Eraker & Politser, 1982).

Subjective clinical judgments can be influenced by many things. A particular practitioner's clinical experience can determine the emphasis that he or she places on certain facts. Experience heavily influenced physicians' decisions to discuss resuscitation efforts with their AIDS patients who had *Pneumocistis carinii* pneumonia, in one study. Physicians who had more experience taking care of these patients (and who thus had a good understanding of the hopelessness of resuscitation efforts) were more likely than those who had less experience to initiate discussion with their patients about the possibility of forgoing intubation and resuscitation (Wachter, Cooke, Hopewell, & Luce, 1988). In other research, estimates of the probabilities of certain clinical outcomes have been found to be affected by physicians' own clinical experience. For example, in cases in which the literature suggested a modest success rate of a particular intervention but most of a physician's patients did well on the treatment, the probability of success with future patients was overestimated (Tversky & Kahneman, 1974; Eraker & Politser, 1982).

Some physicians rely most heavily on *statistical predictions* of outcomes, such as prognosis after cancer therapy. They are concerned only with how many people have received that particular therapy and how many have had various outcomes, such as cure, temporary remission, or death. Other physicians rely more heavily on their *clinical experience*, that is, on what outcomes they themselves have seen occur in their own clinical work (Sawyer, 1966).

Which approach is better is not easy to say. Suppose that a male cancer patient who is young and basically physically robust asks a physician to quote the statistics on long-term survival with treatment for his type of cancer. The average survival rates might be quite low, and the patient might be quite distressed as well as misled if he were to take them as indications of his own chances. The statistics are meaningful in that they are based upon controlled research studies, but they need to be qualified by the fact that the patients in those studies likely were considerably less healthy and robust than the patient himself. Should the physician instead rely solely on his or her own experience and judgment in providing a recommendation to the patient? Probably not. Research suggests instead that the combination of statistical predictions and clinical experience contribute to the best decisions in medicine (Sawyer, 1966). The practitioner may do well to use his or her own experience with the treatment to modify his or her interpretations of what can be found in the literature.

How practitioners process information and make medical decisions can have great implications for patients' preferences as well. For example, how information is presented to patients can significantly affect their choices of various therapies (Tversky & Kahneman, 1981). In one study people were asked to decide between surgery and radiation therapy for lung cancer. Choices depended a great deal upon how the expected outcomes were presented, specifically in terms of the probability of living or dying. For example, respondents favored surgery more when the outcomes were presented in terms of the probability of surviving than when they were presented in terms of the probability of dying, even though the odds were the same in both cases (McNeil, Stephen, Pauker, Sox, & Tversky, 1982).

## ERRORS IN CLINICAL DECISIONS

Research suggests that among medical professionals, differences of opinion may occur because of limitations in their reasoning processes and biases in their subjec-tive judgments. In choosing a diagnosis, many physicians, for example, have been found to make errors that are referred to as *premature closure*. Premature closure tends to occur when a certain amount of information is available, but not enough to make a clear diagnosis. Yet, the physician decides upon an initial course of treatment, presuming (or filling in) the answer to the missing pieces of the diagnostic puzzle (Voytovich, Rippey, & Suffredini, 1985). An initial plan that is wrong, however, may not be able to be remedied by the most carefully determined later steps. In addition, once they have decided upon a diagnosis, no matter how early and prematurely, many physicians establish a cognitive set (a particular way of thinking) and then match subsequent data to their initial formulations, ignoring what does not fit (Elstein, 1976).

Consistent error patterns in diagnostic reasoning have been identified in research on physicians' decision making. It is relatively rare for a physician simply to ignore an important clinical clue, such as a serious symptom or an abnormal test result, or to draw a conclusion that completely contradicts the data. But as mentioned above, premature closure is quite common. The physician diagnoses the patient's condition, but the diagnosis is not justified on the basis of the existing data.

In one study 58 physicians at several levels of training (medical school, residency, and faculty) were given three hypothetical clinical cases with all the relevant data and were asked to indicate what diagnostic conclusions were warranted (Voytovich et al., 1985). Fifty-three of the 58 physicians made at least one error of premature closure (17 on only one case, 15 on two cases, and 21 on all three cases). Surprisingly, the errors were not related to the level of experience; just as many such errors were made by senior residents and faculty as by medical students. Some research shows that as early as the third year of medical school, some students can be identified by faculty as having consistent difficulties with clinical reasoning (Coggan, Macdonald, Camacho, Carline, & Taylor, 1985). Premature closure in diagnosis can, of course, lead to the wrong treatment as well as to a false sense of confidence that the correct treatment has been chosen. There may be a long delay before it is discovered that the wrong pathway is being pursued. In the meantime the patient's real problem is not dealt with, and he or she receives inappropriate therapy.

How can such errors come about? There are several possible explanations. First, most medical decisions are made in a hurry, whether or not they need to be. Although speed is certainly valued in emergency situations, most medical decisions are not emergencies. But physicians tend to make decisions rather quickly because of habit, practice time constraints (for example, an office full of patients), and other pressures and professional demands (May & Revicki, 1985). In their haste, some physicians may be prone to infer information they do not have, and to draw conclusions from incomplete data. Second, physicians vary in their tolerance for uncertainty. Some require certainty (or its approximation given the limitations of testing); others are willing to decide on the basis of a small amount of information. These differences have important implications for the extensiveness of testing to which physicians are willing to subject their patients (Allman et al., 1985). Third, some clinical decisions are complex and not at all routine. Each individual patient has a unique history, laboratory values, and psychosocial and clinical findings, all of which must be integrated to arrive at a decision that is right for that patient. Such integration may be difficult to do effectively, particularly in a brief time frame. Recently, quantitative methods have been developed for incorporating data

about individual patients into clinical decisions. These methods are part of the important new field of *decision analysis* (Pauker & Kassirer, 1987).

In addition, as we see in Box 9–4, medical professionals have certain biases that affect the accuracy of the presumptions they make. These biases can strongly affect the ways that they assess clinical problems.

## STEREOTYPES AS BARRIERS TO CLINICAL DECISIONS

Within the first few minutes of a clinical encounter, a health professional begins to generate hypotheses about what might be wrong with a patient. These hypotheses are typically based upon cues from the patient, on preliminary information that is disclosed by the patient, and on the practitioner's observations. In interpreting this early information, the practitioner may be subtly influenced by the nature of his or her relationship with the patient, and by the patient's characteristics.

In many studies it has been found that perceptions of a patient's social class, economic background, sex, and physical appearance do indeed affect physicians' clinical decisions. *Stereotypes* (that is, exaggerated beliefs, oversimplifications, and uncritical judgments) held about certain patients can strongly influence physicians' clinical decisions (Eisenberg, 1979). In one study the diagnosis of obesity was more than twice as likely to be given to women patients as it was to men patients, although in this study more men than women were actually obese (Franks, Culpepper, & Dickinson, 1982). In other research, students at a school of osteopathy watched videotapes of five different simulated patients, each presenting with the same physical complaint (Johnson, Kurtz, Tomlinson, & Howe, 1986). The students attributed certain positive characteristics to some patients on the basis of irrelevant characteristics, such as the patient's attractiveness and his or her being Caucasian. The characteristics that were attributed had implications for diagnosis, such as the patient's being open and honest and reliable as an information source. Of course, the patient's attractiveness and race do not provide an adequate basis for drawing conclusions about the reliability of his or her reports. However, such decisions could lead a physician to believe information that does not make sense or is clearly inaccurate from a patient who is thought to be reliable, and to doubt information that is accurate and clinically relevant from a patient who is thought to be unreliable.

Stereotyping may be a convenient way to deal with complexity and may even speed up conclusions, but stereotyping can lead to definite problems in clinical reasoning. Stereotyped views that a physician holds about a patient's psychology can strongly influence the conclusions drawn about the origin of the patient's problem and hence about the treatment to be prescribed. For example, in this country, there are over 5 million users of minor tranquilizers prescribed by general practitioners. Over two-thirds of these prescriptions are written for women (Chambers & Griffey, 1975). Research suggests that physicians are more likely to see psychological dis-

BOX
9–4

## THE LAW OF THE KNIFE

When people obtain medical care, they usually think they are getting all the options available for treating them. What they may be unaware of, however, is the important role played by the specialty orientation of their medical practitioners. *The Law of the Knife* refers to the phenomenon in which the tools available define the problem.

Here is an illustration. Recently, on an educational television program for physicians, several surgeons were singing the praises of a new experimental brain operation for patients with Parkinson's disease. *Parkinson's disease* is a neurological disorder that produces progressive muscle rigidity, limitations in movement, and involuntary tremor. The disease progresses for about ten years, leading to death. Parkinson's disease strikes one in every 100 persons over age 60. The experimental surgery involves the placement of fetal tissue deep within the brain of the patient. The procedure had been done on only a few patients so far, many of whom had some improvement in their Parkinsonian symptoms but no data were available on the long-term effects of the surgery. An *internist* (specialist in internal medicine, who treats patients with drugs and other noninvasive techniques) pointed out that the only people who were candidates for the operation were those whose Parkinsonian symptoms were alleviated by the drugs levodopa and carbidopa, which serve to increase levels of dopamine (a brain chemical) that is often in short supply in patients who have this disease. But why conduct dangerous brain surgery, he questioned, when drug treatment worked just as well?

Consider another example. A patient has a lumbar disk herniation (explained in Chapter 6). An orthopedic surgeon automatically recommends surgical treatment. But a sports medicine specialist instead teaches the patient to move correctly and to manage pain with various psychological and physical therapy techniques (Ogden-Niemeyer & Jacobs, 1989).

Keep in mind that medical diagnosis and treatment depend a great deal upon the orientation and experience of the decision makers.

turbance at the root of, or correlated with, the problems of women patients than those of men patients (Fisher, 1986). Physicians are also strongly influenced by their assessments of their patients' motivations and ability to care for themselves, although such assessments are often made rapidly and on the basis of implicit stereotypes rather than on the basis of patients' real capabilities.

Some research suggests that physicians sometimes see what they expect to see, and only what they have been trained to recognize. In a study of 123 residents in five training hospitals, researchers found that despite the unique opportunity that exists for physicians to recognize alcohol problems both from reports of patient behavior and from manifested medical complications, physicians frequently remain unaware of alcohol problems in their patients (Warburg et al., 1987). Even when they are aware, they often undertreat or fail to treat these problems. But training in recognizing and dealing with alcoholism raised their awareness of their patients' alcohol problems and made physicians more likely to refer alcoholics to experts.

Finally, physicians' values can even influence decisions, such as whether a patient is "dead on arrival" at the hospital. Emergency room physicians, for example, have been found to be influenced in their decisions by their inherent values. In one observational study, car accident victims who had been drunk, and destitute old people were more likely to be classified as dead on arrival by emergency room physicians, who made no efforts at resuscitation. Resuscitation was typically attempted on children, even when they appeared to be already dead (Roth, 1972).

Making rational decisions is one of the great challenges of medical practice. Many factors indigenous to the world of medicine can make logical thinking difficult. As we have seen in this chapter, such factors include emotional distress, lack of adequate time, and enormous fatigue, which may promote cognitive deficits (Webb, 1982). Pressures to save time may promote stereotyping as well as premature conclusions that are unwarranted by the data available from the patient. And physicians' values cannot help but affect their evaluations of patients and the decisions they make about patient care.

## Summary

I. In the process of providing patient care, medical professionals experience unusual and sometimes overwhelming pressures.

   A. Medical professionals are required to function effectively in all sorts of physically demanding situations and often under tremendous time pressures. They experience various physical stresses, such as sleep deprivation, irregular schedules for meals, poor nutrition, and few opportunities for relaxation and exercise.

   B. The challenges of being a medical professional are also heavily emotional. Many of the difficulties are so pervasive that they can damage the medical professional's coping mechanisms, affect attitudes toward patients, and limit social support. Family relationships and friendships are often disrupted by training and practice. Particularly during the training years, medical professionals tend to have severely limited time for their spouses and children.

   C. Patients who are noncompliant, demanding, and clinging, and who consistently do not respond to treatment are an important source of stress for medical professionals.

D. Medical professionals sometimes lose their idealistic views of medical practice and are dismayed by the limitations of medical science.

E. Medical professionals are typically expected not to express what they feel and to hide their emotions from their patients, colleagues, and even from themselves. Emotional disowning is a common coping mechanism among medical professionals.

II. The pressures of medical training can have serious consequences.

A. By the end of medical school, over half of graduates need psychotherapy, although only a very small percentage receive it. At least a third of interns have frequent or severe emotional distress. In the first year of residency alone at least 30% of residents experience serious depression, and there is evidence that the emotional impairment of physicians is on the increase. Mild depression is reported by approximately 13% of practicing physicians; 4% report moderate to severe depression; 27% report beyond-normal anxiety; and 13% report moderate or severe anxiety.

B. At least 25% of physicians in training have serious thoughts of committing suicide. The leading cause of death of physicians under 40 is suicide. Suicide among male physicians across all age groups is about 1.5 times the rate of suicide in males in the general population. The rate of suicide among women physicians is 4 times that among females in the general population.

C. Physician impairment is defined as the inability of the physician to practice medicine adequately because of physical or mental illness, including alcoholism or drug dependence. Practicing physicians are prone to alcoholism at rates estimated to range from about 8% to over 12%. Underreporting is suspected. Drug addiction is estimated to be 30 to 100 times more common among physicians than in the general population and even higher compared with persons in socioeconomically matched control groups.

D. There is evidence that health professionals are aware of one another's alcohol and drug use habits. One survey of medical students showed that 25% had on at least one occasion witnessed a faculty member engage in drug or alcohol abuse. Nineteen percent had witnessed drug or alcohol abuse in nurses.

E. Impairment can result in self-destructive actions and can interfere with physicians' ability to carry out effective patient care. Their judgment, memory, and manual dexterity can be severely compromised. Their sensitivity to patients' emotional needs may suffer.

III. The pressure of medical practice can also result in withdrawal from loved ones and retreat from family life. Emotional separation from the family occurs progressively, and eventually the willingness and ability to share feelings are lost. Further, the disowning of their own emotions can cause medical professionals to numb themselves against the feelings of their patients. In denying their own emotions, it is possible for medical professionals to lose their capacity to recognize and to respond to emotions in others.

A. There is also a tendency for health professionals, particularly those overly burdened emotionally, to see patients' problems as the patients' fault.

B. Medical humor is a well-established coping mechanism for physicians and nurses that serves to enhance the cohesiveness of the group of medical professionals who form a team. They demonstrate their recognition of one another's professional identity and acknowledge the stressful nature of their work.

C. Burnout is a negatively valued psychological response that is characterized by physical and emotional exhaustion, an increased cynicism about and dehumanization of patients, a decreased concern and respect for patients, a loss of positive feeling for others, and a tendency to blame others for distress. Burnout results commonly in job change or in ineffective job performance.

IV. Currently, approximately 30% of the medical students in the United States are women. This statistic represents a big change from the 1960s, when the percentage was only about 6%.

A. At least in some realms, women physicians experience somewhat more stress than do men. Although women have been found to have lower stress levels and higher mental health than men during the early years of medical school, later clinical training tends to embody more stressors for females than males. These in-

clude distress over separation from family, friends, and loved ones during clinical training. Women medical students have been found to express more concen about feelings of loneliness, being out of place, and being unable to achieve their goals than have men, and women medical students report more stress-related symptoms than do men.

B. In recent years there has been a recognition of the important contribution that women physicians make to the profession of medicine. Women tend to express the personal characteristics of sensitivity and empathy for patients that we have seen are so valuable in patient care. In their attitudes, they have been found to be on the average more sensitive than male physicians to the doctor-patient relationship, more accepting of patients' feelings, and more open to the social and humanistic aspects of patient care. Women physicians also tend to be more concerned than males about balancing work responsibilities and family life, so that their own emotional needs and social support, as well as the welfare of their families, are not sacrificed.

V. Caring for patients is almost always a matter of dealing with unknowns and probabilities.

A. Finding out what is going on in a person's body involves a process of clinical reasoning. The medical practitioner collects information from the patient during the medical visit and combines the information with that gathered from the examination and from diagnostic tests.

B. The practitioner's job during the clinical reasoning process is to show that the patients' signs and symptoms are more like those that would manifest with a particular disease entity, and are differentiated from those that would manifest with another. This process is called differential diagnosis.

C. Clinical decisions are made on the basis of both statistical predictions and clinical experience.

D. In choosing a diagnosis, many physicians have been found to make errors that are referred to as premature closure. Premature closure tends to occur when a certain amount of information is available but not enough to make a clear diagnosis. The diagnosis is made anyway, and subsequent information is processed only as it fits the diagnosis chosen.

E. In many studies it has been found that perceptions of a patient's social class, economic background, sex, and physical appearance do indeed affect physicians' clinical decisions. Stereotypes (that is, exaggerated beliefs, oversimplifications, and uncritical judgments) held about certain patients can strongly influence physicians' clinical decisions.

# Glossary

**belief in a just world:** an individual's conviction that people get what they deserve and deserve what they get.

**blaming the victim:** a psychological phenomenon that stems from a belief that those who are victimized by life circumstances actually deserve what they get. Thus, someone who is the victim of illness is blamed for doing something that brought that illness on.

**burnout:** a negatively valued psychological response that is characterized by physical and emotional exhaustion, an increased cynicism about and dehumanization of patients, a decreased concern and respect for patients, a loss of positive feeling for others, and a tendency to blame others for their distress.

**clinical experience:** outcomes that medical practitioners have themselves seen occur in their own clinical work.

**clinical reasoning skills:** fundamental to the practice of medicine, clinical reasoning requires logical thinking, incorporation of all the data available, and avoidance of biases.

**clinical years of medical school:** typically the third and fourth years.

**differential diagnosis:** the physician's job during the clinical reasoning process is to show that the patient's signs and symptoms are more like those that would manifest with a particular disease entity and are differentiated from those that would manifest with another.

**emotional disowning:** a relatively common coping mechanism among medical professionals that involves a focus away from emotions and a purposeful avoidance of feelings.

**functional:** having no definable organic basis.

**health-professional impairment:** a general term for the various self-destructive actions in which some medical professionals engage, such as alcohol and drug use. These activities can interfere with their ability to carry out effective patient care, and judgment, memory, and manual dexterity can be severely compromised.

**house officers:** interns and residents in medical training.

**iatrogenic:** caused by medical professionals or resulting directly from medical treatment or diagnostic procedures.

**internist:** a specialist in internal medicine who treats patients with drugs and other noninvasive techniques.

**medical humor:** a well-established coping mechanism for physicians and nurses. Humor serves to enhance the cohesiveness of a group of medical professionals and helps to diffuse the stress of their work.

**nosocomial infections:** hospital-acquired infections that are transmitted to a patient as a result of infractions by hospital personnel in required sterile technique.

**Parkinson's disease:** a neurological disorder that produces progressive muscle rigidity, limitations in movement, and involuntary tremor. The disease can be progressive and eventually fatal.

**premature closure:** a decision-making bias that occurs when a certain amount of information is available, but not enough to make a clear diagnosis. The physician decides upon an initial course of treatment, presuming (or filling in) the answer to the missing pieces of the diagnostic puzzle.

**statistical prediction:** prediction based upon empirical probabilities. For example, statistical prediction of treatment outcomes is based upon the number of people who have received that particular therapy and how many have had various outcomes, such as cure, temporary remission, or death.

**stereotypes:** exaggerated beliefs, oversimplifications, and uncritical judgments held about an individual, object, or phenomenon.

**trivialization of patient distress:** in denying their own emotions, medical professionals lose the capacity to recognize and respond to emotions in others. They may expect patients to deny feelings as they themselves do.

# Psychological Processes, Stress, and Physical Illness

▪ ▪ ▪ ▪ ▪

Things were not going well for Annie. In fact, she had never felt quite so hopeless in her life. Annie tried over and over to get her life on track, but there seemed to be disappointment at every turn. She was having trouble getting up in the morning and had little or no enthusiasm for anything. She had serious problems making decisions because she was afraid that whatever course she chose would be the wrong one. So she went on, day after day, anxious and distressed. Annie's difficulties seemed to start when she broke up with Ken. Throughout high school and most of college, Annie had looked forward to marrying Ken some day. She had never considered what her life would be like without him. Then one day he told her that he was in love with someone else.

A series of academic disasters followed and Annie ended up on academic probation at her college. She was told that if any grade she earned was lower than a "C," she would not be allowed to register for the following semester. Because she was doing so poorly in school, Annie's parents refused to continue supporting her. It was not, however, until her parked car was totaled by a hit-and-run driver that Annie began to have some unusual physical symptoms.

At first she would find herself vaguely off balance once or twice a day. Her "spell" would last for a minute or two and then she would be fine. During it, she would feel the muscles in her legs weaken so that she could not walk. She would trip over her feet as they seemed to buckle under her. Then she began to lose muscular coordination in her arms and face. Initially, Annie attributed the symptoms to her poor care of her own health. After all, she was eating very little and was so anxious and distraught that she couldn't sleep. As the symptoms continued to worsen, however, they became less and less explainable. Finally, she went to the doctor.

The physician she saw at the university health service arranged immediately for Annie to see a neurologist. After many uncomfortable tests, the neurologist diagnosed her condition as *infectious polyneuritis* or Guillain-Barré syndrome. Guillain-Barré syndrome is believed to be a cell-mediated immunologic attack on peripheral nerves in response to a virus. The condition causes inflammation and degenerative changes in nerve roots, resulting in both sensory and motor impairment.

Some patients with acute polyneuritis develop progressive total muscular paralysis and are faced with life-threatening respiratory failure. Because of this, they must be hospitalized and given respiratory support until they recover. Some never again achieve full functioning.

Annie was lucky, however. She had a relatively mild case of Guillain-Barré syndrome, and after a short hospital stay, some rest, and the resolution of some of her more distressing emotional conflicts, she did recover. Annie wondered, however, what role her breakup with Ken and her subsequent academic and financial troubles played in her ill health.

Annie is not the first patient to experience frightening physical symptoms after an emotionally distressing event. One patient described in the early psychological literature was a young woman named Anna O. who was a patient of Joseph Breuer's and later of Sigmund Freud's. Anna O. is credited with having inspired the "discovery" of psychoanalysis (Erdelyi, 1985).

Anna O. became Breuer's patient in 1880, at the age of 21, when she developed some serious symptoms under the pressure of caring for her dying father. These symptoms included a pattern of intermittent, incapacitating paralysis of her limbs, listlessness, anorexia (lack of desire for food), painful coughing fits, and a blinding squint (Erdelyi, 1985). Breuer tried to treat her with hypnosis, which was somewhat successful. However, when her father finally died, she relapsed.

Breuer then treated Anna O. using a technique that resembled the talking cure of "psychotherapy" later developed by Freud. Many of Anna's symptoms were relieved by the analysis of their origin in her unconscious mind. For example, her cough, which was often triggered by music, was finally cured when she remembered how it started. One night while caring for her father in the dark by his bedside, she heard music emanating from a party next door. She found herself wishing that she could go dancing at the lively party instead of attending to her father. She began coughing violently in response to the guilt she felt for such a thought. When Anna recalled the event, with all its painful emotions, her coughing ceased.

The *cathartic technique* developed by Breuer involved reviving inhibited or otherwise difficult to access memories for the purpose of discharging the pathogenic (disease-causing) emotions attached to them. The patient had to recollect (or relive emotionally) the distressing incidents in all their intensity in order for the procedure to work.

Anna O. was treated for two years by Breuer. About a year of that time was spent in cathartic therapy, during which Anna revealed her thoughts and feelings, dreams and recollections. As a result, an intense positive rapport developed between physician and patient. It is said that Breuer was so distressed when he realized the growing emotional connection between himself and his young female patient that he tried to end the therapy abruptly. The patient's distress at her abandonment brought an avalanche of physical symptoms. Sigmund Freud was called in to treat Anna with his newly developed psychoanalysis.

Anna O. was, in real life, a young woman named Bertha Pappenheimer. She went on to become a feminist and the founder of social work in Germany. Her case demonstrates that as early as the 19th century (and even before, cf. Whyte, 1960), physicians were concerned with understanding the role that emotions can play in the development of physical illness.

# Psychophysiological Disorders

Annie and her predecessor, Anna O., each suffered from a *psychophysiological disorder*. A psychophysiological disorder is characterized by physical symptoms and/or dysfunctions that are intimately linked with psychological factors. There is typically a close interplay between the psychological and the physiological processes making separation and analysis of each component impossible.

In Chapter 5 we examined in detail how psychological factors, such as thoughts, beliefs, and feelings, can affect a person's perceptions of his or her bodily state. We saw that distress from loss or anxiety can lead an individual to give more than usual attention to symptoms. In Chapter 6 we examined the manner in which emotional factors can focus attention on pain and exaggerate its effects on the individual. In this chapter we turn to a more general analysis of psychophysiological disorders and examine how psychological variables, particularly emotions, can predispose an individual to disease and even interact with physical variables to exacerbate an already distressed physical condition.

Let us conceptualize a continuum on which we can plot the role of psychological factors in disease states. On one end we have conditions identified or brought about because of purely psychological factors. An example would be very serious illness (or even death) brought about by self-starvation in a person with the psychiatric disorder *anorexia nervosa*. (Anorexia nervosa is "a serious nervous condition in which the patient loses his appetite and systematically takes but little food, so that he becomes greatly emaciated" [*Dorland's Illustrated Medical Dictionary*, 1965, p. 99].) On the other end of the continuum might lie disease conditions that are believed to be little affected or unaffected by psychological states. An example might be acute appendicitis. In between is a vast array of diseases that are influenced in various ways and to varying degrees, by emotions. Let us look at the two examples we considered earlier.

Anna O.'s physical symptoms were conceptualized by Freud and Breuer as the

  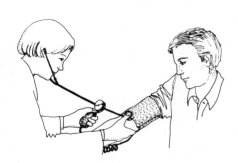 

Asthma:
a suppressed cry in
reaction to the threat
of separation.

Migraine:
bottled-up hostile
impulses exploding
in the head.

High-blood pressure:
feelings of threat from
ever-present danger
or harm.

Hives (urticaria):
taking an unfair
beating.

**FIGURE 10–1**    The Nuclear Conflict Theory and psychoanalytic explanations for specific illnesses.

outward manifestations of her emotional distress. These pioneers of the psychodynamic method proposed a kind of "hydraulic model" of the mind, in which pressure builds up in the psyche and metaphorically "leaks" into another realm (the realm of the body). Freud and Breuer explained Anna O.'s symptoms as expression *through the body* of phenomena of the psyche, namely emotions. Anna's limb paralysis, for example, embodied her anger at her father for restricting her life with his needs for care. With paralyzed limbs, she was helpless to express her anger and could guarantee that she could not run away or strike out at her father and hurt him. Her physical condition was so clearly the result of buried emotional conflicts that when she was treated using the cathartic method and became aware of her emotional conflicts, her physical problems disappeared.

Following from the work of Freud and Breuer, various clinicians and theoreticians have affirmed (unfortunately without any definitive research) that certain emotional states can actually lead to *specific* medical conditions (Alexander, 1950). Based upon observations of people in psychoanalytic treatment, Alexander proposed the *Nuclear*

*Conflict Theory*. The theory holds that each physiological disorder is associated with certain specific unconscious emotional conflicts. This psychoanalytic hypothesis is based upon the belief that an individual's repressed psychic energy can be discharged directly (as in the hydraulic model noted above) to affect the autonomic nervous system, leading to impairment of body functioning.

In this theory, for example, asthma is believed to be caused by unresolved dependency needs, particularly with respect to mother. The obstructed breathing of asthma is believed to *be* (not just to be *like*) a "suppressed cry" for the mother in reaction to the threat of separation. Migraine headaches are believed to be the result of repressed or inhibited hostile impulses (which are "bottled up," and in a sense "exploding" in the head). Note that in this approach the metaphor for the illness becomes its explanation. Figure 10–1 depicts the Nuclear Conflict Theory as well as the psychoanalytic explanations below.

Other psychoanalytically oriented writers have similarly argued that specific physiological disorders result from certain specific attitudes (Graham, 1972). For example, hypertension (high blood pressure) can befall a person who feels threatened by ever-present danger or harm. The person remains constantly on guard and prepared to act. The individual who suffers from hives is one who feels he or she is taking an unfair beating, and while being treated unfairly is helpless to do anything about it. Although these specific relationships between attitudes, emotions, and disease conditions have not been well substantiated by empirical research, they have achieved some popularity among some health professionals and the public because they are intriguing and even entertaining ideas.

Annie's acute polyneuritis was caused by a virus. Current researchers, however, would be quick to point out that her emotional state may very well have predisposed her to that virus in the first place by weakening the ability of her immune system to resist it. Annie's emotional distress led her to unhealthy behaviors, such as skipping meals and sleeping poorly, but these behaviors may not fully account for her increased susceptibility to viral disease. As we will see in this chapter, recent research suggests that emotions may well have a *direct* effect on physiological mechanisms. Emotional factors can lead to a weakened ability to ward off disease.

# Stress

To understand the role that pressures and problems can play in jeopardizing a person's physical health, we need to examine the concept of *stress*. Throughout its history as a concept, stress has proven to be relatively complicated and has inspired considerable confusion.

Stress is really a physical construct, referring to the amount of force acting on a physical object. The term *stress* has been used in the fields of biology, medicine, and psychology to apply to the human orga-

nism. Stress has been used to refer to physical strain (such as taxing an organism beyond its strength) and to psychological strain (such as when an individual experiences negative emotional reactions as a result of conflict in relationships with other people). Unfortunately, in the process of its development, the concept of stress has become more and more imprecise as it has become more and more popular. In fact, these days people tend to say they are under stress (or even "stressed out"!) when they feel almost any form of dysphoria from fatigue to anger. Despite its widespread application and its popular appeal, stress is a surprisingly chaotic construct.

## THE MEANING OF STRESS

To add to the general confusion that exists about the concept of stress, researchers have conceptualized it in at least three ways. Some have looked at stress (or more precisely, a *stressor*) as a *stimulus* that produces feelings of tension. Stressors can include earthshaking events, such as devastating hurricanes and earthquakes; significant life changes, such as the birth of a new baby into a family; and consistently taxing situations, such as living in a dangerous neighborhood. Other researchers have approached stress as the *physical and psychological response to stressors*. In this view, stress is the internal feeling generated in response to certain events or thoughts about those events (Coyne & Holroyd, 1982).

Still other researchers look at stress as a process that involves an *interaction between the person and his or her environment* (Lazarus & Folkman, 1984). The degree of stress an individual feels in response to an environmental event is dependent upon many aspects of the person-environment fit. The person is seen as active in determining the impact of stressors on his or her feelings, thoughts, and behaviors. In this view, stressful events tax the individual's physical makeup and functioning, psychological equilibrium, and relationships with others. Depending upon how extensive his or her resources are, the individual may be more or less able to deal with the demands of the situations presented.

In this third view of stress, what a person *thinks* about the demands of the situation and about his or her own abilities to meet those demands is critically important (Lazarus & Folkman, 1984; Trumbull & Appley, 1986). If an individual believes that the social or physical environment demands more resources than he or she has available, a stress response will be experienced. On the other hand, if the life events are minimally demanding in relation to the person's resources, little or no stress will be experienced. Thus, the experience of stress is dependent upon the individual's *cognitive appraisal* of the events and the resources he or she has available to deal with them (Cohen & Lazarus, 1983).

## THE ROLE OF COGNITIVE APPRAISAL

*Cognitive appraisal* of stress depends upon the thoughtful evaluation of two issues: whether or not an event threatens (both short-term and long-term) well-being and whether or not the resources are available for meeting and dealing with the threat (Cohen & Lazarus, 1983; Lazarus & Launier, 1978). If someone we know responds to us in a hostile manner, we might experience feelings of stress if we like that person, fear losing a friendship, and feel unable to explore with the person the reasons for feelings of hostility toward us. On the other hand, we may feel little or no stress if we care little about maintaining the friendship (that is, do not feel threatened by the loss) and/or if we feel fully able to discuss openly with the person the issues that may have prompted the hostility (that is, we feel able to contend with the challenge).

*Threat* is a key concept in understanding stress. Threat is the subjective appraisal of the potential negative effects of a stressor. The perception of an event as stressful is dependent upon the appraisal of that event as threatening, either as a result of perceptions, expectations, or memory. Threat mobilizes the individual into action. Events are most stressful that are believed or remembered to be negative and uncontrollable, ambiguous and unpredictable, yet that demand adaptation (Lazarus & Folkman, 1984).

There are two phases in the appraisal of a potential stressor. The *primary appraisal* involves the person's determination of whether the event has any potential negative implications for him or her. The person asks: Is the event (or potential event) harmful or dangerous to me or threatening to my future? Is it likely to thwart my values and goals? The *secondary appraisal* involves the individual's determination of whether his or her own abilities are sufficient to overcome the threat of potential harm. Only after such appraisals have been made does the individual react. The reaction might involve physiological, emotional, cognitive, and/or behavioral changes (Lazarus & Folkman, 1984).

This broader theory of stress takes into account the fact that human beings think, and that in doing so they evaluate the meaning of an event before reacting to it. For example, traveling down a hill at breakneck speed in a small car over which one has no control might be a highly stressful event if the car is one's own uninsured subcompact, the streets are in San Francisco, and one has discovered that the car's brakes are defective. On the other hand, if the car and the hill are part of a roller-coaster ride at Disneyland (*and* one likes roller coasters), stress is minimal and excitement is very high. For someone terrified of roller coasters, of course, reactions to the latter situation may be quite similar to reactions to the former!

Researchers have demonstrated that we interpret whatever we encounter, and that our cognitive interpretations determine our responses. In one study, subjects were shown films of gruesome shop accidents (Lazarus, Opton, Nomikos, & Rankin, 1965). Subjects who were told that the events were staged, experienced considerably less subjective stress than did those who believed the accidents were real. Furthermore, subjects who had no available cognitive interpretation (were not told whether the events were staged or had really occurred) experienced the greatest feelings of subjective stress. (Perhaps they wondered whether they themselves were in some kind of danger.) In other studies, individuals who did not have a framework within which they could understand a potentially stressful event interpreted it as threatening (Speisman, Lazarus, Mordkoff, & Davidson, 1964).

In Chapter 11 we will return to this issue of cognitive interpretations and stress because considerable research points to two important facts: (1) psychological factors determine which events are perceived as stressful in the first place, and (2) even when certain events or life situations are indeed appraised as stressful, psychological factors can determine whether these factors will have a negative effect on health.

## ISSUES IN CONCEPTUALIZING STRESS

Researchers have conceptualized stress in many different ways (Stotland, 1987). For example, some researchers have considered stress to be *static*, resulting from an isolated event. Others have looked at stress as a *process* that changes and develops over time. Stress is experienced, adjusted to, enhanced, or diminished, depending upon various mitigating factors. As a process, stress can be studied longitudinally, and

the effects of stress on later behaviors, choices, reactions, and physical conditions can be assessed.

Another important distinction made by stress researchers is that of *objectivity* versus *subjectivity*. Some researchers have measured stress as if it were experienced in the same way by everyone. As we will see below, they have sought to establish an objective measure of the amount of stress associated with various life events. They have averaged the opinions of a large number of people and have compared various stressors with one another. Although there certainly are commonalities among people in their experience of stress, such an approach fails to represent the unique personal experience of stress. Since stress is influenced by psychological factors (as we will see further later), it varies with the experience of each individual. Viewed as subjective, stress can be measured only phenomenologically, that is, from each person's own point of view.

When stress is defined subjectively, the door is left open to examine mediating factors, such as a person's cognitive interpretation of the events experienced or anticipated and the physical, emotional, and social resources the individual can use to help cope with the experience of stress. We do this in detail in Chapter 11.

Recently, researchers have focused on stress as a *dynamic process* (Folkman & Lazarus, 1980; Kobasa, 1979). Stress is conceived as ongoing and pervasive, something that everyone experiences to some degree at any given time. But the person-environment interaction changes character over time, and the individual deals with the stress in various ways. Sometimes it overwhelms him or her, bringing about behaviors that cause new stressors to emerge. Sometimes stressful events can be contended with quite nicely, confidence increases, and he or she proceeds to deal quite well with other aspects of life.

To characterize the stress experience fully, researchers have become concerned with the meaning and the effects of the *chronicity* of stress. Just as certain serious and threatening physical or psychological events can precipitate a stress experience, so too can a series of smaller events. If many stressful occurrences come about in a short period of time, or if irritating, distressing day-to-day events require repeated efforts at adaptation, stress can become chronic. Chronic daily stress can lead not only to dissatisfaction with life but also to some problematic physical symptoms such as rapid heart rate and high blood pressure (Coyne, Aldwin, & Lazarus, 1981).

Let us now examine the three main forms of stressful experiences that have been studied by researchers: chronic stress, day-to-day hassles, and major life changes.

## CHRONIC STRESS

Chronic stress can result from a life situation that requires significant and persistent adaptation. Consider Carolyn, who, as a college student with very limited financial resources, experiences chronic stress. Carolyn works full time in addition to taking a full course load. Her days are spent commuting to her eight-hour job and then commuting to school, much of the time dealing with crowded roads and rush-hour traffic. She must be constantly aware of the passage of time, never wasting a moment that could be spent studying. Carolyn must be extremely organized and juggle her schedule to fit in all of the requirements of the day. She faces financial troubles. Her tuition payments must be the first priority, and so she has little money available for necessities such as food and clothing. Because she can afford only an inexpensive apartment, Carolyn lives in a less than desirable neighborhood that is sometimes dangerous. Coming home alone at night af-

ter class is highly stressful for her because she feels unsafe. Although things are likely to change for her in a few years, right now Carolyn experiences a life of chronic stress.

Chronic stress is typically experienced by an individual who lives in an environment that is inherently stressful. Long-term deprivation and loss, as well as inadequate resources, might cause long-standing, persistent, and debilitating stress responses (Fried, 1982).

One of the greatest sources of chronic stress in modern life is that which comes from the workplace (Quick & Quick, 1984). Occupational stress has been studied rather extensively, and its importance is recognized particularly because people spend such a large proportion of their lives at work. Occupational stress can affect workers' productivity, and stress can result in high levels of job turnover (Quick & Quick, 1984).

One major factor in job stress is work overload (Quick & Quick, 1984). Excessive work loads can result in an increased rate of job-related accidents and health problems. One study of industrial workers, for instance, found that those who worked 48 or more hours a week were twice as likely as those with similar jobs who worked 40 hours a week or less to die from coronary artery disease (Breslow & Buell, 1960).

Individuals who perceive great work pressure, such as being expected to work longer and harder than they wish to, are more likely than those without such perceptions to become ill (Breslow & Buell, 1960). Certain illnesses have also been found more likely to occur in those who have responsibility for other people. For example, studies of air traffic controllers show that they have very high levels of perceived stress. The hypertension rate among air traffic controllers has been found to be *4 times* greater than that among individuals with similar jobs but without responsibility for people's lives. The air traffic controllers were also twice as likely to have diabetes and peptic ulcers (Cobb, 1976). Members of the health professions (as we have seen in Chapter 9) also face job pressures that can lead to emotional exhaustion and the condition called burnout (Maslach & Jackson, 1982).

When workers have little control over what they do (for example, when they cannot control the pace of their work because it is determined by a machine or an assembly line), they are at risk for serious illness (Cottington & House, 1987; House, 1981). Relatedly, people experience considerable job stress when they are given no clear idea what they must do to get ahead and when there are few guidelines or standards of work. Such feelings of lack of control result in chronically elevated blood pressure rates and even in higher rates of cardiovascular disease.

People rely fairly heavily on their work for social contacts and relationships with people with whom they have common interests. Those who have little opportunity to interact with others at work are less satisfied with their jobs and tend to experience more stress than do those who have greater opportunities for social interaction (House, 1981). Relatedly, greater mobility (such as may result among those who must comply with many job transfers) may lead to a sense of uprootedness and to greater psychological distress (Lindheim & Syme, 1983).

Can people adapt to long-term, chronic stress? In some cases individuals can indeed grow accustomed to facing novel stimuli repeatedly. For some, physiological reactions (corticosteroid and catecholamine levels) can eventually return to normal (Rose, 1980). Some long-lasting, negative situations, such as environmental overcrowding, can even be adapted to (Glass & Singer, 1972). However, individu-

als whose resources are already limited and who are already vulnerable, such as the poor, the elderly, and children, may be particularly affected by chronic stress.

## THE HASSLES OF EVERYDAY LIFE

Getting a traffic ticket, misplacing one's keys, and breaking a glass full of milk on the kitchen floor are relatively minor events in the scheme of all the potential problems of human life. Researchers suggest, however, that the cumulative effects of such relatively minor events can, in some cases, be hazardous to an individual's health. Daily *hassles* are events to which we have no automatic, adaptive responses. These events sometimes take us by surprise and always require some degree of adjustment.

Research points out that it is not only major life events that can pose threats to our health. Sometimes the daily hassles of living, if excessive or if not dealt with in an adaptive manner, can, over the long term, have a cumulative negative effect on health (Lazarus & Cohen, 1977; Kanner, Coyne, Schaefer, & Lazarus, 1981). An instrument called the *Hassles Scale* lists 117 of these day-to-day events, many of which are simply unpleasant (such as misplacing or losing things, and having to be near inconsiderate smokers) but some of which are major difficulties (such as having concerns about owing money or about not having enough money for clothing). When completing the scale, the subject indicates which hassles have occurred in the past month and rates each hassle as having been somewhat, moderately, or extremely severe. In one study 100 middle-aged adults completed the Hassles Scale for nine consecutive months and reported their psychological symptoms, including depression and anxiety (Kanner et al., 1981). Hassles were an excellent predictor of these psychological symptoms, even better than were

If not dealt with appropriately, the hassles of everyday life can have a negative effect on our health.
SOURCE: © 1990 Paul Margolies/Research Plus, Inc.

more-major life events. In several other studies, hassles have had a modest but positive association with poor health (that is, the more hassles the individual experienced, the more compromised was the individual's health) (DeLongis, Coyne, Dakof, Folkman, & Lazarus, 1982; Weinberger, Hiner, & Tierney, 1987; Zarski, 1984).

On the basis of our analysis of the role of cognitive interpretation, we might suggest here that the effects on an individual of day-to-day hassles depend to some extent upon how those hassles are *interpreted* by the individual ("that's life" versus "the world is against me"). In addition, researchers have found that other aspects of life (more pleasant experiences called *uplifts*) can help to combat the bad feelings that arise from the experience of hassles. Uplifts are believed to "buffer" (that is, prevent the full impact of) the stress of hassles on an individual's physical and mental condition. Uplifts serve to reduce the effects of annoying, frustrating problems or difficul-

ties, and serve as sources of peace, satisfaction, and even joy (Kanner et al., 1981). Some examples of uplifts are "saving money," "finding something presumed lost," and "liking fellow workers." The subject filling out the *Uplifts Scale* indicates for each of the 135 events listed how often (somewhat, moderately, extremely) each has happened. Evidence suggests that illness can be brought about by chronic day-to-day hassles that are not balanced by uplifts. Illness is expected to be more likely to occur when hassles are frequent and uplifts relatively few (Lazarus & Cohen, 1977; Lazarus, 1980). Some studies generally support this approach (Holahan, Holahan, & Belk, 1984; Weinberger et al., 1987; Zarski, 1984).

What is the relative contribution of chronic stress and daily hassles to ill health? Although they are inherently negative events, hassles may be relatively rare or idiosyncratic and as such may be disregarded by an individual. But when hassles appear continually, particularly if they are not balanced by more satisfying uplifts, they probably derive from a fundamentally negative life situation filled with chronic stressors. Some researchers suggest that chronic stress and deprivation can make a person somewhat less vulnerable to small daily hassles because he or she is less affected by small problems in the face of large ones (Caspi, Bolger, & Eckenrode, 1987). Others argue that hassles are inherently bigger problems for people who are already experiencing chronic stress and deprivation (Lazarus, 1984b). As Lazarus has noted, what may be of most importance are that "powerful hassles that have major significance for a person's long-range values and goals create a particular pattern of vulnerability" (Lazarus, 1984b, p. 376). That vulnerability may then lead, through the mechanisms we will consider later in this chapter, to a compromise of the individual's health.

## STRESS AS A DISCRETE PHENOMENON: STRESSFUL LIFE EVENTS

To date, most of the research on stress and illness has been conducted on the role of specific stressful life events in predicting ill health. This research tradition is a significant part of the history of the field of health psychology. The conceptualization of stress as resulting from a single event or a collection of life-change events represents the first research tradition on this topic.

*Life-change events* are defined as those that bring changes in how the individual lives and require considerable adaptation. Examples are marriage, divorce, the death of one's spouse, and moving to a new part of the country. By far the most extensive research on stress has been conducted using life-change events as the gauge of an individual's stress experience.

Life-change events, such as having one's home destroyed by earthquake, require considerable adaptation and can be very stressful.
SOURCE: © Nourok Jonathan/Tony Stone, Worldwide, Los Angeles, Ltd.

The first large-scale attempt to understand stress was undertaken in the 1960s (Holmes & Rahe, 1967). Researchers began with the hypothesis that the degree of stress an individual experiences can be understood in terms of the number of life changes he or she has recently undergone. The researchers first had hundreds of persons rate the average degree of readjustment required by each of 43 life-change events. The values assigned ranged from 100 points for death of one's spouse down to 11 points for minor violations of the law. Included in the list were positive events, such as getting married and having a vacation, as well as

### TABLE 10–1    Social Readjustment Rating Scale

| Rank | Life event | Mean value |
|------|-----------|-----------|
| 1. | Death of spouse | 100 |
| 2. | Divorce | 73 |
| 3. | Marital separation from mate | 65 |
| 4. | Detention in jail or other institution | 63 |
| 5. | Death of a close family member | 63 |
| 6. | Major personal injury or illness | 53 |
| 7. | Marriage | 50 |
| 8. | Being fired at work | 47 |
| 9. | Marital reconciliation with mate | 45 |
| 10. | Retirement from work | 45 |
| 11. | Major change in health or behavior of a family member | 44 |
| 12. | Pregnancy | 40 |
| 13. | Sexual difficulties | 39 |
| 14. | Gaining a new family member (e.g., through birth, adoption, oldster moving in, etc.) | 39 |
| 15. | Major business readjustment (e.g., merger, reorganization, bankruptcy, etc.) | 39 |
| 16. | Major change in financial state (e.g., a lot worse off or a lot better off than usual) | 38 |
| 17. | Death of a close friend | 37 |
| 18. | Changing to a different line of work | 36 |
| 19. | Major change in the number of arguments with spouse (e.g., either a lot more or a lot less than usual regarding child-rearing, personal habits, etc.) | 35 |
| 20. | Taking out a mortgage or loan for a major purchase (e.g., for a home, business, etc.) | 31 |
| 21. | Foreclosure on a mortgage or loan | 30 |
| 22. | Major change in responsibilities at work (e.g., promotion, demotion, lateral transfer) | 29 |
| 23. | Son or daughter leaving home (e.g., marriage, attending college, etc.) | 29 |
| 24. | Trouble with in-laws | 29 |
| 25. | Outstanding personal achievement | 28 |
| 26. | Wife beginning or ceasing work outside the home | 26 |
| 27. | Beginning or ceasing formal schooling | 26 |
| 28. | Major change in living conditions (e.g., building a new home, remodeling, deterioration of home or neighborhood) | 25 |

| | TABLE 10–1   *(Continued)* | |
|---|---|---|
| *Rank* | *Life event* | *Mean value* |
| 29. | Revision of personal habits (dress, manners, associations, etc.) | 24 |
| 30. | Trouble with boss | 23 |
| 31. | Major change in working hours or conditions | 20 |
| 32. | Change in residence | 20 |
| 33. | Changing to a new school | 20 |
| 34. | Major change in usual type and/or amount of recreation | 19 |
| 35. | Major change in church activities (e.g., a lot more or a lot less than usual) | 19 |
| 36. | Major change in social activities (e.g., clubs, dancing, movies, visiting, etc.) | 18 |
| 37. | Taking out a mortgage or loan for a lesser purchase (e.g., for a car, TV, freezer, etc.) | 17 |
| 38. | Major change in sleeping habits (a lot more or a lot less sleep, or change in part of day when asleep) | 16 |
| 39. | Major change in number of family get-togethers (e.g., a lot more or a lot less than usual) | 15 |
| 40. | Major change in eating habits (a lot more or a lot less food intake, or very different meal hours or surroundings) | 15 |
| 41. | Vacation | 13 |
| 42. | Christmas | 12 |
| 43. | Minor violations of the law (e.g., traffic tickets, jaywalking, disturbing the peace, etc.) | 11 |

SOURCE: From "The Social Readjustment Rating Scale," by T. H. Holmes and R. H. Rahe, *Journal of Psychosomatic Research*, 1967, *11*, 213–218. Copyright © 1967 by Pergamon Press, Inc. Reprinted by permission.

negative events, such as divorce, trouble with the boss, and serving a jail term. The ratings were averaged across raters to determine the seriousness of each life event. The various life events listed in the *Social Readjustment Rating Scale* in Table 10–1 differ among themselves in terms of their judged salience and impact. These differences were measured in *life-change units*.

In studies of thousands of navy recruits, Holmes, Rahe, and colleagues had subjects go through the list of events in the Social Readjustment Rating Scale (SRRS) and check off every event that had occurred in their lives within the past year. (The instrument on which these indications were made is called the *Schedule of Recent Experiences* [SRE].) The number of life-change units that an individual had accumulated in a period of two years (reflecting the number and seriousness of the life-change events the individual had experienced) was found to be positively correlated with the seriousness of illness experienced during that time. A high degree of life change was also positively correlated with mortality (Holmes & Masuda, 1974; Rahe, Mahan, & Arthur, 1970).

Research on life-change events has been criticized as problematic both conceptually and methodologically. First, the earliest studies were retrospective in nature; that is, subjects were asked to recollect both the life events and the illness episodes they had experienced in the previous two years. A correlation between stress and illness could have been the result of the expectations of the respondent, including his or her own belief that personal stress can lead to illness.

In answer to this criticism, prospective studies have been conducted and have shown that life-change scores do indeed predict with some success the experience of illness. For example, in one study the life-events scores were tallied for sailors who were about to embark on a six-month cruise tour of duty. The researchers were able to predict relatively accurately which sailors would get sick during the tour and which would not (Rahe et al., 1970). Other prospective research also supports the role of the SRRS in connecting the occurrence of life-change events and the experience of illness.

The SRE scale itself has come under considerable criticism. In the SRE, stress (that is, the adaptation required by each life-change event) is assessed by the average rating given by the original group of hundreds of raters to each listed event. However, there is generally great variation in how people react to different types of life events. The scale score associated with each event represents an "average" impact that may have little to do with how any given person experiences the event. The SRE scale also includes items that report illness-related problems, such as personal injury and physical symptoms, which of course are redundant with reports of illness. In addition, some of the events listed in the SRE are vague and could be interpreted in many different ways. For example, "change in financial status" could represent a slight change for the better or a tremendous financial disaster.

Research on the SRRS suggests that the undesirable events listed in the SRE are better predictors of illness than are the combined events (both negative and positive) that make up the entire SRE Scale (Ross & Mirowsky, 1979). Furthermore, research indicates that events that are sudden, negative, unexpected, and uncontrollable are more likely to predict illness than are events that are positive, expected, under personal control, or that develop gradually with the opportunity for adjustment (Glass, 1977).

## Mechanisms for the Effects of Stress on Health

How do stress and the need for adaptation affect bodily processes? How might stressful life events lead to illness? Several routes are possible (see Figure 10–2).

First, the experience of (particularly high levels of) stress can prompt an individual to engage in behavior that is compromising to his or her health. Chronic daily stress and/or stressful life events can divert an individual's attention from caring for himself or herself and leave little or no time for exercise, proper diet, and plenty of restful sleep. Even worse, the individual might attempt to cope with the stress by engaging in short-term pleasant but nevertheless unhealthy behaviors, such as drinking alcohol

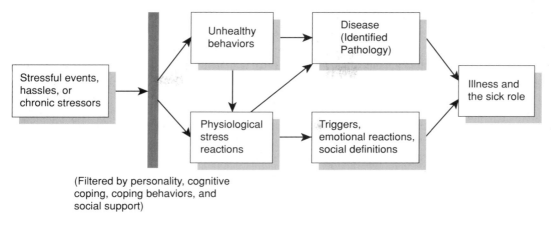

**FIGURE 10–2**  Pathways from stress to illness.

excessively or eating foods that are high in sugar and fat. Indeed, studies of health behavior suggest that people who are under high stress consume more alcohol, cigarettes, and coffee than do people who experience lower levels of stress (Conway, Vickers, Ward, & Rahe, 1981). An individual under stress might be so absent-minded that he or she forgets to wear a safety belt while driving or drives so distractedly as to increase the chances of an accident. Under high levels of stress, people are more likely to be injured on the job, in sports activities, while driving a car, and even in accidents at home (Johnson, 1986; Quick & Quick, 1984).

Second, as we examined in detail in Chapter 5, some people react to stressful conditions in their lives by adopting the "sick role" and seeking health-care services (Mechanic & Volkhart, 1961; Mechanic, 1972). The adoption of illness as the explanation for personal distress allows an individual an excuse for not functioning properly, effectively, and responsibly. Despite such failure, the individual is able to preserve his or her self-concept because illness is a socially acceptable excuse for failing to meet one's obligations. Illness brings secondary gains that allow the individual

legitimately to avoid dealing with the events that cause so much stress in the first place.

A third explanation, which we will pursue in the remainder of this chapter, involves a direct and detrimental effect of stress on bodily processes. As we will see, stress can produce physiological changes that are conducive to the development of disease. Furthermore, physical vulnerability in the form of a preexisting condition can be exacerbated by stress, and certain disease conditions can become considerably worse in the presence of stress.

## Physical Reactions to Stress

As early as the 1850s the term *stress* was applied to humans to mean an outside *force* acting on the body or on mental powers (Mason, 1975). In the early 1900s Walter Cannon described stress not as a stimulus but, rather, as the *response* to a stimulus, particularly to an emergency requiring a person to cope with danger. Cannon named the individual's response to a stressor (stimulus) the *critical stress*, and he identified the now famous *fight-or-flight* response (Cannon, 1932).

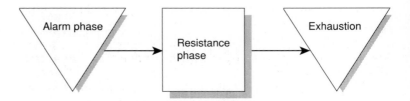

**FIGURE 10–3**    The General Adaptation Syndrome.

The fight-or-flight response is one in which the human organism is readied for fighting or taking flight when in danger. This response is physiologically quite dramatic. The blood pressure rises, heart rate and respiration rate increase, and the blood sugar level rises. There is palmar sweating and the muscles tense (Cannon, 1932). Cannon suggested that the frequent experience of the stress response can break down an individual's physiological homeostasis and increase his or her physical vulnerability. Although the fight-or-flight response can be quite adaptive (for example, it could help a person to run from danger and save his or her own life), continual sympathetic nervous system arousal can be dangerous to the organism because it involves a major disruption in physiological functioning.

## THE GENERAL ADAPTATION SYNDROME

Followers of Cannon's theory, particularly Hans Selye (1956), further examined what happens to the human body in reponse to stressors (which he defined as "demands to which there are no readily available or automatic adaptive responses;" (Antonovsky, 1979, p. 72). Selye developed the theory of the *General Adaptation Syndrome*, which involves three stages in the stress response (illustrated in Figure 10–3).

When faced with a stressor, an organism first becomes mobilized to deal with it. This is called the *Alarm Stage*. The body is made ready to respond and there is an increase in adrenal activity as well as cardiovascular and respiratory function. In the second stage, the *Resistance Stage*, the organism makes efforts to take action to overcome the stressor or learns to adjust to it. Continual resistance to the stressor results in decreased resistance to other stimuli (making the organism, in some ways, more vulnerable). In the third stage, the *Exhaustion Stage*, the organism experiences a depletion of physiological resources in the process of trying to overcome or adjust to the threat. Selye found that the experience of stress results in a general pattern of abnormal hormonal production. In rats, for example, stress reactions resulted in an enlarged adrenal cortex and in atrophied thymus gland and lymphatic structures (important centers of immune functioning). Stress reactions even resulted in stomach ulcers.

Selye's biological model emphasizes the effect of stress on an individual's physiological state (Selye, 1976). Any noxious or aversive event is believed to bring about changes in the adrenal and thymus glands and in the lining of the stomach. In fact, in Selye's research, nearly everything he did to an animal elicited the same physiological pattern (Selye, 1976). He argued that a stressor can be physical, psychological, or both, and that regardless of the cause of a threat, the initial response is precisely the same. Not surprisingly, perhaps, there have been criticisms of Selye's model because of its lack of specificity and its lack of attention to the effects of the appraisal (or evaluation) of threat (Mason, 1975).

It is possible, however, to explain both specific responses and threat appraisal in terms of Selye's three-stage model (Mason, 1975). A stressor can elicit a nonspecific, generalized initial response. Then, because of the character of the stressor and the individual's initial reactions to it, subsequent responses can occur. For the General Adaptation Syndrome to be activated, an organism does not have to be chased by lions and tigers and bears. The daily environment, complete with its traffic jams, midterms, and unreasonable bosses, will do quite nicely. If, for whatever reason, the stress reaction is repeated for a prolonged period of time, according to Selye, the eventual result will be exhaustion, depletion of physical resources, and irreversible physiological damage. Such damage may include exhaustion of the adrenal gland (particularly the adrenal cortex), as well as respiratory and cardiovascular failure, and a reduction in the functioning of the immune system.

The General Adaptation Syndrome is an important model because it depicts the mechanisms by which stress can lead to physiological damage. Early support for the model came from independent research on the physical effects of stress. For example, aggression-provoking stimuli were shown to lead to increased adrenal activity (Levi, 1965). Situations of overload and lack of control as well as major life changes were found to increase physiological responses including catecholamine levels (Theorell, 1974). Early researchers also found that different patterns of physiological reactions occurred in response to stressors that elicited feelings of uncertainty, anger, and fear (Mason, 1975). Epinephrine and norepinephrine were found to be secreted in response to purely psychological stimuli (Frankenhaeuser, 1975). Psycholog-

ical distress was found to precede adrenal-pituitary responses (Mason, 1975).

Such findings were encouraging and led to three lines of research inquiry regarding the role of stress in the development of disease. The first is the exciting new field of *psychoneuroimmunology*. The second is a major field of research on *stress and cardiovascular disease*. And the third deals with *psychophysiological disorders*.

# Psychoneuroimmunology

*Psychoneuroimmunology* (or PNI) is a field of study that examines the relationship between psychosocial processes and nervous, endocrine, and immune system functioning (Ader, 1981; Ader & Cohen, 1985; Buck, 1988). Research has recently demonstrated that the immune system does *not* operate independently of the central nervous system. Rather, there are centers in the brain that are critical to the regulation of hormones and neurotransmitters that affect immune responses. The immune system is subject to modulation by the brain. Because of this effect, mood states can influence an individual's susceptibility to disease and the progression of disease once it has developed.

Until recently, there has been little information available as to why or how emotional factors affect resistance to disease. But lately psychoneuroimmunologists have studied the biochemical interactions between mood and immunity and have found that certain emotions can indeed cause suppression of the immune system (Ader, 1981; Jemmott & Locke, 1984). In this research, for example, depression has been linked to both susceptibility to contracting a disease and to the slower (or limited) recovery from disease (Schmale, 1958; Imboden, Canter, & Cluff, 1961; Levy, 1985b).

Chapter 2 contains a brief explanation of how the immune system works. Reviewing that now may help to make the findings of psychoneuroimmunology research more understandable.

## STRESS AND IMMUNE FUNCTIONING

Stress can affect the immune system in some important ways, and the experience of stress can compromise an organism's ability successfully to defend itself against microbial invaders (Jemmott & Locke, 1984). Severe life stress has been linked to depressed immunologic dysfunction. Lymphocyte production has been found to be depressed in response to the death of a spouse (Bartrop, Lockhurst, Lazarus, Kiloh, & Penny, 1977). The stresses of college life, including examinations, can also lead to immunosuppression, resulting in increased rates of acute respiratory and other infectious diseases (Jemmott & Locke, 1984). Research on astronauts has shown that immunologic deficiencies occur after periods of high stress (Leach & Rambaut, 1974). Uncontrollable stresses appear to produce more adverse effects than do controllable ones. And immunologic responses seem to depend partly upon the individual's ability to cope with the stressor (Jemmott & Locke, 1984). For example, in one study blood samples were taken from married, separated, and divorced women. While there were no across-group differences in immune functioning, certain characteristics within the groups did predict blood test results. There was a positive correlation between marital satisfaction and immune functioning such that those less satisfied showed poorer immune functioning than did those with greater marital satisfaction. Among the separated and divorced women, those with poorer adjustment to the separation from their husbands had poorer immune functioning than did

those who accepted the fact of the separation and divorce and did not spend much time thinking about their husbands (Kiecolt-Glaser et al., 1987).

Moods and emotions can affect the immune system. Depression has been linked both to suppressed T-cell levels and to suppressed lymphocyte activity (Kronfol et al., 1983; Levy, 1985a, 1985b). Anxiety, anger, and hostility have also been found to bring about elevated levels of corticosteroids (such as cortisol) and catecholamines (such as epinephrine), causing immunosuppression and even metabolic disorders (Krantz, Baum, & Singer, 1983). Research on animals demonstrates that experimentally induced stressors can alter immunologic regulation, and studies of humans show decreased phagocyte activity and immunological suppression during times of emotional excitement (Borysenko & Borysenko, 1982).

Precisely how does stress affect immunocompetence? No complete answer is yet available, but it is believed that stress causes the adrenal glands to produce epinephrine and cortisol, which in turn affect immune cells. Catecholamines (epinephrine and norepinephrine) appear to have a variety of immunosuppressive effects. Specifically, epinephrine may increase suppressor T cells and decrease helper T cells (Antoni, 1987; Borysenko, 1984). Corticosteroids, secreted as anti-inflammatory agents, have an immunosuppressive effect as well, and cortisol inhibits the functioning of phagocytes and lymphocytes (Antoni, 1987; Borysenko, 1984). The connection between stress and suppressed immune functioning may also occur because of stress-stimulated changes in endorphine responses.

Kiecolt-Glaser and colleagues have attempted to explain the effects of stress on the immune system and the physiological mechanisms by which these effects appear to come about (Kiecolt-Glaser et al., 1984; Kiecolt-Glaser & Glaser, 1986; Kiecolt-Glaser, Stephens, Lipetz, Speicher, & Glaser, 1985). In one study (Kiecolt-Glaser et al., 1984) blood samples were taken from first-year medical students during low- and high-stress times in their scheduling of examinations. The blood samples were analyzed for killer T-cell activity and for concentrations of antibodies. Although antibody levels were not found to vary with stress levels, killer T-cell activity was lower during high-stress times than during lower-stress periods. Killer T-cell activity was also negatively correlated with the medical students' self-reported levels of stress and loneliness.

The relationship between stress and immune functioning is not yet fully understood. Theories abound but studies are difficult and expensive to carry out. Research over the next several years is likely to shed considerable light on the role of stress responses in resistance to disease.

# Stress and Cardiovascular Disease

The second major line of research on the role of stress in the development of disease involves work on *cardiovascular disorders*. Cardiovascular disorders are the number-one cause of death in the United States today, and stress has been implicated in their direct cause. The evidence is particularly strong for two types of cardiovascular disorders: hypertension and coronary heart disease (CHD).

### HYPERTENSION

Hypertension involves having consistently high blood pressure (over 140 systolic and/or 90 diastolic) (usually over several weeks or months). About 30% of Americans have hypertension, which is a major risk factor for CHD as well as for other diseases, such as stroke and kidney disease (Shapiro & Goldstein, 1982). Most hypertension (over 85% of cases) seems to be determined by several risk factors, many of which we examined in detail in Chapter 3. These include obesity, sedentary lifestyle, diet, and alcohol use, as well as family history and various psychosocial factors. Although hypertension is unlikely to be caused solely by emotional factors, there is some evidence that stress, anger, and hostility may play an important role in the development and maintenance of hypertension. Hypertensives have been found to be more likely to experience chronic hostility than have individuals with normal blood pressure (Diamond, 1982). Both men and women high in hostility have been found to achieve higher reactive blood pressure levels in response to a situation evoking suspiciousness and mistrust than have subjects with lower levels of hostility (Weidner, Friend, Ficarrotto, & Mendell, 1989). People in high-stress jobs who suppress their anger have been found to have higher blood pressure than do those who have lower-stress jobs or who express their anger (Cottington, Matthews, Talbott, & Kuller, 1986). Blood pressure rates among air traffic controllers have been found to be positively correlated with both their ages and the job stress they experienced (Cobb & Rose, 1973). Both heart rate and blood pressure have been found to increase under conditions of physical over-crowding (Fleming, Baum, Davidson, Rectanus, & McArdle, 1987) and seem to be correlated with living in high-stress urban areas, particularly among Blacks (Harburg et al., 1973). Blood pressure also seems to be higher among those who have higher cardiovascular reactivity (that is, whose heart rate is affected by emotional factors) (Rose & Chesney, 1986).

## CORONARY HEART DISEASE

CHD is a category of diseases that result from the narrowing or blocking of coronary arteries, which supply oxygen-rich blood to the heart muscle. CHD includes angina, arteriosclerosis, and myocardial infarction. *Arteriosclerosis* is a condition in which the walls of the coronary (or other) arteries narrow and harden because of the formation of fatty patches or plaques. The plaques are composed of cholesterol (the fatty substance in the blood both manufactured by the body and introduced with saturated fat foods) and can occur throughout the body. When the plaques forming in the coronary arteries obstruct blood flow, insufficient oxygen is supplied to the muscle of the heart, which can result in angina pectoris (chest pain) and myocardial infarction (heart attack). *Angina pectoris* (also called angina) is a form of heart disease in which the sufferer feels pain and tightness in his or her chest because of brief or incomplete blockages of oxygenated blood to the heart. *Myocardial infarction* ("heart attack") involves a severe or prolonged blockage of blood to the heart that results in the destruction of muscle tissue (myocardium). About 1.5 million Americans suffer a myocardial infarction each year and more than a third of them die (Krantz & Deckel, 1983).

As we noted in detail in Chapter 3, CHD has many risk factors, such as cigarette smoking, obesity, sedentary lifestyle, uncontrolled diabetes, hypertension, high serum cholesterol, and family history. Included in the list is psychological stress, particularly the individual's pattern of responses to stress. In general, researchers have found that in the realm of occupational stress, workers with unsatisfying yet demanding jobs requiring a great deal of responsibility have a higher incidence of CHD than do those whose jobs are less demanding (Quick & Quick, 1984). A buildup in stressful life-change events also appears to be associated with a first and repeat myocardial infarction (Garrity & Marx, 1979; Theorell & Rahe, 1975).

The critical factor in determining the effect of stress on CHD may be how the individual *reacts* to stressful situations. Let us turn to an examination of the Type A behavior pattern in an effort to understand reactions to stress as they affect cardiovascular disease.

# Type A Behavior and Heart Disease

One major area of research that has linked psychological factors with disease is that on the *Type A Behavior Pattern* (TABP). TABP is more than just a way of behaving. It involves a predisposition to think, feel, and act in a particular way in response to environmental demands and conditions. These predispositions remain fairly consistent over time, and there are definable differences between people who exhibit the Type A behavior pattern and those who do not. Let us explore the many fascinating aspects of the TABP and see how this purely psychological construct has come to be accepted by the medical community as a significant risk factor for heart disease, the leading killer of Americans today.

The Type A behavior pattern was first identified by cardiologists Meyer Friedman and Ray Rosenman in the 1950s. These physicians noted a particular way of behaving that seemed to be common to many of their patients with heart disease. The patients (nearly all men) exhibited persistently agitated behavior and tended to sit at the edge of their chairs as if ready to bolt away. They were very ill at ease in the doctor's office. In fact, Friedman and Rosenman reported that this way of sitting was so common among these patients that when the chairs in the office waiting room were reupholstered, the man doing the work commented on the unusual pattern of wear on the front edges of the chairs (Friedman & Rosenman, 1974).

In the late 1950s Rosenman and Friedman applied to the federal government for a grant to study the unusual behavior pattern of their cardiac patients. The researchers were turned down twice for a grant to study "emotional stress" and its possible relationship to coronary heart disease. They were advised that their use of the term *emotional stress* meant that automatically the grant proposals had been reviewed by psychiatrists, who doubted that two cardiologists could successfully study emotional matters. So they changed the label to the innocuous "Type A behavior pattern" (with its opposite called "Type B behavior pattern"), and on its third submission, the grant application was funded (Friedman & Ulmer, 1984).

The major elements of TABP involve an individual's aggressive and incessant struggle to achieve more and more in less and less time (Friedman & Rosenman, 1974). The person who is Type A is competitive and strives for achievement. He or she has a sense of time urgency and impatience, and acts aggressively toward others. The Type A person is easily aroused to hostility. Type A behavior pattern involves a personal style that includes how the individual communicates, how he or she copes with emotions and expresses emotions. This collection of cognitive, emotional, and behavioral predispositions has been found in over 30 years of research to be predictive of coronary heart disease (CHD) (Booth-Kewley & Friedman, 1987).

The Type A concept, although formally described in the 1950s and empirically tested in the 1960s, did not receive wide acceptance until the 1970s (Booth-Kewley & Friedman, 1987). By 1978 the TABP was accepted by the National Heart, Lung and Blood Institute as being an independent risk factor for coronary heart disease on par with serum cholesterol, blood pressure, and heredity. The TABP was an exciting breakthrough for psychology, of course, for here was a psychological construct that had some serious implications for debilitating disease and death.

## THE TYPE A CONSTRUCT

The TABP is a behavioral style. Much of the behavior that defines Type A is nonverbal in nature, but Type A also involves an underlying cognitive disposition—that is, a way of thinking. The Type A person is "overly mobilized" not only in response to physical tasks but in response to psychological tasks as well. Psychologically, this mobilization takes the form of time urgency as well as anger at those who waste (particularly the person's) time. The Type A person is chronically activated and often tries to do two or more things at once. He or she may remain keyed up all day, every day. The Type A person tends to be constantly impatient and has a great deal of trouble relaxing (Chesney, Frautschi, & Rosenman, 1985).

How are these psychological characteristics translated into physical problems? There are at least two possible ways. One explanation is mechanical and uses the analogy of a car with its accelerator pushed to the floor and its brakes on. Reactions of emotional distress cause the peripheral blood vessels to narrow while an accelerated heart rate attempts to pump blood through them, producing chronic wear and tear on the coronary arteries.

The second explanation comes from classical conditioning and involves hormones. As we noted earlier in this chapter, an individual's perception of an emergency situation causes a discharge of certain hormones, specifically catecholamines and cortisol, which when discharged are rarely harmless. However, the Type A person perceives and reacts to nearly everything as an emergency, including bumper-to-bumper traffic and a long checkout line at the supermarket. Simple, day-to-day, common stimuli trigger enormously complex physiological reactions that because of the frequency with which they occur, may have detrimental effects on the body.

Recent research on the Type A construct has attempted to sort out which aspects of the TABP are the most dangerous in their contribution to CHD. For example, Type A people who are energetic, expressive, and animated do not have an elevated risk for CHD. Rather, those in most danger of heart disease are the individuals who experience the emotions of chronic hostility, anger, and aggression (Barefoot, Dahlstrom, & Williams, 1983; Chesney & Rosenman, 1985), particularly those who have a basic distrust of others (Barefoot et al., 1987; Weidner, Sexton, McLellarn, Connor, & Matarazzo, 1987).

## THE MEASUREMENT OF
## TYPE A AND CORONARY DISEASE

There are two primary methods of assessing TABP: the *Structured Interview* (SI) (Rosenman, 1978; Friedman & Powell, 1984) and the *Jenkins Activity Survey* (JAS) (Jenkins, Zyzanski, & Rosenman, 1971). In the SI an interviewer has the subject respond to situations that potentially elicit impatience, competitiveness, and hostility. The actual content of the subject's responses is less important than *how* he or she responds. The interviewer, for example, will do things such as stutter and ask questions very slowly, allowing the subject's impatience to surface. In the SI, nonverbal cues such as vocal speed, explosiveness, and vocal volume are measured (Rosenman, Swan, & Carmelli, 1988).

The JAS is very different. As a pencil-and-paper measure, it involves the self-report of behavior. The measure is easily administered and of very low cost. Yet, this self-report may be affected by the subject's need to give socially desirable responses as well as by other response biases, such as the subject's unawareness of his or her own behavioral style and feelings of hostility, both of which are important components of the TABP (Friedman, Harris, & Hall, 1984). Although the SI and the JAS are adequately reliable, they do not correlate very highly with each other. (There tends to be agreement at the extremes of Type A—or the opposite, Type B—but in general the two approaches to measurement give different results.)

The two measures of TABP also differ in their content. The SI measures nonverbal behaviors and general responsiveness to provocation. The JAS, on the other hand, asks about time urgency and pressure to achieve, and so measures some aspects of self-concept. The JAS has three subscales: Speed and Impatience, Job Involvement, and Hard-Driving Competitiveness.

TABP has been studied not only as a predictor of heart attacks per se but also as a predictor of other coronary heart disease conditions.

## TYPE A AS A PREDICTOR OF CHD

In a review of hundreds of studies of CHD and the Type A construct, a technique called *meta-analysis* has been used to combine statistically the results of many independent studies. A highly significant average association has been found between TABP and CHD (Friedman & Booth-Kewley, 1987). When TABP is measured by the Structured Interview, its prediction of CHD is considerably better than when TABP is measured by the JAS. In the JAS, the scale measuring Hard-Driving Competitiveness seems to have the strongest association with CHD and atherosclerosis, whereas Job Involvement appears to have a negligible relationship to disease. Speed and Impatience has a weak but reliable association. It appears that the JAS and the SI classify individuals on different aspects of the Type A pattern, and that the components of TABP tapped by the Structured Interview are the most predictive of CHD and atherosclerosis. Let us examine these components in detail in order to understand more fully the role played by behavioral factors in coronary disease.

## THE DISCRIMINATING TYPE A CONSTRUCT

"Slow down, you'll get a heart attack" may be a popular warning, but health psychologists are learning that such a warning may indeed be misleading and inaccurate. Working hard and being energetic do not cause heart attacks. Only certain very specific reactions to stressful situations may actually contribute to coronary disease.

From its earliest descriptions TABP has been associated with what researchers call *expressive style*. Expressive style is a quantifiable patterning in the individual's expression of nonverbal cues. The Type A person was originally identified as one who walks briskly, has an alert face and eyes, appears tense, clenches his or her jaw, grinds his or her teeth, laughs tensely, makes eye contact, sits on the edge of the chair, makes hand gestures with a fist or pointed finger, squirms or moves about with impatience, and has a loud, explosive voice, accelerated speech with clipped words, a firm handshake, and a general nonverbal expression of vigor (Rosenman, 1978). These descriptions came from clinical observations, and until lately were only clinical impressions. Recent research has demonstrated, however, that it is possible to quantify them.

As we noted above, the Structured Interview is designed to elicit nonverbal behaviors from the individual who is asked a series of factual questions. Interviewees are asked whether they are hard driving and competitive while being challenged by a stern interviewer who takes a long time to ask the question. The goal is to elicit the individual's impatience, hostility, loud accelerated speech, and other nonverbal cues that are indicative of Type A. In studies using the SI, a person's "potential for hostility" (derived from a judgment of the individual's nonverbal style) is the most strongly predictive of CHD. However, researchers have had difficulty understanding the health implications of simply being enthusiastic, fast paced, and expressive but *not* hostile, aggressive, and impatient (Friedman et al., 1984).

Studies of nonverbal expressiveness show that some people are nonverbally expressive and charismatic (Riggio & Friedman, 1983). They appear animated, speak rapidly, move their heads a great deal, and smile. People who are emotionally expressive tend to influence others and are quite popular. Those who have a great deal of personal charisma do share some characteristics with the Type A (as determined by the SI): they are dominant, impulsive, extraverted, colorful, dramatic, and showy. But they are not necessarily unhealthy. Thus, it is important to distinguish between the healthy expressive charismatics and the unhealthy aggressive, hostile Type A's (Friedman et al., 1984).

Popular stereotypes of the harried executive suggest that someone who is intensely involved in his or her job is at risk for heart disease. Yet, research shows that it is not the involvement per se but the character of the involvement that seems to affect health. Being hard driving and *competitive*, with a need to get ahead of other people, seems to be related to heart disease. In fact, in eight studies the personality characteristics of competitiveness and hard-driving aggressiveness were correlated with CHD and atherosclerosis (Booth-

Kewley & Friedman, 1987). Furthermore, being hostile, suspicious, and mistrusting of other people seems to be consistently related to coronary heart disease and CHD mortality (Barefoot et al., 1983; Shekelle, Gayle, Ostfeld, & Paul, 1983; Williams et al., 1980; Barefoot et al., 1987; Weidner et al., 1987). And although stereotypes suggest that suppressed emotion can play a role in CHD, for the most part the research consensus is that coronary-prone people exhibit exactly the opposite tendency. They do not suffer in silence but, rather, explode with frequent, open displays of hostility (Dunbar, 1943; Cady, Gertler, Gotsch, & Woodbury, 1961).

In an important prospective study of hostility as a risk factor for CHD, 255 medical students filled out a multidimensional psychological test (the MMPI), which includes a measure of hostility. Almost 30 years later the health status of these physicians was assessed (Barefoot et al., 1983).

There was a nearly five times greater incidence of CHD among the physicians with hostility scores above the median than among those with hostility scores below the median. Interestingly, hostility predicted mortality from *all causes*. The number of deaths was 6.4 times greater among those with the higher hostility scores than among those with the lower hostility scores. Research attempting to explain this connection between hostility and CHD has suggested that hostility and Type A behavior (as measured by the JAS) together predict elevated levels of plasma and low-density lipoprotein (LDL) cholesterol, which are well-known risk factors for CHD (Weidner et al., 1987). Thus, hostile competitiveness may be the component of TABP that best predicts CHD (Booth-Kewley & Friedman, 1987). Indeed, as we will see in the next chapter, dislike and distrust of other people may prevent a person from achieving a level of social support from oth-

**BOX 10–1**

## SELF-CONCEPT AND HEART DISEASE

An individual's self-concept (perception and evaluation of himself or herself) may be an important predictor of health. For over a century psychologists have used the construct *self* to organize and explain people's thoughts, feelings, and actions. When experiencing the world, a person does so in relation to the construct of self. Some research has begun to show that excessive self-involvement and a narrow self-concept may actually increase one's risk for heart disease.

Researchers interviewed 59 students who had been classified by the Structured Interview as Type A or B (Scherwitz, Berton, & Leventhal, 1978). Each student was asked to recall an incident that had made him or her quite angry and to discuss it as if telling it to a sympathetic friend. The student's blood pressure was taken while the story was being recorded. Blood pressure readings were much higher among the students who frequently used self-references, such as *I, me, mine,* and *my*. Researchers counted all the self-references in each recounting and rated the intensity of the student's expressed anger. The Type A students used twice as many self-references as did the Type B's, and self-references were highly correlated with both anger intensity and blood pressure. In fact, when highly self-involved Type A's described anger-inducing episodes, their blood pressures reached hypertensive levels (150 systolic and 95 diastolic). Less-self-involved Type A's showed

ers necessary to help reduce some of the effects of distressing life conditions. Also see Box 10–1 for a discussion of self-concept and heart disease.

## Psychophysiological Disorders and Stress

Now we turn to the third realm of research in which psychological distress has been linked to disease. In a sense this is the most frustrating realm of inquiry because of the paucity of research studies that directly address the role of psychological factors in the development and exacerbation of these diseases. Yet, there is evidence that a link exists between physiological and psychological variables and there continues to be considerable clinical interest in the psychological components of these diseases.

At the beginning of this chapter we defined a psychophysiological disorder as one that is characterized by physical symptoms and/or dysfunctions that are intimately aligned with psychological factors. Psychological and physiological processes interconnect so closely in such a disorder that it is impossible to separate them. Throughout this chapter we have been examining psychophysiological disorders in the form of cardiovascular diseases and diseases that result from impaired immune functioning. There is yet an additional set of disorders that appear to have a rather strong connection to psychological factors, although the precise character of the connection and mechanisms of effect are not known.

Many of these diseases were once referred to as *psychosomatic disorders*, diseases believed to have psychological factors as their causative agents. The implication was that these diseases, or at least their symptoms, were *caused* by psychological factors. Now we recognize the complexity of the interplay of psychological and physical processes and have evidence that

considerably lower peak blood pressures (134 systolic and 82 diastolic on the average) (Scherwitz, Graham, & Ornish, 1985). And students who made more self-references in this study were more likely to be Type A than Type B.

Prospective research has also demonstrated the connection between self-involvement and heart disease. Subjects who made more self-references in interviews were more likely if they later had a heart attack to die from it than were those who made fewer self-references (Scherwitz et al., 1985). In addition, more extreme Type A individuals with high self-references had more than twice the heart disease risk of extreme Type A's with low self-references. Smoking was an even higher risk factor for heart disease among high self-referencers than among low self-referencers. Thus, self-involvement seems to increase heart disease risk for many, both independently and in interaction with other risks, such as Type A and smoking.

The realm of self-concept is emerging as a potentially important general construct in the search for a bridge between psychological and physical factors in disease. A person with a poor self-concept, for example, may define himself or herself in very narrow terms (such as work) and see self-worth tied solely to work accomplishments. He or she may feel personally responsible when things go wrong, may strive compulsively to achieve higher status in the eyes of others, and may see other people as threats rather than as emotional resources. In doing so, he or she experiences hostility in the struggle to prove himself or herself (Scherwitz et al., 1985).

straightforward causal explanations may be too simplistic and inaccurate.

Reviews of the psychological, psychiatric, and medical literature from the past several decades suggest that there is research evidence linking psychological factors (specifically the experience of chronic negative emotions) to specific, classically identified psychosomatic diseases. These diseases include ulcers, rheumatoid arthritis, asthma, and headaches (Friedman & Booth-Kewley, 1987). Each disease is widespread and chronic, and its etiology is not well understood. Yet, each can be identified with some objective physical findings upon examination and each is commonly believed to be influenced by psychological factors.

*Ulcers* are circumscribed lesions in the digestive tract (usually the esophagus, stomach, and duodenum) that are caused by contact of its lining with hydrochloric acid and pepsin in the stomach. Certain ulcers seem to be caused by hyperacidic conditions. Hyperacidity is believed to be contributed to at least partly by psychosocial factors, such as hostility, anxiety, and rage (Wolf & Wolff, 1947; Engel, Reichsman & Segal, 1956; Weiss, 1984). Ulcers are diagnosed not only on the basis of history and the report of symptoms but are confirmed by evidence on X rays.

*Rheumatoid arthritis* is a chronic, inflammatory disease (or more accurately, category of conditions) characterized by peripheral joint inflammation, pain, swelling, stiffness, and limitations in movement (Achterberg-Lawlis, 1988). There are several types of arthritis, but the rheumatoid type is potentially the most serious and crippling. A diagnosis of rheumatoid arthritis is typically determined on the basis of objective measures, such as rheumatoid factor (in the patient's blood), radiological findings, and joint swelling.

*Asthma* is a chronic reactive airway disorder that can cause wheezing, consid-

Anxiety is one of the negative emotions found to be related to many kinds of diseases.
SOURCE: Suzanne Szasz/Photo Researchers

erable difficulty breathing, and even life-threatening respiratory failure. Most cases of asthma appear to be caused by sensitivity to external allergens, such as pollens, animal dander, and house dust. Obstruction of air exchange is caused by bronchial spasms and tissue swelling that narrows the bronchial tubes.

*Headaches*, as described in detail in Chapter 6, can be of several types. Tension headaches are caused by muscle contractions and muscle spasms. Migraine headaches are caused by abnormally dilated muscles in the head. Cluster headaches are vascular in origin and are sometimes associated with nasal congestion.

In research by Friedman & Booth-Kewley (1987), the technique of *meta-analysis* was employed to combine the results of independent studies using quantitative techniques (Rosenthal, 1984). The correlation of headaches, asthma, arthritis, and ulcers with five chronic emotions was assessed. These emotions were anger (negative reaction to a perceived wrong), hostility (an enduring attitude involving negative feelings and evaluations of other people), aggression (the actual or intended harming of others), depression, and anxiety. The negative emotions and the diseases studied were found to be significantly and positively related. Furthermore, contrary to the psychoanalytic approach detailed in the early sections of this chapter (Graham, 1972), there were no significant associations of specific diseases with specific emotions. Rather, *all kinds* of negative emotions, from depression and anxiety to anger and hostility, appeared to be related to many kinds of diseases such as ulcers, rheumatoid arthritis, headaches, and asthma. (See Box 10–2 for a discussion of the functional impairment of depression.)

BOX
10–2

**EMOTION AND ILLNESS:
THE FUNCTIONAL IMPAIRMENT OF DEPRESSION**

Further evidence for the strong covariation of emotion and illness is provided by an important recent study of over 11,000 patients in three United States cities (Wells et al., 1989). In the Medical Outcomes Study (MOS) researchers measured patients' self-reported physical, social, and role functioning, as well as their self-reported number of days in bed due to health problems (in 30 days), perceived well-being, and amount of pain experienced. They also assessed patients' self-reported depression. This last measurement was done in two ways. Patients reported any diagnoses of depressive disorder, and they also reported on their experience of symptoms (such as feeling sad or having crying spells) on an index of depressive symptoms.

Although some research in the past has linked depression with limitations in social and role functioning, the MOS is the first study to examine the physical functioning and overall well-being of depressed patients. In addition, the MOS researchers were able to compare the functional limitations of depression with those of other chronic physical conditions, such as hypertension, diabetes, advanced coronary artery disease, angina, arthritis, back (including disk or spine) problems, lung problems (including asthma, chronic bronchitis, and emphysema), and gastrointestinal problems (including ulcers and chronically inflamed bowel).

The well-being and functioning of depressed patients was found to be surprisingly poor. The physical functioning of patients with depressive symptoms was significantly worse than that of patients with all medical conditions except advanced coronary artery disease and angina. Patients with depressive symptoms had significantly worse social functioning than did patients with the eight listed chronic medical conditions. Role functioning (work, housework, schoolwork) was worse for depressed patients than for any others except those who had advanced coronary artery disease. Depressed patients spent significantly more recent days in bed than did patients with six of the chronic conditions, although they had fewer days in bed than those with advanced coronary disease. Patients with depressive symptoms also had more bodily pain than did all other patients except those with arthritis.

## THE DIFFICULTIES OF ASSUMING CAUSATION

Despite our temptations to do so, we cannot, on the basis of the research described above, conclude that chronic negative emotions *cause* illness. This research examined associations, not causal relationships. In fact, the emotions could just as easily have been caused by illness as vice versa. Finding an association between asthma and anxiety, for example, means that although anxiety may have contributed to the development of asthma, asthma may just as likely have contributed to the development of anxiety. (Gasping for air in the throes of an asthma attack would probably make anyone consistently anxious.)

Of course, researchers note that a biological third variable could be the cause of both emotion and disease and could account for the relationship between the two. For example, a hyperresponsive nervous system could be the cause of chronic anxiety *and* of asthma (Friedman & Booth-Kewley, 1987). Chronic anxiety could in that case be the "marker" for asthma, but it would fail to play a role in its development. Thus, negative emotion may be related to disease but not cause it (Buck, 1988).

Much has yet to be learned about psychophysiological disorders, particularly about the physiological mechanisms that connect emotions with various disease processes. This realm of research is an exciting element of the fast-growing field of health psychology. Stay tuned!

In the next chapter we will examine the many ways in which individuals under stress try to deal effectively with it. We will consider the consequences of their attempts to prevent stress from adversely affecting their physical and their mental health. We will examine the most and least effective methods of combating stress, as well as the theories and research that support current thinking about the concept of coping.

# Summary

In Chapter 10 psychophysiological disorders are examined.

I. A continuum of psychophysiological disorders has at one end conditions identified as brought about mainly by psychological factors (for example, anorexia nervosa) and at the other end conditions that probably have little psychological origin (for example, appendicitis).
   A. The Nuclear Conflict Theory holds that each physiological disorder is associated with certain specific unconscious emotional conflicts. This psychoanalytic hypothesis is based upon the belief that an individual's psychic energy is directly expressed through specific bodily symptoms.

II. To understand the role that pressures and problems can play in jeopardizing a person's physical health, the concept of stress is examined. Stress has proven to be a relatively complicated concept and has inspired considerable confusion. Stress has been used to refer to physical strain (such as taxing an organism beyond its strength) and to psychological strain (such as when an individual experiences negative emotional reactions as a result of conflict in relationships with other people).
   A. Stress is looked at in three ways: as a stimulus that produces feelings of tension; as a physical and psychological response to a stressor; and as an interaction between the person and his or her environment.

B. The experience of stress is dependent upon the individual's cognitive appraisal of the events and the resources he or she has available to deal with them. The primary appraisal of stress involves the person's determination of whether the event has any potential negative implications for him or her. The secondary appraisal involves the individual's determination of whether his or her own abilities are sufficient to overcome the threat of potential harm.

C. Most researchers look at stress as a process that changes and develops over time.

D. Chronic stress can result from a life situation that requires significant and persistent adaptation.

E. Hassles are stressful events (usually minor) for which we have no automatic, adaptive responses. They can be balanced by uplifts, which are pleasant experiences.

F. Life-change events are defined as those that bring changes in how the individual lives and require considerable adjustment.

III. Stress can significantly affect physical health.

A. The fight-or-flight response is a reaction in which the human organism is readied for fighting or taking flight when in danger. This response involves a rise in blood pressure, heart rate, respiration rate, and blood sugar levels.

B. The General Adaptation Syndrome involves three stages in the stress response. When faced with a stressor, an organism first becomes mobilized to deal with it (the Alarm Stage). In the second stage, the Resistance Stage, the organism makes efforts to take ac-tion to overcome the stressor or learns to adjust to it but has decreased resistance to other stressors. In the third stage, the Exhaustion Stage, the organism becomes physically impaired.

IV. Psychoneuroimmunology (PNI) is a field of study that examines the relationship between psychosocial processes and nervous, endocrine, and immune system functioning. Stress can affect the immune system in some important ways, and the experience of stress can compromise an organism's ability successfully to defend itself against microbial invaders. Moods and emotions can also affect the immune system.

V. Another realm of research on the role of stress in the development of disease involves the cardiovascular disorders. Stress has been implicated in their cause. The evidence is particularly strong for two types of cardiovascular disorders: hypertension and coronary heart disease (CHD).

A. One major area of research on CHD is on the Type A Behavior Pattern (TABP). TABP is more than just a way of behaving. It involves a predisposition to think, feel, and act in a particular way in response to environmental demands and conditions. The Type A person is "overly mobilized." TABP is measured by the Structured Interview and by the Jenkins Activity Survey.

B. The personality characteristics that seem to predict CHD best are competitiveness, hard-driving aggressiveness, and particularly suspiciousness and mistrust of other people.

VI. Research on psychosomatic disease (or psychophysiological disorder) tends to demonstrate that negative emotions, including depression, anxiety, anger, hostility, and aggression tend to be correlated with the diseases of ulcers, rheumatoid arthritis, headaches, and asthma. This research, however, is correlational, and causal explanations may be unfounded.

# Glossary

**Alarm Stage:** the first stage in the General Adaptation Syndrome, during which the body is made ready to respond to threat, and there is an increase in adrenal activity as well as cardiovascular and respiratory function.

**angina pectoris** (also called angina): a form of heart disease in which the sufferer feels pain and tightness in his or her chest because of brief or incomplete blockages of oxygenated blood to the heart.

**anorexia nervosa:** a serious psychiatric condition in which the patient loses his or her appetite and systematically ingests very little food, so that he or she becomes greatly emaciated.

**asthma:** a chronic reactive airway disorder that can cause wheezing, considerable difficulty breathing, and even life-threatening respiratory failure.

**atherosclerosis:** a disease process that involves the formation of fatty plaques in the arteries throughout the body. When the plaques form in the coronary arteries, they obstruct blood flow and insufficient oxygen is supplied to the muscle of the heart, which can result in angina pectoris (chest pain), cardiac insufficiency (inability of the heart to perform its function properly), and myocardial infarction (heart attack).

**catecholamines:** one of a group of compounds having a sympathomimetic action. Such compounds include dopamine, norepinephrine, and epinephrine.

**cathartic technique:** a technique of psychological treatment developed by Breuer that involves reviving inhibited or otherwise inaccessible memories for the purpose of discharging the pathogenic emotions attached to them.

**cell-mediated immunity:** an immune response that involves T lymphocytes from the thymus gland. When stimulated by an antigen, T cells secrete chemicals that attack microorganisms by a process called phagocytosis.

**chronicity of stress:** the chronic character of stress.

**cognitive mediators:** cognitive interpretations that affect the degree to which an individual experiences physiological stress reactions.

**coronary heart disease:** a category of disease that includes myocardial infarction (heart attack), angina (chest pain caused by restriction of oxygen to the heart muscle as a result of occluded coronary arteries), sudden cardiac death, cardiac insufficiency (inability of the heart to perform its function properly), and electrocardiogram abnormalities.

**corticosteroids:** adrenal cortical hormones that have physiological effects similar to those of cortisone.

**dynamic process of stress:** the conception of stress as ongoing and pervasive, occurring to some degree at any given time in an individual's life.

**Exhaustion Stage:** the third stage in the General Adaptation Syndrome. The organism experiences a depletion of physiological resources in the process of trying to overcome or adjust to a threat.

**expressive style:** a quantifiable patterning in an individual's use of nonverbal cues.

**fight-or-flight response:** a response whereby the human organism is readied for fighting or taking flight when in danger. This response is physiologically quite dramatic: blood pressure rises, heart rate and respiration rate increase, blood sugar level rises, there is palmar sweating, and the muscles tense.

**General Adaptation Syndrome:** Selye's theory of stress, which involves three stages of reaction in the stress response.

**hassles:** daily events for which an individual may have no automatic, adaptive responses and to which adjustment is required. Researchers have recently recognized that not only major life events can pose threats to health; sometimes the daily hassles of living, if excessive or if not dealt with in an adaptive manner, can have a cumulative negative effect on health.

**humoral immunity:** an immune response that occurs when an antigen stimulates B lymphocytes to differentiate into cells that secrete antibodies to fight the foreign invader.

**infectious polyneuritis,** or Guillain-Barré syndrome: believed to be a cell-mediated immunologic attack on peripheral nerves in response to a virus. The condition causes inflammation and degenerative changes in nerve roots, causing both sensory and motor impairment.

**Jenkins Activity Survey** (JAS): a pencil-and-paper self-report of behavior that is easily administered and of very low cost. This self-report may be affected by the subject's need to give socially desirable responses as well as by other response biases, such as unawareness of his or her own nonverbal style and hostility, which may be important components of TABP.

**life-change events:** life events that bring changes in how the individual lives and that require considerable adaptation.

**lymphocytes:** white blood corpuscles that arise in the reticular tissue of the lymph glands and play a key role in immune system functioning.

**meta-analysis:** a methodological tool for combining the results of independent research studies using quantitative techniques. Meta-analysis can reveal specific patterns of findings in a series of studies in the research literature. The technique involves statistically combining the results of many similar studies in order to determine the overall size and significance of the findings.

**myocardial infarction** ("heart attack"): involves a severe or prolonged blockage of blood to the heart, which results in the destruction of the muscle tissue (myocardium).

**Nuclear Conflict Theory** (proposed by Alexander): a theory that holds that each specific physiological disorder is associated with specific unconscious emotional conflicts. This psychoanalytic hypothesis is based upon the belief that an individual's repressed psychic energy can be discharged directly to affect the autonomic nervous system, leading to impairment of visceral functioning.

**primary appraisal of stress:** involves the person's determination of whether the event has any potential negative implications for him or her.

**process stress:** stress that changes and develops over time. In the stress process, stress is experienced, adjusted to, enhanced, or diminished, depending upon various intervening factors. As a process, stress can be studied longitudinally and the effects of stress on later behaviors, choices, reactions, and physical conditions can be assessed.

**Psychoneuroimmunology (PNI):** a field of study that examines the direct effects of psychological factors and the nervous system on the immune system.

**psychophysiological disorder:** a disorder that is characterized by physical symptoms and/or dysfunctions that are intimately linked with psychological factors. There is typically a close interplay between the psychological and physiological processes, sometimes making separation and analysis of each component quite difficult.

**Resistance Stage:** the second stage in the General Adaptation Syndrome, during which an organism attempts to take action to overcome a stressor or learns to adjust to it. Constant resistance to the stressor results in decreased resistance to other stimuli.

**rheumatoid arthritis:** a chronic, inflammatory disease (or more accurately, category of conditions) characterized by peripheral joint inflammation, pain, swelling, stiffness, and limitations in movement.

**secondary appraisal of stress:** involves the individual's determination of whether his or her own abilities are sufficient to overcome the threat of potential harm from a stressful event.

**Social Readjustment Rating Scale** (Table 10–1): a measure of the differences among various life events in terms of their judged salience and impact. These differences are measured in *life-change units*, with the most serious being the death of a spouse at 100 life-change units.

**static stress:** stress that results from isolated events.

**stress:** a physical construct referring to the amount of force acting on a physical object. The term *stress* has been used in the fields of biology, medicine, and psychology, as well to apply to the human organism. *Stress* is used to refer to physical strain (such as taxing an organism beyond its strength) and to psychological strain (such as when an individual experiences emotional distress from a lack of meaningful relationships with others).

**Structured Interview** (SI): an interview measure of an individual's TABP. In the SI an interviewer has a subject respond to situations that potentially elicit impatience.

**T cell:** a type of infection-fighting white blood cell that is a key element in immune functioning.

**threat:** the subjective appraisal of the potential negative effects of a stressor. The perception of an event as stressful is entirely dependent upon appraisal of that event as threatening, either as a result of perceptions, expectations, or memory. Threat mobilizes an individual into action.

**Type A Behavior Pattern** (TABP): a predisposition to think, feel, and act in a particular way in response to stress. The major elements of TABP are an aggressive and incessant struggle to achieve more and more in less and less time. The person who is Type A is competitive and strives to achieve, has a sense of time urgency and impatience, and is aggressive toward others. The Type A person is easily aroused to hostility. This collection of cognitive, emotional and behavioral predispositions has been found in over 30 years of research to be predictive of coronary heart disease (CHD).

**ulcers:** circumscribed lesions in the digestive tract (usually the esophagus, stomach, and duodenum) that are caused by contact of its lining with hydrochloric acid and pepsin in the stomach.

**uplifts:** positive daily events that can be used to combat negative feelings and to cope successfully. Uplifts can "buffer" (prevent the full impact of) the effects of stress on an individual's physical and mental condition. Uplifts can serve to reduce the effects of annoying, frustrating problems or difficulties, and can serve as a source of peace, satisfaction, and even joy.

# Coping with Stress: The Role of Psychological Processes in Staying Healthy

. . . . .

"Mr. Haynes, your notes on the Rutherford report are missing," his secretary called out as Bob Haynes was about to leave for the meeting to discuss this very report. His secretary was usually very competent. How could she have lost the file? Was it discarded by mistake?

Adrenalin poured into Bob Haynes's bloodstream. He began to breathe faster. His heart pounded. The "fight-or-flight" response was upon him. He felt like his body was running the 100-yard dash as he stood still. And all he could think of was that he was going to be late for the meeting, and without his notes he probably couldn't discuss the proposal intelligently.

Bob realized at that moment that he had a few choices. He could continue to panic, get angry at his secretary, and focus his mind on all the terrible things that would happen if he performed poorly at the meeting. He could sit still and feel helpless as his secretary searched for the missing notes, and he could berate himself for making mistakes.

But Bob Haynes chose to cope effectively with the stressful minidrama before him. First, he breathed deeply and shrugged his shoulders a few times to relieve some of the muscle tension building in his body. He thought to himself that his rapid heart rate and respiration were perfectly familiar feelings, quite similar to what he experienced every day on his morning run and when he played racketball with his partner. And he focused his mind not on impending doom but instead on something useful. He thought about the last time he had seen the notes. Remembering that he had never taken them out of his briefcase that morning, Bob decided to check. The file was right where he had left it.

As he walked briskly out of his office, Bob nodded and smiled at his secretary. He held the notes high in the air to show her that he had found them. Then he walked faster than usual down the hall, inhaling deeply with each long stride, letting his body catch up in its race with itself. "Might as well get some exercise" he thought to himself as he strode with energy and purpose.

One of the most intriguing aspects of the phenomenon of stress is the fact that people who are exposed to precisely the same stressful life event experience it in very different ways. One person may be overwhelmed physically and psychologically; another barely notices the event and proceeds relatively unconcerned. One person might instantly tackle the source of the stress; another does little but worry about it for days. One person may be able to relax and put the problem out of mind; another is so distressed that restful sleep is out of the question. The character of a stressor is not a reliable indicator of the degree of stress an individual feels or of how that stress will affect the individual's physical and psychological health. Many factors can alter or even completely filter out the negative effects of stress. In doing so, these factors may prevent the potentially debilitating effects of stress on health.

Psychologists have long recognized, for example, that what people think and the meaning they attach to the events they experience can influence their reactions and subsequently their adjustment (Lazarus & Launier, 1978). As we noted in Chapter 10, cognitive evaluations of potential stressors are extremely important in determining reactions to them. Stress depends upon the perception of threat of harm to the individual as well as upon the discrepancy he or she perceives between the demands of the situation and his or her ability to meet them. One person who is given a job transfer across the country may view the change as very stressful and may encounter many emotional difficulties attempting to adjust to it. These difficulties may, in turn, compromise his or her health. Another person might view the job change and the cross-country move as an exciting adventure to be enjoyed and as an opportunity for learning. As we will see in this chapter, how a challenging situation is approached and dealt with can make a great deal of difference in how it affects the individual's life.

In this chapter we will examine several psychological factors that have been found to mediate the connection between stress (stressful life events, hassles, or chronic stressors) and physical illness. We will consider cognitive factors that affect people's interpretations of what is happening to them and we will examine the sense of control that people have over what they are experiencing. We will look at long-standing patterns of cognition and emotion in response to stress as well as methods for altering thought patterns about stressful events. We will broaden the cognitive realm to examine training in cognitive coping methods (such as stress-inoculation) and will consider problem-solving approaches to stress, such as cognitive behavior modification.

In this chapter we will go beyond the cognitive realm to examine other successful approaches to coping that rely on methods to reduce the impact of the stressor on the individual's physical well-being. We will look at methods aimed at minimizing the physiological arousal that accompanies stress reactions and examine the effectiveness of specific behaviors (such as exercise) that can help to bring about adjustment. We will also examine the role of more technical psychological interventions, such as progressive muscle relaxation and biofeedback techniques in the quest for stress management. Finally, we will examine the role of assistance and encouragement from other people—that is, social support.

In this chapter we consider methods for accomplishing two goals: (1) the reduction of the individual's potential for experiencing stress in the face of potentially stressful situations, and (2) the management and reduction of stress once it has been experienced. These goals are interrelated, of course. Having ways to manage stress may make it more difficult for stressful events to affect the individual in the first place. Reducing the potential for stress obviates the need to reduce stress itself.

If this chapter has a primary message, it is that stress can be dealt with successfully. A human being's health is not at the mercy of life's events. Stress jeopardizes health only when it is not contended with effectively. This chapter presents the many options that are available for people to meet the challenges of stress and to remain healthy both physically and psychologically despite the vexations and vicissitudes of life.

# Coping

*Coping* is a term that has made its way into popular culture. People talk about trying to cope with their problems; they may say that they cannot cope with one another. Although the psychological definition of *coping* is not far from the popular usage of the term, a precise definition is essential for our examination of coping:

> Coping consists of efforts, both action-oriented and intrapsychic, to manage (i.e., master, tolerate, reduce, or minimize) environmental and internal demands and conflicts among them. (Lazarus & Launier, 1978, p. 311)

When they attempt to cope, people try to deal with the discrepancies they perceive between the demands of a stressful situation and their ability to meet those demands. Ideally, people focus their efforts on trying to correct the problems they face, but in trying to deal with (or manage, master, tolerate, reduce, or minimize) discrepancies between situational demands and their own abilities, they sometimes try to escape from or avoid the things they find threatening (such as by getting drunk). They may also try passively to accept situations they find untenable. Although technically the definition of *coping* can include all attempts (however self-destructive) to deal with stressful situations, here we focus on active coping efforts that can be expected to leave the individual better off physically and psychologically after employing them.

What is meant by *better off*? Efforts to cope are typically successful if they accomplish five general tasks (Cohen & Lazarus, 1979). The first and primary task involves contending realistically with the problem. When faced with a stressful experience, an individual who is coping successfully must engage in all possible efforts to reduce the harmful environmental conditions and to enhance prospects for survival and recovery. The individual's efforts are oriented toward this critically important task of contending with the realistic demands of the stressful situation. The second, third, and fourth tasks focus on the individual's emotions and thoughts. The individual attempts to tolerate or to adjust emotionally to the negative events or realities; tries to maintain a positive self-image; and tries to maintain his or her emotional equilibrium. The final task is concerned with the social environment: the individual tries to continue satisfying relationships with other people (Cohen & Lazarus, 1979).

Coping is a *dynamic process*. Various coping efforts may be attempted by an individual, and feedback about the success of one type of effort typically spurs the person on to try it again. Failure, on the other hand, brings a shift to another approach. The individual continually appraises and reappraises the environment and his or her efforts at coping with it (Lazarus & Folkman, 1984).

How do we know when an individual has coped successfully with a stressor? A precise answer to this question has not yet been found, although we can use what we know about stress to suggest one. The most adequate measures of successful coping are likely to be multifaceted. When coping well, an individual would report a reduction in his or her feelings of psychological distress (including anxiety and depression). He or she would return to prestress behaviors. Physiological measures would also show less distress. Successful coping should reduce heart rate, breathing rate, skin conductivity, and muscular tension. Blood or urine levels of catecholamines (epinephrine and norepinephrine which may affect the heart through chronic arousal) and corticosteroids (which may impair immune functioning) should drop. Complex,

multifaceted measures are necessary to give an accurate picture of the quality and effectiveness of coping.

## PROBLEM SOLVING AND EMOTIONAL REGULATION

Coping efforts fall into two major functional categories: problem-solving efforts and efforts at emotional regulation (Pearlin & Schooler, 1978; Leventhal & Nerenz, 1982; Lazarus & Folkman, 1984).

*Problem-solving efforts* (also known as problem-focused coping efforts) involve taking direct action to change a stressful situation or to prevent or reduce its effects. The goal of problem-focused coping is to reduce the demands of the situation or enhance one's resources to deal with it. Applying for a loan to pay overdue bills is a good example. A person may even seek information in order to cope with a problem (such as learning to do basic automobile repairs on a car that breaks down continually). People tend to use problem-focused coping when they believe that there is something that they can do about the stressful situation they face (Lazarus & Folkman, 1984).

*Efforts at emotional regulation* (also known as emotion-focused coping), involve attempts to regulate or reduce the emotional (and relatedly social) consequences of the stressful event. When faced with the breakup of a romantic relationship, for example, a person may try to cope by focusing on distracting day-to-day activities. In response to stressful events, the emotion-focused coping response may also involve cognitively reevaluating the situation ("The relationship was not very good from the start, so breaking up is the best thing"), seeking emotional support and reassurance from other people, trying to accept the problem if one can do nothing about it, and

Problem-focused coping involves taking direct action to deal with a stressful situation.
SOURCE: © Betsy Williamson 1979/Photo Researchers

discharging emotion (by crying, or by joking and using "gallows" humor).

While both forms of coping are necessary when faced with stressful situations, research suggests that people generally tend to use more problem-focused than emotion-focused coping (Billings & Moos, 1981). Emotion-focused coping is used primarily after events, such as death of a loved one, when the situation cannot be changed. Women tend to use more emotion-focused coping strategies than do men (Billings & Moos, 1981). In most cases, however, both problem-solving and emotion-focused approaches are necessary for effective long-term coping. Although coping with the emotional aspects of a stressful event can

be extremely important, emotion-focused coping efforts do not deal with the reality of a problem and bring about a long-term solution. Likewise, continuous effort to solve a problem without concern for its psychological impact on the individual may place him or her in jeopardy. A long-term realistic solution may come at the expense of the individual's psychological health, and long-term problem solving efforts may fail without the short-term relief of emotion-focused coping.

Consider, for example, the woman who has accepted a new sales position with a high-profile company. The position requires considerably more effort and expertise than did her last, and during the first several weeks she experiences considerable stress as a result. She is unsure of whether or not she can do her job well enough to succeed or even to keep from being fired. She decides to maintain her emotional equilibrium by visiting with friends. This is a wise choice in general. However, she takes emotion-focused coping to an extreme. Each day she leaves work early to get together with people she likes. She spends hours a day having lunch with friends. But she makes no effort to change the problem, which is her lack of knowledge and expertise in the job situation. She does not learn what she needs to do to become competent. She does not get a new job at which she can excel. So the stress continues, relieved temporarily by her pleasant interactions with supportive people. Moreover, further sources of stress begin to emerge, such as co-workers' criticism of her unavailability and her own recognition that she is avoid-ing the problem. (See Box 11–1 in which five broad categories of coping strategies are discussed.)

## Cognitions and Coping

*Cognitions* refer to one's thoughts about and interpretations of events or oneself in relation to those events. Cognitions include an individual's view of his or her own life and its meaning.

Cognitions can have an important effect on how an individual views a stressful situation. For example, the stress of losing his job is likely to be much higher if a man views the job loss as a failure than if he does not. He is likely to experience a higher level of stress if he views his future with pessimism than if he sees a job change as a new opportunity. Not surprisingly then, the individual's efforts to manage the distressing

BOX
11–1

### COPING STRATEGIES

Five broad categories of coping strategies or actions have been identified by researchers (Cohen & Lazarus, 1979). When faced with a situation demanding action or adjustment, an individual has various options. (1) *Seeking information* (considering what courses of action are open and the probable outcome of each, as well as learning precisely what to do if one were to follow a particular course of action). (2) *Taking direct action* (using specific measures to deal directly with the stressor). When direct action is possible (such is not always the case), this coping strategy is likely to be much more adaptive emotionally as well as physically than taking no action at all. Taking direct action promotes a sense of mastery and control, and allows the person to discharge physiological arousal (Gal & Lazarus, 1975). (3) *Inhibiting action,* which under some circumstances may be the best course. Suppressing the desire to scream at one's boss for example, probably contributes more to one's long-term interests than does giving into the impulse. (4) *Engaging intrapsychic efforts,* such as suppressing upsetting thoughts and trying to ignore them. And (5) *Calling on others* for both physical and emotional support. The coping strategies that an individual chooses depend a great deal upon the situation and upon the unique interaction of the individual and the situation.

thoughts and feelings that arise in response to a problem can reduce the experience of stress.

What kinds of cognitions contribute to successful coping with stress? This important question is being answered in many interesting ways. Let's consider various aspects of research on cognitive coping with stress.

## Cognitive Coping Style

An individual's *coping style* refers to the manner and the amount that he or she thinks about stressful life events. People can exhibit vastly different coping styles. For example, some may minimize and others completely avoid the implications of a threatening event. Still others may confront the trouble directly by gathering information and even by taking direct preventive action (Goldstein, 1973). Which coping style is the better approach depends a great deal upon the situation. For example, an "avoider/minimizer" student may ignore recommendations to preregister for courses and instead merely show up on the first day of school and take whatever courses are still open for enrollment. The "vigilant" student, on the other hand, confronts problems directly. He or she prepares for preregistration several days ahead of time by consulting the course catalogue and the list of course requirements. He or she may know as early as the sophomore year precisely which courses are needed for graduation, and is careful to take all the necessary prerequisites early for each upper-division course. Nothing is left to chance. Things usually work out right for the vigilant individual, but often a price is paid in anxiety because of the need to anticipate each next necessary action. The avoider tends to be considerably more relaxed but sometimes fails to carry out the actions necessary to achieve his or her goals. For example, the courses needed for graduation may be filled and he or she may be unable to graduate according to plan.

Relatedly, reactions to stressful events can be influenced by an individual's need for and tolerance of stimulating experiences. Some people find new experiences and a varied routine absolutely necessary for happiness, whereas others experience distress when their familiar routine is even mildly interrupted. Research demonstrates that individuals with a high need for stimulation adjust better to stressful life events than do those who have a low need for stimulation (Johnson, Sarason, & Siegel, 1979). Of course, we are unsure whether these coping styles *directly* influence the experience of stress so that, for example, the individual who seeks out sensations does not even think of a "stressful event" as stressful. These coping styles may instead influence the presence or absence of immediate coping measures, such as the recognition of *self-efficacy* (the belief that one can indeed accomplish a particular goal) (Bandura, 1977; Wheaton, 1983).

## A Sense of Control

Cognitions determine how events are interpreted, whether they are threatening or not, and how much adaptation they require. If an individual regards change as exciting and himself or herself as capable of handling it, the reaction is likely to be more positive and the stress level lower than if change is viewed as frightening and himself or herself as incapable. More specifically, psychologists have found that human beings have a fundamental need for *control*. Since human survival depends to a great extent upon control of the environment and the expression of one's reasoning processes in action, it may not be surprising to find that when people are put into situations in which their control is jeopardized, they try very hard to gain and maintain it. If all their efforts fail, they become anxious or eventually helpless and depressed (Seligman, 1975).

Coping with a stressful event can be greatly enhanced by a sense of control (Thompson, 1981). Such control can take several forms, including the way the individual thinks about the stressful event. Thoughts of control are referred to generally as *cognitive control* and focus on whether the individual believes that he or she guides the events in his or her life, or vice versa. One form of cognitive control, *distraction*, involves the person's consciously attending to something other than the phenomenon that is distressing. A second type of cognitive-control strategy involves selectively attending to or focusing on some aspects of a situation but not on others (that is, *cognitively restructuring* the event). (As we will see later in this chapter, these cognitive interventions are somewhat complex and there are several methods for gaining cognitive control.)

One realm in which cognitive control can significantly help reduce stress is in the medical situation. For example, the patient who must undergo frequent painful examinations might try to think about being somewhere else (such as lying on the sand at the ocean). Thinking about a peaceful environment will serve to focus attention away from the pain and discomfort being experienced. A patient receiving chemotherapy, for example, might try to avoid focusing on the nausea, pain, chills, and fever that result from the powerful drugs and instead focus on positive images of healing (Simonton, Matthews-Simonton, & Creighton, 1978). These two aspects of cognitive control can significantly improve an individual's adjustment to aversive events.

Relatedly, *informational control* can be extremely valuable in helping a person to cope with a stressful event. Particularly in the medical realm, gaining information about procedures and what sensations will be experienced can help to promote effective coping as well as later adjustment and recovery (Thompson, 1981; Anderson & Masur, 1983).

Although not a cognitive coping mechanism, another form of control is valuable in helping an individual to cope with stress. The specific behaviors that the individual enacts to control his or her environment determine his or her *behavioral control*. In the medical realm behavioral control allows the patient to lessen the aversiveness of the medical event or to influence it in some way.

When my daughter had her first throat culture at the age of 3, she sought to lessen her distress by exerting behavioral control. The nurse had asked her to sit on the examining table and instructed her to open her mouth wide. My assertive, good-natured little girl had her own ideas, however. "Wait," she responded. Then she proceeded to lie down on the examining table. When comfortable, she said, "Okay, . . . now," and opened her mouth wide, as she had been instructed to do for the throat culture.

Adult patients who are similarly given the opportunity to control some aspect, however small, of their experience, are better able to tolerate unpleasant medical procedures. Examples of such control include allowing a patient to vary the volume of sound or music to distract himself or herself from discomfort in the dentist's chair, and teaching a patient to reduce discomfort by relaxing his or her muscles and swallowing when undergoing *endoscopy*, a procedure in which a tube is passed through the throat into the stomach to allow its examination (Johnson & Leventhal, 1974). Behavioral control helps people tolerate the stress of uncomfortable and/or frightening medical procedures, probably because it enables them to reduce their anxiety in anticipation of and during these noxious events (Thompson, 1981).

# Learned Helplessness and Explanatory Style

As we saw in Chapter 10, uncontrollable events are perceived as more stressful than are controllable ones. The belief in one's ability to modify or to put an end to an aversive event reduces the degree to which it imposes stress on the individual (Thompson, 1981). Lack of control, on the other hand, can raise stress and increase levels of epinephrine and norepinephrine (Frankenhaeuser, 1986). What happens when an individual is unable to exert even the smallest amount of behavioral control and is likewise unable to change how he or she thinks about the stressful events being experienced? The individual experiences *helplessness*.

Research on the phenomenon of *helplessness* has shed considerable light on the experience of stress (Seligman, 1975). *Learned helplessness* occurs when our efforts at control continually come to no avail and we are unable to change an intolerable situation. After repeated failures to exert some kind of control, we become helpless in three specific realms (Maier & Seligman, 1976): *motivational* (we stop making efforts to change the outcome), *cognitive* (we fail to learn new responses that could help us to avoid aversive outcomes in the future), and *emotional* (we become depressed). Newer versions of the model of helplessness suggest that cognitive factors play a very important role in its development and determine how chronic and pervasive the individual's degree of helplessness will be (Abramson, Garber, & Seligman, 1980).

How an individual understands and explains (particularly unfortunate) events in his or her life will influence his or her degree of helplessness in the face of those events. Attributing cause *internally* versus *externally* (example: "I was unable to succeed" versus "The task was very difficult") can cause greater helplessness. Attributing cause to a *stable* versus a *temporary* or *unstable* problem ("I fail to solve all problems like this" versus "I failed to solve this problem") can cause greater helplessness. Finally, attributing cause to a *global* problem versus a *specific* one ("I can't do anything right" versus "I can't do this") can cause greater helplessness. Perceived causes of stressful events that are internal, global, and stable can result in the greatest threats to motivational, cognitive, and emotional control (Peterson & Seligman, 1987).

Using this model of helplessness, researchers have attempted to examine how people explain disappointments, misfortunes, and tragedies (their explanatory style), and what effect this style can have on their health. The research suggests that how *optimistically* versus *pessimistically* an individual explains and understands negative events can have a very important influence on his or her ability to cope with stress. Optimistic explanations are those that invoke external, temporary, and specific explanations for things that happen. Pessimistic explanations are those that invoke internal, stable, and global explanations (Peterson & Seligman, 1987; Peterson, Seligman, & Vaillant, 1988).

A longitudinal study that began in 1946 followed 99 young men for over 40 years. They were roughly 25 years old when the study began and had just graduated from Harvard University. Their illness status at age 45 was one of the variables assessed. Those who early in their adulthood (at the beginning of the study) had explained bad events pessimistically developed poorer health by age 45 than did those who had explained events in an optimistic way. The results showed a significant effect on their health even up to age 60 (Peterson et al., 1988).

The researchers analyzed responses that the subjects as young men had given to the questionnaire items. The researchers assessed three elements of what they called "pessimism" in their explanatory style: (1) invoking a *stable*, long-lasting cause for the misfortune (for example, "Things always go wrong; I never get what I want"); (2) assuming the cause of the bad event will have a *global* effect on most areas of one's life ("I can't be a successful writer and I can't be anything else either"); and (3) identifying the cause as *internal* to oneself versus external, such as other people or circumstances ("I was not able to get the job" instead of "They wanted someone with skills different from mine"). Because this was a longitudinal study, it was possible to make some statements about causality. Explanatory style at age 25 may very well have caused ill health at 45, but not vice versa. Additional research corroborates this finding. In a study by Scheier & Carver (1987), optimism was assessed in surgical candidates for coronary bypass (installation of arterial grafts in the heart to bypass coronary arteries that are blocked by atherosclerotic plaques). The assessment was made on the day before this major open heart surgery. The hospital staff judged the optimists as achieving a faster recovery than the nonoptimists, and the optimists were ambulatory sooner than the nonoptimists.

Why might explanatory style and health be associated? Several interpretations are possible. First, developing disease may contribute to developing explanatory style. For example, pessimistic people may be pessimistic because they feel bad physically. The cognitive and emotional manifestations of disease may become apparent long before the physical manifestations do, and so pessimism appears first and physi-

cal illness develops later. It is possible too that people who offer stable, global, internal explanations become passive in the face of illness and are less likely than optimists to take action to enhance their health. One study, for example, showed that college students with a pessimistic style who developed colds or flu did not take even the simplest of precautions (such as resting) to help themselves (Peterson & Seligman, 1987). In general, pessimistic explanatory style may result in failing to seek medical advice or in not following such advice once it is obtained (Peterson & Seligman, 1987; Seligman, 1975). Of course, regularly explaining events pessimistically might cause an individual to experience chronically negative emotions, which, as we saw in Chapter 10, may precipitate or exacerbate certain chronic diseases. Chronically negative emotional states may bring about negative health status. Finally, research suggests that people who generate pessimistic explanations for bad events show increased immunosuppression and less effective immune system functioning than do those whose explanations are optimistic (Jemmott & Locke, 1984; Peterson et al., 1988).

It is important to recognize that optimism does not refer to superficial positiveness. Optimists are problem solvers. They make plans of action and follow them. They expect things generally to go their way, and they have a favorable outlook on life. Their expectation that things will eventually work out inspires them to keep trying. Pessimists, on the other hand, cope with stressful negative events by focusing on their feelings or by trying to escape through fantasy. Pessimists, convinced that things will turn out badly for them anyway, give up and stop trying. In giving up, they succumb to the setbacks and obstacles they encounter and may have great difficulty attaining their goals (Peterson & Seligman, 1987).

# Hardiness

Research in the realm of existential personality theory has sought to explain why some people, despite highly stressful conditions, are able to enjoy their lives and maintain or even improve their health. Focusing on the individual's perspective and the meaning he or she attributes to life events, psychologists Salvatore Maddi and Suzanne Kobasa developed the concept of *hardiness*. Hardiness is a psychological construct that refers to an individual's stable, characteristic way of responding to life events. Individuals who exhibit hardiness have been found to be less susceptible than are those who do not exhibit hardiness to experiencing illness in response to stressful conditions in their lives (Kobasa, 1979, 1982).

Hardiness involves three intertwined components: *commitment*, *control*, and *challenge*. Individuals exhibiting hardiness approach life-change events from these perspectives. Let us analyze them in detail.

Persons high in *commitment* become intensely involved in what they are doing and believe in the importance and value of their work. They tend to involve themselves deeply in many aspects of their lives, from work to family interactions to social relationships. They believe that there is an overall purpose to the actions of their day-to-day lives. On the other hand, people low on this dimension of commitment tend to be alienated from other people and feel there is little meaning in their lives. In Kobasa's research those low in commitment tended to experience a sense of alienation from themselves and from their work. They agreed with statements such as "I wonder why I work at all" and "Most of my life is wasted in meaningless activity."

Persons high in *control* believe (and act as if) they indeed can influence events that they encounter rather than remain powerless in the face of outside forces. They place considerable emphasis on their own responsibility for their lives and feel that they are capable of acting on their own, without direction from other people. Those who approach their lives with a low degree of control, on the other hand, feel powerless and believe that most of their activities are determined by the demands of others and of society. They believe that luck or chance controls their destinies.

Finally, people who have a sense of *challenge* regard life changes to be the norm and are not threatened by them. They anticipate and welcome life change as a stimulus to and opportunity for personal growth. They are open and flexible in their ways of thinking, and they are able to tolerate ambiguous situations.

Hardiness was initially examined only in retrospective research and the results were open to several interpretations. However, more recently the hardiness construct has held up in prospective research as well to be a good predictor of health, even in the face of quite stressful life events (Kobasa, Maddi, & Kahn, 1982; Kobasa, Maddi, Puccetti & Zola, 1985).

## WORLDVIEW AND A SENSE OF COHERENCE

Another existential theory of coping, the theory of a *Sense of Coherence*, arose out of studies of concentration-camp survivors who managed, despite terrible life experiences, to remain healthy both physically and psychologically (Antonovsky, 1987). This theory helps to explain how people can cope with very stressful and chaotic circumstances, even when they have no control over events in their lives.

In the theory of a Sense of Coherence, life stressors are conceptualized as ranging from the microbiological to the sociocultural. One's family situation and one's job

Antonovsky's theory of a *Sense of Coherence* grew out of his studies of concentration camp survivors who remained physically and psychologically healthy.
SOURCE:  Wide World Photos

can be significant sources of life stress and so too can the social and cultural environment in which one lives. As we noted in Chapter 10, existing in poverty, living in an unsafe neighborhood, and functioning in an oppressive cultural environment can be extremely stressful. In the nature of human existence, stressors are inevitable and omnipresent. Yet, some people carry an extremely high stress load. The theory of a Sense of Coherence attempts to understand how these people manage to survive and even to flourish.

According to Antonovsky, it is incorrect to assume that stressful life experiences are inherently bad. Stressors *do* cause a state of tension in an individual, but the physical outcome of that tension is dependent upon the adequacy of the individual's tension management. Inadequately managed tension may result in a long-term perception of stress and subsequently in the individual's ill health. But ill health is not the *nec-*

*essary* outcome of life events that require adaptation. Though significant to the individual, stress, in statistical terms, does not account for a high proportion of the variance in people's health. In fact, despite terrible circumstances in their lives, many people remain quite healthy. Antonovsky argues that if we really want to understand the interplay of mind and body, of stress and physical illness, we must learn to understand precisely how some people are able actually to avoid illness and remain quite healthy despite significant stress.

Antonovsky has contended that research on stress and illness focuses, to its detriment, on a *pathogenic* model. A pathogenic model of research posits a direct effect of some psychological or physical variable on disease. Current examples of this approach are the effect of Type A behavior on coronary disease, and the effect of learned helplessness on depression. A *salutogenic* orientation, on the other hand, allows us to examine the factors that promote movement toward health rather than toward illness. It is as important to study what causes health as it is to study what causes threats to health.

The salutogenic approach leads the way to the formulation and development of a theory of coping. Using a salutogenic approach, we ask how it is that some people do well and feel good *despite* life problems, impediments to their goals, and even tragedies. An individual's Sense of Coherence, according to Antonovsky, is a major determinant of the individual's ability to maintain health and avoid illness. Why?

According to Antonovksy, a Sense of Coherence is a *General Resistance Resource* (GRR). GRRs are resources (such as money, ego strength, social support, and cultural stability) that help to protect a person against the ill effects of stress. Money is a physical GRR because it can alleviate or minimize the effects of a stressful event. If one has enough money to solve a practical problem that causes feelings of stress, the problem can be eliminated and the stress reduced. Of course, money is a GRR only with regard to the financial effects of a problem. Money can purchase a new car to replace the one that was "totaled" in an accident, but money cannot bring back the loved one who was killed. Likewise, emotional support from others can make one feel much better but may do nothing to get one a badly needed replacement car. So, an individual's Sense of Coherence is a General Resistance Resource because this worldview can "buffer" the effects of stressful events so that they are not felt so intensely by the individual. Sense of Coherence is an

> enduring though dynamic, feeling of confidence that: (1) the stimuli deriving from one's internal and external environments in the course of living are structured, predictable, and explicable; (2) the resources are available to one to meet the demands posed by these stimuli; and (3) these demands are challenges worthy of investment and engagement. (Antonovsky, 1987, p. 19)

This was how Antonovsky characterized the people he interviewed who had experienced major trauma but who nevertheless coped exceedingly well. They were people who remained physically healthy despite significant psychological stress. Antonovsky asked these individuals how they viewed their lives. Three characteristics emerged. (1) They saw the world as comprehensible and as making cognitive sense to them. These people expected that the stimuli they would encounter (for example, other people or natural phenomena) would be ordered and explicable. Although certain events were not at all desirable to them, such as career failure, the death of a loved one, or war, they felt they could make sense of them. They explained accidents in terms of certain physical forces; job failure in terms of a lack of key knowledge or a personality clash with the boss; war as the result of a variety of political forces. Such explicability stood in contrast to the more magical beliefs of those without a Sense of Coherence (such as that one's loved one was torn from one's grasp by a malevolent universe, or that jobs are lost for no understandable reason). (2) Those with a Sense of Coherence saw the world as manageable, and had a solid belief that things would work out as well as can be reasonably expected. This emphasis is a cognitive one that involves a solid capacity to judge reality. Events in life were seen by those with a Sense of Coherence as experiences that can be coped with. People with a Sense of Coherence recognize that unfortunate things do happen in life but that such experiences can indeed be survived. (3) Those with a Sense of Coherence believed that events in life have meaning. They valued life on a deep emotional level and believed that, for the most part, the problems and demands posed by life are worth the investment of their energy.

Although people with a Sense of Coherence certainly did not welcome troubles, they faced life's burdens with a sense of challenge and sought to find meaning in them.

# Social Resources and Social Support

One of the most potent factors in helping an individual to deal with stressful life conditions and events is *social support*. Social support is support or help from other human beings such as friends, family, neighbors, co-workers, and acquaintances. It can come in the form of physical assistance, and can also involve reminders that one is an esteemed and valued person.

Social support is believed to help in three ways to deal with stress (House, 1981; Coyne & Holroyd, 1982; Wills, 1984). First, family members, friends, and others can directly provide *tangible support* in the form of physical resources (for example, lending money, doing the grocery shopping, taking care of the children). Second, members of one's social network can provide *information support* by suggesting alternative actions that may help to solve the stress-producing problem. These suggestions may help the person to look at the problem in a new way and thus help him or her to solve it or to minimize its impact. Third, persons in the social network can provide *emotional support* by reassuring the individual that he or she is a cared-for, valued, and esteemed person. Supportive individuals can provide nurturance.

Social support can be very valuable in the work setting, where fellow employees can provide one another with tangible help, information, and personal esteem (House,

1981; Billings & Moos, 1981). Social support has been found to be associated with reduced job stress (Cottington & House, 1987) and can also be critically important in helping an individual to cope with the demands of serious illness (Wortman & Dunkel-Schetter, 1987).

Evidence suggests that people who receive social support enjoy better health than do those who do not receive social support. Individuals with more extensive social contacts and community ties have been found to live longer than do those who have few such ties to others (Berkman & Syme, 1979; House, Robbins, & Metzner, 1982). Receiving social support has been found in research to be associated with lower rates of myocardial infarction (heart attack), with reduced incidence of tuberculosis, with fewer complications during pregnancy, and with lower rates of psychological distress (Williams, Ware, & Donald, 1981; Billings & Moos, 1981).

How and under what circumstances social support helps an individual is not entirely clear and must be explored in more detail in research. It may be the case that social support "buffers" the effects of stress by making situations less likely to be appraised as threatening (Cohen & Wills, 1985) and by rendering stress less likely to trigger deleterious physical responses (such as poor health habits or chronic, exhausting physiological arousal) (Kaplan, Cassell, & Gore, 1977). It is also possible that social support actually makes potentially stressful events more benign by diffusing or minimizing their initial impact. For example, having a loving and supportive romantic partner may make it much less likely that one will interpret a course grade that is lower than one expected as evidence of personal failure. The person who enjoys a high level of social support may even approach each examination in a course with much less anxiety and distress than he or she might otherwise. Researchers still do not know, however, precisely how social support operates to help an individual cope with stressful situations. Some suggest that social support has a direct effect on health regardless of the amount of stress an individual experiences. Social support may give an individual a more positive outlook on life as well as a greater sense of self-esteem. These positive psychological outcomes may manifest themselves in the individual's greater resistance to disease and engagement in more positive preventive health habits (Cohen & Wills, 1985; Wortman & Dunkel-Schetter, 1987).

Not all kinds of social support can help under all circumstances, however. In fact, the role of social support in helping to maintain and promote health is emerging as rather specific. Under certain circumstances, for example, only *one* kind of support will be helpful to an individual. In research on younger, widowed people, it was found that the stress of their loss was best buffered by social support from their parents, particularly emotional support. Among working women with newborn babies, however, the only significant source of social support was their spouse (Lieberman, 1982). Obviously, the form of social support received can matter a great deal as well. If one really needs tangible support but receives only encouragement, one may begin to feel frustration and further stress (Cohen & McKay, 1983).

Finally, social support may affect an individual's *subjective* feelings of stress but do nothing to change his or her bodily experience of stress. Although people who receive social support report *feeling* fewer negative effects of stressful situations, their physiological indicators of stress tend to remain unaffected. For example, in a study of residents near Three Mile Island after the nuclear accident, people with high levels of social support *felt* less distress than did those who had little social support, but the physiological indicators of stress in the two groups did not differ (Fleming, Baum, Gisriel, & Gatchel, 1982).

Of course, receiving social support may have some risks. Such help may carry with it the implicit requirement to reciprocate, and it is possible that those who try to help will instead become intrusive. For example, receiving suggestions from others may be quite helpful, but having another's solutions forced upon one vigorously (with accompanying distress if they are not followed) may in itself become a burden and a source of further stress. Overly intrusive members of the social network might actually make things worse (Lieberman, 1982). And some may encourage the individual to engage in health-compromising instead of health-enhancing behaviors (Suls, 1982).

# Helping People Cope: Interventions That Work

## EXERCISE

■ ■ ■ ■ ■

I was upset. It was not even clear precisely why. Something my boss had said during our meeting left me feeling unsure of where I stood in his estimation. My hopes for a promotion seemed threatened. My heart was beating faster than usual after the meeting. My body felt strangely exhausted and my chest felt tight.

When I got to the gym, I was distracted and anxious. But this was my time to work out, I told myself, and I was not going to miss it. I had faith based on years of experience working out "hard" that while my problems would still be there after my workout, my ability to deal with them would be greatly improved. My body would feel relaxed and strong, and I would be much better able to think.

And that is exactly what happened. After a few minutes on the treadmill, my body

Exercise can help to decrease both the organismic and the emotional strains resulting from stress.
SOURCE: © Bob Clay/Clay Images

felt warm as blood rushed to my muscles. After several sets on the weight machine, my chest felt strong. Thirty minutes into my workout with weights I felt hopeful. I believed in myself again.

The aerobics class gave me the chance to jump around like a kid. At first I did not really feel like doing it, but my optimistic fellow classmates made the mood light. The rock music pounded. Although my problems did not disappear, I was able to put them into perspective. I experienced a certain physical euphoria that helped me to feel very clearly that my job was not my whole life. For a short time, I felt good. I focused all my attention on getting the aerobic dance combinations right and I entered a kind of meditative state in which the repetitive movements occupied my entire consciousness. My irrational fears disappeared; my breathing became regular. I felt genuinely happy.

Research suggests that exercise can serve two important functions in helping people to cope with stress. Exercise helps to decrease the organismic strain that can result from stressful events, and exercise can help to reduce emotional strain that has already manifested itself in an individual's life.

First of all, people who exercise regularly and are generally physically fit experience significantly lower levels of anxiety than do people who do not exercise (Blumenthal & McCubbin, 1987). This relationship has been supported by both correlational and experimental research (Goldwater & Collis, 1985). In the latter, subjects who had been randomly assigned to obtain vigorous exercise were found to have significantly lower anxiety as well as greater cardiovascular fitness than did those who did not exercise vigorously. Such lowered anxiety is likely to reduce the initial impact of a potentially stressful event and may minimize the perception of environmental threat.

Exercise appears to reduce blood pressure and heart rate, and particularly to reduce cardiovascular reactivity (Dimsdale, Alper, & Schneiderman, 1986; Jennings et al., 1986). Studies suggest that exercise can provide an active outlet for the physiological arousal experienced in response to stress. Regular physical exercise can help to protect health in the face of stressful life events and chronic daily stressors. Vigorous physical exercise is particularly valuable in preventing cardiovascular disease. In general, exercise has been found to increase the efficiency of cardiac action and slow the heart and regulate its rhythm, as well as decrease the likelihood of a heart attack (Paffenberger & Hale, 1975; Epstein, Miller, Stitt, & Morris, 1976). Recent research links exercise with reduced mortality from not only cardiovascular disease but all causes (Blair et al., 1989).

Some research has directly examined the role of physical fitness in the link between stress and health. One study found that individuals with poor fitness levels tended to be more susceptible to illness under stress than did those who were physically fit (Roth & Holmes, 1985). Similarly, in research on executives under stress, exercise was associated with lower overall illness scores, and this buffering effect was found to be *distinct* from the personality characteristic of hardiness (Kobasa et al., 1982). Whereas hardiness was found to help limit the stressfulness of events, thereby decreasing their ability to produce sympathetic arousal or organismic strain, exercise had a general buffering effect that directly *relieved* organismic strain on the executives. In subsequent studies of male executives who faced highly stressful conditions, researchers found that exercise worked in conjunction with other resources to help these men increase their resistance to illness (Kobasa et al., 1985). Taken together, hardiness, social support, and exercise *substantially* decreased their likelihood of becoming ill. In this research, hardiness emerged as having a somewhat stronger buffering effect on stress than did exercise and social support, but the latter two were still extremely important.

# Behavioral and Cognitive Coping Techniques

## COGNITIVE APPROACHES

As we noted in Chapter 10, stress arises from one's cognitive interpretations of events. If an experience is evaluated as threatening to the individual's well-being and the individual believes that he or she does not have the appropriate resources to cope with it, a stress response (complete with its physiological and psychological threats to homeostasis) will ensue.

Earlier in this chapter we examined how people's patterns of cognitive interpretation can affect their experience of stress. For example, a hardy person interprets life changes as challenges instead of problems, experiences himself or herself in control of life, and views the pressures encountered as part of the commitment to a meaningful job, family, and community. Likewise, people who view the world as a coherent, understandable place are able to weather very stressful experiences without becoming ill.

Some people may develop health-enhancing cognitions quite early in their lives. Others may need to change how they think about themselves and the events in their lives and can even eliminate cognitive patterns that are destructive to their physical and emotional well-being. *Cognitive therapy for stress management* is based upon the view that the cognitive representation of the environment, rather than the environment itself, determines stress responses. If the cognitions are changed, stress responses can be reduced. Let us examine several approaches in the field of cognitive therapy that are particularly relevent to the management of stress.

*Cognitive restructuring* is a widely used technique for changing stress-provoking thoughts or beliefs so that they promote, rather than detract from, the individual's well-being (Mahoney, 1977). If a student believes that one particular test will make or break his or her entire career, it is likely that the experience of stress while preparing for the test will be extremely high. It is also likely that the belief is irrational—that is, not based on a rational analysis of the facts. The test is likely to be one out of many. And few if any careers are destroyed on the basis of one course grade. Yet, unless the student's irrational beliefs are changed, he or she is likely to experience considerable stress in response to the test.

An important technique for changing irrational cognitions was developed many years ago by the psychologist Albert Ellis (1962, 1977). Ellis's approach to cognitive restructuring is called *rational emotive therapy* or RET. According to RET, stress-appraisal processes, such as we examined early in Chapter 10, tend to go awry when people engage in irrational thinking. Such irrational beliefs may involve *catastrophizing*. Catastrophizing involves believing that an event that has not gone according to plan is not simply inconvenient but is truly a catastrophe of major proportions from which one may never recover. Irrational beliefs may also include the individual's vast underestimation of his or her ability to accept the consequences of the inconvenient event ("I won't be able to stand it if I get a 'B' on this test"). The individual might also judge his or her own personal worth on the basis of something like school performance (for example, "I am a worthless person if I do not get an 'A'"). Such irrational thoughts can be replaced with rational thoughts (for example, "If I do poorly on this test, I will simply have to try harder next time" or "My grade in this test does not reflect my worth as a person").

Cognitive therapies such as RET and the cognitive therapy of Aaron Beck (Beck, 1976) can help in the management of stress. Changing one's interpretations of events can change the subjective reaction to those events and the associated physiological responses as well. The success of the cognitive approach to the clinical treatment of stress-related problems, such as anxiety and depression, has been encouraging (Hamberger & Lohr, 1984; Beck, 1976).

*Stress-inoculation training* is a somewhat different cognitive approach to the management of stress (Meichenbaum & Cameron, 1983; Meichenbaum, 1985). Stress-inoculation training is based upon the theory that the stress experience can be reduced if a person is cognitively prepared. Stress inoculation occurs in three steps. During *conceptualization*, the client and therapist work together to understand the problems facing the client and to analyze the details of the client's stress experience. During the stage of *skill acquisition and rehearsal*, the individual may learn relaxation and desensitization techniques (such as described below), as well as ways to redefine his or her situation in cognitive terms. The client may also incorporate into the program practical aids to overcoming stress-producing problems, such as social-skills training for the individual who experiences interactions with other people as stressful. Finally, in the phase of *application and follow-through*, behavioral and cognitive techniques are used to bring about behavior change. For example, client and therapist might use role-playing to simulate a stress-producing situation so that the client can practice the skills he or she has acquired. Or client and therapist may practice or rehearse upcoming situations expected to be stressful so that the client can apply new abilities.

## RELAXATION TECHNIQUES

In Chapter 6 we examined relaxation as a method for controlling pain and saw that the reduction of muscular tension can be tremendously helpful in reducing the intensity of the pain experience. In the realm of stress management, relaxation has been found to reduce effectively not only muscle tension but also heart rate and blood pressure (English & Baker, 1983; Lavey & Taylor, 1985).

Two forms of relaxation work particularly well to deal with stress. *Progressive muscle relaxation* is a technique in which the individual focuses his or her attention on specific muscle groups and alternately tenses and relaxes the muscles. The individual might begin with feet and leg muscles and work up through the torso to his or her head, shoulders, and arms. With each muscle group, the individual tenses the muscles for about ten seconds and then relaxes them for about the same amount of time. During the relaxation phase, the individual might be asked to think a pleasant thought, such as how pleasant the relaxation feels. The alternation of tensing and relaxing allows the individual to become aware of the experience of tension in each muscle group and to contrast it with the experience of relaxation. After some training in this technique, an individual is usually able to achieve the experience of relaxation by remembering the feelings and thoughts he or she had during the training.

A second method of relaxation for stress management was developed by cardiologist Herbert Benson (Benson, 1974; Benson, Beary, & Carol, 1974). This technique has been particularly popular with executives because it is fairly easy to accomplish and can be worked into a normal business day routine. The technique combines muscle relaxation with a comfortable position, a passive attitude, a quiet environment, and a repetitive sound in the same manner as does meditation (see below). The individual sits with his or her eyes closed for about 20 minutes and silently repeats the word "one" (or whatever word he or she has chosen). During repetition of the single word, the individual is prevented from having distracting thoughts interfere with the relaxation. In fact, the individual's goal is to "let go of" any distracting thoughts that enter his or her awareness during the relaxation experience.

Relaxation has been a very successful technique in helping people under stress to cope with their experience and to prevent or control stress-related disorders (Lavey & Taylor, 1985; Rimm & Masters, 1979).

Relatedly, *meditation* involves several techniques that attempt to focus an individual's attention on a single thought or image in an effort not to be distracted by other thoughts, particularly ones of an evaluative or analytic nature (Shapiro, 1985). Although meditation has been associated over the years with various spiritual frameworks, particularly those from the Far East and India, it can involve purely psychological techniques for being aware of one's thoughts as they come and go. The practice of meditation has been found to be effective in reducing stress and anxiety, as well as in reducing hypertension and even eliminating certain phobias (Shapiro, 1985), although the degree and type of benefit achieved by meditation is very similar to that achieved by relaxation training.

## SYSTEMATIC DESENSITIZATION

In the realm of stress management, relaxation techniques are often used as part of a program of *systematic desensitization*. Systematic desensitization is a method for reducing stress (particularly stress that is generated from fear of or anxiety about something specific). The method is based upon the stimulus-response associations of classical conditioning. Systematic desensitization involves a process of undoing the associations that have been established in the past between some environmental event and the stress response (Rimm & Masters, 1979). For example, a young man who is an advertising executive may begin to experience a frighteningly powerful stress (fight-or-flight) response whenever he has to give a presentation to his bosses. The counterconditioning of systematic desensitization could help him to replace the stress response with calmness and relaxation. Here is how it might be done.

A psychologist working with this executive would use a method that involves a *stimulus hierarchy*. The situation that elicits the stress response, specifically a presentation to the boss, would be approximated in the executive's imagination as he engages in progressive relaxation as described above. For example, the executive might first sit in the psychologist's office and learn to associate a relaxed state with thoughts of being asked to do a presentation sometime in the future. The next steps might involve the executive's associating his relaxed state with images of preparing materials for the presentation and writing out what he plans to say during the presentation. The next step may involve associating a relaxed physical and mental state with thoughts of walking into the conference room in which the presentation will take place. The executive might then imagine himself opening up his briefcase and arranging his graphs for the presentation. He might imagine the sounds and sights of his colleagues and then his boss coming into the room. Finally, he would imagine himself talking in front of the group. He would imagine each of these scenes while feeling comfortable and calm. As the executive climbs the hierarchy and more closely approaches the stress-producing activity, he may become more and more uncomfortable and begin to experience the stress response. If he does, the psychologist would likely stop at that point and work intensively on the association of that particular step with relaxation until it has been accomplished successfully. Then the next step on the hierarchy would be approached.

Depending upon how strong the individual's fear and how intense the stress reaction, the entire process of systematic desensitization may take several sessions with a psychologist, as well as the individual's own personal follow-up and reinforcement of the achieved associations. In addition, basing the systematic desensitization on images of the stressful situation may not be enough to quiet the distressing response as it happens in the real world. Some therapists use symbolic contacts with the feared object or event (such as tangible representations or pictures), and some even use *in vivo* contacts (which involve experiencing the actual stress-provoking situation). Thus, the therapist might accompany the executive to the conference room where the presentation will take place and help him to achieve a relaxed state when he is actually there.

Systematic desensitization works very well to reduce the stress responses that people have to such things as flying in an airplane, going to the dentist, public speaking, being in high places, and taking tests (Gelfand, 1978; Rimm & Masters, 1979).

## BIOFEEDBACK

In Chapter 6 we examined biofeedback in detail as an effective technique for pain control. Biofeedback, as we noted, can be a very useful method for helping people to relax specific muscles or muscle groups, as well as for generally decreasing their state of emotional arousal.

Biofeedback involves an electromechanical device that emits a signal (a light or a buzzer or a sound of varying frequency) to "feed back" to the individual some information about the state of his or her body. Typically, the information fed back is the degree of tension in specific muscles or the general state of arousal of the individual's sympathetic or parasympathetic nervous system. When the individual achieves the desired physical state (relaxed muscles or a slowed down heart rate, for example) the device emits a signal and through the process of operant conditioning, reinforces the individual's efforts.

Biofeedback has been useful, as we noted in Chapter 6, in treating certain stress-related disorders, such as muscle-tension headaches. As we noted in Chapter 6, biofeedback appears to have the same level of effectiveness as progressive muscle relaxation for treating headaches (Blanchard & Andrasik, 1985). In general, although biofeedback can be quite helpful in treating stress and stress-related disorders in some people, the gains over simpler methods such as self-induced relaxation have not been enough to justify the considerable costs of biofeedback.

| TABLE 11–1   Summary of Ways to Cope |
|---|
| 1. Try to solve the problem |
| 2. Regulate emotional reactions |
| 3. Try to maintain a sense of cognitive and behavioral control |
| 4. Approach the task with a sense of challenge |
| 5. Have a strong commitment to what is being accomplished |
| 6. See the big picture; view the world as making sense |
| 7. Ask for and rely on social support |
| 8. Exercise regularly |
| 9. Eat a healthful diet |
| 10. Get enough sleep |

## Learning to Cope: Effective Stress Management

The stresses of modern life, the intensity of daily work commitments, pressures to succeed financially, and loosening family and community bonds make successful coping difficult to achieve. For many people, stress management consists of hitting the bars after work or taking Valium (diazepam) to get to sleep. Although over 5 million people in this country regularly take addicting minor tranquilizers and about 12% abuse alcohol, substance use is a poor method of stress management. Alcohol and drugs and even more benign avoidance measures such as hypersomnia (sleeping too much), binge eating, and chronic television "addiction" may serve as short-term remedies for stress but in the long run cause more problems than they solve. The ability to function effectively in the long run can become severely jeopardized by the means chosen in the short run to deal with problems. (A summary of the most effective coping methods is provided in Table 11–1.)

Research on stress management demonstrates that people can *learn* to cope effectively with and manage their stress to prevent the development of both psycho-

logical and physical difficulties. Some learn stress management from individual therapists, others from participation in workshops. Others receive training in the workplace. Currently, many corporations assist their workers to develop effective means to cope with stress. Such efforts are beneficial to the corporations themselves because stress-related illnesses may cause employees to miss work, perform poorly, and even suffer work-related injuries. Since the monetary cost of work stress in the United States is estimated to be as high as $17 billion a year (Adams, 1978), stress-management assistance is indeed a cost-effective endeavor.

Research suggests that some multidimensional stress-management programs have been especially effective in helping to minimize or eliminate the negative physical consequences of stress. For example, stress-management programs have helped people with stress-related disorders, such as muscle-contraction headaches (Holroyd, Andrasik, & Westbrook, 1977) and chronically high blood pressure (Shapiro, Schwartz, Ferguson, Redmond, & Weiss,

1977). Stress management has also been successful in modifying extreme Type A Behavior (Chesney, Frautschi, & Rosenman, 1985) and in reducing morbidity (disease) and mortality (death) from coronary heart disease (Chesney et al., 1985). Psychotherapy and behavior modification approaches have been used to change the behavioral patterns believed to contribute to CHD (Roskies, Spevack, Surkis, Cohen, & Gilman, 1978).

Psychologists have been very successful in designing programs to help people manage stress. These programs involve interventions to control the physical manifestations of stress and include such activities as relaxation training and exercise. These programs also involve instruction in how to recognize and change the factors in daily life that cause the stress.

Several points are worth noting about stress-management programs. First, a successful, multidimensional approach to stress management must involve recognizing the sources of stress in one's life and examining the factors that contribute to feelings of stress. As we noted in this chapter, stress may arise from (among other things) irrational cognitions ("If I don't succeed at this job, I will never succeed at anything"), from a great perceived discrepancy between one's abilities and resources and the demands of the situation, and from ways of thinking about life that leave one feeling vulnerable instead of in control. Adjustments in the source of the stress experience are necessary, as we have considered in some detail in this chapter.

Second, learning to cope with stress requires learning to modify the physiological effects of the stress reaction. This modification might best be achieved by a combination of exercise and other physical interventions, such as deep breathing, deep muscle relaxation, certain forms of meditation, as well as yoga and hypnosis. These methods have been found to reduce heart rate, skin conductance measures of stress, muscle tension, and blood pressure, as well as subjects' self-reported feelings of tension (English & Baker, 1983).

Third, successful stress-management programs teach people to figure out which components of a stressful situation are causing their stress reactions and, if possible, to alter those components. It can be very valuable for an individual to learn to distinguish among potentially stressful experiences and to determine which can be avoided, which must be tolerated, and which can be appropriately modified to reduce the experience of stress.

And finally, stress-management techniques must be incorporated into an individual's daily life and practiced regularly in order to maintain their effectiveness.

In this chapter we have discussed how people can and do cope with stress. We have examined factors that affect the evaluation of stressful stimuli and modify the experience of stress. We have also considered approaches to changing the psychological and physiological reactions to events once they have been perceived as stressful. In essence, we have examined the ways in which the tie between stress and illness can be modified and even broken. The study of stress and its management is one of the most promising and potentially applicable realms of research in the exciting field of health psychology.

In the next chapter we look in detail at a specific kind of stress, the experience of serious illness, and we examine the unique ways in which patients attempt to cope with what are sometimes the greatest crises of their lives.

## Summary

Different people experience stressful life events in very different ways. In this chapter we examine several psychological factors that have been found to mediate the connection between stress and physical illness. These include: cognitive responses (including adaptive thinking and personality), general resistance resources (including social support), and coping behaviors (including exercise and psychotherapy for stress management).

I. Coping consists of efforts, both action-oriented and intrapsychic, to manage (that is, master, tolerate, reduce, or minimize) environmental and internal demands, and conflicts among them.
   A. Coping is a dynamic process.
   B. Efforts to cope with stressful experiences are typically focused on accomplishing five main tasks: contending realistically with the problem; tolerating or adjusting emotionally to the negative events or realities; attempting to maintain a positive self-image; attempting to maintain emotional equilibrium; and attempting to continue satisfying relationships with other people.
   C. There are two types of coping efforts: problem-solving efforts and efforts at emotional regulation. Problem-solving efforts involve taking action to change a stressful situation or to prevent or reduce its effects. Efforts at emotion-focused coping involve attempts to regulate or reduce distressing emotions.
II. Coping style refers to an individual's manner and the amount that he or she thinks about stressful life events.
   A. One categorization of coping styles involves avoiding/minimizing versus being vigilant. Each style has costs and benefits.
   B. Self-efficacy involves the belief that one can indeed accomplish a

particular goal. Self-efficacy may promote positive coping.
III. Psychologists have found that human beings have a fundamental need for control. If all their efforts at control fail, people tend to become anxious or eventually helpless and depressed.
   A. Thoughts of control are referred to generally as cognitive control. Behaviors enacted to enhance control come under the heading of behavioral control.
   B. Cognitive control may involve cognitively restructuring an event.
   C. Research on the phenomenon of helplessness has shed considerable light on the phenomenon of stress. Learned helplessness occurs when efforts at control continually are frustrated and come to no avail. One may become helpless in three specific realms: motivational (by failing to make any efforts to change the outcome); cognitive (by failing to learn new responses that could help avoid aversive outcomes in the future); and emotional (by becoming depressed).
   D. Newer versions of the model of helplessness suggest that cognitive factors play a very important role in its development and determine how chronic and pervasive the individual's degree of helplessness will be. Attributing cause internally versus externally can cause greater helplessness. Attributing cause to a stable versus a temporary or unstable problem can cause greater helplessness. Finally, attributing cause to a global problem versus a specific one can cause greater helplessness. Perceived causes of stressful events that are internal, global, and stable can result in the greatest

threats to motivation, cognition, and emotion.

E. Optimism is defined as a cognitive style. Optimists are problem solvers. Pessimists, convinced that things will turn out badly for them anyway, tend to give up and stop trying.

F. Hardiness involves three intertwined components: commitment, control, and challenge. Individuals exhibiting hardiness approach life's challenges from these perspectives and are less likely than those who do not exhibit hardiness to remain healthy in the face of stressful events.

IV. Antonovsky has proposed the Sense of Coherence as a model to explain successful coping with stress and the maintenance of health.

A. Research on stress and illness has focused to its detriment on a pathogenic model that posits a direct effect of some psychological or physical variable on disease. A salutogenic orientation, on the other hand, allows us to examine the factors that promote movement toward health rather than toward illness.

B. The salutogenic approach leads the way to formulation and development of a theory of coping. Several characteristics emerged in the study of successful copers: they see the world as comprehensible and as making cognitive sense; they see the world as manageable and have a solid belief that things will work out as well as can be reasonably expected. Those with a Sense of Coherence believe that events in life have meaning, and life "makes sense" to them on a deep emotional level.

V. The resources available to individuals to deal with stress can significantly affect their success.

A. Those in the lowest socioeconomic positions in society have been found to suffer the highest rates of illness and mortality in response to stress.

B. Social support can be very important in helping an individual to deal with stressful life conditions and events. Social support is support or help from other human beings. Social support is believed to help in three ways: people can directly provide tangible support in the form of physical resources, information support by suggesting alternative actions that may help to solve the stress-producing problem, and emotional support by reassuring the individual that he or she is a cared-for, valued, and esteemed person. Supportive individuals can also provide nurturance.

C. Exercise can provide an active outlet for the physiological arousal experienced in response to stress. Research suggests that regular physical exercise can help to protect health in the face of stressful life events and chronic daily stressors. Vigorous physical exercise is particularly valuable in preventing cardiovascular disease.

D. Cognitive therapy for stress management is based upon the view that the cognitive representation of the environment, rather than the environment itself, determines stress responses. If the cognitions are changed, stress responses can be reduced. Cognitive restructuring is a widely used technique for changing stress-provoking thoughts or beliefs so that they promote, rather than detract from, the individual's well-being. One method of restructuring that attempts to change irrational thoughts is called rational emotive therapy, or RET. Stress-inoculation training is another cognitive approach to the management of stress.

    E. Relaxation works particularly well to help an individual deal with stress. Progressive muscle relaxation is a technique in which the individual focuses his or her attention on specific muscles and alternately tenses and relaxes them. Relatedly, meditation involves several techniques that focus an individual's attention on a single thought or image. In the realm of stress management, relaxation techniques are often used as part of a program of *systematic desensitization*. Biofeedback is also used in stress management.

VI. Research on stress management demonstrates that people can learn to cope effectively with and manage their stress to prevent the development of both psychological and physical difficulties.

    A. People can learn stress management from individual therapists as well as from participation in workshops. Others receive training in the workplace.

    B. A successful, multidimensional approach to stress management must involve recognizing the sources of stress as well as the factors that contribute to feelings of stress; learning to modify the physiological effects of stress reactions; and learning to remedy the factors that contribute to stress.

# Glossary

**behavioral control:** the specific behaviors that the individual enacts to control his or her environment in order to cope with stress.

**biofeedback:** a technique involving an electromechanical device that emits a signal (a light or a buzzer or a sound of varying frequency) to "feed back" to the individual some information about the state of his or her body. Typically, the information fed back is the degree of tension in specific muscles or the general state of arousal of the individual's sympathetic or parasympathetic nervous system.

**catastrophizing:** believing that an event that has not gone according to plan is not simply inconvenient but is truly a catastrophe of major proportions from which one may never recover.

**cognitions:** one's thoughts about and interpretations of events or about oneself in relation to those events. Cognitions include an individual's view of his or her own life and its meaning.

**cognitive control:** control over thoughts and other psychological activities.

**cognitive restructuring:** a widely used technique for changing stress-provoking thoughts or beliefs so that they promote, rather than detract from, the individual's well-being.

**coping:** efforts by an individual, both action-oriented and intrapsychic, to manage (that is, master, tolerate, reduce, or minimize) environmental and internal demands and conflicts among them. Coping is a dynamic process.

**coping style:** the manner and the amount

that an individual thinks about stressful life events.

**coronary bypass:** installation of arterial grafts in the heart to bypass coronary arteries that are blocked by atherosclerotic plaques.

**efforts at emotional regulation:** actions undertaken to change or reduce the emotional distress resulting from a stressful situation.

**emotional support:** help from members of the social network to reassure the individual that he or she is a cared-for, valued, and esteemed person.

**endoscopy:** a procedure in which a tube is passed through the throat into the stomach to allow its examination.

**General Resistance Resource** (GRR): resources (such as money, ego strength, social support, and cultural stability) that help to protect a person against the ill effects of stress.

**hardiness:** a psychological construct that refers to an individual's stable, characteristic way of responding to life events. Individuals who exhibit hardiness have been found to be less susceptible than those who do not to experiencing illness in response to stressful conditions in their lives. Hardiness involves commitment, control, and a sense of challenge.

**information support:** help from members of the social network in which they suggest alternative actions that may help to solve the stress-producing problem. These suggestions may help the person to look at his or her problems in a new way and thus help to solve those problems or at least to minimize their impact.

**informational control:** a valuable element in coping, informational control occurs when an individual has knowledge about ways in which to deal with the stressful event.

**in vivo contacts:** the experiencing of the actual stress-provoking events or circumstances in the real-life situation.

**learned helplessness:** a condition that occurs when an individual's efforts at control are continually unavailing and he or she is unable to change an intolerable situation. Learned helplessness is manifested in three specific realms: motivational, cognitive, and emotional.

**meditation:** reflection brought about by one of several techniques that attempt to focus an individual's attention on a single thought or image in an effort to prevent distraction by other thoughts, particularly those of an evaluative or analytic nature. The practice of meditation has been found to be effective in reducing stress and anxiety, as well as in reducing hypertension and even eliminating certain phobias.

**optimistic explanations for events:** explanations that invoke external, temporary, and specific rationales or bases for things that happen.

**pathogenic model:** a model that posits a direct effect of some psychological or physical variable on disease. Current examples are the effect of Type A behavior on coronary disease, and the effect of learned helplessness on depression.

**pessimistic explanations for events:** explanations that invoke internal, stable, and global rationales or bases for things that happen.

**problem-solving efforts:** actions taken to change a stressful situation or to prevent or reduce its effects.

**progressive muscle relaxation:** a technique in which the individual focuses his or her attention on specific muscle groups and alternately tenses and relaxes the muscles.

**restructuring:** a type of cognitive strategy that involves selectively attending to or focusing on some aspects of a situation but not on others.

**salutogenic orientation:** an approach to research that allows examination of the factors that promote movement toward health rather than toward illness.

**self-efficacy:** the belief that one can indeed accomplish a particular goal; self-efficacy may promote positive coping.

**Sense of Coherence:** an existential theory of stress that addresses how people who experience very stressful and chaotic existences can still remain healthy.

**social support:** help from other human beings, such as friends, family, neighbors, co-workers, and acquaintances. Social support can come in the form of physical assistance and can also involve reminders that one is an esteemed and valued person.

**stress-inoculation training:** a cognitive approach to the management of stress based upon the theory that the stress experience can be reduced if a person is cognitively prepared. Stress inoculation occurs in three steps: conceptualization, skill acquisition and rehearsal, and application.

**systematic desensitization:** a method for reducing stress (particularly stress that is generated from fear of or anxiety about something specific). The method is based upon stimulus-response associations.

**tangible support:** help in the form of physical resources (for example, lending money, doing the grocery shopping, taking care of the children).

# 12

# Serious Illness: The Patient's Perspective

· · · · ·

Catherine had the strange, simple thought that this was real and it was serious. She felt as if she had somehow failed and there would be a huge price to pay. She was amazed that she felt no pain, as if her body were not really "her." Then she blacked out.

Police Officer Catherine Parker awoke in the recovery room after surgery. Someone was calling her name. A woman she didn't know was talking to her. "You had an accident," said the woman. "You're at Metropolitan Hospital. You've just had surgery. You have some burns, and your right arm was severed. But you are going to recover. Are you in pain right now?"

Catherine struggled to remember what had happened. She and her partner were trying to pull two children from a car that had crashed on the highway. There was an unexpected explosion.

Catherine lost consciousness again. This time she had a bizarre dream. A huge dog, vicious and wild, pursued her. He leapt at her and dug his fangs into her arm. He was tearing it off. She was screaming, but no sound would come out of her mouth.

The pain was overwhelming. Her chest and her face felt searing hot. Catherine was awake. She looked at the bandage attached to her shoulder. "Where's my arm?" She was pleading with the nurse, as if this unknown woman held the power to return it. "It was severed in the explosion, Catherine," the nurse said gently. "I'll get you something for the pain."

Catherine was screaming into a long, dark tunnel. She heard the echo of her own voice resounding over and over, but she couldn't make sense of the words. She was searching for something vitally important. In the dream she used her two arms to grope in the darkness.

Awake again, Catherine heard more bits of the reality she would be facing for months to come and for the rest of her life. One arm was amputated. She had second and third degree burns on her face, neck, and chest. She would survive, but she would endure extreme pain in the next few months of hospitalization. Her burns would heal as heavy scar tissue. Even after plastic surgery, she would never look the same again.

■ ■ ■ ■ ■

Fitzhugh Mullan, M.D., looked at an X-ray of his own chest and saw a cancerous tumor. It was large and infiltrated structures that were vital to his life. He was 32 years old, with a wife and a 3-year-old daughter. The treatment of his cancer took years, and permanently changed his life. He wrote candidly about his experience with serious illness in a moving book called *Vital Signs* (Mullan, 1983).

The story goes something like this. Within a week of seeing his cancer on a rou-

tine X-ray, Dr. Mullan became a surgical patient. A biopsy of the mass in his chest was attempted, but the biopsy procedure was disastrous. A major vein in his chest was inadvertently cut, and the surgeons had to split open his chest in a matter of moments to save his life. With his chest open and the bleeding controlled, the surgeons removed about 60% of the huge tumor. It was a seminoma, a kind of cancer that is amenable to cure.

During the weeks after surgery, Mullan was severely ill. He suffered considerable pain from the chest surgery. He was subjected to extensive X ray studies to determine whether the cancer had spread to other parts of his body. Since it had not, he was given radiation and chemotherapy treatments. In themselves, these treatments would be very debilitating, but even before they could be started, Mullan experienced massive swelling of his upper body. The *superior vena cava*, the major blood vessel that carries blood from the upper body to the heart, was obstructed by the remaining tumor and by the tissues that were swollen as a result of the surgery. His upper body puffed up so much that his hands were grotesquely swollen. He had the sensation that his head was bloated, and his eyes protruded. He was very frightened.

The chemotherapy came each week. Drugs designed to kill cancer tissue were injected into Mullan's veins. Cancerous cells grow faster than normal cells do and are more susceptible to these chemicals. But the chemicals still act as poisons in the body and can cause terrible reactions. Mullan suffered for hours with violent shivering and fevers of 104° F. He was severely weakened and nauseated. He vomited for two or three days after each drug administration. This went on for many weeks, leaving him with few reasonably "good" days in between treatments. Daily radiation therapy necessary to destroy the tumor in his chest eventually burned his esophagus as well, so that eating became extremely painful. He lost a great deal of weight.

Mullan's physical difficulties and limitations were not his only problems. He suffered psychologically as well. Being a cancer patient at age 32 was a very lonely experience. Most people who get cancer are in their retirement years, with many of their hoped-for accomplishments behind them. Mullan, on the other hand, was the father in a fledgling family. He had extensive emotional and financial obligations. He was a physician who could not take care of anyone, including himself, and his self-esteem suffered severely. He remained exceedingly weak for a long time, and found it very difficult to stay emotionally connected to those he loved. He was haunted by the possibility of a recurrence of the cancer and of his death. For a long time, his dominant emotion was depression.

Accidents and serious illness have the potential to transform an individual's life instantly and completely. Illness and injury happen not only to a body but also to a mind, a consciousness. It is a thinking, feeling human being who suffers. Officer Parker and Dr. Mullan face both physical and emotional traumas. Their conditions threaten their emotional balance as well as their survival.

In this chapter we are going to examine in detail what it is like to be seriously ill or injured. We will explore patients' thoughts and concerns. We will examine what patients feel about themselves and about their own lives and prospects for the future. We will examine the difficulties faced in making decisions about diagnosis and treatment and in fighting for control of their own lives. We will see how patients cope with feelings of helplessness and alienation. We will also examine how patients learn to cope with the tragic circumstances of illness and injury. We will explore some of the conditions under which patients find hope for a future, however different that future might be from what they once expected. We will see the value in patients' setting limited, concrete goals and taking small but regular steps toward achieving independence and rebuilding their lives in new ways. Finally, we will continue this examination in Chapter 13, where we consider the chronic phase of illness in which patients must learn to adjust to permanent limitations and find ways to lead meaningful lives.

## STAGES OF ILLNESS

Different demands are made on an individual at different stages of illness or physical injury. During the first phase, the *acute phase*, the primary concern of both patient and medical personnel is survival. Moment to moment, or day to day, the individual's chances of survival depend upon the immediate measures taken to deal with the physical trauma or disease. For the heart attack patient, intervention is initially provided within moments of arrival at the hospital and the effectiveness of that intervention can determine both immediate and long-term survival (Gentry, 1979). In other cases short-term survival (months, or a few years) may be relatively certain. But beyond the short term, the length and quality of the individual's life will depend upon appropriate and timely treatment. A person with a newly discovered cancerous tumor might receive swift surgical intervention to remove the tumor and timely chemotherapy to prevent *metastasis* (spread to other organs). Thus, the choices that are made in the acute stages of illness or injury can have a lasting impact on the individual's long-term survival and on the quality of his or her future life. Therefore, the imperative exists for professionals to make the correct diagnostic and treatment decisions.

The acute phase of care is also likely to be accompanied by pain, confusion, and fear on the part of patients. These emotions can influence patients' decisions regarding treatment. Dr. Mullan, whom we encountered at the beginning of this chapter, felt many of these emotions as he underwent surgery, chemotherapy, and radiation in the acute phase of his cancer treatment. These emotions sometimes threatened his decision to undergo the initial physical and emotional suffering of cancer treatments in an effort to eradicate the cancer from his body and thereby increase significantly his chances for survival (Mullan, 1983).

During the next phase of *rehabilitation* a person who has been bedridden or has been passively cared for by medical profes-

**BOX 12–1**

## REHABILITATION

The cost of illness and disability can be staggering. Not only is treatment a huge expense but human potential for productive labor is lost. The *process of rehabilitation* can aid in reducing these costs significantly by helping a person to attain his or her maximum potential for normal living in physical, psychological, social, and vocational realms.

Rehabilitation has a fairly recent history. In ancient times there was little tolerance for physical infirmity. The Greeks, for example, were so enamored of physical perfection that they killed defective children by throwing them from a precipice or abandoning them on the side of a mountain. Any enlightenment that occurred after that was halted in the Middle Ages when the emphasis on spirits and demons as the cause of illness stood in the way of the humane treatment of persons afflicted (Goldenson, 1978a; Goldenson, Dunham, & Dunham, 1978). During the 1800s several institutes for the care of those ill and crippled were opened in Europe and in the United States. It was not until after World War I, however, that the rehabilitation movement took hold and began to develop. Emphasis was on the physical restoration and rehabilitation of those injured in war. The greatest strides in the clinical care of the chronically ill and disabled have come since World War II.

Today rehabilitation is a *dynamic* process that is geared to the needs of the whole person. It is not limited to restoration of the individual's physical capacities alone but is targeted at several realms. Physical treatments, such as medication and surgery, are instituted to reduce as much as possible the impact of the individual's physical problems. Rehabilitation may also involve acquisition and training in the use of a prosthetic device (or a prosthesis, which is an artificial substitute for a missing body part). The use of a prosthesis can often bring a person to near-normal functioning, such as when an amputee learns to ski with a leg prosthesis.

Current rehabilitation methods also include: (a) vocational rehabilitation, which involves counseling, testing, and training toward the goal of job placement or independent self-employment; (b) psychological rehabilitation, which consists of personal counseling and psychotherapy, and supportive measures toward the goal of increased self-acceptance and self-esteem; and (c) social rehabilitation, which includes help in developing and maintaining social relationships and recreational pastimes. Sexual counseling is also provided, so that with some relearning, a handicapped individual can enjoy a fulfilling sex life.

sionals must work toward achieving as high a level of health and independent functioning as his or her condition makes possible. Tremendous efforts may be required for the patient to walk unassisted, for example, or to talk coherently, or to get dressed and to eat. A rehabilitation patient must learn to adjust to these limitations and to come to terms with an altered self-image. As described further in Box 12–1, specialists in medical rehabilitation can help the patient to maximize his or her remaining potential (Goldenson, 1978b; Goldenson, Dunham, & Dunham, 1978).

As diagrammed in Figure 12–1, rehabilitation may lead to recovery. Often, however when an individual has accomplished as much as possible toward rehabilitation, he or she often must accept the remaining disabilities and limitations as *chronic* and go on with life. Chronic conditions (considered in detail in Chapter 13) are those from which patients are not expected to recover. Facial disfigurement, a limp, or life in a wheelchair may be inescapable realities.

In some cases an illness progresses to the point at which it cannot be cured and the condition is *terminal*. Cancer may metastasize, for example, as neoplastic cells escape from the initial tumor site and travel to other parts of the body, such as the bones, lungs, brain, or liver. A heart attack, or a series of heart attacks, may cause irreparable damage, making it impossible for the heart to sustain the patient's life. In Chapter 14 we examine in detail the wide range of emotional reactions that patients experience in attempting to come to terms with their terminal conditions and the prospect of death.

### THE IMPORTANCE OF FOCUSING ON PSYCHOSOCIAL ISSUES

In this chapter we will see that serious illness and injury threaten virtually every aspect of an individual's life. Thoughts and

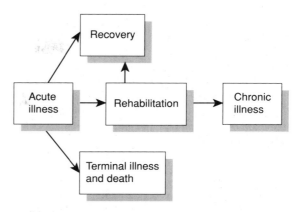

**FIGURE 12–1**   The stages of illness.

feelings inevitably arise from serious threats to a person's well-being and change with the current stage of the person's condition. It is important for medical and psychological professionals, as well as for patients and their families, to understand the psychological outcomes of serious illness and injury. The character of a patient's thoughts and feelings may not only be affected by but also affect his or her physical condition. For example, a patient's anxiety and fear may deplete the energy he or she needs for healing. Depression and hopelessness may translate into an unwillingness or inability to take the necessary steps toward health and well-being. Knowledge and understanding of these psychological factors can be critical to the patient's achievement of long-term goals (Gulledge, 1979; Wishnie, Hackett, & Cassem, 1977).

## Serious Illness: The Losses

I submit to you that, in the entire dictionary, in any language, you will not find a single word that carries with it such emotional impact as cancer. Lawrence Le Shan [a specialist on the psychological aspects of cancer] once defined the elements of a nightmare. 1. Someone or something is doing something terrible to you. 2. You have no idea how long it will last. 3. You have no control over it. That definition fits nicely for cancer. (Shlain, 1979, p. 177)

More recently, this definition also applies to the dreaded killer, AIDS. Life with a serious illness or injury can be unpredictable and at times can seem to make little sense. It can be filled with threats to self-image and losses of self-esteem, of freedom, of day-to-day activities, of feelings of physical comfort, and of the possibilities of the future.

## THREATS TO SELF-IMAGE

The weakness and limitations of heart disease, the physical disfigurements of burns and amputations, and particularly the debilitating treatments of cancer can drastically change an individual's self-image (Curbow, Somerfield, Legro, & Sonnega, 1990). A man's sense of his strength and masculinity may be seriously threatened by the exhaustion and forced dependency of sickness and disability. A woman's sense of her femininity and attractiveness may be drastically altered by a facial disfigurement or by the loss of a breast to cancer (Berger & Bostwick, 1984; Bernstein, 1976; Taylor, Lichtman, & Wood, 1985).

> Mastectomy is so shattering to a woman's self-image that she may feel she is only "passing" for normal. Attention from a man, particularly a man she did not know "before," will overwhelm her with feelings of fraudulence; she knows what he doesn't —that beneath her sweater are scars and a missing breast. (Dackman, 1987, p. 420)

In general, diseases such as cancer of the reproductive organs or disabilities that interfere with sexual activity have the potential to threaten seriously an individual's self-image as a sexual being. The individual may doubt his or her ability to be a loved and desired partner (Dunham, 1978).

Overall, one's self-image as a whole and independent person may be seriously challenged by the forced dependency of illness and injury (Cohen & Lazarus, 1979). This may be particularly true when survival depends upon artificial devices (such as ventilator equipment or cardiac pacemakers) (Abram, 1977).

> Upon hearing his diagnosis of cancer, a 37-year-old surgeon reported . . . "At that moment . . . I was consumed by fear. . . . No one ever said that fear was rational. It was the thought of suffering, of dying slowly, and in the end dying, not as I was in life but rather as a shriveled ghost of myself. My vanity loathed the idea that my children, my wife, my friends would see me thus. I feared I would be the object of pity and that people would be afraid of me and withdraw." (Shlain, 1979, p. 177)

## LOSS OF BODY INTEGRITY

The physical alteration of one's body can be disorienting and terrifying. Watching one's own blood pour from a serious wound, or recognizing that a body part has been amputated and is permanently gone may at first bring *dissociation*, the experience "This body isn't me." *Integration* of an altered body image, the perception and evaluation of one's new physical appearance and functioning, may take some time (Fischer & Cleveland, 1958). Even when a bodily change is for the better, and comes from cosmetic or reconstructive surgery, adjustment may be very slow. When a permanent change in physical reality is for the worse, however, as is usually the case in serious injuries, reality is not faced easily, and often not right away (Schwab & Hameling, 1968; Curbow et al., 1990).

The patient who has lost a breast to cancer, for example, may wait a long time before looking at the results of her surgery. Many women report that the initial viewing was a tremendous shock and that the incorporation of the reality of the amputation into body image took considerable time. For some, it is never done completely, and the only solution is breast reconstruction (Berger & Bostwick, 1984). Likewise, a burn patient may deny the existence of a severe facial disfigurement by avoiding mirrors. Some patients with facial burns delay looking at themselves for a very long time. The patient's altered appearance is almost always a considerable shock that challenges his or her entire sense of identity (Andreasen & Norris, 1977). Those who are facially disfigured tend to have the most difficulty adjusting, probably because of their inability to hide the disfigurement, the reactions of other people to them, and the role that the face plays in their establishment of self-concept (Richardson, Goodman, Hastorf, & Dornbusch, 1961). Burn patients typically cope with this stress by minimizing the importance of physical appearance and even of physical functioning. In a self-protective manner, they tend to emphasize the value of intellectual and character development (Andreasen & Norris, 1977).

*Denial*, of course, can be a very effective short-term defense mechanism. It allows the individual slowly to come to terms emotionally with the full meaning of the altered body image. Most people who must deal with such major adjustments in their lives tend, initially at least, to defend themselves emotionally against the full meaning of their deformities. Denial is a common response of patients to such conditions as heart attack, strokes, and cancer (Krantz & Deckel, 1983; Diller, 1976; Katz, Weiner, Gallagher, & Hellman, 1970), as well as burns (Andreasen & Norris, 1977). Denial, although self-deceptive, can serve to help maintain the individual's identity and self-esteem, particularly in the face of negative reactions from other people (Hamburg, Hamburg, & DeGoza, 1953).

Major physical change can have a significant emotional effect even when it comes on slowly, such as when long-term illness depletes capacities and appearance. After months of cancer treatment, Dr. Mullan found his body altered in a way that made salient the profound physical losses he had experienced because of his cancer.

> There were no mirrors in my hospital room, and while I knew I was losing weight, I had had no opportunity to see my body. Daily, to be sure, I showered and ran my hands over the increasingly bony prominences of myself, but somehow that didn't add up to what had really happened until I came home and saw myself in a full-length mirror. I was staggered. My arms, once strong, stuck into the sides of my chest like broomsticks on a scarecrow. My buttocks had turned soft and fleshless and my leg muscles—the legs I had once been proud of—had been replaced by loose hanging flesh. My waist was concave, sucked in over the immutable hip bones. . . . I had *felt* sick. Now I saw what it was like to *look* sick. (Mullan, 1983, p. 60)

When an individual's body is altered due to accident, or to a disease such as cancer, he or she may fear that relationships with others, particularly with loved ones, will be changed drastically because of the new physical appearance (Lichtman, 1982; Shlain, 1979). They fear that they will be rejected or become an object of revulsion or pity. Thus, the reactions that these loved ones actually have can profoundly influence the individual's self-definition. A woman who had had a mastectomy allowed her lover to see the results of her surgery: " 'It's not that bad,' Tom said. He lied. I know because he squeezed me tightly and whispered, 'Oh, you poor darling.' I heard his words of sympathy, and then I heard

myself wail as I had wailed only once before—when I thought my life might shortly
end" (Dackman, 1987, p. 436).

## INTERRUPTION OF WORK

Many people derive a strong sense of identity from the work that they do, for example, from their role as student or their
devotion to a career. Work is the outlet for
creative ideas. It provides a view of oneself
as a productive person. The ability to support oneself and one's dependents can
figure prominently in an individual's self-
esteem (Branden, 1969). Thus, self-esteem
may be threatened by the need to rely on
others for financial, physical, and emotional support.

When people are seriously ill, their
schoolwork and careers must be put on
hold. Opportunities for advancement may
vanish. The likelihood of returning to
school or career may remain unclear for
a long time. Resumption of former activities may become impossible. New self-
definitions may be slow in coming, as new
opportunities for productivity must be discovered or learned (Gulledge, 1979).

Relatedly, the financial costs of serious
illness can be tremendous. Family resources may be taxed beyond their capacity. Even with medical insurance coverage,
which is likely to vanish if the patient loses
his or her job, the costs (such as deductibles
and copayments) can be considerable.
Without insurance, these costs can be
astronomical.

## LOSS OF INDEPENDENCE

My greatest fear was loss of control over
my own destiny. I would have to hand it
over to faceless X ray technicians and people I did not know. (Shlain, 1979, p. 177)

Helplessness and forced dependency are
the realities of many serious medical conditions. Because of the limitations that re-

sult from illness and injury, a patient must
rely on other people such as family members, medical professionals, and attendents
for his or her most basic needs. Walking,
eating, using the bathroom, and other simple tasks may be impossible to face alone,
and their accomplishment depends entirely
on the assistance of others. Illness and injury bring limitations and restrictions that
may be frustrating and overwhelming to
the person who is trapped in a damaged
body.

Paradoxically, the best adjustment to
the enforced passivity of illness may involve fighting it (Mullan, 1983). A patient
who relinquishes independence and control
too readily may find that dependence and
passivity become a habit. Even the things
he or she really *can* do alone may come to
require assistance. On the other hand, the
patient who, within the confines of medical
recommendations, tests his or her capacities continuously will be able to maintain
an accurate assessment of what can and
cannot be accomplished alone. In this way,
the limits of independence are defined and
redefined. Goals for accomplishment can be
adjusted and readjusted. "They had an elevator to transport stretchers and wheel-
chairs to the treatment level. I refused to
use it, determined to walk the eight steps
downward. With Aunt Pat steering me from
behind, I made it" (Mullan, 1983, p. 32).
Such emphasis on maintaining some independent action, however minimal, is valuable in preventing the depression that can
result from helplessness (Seligman, 1975).

Sometimes, however, a patient will
fight passivity at a significant cost to his or
her own well-being (Gulledge, 1979). The
male heart attack patient for whom bedrest
is essential may do pushups on the floor of
his hospital room to prove he's still robust
and strong (Olin & Hackett, 1964). Although it can be valuable for a patient to
do as many things as possible for himself or
herself, independent actions must be car-

ried out within medically recommended guidelines.

## THREATS TO COGNITIVE FUNCTIONING

Certain medical conditions can interfere directly with cognitive functioning. For example, partly because of the peculiar nature of intensive or coronary care units and partly because of the direct effects of certain physical treatments, patients may become completely disoriented for significant periods of time. After open-heart surgery, for example, a patient's delirium may last for several days. This is a well-known condition that has been termed *cardiac delirium* or *cardiac psychosis* (Kimball, 1977). Some cardiac surgery patients experience only transient intellectual deficits; others have gross impairment of their cognitive functioning. Some experience hallucinations and even *paranoid ideations* (mental representations and thoughts of being the target of persecution). To the patient with cardiac psychosis, all environmental stimuli seem equally important and threatening. Stimuli that are normally tuned out remain quite salient. Cardiac psychosis is believed to be caused by small cerebral emboli (blood clots that go to the brain) following surgery. Cardiac psychosis is an example of a specific psychobiological reaction to the assault of illness and surgical treatment. Obviously, it is important for those who must deal with and care for the patient to know that such reactions are common and temporary.

## A THREATENED FUTURE

The phenomena of illness and injury underscore the fact that life is unpredictable. A hoped-for future and distant goals can suddenly vanish from the realm of possibility when serious illness and injury occur. Plans to have children may be destroyed by the discovery of cancer of the reproductive organs (cervical or testicular cancer, for example). Even short-range goals, such as finishing college, running in a marathon, or writing a book, may be thwarted temporarily or forever by serious medical problems.

Despite the uncertainties inherent in anticipating and planning for a future, present actions are usually undertaken in anticipation of their long-term goals. Planning assumes that there is a future to work toward, and that the future is as one has envisioned it. In the context of serious illness, of course, such assumptions may be incorrect.

Would people spend their time differently if they knew a serious illness or injury would befall them and change their lives forever? People whose lives *have* been changed by serious illness or disabling injury do in fact focus on precisely this issue. In attempting to find meaning in their lives, they look back: How have I spent my time? Were my choices wise, given what I know now? What are the things that were and are really important to me? If I had another chance at a healthy life, how would I live it?

Dr. Mullan, the cancer patient we met earlier, looked back on the time just before his diagnosis and the terrible events that followed:

> It was about five o'clock on a Sunday afternoon. The sun was brilliant gold, illuminating Santa Fe and the Rio Grande Valley stretching to the west. With two beers and a basketball game under my belt, I felt euphoric. . . . It was a moment of exquisite happiness. . . . I could not possibly have had any inkling of the problems to come and yet that is what euphoria is all about. It ignores the possibility of catastrophe and unhappiness. It is a moment of freedom, a moment of perfect flight, that belies, discounts, forgets, and denies all other possibilities. In the time that followed that early March afternoon I thought frequently of that moment. I clung

to its memory as proof that happiness exists. My body was to become a vessel of pain, nausea, depression, and despair. I clung to the memory of that golden twilight in the belief that bodies were made for something better than what I felt. (Mullan, 1983, p. 26)

In no way do I mean to recommend or endorse serious sickness, but living through it has, I think, left me with a fuller sense of life. This sense includes the inevitability of death attended by some quantity of pain and despair as well as the richness of life in the years that are ours. The predictable is not life and health but rather death. I say that not in any spirit of morosity but rather with a reinforced sense of the muscularity and mischief, the loyalty and generosity, the sensuality and humor that are ours for the time that we are here. (Mullan, 1983, p. 203)

## STRAIN ON
## RELATIONSHIPS WITH LOVED ONES

Hospitalization and the invasive, debilitating treatments of illness and injury can bring both physical separation and emotional alienation from other people. Hospitalized patients, as well as those disabled at home, are very often terribly lonely. Visiting hours may be restricted, and busy schedules of work, school, and household duties may make it difficult for family and friends to visit the patient (McCubbin et al., 1980; Lewis, 1986).

Even when loved ones do see the patient regularly and often, the circumstances of hospitalization can prevent normal interactions. Hospital roommates, nurses, and other medical personnel, for example, can severely limit privacy. When such a situation exists for a long period of time, marital and family relationships may become quite strained (Croog & Fitzgerald, 1978).

Many obligations fall on the loved ones of a person who is ill. Family members typ-

ically must carry out many of the tasks that were once the patient's responsibility. The patient may begin to feel like an outsider in the family. During his years fighting cancer, for example, Dr. Mullan watched the relationship between his wife and daughter grow very strong and at times appear to exclude him. He knew that the exclusion was not intentional, and that it came about as a result of his long absence in the hospital. He also recognized that were he to die, the closeness that his wife and daughter developed would be extremely important to them both. Yet, he still felt sadly left out (Mullan, 1983).

Illness can challenge the cohesiveness of a family. It has been suggested that the stresses of a serious illness, such as cancer, typically make a solid, strong marriage much better, and a weak, troubled one considerably worse (Shlain, 1979). The crisis of illness brings many opportunities for intense emotional intimacy and for the expression of concern and devotion. Illness also presents a tremendous challenge to maintaining trust and open communication (Klein, Dean, & Bogdonoff, 1967; Chekryn, 1984).

Finally, an individual's role in his or her family may change, temporarily or permanently, as a result of illness or disability (Glasser & Glasser, 1969; Kaplan, Smith, Grobstein, & Fischman, 1977). When someone is absent from his or her family while severely ill and hospitalized, other family members must carry on in whatever way they can. For example, a woman who was once dependent upon her husband is forced to become self-sufficient when he is ill. Unless their communication is open and intimate, he may come to feel unneeded. In an effort to forestall such a loss, one woman whose husband was seriously ill with *amyotrophic lateral sclerosis* (or Lou Gehrig's disease, which is an incurable, degenerative disease of the nervous system) made it a point to send the children to their father whenever he was well enough to help them with their problems. This action underscored his continued role as a parent and co-decision maker of the household (Safran, 1977). In some cases role changes may be for the better. The disruption of dysfunctional patterns may give rise to new and better ways for family members to relate to one another.

BOX 12–2

## SOCIAL SUPPORT AND ILLNESS

Adjustment to illness and disability can be strongly influenced by the resources available. *Social support* is particularly important, and comes in two forms: *physical assistance* (tangible aids such as going grocery shopping and driving the children to school), and *psychological* or emotional support (such as providing acceptance and encouragement, and listening to expressions of frustration) (Caplan, 1979). Although there has been no experimental research regarding the importance of social support (that is, research with control groups and random assignment of subjects to conditions has not been done), there has been considerable research on naturally occurring social support and the outcomes of illness and injury. Generally, researchers have found that people who receive both tangible and emotional support from friends and extended family tend to cope better than those who do not (Wortman, 1984; Dunkel-Schetter & Wortman, 1982; Wortman & Dunkel-Schetter, 1979).

Of course, furnishing the necessary support for a loved one can be quite a burden. At the very least, providing physical and emotional care to someone who is ill can be exhausting. The tremendous emotional demands of care may leave the caregiver with little time to focus on his or her own needs. Also, a caregiver's negative emotional state might actually be detrimental to the emotional life of the patient. Therefore, it is especially important that caregivers themselves receive social support. In addition, for a family member or friend who provides support to maintain a relationship with the patient, there must be some reciprocity. The patient must provide whatever support he or she can to the caregiver, for example, by being involved in the caregiver's concerns and being emotionally available.

Social support is a potentially complicated issue. People stricken by illness usually receive social support as long as they are optimistic and try to maintain their social network. Some may feel great pressure to do so, lest they be abandoned. Depression and uncommunicativeness may lead to a complete loss of social support. In addition, while tangible social support is fairly straightforward, psychological supports can be quite complex. For example, what feels like concern to one person may feel like overprotection and control to another. People who are overprotected by their families may fail to test and develop their own abilities.

It is not unusual for those providing support to an ill or disabled loved one to be confronted with major emotional adjustments. Family alliances may shift and once-stable bonds may be threatened. Family counseling may be imperative in assisting all those affected to make needed role adjustments in the context of disability and illness.

# Facing The Emotional Challenges of Serious Illness

A patient who is seriously ill or injured faces many challenging tasks. Among the greatest of these is to remain an emotionally healthy person in the face of the demands of a serious medical condition.

As we have seen so far in this chapter, there are many aspects of serious illness and injury that can be psychologically extremely stressful to patients. Several important emotional challenges must be dealt with successfully.

## MAINTAINING IDENTITY AND SOCIAL SUPPORT

Serious illness and injury have the capacity to change people significantly, and one of the greatest challenges confronting the patient is to maintain his or her own identity. As a result of the physical and emotional demands upon them, happy, optimistic people can become severely depressed. Intelligent, energetic people can lose their ability and their willingness to direct their lives. Mature, reasonable people can become petulant and childish. How extensively a person is changed depends upon the conditions of the illness, the precise experiences of treatment, the individual's emotional resiliency, and a host of other factors (Moos & Tsu, 1977a). But illness and injury often bring challenges to, and losses of, the very things that make each person unique, such as his or her appearance and bodily functioning, physical and mental capabilities, plans and future possibilities, personal philosophy, and relationships with others. When many of his or her own unique characteristics are changed or can no longer find expression, the ill person must work to develop new aspects of identity and strive to accept and maintain social support from others (Wortman, 1984; Wortman & Dunkel-Schetter, 1979).

## EMOTIONAL DEVELOPMENT

Another challenge is for the individual to continue developing psychologically and emotionally despite the interference of illness. Amidst the impediments and limitations of a serious threat to his or her physical well-being, an individual may find himself or herself struggling to continue growing psychologically. For the young cancer patient with a wife and children, for example, such development involves continuing to pursue trust and intimacy with his wife, and learning to be consistently supportive and emotionally open and available to his children (Mullan, 1983).

The demands of a medical crisis can make it relatively easy for medical practitioners, loved ones, and the patient himself or herself to lose sight of the need to maintain and support the patient's identity and development. During the initial phase of an acute illness or injury, all attention may need to be focused on actions that will insure the patient's survival and minimize long-term disabilities. But eventually the crisis is over and the patient must face the normal challenges of living. Even in the face of physical limitations, emotional development continues (Moos & Tsu, 1977a, 1977b).

## EXPLAINING ILLNESS AND INJURY

Patients who develop life-threatening illnesses such as cancer often try to understand just how their disease came about; they seek an explanation (Curbow et al., 1990). Several researchers have examined how patients organize their thoughts and beliefs about illness (Garrity, 1975; Lau & Hartman, 1983). Typically, people form cognitions about the identity, the cause, the duration, and the consequences of their conditions (Nerenz & Leventhal, 1983). Of these beliefs, what people think about the causes and the consequences of their

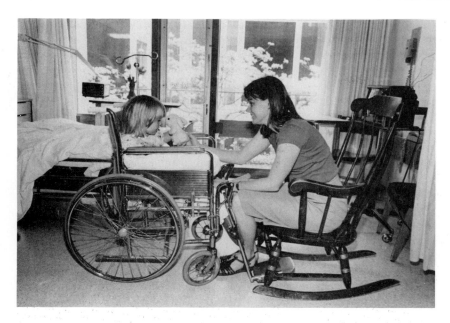

The demands of a medical crisis should not obscure the need to support the patient's identity and development.
SOURCE: © Jerry Howard/Stock, Boston

illnesses may be the most important in predicting how well they will adjust (Meyerowitz, 1983).

Self-blame is common. In clinical studies several researchers found that one-third to one-half of cancer patients blame *themselves*, particularly their own past "sins," for the cancer (Hinton, 1977; Moses & Cividali, 1966). Many others blame someone else, and believe that the cancer was caught through contagion or developed because of something another person had done. Since these explanations are typically held implicitly, and without awareness, they may affect the patient's feelings about himself or herself. Such explanations may be rather destructive to an individual's emotional well-being. Some research has suggested that self-blame can lead to guilt and self-recrimination, and that patients may feel they should have been able to prevent their illness or accident (Krantz & Deckel, 1983). Other research does suggest, however, that

self-blame may at times be adaptive (Bulman & Wortman, 1977). Those who took responsibility for their spinal cord injuries adjusted better than did those who would not take such responsibility. Presumably, those who felt responsible were also better able to feel in control of their lives and to come to terms with their tragedy. Research uniformly suggests, however, that blaming another person for one's disorder is maladaptive (Bulman & Wortman, 1977; Taylor et al., 1984). Blaming others may reflect either a general tendency to avoid taking responsibility for one's life, or an unresolved hostility that may make adjustment to illness or injury considerably more difficult.

## FACING EMOTIONAL CONFLICTS

Consider this example. A breast cancer patient is convinced that she is unaffected emotionally by the loss of her breast. She tells everyone, "It's not a big deal." She never allows herself to feel sadness, anxiety, or anger about the change in her image. She acts almost as if nothing had happened. Yet, the loss affects her in other ways. She suddenly becomes very dissatisfied with other aspects of her life. She has terrible fights with her husband. She begins to despise a job that once gave her a great deal of satisfaction. She remains unaware that her emotional amnesia surrounding the loss of her breast is adversely affecting the rest of her life.

Consider another patient who develops fearful associations when she encounters the site or circumstances of an earlier accident. She has intense *phobic reactions*, which are negative emotional responses that can cause the victim to avoid the accident situation, or anything resembling it, whenever possible. A victim of an automobile crash, for example, may develop a phobia and remain unable to ride in an automobile again. The successful maintenance of emotional balance in the face of illness and injury would certainly involve overcoming such a phobia and working through the emotional impact of the devastating event. Although the *repression of emotion* (forcing it out of conscious awareness) might protect the individual from immediate distress in the short term, repression is not a long-term solution (Branden, 1971).

These examples illustrate how important it is for an individual to face the impact of illness and injury, and to understand fully the effect it can have on his or her thoughts and emotions.

## FACING STRESSFUL MEDICAL TREATMENTS

Despite their promise of another chance at life and health, medical treatments for serious illness and injury can present a major source of stress to a patient. Cancer treatment is a good example.

Many cancer patients are treated with surgery as well as with radiation and chemotherapy. The surgical excision (removal) of a tumor, if it is successful, removes most or nearly all of the neoplastic (malignant) cells in the patient's body. Cure necessitates, however, the removal of *all* cancerous cells because such cells can cause recurrence of the disease. Therefore, radiation treatment and/or chemotherapy may be needed to destroy any remaining malignant cells in the patient's body. The physical effects of these treatments are often very unpleasant and sometimes intolerable. Radiation treatment can bring nausea, vomiting, and severe weakness. Chemotherapy can bring the same, along with chills and high fever.

The physical effects of cancer treatment can be debilitating, but the psychological effects can be disquieting as well. Radiation treatments, for example, require a huge commitment of time and energy. They usually must be taken every day for several weeks, and are administered by a huge, faceless cobalt machine. Positioned on the table, the patient is left in total isolation, separated from everyone else by heavy lead doors. The cobalt machine might display a light, or sound a discordant buzzer, or emit no signal at all. The patient is told not to move while the machine directs its radiation to designated parts of the patient's body. The patient knows that the machine is emitting X rays that destroy both healthy and malignant tissue. Even medically sophisticated patients can be frightened and awed by a machine that dispenses a potentially lethal yet imperceptible substance.

A surgeon who received radiation treatments for cancer of the lymph nodes wrote:

> Since this went on for 5 months, it was interesting for me to watch my feelings

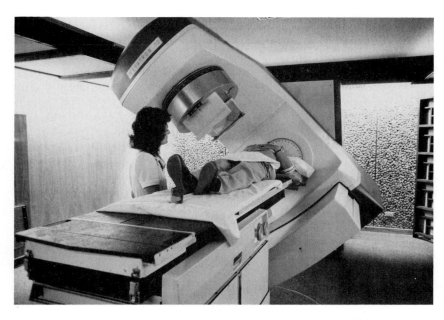

Radiation treatments for cancer can be both physically debilitating and psychologically distressing.
SOURCE: © David Powers, 1985/Stock, Boston

toward this machine change. After a while, I came to develop a certain affection for it. I considered it my daily journey to a center of a star. How ironic that I had to drive an hour each day to find this machine that emitted the stuff of the universe. After all, this kind of radiation fills the interstellar spaces and is inimitable in life. Yet I was depending on it to cure me. (Shlain, 1979, p. 180)

This patient's way of successfully adapting to the necessary treatments was to acknowledge his fear of the machine, accede its power, and recognize that the power was being harnessed in his own best interest.

In addition to discomfort and pain, treatments for some serious illnesses and injuries can call forth a host of dysphoric emotions, such as fear, anger, and confusion. Being around other patients, particularly those who are gravely ill, can be depressing. Seeing a fellow patient resusci-

tated in an emergency because heart or breathing have stopped can cause feelings of terror. Recognizing one's own dependency can even call forth embarrassment (Mullan, 1983).

## FACING THE STRESSES OF HOSPITALIZATION

■ ■ ■ ■ ■

John Martin felt a huge wave of relief as the ambulance pulled into the parking lot of the emergency room. He was at the hospital, about to be cared for by the best of cardiac specialists. He was also relieved that he had survived the ambulance ride. The blaring sirens and wild maneuvers through rush-hour traffic made him wonder whether they would make it to the hospital at all.

In the emergency room John was surrounded by machines that beeped and whirred. He was aware that several doctors and nurses were standing near him, watching the screen that displayed his *electrocardiogram*, a continuous graphing of the electrical patterns of his heart. They talked about him in words that he did not understand. Nobody talked *to* him. Then John was given some medication and transferred to the Coronary Care Unit, known to the medical staff as the "CCU."

John's myocardial infarction had been a fairly mild one, but for a few days he was to be observed in CCU. This was a strange and distressing place. The CCU was a large room that held ten beds, each with an imposing collection of high technology. Each patient was hooked up to several machines at once. There was a central station for nurses and doctors. No privacy was to be had. The lights remained on all day and night, and the machines made such ominous sounds that John found it very difficult to rest. John's condition required constant surveillance because of the probability of another heart attack, but John was unnerved by the stresses of the CCU. He felt like a "case" being managed by the machinery that surrounded him.

John was more than a heart muscle, however. He was more than a pump that needed servicing. He was a terrified human being, and his emotional distress was having an adverse effect on his medical condition.

Apart from all the difficulties and discomforts of illness and treatment, hospitalization itself is generally considered stressful (Lorber, 1975). Maintaining one's individuality in the midst of hospital routine can be a very difficult undertaking. To most staff members, one's identity becomes that of the patient in room 306. Additional characteristics, such as "surgical patient," or "critically ill patient," or "demanding patient," may be applied, but the core identity of patient remains, no matter what.

Few people are happy with the role of patient, and there are good reasons for their lack of enthusiasm. Hospital routine typically takes over virtually every aspect of an individual's day-to-day life. A normally late sleeper may be awakened each morning at 6 o'clock by the cleaning crew, and again at 7 o'clock for breakfast. During the day, the patient remains dependent upon everyone else's schedule. Hospital personnel enter at will, giving medication and checking dressings. Doctors, nurses, and laboratory technicians come and go seemingly as they please, and the patient spends each day waiting and adapting. The patient has no schedule of his or her own choosing.

Such routine is obviously necessary for the smooth functioning of a complex institution. Most patients recognize and accept that necessity and try to accommodate it, but acceptance can have its drawbacks. The process of adapting, particularly if one is hospitalized for a long period of time, can result in alienation from one's own needs and wants. The hospital routine becomes the patient's routine, and he or she begins to forget that there is a world outside where one schedules one's own time and controls one's own destiny. To the well-adapted *good patient*, freedom begins to look terribly frightening (Taylor, 1982). Doing what one is told, not asking questions, and not making trouble become priority behaviors for the good patient. In addition, the good patient suppresses his or her emotions, and as a result may feel numb, emotionally alienated, and even seriously depressed.

Of course, the oppressive routines and the restriction of freedoms can cause some patients to react in an opposite manner: they become cantankerous and quite troublesome. These "bad" patients may try to hold onto their individuality by demanding attention and special changes in routine. They may refuse treatment, not because they have carefully thought about their options but for the sake of asserting control. Such patients are often very anxious and angry, and they use a considerable amount of their energy rebelling for the sake of rebelling. They may fight a system that, although sometimes oppressive and uncomfortable, may actually be working in their own best interest.

Taylor (1982) has suggested that patients caught in the maze of hospitalization must act rather than react. It is in a patient's best interest to make his or her wishes known to the medical caretakers. He or she must assert the need for information, not only about diagnosis and treatment but also about the events to be experienced (the tests to be done, when, what they will be like, and so on). Norman Cousins (1979) has gone further, saying that a fully active patient must make his or her own informed decisions. This may involve electing treatment that differs from the standard protocol, or specifically requesting that the doctor write orders to deviate from hospital routine (for example, for the patient to receive no medication at night so sleep will be undisturbed).

By being assertive and asking for what he or she wants and needs, a patient works in the interests of preserving identity and individuality. Such assertiveness may be critically important to the patient's emotional well-being in the face of serious illness (Cousins, 1979). Of course, the passivity of patienthood is underscored when one is in a position that makes taking such control difficult or impossible. The patient on a respirator cannot talk. One who is on pain medications may be unable to think clearly. Another may be so stricken with panic that he does not know what he wants. In such cases the advocacy of a friend or family member who is comfortable being assertive in a medical setting can be invaluable. (The role of social support in helping the hospitalized patient is discussed in Box 12–2.)

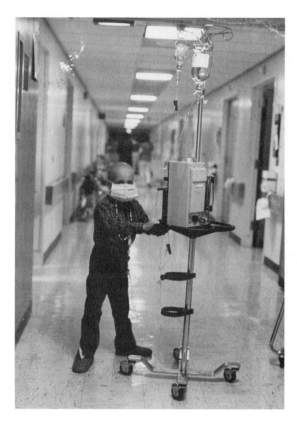

A young patient undergoing chemotherapy tries to maintain some independence despite the restrictions imposed by his treatment.
SOURCE: © Peggy Fox

## COMMUNICATING WITH MEDICAL PROFESSIONALS

As we saw in Chapter 7, many medical professionals have a habit of telling patients as little as possible. If information is given at all, it is often too simplistic or too jargon-laden to be very helpful. Probably not intentionally but nonetheless often completely, they keep patients in the dark. As we also saw in Chapters 7 and 8, the communication of information and understanding between medical professionals and their patients can be quite difficult to achieve.

The inability to obtain complete information about their conditions and plans for treatment can·be a source of great stress for many patients and can leave them angry, discouraged, frustrated, and fearful that they are losing control over their lives. Such fears are not unfounded, of course. Only with the necessary information can patients make weighty treatment decisions in light of their own values, needs, and life plans.

It is possible, of course, that on a deep emotional level patients who wish to remain in control of their situation *also* harbor a desire to be cared for when they are ill.

> When you take people who have a strong sense of themselves and put them in a hospital bed with a life-threatening illness, they find themselves in a relationship with their doctor much like a child and his parents. During serious illness patients must give up control over their lives. . . . Most people react to this kind of helplessness and authority just like they did as a child, with a great deal of ambivalence. They put their faith in the attending physician, hoping that he will make them well, but they also harbor a great feeling of anger for being put in their dependent position in the first place. (Shlain, 1979, p. 179)

## FACING PAIN

As we saw in Chapter 6, pain is one of the most terrifying aspects of serious illness and injury. Even when they are comfortable, many patients worry about the possibility that they will be in pain in the future. Cancer patients, for example, typically express tremendous fear that their pain will become overwhelming, debilitating, and uncontrolled. They anticipate helplessness. Their anxiety is not groundless. The pain of severe burns is a good example. Such pain can be excruciating for the patient, and continue unabated for weeks and even months (Andreasen & Norris, 1977).

A physician assigned to take care of patients with severe burns underscores the suffering they experience:

> It is a semiprivate room set up for burn care. . . . The two men here are naked, scraped raw. Their pain stops me, fogs my glasses, raises up sweat between my shoulder blades, under my mask and gown, its presence as strong as the dead-flesh smell that permeates the Burn Unit. (Hellerstein, 1986, p. 185)

Emotions can influence the perception of pain, as described in detail in Chapter 6. Negative emotions tend to intensify pain; positive emotions tend to minimize it. Thus, health psychologists are recognizing that even serious, acute pain can be modified by one's thoughts and feelings about it.

Norman Cousins, the former editor of the *Saturday Review,* was considered by his doctors to be terminally ill with a severe collagen disease. As he described it, the pain in his spine and joints was overwhelming and debilitating. As a patient active in his own care, Cousins did a considerable amount of reading about his condition and determined that some of the medications that were being given to him to ease his pain were actually detrimental to his chances of recovering, so he chose to stop taking them. But his pain was very intense, and he had to do something. Cousins reasoned that the perception of pain was partly a function of attitudes, and that he could stand his pain if he felt that he was making progress in meeting his body's needs. He established a setup whereby he could view humorous movies and have humorous books read to him. "I made the joyous discovery that 10 minutes of genuine belly laughter has an anesthetic effect and would give me at least two hours of pain-free sleep" (Cousins, 1976, p. 1261).

Psychological factors can figure prominently in treatment difficulties as well. Chemotherapy, used in the treatment of cancer, can often bring serious and discomforting side effects, such as nausea and vomiting. These can be very debilitating and last for hours or even days after treatment. Psychological and emotional factors can influence the severity of these side effects as well. For example, after a few courses of chemotherapy, a patient may begin to anticipate the upcoming discomfort. The expectations influence the onset of nausea and vomiting. In one study 33% of chemotherapy patients reported having anticipatory nausea, and 11% reported having anticipatory vomiting (Van Komen & Redd, 1985). Like a conditioned response (Pavlov, 1927), the reaction comes on even before the drugs are administered, such as when the patient is traveling to the hospital or entering the hospital building. These distressing anticipatory reactions have been found to occur more often in patients who are anxious, despairing, socially isolated, and depressed.

Some researchers have found that anticipatory nausea and vomiting can be reduced and even eliminated by the use of certain well-established conditioning principles, such as *systematic relaxation and desensitization* (Wolpe, 1958; Rimm & Masters, 1974). Through the process of pairing relaxation with thoughts of the upcoming distressing event (say, chemotherapy), the patient learns to associate a relaxed and comfortable state with instigation of the treatment. Typically, the patient starts with imagining scenes that provoke low anxiety and builds to associating a relaxed state with scenes that provoke high anxiety. This procedure results in an enhanced ability to tolerate the rigors of chemotherapy.

## FACING THE POSSIBILITY OF DEATH

As we examined earlier, the possibility of death hangs over every seriously ill person. Any illness that carries more than a negligible chance of mortality brings a terrify-

---

| TABLE 12–1    Tasks of Serious Illness: Facing the Challenges |
|---|
| 1. Maintaining identity in the face of:<br>    Threatened self-image<br>    Loss of body integrity<br>    Interruption of work<br>    Loss of independence<br>    Cognitive deficits<br>    Threatened future<br>    Strain on relationships with loved ones |
| 2. Continuing to develop emotionally |
| 3. Understanding how illness and injury came about: explaining them in the context of one's life |
| 4. Facing complex, conflicting emotions |
| 5. Facing the stresses of modern medicine:<br>    Medical treatments<br>    Communication with medical<br>        professionals<br>    Hospitalization |
| 6. Facing the existential issues:<br>    Pain and suffering<br>    Death |

ing confrontation with the possibility that life may be cut short. When the future is threatened by serious illness, the individual may find it difficult or impossible to maintain hope.

In Chapter 14 we discuss the specific reactions that people have when they face death, and we examine the psychological aspects of coming to terms with terminal illness.

Table 12–1 summarizes the tasks of facing serious illness.

## THE ROLE OF EMOTIONS IN HEALING

As we have seen so far in this chapter, the emotions that attend serious illness can be complicated and terrifying. Many patients feel that their emotions are out of control. They experience self-blame, a sense of failure, anxiety, apprehension, and confusion.

One of the most important tasks facing a patient is to maintain emotional equilibrium. Several studies have emphasized the central role of keeping emotions in balance in coping successfully with illness and injury (Cohen & Lazarus, 1979). Depression is believed to contribute to more lengthy recovery from serious illness. Low psychological morale is thought to affect physiological processes directly in deleterious ways (Cohen & Lazarus, 1979).

This is not to say that patients must "put on a happy face" in order to recover. As we consider in Box 12–3, such expectations for a patient can be detrimental to his or her well-being. While a patient should be helped to deal with negative emotions and to avoid becoming overwhelmed and incapacitated by them, some concern and worry on the part of the patient may actually be valuable. Worry that is not paralyzing or debilitating can serve to motivate

**BOX 12–3**

## CAN POSITIVE EMOTIONS BRING RECOVERY?

When they are faced with life-threatening illness, people try to cope. Although some psychologists have developed elaborate definitions of coping (as we saw in Chapter 11), here let us consider coping as something that people do every day when they try to accommodate to stressful and disruptive life events.

In attempting to cope with serious illness, people may do one or several of the following things: (1) focus on the problems that need to be solved and deal with them alone; (2) try to minimize their emotional distress by detaching themselves from disturbing thoughts and remaining composed, and by maintaining some sense of self-esteem and happiness; and (3) turn to others for assistance, information, clarification, and emotional support.

Much attention has recently been focused on the second type of coping, that which involves "positive thinking." Positive thinking requires one's efforts to avoid or divert thoughts from negative things on which it may be pointless to dwell, such as poor prognoses and what can go wrong. Sometimes positive thinking can make a person's life more pleasant, at least in the short run. Partly because the power of positive thinking is such an intuitively appealing notion, however, many people have come to believe that positive thinking might actually make people not only happier but physically better as well.

Pointing to the indisputable connection between the mind and the body, some hold that positive thinking can cure life-threatening illness. One approach, called the *Simonton Technique* (Simonton, Matthews-Simonton, & Creighton, 1978), uses a technique of visualization, in which a seriously ill cancer patient learns to relax deeply and to imagine his or her body's natural defenses fighting the cancer cells. This technique is typically used in conjunction with standard medical treatments, or after all medical interventions have failed. While the Simontons presented considerable anecdotal evidence for the value of their technique in prolonging people's lives, there still is no empirical research evidence to back up their assertion. Certainly, many cancer patients may come to feel greater control over their lives as a result of their positive imaging, but the role of such an approach in actually improving a person's chances of survival remains doubtful. In fact, at least one major methodologically sound study found no relationship whatsoever between pos-the patient to follow necessary treatments, to ask questions, and to make sure he or she is getting the best care available. In fact, according to Janis (1958), the *work of worrying*—that is, mentally rehearsing potentially unpleasant events and gaining information about what to expect—can help a person.

The expression of feelings, whatever they are, may be best for a patient. Bottling up feelings has been associated with shorter survival, and expressing emotions with longer survival (Cohen & Lazarus, 1979). Research has found that the patients who survive longer are those who more frequently express their emotions, including their negative ones (Derogatis, Abeloff, & Melasaratos, 1979). Those who ask for what they want, including emotional support from others, and who express what they are feeling tend to fare better than do patients who keep their wishes hidden.

itive attitudes and survival or recurrence among 359 cancer patients (Cassileth, Lusk, Miller, Brown, & Miller, 1985). Relatedly, it has not been established in any scientific way that seriously ill patients can improve their chances for survival by learning to enjoy life more or by refusing to think about the negative aspects of their situation.

There may, of course, be no harm in thinking positive thoughts, whether or not these thoughts promote healing. But the expectations that surround those who are seriously ill may prove to be destructive. For example, those who are ill may admonish themselves when they feel understandably distressed and sad. Other people may tell them that if they would only change their attitudes, they might recover from their disease. In some unfortunate cases, people with serious illnesses may even be blamed for thinking negatively and accused of bringing on their disease. Patients who fail to respond to treatment may be thought to lack the will to live. In fact, those close to a patient (or even the patient himself or herself) may have such a strong need to believe in this mind-body connection that the patient who is sad and realistically pessimistic may even be blamed for the illness. Patients who already have tremendous anxiety and depression may end up also experiencing tremendous guilt.

The psychological phenomenon in question here is called *blaming the victim* (Ryan, 1971). In an effort to deal with their outrage and sense of powerlessness when someone they love is very ill, some people develop an exaggerated belief in the victim's own power to get well again or to have avoided the illness in the first place. The patient may feel subtly blamed for the misfortune and admonished to fix himself or herself. In the extreme, a patient who is very sad because of all the losses experienced in the face of serious illness may be forced to hide his or her true feelings and act happy, or "make nice."

It is important to recognize that the phenomenon of blaming the victim is insidious and often goes unrecognized. Yet, such a reaction to a seriously ill person can have devastating effects on his or her self-image, sense of worth, and feelings of being loved and cared for by those close to him or her. The seriously ill person might even avoid attempting new treatments because of fear that failure to recover may bring more blame.

# Summary

Chapter 12 examines the psychological challenges faced by victims of serious illness and injury.

I. Different demands are made on an individual at different stages of illness or physical injury.

   A. During the acute phase the primary concern of both patient and medical personnel is survival. Beyond the short term, the length and quality of the individual's life will depend upon appropriate and timely treatment. The acute phase of care is also likely to be accompanied by pain, confusion, and fear on the part of the patient. These emotions can influence the patient's decisions regarding treatment.

   B. During the second phase, rehabilitation, a person must work toward achieving as high a level of health and independent functioning as his or her condition makes possible.

   C. When an individual has accomplished as much as possible toward rehabilitation, he or she often must accept any remaining disabilities and limitations as chronic. Chronic conditions (considered in detail in Chapter 13) are those from which patients are not expected to recover.

   D. In some cases an illness progresses to the point at which it cannot be cured and the condition is terminal.

II. In this chapter we see that serious illness and injury threaten virtually every aspect of an individual's life. Thoughts and feelings inevitably arise from serious threats to the person's well-being and change with the current stage of the person's condition. The character of these thoughts and feelings may not only be affected by but also affect the patient's physical condition. For example, the patient's anxiety and fear may deplete the energy he or she needs for healing. Depression and hopelessness may translate into an unwillingness or inability to take the necessary steps toward health and well-being.

   A. Life with a serious illness or injury is unpredictable; it makes little sense. It is filled with threats to self-image and losses of self-esteem, of freedom, of day-to-day activities, of feelings of physical comfort, and of the possibilities of the future.

   B. The physical alteration of one's body can be disorienting and terrifying, and can bring a sense of dissociation. Integration of an altered body image, the perception and evaluation of one's new physical appearance and functioning, may take some time.

   C. Denial can be a very effective short-term defense mechanism. It allows the individual slowly to come to terms emotionally with the full meaning of the altered body image.

   D. A seriously ill or injured person may fear that his or her relationships with others, particularly with loved ones, will be changed drastically because of the new physical appearance. He or she may fear rejection or becoming an object of revulsion or pity.

   E. Many people derive a strong sense of identity from the work that they do, for example, from their role as student or their devotion to a career. Work is the outlet for creative ideas. The ability to support oneself and one's dependents can figure prominently in an individual's self-esteem. Thus, self-esteem may be threatened by the need to rely on others for financial, physical, and emotional support.

F. Helplessness and forced dependency are the realities of many serious medical conditions. Maintaining some independent action, however minimal, is valuable in preventing the depression that can result from helplessness.

G. Certain medical conditions can interfere directly with cognitive functioning. A well-known condition termed cardiac delirium or cardiac psychosis can occur after open-heart surgery. Some cardiac-surgery patients experience only transient intellectual deficits; others have gross impairment of their cognitive functioning; and some experience hallucinations and even paranoid ideations.

H. The phenomena of illness and injury underscore the fact that life is unpredictable. A hoped-for future and distant goals can suddenly vanish from the realm of possibility when serious illness and injury occur.

I. Hospitalization and the invasive, debilitating treatments of illness and injury can bring both physical separation and emotional alienation from other people and strain relationships with loved ones. Many obligations fall on the loved ones of a person who is ill. The patient may begin to feel like an outsider in his or her own family. The severe stress that illness

places on a family can challenge its cohesiveness.

III. Serious illness requires the fulfillment of many challenging tasks. Among the greatest of these is to remain an emotionally healthy person in the face of the demands of a serious medical condition. Several important emotional challenges must be dealt with successfully.

A. When many of his or her own unique characteristics are changed or can no longer find expression, the ill individual must work to develop new aspects of identity.

B. Another challenge is for the individual to continue developing psychologically and emotionally despite the interference of illness.

C. Patients who develop life-threatening illnesses, such as cancer, often try to understand just how their disease came about. Self-blame is common.

D. Patients who are ill must face the difficulties of receiving stressful medical treatments. In addition to discomfort and pain, treatments for some serious illnesses and injuries can call forth a host of dysphoric emotions, such as fear, anger, and confusion. Being around other patients, particularly those who are gravely ill, can be depressing.

E. Hospitalization itself is generally considered stressful. Maintaining one's individuality in the midst of hospital routine can be a very difficult undertaking. To the well-adapted good patient, freedom begins to look terribly frightening. Doing what one is told, not asking questions, and not making trouble become priority behaviors for the good patient. The good patient suppresses emotion, and as a result may feel numb, emotionally alienated, and even seriously depressed. Bad patients try to hold onto their individuality by demanding attention. They are often very anxious and angry.

F. Communicating with medical professionals can be very difficult. Many medical professionals have a habit of telling patients as little as possible. If information is given at all, it is often too simplistic or too jargon-laden to be very helpful to the patient.

G. Facing pain can be a tremendous challenge.

H. Serious illness and injury may require the patient to face the possibility of death. When the future is threatened by serious illness, the individual may find it difficult or impossible to maintain hope.

IV. The expression of feelings, whatever they are, may be best for a patient. Bottling up feelings has been associated with shorter survival; expressing emotions, with longer survival. Those who ask for what they want, including emotional support from others, and who express what they are feeling tend to fare better than do patients who keep their wishes hidden.

# Glossary

**acute phase of illness:** the period of illness (or the period following injury) in which the primary concern of both patient and medical personnel is the patient's survival. Moment to moment, or day to day, the individual's chances of survival depend upon the immediate measures taken to deal with the physical trauma or disease.

**amyotrophic lateral sclerosis** (or Lou Gehrig's disease): an incurable, degenerative disease of the nervous system.

**blaming the victim:** a psychological phenomenon in which the victim of an unfortunate event is held to blame for his or her experience.

**cardiac delirium or cardiac psychosis:** a condition in which some cardiac-surgery patients experience only transient intellectual deficits and others have gross impairment of their cognitive functioning and even hallucinations. To the patient with cardiac psychosis, all environmental stimuli seem equally important and threatening. Cardiac psychosis is believed to be caused by small cerebral emboli (blood clots that go to the brain) following surgery.

**chronic conditions:** conditions that are not terminal but from which patients are not expected ever to recover.

**denial:** a psychological defense mechanism that can serve to help maintain the individual's identity and self-esteem, particularly in the face of negative reactions from other people.

**dissociation:** the experience of being outside one's body, that "This body isn't me."

**electrocardiogram:** a continuous graphing of the electrical patterns of an individual's heart.

**metastasis:** spread (usually of cancer) to organs other than that of the primary site. Neoplastic cells escape from the initial tumor site and travel to other parts of the body, such as the bones, lungs, brain, or liver.

**paranoid ideations:** mental representations and thoughts of being the target of persecution.

**phobic reactions:** negative emotional responses that can cause an individual to avoid certain stimuli.

**rehabilitation phase of illness:** the phase of illness during which the patient must learn to adjust to the limitations of illness and work toward achieving as high a level of health and independent functioning as his or her condition makes possible.

**repression of emotion:** the forcing of emotion out of conscious awareness in an attempt to avoid immediate, short-term emotional distress.

**Simonton Technique:** a technique of visualization in which a seriously ill cancer patient learns to relax deeply and to imagine his or her body's natural defenses fighting the cancer cells. This technique is typically used in conjunction with standard medical treatments, or after all medical interventions have failed.

**superior vena cava:** the major blood vessel that carries blood from the upper body to the heart.

**systematic relaxation and desensitization:** the process of pairing relaxation with thoughts of an upcoming distressing event so that a patient learns to associate the event with a relaxed and comfortable state. Typically, the patient starts with imagining scenes that provoke low anxiety and builds to associating his or her relaxed state with scenes that provoke high anxiety.

**work of worrying:** the mental rehearsal of potentially unpleasant events, together with the consideration of what to expect in the future.

# A Life-Span Perspective on Chronic Illness

After losing her arm and suffering severe burns on her face and chest, Officer Catherine Parker faced years of rehabilitation and the certain knowledge that her life was changed forever. She would no longer be able to serve as a police officer in the field, although she was given a challenging desk job in the area of police investigation. She learned to function well with one arm, and she had the option of obtaining a prosthetic device to replace it. Either choice required adjustment and relearning. Catherine's burns presented a bigger problem, however. Once healed, her face and chest were covered with scar tissue. Her movements were restricted and her appearance was, to people who did not know her, frankly grotesque and initially somewhat frightening. So, Catherine strictly limited her contact with others. At work she saw her colleagues but avoided contact with the public. She socialized only with her close friends, and she was extremely hesitant about meeting new people. Understandably, she became acutely lonely. Catherine's accident left her with severe psychological and social limitations, as well as physical ones.

John Martin, the heart attack victim introduced in Chapter 12, eventually went home and back to work. Yet, he was never again free of the threat of another heart attack. He had no choice but to adopt a new and healthier lifestyle and to maintain constant vigilance lest he lapse into his old, life-threatening habits. He tried to live normally, yet he remained acutely sensitive to his physical condition. He often felt tremendous anxiety because his heart was damaged and he was at risk for another heart attack.

Fitzhugh Mullan was very sick for several years, battling the cancer that invaded his chest and dealing with the physical problems that accompanied his treatment. His body was permanently altered, both in appearance and in functioning. His limited lung capacity restricted his physical activity. He tired easily. Because of his extensive radiation treatments, he and his wife decided to adopt a child rather than risk conceiving one with birth defects. Although his treatment was considered successful, Mullan lived every day with the possibility of recurrence. Every simple ache or pain caused him to panic at the possibilities they might represent.

The aftermath of serious illness and injury is not always the full recovery of health and the return to life as it once had been. Like those who are born with or develop chronic disorders, many victims of serious illness and accidents face a lifetime of limitation, such as physical impairment, demanding routines of care, and even social isolation. For the chronically ill patient who never

really gets better, a medical crisis is always imminent. Further limitations loom, and the fear that the condition may become life threatening can be a constant. Despite precautions, medical crises may become regular events and absorb tremendous amounts of time, money, and energy. Further, the day-to-day reminders of physical illness and impairment force many victims of illness and injury to live lives that are radically different from the ones they had once planned and hoped for.

## What Are Chronic Illness and Disability?

Catherine Parker, John Martin, and Fitzhugh Mullan each suffer what is referred to as a *chronic* condition. Chronic illness or handicap involves one or more impairments or deviations from normal structure and functioning that, whether extensive or not, remain permanent. Chronic conditions are caused by pathological alterations that are not reversible, and they are usually accompanied by some sort of residual disability. Contending with a chronic condition typically requires treatment, supervision, and special training.

Unlike the acutely ill or injured person who remains hospitalized to receive treatment, the chronically ill patient tries to incorporate his or her limitations into a relatively normal life at home. Whether living alone or with a family, the chronically ill person may attempt to maintain some degree of independence and achieve as high a quality of life as possible within the constraints of the medical condition (Revicki, 1989).

Chronic illness is surprisingly common. Surveys have found that approximately 50% of the population of the United States (not including those in institutions) have at least one chronic condition that involves some form of mobility restriction or activity limitation (Moos & Tsu, 1977a; Strauss & Glaser, 1975). Some of these conditions represent the aftermath of a serious acute illness or accident, and others are gradually degenerative, such as rheumatoid arthritis. Chronic illnesses include such conditions as heart disease, arthritis, back or spine impairments, ulcerative colitis, diabetes, leg or hip impairments, visual impairments, and even psychiatric conditions. The most common chronic conditions of people under 45 are paralysis and limitations of the lower extremities (usually the result of accidents). For people over 45, the most common chronic conditions are arthritis and rheumatism, and heart disease. The older a person is, the more likely he or she is to have one or more chronic conditions that limit major activities such as work, housework, school, or recreation. Chronic conditions are not limited to older persons, however, for, as we shall see, chronic illness and disability strike young persons with surprising frequency (Strauss & Glaser, 1975).

Many patients in acute-care hospitals today are being treated either for conditions that likely will eventually become chronic or for medical crises that arise from ongoing chronic illnesses. Examples of the former conditions are heart attacks, cancer, and accidental injuries that result in paralysis. Examples of the latter are repeat heart attacks, diabetic coma, and complications that arise from the treatment of kidney failure with hemodialysis.

Of course, some chronic conditions typically require no hospitalization but, rather, are diagnosed and treated on an outpatient basis. These may be insidious illnesses, like arthritis, that slowly rob the individual of health and vitality and bring gradual deterioration over the course of many years.

Our discussion of chronic illness applies to the many and varied conditions noted so far. Although these conditions may vary widely, they have one very important characteristic in common. Chronic conditions, by definition, *have no cure*. This one fact has many important implications for the psychological and social adjustment of the person stricken with a chronic condition (Kleinman, 1988; Anderson & Bury, 1988).

# Dealing with Chronic Illness

The stresses of chronic illness and handicap can severely tax the emotional resources of the most patient and optimistic person. Chronic illness and handicap must be dealt with day after day, year after year, without the possibility of cure. While chronic conditions do vary in their severity and in the extent to which they interfere with "normal" life, each chronic condition brings with it at least some of the following problems and challenges. Typically, the more disabling the condition, the more problems there are to face.

## MANAGING MEDICAL CRISES

When things are going well, a chronically ill person's physical functioning may be quite good. Certain limitations may be imposed, but with effort these limitations may be incorporated into day-to-day routine and even concealed from the scrutiny of others. When things go badly for the chronically ill person, however, he or she can be quite ill and even in significant danger. A person with emphysema, for example, can become so short of breath that he or she collapses in the street. A diabetic can self-administer the wrong dosage of insulin and fall into a coma. The chronically ill individual (and those who are close to him or her, such as the parents of a diabetic child) often must remain ever-vigilant to recognize the signs of an oncoming medical crisis. Many chronically ill people must wear identification bracelets so that their conditions can be interpreted correctly if, during a medical crisis, they are unable to communicate. Some must carry with them at all times the necessary treatments should a medical crisis arise. A heart disease patient may need to carry nitroglycerine pills, for example, to take for chest pain. Other patients may need to avoid certain situations and environments altogether, lest these precipitate a medical crisis. To protect themselves, some chronically ill persons may need to formulate elaborate plans (Croog & Levine, 1973). A cardiac patient, for example, may need to make certain that, when alone, he or she can get to a phone to reach medical personnel. The emphysema patient might completely avoid social interaction in order to reduce the chances of becoming emotionally upset and experiencing impaired breathing. Such vigilance can, in itself, be quite taxing for the chronically ill individual and require him or her to learn a considerable amount about self-care in an effort to lead a relatively independent life (Strauss & Glaser, 1975).

## CONTROLLING THE SYMPTOMS

Nearly all chronic illnesses present some distressing symptoms with which their victims must cope. These symptoms may be as mild as midday fatigue or as debilitating as daily, intractable diarrhea that causes physical exhaustion and social isolation. Certainly, the more debilitating an individual's symptoms, the greater the adjustment that may be necessary to live with a chronic illness. However, debilitation is not the only characteristic that determines the undesirability of symptoms. The *social acceptability* of the symptoms also influences what measures people will take to control them and how well people are able to adjust. Symptoms that limit the ability to

speak coherently, or that make salient bodily processes that are normally private (such as elimination), are likely to be quite difficult to adjust to (Strauss & Glaser, 1975; Kelly, 1986).

Let's consider the adjustments that have been made by one chronically ill person:

■ ■ ■ ■ ■

Mr. Springer is 52 years old, and has *emphysema*, a chronic obstructive lung disease. He developed emphysema as a result of many years of smoking cigarettes, and though he has finally quit smoking, his lungs are severely damaged. Even with medication, he can walk less than 100 yards before he becomes short of breath and needs to rest. His airways are so damaged that he is literally being starved of oxygen.

Mr. Springer's children worry that he will collapse in the streets of New York City, where he lives and works. They want him to move to the suburbs to live with one of them, but he wants to remain independent and to continue to live in the city that he loves. In order to remain independent, he must work out a way to take care of himself and avoid a medical crisis that could jeopardize his life.

Mr. Springer takes many precautions. He carries identification, in case he falls down helpless while out of doors and must be taken to the hospital. The identification clearly indicates his medical condition, and provides information so that both his family and his doctors can be reached. Second, Mr. Springer redesigns his activities and movement patterns to accommodate his condition. When he goes out, he tries to estimate how far he can walk before becoming too tired. He rests against a pole or on a bench and pretends to watch the passersby. He is careful not to become so weak that he must sit on the curb or sidewalk, lest he be taken for a drunk or a derelict. Mr. Springer has memorized many of the bus routes, and always carries plenty of change with him so that he can take a bus whenever he needs to. He allows a good deal of time to get wherever he wants to go.

Mr. Springer must plan his every move. He must think ahead whenever he goes somewhere so that his route can avoid stairs or long stretches with nowhere to rest. He can shop only if he has taken along his rolling cart for carrying parcels. Whenever he is with people, he must remain somewhat detached emotionally, because his limited capacity to breathe requires that he avoid becoming excited or upset. Through smoking cessation, regular use of medications, and walking, Mr. Springer is gradually increasing his lung capacity and he is becoming more and more capable of living his life independently. Although he will never be totally free of disease, he is able to do many of the things he wants to do.

Mr. Springer's experience is not unusual (Fagerhaugh, 1973). Many people with chronic conditions spend a great deal of their time and energy trying to *pass* as normal or unimpaired (Goffman, 1963). They are continually challenged to find ways to hide their symptoms and limitations and to live a relatively independent life (Schneider & Conrad, 1980). Understandably, some chronically ill persons fear that they will be rejected by other people because of their disfigurements. Indeed, research shows that many people with obvious physical alterations and limitations meet with expressions of pity and disdain from others (Kleck, 1968). Therefore, many work to conceal or minimize the intrusiveness of deformities in their bodies and limitations in their abilities. When symptoms of chronic illnesses are under control, victims can live enjoyable, productive lives.

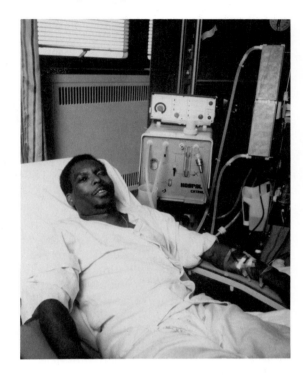

Hospital-based hemodialysis can require the patient with kidney failure to spend up to 4 or 5 hours, 3 or 4 times a week hooked up to a dialysis machine.
SOURCE: © 1982 Robert Houser/Comstock

## CARRYING OUT TREATMENT REGIMENS

As we saw in Chapter 4, despite the importance of symptom control and the established effectiveness of treatments for many chronic illnesses, compliance with medical regimens is surprisingly poor. Noncompliance probably results from both the difficulty and the intrusiveness of many regimens and from the fact that these regimens must be carried out forever, typically over the course of the individual's entire life.

Consider, for example, the patient who has chosen at-home *peritoneal dialysis* instead of hospital based hemodialysis. (Dialysis involves the process of cleansing the blood of impurities, a task carried out by the kidneys unless they have been damaged in some way [Abram, 1977]). Peritoneal dialysis involves the installation of a solution in the abdominal cavity overnight and connection of the patient to a machine by means of tubes that have been surgically implanted in the patient's abdomen. Peritoneal dialysis requires elaborate sterile technique for connection up to the dialysis machine so that dialysis can take place while the patient sleeps. The procedures for connection can take an hour or more, and require considerable concentration lest mistakes be made. Errors in the sterile procedure can cause bacteria to be introduced into the abdominal cavity resulting in a serious, life-threatening infection called *peritonitis*. Many of us have trouble washing our faces and brushing our teeth before bed when we are tired or deeply engrossed in a novel or a television program. Imagine incorporating the elaborate preparations for peritoneal dialysis into each evening's routine (Gerhardt, 1990)!

The complex arrangements that many chronic illnesses demand may be lifelong. As we saw in Chapter 4, patients who fail to carry out treatment regimens for chronic conditions often try to manage their daily lives within the confines of many practical, social, and financial constraints. Some treatment regimens may cause the patient a certain amount of emotional distress as well (for example, the self-administration of injections for the control of diabetes, or the application of bad-smelling creams and ointments for the control of dermatologic conditions). Some regimens cause side effects, such as pain or discomfort. Others lead to social isolation or tremendous financial stress. Obviously, the more a treatment regimen interferes with daily activities and personal identity, and the less it improves physical functioning, the more likely it is that the individual will fail to follow the regimen, or will follow it inconsistently or incorrectly (DiMatteo & DiNicola, 1982).

Patients who take an active part in their medical care typically achieve better control of their chronic illnesses than do those who are passive (Schulman, 1979). Persons with chronic conditions who learn what they must do and who design their day-to-day lifestyle and environment to meet the requirements of the treatment regimen as well as their personal needs and values are best able to achieve a satisfying life despite their illnesses (Gulledge, 1979).

Self-help groups, consisting of patients with the same disease who get together for regular meetings, can be an important source of information and support for many chronically ill people (Lieberman, 1979). Often these groups provide more information and better suggestions for disease control than do physicians, who may lack the time, communication skills, and experience required to train patients to carry out complex treatments. These groups can provide practical help and information, such as where to buy or rent special equipment or appliances required for home care. They may provide ideas for management of symptoms and for "passing" (avoiding detection of their infirmities), as well as assistance in dealing with financial matters, such as health insurance. Box 13–1 contains a partial list of national self-help organizations.

## COPING WITH AN
## UNCERTAIN PROGNOSIS:
## THE CASE OF MULTIPLE SCLEROSIS

■ ■ ■ ■ ■

The young woman was stunned by the doctor's words.

"Well, what's going to happen next?" she asked the neurologist. She was tremendously impatient after all the tests she had been through and all the distressing symptoms she had dealt with over the course of her three weeks in the hospital.

"Well, actually, we don't really know," he answered her. "Multiple sclerosis is such a variable disease that we cannot predict what the precise course will be in your case. Most likely, it won't be fatal. But we are not even totally certain of that. You will probably be limited in some ways by your disease."

"Will I be able to walk again?" she asked. "Will my vision improve? Will I ever stop feeling so weak?"

"Probably you'll have ups and downs, some relatively healthy times as well as some bad times. But I can't predict when, or to what degree."

Approximately 250,000 Americans currently suffer from multiple sclerosis (MS). MS is a major cause of chronic disability in young adults. In this disease cellular changes in the brain and spinal cord disrupt proper nerve transmission. Scarlike areas form, destroying the fatty sheaths of myelin that cover the nerve-cell extensions called axons. Myelin is essential to the synaptic transmission of nerve impulses, and its destruction causes symptoms that are in some cases transient, in others chronic, and in others severely degenerative (Hamilton & Rose, 1982; Robinson, 1990).

The symptoms of MS may last for hours or for weeks, coming and going with no particular pattern, and varying from day to day. The symptoms are often bizarre and difficult to understand. They include some or all of the following: muscle dysfunction; weakness; paralysis; spasticity; tremor; ocular dysfunction, including double vision and blurred vision; urinary disturbances, including incontinence; and emotional lability, including mood swings, irritability, euphoria, and depression. There may also be slurred speech and numbness or tingling sensations in various parts of the body.

The average age of onset of MS is 27, striking slightly more women than men and tending to run in families. MS is usually not fatal. Its cause is unknown; theories suggest a slow-acting viral infection, an autoimmune response of the nervous sys-

BOX
13-1

## SOME NATIONAL ORGANIZATIONS: SOURCES OF INFORMATION AND HELP

*Arthritis*   Arthritis Foundation, 3400 Peachtree Road, N.E., Atlanta, GA 30326

*Birth defects*   March of Dimes, 1275 Mamaronek Ave., White Plains, NY 10605

*Burns*   Phoenix Society, 11 Rust Hill Road, Leavittown, PA 19056

*Cancer*   American Cancer Society, 777 Third Avenue, New York, NY 10017

*Diabetes*   American Diabetes Association, 600 Fifth Avenue, New York, NY 10020
Juvenile Diabetes Foundation, 23 E. 26th St., New York, NY 10010

*Epilepsy*   Epilepsy Foundation of America, 1828 L St., N.W., Suite 406, Washington, DC 20036

*Multiple Sclerosis*   National Multiple Sclerosis Society, 205 E. 42d St., New York, NY 10017

*Sudden Infant Death Syndrome*   National Sudden Infant Death Syndrome Foundation, 310 S. Michigan Ave., Suite 1904, Chicago, IL 60604

tem, or an allergic response to an infectious agent.

There is no cure for MS. Corticosteroids and the drug ACTH have been found to reduce symptoms and to hasten remission from an attack of serious symptoms. But future attacks are not prevented. MS patients must learn to adjust to the disease, although adjustment is a tremendous task, considering the monumental problems that the disease presents. During a period of remission, the MS patient might be able to live a normal life. During exacerbations of the illness, however, he or she might be totally paralyzed, incontinent, and unable to see.

To live a productive, satisfying life, the person with MS is required to take certain steps to prevent progressive debilitation and manage the symptoms of the illness. For example, to maintain muscle tone, he or she must do special exercises every day, must be consistently vigilant to avoid infections, and must always get adequate rest because fatigue and stress can worsen the symptoms. In order to maintain independence, the MS victim must develop new ways to perform daily activities. Since exacerbations of the disease are unpredictable, the patient usually has to make many physical and emotional adjustments in lifestyle (Robinson, 1990).

Although most chronic conditions are not nearly so unpredictable as MS, many do tend to vary over time in their effects on the patient's life. Someone with rheumatoid arthritis, for example, might be quite energetic and mobile for several days and then experience yet another round of pain and limitation (Weiner, 1975). One of the major difficulties experienced by many victims of chronic illness is the fact that they cannot plan many aspects of their lives because illness makes it impossible to predict what kind of physical state they will be in at any point in the future.

Box 13–2 describes the difficulties of caring for another kind of chronic illness—childhood diabetes.

## AVOIDING OR ADJUSTING TO SOCIAL ISOLATION

Chronic illness often brings serious social consequences (Anderson & Bury, 1988). The practical limitations of a debilitating physical condition can make it all but impossible to maintain social ties. Contact with friends may diminish considerably, to the point where the patient rarely has contact with anyone outside the immediate family (Brodland & Andreasen, 1974). The person with cancer, for example, may have too little energy to attend social functions or to organize get-togethers with friends. The complex scheduling of dialysis, for example, may leave little free time during which to socialize. Medical limitations and requirements may be such that the character of time spent with others must be controlled. The severe diabetic, for example, might avoid parties or dinner with friends in order to stay out of the way of temptations to deviate from the strict diet necessitated by the illness (Benoliel, 1975). The cardiac patient may avoid coffee breaks with co-workers because these situations are conducive to smoking (Gulledge, 1979).

Some victims of chronic illness must work to *normalize* their conditions as much as possible. Normalizing involves hiding symptoms, such as limbs twisted by arthritis or polio and offensive smells from a colostomy. Normalizing also involves adjusting the routines of care so that they will remain unnoticed by others (Goffman, 1963). Sometimes the arrangements must be ingenious and elaborate.

Normalizing may be necessary in order to avoid the problem of *identity spread* (Strauss & Glaser, 1975). When others are unfamiliar with the capabilities of the chronically ill or handicapped person, they tend to overgeneralize from the actual limitations. A blind person is addressed loudly and slowly as if he or she were unable not only to see but also hear and comprehend.

A handicapped person may be given little chance to show what he or she really can do, while emphasis is placed on what he or she cannot do. Chronically ill and disabled people sometimes must avoid social con-

**BOX
13–2**

## CHILDREN WITH DIABETES

Insulin-dependent diabetes mellitus (IDDM) is one of the four most prevalent chronic illnesses of childhood. It affects about 150,000 children and their families. Referred to also as juvenile diabetes, IDDM is a chronic metabolic disorder that is treatable but not curable.

Juvenile diabetes must be controlled through careful adherence to a complex regimen of care that involves strict control of food intake and physical activity, and the routine, balanced use of insulin replacement. Much attention must be paid to the management of time. The diabetic child's behavior must be monitored constantly to control aspects of life (such as food intake) that most people take for granted. For example, the diabetic child cannot spontaneously eat cookies and candy and other sweets because his or her insulin level will be significantly affected. A great deal of responsibility must fall on the child and the family in order for the child to survive and lead a reasonably normal life (Wertlieb, Hauser, & Jacobson, 1986).

Parents of a diabetic child carry a heavy responsibility for their child's welfare (Drotar, 1981). Just as they try to maintain the child's adherence to rules of social conduct, they attempt to bring about adherence to the management demands of insulin injections, blood or urine monitoring, dietary regimens, and exercise (Wertlieb et al., 1986). All the activities must be done according to schedule and carried out correctly. Organization is a paramount concern. Rebelliousness and failure to follow rules can be annoying and frustrating for parents of a healthy child. But parents of a diabetic child know that their child's refusal or inability to follow the required course of treatment could jeopardize his or her life. Something done wrong could kill the child.

Diabetes presents a significant challenge not only to a child's health but also to his or her development and the family's emotional adaptation. As the young diabetic assumes increasing independence and responsibility, the parents must help him or her to take over more and more of self-care. Studies have shown that a supportive family environment is associated with favorable treatment adherence and metabolic control (Jay, Litt, & Durant, 1984). In families in which there is avoidance of conflict or lack of conflict resolution, the diabetic child may express rebellion by poorly caring for his or her disease. He or she may use treatment lapses to control the parents. Further, research has shown that diabetic adolescents who are independent and can express their feelings are able to maintain metabolic control better than are those who have high levels of conflict in their families. Greater behavioral symptoms and more problems in disease control have been found in diabetic children whose parents are unsupportive of their independence and self-sufficiency (Wertlieb et al., 1986).

This artist adjusts to the limitations imposed by her congenital deformity which resulted from prenatal exposure to the drug Thalidomide.
SOURCE: © Alan Carey/The Image Works

tact to maintain their self-image. They may be embarrassed by their required therapeutic nostrums. Or they might fear the initial rejecting responses of others to their disfigurements. Even close friends who eventually make the necessary adjustments to the chronically ill individual's altered appearance and abilities might initially be taken aback. The reactions of friends can have a very strong impact on the patient (Andreasen & Norris, 1977; Moos & Tsu, 1977; Dunkel-Schetter, 1984).

Many victims of chronic illness and disability eventually do adjust socially. They develop ways to continue relationships with their understanding friends under conditions that they and the disease can tolerate. Many find that as a result of the necessary adjustments, they and their friends are able to form deeper and more meaningful relationships (Mages & Mendelsohn, 1979). The stresses of illness and the experience of crises together may lead patients and their loved ones to a strengthening and deepening of their relationships and a keener appreciation of what is important in their lives (Mullan, 1983).

## SETTING CONCRETE GOALS AND MAKING PLANS FOR THE FUTURE

Regardless of their health status, human beings have a need to conceive of their own future and orient themselves toward goals that they value, but chronic illness has the power to impose an orientation to the here and now. Because chronic illness renders prospects so uncertain, it may severely compromise the ability to plan and strive for future goals (Riessman, 1990).

Paradoxically, those who cope most successfully with chronic illness tend to be those who *do* plan, those who set goals that are of value to them and work toward achieving those goals (Moos & Tsu, 1977). Granted, the goals often must remain short-term and limited, such as doing grocery shopping alone, or walking in the academic procession at graduation. The goals that are chosen must be simple enough to produce initial success, after which tasks can be gradually increased in difficulty. For example, those with disfigurements might first try to appear in public among close friends, and then later try to be near strangers. Only after considerable time might they be ready to meet new people (Andreasen & Norris, 1977).

In making plans for the future, the chronically ill person must have in mind many possible outcomes. For example, as graduation approaches, the disabled person may choose to make arrangements to use a walker or a wheelchair at the commencement ceremonies if the goal of walking unassisted cannot be achieved. The chronically ill or handicapped person may need to consider various contingency arrangements for the course of an illness, such as what will be done if there is a recurrence of cancer or if a donor kidney is rejected (Adler, 1972; Gerhardt, 1990). The individual may need to devise ways in which an independent lifestyle can be maintained if movements become restricted and/or the environment becomes inaccessible. Many chronic conditions necessitate the continual formulation and revision of long-range and alternative plans.

As we noted earlier, the process of rehearsing various alternative plans and courses of action is referred to by psychologists as *the work of worrying* (Janis, 1958). The individual must think through several courses of action and their results, and take into account how his or her life might be affected by a range of uncontrollable factors. The work of worrying allows the individual to come to grips emotionally with the various outcomes he or she might face (Gulledge, 1979). (The work of worrying is also referred to as the conceptualization phase of Stress-Inoculation Training [Meichenbaum, 1985]; see Chapter 11.)

Chronic illness permanently alters an individual's life and provides him or her with the immutable requirement of coping with and adjusting to restricted life choices. Limitations in certain choices may, however, open up other possibilities. For example, unable to pursue physical endeavors, the chronically disabled individual might choose the intellectual life and go back to school or might settle on beginning a new career. Or the individual might discover artistic talents that might never have been recognized and developed had not disability intervened. Sometimes the changes that occur in the individual's self-image may even be for the better.

**TABLE 13–1   Dealing with Chronic Illness and Disability: What the Patient Must Do**

1. Control the physical symptoms of chronic illness (passing)
2. Carry out complex, uncomfortable treatment regimens (maintain patient compliance)
3. Cope with an uncertain medical prognosis
4. Avoid social isolation and maintain a social network (or adjust to diminished social contact)
5. Set concrete goals and make plans for specific, achievable future goals

So far we have examined many general aspects of chronic illness and disability. (A summary of tasks for dealing with chronic illness and disability is presented in Table 13–1.) Now we turn to an examination of developmental issues and their effect on chronic illness. We will look at the role played by chronic conditions in the emotional growth and development of children, adolescents, and young adults, and we will see how chronic conditions can alter the lives of middle-aged adults and their families. Finally, we will look at the difficulties faced by the aged, who are most commonly the victims of chronic illness.

# Chronic Illness in Children and Adolescents

About 10% of children in the United States have some kind of physical disorder that brings serious concerns about their future as well as limitations in their current activities (Strauss & Glaser, 1975; U.S. Public Health Service, 1971; Davis, 1973). Many of these disorders require special treatment, such as a restricted diet or regular medication. In addition, increasing numbers of children with long-term illnesses are remaining at home with their families instead of staying in a hospital (Anderson & Bury, 1988). Thus, there is considerable developing interest among health professionals and parents of these children in the impact and management of the chronic conditions of childhood.

Diseases that were once fatal among children, such as diabetes and severe bronchial asthma, are now survivable and manageable because of advances in medicine and related sciences. While children with chronic diseases are never actually cured, they are able to live relatively normal lives as long as they maintain a regimen of care for their chronic life-threatening conditions. In addition, in current times children who once would have died from leukemia and various forms of childhood cancer now survive longer than ever before and a great many are eventually cured (though they may be left with some residual impairments). Their process of recovery, however, can be extremely long and emotionally draining for the family. Typically, the physical, emotional, social, and financial demands of caring for an ill or disabled child can affect all members of the family in some very profound and complex ways (Mattsson, 1977).

■ ■ ■ ■ ■

Jeffrey is a normal, happy eight-year-old—as normal as can be expected, of course, since he has *bronchial asthma.*

Jeffrey's asthma is severe enough at times to endanger his life. In the midst of an asthma attack, for example, he is literally suffocating. Because of swollen and spasming bronchial passages, he cannot expel the carbon dioxide in his lungs quickly enough to be able to breathe again and take in needed oxygen. Several times a month his parents must rush him to the local emergency room to receive oxygen and an

injection of adrenalin. His parents never know when an attack will occur, so they keep extra close watch on him at all times. Even Jeffrey's ten-year-old sister is required to keep track of him when they are out playing or at school, in case he begins to develop difficulty breathing.

Jeffrey's environment and activities are quite restricted by his asthma. For example, he must never even taste chocolate because it is a suspected allergen. He must avoid other allergens too, such as pollen, animal dander, dust, and molds. This means that his parents must keep their home absolutely spotless at all times. They cannot have carpeting in their house but have had to install linoleum flooring that can be mopped every day. They have minimal furniture, so that dusting every day will be easier. They cannot have a pet, much to the distress of Jeffrey and his sister. Jeffrey is not allowed to visit the homes of his friends because the necessary precautions have not been taken there. And because dampness and humidity are so detrimental to Jeffrey's condition, his parents are planning to move the family from the East Coast to Arizona, where the air is very dry.

Jeffrey typically misses several days of school after an asthma attack. Unlike the other children, he cannot participate in physical education classes because the exertion of exercise can bring on another attack. Jeffrey must control or avoid all emotions that could trigger an attack, such as fear, anxiety, anger, and even excitement. Hence, his life has become very restricted and the burden on his family to control the emotional stimuli to which he is exposed has become tremendous.

Jeffrey must take preventive medication routinely. He and his family must learn to anticipate his asthma attacks and to use various means, such as medication, to avert them. Jeffrey, his sister, and his parents must become competent at dealing with his attacks. They must administer medication, physical support for coughing, and help to rest and use relaxation techniques.

Jeffrey cannot always be with his parents or his sister, of course. To gain the independence that is normal for a developing eight-year-old, Jeffrey must learn to take more and more responsibility for his own care. This responsibilty takes considerable time to develop and tends to be quite stressful for him. Jeffrey's parents worry that if he makes a mistake, he could die. So they tend to be overcontrolling of him. They also place some of the responsibility for Jeffrey's life on his ten-year-old sister. Family dynamics are very much influenced by Jeffrey's illness, sometimes in a negative manner.

## DEVELOPMENTAL TASKS AND ILLNESS

Many psychologists use a developmental approach in order to understand how an individual grows and changes psychologically throughout his or her life span. Early psychodynamic theorists, such as Sigmund Freud, proposed that development is confined to childhood. But the theorist Erik Erikson speculated that each life stage presents a variety of tasks to be mastered before an individual can move on to the next psychological stage (Erikson, 1963). This formulation is particularly relevant to the understanding of illness. Because of certain uncontrollable life events, such as illness, a person may fail to master the psychological tasks necessary at each stage of development. Erikson's theory holds that competence at each stage is necessary to move on and meet the challenges of the next stages. (These stages are summarized in Table 13–2.)

A person's adaptation to illness or disability depends a great deal upon the stage at which it first appears. A particular limitation may have a huge impact at one stage of development but a much smaller impact at another. Also, the accomplishments of the previous stage may make adjustment

more or less possible when illness or disability appear. The patient's developmental level will also affect the number and type of demands he or she places on family members. And within a family the developmental levels of the various other members may affect the reactions and adjustment of each to the patient's limitations.

Briefly, Erikson described the major task of *infancy* as the attainment of a sense of basic trust. Such trust comes from perceiving the caretaker as consistent and reliable. Serious illness at this stage can interfere with such attainment because illness may require separation from parents and the frustration of basic needs. Illness of the infant may interfere with the mother-child and father-child bonds and other important early attachments.

In *early childhood*, the main task is to strive for autonomy, particularly in controlling bodily functions. Successful toilet training is a source of pride for the young child, who feels that he or she has accomplished something important when such mastery is achieved. Success leads to further development. Illness and disability however, may bring considerable restriction in activity and the curtailment of efforts toward independence. Particularly when illness interferes with control of bowel and bladder functions, the child's confidence and sense of competence may falter. Contributing to a faltering self-confidence may be feelings of shame and doubt to which the child is vulnerable by virtue of his or her physical defects.

Chronically ill children under age 4 typically react with willfulness and attempt to test the boundaries of the control their parents exert over them. Sometimes when a child is ill or disabled, parents tend to be more permissive than they otherwise would and to favor the child, allowing him or her to develop problems in behavioral control. *School-age children* (age 5 to puberty) typically attempt to develop a sense of industry and competence, as well as the

| TABLE 13–2 | Stages of Personality Development, According to Erik Erikson | |
|---|---|---|
| Stage | Age of person (years) | Tasks of development |
| Trust v. mistrust | birth–1 | Trust in primary caretakers (parents), and perception of world as safe. |
| Autonomy v. shame | 1–3 | Sense of competence gained from successful toilet training, learning to feed self, and so on. |
| Initiative v. guilt | 3–5 | Living within the bounds of caretakers' limits; learning to depend upon own initiative for action. |
| Industry v. inferiority | 5–11 | Meeting demands of school and home responsibilities and requirements for accomplishment. |
| Identity v. role confusion | 11–18 | Developing of sense of identity and role in life. |
| Intimacy v. isolation | 18–40 | Building and maintaining intimacy in relationship with another person. |
| Generativity v. stagnation | 40–65 | Contributing to future generations through work, care of children, community responsibility. |
| Integrity v. despair | 65 + | Accepting the meaning of mortality; finding meaning in one's life. |

capacity for sustained effort. The opinions of peers can take on greater significance than the opinions of family. If a child is ill or disabled, responses from peers can be quite negative and severely affect the child's self-image. Parents and siblings may try to protect the child from such criticism.

Boxes 13–3 and 13–4 examine children's understanding of illness and adjustment to hospitalization respectively.

*Adolescents* typically question parental values and attempt to formulate their own values, giving rise to a separate and unique identity. For appropriate development to occur, adolescents need the opportunity for their own unique self-expression, as well as the opportunity to form close relationships with individuals outside the family. An illness or disability that occurs during adolescence may not only interfere with these pursuits but also threaten what was accomplished at earlier stages of development (such as when bowel and bladder control are lost, or independent action becomes impossible). It may be very difficult for the parent of an ill or disabled adolescent to provide the required physical care and at the same time devise an environment in which the adolescent can express his or her individuality, receive needed emancipation from parental control, establish rewarding peer relationships, and develop values that are independent of those of his or her parents.

## I'M THE DOCTOR, AND I'M GONNA CHECK YOU

At the age of 3, my little girl was sure that doctors can make you better just by "checking" you. When I had a terrible headache, or when I had dropped something heavy on my foot and was howling in pain, she would tell me to lie down and be examined. She played the doctor and I was the patient. To add realism, she put on a pair of my high heels. (Since the most salient physicians in her life were women, this part of the outfit was apparently essential.) Like most children her age, she believed in a kind of "abracadabra" magic in which the doctor could make everything better with a wave of her stethoscope.

Exploring the ways in which children attempt to make sense of their medical-care experiences can be enlightening and amusing. Understanding these issues can also be absolutely essential if children's confusions and fears are to be taken seriously.

Consider this example. Many 4- and 5-year-old children are afraid of the stethoscope. In one study children were initially thought to be distressed because the stethoscope is cold. However, on closer inspection, it was found that the children were concerned about something much more complicated. They believed that the purpose of the stethoscope is to discover whether or not they have a heart. They also believed that the heart is what makes them live. Thus, "a negative finding by the physician, then, as the child sees it, could result in the child's being dead" (Bibace & Walsh, 1979, p. 286).

In another study 4-year-old children gave fanciful explanations of how illness is transmitted. For example, some said that measles can be transmitted by taking a bite of snow. "Measles come out of the snow, it comes into your body and turns to ice and then comes out" (Haight, Black, & DiMatteo, 1985, p. 36). Ritual behaviors were used to explain recovery. When asked how one gets well, answers involved personal experiences, such as going to the doctor and then sliding down the slide.

Children as young as 4 can act out the roles of doctor and patient quite well. When asked by a researcher to work a doctor puppet and a patient puppet, children had the doctor puppet ask a lot of questions and the patient puppet ask very few but disclose a great deal of information (a pattern that is shown in the literature to be what actually happens in doctor-patient interactions) (Haight et al., 1985). These children were not aware, however, that doctors receive medical training. They believed that one gets to be a doctor simply by donning a white coat. Interestingly, some of them believed that someone who does not wear a white coat cannot be a doctor! This may be important information for a medical professional to have.

Researchers who study children's understanding of illness examine how that understanding changes as children mature through various stages of their development. As children become more sophisticated in understanding the world in general, their appraisals of what is happening to them when they are sick or receiving medical care become more realistic.

## IMPAIRED SOCIAL RELATIONSHIPS WITH PEERS AND SIBLINGS

The difficulties of illness do not stop with the chronically ill child. Peers and siblings both affect and are affected by the psycho-logical and social concomitants of illness and disability.

Because of the limitations placed on the entire family, siblings of a chronically ill child may be deprived of a family atmosphere that is suitable to their own devel-

**BOX 13–4**

### CHILDREN IN THE HOSPITAL

The developmental stage that an individual has reached is an important determinant of how he or she will react to illness and hospitalization. This is especially true when the patient is a child.

Hospitalization can be a terrifying experience for a child. Frequently, the younger the child, the less able he or she is to take in what is happening and the more frightened he or she may become. Uncertainty and lack of understanding about one's experience of illness is stressful for most people regardless of age. Children are more susceptible to this stress because they typically have a limited grasp of the phenomenon of illness and its causes, and they are usually not provided with enlightening information.

Children usually know little about what caused their pain and illness. They may interpret "feeling bad" as a punishment for having behaved badly. They might also think that they became sick or hurt because their family members didn't protect them. In the hospital they may feel abandoned by parents and left alone to face a confusing array of health professionals. They may be terrified by the strange and uncomfortable medical procedures to which they are subjected.

Children who are hospitalized often experience anger, humiliation, and considerable anxiety. Some respond by regressing to babyish behavior. Some children lose their recent gains, such as toilet training, or the ability to dress themselves or to brush their teeth. Some children, out of panic, carry on with temper tantrums.

Several decades ago few if any hospitals would allow a parent to stay with a hospitalized child. This rule was adhered to despite the tremendous difficulties encountered by toddlers and young children in being separated from their parents. Now most hospitals permit parents to "room-in" with their sick children and even to participate in delivering their care. Older children and adolescents are given the opportunity to reduce their separation and loneliness with peer contact. Many hospitals have programs to provide parents and children with adequate information and preparation for what will be experienced. Explanations are given in language that children can understand. Children are found to be more likely to comply with treatment regimens when given a chance to participate in their own care and to take some control. One child for example, was able to tolerate painful bone marrow aspirations when the physician followed the child's orders first to count to 10. Another was able to tolerate an uncomfortable diagnostic examination when she was able to choose whether she would sit up or lie down for the procedure. Children do best when they are given the opportunity to verbalize their feelings and to exert some control over what is happening to them (Koocher, 1985).

opment. They may become jealous of the increased attention and special privileges given to the ill child (Boone & Hartman, 1972). The ill sibling who receives medications and special diets may appear to be overindulged. Often siblings experience decreased parental tolerance for them, as well as increased parental expectations for their maturity and independence, and a lack of positive emotional expression toward them. The ill sibling may have significantly diminished energy, making normal sibling interactions impossible. Many siblings of chronically ill children experience confusion and anxiety from a lack of information about what is happening to their sibling. They experience loneliness from decreased parental involvement, feelings of parental rejection, sadness at the loss of former family interactions, embarrassment about and unwillingness to express their own negative reactions, and even *survivor guilt* at witnessing the ill child's physical deterioration and pain while they themselves remain healthy. Siblings of ill children experience fears of loss: loss of the sibling whom they love, as well as loss of one or both parents who are often separated from the rest of the family while caring for the ill and sometimes hospitalized child. As a result, siblings may develop behavioral problems at home and in school (Kramer, 1987).

Their peers have a tendency to reject children with chronic illnesses, and because of difficulties gaining peer acceptance, chronically ill children often experience loneliness (Krulik, 1987). "Being different" can expose them to ridicule. Among school-age children, acceptance and popularity often depend upon physical appearance, and so the degree of rejection experienced is usually influenced by how much the condition interferes with normal classroom and play activities, how noticeable the defect is, and the level of cognitive development and maturity of the ill child's peers (Roberts, 1986). Efforts to help peers

(for example, members of the child's class) to understand the child's condition and to deal with their own fears and anxieties regarding their friend's illness, can help peers to be supportive of the ill child.

Children with chronic illnesses have many experiences that have the potential to impede their social development. Friendships may be difficult to maintain because of interruptions by illness crises and treatment. Children who are chronically ill sometimes develop characteristics that separate them from other people, such as shyness and avoidance of other people, stemming from embarrassment about their symptoms and treatments.

## THE EMOTIONAL AND PHYSICAL ADJUSTMENT OF THE FAMILY

There is no one pattern of stress faced by families with children who have long-term chronic illnesses. Rather, the quantity and the quality of stress depend upon the type and extent of the child's limitations. For example, some children may be wheelchair-bound or even totally dependent upon their parents for physical care. Their capacities may slowly deteriorate over time. Others may experience periods of poor functioning that alternate with relatively active and healthy periods during which they can develop normally. Inconsistencies in and uncertainties about the child's abilities may be particularly difficult to deal with since patients and their families must adapt to continually changing conditions. For example, just when they become accustomed to the child's good health, there may be yet another exacerbation of the disease, causing tensions to mount again. Partly because of the tremendous stress placed on the entire family, compliance with recommended treatments can become very difficult. In one study of children with cancer, for example, it was found that 67% had stopped taking their medication before they were

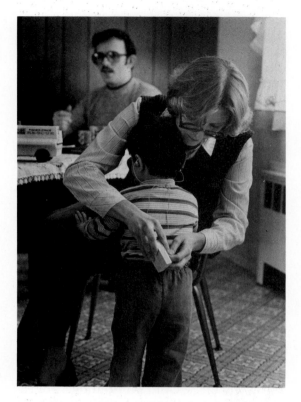

Maternal psychological and physical adjustment correlate highly with overall family response to a chronically
ill or handicapped child.
SOURCE: © Alan Carey/The Image Works

told to do so by their physicians (Roberts,
1986). Some ill or disabled children become
passive, dependent, and overprotected by
their parents and do not learn to take responsibility for their own care. Others re-
sent the restrictions placed on them and
rebel, becoming excessively independent
and even daring to risk serious medical
consequences. Thus, there is evidence that
families experiencing the distress of coping
with a serious illness may not be functioning in an optimal way to support adherence
to the treatment regimen (Jay, Litt, & Durant, 1984).

The type of disability the child experiences is also an important factor in family
adjustment. Mental slowness and retardation, such as can accompany neuromuscular disease, tend to be more difficult to cope
with than physical difficulties. Of course,
even when there is no effect on the child's
mind, the physical limitations and financial pressures of many chronic conditions
(renal disease, for example) can seriously
affect a family's ability to cope. Many aspects of day-to-day life may be altered because of the requirements of the ill child's
care. Much attention may be required by
the schedules of medical visits and the timing of exercise, meals, and travel. The desires of the other children in the family (for
example, to have a pet) may be thwarted
by requirements for the ill child's care
(Wilson-Pessano & McNabb, 1985).

Psychologists do not yet have enough
information about why some families rise
to the challenge of a crisis of illness or disability while others fall apart. Certainly the
strength of the family bonds, including the
viability of the marriage, are important
factors, as are the degree of adjustment and
emotional health enjoyed by the individual
parents. One researcher found that maternal psychological and physical adjustment
correlated highly with overall family response to a handicapped child (Shapiro,
1986). If the mother was depressed or ill
herself, the family was seriously disrupted
by the presence of the ill child. Under these
circumstances the family members tended
to have angry or prolonged negative feelings toward the chronically ill child or to
perceive him or her to be a burden. On the
other hand, mothers who were able to seek
emotional support from a variety of
sources, who felt in control of the problem,
who were not depressed, and who were
themselves in good health had families who
adjusted better to the chronic illness of one
of the children (Shapiro, 1986).

Finally, in this research, mothers who
tried to normalize family life as much as
possible (for example, matter-of-factly giving the ill child medication at the same

time the other children take their vitamins) achieved higher levels of functioning. On the other hand, those who avoided facing their feelings about their child's illness and who blamed themselves were depressed, were in poor health, had lower levels of personal functioning, and had families that experienced poorer adjustment. It is important to remember, of course, that it is quite difficult to decide which factor causes which (Shapiro, 1986). Causal inference is not possible in this research. For example, did the mother's good health and emotional stability cause good family adjustment or vice versa?

In general, clinicians have noted that more negative family and individual outcomes are likely to result if family members cannot talk openly about the child's condition (Shapiro, 1986). Destructive coping mechanisms, such as denial, might be chosen, making communication about the illness among family members impossible. Feelings of self-blame, which parents may find preferable to facing the random tragedies of illness, may cause further harm by alienating family members from one another (Shapiro, 1986).

The entire family environment can be affected by the limitations that accompany the illness or disability of one child. Because of this, medical practitioners now recognize that they must work with the family as a whole unit whenever they treat a child. They must focus on interaction patterns and the ability of family members to communicate with one another and express and deal with their feelings (Minuchin, Rosman, & Baker, 1978).

## SOME SOLUTIONS

With the support of their health professionals, parents of chronically ill children can do a great deal to help them develop as normally as possible (Roberts, 1986). For example, parents can work within the family to minimize the differences between the chronically ill child and his or her peers and siblings. Within the bounds of the required treatment regimens, parents can provide the child with opportunities for normal peer contacts and with help to avoid social isolation (Krulik, 1987). Extra effort on the part of the parent may be required to find activities in which the child can successfully participate. Parents can help the child to solidify sibling relationships by avoiding overprotection, overindulgence, and permissiveness. They may also prevent sibling resentment and anger by avoiding suggesting that the ill child is somehow the favored one (Boone & Hartman, 1972).

Parents can help their chronically ill child by communicating honestly and focusing on the child's feelings. Some parents may try to avoid answering their child's questions about the illness, or they may be willing to discuss only day-to-day care but not the child's feelings about being ill. The child may learn that certain topics are taboo and may become isolated in private fears.

Chronically ill and handicapped children can be helped to develop normally and to be quite well adjusted. There may be many problems to overcome, but the demands of chronic illness and disability can be incorporated into a rewarding family life. Psychologists and other health professionals can help the child and the family to achieve confidence and the competence to cope effectively.

# Chronic Illness in Adulthood

## YOUNG ADULTHOOD

Illness and disability can have a profound impact upon young adults and can significantly affect the people in the patient's *family of origin* (parents, siblings), *family of commitment* (spouse and children), and *close social network* (extended family and close friends). Social and emotional development do not stop in adolescence but continue throughout the life span. At all ages illness and disability can interfere (Lewis, 1986; Wellisch, Fawzy, Landsverk, Pasnau, & Walcott, 1983).

During *early adulthood* (roughly ages 20 to 39) an individual usually strives to develop both a career and an intimate relationship with another person (Erikson, 1963). Chronic illness and disability can significantly interfere with these goals. Preferred career choices may become unavailable, and alternative plans must be developed. Physical limitations can alter the patient's ability to relate to an intimate partner. For example, a young couple may be starting their life together when one of them is suddenly propelled by the dependency of illness to an earlier stage of development. The demands of illness may cause the couple to lose the autonomy they had just begun to develop. The spouse or partner of the ill or disabled patient may not yet have matured enough emotionally to withstand the stresses that challenge his or her commitment to stay with the partner.

The patient's physical limitations can also limit a couple's sexual expression. Illness and bodily disfigurement or disability, and some required medication treatments, may bring certain physiological changes that make sexual functioning difficult or impossible. Psychological factors, such as changes in body image and alterations in social environment, may bring a lowered self-concept for the patient and restrict opportunities for and comfort with intimacy (Glueckauf & Quittner, 1984) (see Box 13–5).

During young adulthood, chronic illness may place close relationships in serious jeopardy. After the onset of illness or disability, a young couple may need to renegotiate the terms of their relationship. New pressures may have been placed on the able-bodied spouse that were never expected when the commitment took place. Very often the patient has gone through experiences that the spouse cannot understand. Sometimes the partners have become so alienated from one another emotionally that parting is the only alternative (Ireys & Burr, 1984). In all cases young adults whose lives have been changed by chronic illness must struggle to redefine their roles and relationships with regard to their partners.

Many young adults who do not have partners are forced by their disabilities to move back to their families of origin (Ireys & Burr, 1984). Such a move often has a negative effect on the patient's self-image. Parents, who may have already reached their retirement years, are placed back into the role of providing care for their young-adult children.

When a disabled young adult who has lived on his or her own for a time returns to the family of origin, certain tasks must be undertaken and certain important goals achieved. Parents and siblings must maintain the opportunity to continue with their own developmental tasks. New patterns of relating must be developed that do not simply repeat the old patterns that existed in the family at an earlier time. For example, siblings in the household must learn to abandon the relationships they had as children and develop new adult patterns of interaction.

## MIDDLE AGE

Chronic illness can bring serious problems even among *middle-aged patients* (roughly ages 40 to 65) who have strong family ties and considerable emotional support (Cassileth, 1979). A significant alteration in roles and lifestyles within the family may occur. A spouse may have to accept total responsibility for earning the monetary support of the family as well as for all domestic chores and care of the children. The chronically ill adult who was once a nurturer may become the one who needs nurturing (Rustad, 1984).

Chronic illness and disability can challenge the financial stability of the family. Blue-collar workers, for example, whose work involves physical strain may be unable to continue in their jobs and as a result lose their health insurance and retirement and disability benefits. Such financial constraints can significantly limit the opportunities afforded other family members (such as to go to college) and can challenge the ill person's conception of himself or herself as a provider for the family.

Illness interferes with many of the normal tasks of midlife, such as helping teen-age children to grow into responsible and happy adults, developing adult leisure activities, and caring for aged parents. By the time they have reached their 40s and 50s, people have typically gained a sense of mastery over their lives. They may have developed more equal relationships with their spouses than they had been able to have in the past when a division of labor may have been required to care for small children. Unfortunately, illness and disability may once again bring the need for rigid roles, sometimes quite different from what the family is accustomed to. For example, when a wife is disabled, her husband may be thrust into the role of nurturer and caretaker, a role he may never have played before. Likewise, when a hus-

## SEX AND CHRONIC ILLNESS

Among patients with chronic illness and disability, the pleasures of sexual expression may be severely threatened. There is considerable research showing that sexual behavior becomes limited or nonexistent among those who have suffered from various chronic medical conditions. Some patients may become impotent or nonorgasmic. Even after they have recovered and are doing well on many other dimensions of their lives, they may avoid sexual activity. Often their problems are not physiological but psychological in origin (Zilbergeld, 1979).

Certainly patients with serious medical problems have many concerns besides sex. But threats to their sexuality affect other dimensions of their lives as well: their feelings of attractiveness, their self-esteem, and their feelings of physical and emotional support from another. Although some patients are certainly comfortable forgoing sexual activity altogether, most of them very much want to regain their ability to redevelop and maintain this means of closeness with their partner. If sex becomes problematic because of the medical conditions or treatments, the person facing illness and disability finds additional frustrations with which he or she must deal. The relationship between the patient and his or her partner can be threatened.

Medical professionals can do a great deal to help patients and their partners to overcome the difficulties they face in resuming sexual activity. Medical professionals typically fail to provide even the most rudimentary information to their patients, yet information about the impact of a medical condition on sexuality is essential. Enlightened medical professionals provide such information as a matter of course and are careful to deal with all of their patients' concerns in the realm of sexuality. Sensitivity and attention to patients' sexual difficulties can foster recovery on emotional and social dimensions.

band is disabled, a wife who was always dependent in the realm of financial matters may be required to learn to do these things herself.

Typically, chronic illness causes a change in the couple's sexual relationship. They may even cease sexual relations altogether. Sexual activity may be particularly problematic if there is anxiety that sex might jeopardize the patient's condition (for example, if the husband has had a heart attack). By interfering with sexual expression, chronic illness may jeopardize all of the couple's opportunities for emotional intimacy (Gotay, 1984; Steele, Finkelstein, & Finkelstein, 1976).

## THE EFFECT ON THE PATIENT'S CHILDREN

The children of a chronically ill or disabled patient are likely to be affected in significant ways. If alternative methods are not found for a parent to fulfill the children's needs, the long-term effects of such illness or disability may be quite profound. Illness and disability may interfere with two important roles that a parent plays with respect to his or her child: teacher and protector. Because of limitations in a parent's physical condition, for example, a child may not have appropriate controls and boundaries placed on his or her behavior. Or the child may feel insecure because he or she sees the disabled parent as unable to provide protection (Peters & Esses, 1985; Rutter, 1966).

The period after onset of illness and disability is likely to be particularly stressful, and children may feel exceptionally vulnerable and in need of support. Hospitalization may deprive them of much-needed contact with their parents. Both the ill and the caretaking parent may become so absorbed in physical care and in their own adjustment that they remain emotionally unavailable to the children. Younger children may experience considerable anxiety, which is fueled by their fears and fantasies of losing the parent and being abandoned. Older children who have a better understanding of the situation may experience more realistic but no less terrifying fears (Stetz, Lewis, & Primomo, 1986).

When children are forced to care for their disabled parents (for example, to stay in the home at an age when they should be establishing their own separate identities), their own development can be severely disrupted. Children with a disabled parent may be thrust into a situation that is well beyond their current developmental stage. Concern for the physical care of a parent is part of middle-age adult development (in the 40s and 50s), not of development in the adolescent and young adult years. Offspring in their late teens and early 20s who are old enough to leave the family to make their own lives may feel conflict between their own desire for freedom and independence and parental demands (real or implicit) for physical and emotional support. Because of parental chronic illness, the accomplishment of normal developmental tasks of offspring may be seriously inhibited.

Of course, the difficulties of parental chronic illness can be overcome and alternative ways for parent and child to interact can be found. Intervention by psychologists and other medical professionals can help to prevent many of the difficulties that the children of chronically ill parents encounter.

## HOW FAMILIES COPE

Families cope with chronic illness in many different ways. Some are brought closer together as a result of their open expression of feelings. Others develop considerable resentment, and the patient becomes a source of chronic stress and a burden on the family. The character of family adjustment prior to the illness can be a very important factor in postillness coping. The pressures of illness and disability can cause a basically stable family unit to mobilize resources to deal with the crisis and to adjust to the long-term effects of the life changes brought about by the illness. In a well-functioning family system, individuals adjust their roles in relation to one another in order to cope with the difficulties that illness and disability bring (Lavee, McCubbin & Patterson, 1985; Schwenk & Hughes, 1983; Thorne, 1985).

Illness can have pervasive consequences for families, consequences that must be recognized and dealt with, or prevented if possible (Minuchin, 1974). Rigid defenses, denial, and lack of conflict resolution fail to serve the interests of the family as a social unit.

# Chronic Illness and the Aged

■ ■ ■ ■ ■

Kate Quinton is an 80-year-old widow who lives in Brooklyn, New York, with Claire, one of her two daughters. Claire Quinton is unmarried, in her 50s, and has lived with and cared for her aging mother for many years. Kate's other daughter, Barbara, lives in New Jersey with her husband and is in conspicuous conflict with Claire about how their mother should be cared for. From her vantage point in the suburbs, uninvolved with her mother's day-to-day care and emotionally distant from her mother and sister, Barbara believes that her mother belongs in a nursing home. But Claire, who cares for all of her mother's needs despite her own extensive spine problems, believes that her mother should remain at home where she can maintain her spirits and have a fairly independent life.

The Quintons are a real family, subjects of a book by Susan Sheehan called *Kate Quinton's Days*. The book clearly describes the plight of many elderly people and their families and the huge burden that is placed upon the caregivers of the elderly. The story of the Quintons also demonstrates how difficult it can be for an elderly, chronically ill person to avoid being committed to a nursing home.

One incident in the winter of 1982 starts the process that brings Kate to the brink of being put into a nursing home and begins Claire's struggles to care adequately for her mother. Kate has severe abdominal pain, and unable to reach their family physician, Claire calls a physician service, which sends a doctor to make a house call. The doctor visits, charges $40, and advises that Kate be taken to the emergency room of the hospital. He recommends an ambulance service, for which Claire pays $90. Kate and Claire live on only $271.10 a month, which constitutes Kate's monthly Social Security benefit. Claire is unemployed. This single incident has cost them roughly half their monthly subsistence.

The hospital bill is paid by Medicare, but the elderly Kate is subjected to extensive testing *even after* the source of her problem, a urinary tract infection, has been identified and treated. The doctors test her to check for malignancies, even though Kate may not even want to be treated for cancer were it to be found. Kate is considerably weakened and debilitated by these tests, and within a few weeks the doctors and nurses suggest that she be transferred to a nursing home. They tell Claire that the nursing home stay will be temporary, "to regain her strength," but as Sheehan notes, most old people who go to nursing homes stay there permanently.

Claire considers the nursing home because she herself has a severe, painful back problem after having had several unsuccessful back surgeries. But she rejects the nursing home suggestion and is glad to learn that her mother is eligible for a home-care program sponsored by New York City. The program is designed to help people in circumstances like the Quinton's, and involves attendants who will clean up the house and care for Kate, lifting her when necessary and generally doing things that Claire cannot do. In practice, however, Claire finds the program lacking in many ways. The home-care attendants mess up the house more than they clean it, and they are not careful to prevent the aged Mrs. Quinton from being injured. Paid minimum wage by the city, they arrive late, leave early, and quit after only a few weeks.

Kate's medical bills are paid by Medicaid because she is so poor that she qualifies for government health care assistance. Yet the care is extremely limited. She needs special shoes because of her severe arthritis, but she must wait over six weeks to get them. Claire spends weeks trying to find an optometrist who will take the reduced payments from Medicaid so that her mother can have glasses, and several more weeks finding a dentist who will make Kate's dentures for the Medicaid payment.

Claire persists in caring for her mother, although her own life is severely restricted. She is constantly fearful that her mother will have another medical crisis. Her one enjoyable weekend in years was spent when a friend came to visit her and they went to the movies twice in a weekend. Faced with the choice of institutionalizing a mother whose intellectual faculties are quite intact, Claire chooses the difficult route of home care, at great cost to herself.

There are many myths about those over age 65, individuals whom many term *the elderly*. Perhaps one of the most prevalent of those myths is that most old people are shut off in nursing homes, alone and uncared for by their families, but that is far from the truth. As we will see in this section, although many older people do have certain physical, social, and financial limitations and handicaps, most are able to live gratifying, independent lives (Pearlman & Uhlmann, 1988). Furthermore, their loved ones, particularly their spouses and children, do a great deal to care for most elderly. Sometimes, as we see in the case of Claire Quinton, above, these loved ones deliver such care at great personal sacrifice.

## THE LOSSES OF OLD AGE

One of the major tasks of old age is adapting to the many losses that accompany the last decades of life. For example, physical infirmities are common among the aged. Eighty-five percent of the elderly suffer from at least one chronic physical condition (Schienle & Eiler, 1984). Forty-one percent are severely limited by a chronic, disabling condition, such as heart disease, cancer, stroke, or respiratory disease. In addition, the activities of about 25% of the elderly are limited by arthritis, rheumatism, and sensory impairments (such as limitations in eyesight and hearing). About 10% have major health problems that require continuous medical care. Four to five percent have organic brain damage that causes chronic cognitive impairment.

Socially, the elderly tend to be hampered by the negative stereotypes held by members of the younger generations about older people. The elderly are often seen by younger people as very different from themselves. Certain stereotypes about what the elderly can and cannot do may significantly limit their employment possibilities and interfere with their interpersonal relationships. Stereotypes can even affect caregivers, such as physicians, nurses, counselors, and therapists. Less may be expected of the elderly than of younger people, and the concerns of elderly patients may be downplayed or ignored.

Many elderly people face financial difficulties. Those who are not affluent may be forced to live on fixed incomes from Social

Most elderly persons in the United States are able to live independent and gratifying lives. Those who stay physically active can significantly extend their healthy life span.
SOURCE: © Bob Clay/Clay Images

Security. Many have no pensions. With no private health insurance, they must rely on Medicaid and Medicare, government health-care reimbursement systems that provide the poor and aged with coverage of their health care costs but severely limit the services available. Many elderly meet with the frustrations described above in the story of the Quintons. These frustrations include long waits for inadequate services and sometimes inappropriate medical treatment (Brook et al., 1989).

Many elderly also must cope with such emotional losses as the deaths of their spouse and friends. Some have very limited contact with their children who have moved away to live their own independent lives. Partly because of a narrowing of their social networks, about a quarter of the elderly report being quite lonely (Hendrick, Wells, & Faletti, 1982; Revenson, 1986).

## CARE BY THE FAMILY

Despite their physical limitations, most people over 65 are independent and with limited help are able to take care of themselves. Most can depend upon members of their extended families for both tangible support (such as, to make home repairs or do shopping) and emotional support (such as calling on the telephone to alleviate loneliness) (Zarit & Zarit, 1984). Contrary to the stereotypes some hold of the abandoned and rejected elderly person, most older people can successfully rely on their families for assistance. In most cases, such help is provided by the children and the spouse of the older person. Oftentimes, elderly siblings help one another and many even live together and provide mutual care (Stone, Cafferata, & Sangl, 1987).

As we saw in the case of Kate Quinton, above, a family member's help can mean the difference between institutionalization in a nursing facility and independent living at home. Only about 5% to 7% of the elderly in this country actually reside in nursing homes (Stone et al., 1987). A large number of these institutionalized people suffer from significant cognitive impairments due to organic brain damage. These individuals (about 4% to 5% of the elderly) cannot engage in self-care activities, such as dressing themselves, going to the bathroom, washing, and eating.

An elderly person's inability to engage in self-care is not the sole determinant of the decision to institutionalize him or her in a nursing home. Many families do take care of their helpless elderly persons as long as they can do so. Institutionalization is finally chosen, however, when circumstances threaten the caregiver's ability to provide assistance (rather than because the older person's physical or mental condition has worsened). In other words, the degree of burden imposed upon the caregiver and his or her ability to cope with the many demands placed on him or her typically determine whether the elderly person can remain at home or must be institutionalized (Brody, 1985).

Many caregivers become physically, emotionally, and/or financially exhausted from their day-to-day care of a dependent elderly relative (Brody, 1985). In many cases, the primary caretaker of the elderly person is also the wife and mother in her own family and she is employed part or full time. Her duties may be both physically and emotionally overwhelming (Montgomery, Gonyea, & Hooyman, 1985; Pratt, Schmall, Wright, & Cleland, 1985). Researchers and clinicians now recognize that the ability of a family to care for an impaired older person at home requires early intervention to relieve some of the burden on the caregivers. Such help might come from members of the extended family or from outside agencies. Without this help, the detrimental effects on caregivers and family members can be quite extensive (Pinkston & Linsk, 1984).

## CONTROL OF THE ENVIRONMENT IN NURSING HOME CARE

In most nursing homes, custodial care, control, and safekeeping of the elderly tends to be the norm. Elderly people with disabilities are usually not rehabilitated, as are younger people with similar limitations. Rather, the nursing home is "the end of the line" for the elderly person. He or she is not expected to return home, as might be possible with rehabilitation. Instead, because of limited financial resources for nursing care and the need to achieve both safety and control of the impaired elderly, considerable regimentation is required. Tolerance for individual variation among elderly persons may be quite low.

Nursing home care typically involves the provision of all aspects of care for the elderly client; for example, he or she is bathed, dressed, and fed. But provision of these services may not always be to the benefit of the elderly person. For example, someone who can maintain independence by dressing, washing, and self-feeding may cease to attempt such activities when these are carried out for him or her. In such an atmosphere of complete care, the elderly person can learn to become completely helpless and then may become depressed (Abeles, 1990; Lachman, 1986).

Dependency and depression can be minimized or avoided when the elderly person is able to exert some control over his or her environment and to carry out responsible actions. One study examined the effect of the introduction of an element of control on the morale and health of the institutionalized elderly (Langer & Rodin, 1976). Patients on one floor of a nursing home (the experimental group patients) were given a plant to care for and were asked to choose when they would like to participate in some of the activities available to them in the nursing home. Patients on another floor (the comparison group patients) were also given a plant but were told that the staff of the home would take care of it for them. They participated in the same activities as the first group, but were not allowed to choose when they would do so. Several weeks later nurses rated the mood and activity level of the patients. The patients who had experienced the intervention were rated as more active and as having greater psychological well-being than were the control group patients. A year later patients who had been given control in the experiment were still healthier than their counterparts both physically and mentally, and more of them were still alive (Rodin & Langer, 1977).

Further research evidence shows that the possibility of control must remain in effect in order for a successful outcome to be maintained. If nursing home patients are first given a chance to control their environment and then that control is taken away (and the old regimentation reinstated), patients may be worse off than they would have been without the intervention (Schulz, 1976; Rodin, 1986).

# Summary

Chapter 13 examines chronic illness and handicap which involve permanent impairments or deviations from normal structure and functioning.

  I. Chronic conditions are caused by pathological alterations that are not reversible, and they are usually accompanied by some sort of residual disability.
  A. Chronic illness is surprisingly common. Surveys have found that approximately 50% of people in the United States have at least one chronic condition. Examples are mobility restriction or activity limitation from such conditions as heart disease, arthritis, back or spine impairments, ulcerative colitis, diabetes, leg or hip impairments, visual impairments, and even psychiatric conditions.
  B. Chronic conditions by definition have no cure. This one fact has many important implications for the psychological and social adjustment of the person stricken with a chronic condition.
 II. The stresses of chronic illness and handicap can severely tax the emotional resources of the most uncomplaining and optimistic person.
  A. The social acceptability of the symptoms can influence what measures people will take to control them and how well people are able to adjust.
  B. People with chronic conditions spend a great deal of their time and energy trying to pass as normal or unimpaired.
  C. Noncompliance can result from the difficulty and the intrusiveness of many regimens, and from the fact that these regimens must be carried out over the course of the individual's entire life.
  D. The practical limitations of a debilitating physical condition can make it all but impossible to maintain social ties. Contact with friends may diminish consider-

ably, to the point where the patient rarely has contact with anyone outside his or her immediate family.

E. Some victims of chronic illness must work to normalize their conditions as much as possible. Normalizing involves hiding symptoms and adjusting the routines of care so that they will remain unnoticed by others.

F. Because chronic illness is so uncertain, the ability to plan and strive for future goals may be severely compromised.

III. About 10% of children in the United States have some kind of physical disorder that brings serious concerns about their future, as well as limitations on their current activities. Diseases that were once fatal among children, such as diabetes and severe bronchial asthma, are now survivable and manageable because of advances in medicine and related sciences. Although children with chronic diseases are never actually cured, they are able to live relatively normal lives as long as they maintain a regimen of care for their chronic life-threatening conditions.

A. The physical, emotional, social, and financial demands of caring for an ill or disabled child can affect all members of the family in some very profound and complex ways.

B. Adjustment to chronic illness can be examined in light of its effect on normal developmental tasks.

C. Siblings both affect and are affected by the psychological and social concomitants of illness and disability. They experience loneliness from decreased parental involvement, feelings of parental rejection, sadness at the loss of former family interactions, embarrassment about and unwillingness to express their own negative reactions, and even survivor guilt at witnessing the ill child's physical deterioration and pain as they themselves remain healthy.

D. There is no one pattern of stress faced by families with children who have long-term chronic illnesses. Rather, the quantity and the quality of stress depends upon the type and extent of the child's limitations and upon characteristics of the family.

IV. Chronic illness and disability can significantly interfere with the goals of early adult development. During young adulthood, chronic illness may place close relationships in serious jeopardy. After the onset of illness or disability, a young couple may need to renegotiate the terms of their relationship.

V. Chronic illness can bring serious problems even among middle-aged patients (roughly ages 40 to 65) who have strong family ties and considerable emotional support. Chronic illness and disability can challenge the financial stability of the family. The children of a chronically ill or disabled patient may be significantly affected emotionally and developmentally.

VI. Families cope with chronic illness in many different ways. Some are brought closer together as a result of their open expression of feelings. Others develop considerable resentment, and the patient becomes a source of chronic stress and a burden on the family.

VII. One of the major tasks of old age is adapting to the losses that accompany the last decades of life. For example, physical infirmities are common among the aged. Eighty-five percent of the elderly suffer from at least one chronic physical condition. Forty-one percent are limited by a chronic, disabling condition, such as heart disease, cancer, stroke, or respiratory disease. In addition, the activities of about 25% of the elderly are limited by arthritis, rheumatism, and sensory impairments (such as limitations in eyesight and hearing). About 10% have major health problems that require continuous medical care. Four to five percent have organic brain damage that causes chronic cognitive impairment.

A. Many elderly also must cope with such emotional losses as the deaths of their spouses and friends. Some have very limited contact with their children who have moved away to live their own independent lives. Because of a narrowing of their social network, many elderly people are lonely. Research has found that about a quarter of the elderly are severely lonely.

B. Despite their physical limitations, most people over 65 are quite independent and with limited help are able to take care of themselves. Most can depend upon members of their extended families for both tangible support (such as to make home repairs or do shopping) and emotional support (such as calling on the telephone to alleviate loneliness).

C. An elderly person's inability to engage in self-care is not the sole determinant of the decision to institutionalize him or her in a nursing home. Many families do take care of their helpless elderly persons as long as they can do so. Institutionalization is finally chosen, however, when circumstances threaten the caregiver's ability to provide assistance (rather than because the older person's physical or mental condition has worsened). In other words, the degree of burden imposed upon the caregiver and his or her ability to cope with the many demands placed on him or her typically determine whether the elderly person can remain at home or must be institutionalized.

D. In most nursing homes custodial care, control, and safekeeping of the elderly tends to be the norm. Nursing home care typically involves the provision of all aspects of care for the elderly client. But provision of these services may not always be to the benefit of the elderly person. Dependency and depression can be minimized or avoided when the elderly person is able to exert some control over his or her environment and carry out responsible actions.

# Glossary

**bronchial asthma:** a respiratory condition marked by swelling and spasming of the bronchial passages, making it difficult for an individual to exhale carbon dioxide quickly enough to be able to breathe again and take in needed oxygen.

**chronic illness or handicap:** impairment or deviation from normal physical structure and functioning that, whether extensive or not, remains permanent. Chronic conditions are caused by pathological alterations that are not reversible and are usually accompanied by some sort of residual disability.

**emphysema:** a chronic lung condition characterized by swelling and inflammation in the air spaces due to destruction of the alveolar walls.

**family of commitment:** an individual's spouse and children; the family that the individual forms as a result of marriage and childbearing.

**family of origin:** an individual's parents and siblings; the family in which the individual grew up.

**identity spread:** the overgeneralization from an individual's actual limitations by others when they are unfamiliar with the capabilites of the chronically ill or handicapped person.

**insulin-dependent diabetes mellitus (IDDM):** one of the four most prevalent chronic illnesses of childhood. It affects about 150,000 children and their families. Referred to also as juvenile diabetes, IDDM is a chronic metabolic disorder that is treatable but not curable. It must be controlled through careful adherence to a complex regimen of diet and physical activity, as well as insulin replacement.

**multiple sclerosis (MS):** a disease in which cellular changes in the brain and spinal cord disrupt proper nerve transmission. Scarlike areas form, destroying the fatty sheaths of myelin that cover the nerve-cell extensions called axons. Approximately 250,000 Americans currently suffer from multiple sclerosis. MS is a major cause of chronic disability in young adults.

**myelin:** material essential to the synaptic transmission of nerve impulses. The destruction of myelin can cause neurological symptoms that are in some cases transient, in others chronic, and in others severely degenerative.

**normalization:** the process of hiding symptoms as much as possible so that they remain unnoticed by others. Sometimes arrangements to normalize must be ingenious and elaborate.

**passing:** efforts by an ill or impaired individual to find ways to hide symptoms and limitations and to live a relatively independent life.

**peritoneal dialysis:** dialysis involves the process of cleansing the blood of impurities, a task carried out by the kidneys unless they have been damaged in some way. Peritoneal dialysis involves the installation of a solution in the abdominal cavity overnight and connection of the patient to a machine by means of tubes that have been surgically implanted in the patient's abdomen. Peritoneal dialysis requires elaborate sterile technique.

**survivor guilt:** feelings of guilt at witnessing the suffering or death of another person, particularly a loved one. The guilt arises because one has survived (or avoided suffering) but the other person has not.

**work of worrying:** the process of rehearsing several alternative plans and courses of action when faced with a life change or stressful life event. During the process of worrying, the individual plans several courses of action and their outcomes, and considers how his or her life might be affected by various uncontrollable factors. The work of worrying allows the individual to come to grips emotionally with the outcomes he or she might face.

# 14

# Terminal Illness and Bereavement

A serious illness or injury can follow several possible courses. One course is recovery. After the tremendous stresses and limitations of acute illness, the individual returns to life as it had been in the past. Another course is chronic illness or handicap. Although the patient is unable ever to return to normal, he or she is quite certain of surviving. A third possibility, of course, is that the patient's survival remains continually in jeopardy, and in all likelihood the final outcome of the condition will be death.

In this chapter we turn our attention to that terminal phase as we examine terminal illness from the perspective of the patient. We attempt to understand the internal struggle that attends the patient's efforts to come to terms with death. We examine the patient's struggle in the context of his or her relationships with family and friends, and we consider the emotional adjustment of those who must face the loss of someone they love.

Here a young woman named Karen talks about her sister's terminal illness:

■ ■ ■ ■ ■

I know that I'll never forget what I felt as I watched my sister dying. It all makes so little sense to me, even today. She had been so healthy and energetic, enjoying school, her friends, and the whole family. She always seemed to be moving, playing volley-ball, or running. It seems like an instant between the day she ran her first marathon and the day we buried her. But I know it was a long and heartbreaking time for all of us.

I remember very clearly the night I saw Debby in Intensive Care after her surgery. Her head was bandaged and her face looked bruised. There was a large tube down her throat connected to a machine that breathed for her. She was intubated, they said, and on a respirator. All I could tell was that her life seemed not to be her own but belonged to some mechanical monster. When she looked at me, she was clearly terrified.

I moved closer to her and she looked right at me with horror in her eyes, as if she could not imagine spending another moment in that situation. I took her hand and she squeezed mine weakly. "Mom and Dad are sleeping in the lounge," I told her. "I'll sit here. Why don't you try to sleep. I love you Debby," I said quietly as I kissed her eyelids. For the first time since the whole mess started it occurred to me that she would probably die.

The events leading to Debby's diagnosis of a malignant brain tumor were so strange and troublesome that the diagnosis itself was almost a relief. We felt better, in some bizarre way, when we found out what was going on—at least until we all realized what was going to happen next.

Debby and I were home for summer vacation. I had just completed my fresh-man year, and she her junior year, at col-lege. Working in town gave us a chance to be together for the first time in years. It turned out that there was little choice for Debby. She had been having debilitating headaches for three or four months and after visiting the college health service and our family doctor, she was sure the problem was stress. She decided that she needed to relax. Debby had been taking a very full course load at college and she had recently broken up with her boyfriend, whom she had been seeing for three years. It was a logical explanation, but it wasn't right.

One day she had a seizure, and every-thing changed. The neurologist said the CT scan showed a large tumor and the neuro-surgeon said it would probably prove to be malignant. With surgery and radiation therapy, Debby might live. If she did, there was a good chance she would be paralyzed and unable to talk. Her rehabilitation would be very slow and she would require a great deal of support. All we hoped for was that she would have a chance to face the rehabilitation.

## FACING DEATH

The possibility of death hangs over every-one, but death is particularly salient to those who are ill. Any illness or injury that carries more than a negligible chance of mortality brings a terrifying confrontation with the fact that one's life may be cut short. In some cases death can be almost a certain outcome.

Facing his or her own death is probably the most difficult task of an individual's de-velopment. Death brings the loss of every-one and everything that a person loves. Every aspect of life that one has taken for granted may suddenly seem intensely valuable. The certainty of its loss is acutely painful (Kübler-Ross, 1969).

Certainly, one's feelings about death depend partly upon how one conceives of death in the first place, and particularly upon how much one fears death. Those with a strong spiritual orientation are often very much at peace in the last days of their lives because their worldview holds that there is an afterlife during which they will be happy (Kübler-Ross, 1969). Often fear of death reflects an individual's inability to face the incompleteness of his or her life. Death may seem like a premature and unfair revoking of one's potential (Kübler-Ross, 1969).

A surgeon stricken with Hodgkins disease faced the possibility of a premature death: "Mixed into all this fear was the overwhelming grief of the knowledge that I might not have a chance to see how it all turned out. . . . To be absent from all the important milestones in my wife's and children's lives was a sad thing to contemplate" (Shlain, 1979, p. 177).

## THE RESEARCH ON DYING

Until only about two decades ago, the psychological reactions of the terminally ill were virtually ignored by medical professionals. Even when a patient's condition was obviously hopeless, most physicians would act as if the issue of dying were irrelevant. They would continue to fight the disease (on the battleground of the patient's body) long past the point of any hope for recovery. At best, the family might be told to get the patient's affairs in order. But the patient would face a conspiracy of silence, denied the truth and denied the chance to choose the way he or she preferred to spend the last days of life.

The pioneering work of psychiatrist Elizabeth Kübler-Ross changed this situation a great deal (Kübler-Ross, 1969). She

Dr. Elizabeth Kübler-Ross.
SOURCE: Kathy Haas

demonstrated clearly that most dying patients were already well aware that they were terminally ill, even though no one had told them explicitly. They knew that they were not getting better, and they received many clues from the behavior of others toward them. Their physicians would avoid their questions and spend very little time with them. Their family members would try to smile but have tears in their eyes. Kübler-Ross found that not only were dying people able to hear the truth, they desperately wanted to talk about their feelings about dying.

Thanks to the work of Kübler-Ross, attitudes toward dying patients have changed dramatically. Now almost all physicians tell patients the complete truth about their medical conditions. They tell them the likely prognosis and what is the best and the worst that can be expected. Many physicians try hard to do this in a compassionate and supportive manner. Nurses and other medical professionals, such as psychologists and social workers, are also available to terminally ill patients to help them accept and deal emotionally with their prognosis.

Researchers in the field of *thanatology* (the study of death and dying) have learned a great deal about how people react psychologically to terminal illness (Kastenbaum, 1977; Kastenbaum & Aisenberg, 1972; Kübler-Ross, 1969). Initially, many people attempt to deny the facts they have learned or else to deny the meaning of those facts. For example, a patient may be told that he is suffering a recurrence of his leukemia and that the chance of experiencing another remission (temporary arresting of the disease) is very low. The patient's reaction, however, is *denial*. The day after hearing the news, he asks his doctors when he can leave the hospital to go back to work. When questioned, he can remember nothing of what he was told. When told again, he laughs as if he were hearing a joke. He explains to the doctors that his chart was mixed up with that of a person who is really dying, *and he believes it*. He takes actions that do not follow from the information he has been given, such as making commitments to do things many months or years hence. The patient's denial stems from tremendous anxiety and represents an attempt to keep the threatening facts from entering his consciousness.

Denial can be easily mislabeled, however. The patient who knows and acknowledges the truth but prefers to put it out of his or her mind while trying to do all he or she can to improve the chances of survival is not exhibiting denial but taking positive action.

The patient's immersion in denial may wax and wane. Sometimes he or she will gradually allow into consciousness the threatening details of the condition and the meaning of those details. As time passes, more and more of the information may be accepted and incorporated into his or her emotional life.

Some patients become extremely angry when they receive a diagnosis of terminal illness. *Anger* sometimes follows denial as the individual becomes overwhelmed with anxiety. The angry terminally ill patient may threaten to sue the doctor or make accusations of incompetence. An angry patient may seek second, third, and fourth opinions. Such anger can have both good and bad consequences. The angry patient may be motivated to find the best health professionals available to treat the problem. He or she may insist on the best treatments, and because of active involvement in getting the things needed, may actually survive longer (Derogatis, Abeloff, & Melasaratos, 1979). The anger may be a manifestation of the will to live and to fight for life. But expressions of anger can alienate those close to the patient and drive them away.

Some patients engage in *bargaining* in an effort to survive. A patient might volunteer to participate in a research project and serve as a subject to test a new drug. The patient assumes the role of a "guinea pig" in an effort to achieve a cure. This kind of behavior may be quite rational, for it may actually increase the patient's chances of surviving. Other forms of bargaining may have a less direct effect. The religious patient might promise to be a better person and lead a perfect life if only given another chance. Such thoughts might make him or her feel better emotionally but may prevent taking truly effective action to increase the chances of survival.

*Depression* is a likely response to a terminal prognosis. Depression may occur immediately or it may take some time to set in. Usually, after many failed efforts to change the course of the terminal illness, a patient whose prognosis remains poor is likely to become quite depressed. Depression, of course, might be the initial reaction of a patient who has given up without a fight. Some mental health professionals argue that depression is an inevitable, and perhaps even necessary, state for the terminally ill patient to experience. But depression comes at great cost: it involves giving up. Depressed people no longer fight for survival, and they may miss opportunities to live the remainder of their lives in the best way that they can.

Some patients arrive at *acceptance* of the inevitability of death in a peaceful manner and strive to understand the meaning of their own lives. The patient who arrives at an acceptance of inevitable death usually withdraws emotionally from the world and becomes less and less involved in life. After experiencing considerable pain and exhaustion fighting for life, the patient might finally come to see death as a welcome relief.

The five reactions examined above are exhibited by many, though by no means all, dying patients. The reactions were originally proposed by Dr. Kübler-Ross as stages, although the theory has been revised by others who have followed her in the study of death and dying. Clinical observation has shown that although some patients do experience these five reactions in the order they have been described— denial, anger, bargaining, depression, and acceptance—many patients do not. The order of reactions, and indeed whether they appear at all, can be influenced by, among other things, the characteristics of the terminal disease or condition. For example, a remission may bring the patient who has accepted the inevitability of death back to the stage of denial that he or she has a serious disease at all. Consider, too, the reactions of the following patient who has progressed rapidly to an acceptance of death.

■ ■ ■ ■ ■

The partner of Officer Catherine Parker suffered third-degree burns over almost all of his body. Shortly after the trauma of the explosion, his nerve endings and his brain did not yet register the excruciating pain that was to come. He was conscious and aware of what the burn specialist said to him. He had a relatively small chance of surviving, but if everything possible was done for him, he might make it. The treatment would involve constant, horrible pain, mostly unrelieved by even the most powerful painkillers. He would never again be close to what one would call "normal." His entire body would be covered with scar tissue. He might never be able to walk again. But he would be alive. If no heroic measures were taken, he would die soon and fairly peacefully. Which way did he want to go?

Ken had no family. His work was his life, and he would never be able to be a police officer again. If he could not live his life on his own terms, he said, he did not want to compromise.

Although patients' reactions to terminal illness can be quite idiosyncratic, understanding the range of reactions that people have to a terminal prognosis can be very helpful. Such knowledge can help family members, health professionals, and patients themselves who are confused or distressed by such reactions.

## PHYSICAL LIMITATIONS IN THE PROCESS OF DYING

So far we have examined what goes on in the mind of the patient who is facing terminal illness. In a sense we have looked only at the abstract psychological issues, without taking into account the practical limitations that inevitably occur when we deal with real people and real illness. This point can be best illustrated with an example.

Suppose you knew for sure that you had six months to live. Most likely you would try to spend the time in a way that is enjoyable and meaningful for you. You might quit school and take a trip around the world, pay off old debts, or even run up new ones. You might do things you had always been afraid to try.

This, of course, is an abstract consideration. It assumes that your physical condition makes it possible to carry out your plans. However, by its very nature terminal illness often prevents the patient from spending the remaining time in ways that he or she wishes. The patient may be very weak and sick, requiring a great deal of medical and nursing care. Attempts to "buy more time" with treatments may mean hospitalization, which significantly limits freedom. By and large, people who are seriously ill are not able to enjoy all of their remaining time. Relatively healthy and functional time remaining between diagnosis and the end of life may be extremely limited and precious.

## UNCERTAINTY

For those who are in remission from a fatal disease, and who do feel relatively (albeit possibly temporarily) well, there are different problems. The physical tortures give way to the psychological ones. People in remission are plagued by tremendous uncertainty about the most important of issues: their own survival.

How should one spend one's time? Should one go back to work, seeing one's children only evenings and weekends, or quit work and take them around the world? Almost invariably there are differing opinions from doctors about when one is likely to die. There are no certainties. The patient "plays the odds" and takes risk with the time, not knowing how much of it remains.

A patient whose cancer was technically in remission, perhaps soon to recur, perhaps to be gone forever, noted:

> Suppose I live my life as if everything is going to be fine. In that case, if it isn't . . . I will have done the wrong thing. So my mind travels on two tracks. The main one is that I'm all right, but the other one is always there cautioning me to be prudent, spend time with my family, take many vacations and try to live a quality life, and God knows that's hard enough to do. (Shlain, 1979, p. 182)

## LONELINESS

Dr. Elizabeth Kübler-Ross once pointed out that of all the fears that dying patients have, the greatest one is the fear of being left alone and abandoned. Such a fear is well founded, for social isolation and loneliness are indeed major problems for the terminally ill. Their isolation stems from several sources. First, those who are dying are often afraid to talk with their loved ones about what is foremost on their minds. They may be afraid to burden their loved ones, or to "break down" emotionally. Terminally ill people also have difficulty maintaining normal social relationships because they take on a very distressing identity, that of a dying person. Sometimes other people even display impatience, as if it were too much for them to bear the emotional burden of having someone around who reminds them of their own mortality.

Box 14–1 describes children's experiences of terminal illness.

Let us turn now to examine in more detail the interpersonal aspects of serious illness and dying. So far, we have examined principally what the terminally ill patient thinks and feels. But while the process of dying is a very personal event, it is an interpersonal event as well. Death and dying carry tremendous meaning for the members of the patient's family and network of close friends. Death and dying are closely entwined with interpersonal relationships.

# Death and the Family

Loss of a loved one through death can be emotionally devastating. The death of a family member or close friend is one of the most stressful life events that a person can experience and the recovery process can be long and very painful.

An important topic in the field of health psychology is the study of the impact, both psychological and physical, of loss through death. Because such loss represents a naturally stressful event, psychologists can even begin to unravel some of the mysteries

**BOX 14–1**

## TERMINALLY ILL CHILDREN

Can a child really understand what it means to die? What is the process of dying like for a child?

These are important questions to ask if the psychological needs of a terminally ill child are to be met by the parents and medical professionals. Misconceptions about his or her psychological state and understanding of death can leave the child who is dying quite lonely and emotionally abandoned. What the child can be told, however, is partly dependent upon his or her level of development and upon what he or she can understand.

Very young children, particularly those under age 5, conceive of death inaccurately. Perhaps because they see cartoon characters blown to bits one minute and running around the next, they believe that death is not permanent. Death seems to be an event that happens ("I'll shoot you dead") and then life goes on as usual. Death may be associated with something scary because of Halloween ghosts and the terrifying presentation of death in horror movies. Those who are somewhat older, say between 5 and 9, are more convinced that death is permanent but cannot accept that it is inevitable. They believe that death can be fought or escaped (Kastenbaum, 1977; Nagy, 1948). Although the full meaning of their own death is not yet grasped by young children, those who are terminally ill are indeed affected psychologically. The behavior of others toward them can influence their feelings quite significantly.

Finally, by the age of 9 or 10, children develop a clearer understanding of the permanence and the inevitability of death. Their concept of death is much closer to that held by an adult.

Despite the limitations in their concept of death, many children recognize that their own death will involve separation from their loved ones and protectors. They need a tremendous amount of reassurance that their parents and other people they depend upon will not abandon them. Often this involves allowing them to express their dependency and to have constant companionship. Terminally ill children may regress in their emotional development and become extremely dependent. For parents, siblings, and other family members, the child's need for closeness and dependency may be painful and difficult to maintain because of their own anticipation of the loss of the child. Yet, for the child's sake they must continue to treat him or her in a loving and consistent manner for as long as he or she is alive. Every attempt must be made to provide the information the child desires in an understandable form, and to aid the child in reducing his or her anxiety and fear of the unknown.

of psychoneuroimmunology examined in Chapter 10. Psychologists who study the aftereffects of a death are also able to learn what constitutes the normal and the abnormal aspects of the process of coping, and to determine when intervention in the form of supportive therapy may be needed. They also provide important information and training to medical professionals who encounter death nearly every day.

Understanding the effects of death on survivors is also essential if medical professionals are to intervene in an effective manner to help survivors cope. Medical professionals are typically closely involved when someone dies. These days about 80% of deaths in the United States occur with at least several weeks warning, and in most cases health-care professionals are involved with the patient and with the patient's family (Osterweis, Solomon, & Green, 1984). Medical professionals typically serve some function even when a death occurs suddenly. Victims of automobile and other vehicle accidents, drownings, and violent assaults are usually brought to hospitals, where, if they cannot be resuscitated, they are pronounced dead. The family is usually informed of the death by a physician or nurse. Thus, in most cases, health professionals have at least some contact with those who experience a loss through death of a loved one.

The extent of a health professional's contribution, of course, depends upon the nature of his or her relationship to the patient's family members and other loved ones. At the very least, health professionals can provide information and education. In many cases they can provide emotional support as well. They can help to recognize clinically abnormal patterns of reactions and adjustment in those who have suffered a loss so that those who need help can be given referrals to mental health professionals.

During a patient's terminal illness, staff members, physicians, and nurses who care for him or her can effectively establish themselves as resource persons for the family and friends of the patient. Much can be done during the period of terminal illness to facilitate the adjustment of those to be left behind. Clarification of the patient's physical situation, accurate information about the cause of the condition, as well as ongoing updates of the patient's care, can be extremely important. Physicians can arrange for extended visiting hours and time without instrusions by the bureaucracy of the hospital so that patient and family can have privacy to talk openly with one another.

Thus, it is important for health-care professionals to understand the experience of survivors, as well as to learn ways to help survivors cope with their own physical and emotional reactions. Often preparation can do much to help the surviving person cope with the complex and often distressing outcomes of a death. (See Box 14–2 on hospice care.)

# Bereavement and Grieving

## DEFINITIONS AND INCIDENCE

Let us first define some important terms that we will be using in this section. *Bereavement* is the fact of loss through death. A person who survives the death of a loved one is bereaved. *Bereavement reactions* are psychological, physical, or behavioral responses to bereavement. As bereavement reactions emerge over time, there is a *process of bereavement* that unfolds. *Grief* is the feeling or affective state associated with the condition of bereavement.

How common is bereavement? In any given year, between 5% and 9% of the general population is bereaved (Osterweis et al., 1984). In one survey of 455 men with an average age of 35, 8.9% had lost a family member to death sometime in the previous year (Imboden, Canter, & Cluff, 1961). Annually, roughly 5% of the general population experiences bereavement from the death of a parent (Pearlin & Lieberman, 1979).

## THE GRIEF EXPERIENCE

■ ■ ■ ■ ■

Claire Franklin's husband died suddenly of a heart attack. Although she knew he had heart disease, his death came as a tremendous shock to her. Claire felt like she was losing her mind. She expressed fears that she was going crazy, yet what she experienced was well within the range of normal acute grief reactions. She ate almost nothing. The thought of food repulsed her. Her sleep was seriously affected; if she was lucky, she slept fitfully for three or four hours a night. Many nights she could not sleep at all. She walked around for weeks feeling numb and dazed, remembering little if anything of what people said to her.

BOX
14–2

## HOSPICES

Earlier in this century most terminally ill people died at home amidst their family members and friends, close to the day-to-day routines they enjoyed and with which they were familiar. Opportunities presented themselves constantly for loved ones to visit, express their deep feelings, and say goodbye. Children naturally learned the meaning of death and watched the transition of grandparents and other people they loved through old age to final peace.

But since the advent of technological medicine (roughly the 1950s), the process of dying has become hidden away in acute-care hospitals where there may be little if any acknowledgment that a patient's death is soon to come. Efforts are undertaken to resuscitate patients who will never get well. Death occurs amidst machines and strangers.

In the midst of the modern hospital's approach to dying, a powerful grassroots movement began in about 1975 in the United States. Proponents argued for and helped to promote an alternative to aggressive hospital care for the terminally ill. This alternative is called the *hospice*. The number of hospices in the United States has grown in the past ten years from under 100 to several thousand.

In a hospice, it is not the patient alone who is treated but the patient and the family. The focus is not on cure but on alleviation of symptoms, particularly pain. The atmosphere is homelike, and patients have considerable autonomy in making decisions about their care. Attention is given not only to the requirements for physical care but also to the emotional, social, and spiritual needs of the patient and family.

Hospice care is available in this country in inpatient settings as well as in home care (which involves visits from the staff daily or several times a week). Hospice services are provided by multidisciplinary teams of physicians, nurses, social workers, psychiatrists, psychologists, and physical therapists. Many hospices also provide some bereavement intervention, in preparation for the death as well as after the death, in an effort to promote adjustment among loved ones of the deceased. In all hospices a great deal of attention is paid to the quality of the patient's life. Family members are encouraged to speak openly with the terminally ill loved one. There is an effort, in a supportive atmosphere, to promote closeness and expressions of love while the opportunity still exists to do so.

She had almost no recollection of the funeral or who was in attendance.

What disturbed her most were the recurring dreams and hallucinations she had of her late husband. She awakened several times at three or four o'clock in the morning to a vision of him sitting next to her. She thought she heard his voice. Sometimes she felt him sleeping near her. Once she was fully awake and aware of her surroundings, however, each hallucination disappeared.

The grief reaction can be overwhelming to a person, both psychologically and physically. Not only is a person's mind affected but his or her biological homeostasis is interrupted as well. Researchers have systematically observed and measured changes in emotions, thought patterns, and behaviors during grief. They have witnessed intense physical and psychological reactions. Although there is substantial individual variation in grief reactions, there are also many commonalities (Parkes, 1970; Parkes & Weiss, 1983; Raphael, 1983).

One of the most frequent responses following death, regardless of whether or not the loss was anticipated, is shock, numbness, and a sense of disbelief. Initially, those left behind feel as though things around them are unreal. They may express no emotion and appear to be holding up quite well. Illusions and misperceptions appear often in this early stage. There may be dreams in which the deceased person is still alive, and terrifying hallucinations. However, once the bereaved person comes to an emotional acceptance that the deceased person is really gone, these illusions usually diminish in frequency and eventually cease to occur. Then the grieving person experiences difficulty concentrating, feelings of anger, guilt, irritability, restlessness, extreme sadness, and a severely depressed mood.

During the period of acute grief the bereaved person's movements are often slowed down, and he or she may have a slumped posture. Sometimes there is alternating agitation, restlessness, and increased motor activity. During periods of despair the bereaved person may give up favorite activities and avoid socializing. Some may engage in excessive smoking and drinking and other health-compromising behaviors, particularly if they had been users of such substances before the death. These and other risk-taking behaviors likely represent an attempt to defend against the painful feelings of grief rather than to accept and work through them. It is important to note that although grief and depression appear similar in terms of the individual's behavior, they are quite different in an important way. Both depression and grief involve sadness and vegetative signs, but in depression there are feelings of unworthiness, or worthlessness, and negative beliefs and thoughts about the self.

Certain biological events occur during the grieving process as well. Like many other severe stressors, grief frequently leads to changes in the endocrine, immune, autonomic nervous, and cardiovascular systems. There have been some important studies of biological variables in grieving human beings (Lindemann, 1944; Parkes, 1972; Clayton, 1974). These studies give a picture of the physiological and behavioral symptoms of grief. The acute symptoms come in waves of distress lasting minutes and including agitation, crying, aimless activity, preoccupation with an image of the deceased, tears, sighing respirations, and muscular weakness. Chronic disturbances lasting weeks to months include decreased concentration, anxiety, altered food intake, changes in body weight, sleep disturbances, muscular weakness, and endocrine and immunologic changes. Studies show, for example, that those most distressed by their loss had greater plasma levels of hormones that are triggered by stress (prolactin, growth hormone, and ACTH). Although no connection has yet been firmly established on empirical grounds, a few studies have begun to show that in the immune system, grief results in impaired functioning of T lymphocytes, the agents of cell-mediated immunity (Bartrop et al., 1977). Such hormonal changes and disturbances in immune functioning are believed to pave the way for greater susceptibility to bacterial and viral infections, as well as to the development of neoplasms (cancers) (see Chapter 10).

The strongest effects of bereavement seem to be on the cardiovascular system. Sudden cardiac death, cardiac arrhythmias, myocardial infarction, and congestive heart failure are the most frequent life-threatening conditions associated with grief. They are thought to be accounted for by disturbances in autonomic cardiovascular regulation and in circulating catecholamines (such as adrenalin), which may exaggerate danger and risk in patients who have preexisting cardiovascular regulation problems about which they may not even have been aware. Patients with heart conditions and hypertension are particularly prone to exacerbation of these conditions in response to threatened or actual loss of a human relationship (Osterweis et al., 1984).

The process of grieving involves development from a state of disbelief to one of gradual acceptance. This change does not occur in a straightforward fashion, however. The grieving person may go back and forth many times from avoidance of thinking about the deceased to cultivation of the person's memory, from acceptance of the passing to immersion in a world of fantasies and dreams in which the deceased person is still alive. It may take a bereaved person several months, or even more than a year, to control his or her depression and mood swings and to become settled emotionally. It may be a long time before there is an emotional acceptance that the loved one is really dead. Eventually, the grieving

person is able to recall the deceased without being overwhelmed by sadness or other distressing emotions, and for him or her to feel ready to become involved in the world again. Close to complete recovery may take as long as two and a half years in the normal process of adjustment (Shlain, 1979).

Bereavement, of course, can bring changes in a person's social status, (for example, from being married to being widowed, or from being a parent to being childless). The bereaved person may have had opportunities to socialize as part of a couple but finds no such opportunities as a single person. If friendships involved the person who is deceased, making new friends may be very difficult.

The end of the grieving process can be called *recovery* or *adaptation*. The person is certainly changed by the loss, so recovery is never complete. The word *adaptation* suggests that the bereaved person makes the best of an unpleasant situation. There may be investment in current life, renewed hopefulness, the capacity to experience gratification, and adjustment to new roles, but the sense of loss may never be completely overcome.

## THE OUTCOMES OF GRIEVING

The process of grieving sometimes results in outcomes that threaten the bereaved individual's stability and forestall his or her recovery. Sometimes a person who has been bereaved may, many years after the death, express his or her psychological pain in physical symptoms. Acute grief is often associated with physical complaints including pain, gastrointestinal disturbances, and vegetative symptoms such as loss of energy, sleep disturbances, and appetite disturbances. Beyond these physical complaints, some bereaved persons identify with the deceased by taking on the symptoms that contributed to the loved one's death. One study found that 15% of bereaved persons reported feeling "just like" the person who died. Eight percent had acquired habits of the deceased, 12% felt they had the same illness, and 9% had pains in the same area of the body as did the person who died (Zisook, Devand, & Click, 1982). Such physical symptoms may arise soon after, or many years after, the death and may reflect unresolved feelings of grief. When and if the grief is resolved, the symptoms usually disappear.

Anniversary reactions can be particularly troubling. The feelings and symptoms triggered by bereavement can recur around birthdays, anniversaries, holidays, and circumstances that are reminders of the deceased. Anniversaries can even trigger serious pathological reactions in vulnerable persons (Pollock, 1970).

Reinvestment in new relationships, particularly remarriage, seem to signal acceptance and adjustment to the death. Sometimes, however, even though such apparent social adaptation has occurred, emotional adaptation may still be far behind. For example, many widowed men seemingly recover socially and even remarry well before they have emotionally recovered from their loss. Women, on the other hand, tend to delay social reinvestment, avoiding dating and remarriage until they have healed emotionally (Parkes & Weiss, 1983).

Not all outcomes of bereavement are negative. Bereavement can have positive, growth-producing effects. For example, successful completion of grieving can result, for creative people, in increased creativity and productivity (Pollock, 1982). Some older women who have been in traditional marriages and are suddenly widowed can develop their potential substantially, assuming responsibility for their own lives and carrying out activities they had never been able to do before their loss.

The character of the relationship that the bereaved person had with the deceased is one of the best predictors of bereavement adjustment (Parkes & Weiss, 1983). If the bereaved felt a significant amount of hostility before the death, there is often a sense of remorse when the loved one dies. After marriages that were happy, bereaved persons are more likely to recover well. Those who had been in relationships with a high level of marital conflict were found to be twice as likely as others in low conflict relationships to be depressed, anxious, guilty, in poor health, and yearning for their deceased spouses as much as two to four years after the death (Parkes & Weiss, 1983).

## PATHOLOGICAL GRIEF

There are, of course, pathological outcomes of bereavement. Researchers have found that some people persist in the intensity of their grief reactions despite the passage of a great deal of time. They become mired in the grieving process, unable to diminish the intensity of their relationship with the deceased. Some experience excessive anger, guilt, self-blame, and depression far longer than usual. A person experiencing long-term, chronic grief may feel there is nothing left to look forward to. Roughly 12% to 15% of widowed people are still severely clinically depressed a year after the death (Parkes & Weiss, 1983).

Complete lack of involvement is a related problematic pattern for the bereaved person. Some individuals have a total absence of feeling after a death. They experience neither distress nor the typical symptoms of grief. They deny their feelings, and may even prevent other people from making references to the loss. They fend off threatening emotions that are too painful to bear. Typically, those who struggle with chronic grief feel too weak to undertake the tremendous emotional work of grieving. Instead, they may develop persistent symptoms of depression, sometimes masked for several years by a multitude of physical complaints (Baur, 1988).

## ANTICIPATORY GRIEVING VERSUS SUDDEN DEATH

Is it easier to cope with a death that has been anticipated or one that has happened suddenly? After which type of death do survivors cope better? There is disagreement among experts about whether emotional responses to the *impending* death of a loved one are comparable to grief and therefore allow the individual to adjust gradually to the impending loss (Sweeting & Gilhooly, 1990). Some researchers argue that anticipatory grieving follows the same patterns of postdeath reactions. They note that during this anticipatory period, the person who will be left behind has a chance to disengage emotionally from the dying individual (Brown & Stoudemire, 1983). But other researchers have found that persons threatened with loss typically develop even more intense attachment to their loved ones who are dying, making it even more difficult to separate later (Parkes & Weiss, 1983). This result may depend partly on the age of the bereaved. Research on spousal death shows, for example, that for younger people, sudden death (with less than two weeks' warning) is very traumatic and extremely difficult to adjust to. Younger people adjust better once bereaved if they have had considerable time to become accustomed to the idea of the loss. On the other hand, elderly people, many of whom are accustomed to the death of friends and relatives, adjust better to the sudden death of their spouses than to prolonged death. This may be because prolonged death can leave older survivors drained physically, financially, and emotionally from caring for their aged spouses (Parkes & Weiss, 1983).

# Bereavement in Adulthood

## BEING WIDOWED

Of all the conditions of bereavement, widowhood has received the most research attention. This research has looked not only at the special emotional difficulties of widowhood but also at the physical outcomes of spousal bereavement.

Researchers have found that the death of one's spouse is considered by most people to be among the most stressful of life events. Such a change in one's life is thought to bring tremendous difficulties and to require significant adjustment of life circumstances and expectations (Holmes & Masuda, 1974; Raphael, 1983).

Although several studies have certain methodological limitations (such as being retrospective or lacking a perfectly comparable control group), the evidence is quite strong that some people are at increased risk for mortality after the death of a spouse. One of the earliest studies on this topic examined death records and found that among people of younger ages (20s and 30s), the mortality rate of widowed people was strikingly higher than that of married people. The gap narrowed with increasing age of the widowed person, until in old age there was little difference between those married and those widowed in how likely they were to die (Kraus & Lilienfeld, 1959). Among persons under age 45, mortality of the widowed was found to be at least 7 times higher than mortality of those married. And mortality rates for widowed males were significantly higher than for widowed females. Widowed men were most likely to die of heart conditions, such as arteriosclerosis and myocardial degeneration, stroke, and respiratory diseases, such as tuberculosis and pneumonia. These are relatively unusual diseases for a young population. Death from cardiovascular disease was 10 times greater in widowed men than in married men of the same age.

A major prospective study of almost 92,000 persons was conducted in Maryland from 1963 to 1975. A group of individuals who became widowed during that time was matched to a married, nonwidowed group on race, sex, age, and many other factors, such as geographic location of residence

(Helsing, Szklo, & Comstock, 1981). Particularly among younger men there was greater mortality in the widowed group. This difference also occurred among middle-aged men, but not among those widowed after age 75. Mortality rates were found to be somewhat lower in those who remarried than in those who did not. The risk of death was also found to be greatest in the first year of widowhood. In addition, suicide rates were higher among widowed than among married men. In general, suicide among the widowed population was found to be 2.5 times higher than that among the married population in the first six months of bereavement and 1.5 times higher in the first, second, and third years of bereavement. Men were found to have a higher suicide rate than women.

There is little evidence, none of it conclusive, to link bereavement with subsequent psychiatric illness (Osterweis et al., 1984). There are somewhat higher rates of depression and use of counseling services, particularly among the younger bereaved than among comparable age groups of persons who are not bereaved (Parkes & Brown, 1972). It is estimated that approximately 15% of the bereaved still have a constellation of depressive symptoms a year after the death. Loss of a spouse is a huge life stressor likely to precipitate depression in those who are predisposed by virtue of family history or personality (Clayton, 1979).

Physicians are very likely to prescribe psychotropic (mood-altering) or sleeping medications to women who have been bereaved. One study found that after the death of a husband, women under 65 were 7 times more likely to get such a prescription than before the death (Parkes, 1964; Parkes & Weiss, 1983). The tranquilizers and hypnotic medications presented an opportunity for abuse and addiction. They also contributed to emotionally numbing the bereaved person and possibly preventing her from fully resolving her distress.

Studies of the effects of bereavement on illness behavior document somewhat less immediate physical expression of distress than one might expect. Although the widowed (particularly the young) tend to have more anxiety than do those who are married, resulting in a somewhat greater focus on some physical symptoms, no major changes or differences have been found between the groups in their use of health-care services or in their physical complaints for which no organic basis can be found (Osterweis et al., 1984.)

Certain existing physical problems can be seriously affected by the emotional stresses of bereavement, however. Patients with hypertension and congestive heart failure, for example, are especially prone to an exacerbation of their poor physical condition in response to bereavement (Osterweis et al., 1984). Of course, illness and death among the bereaved can be accounted for in many cases by a significant increase in poor health habits, such as failing to take necessary medications, smoking heavily, and drinking considerable alcohol. Alcohol use tends to increase among bereaved persons who are already at risk for alcohol abuse and alcoholism. Relatedly, bereaved persons, particularly men, report a significant increase in their use of tobacco and alcohol during the first 13 months after bereavement.

## THE SOCIAL IMPACT OF WIDOWHOOD

Why is the death of a spouse so stressful? The reason probably has to do with how intertwined the lives of married people often become. Spouses are co-managers of home and family. They jointly set family policy and either participate jointly in all aspects of running the family, or divide the tasks so that one person is primarily breadwinner while the other takes care of the household and the daily needs of the children. Spouses are sexual partners, and if the relationship is close, best friends to and emotionally supportive of one another as well. The spouses are fellow members of larger social units, such as the extended family, the community of parents in their children's school, their circle of friends, and perhaps their church or community organization. Because of these social connections, the death of a spouse sometimes leaves the widowed person excluded from the sociability of couples. He or she may feel abandoned and left to function without the help of a partner. Responsibilities that were once shared become the sole responsibility of the survivor. In many cases the individual left behind is not prepared to take over certain activities because he or she may know nothing about how to do them. Further, widowed parents are often overwhelmed with their children's demands for attention and understanding. The widowed parent sometimes must subordinate his or her own grief reactions in order to help children deal with their own feelings at having lost a parent.

Compared to the research on widowhood, little has been done on other forms of bereavement in adulthood. Let us turn to an examination of these other losses, of a parent, a sibling, and a child.

## DEATH OF A PARENT

Losing a parent to death is a common phenomenon. As noted earlier, at any given time, approximately 5% of the U.S. adult population has suffered parental bereavement within the previous year. Losing a parent can affect some people quite intensely. In one study half of the 75 people who committed suicide in West Sussex, Great Britain, had experienced maternal bereavement in the previous three years (Bunch, Barraclough, Nelson, & Sainsbury, 1971). Single men were found to be at highest risk for suicide following the deaths of their mothers. This may be because men are more likely to "act out" their distress, whereas women seek medical and psychi-

atric help following the death of a parent. Although there has been little systematic research on the subject, clinicians agree that the death of a parent is a serious life event that leads in many cases to measurable distress (Osterweis et al., 1984). It is noted by clinicians that more often the death of a mother is harder to sustain than the death of a father, possibly because of the mother's early role as nurturer. This may be the case, too, because in 75% of couples, the husband dies first. The bereaved children may be most upset with the second loss (more often the mother) because both parents are then deceased.

Although the death of one's parents during one's adulthood may be preferable to such a loss during one's childhood, the death of a parent can still be quite difficult to cope with. Such a death may mean the loss of the only person in the world who accepts one unconditionally. Such a death may be perceived as a developmental push to the next stage of adulthood in which one becomes a member of the oldest generation in the family (Osterweis et al., 1984).

## DEATH OF A SIBLING

There is a striking absence of data about adults' reactions to the death of a brother or sister. In many cases, however, the empathy that siblings develop for one another in childhood continues into adulthood and the loss is quite significant. Sibling relationships tend to assume greater importance in old age than they did in earlier life. Many elderly siblings live together or at least maintain close contact. Such a loss in old age can be a devastating event (Osterweis et al., 1984). Loss of a sibling tends to increase an individual's fears of his or her own mortality. The death of a sibling who had most responsibility for aging parents or for other duties, such as maintaining contact among members of the family, can cause significant shifts in the responsibilities of others. Also, the death of a sibling may cause those who remain to develop closer bonds and to appreciate one another more.

## DEATH OF A CHILD

Death of any loved one is difficult to deal with, but researchers and clinicians agree that the death of one's child is by far the most painful. These days people expect that their children will live to adulthood. Nevertheless, 400,000 children (under age 25) die each year in the United States, most often from accidents, suicide, murder, and some devastating diseases, such as cancer. Further, as more and more parents live to very old age, the experience of premature death of their middle-aged children is becoming more common.

When a person outlives his or her child, he or she is faced with loss of a major investment in the life and happiness of another person of the next generation. Consciously or not, people have dreams, wishes, and hopes for their children's futures. Their feelings of guilt and self-blame are also very prominent because people feel responsible for keeping their children well and safe and protecting them from harm (Gorer, 1965; Videka-Sherman, 1982).

Let us consider the deaths of children at different ages, for they typically generate different reactions in parents.

A *stillbirth*, in which a fetus dies *in utero* late in pregnancy or during labor and delivery, can be an extremely painful emotional experience for young parents. Typically the mother, and in many cases both parents, have bonded closely to the new life and the loss can be very traumatic. The grieving process for those who have experienced stillbirth is, however, a "conspiracy of silence" (Osterweis et al., 1984). Until recently medical professionals believed that it was better for a mother not to discuss her loss. Many physicians sedated the mother so much that she could not feel anything

emotionally, and could not even cry. She was not allowed to see her baby. Recent research has shown, however, that the silence surrounding a bereaved mother intensifies her feelings of guilt and makes the death "unspeakable," confirming, in a sense, that it is too terrible to talk about (Stringham, Riley, & Ross, 1982). Mothers who have lost babies confirm the loneliness they feel because they alone have known the baby intimately. They feel tremendous guilt that they may have been responsible, and a loss of self-esteem that they could not produce a healthy baby. Recently, medical professionals have learned that it is best if parents have visual and physical contact with the dead infant to facilitate the process of grieving. It is even helpful for them to take pictures of and gather locks of hair from the infant to remind themselves later that the baby really existed as a member of their family.

*Miscarriage* (death of the fetus in the earlier months of pregnancy, before it can be expected to live outside the mother's body) presents a variation of the loss from stillbirth. Although the parents may have had less time to become attached to the fetus, the reactions they have after such a loss are usually quite intense. Fetal loss, even as early as six or eight weeks of gestation, can have a significant emotional impact on parents. As soon as the pregnancy is confirmed, there is investment in the future and in fantasies of the new life. Miscarriage involves lost hope for a particular future and loss of a potential family member.

Unlike stillborns, babies who live for a few days or a few weeks are accorded personhood, given names, held, talked to, talked about, and visited by members of the extended family. Such a death can be quite traumatic for parents, who may need to be involved in complex decisions about care during the perinatal period. They may be required to approve interventions that have only a small chance of saving their infants and that carry tremendous risk. Although there may be somewhat more support for parents who experience perinatal death than for those who suffer after a stillbirth, many people in the parents' social network may ignore the death and try to avoid discussing it. The parents are left alone to deal with their complex emotions of guilt, anger, sadness, and relief.

Crib death (*sudden infant death syndrome*, or *SIDS*) is the most common cause of death in the first year of an infant's life after the perinatal period. SIDS accounts for one-third of all deaths of infants between one week and one year of age. It occurs in two to three babies per 1000 in the United States; nearly 10,000 babies die of SIDS each year. The peak incidence of death is between 2 and 4 months of age. Almost all SIDS deaths occur before 6 months of age. Babies with SIDS die in their sleep with no forewarning and no audible noise. Babies have died with an adult right near them in the room, unaware that anything was happening. Parents report that their baby who has died was perfectly fine just moments before the death. Although early theories about the cause of SIDS have ranged from the type of feeding (breast versus bottle) to the type of bedclothes used and the temperature of the room, all such theories have been overthrown by empirical data. Currently, researchers believe that the cause of SIDS is a problem with the brain mechanism that controls breathing and sleep. Although autopsies of these infants show pulmonary congestion and swelling, there has been no established connection with a viral or bacterial agent.

The family that loses a baby to SIDS suffers a tremendous tragedy. The parents usually feel terribly guilty and personally responsible for the death. Emergency personnel, neighbors, and even the police and press may add to parents' feelings of guilt and blame by questioning the circumstances that surround the death. Parents are most helped by those who recognize the SIDS condition and are careful to tell parents clearly that there was nothing they could have done to prevent the death. Without action to forestall their feelings of responsibility and their fears, parents may suffer tremendously.

Although deaths are less common among older children than among infants, accidents are the most frequent cause (45%), followed by leukemia and other cancers (18%). Children and adolescents who die have well-formed personalities and represent more "real loss" than "fantasy loss" to their parents. They leave a large store of memories. Not surprisingly, a commonly expressed emotion among bereaved parents is anger. The loss of a child compared with loss of other family members results in more intense grief reactions of the somatic type as well as more feelings of depression and despair. Bizarre responses and suicidal thoughts have been found to be common. Parents report feeling totally vulnerable, having suffered a blow from which they believe they may never recover (Osterweis et al., 1984). The course of bereavement for parents can be considerably longer than for those otherwise bereaved (Osterweis et al., 1984). Grief sometimes intensifies rather than diminishes over time, and may last for several years.

The parents of children dying of a terminal illness tend to recover better when they feel they have participated in the care of the terminally ill child. Research has shown somewhat less difficulty among parents whose children have died at home rather than at a hospital. Such parents are far less likely to experience marital strain (Lauer, Mulhern, Wallskog, & Camitta, 1983). Of course, the determining factor may not have been the hospital versus the home environment at all but, rather, a selection factor. Preexisting personality and attitude factors probably influenced some parents to choose home instead of hospital care for their children.

Parents generally experience significant problems in grieving for a child. "Having a child die can have a devastating effect on a marriage" (Osterweis et al., 1984, p. 81). A good marriage with strong communication can become stronger with the terminal illness or sudden death of a child, but it is not uncommon for marriages to break down under the strain. For example, marital discord and divorce occur in 50% to 70% of families in which a child dies of cancer. One reason for the discord may be the fact that the two parents often have different styles of grieving, and the spouses may not understand one another. For example, mothers tend to express more outward signs of sorrow, such as crying and appearing depressed; fathers express more anger but typically attempt to control and to hide their feelings and "take things like a man." In doing so, however, they may appear to their wives as cold and unsupportive, and as unaffected by the loss of the child. Medical and psychological professionals can do a great deal to help bereaved parents understand their own and each other's emotional reactions to their loss.

# Bereavement During Childhood and Adolescence

Bereavement during childhood or adolescence can be an important factor in later emotional and personality development. A child's understanding of the meaning of death varies with age, and a full understanding of death may not be arrived at until roughly age 9. Therefore, the precise effect that bereavement has on a child depends upon level of development and therefore on degree of understanding of the loss.

Bereavement during childhood or adolescence does not automatically result in difficulties. The full impact of the loss of a loved one hinges upon a variety of factors: the closeness of the relationship, the degree of disruption in the child's day-to-day life, the emotional reactions of others around him or her, including the continued ability of remaining loved ones to provide the child with emotional support. Early research that showed the effects of parental loss to be devastating (for example, Bowlby, 1961) focused on children who, upon the loss of their parents, were placed in institutions. Their losses were multiple, including loss of familiar persons, removal from the home environment, and unfamiliar and sometimes chaotic circumstances of institutional placement. But, as we will see, current research suggests that the effects of loss need not be devastating, and under certain circumstances can be minimized.

Children typically experience a wide range of emotions and behaviors following the death of a parent, sibling, or grandparent who was involved in the child's life. After such a death, young children often become sad, angry, and fearful. They experience appetite and sleep disturbances, difficulty concentrating, withdrawal, dependency, restlessness, aggressiveness, learning difficulties, and/or regression to an earlier stage of development. There is often a marked effect on their school performance. After loss of a sibling, children have been found to exhibit guilt reactions, most likely because they fear that their rivalrous feelings and aggressive wishes toward the sibling have actually come true. Some children exhibit crying and sadness as many as five or more years after the death. Forty percent of children in one study had prolonged or "anniversary" hysterical identification with the prominent symptoms of the dead sibling (Cain, Fast, & Erickson, 1964). Delinquency is not an uncommon reaction of children who are parentally bereaved, particularly in adolescence. Many experience a marked decrease in interest in school activities (Raphael, 1983). Some researchers suggest that there is an increase in neurosis and depression during adulthood among those who were bereaved in childhood or adolescence; however, this connection is not well established and is still being debated (Osterweis et al., 1984). Initial research is biased by the special characteristics of the clinical population studied (those who had already developed neurosis and depression).

It is important to understand the grieving process in children. One major research project studied children whose fathers had died. During the first year, they typically experienced tremendous pain, sadness, and anger. Depending upon their developmental level, some tried to explore the implications of the loss and tried to understand the concept of "dead." During the second year, they showed significant anxiety, as well as demanding, aggressive behavior. Some became restless and exhibited discipline problems. In subsequent years they manifested considerable overdependency on their mothers (Elizur & Kaffman, 1982). Thirty-nine percent of the previously normal sample continued to show signs of emotional distress four years after the deaths of their fathers.

Children often assess themselves more negatively after a parent's death than before (Rochlin, 1965). Some children interpret a parent's death as desertion because the parent did not love them. They may believe that they are unlovable. Some develop a persistent low self-esteem. Following loss of a major relationship, such as a parent, sibling, or grandparent, children may see themselves as helpless, vulnerable, and frighteningly small. They may attempt to blame themselves for the loss in an effort to make the world appear more predictable

and controllable and less random than it would seem if the death occurred for reasons beyond their control (Furman, 1974).

Some children try to identify with the deceased, taking on his or her characteristics. For example, a boy whose father has died may try to become the "man of the house." Such activity can be both a reflection of and a cause of disturbance. The identification may result from the child's defending against normal feelings of grief. In addition, identification with an adult may cause the child to be rejected by his or her peer group. A child who tries to serve as a replacement for a deceased sibling might seriously interfere with his or her own natural course of development.

How can children be helped to deal with their grief? First of all, one must recognize that children who are bereaved often exhibit emotional expressions that are frightening or distressing to their parents. Children may become angry, anxious, clinging, and obstinate. Bereaved children may behave as if they trust no one. The world may seem to them unpredictable and unsafe, and they may need considerable help to rebuild their trust in relationships with others. Sometimes, a child idealizes the lost parent in fantasy and projects hostility onto the surviving parent. The surviving parent may even be accused of causing the death, or berated for not preventing it.

Most bereaved children have the following three questions in their minds, although they may not articulate them: Did I cause this to happen? Will it happen to me? Who will take care of me now? Someone close to the child, the surviving parent if the child is parentally bereaved, or both parents if the child has lost a sibling, must answer these questions in a sensitive and loving way. What the child understands must be carefully checked to be sure that there are no misconceptions that can cause harm.

Note that children go through the process of grief in stages just as adults do, but because of the effects of their developmental stages as well as their more "primitive" defenses (particularly the use of denial and regression) they have more difficulty coping with grief. For example, the continued fantasy that the dead parent really is still alive and waiting somewhere for the child will prevent the child from working through his or her feelings and coming to terms with the loss.

One of the best ways to help children cope with their grief is to help the surviving parents who are caretakers of those children. Parents need to know what to expect when children display their grief. Children often want to keep photographs and clothing of the deceased to remember him or her and to represent the relationship. Children also sometimes work through their understanding of a death by playing "funeral" or "undertaker." Such behavior can unnerve adults who are also suffering intensely from the loss. Children may tell strangers and relatives over and over again about the death, in an effort to master the situation. They may appear to have a light attitude toward something so serious, but children must alternate between sadness and less negative feelings in order not to be overwhelmed by emotions that are too intense for them to feel. They give up their attachments to people slowly and may take years before they have fully accepted the loss.

# Suicide

The loss of a close friend or family member is certainly very painful, but it can be even more so when the death was caused by suicide. More than 27,000 people commit suicide in the United States every year. This is a conservative estimate, of course, because many deaths of an ambiguous nature, such

as accidents, could easily have been suicide but are not labeled as such. Elderly white men have the highest suicide rates of all groups, but suicide cuts across all economic classes (Butler & Lewis, 1977).

As a result of suicide, many survivors are left to deal with some very complex feelings. Survivors are typically at greater risk for physical and mental health problems than are those who are bereaved in a nonsuicidal fashion. Suicide survivors often display bereavement reactions in exaggerated form. They may blame themselves or others for the death, insisting that they should have known about the impending act or done something to prevent it. Of course, sometimes those who commit suicide leave notes or other communications that directly blame survivors, who are then at considerable risk for guilt and unresolved distress. Survivors often fear that their own deaths will inevitably be caused by suicide because they too are vulnerable. Feelings of inevitability are unconscious, of course, and for children of suicide victims these feelings usually arise as they approach the age at which their parent committed suicide. The very fact that someone close has used suicide as a solution to overwhelming problems may legitimize it as a choice.

Children who have lost a significant person (parent, sibling, or grandparent) to suicide may be at risk for lifelong vulnerability to mental health problems as well as for suicide itself (Shepherd & Barraclough, 1976). Parental suicide may render children particularly vulnerable to suicidal thoughts and impulses, fearing that they too will die by suicide.

Probably more than any other bereaved group, survivors of suicide may need professional help. Unless the suicide was straightforwardly ascribed to an outside cause (such as the victim's terminal illness), professional psychotherapeutic intervention may be needed to help survivors to resolve their own conflicting and sometimes terrifying feelings about the deceased (Cain, 1972; Osterweis et al., 1984).

## IS SUICIDE PREVENTABLE?

Some suicides can actually be prevented if surrounding loved ones know what to look for in the behavior of the person. Researchers have been working to understand people who commit (or try to commit) suicide in order to learn why they do it and at what point they might have been stopped (Shneidman, 1985). The important new findings are based on information left behind (notes, diaries) by people who have been successful at committing suicide, on interviews with those who tried to kill themselves but survived, and on interviews with the bereaved.

Suicide is not a bizarre or incomprehensible act of self-destruction. Suicidal people have a particular style of thinking that brings them to the conclusion that death is the only answer to their problems. Steps can be taken to stop a suicide if one knows how and when to intervene.

Knowledge of the following ten common characteristics of a suicidal person (Shneidman, 1985) may actually be the most effective means of preventing suicide.

*1. Unendurable psychological pain.* Death represents an attempt to escape pain. Suicide might be prevented if the individual's pain can be reduced in whatever way possible, even just a little. With a lower level of suffering, a suicidal person will choose to live.

*2. Frustrated psychological needs.* The inner life of the suicidal person is desperately in need of something, such as security, achievement, trust, love, or friendship. The helper must find out what that is, and assist the person to see a way to get it.

*3. The need for a solution.* The suicidal person really thinks that death is the only way out of a problem or crisis. Other solutions might be suggested.

*4. A desire to end consciousness.* Suicide is often a move to stop awareness of a painful existence.

*5. Helplessness and hopelessness.* Underlying all the negative emotions felt by the individual is a sense of powerlessness and a belief that nobody can help. The last rays of hope are gone and there is nothing left to do but die.

*6. Constriction of options.* The suicidal person does not look for several ways he or she might solve the overwhelming problems. He or she sees dying as the only method.

*7. Ambivalence.* The suicidal person both wants and does not want to die; that is, at the same time that he or she may be trying to commit suicide, he or she is likely to be crying out in some way for help.

*8. Communication of intent.* About 80% of suicidal people give friends and family very clear clues that they intend to kill themselves. Many essentially say goodbye, put their affairs in order, even state that they can no longer endure their pain and intend to die. There is often a clear chance for intervention, particularly by preventing the person from obtaining the means to destroy himself or herself.

*9. Departure.* Suicidal people express a desire to escape. A helper can aid them to distinguish between the need to get away from everything (for example, leave a marriage, leave school) and the desire to die.

*10. Lifelong coping pattern.* How did the person endure psychological pain in the past? People who commit suicide are more likely to have a style of problem solving known as "cut and run." They end a marriage by walking out, end a job by quitting abruptly. Such actions suggest a need to

Rituals that surround death, such as the funeral, can help in adjustment to and recovery from loss.
SOURCE: © Michael Grecco/Stock, Boston

maintain control, which may be at the heart of the decision to commit suicide.

With information about why a person would choose to end his or her life, others may be able to help the person try a different approach to getting what is wanted and needed emotionally (Shneidman, 1981, 1985).

## Social and Cultural Influences on Bereavement

Bereavement is a social and cultural as well as a psychobiological phenomenon (Osterweis et al., 1984, p. 199).

Bereavement typically affects not just one individual but an entire group of persons. This was probably more true in the past, when societies were organized with great emphasis on kinship, extended family

households, and religion. Communities were small and kinship units tightly integrated. The death of an individual affected an entire community. Today the effect of one death is somewhat less pervasive. Yet one death can affect many people and bring them from different ends of a continent to share their common grief.

*Mourning* is the social expression of grief. In every society there are mourning rituals and associated behaviors. The wearing of black by the bereaved is an example. Because ethnic ties and religious ties today are so much less strong than they were several decades ago, there are fewer social prescriptions regarding behavior appropriate to grieving and mourning.

Rituals that surround death, such as the wake and funeral, can help in adjustment to and recovery from the loss and can help families to express their grief. Mourning rituals can help the bereaved to cope with their loss. For example, the funeral represents a coming together of those who knew the deceased to confirm the death and to validate it. People express support for one another and especially for those closest to the deceased. The mourning rituals, in fact, signal changes in self-concept and transitions to new stages of personal identity (for example, from wife to widow). These rituals provide for public articulation of private distress and a reassertion of values, such as family and friendship. Rituals help to remoralize, through the expression of support from others, those who have been demoralized by loss.

Health professionals can play a significant role in the adjustment of persons who lose a loved one through death. Those who establish an alliance with the family of an ill patient have the opportunity to continue the relationship with the bereaved after the death has occurred. If necessary, referrals can be made to appropriate mental health professionals.

# Summary

Chapter 14 examines terminal illness from the perspective of the patient. The chapter also deals with the internal struggles that accompany people's attempts to come to terms with bereavement.

I. Facing death, particularly in the throes of physical illness, is probably the most difficult of life's tasks. Impending death brings loss of family and friends, as well as of the most treasured aspects of existence. Reactions to impending death typically depend upon an individual's life philosophy as well as his or her fear of death.

II. Research findings by Dr. Elizabeth Kübler-Ross have changed attitudes about dying patients.

A. Patients typically know that they are dying even when no one has told them directly. Physicians now usually tell their patients the complete truth about their terminal conditions and try to be as compassionate and sympathetic as possible.

B. Some patients try to deny the facts they have learned about their terminal illnesses. They engage in denial in order to reduce anxiety and sometimes to take positive action and continue enjoying life despite terminal illness. Anger may follow denial, as the dying person becomes overwhelmed emotionally. Some patients may try to "bargain" in an effort to survive. Depression may occur among terminal patients who give up fighting for survival. Some patients are able to arrive at an acceptance of their impending death.

C. People vary a great deal in whether they experience the various stages of adjustment to terminal illness, and the order in which they experience those stages. Dying is a very individualistic process.

III. The death of a loved one can have a serious effect on an individual. Understanding the effects of loss is essential if a health professional is to help survivors.

A. The extent of a health professional's contribution to helping individuals who have lost a loved one through death probably depends upon the nature of the relationship he or she has with those persons. The health professional can provide information and emotional support.

B. Bereavement is the fact of loss through death. People respond psychologically, physically, and behaviorally to bereavement. Through the course of time, the process of bereavement becomes evident. Grief is the feeling or emotion associated with bereavement.

1. Following death, a survivor will usually feel shock, numbness, and a sense of disbelief. Once a person recovers from shock, he or she may experience a variety of frightening emotions.

2. The grieving process may affect biological functioning, leading to changes in many systems, most strongly the cardiovascular system.

3. Bereavement may also bring changes in one's social status.

4. Anniversary reactions can be troubling. Reminders of the deceased can be triggered by birthdays, anniversaries, and holidays.

5. Investing in new relationships may seem to signal acceptance and adjustment to death. Women, however, tend to delay social reinvestment until they are emotionally healed, whereas men are more likely to "recover" socially and even to remarry before they have resolved the death emotionally.

C. There are also pathological outcomes to bereavement. Some people remain "stuck" in the grieving process, experiencing intense emotions, such as anger and depression far longer than is usual with bereaved persons. Physical complaints may also be involved.

IV. The death of one's spouse is considered to be among the most stressful of life events. It brings about tremendous difficulties and great adjustment of circumstances and expectations. The intertwining of the two lives of the married couple is a major factor in the devastating effects of a spouse's death.

V. The loss of a parent through death is also a common phenomenon, although there is not much research available on the subject. It has been noted that probably due to the mother's early role as nurturer, her death is often more difficult to sustain than that of the father.

VI. The deaths of other relatives, such as of a sibling or one's child, can be emotionally devastating to the individual. The impact of these deaths depends a great deal upon the timing and circumstances under which they occur.

VII. A child's or adolescent's understanding of death is an important factor in development. Bereavement does not always automatically cause difficulties. Children can experience a wide spectrum of emotions and behaviors following a death. However, the grieving process in children is different from that in adults. Children often have feelings of self-blame and anxiety about who will take care of them, particularly if the death was of a parent.

VIII. Suicide, death at one's own hands, can leave survivors with very complex feelings, leading to a greater risk for physical and mental health problems. People who have suicidal thoughts need professional help to recognize that their problems can be solved in other ways. Any threats of suicide should always be taken very seriously.

IX. Bereavement affects an entire social network. Mourning rituals, such as funerals and the wearing of black by the bereaved, tend to aid in recovery from the loss.

# Glossary

**bereavement:** the fact of loss through death. A person who survives the death of a loved one is bereaved.

**bereavement reactions:** psychological, physical, or behavioral responses to bereavement.

**grief:** the feeling or affective state associated with the condition of bereavement.

**miscarriage:** a variation of the loss with stillbirth. Fetal loss, even as early as six or eight weeks of gestation, can have a significant emotional impact on parents. Loss through miscarriage involves diminishment of hope for a particular future and loss of a potential family member.

**mourning:** the social expression of grief.

**recovery or adaptation:** the end of the grieving process.

**stillbirth:** the condition in which a fetus dies late in pregnancy *in utero* or during labor and delivery.

**sudden infant death syndrome,** or *SIDS* (also known as crib death): the most common cause of death in the first year of an infant's life after the perinatal period. SIDS occurs in two to three babies per 1000 in the United States. Nearly 10,000 babies die of SIDS each year. The peak incidence of death is between 2 and 4 months of age. Almost all SIDS deaths occur before 6 months of age. Babies with SIDS die in their sleep, with no forewarning, and no audible noise.

**thanatology:** the study of death and dying.

# Afterword

On the last day of class in health psychology, my students usually ask me to sum up briefly the main message of the course. Although a short summary cannot possibly do justice to the complexities of the material we have examined in this book, I would like to try to point out a few primary messages that I hope have gotten across.

Throughout this book we have examined issues of health, illness, and medical care from the perspective of the individual. We have seen that although they can be looked at as societal problems, issues of health and illness can also be seen to be very private and to affect individuals and their loved ones in very personal as well as very powerful ways. In this book, I have chosen to focus on the *intrapersonal* and the *interpersonal* aspects of maintaining health and preventing disease, and of adjusting to and coming to terms with pain, life stress, acute and chronic illness, and even death.

My first message, then, is that issues of health and illness both are guided by and affect individual psychology. While there are commonalities among people in their reactions to these important aspects of life, people are unique, and issues of health and illness have very personal effects.

My second message is that individuals continually make choices and must face the consequences of their choices. They may choose to relapse and have a cigarette or to take a drink and drive without a safety belt. They may choose to ignore the warning signs of impending heart attack. They may choose to avoid screening for cancer. Those are personal choices that no person and no law can completely control. People make these choices every day and they must be respected. Knowing something about health psychology, however, can help a health professional to be an agent of change. Health professionals with training in health psychology can help to change attitudes and beliefs, as well as assist in the practical issues involved in helping people to approach more closely an ideal of health.

A third message, and one that is based on my own personal philosophy, is that, to a great extent, we each create our lives and our destinies. We make the decisions and choices, and take the steps. Certainly, we do not control all of our outcomes. Things hap-

pen that we could not predict. But although we may not be able to guarantee each outcome, we can choose how we react to it. We can choose to take the next step, to try again, or to give up. Knowing something about health psychology, a health professional can help patients to choose one way of thinking over another, to manage their pain instead of give into it, to choose to remain connected and emotionally open to loved ones rather than to withdraw, to assert their wishes to their medical professionals. People can be helped to choose and to act in ways that serve the beauty and magnificence of their lives rather than head them toward depression and hopelessness. The choices are not often easy; some are gut-wrenching compromises. But they are free choices.

For those who have read this book in preparation for a career in the health professions, there will be hundreds, perhaps thousands, of opportunities to apply the psychological principles contained here in future work with patients. For those who have a more personal interest in health psychology issues, it may be surprising just how many opportunities there will be to apply what has been learned. Pain, illness, and death are part of life. And so is striving to prevent illness and to be healthy and happy!

# References

**Abeles, R. P.** (1990). Schemas, sense of control, and aging. In C. Schooler, J. Rodin, & K. W. Schaie (Eds.), *Self-directedness and efficacy: Causes and effects throughout the life course.* Hillsdale, NJ: Erlbaum.

**Abram, H. S.** (1977). Survival by machine: The psychological stress of chronic hemodialysis. In R. H. Moos (Ed.), *Coping with physical illness* (pp. 295–310). New York: Plenum.

**Abrams, D. B., & Wilson, G. T.** (1986). Habit disorders: Alcohol and tobacco dependence. In A. J. Frances & R. E. Hales (Eds.), *American Psychiatric Association Annual Review, 5,* 606–626. Washington, DC: American Psychiatric Association.

**Abramson, L. Y., Garber, J., & Seligman, M. E. P.** (1980). Learned helplessness in humans: An attributional analysis. In J. Garber and M. E. P. Seligman (Eds.), *Human helplessness: Theory and application.* New York: Academic Press.

**Achterberg-Lawlis, J.** (1988). Musculoskeletal disorders. In E. A. Blechman & K. D. Brownell (Eds.), *Handbook of behavioral medicine for women.* New York: Pergamon Press.

**Adams, J. D.** (1978). Improving stress management: An action-research based O.D. intervention. In W. W. Burke (Ed.), *The cutting edge.* La Jolla, CA: University Associates.

**Aday, L. A., & Andersen, R.** (1974). A framework for the study of access to medical care. *Health Services Research, 9,* 208–220.

**Aday, L. A., & Andersen, R.** (1975). *Access to medical care.* Ann Arbor, MI: Health Administration Press.

**Ader, R.** (Ed). (1981). *Psychoneuroimmunology.* New York: Academic Press.

**Ader, R., & Cohen, N.** (1985). CNS-immune system interactions: Conditioning phenomena. *Behavioral and Brain Sciences, 8,* 379–395.

**Adler, M. L.** (1972). Kidney transplantation and coping mechanisms. *Psychosomatics, 13,* 337–341.

**Agran, P. F.** (1981). Motor vehicle occupant injuries in noncrash events. *Pediatrics, 67,* 838–840.

**Agran, P. F., & Dunkle, D. E.** (1982). Motor vehicle occupant injuries to children in crash and noncrash events. *Pediatrics, 70,* 993–996.

**Aiken, L. H.** (1983). Nurses. In D. Mechanic (Ed.), *Handbook of health, health care, and the health professions.* New York: Free Press.

**Ajzen, I., & Fishbein, M.** (1977). Attitude-behavior relations: A theoretical analysis and review of empirical research. *Psychological Bulletin, 84*, 888–918.

**Ajzen, I., & Fishbein, M.** (1980). *Understanding attitudes and predicting social behavior.* Englewood Cliffs, NJ: Prentice-Hall.

**Akil, H., Watson, S. J., Young, E., Lewis, M. E., Khachaturian, H., & Walker, J. M.** (1984). Endogenous opioids: Biology and function. *Annual Review of Neuroscience, 7,* 223–255.

**Alberman, E.** (1986). Prevention and health promotion. *British Medical Bulletin, 42*(2), 212–216.

**Alden, L.** (1980). Preventive strategies in the treatment of alcohol abuse: A review and a proposal. In P. O. Davidson & S. M. Davidson (Eds.), *Behavioral medicine: Changing health lifestyles* (pp. 256–278). New York: Brunner/Mazel.

**Alexander, F.** (1950). *Psychosomatic medicine.* New York: Norton.

**Allman, R. M., Steinberg, E. P., Keruly, J. C., & Dans, P. E.** (1985). Physician tolerance for uncertainty: Use of liver-spleen scans to detect metastases. *Journal of the American Medical Association, 254*(2), 246–248.

**Allport, G. W.** (1935). Attitudes. In C. Murchinson (Ed.), *Handbook of social psychology* (pp. 798–844). Worcester, MA: Clark University Press.

**Alpert, J. J.** (1964). Broken appointments. *Pediatrics, 34,* 127–132.

**American Cancer Society.** (1989). *Cancer facts and figures, 1989.* Atlanta: Author.

**American Cancer Society.** (1985). *Annual Report.* Atlanta: Author.

**American Diabetes Association.** (1976) *What you need to know about diabetes.* New York: Author.

**American Diabetes Association.** (1979). *What you need to know about diabetes.* New York: Author.

**American Diabetes Association.** (1986). *Facts and figures.* Alexandria, VA: Author.

**American Heart Association.** (1984). *Heart facts, 1984.* Dallas: Author.

**Anda, R. F., Remington, P. L., Sienko, D. G., & Davis, R. M.** (1987). Are physicians advising smokers to quit? The patient's perspective. *Journal of the American Medical Association, 257*(14), 1916–1919.

**Anderson, K. O., & Masur, F. T.** (1983). Psychological preparation for invasive medical and dental procedures. *Journal of Behavioral Medicine, 6,* 1–40.

**Anderson, R., & Bury, M.** (Eds.). (1988). *Living with chronic illness: The experience of patients and their families.* London: Unwin Hyman.

**Andrasik, F., & Holroyd, K. A.** (1980). A test of specific and non-specific effects in the biofeedback treatment of tension headache. *Journal of Consulting & Clinical Psychology, 48,* 575–586.

**Andreasen, N. J. C., & Norris, A. S.** (1977). Long-term adjustment and adaptation mechanisms in severely burned adults. In R. H. Moos (Ed.), *Coping with physical illness* (pp. 149–166). New York: Plenum.

**Angell, M.** (1982). The quality of mercy. *New England Journal of Medicine, 306*(2), 98–99.

**Antoni, M. H.** (1987). Neuroendocrine influences in psychoimmunology and neoplasia: A review. *Psychology and Health, 1,* 3–24.

**Antonovsky, A.** (1979). *Health, stress, and coping: New perspectives on mental and physical well-being.* San Francisco: Jossey-Bass.

**Antonovsky, A.** (1987). *Unraveling the mystery of health: How people manage stress and stay well.* San Francisco: Jossey-Bass.

**Aronoff, G. M., Wagner, J. M., & Spangler, A. S.** (1986). Chemical interventions for pain. *Journal of Consulting and Clinical Psychology, 54,* 769–775.

**Ary, D. V., & Biglan, A.** (1988). Longitudinal changes in adolescent cigarette smoking behavior: Onset and cessation. *Journal of Behavioral Medicine, 11,* 361–382.

**Ashley, M. J., & Rankin, J. G.** (1988). A public health approach to the prevention of alcohol-related health problems. In L. Breslow, J. E. Fieldings, & L. B. Lave (Eds.), *Annual review of public health* (Vol 9). Palo Alto, CA: Annual Reviews.

**Atkins, C. J.** (1981, April 12). *Improving exercise compliance among chronic lung patients: A comparison of cognitive and behavioral approaches.* Paper presented at the meeting of the Western Psychological Association, Los Angeles.

Awbrey, B. J. (1985). Reflections on medical education: Concerns of the student. *Journal of Medical Education, 60,* 98–105.

Bain, D. J. G. (1976). Doctor-patient communication in general practice consultations. *Medical Education, 10,* 125–131.

Bakal, D. A. (1979). *Psychology and medicine: Psychological dimensions of health and illness.* New York: Springer.

Balint, M. (1957). *The doctor, his patient, and the illness.* New York: International Universities Press.

Bandura, A. (1969). *Principles of behavior modification.* New York: Holt, Rinehart & Winston.

Bandura, A. (1977). Self-efficacy: Toward a unifying theory of behavioral change. *Psychological Review, 84,* 191–215.

Barber, J. (1986). Hypnotic analgesia. In A. D. Holzman & D. C. Turk (Eds.), *Pain management: A handbook of psychological treatment approaches.* New York: Pergamon Press.

Barber, T. X. (1982). Hypnosuggestive procedures in the treatment of clinical pain: Implications for theories of hypnosis and suggestive therapy. In T. Millon, C. J. Green, & R. B. Meagher, Jr. (Eds.), *Handbook of clinical health psychology.* New York: Plenum.

Barefoot, J. C., Dahlstrom, W. G., & Williams, R. B. (1983). Hostility, CHD incidence, and total mortality: A 25-year follow-up study of 255 physicians. *Psychosomatic Medicine, 45*(1), 59–63.

Barefoot, J. C., Siegler, J. C., Nowlin, J. B., Peterson, B. L., Haney, T. L., & Williams, R. B. (1987). Suspiciousness, health, and mortality: A follow-up study of 500 older adults. *Psychosomatic Medicine, 49,* 450–457.

Barnlund, D. C. (1976). The mystification of meaning: Doctor-patient encounters. *Journal of Medical Education, 51,* 716–725.

Barron-McBride, A. (1976). *Living with contradictions.* New York: Harper-Colophon.

Barsky, A. J. (1988). The paradox of health. *New England Journal of Medicine, 318,* 414–418.

Bart, P. B. (1968). Social structure and vocabularies of discomfort: What happened to female hysteria. *Journal of Health and Social Behavior, 9,* 188–193.

Bartrop, R. W., Lockhurst, E., Lazarus, L., Kiloh, L. G., & Penny, R. (1977). Depressed lymphocyte function after bereavement. *Lancet, 1,* 834–836.

Batchelor, W. F. (1988). AIDS 1988: The science and the limits of science. *American Psychologist, 43,* 853–858.

Battista, R. N., & Fletcher, S. W. (1988). Making recommendations on preventive practices: Methodological issues. In R. N. Battista & R. S. Lawrence (Eds.). *Implementing preventive services* (pp. 53–67). New York: Oxford University Press.

Baumann, B. (1961). Diversities of conceptions of health and physical fitness. *Journal of Health and Human Behavior, 2,* 39–46.

Baur, S. (1988). *Hypochondria.* Berkeley: University of California Press.

Beck, A. T. (1976). *Cognitive therapy and the emotional disorders.* New York: International Universities Press.

Beck, K. H., & Frankel, A. (1981). A conceptualization of threat communications and protective health behavior. *Social Psychology Quarterly, 44*(3), 204–217.

Becker, H. S., & Geer, B. (1958). The fate of idealism in medical school. *American Sociological Review, 23,* 50–56.

Becker, M. H. (1974). The health belief model and sick role behavior. *Health Education Monographs, 2,* 409–419.

Becker, M. H. (1979). Understanding patient compliance: The contribution of attitudes and other psychosocial factors. In S. J. Cohen (Ed.), *New directions in patient compliance* (pp. 1–31). Lexington, MA: Heath.

Becker, M. H., & Joseph, J. G. (1988). AIDS and behavioral change to reduce risk: A review. *American Journal of Public Health, 78*(4), 394–410.

Becker, M. H., & Maiman, L. A. (1980). Strategies for enhancing patient compliance. *Journal of Community Health, 6,* 113–135.

Beecher, H. K. (1955). The powerful placebo. *Journal of the American Medical Association, 159,* 1602–1606.

Beecher, H. K. (1956). Relationship of significance of wound to pain experienced. *Journal of the American Medical Association, 161,* 1609–1613.

**Beecher, H. K.** (1959). *Measurement of subjective responses.* New York: Oxford University Press.

**Beecher, H. K.** (1972). The placebo effect as a non-specific force surrounding disease and the treatment of disease. In R. Janzen, W. D. Keidel, A. Herz, C. Steichele, J. P. Payne, & R. A. P. Burt (Eds.), *Pain: Basic principles, pharmacology, therapy.* Stuttgart, West Germany: Georg Thieme.

**Beisecker, A. E., & Beisecker, T. D.** (1990). Patient information-seeking behaviors when communicating with doctors. *Medical Care, 28*(1), 19–28.

**Belloc, N.** (1973). Relationship of health practices and mortality. *Preventive Medicine, 2,* 67–81.

**Belsky, M. S., & Gross, L.** (1975). *How to choose and use your doctor.* Greenwich, CT: Fawcett.

**Benoliel, J. Q.** (1975). Childhood diabetes: The commonplace in living becomes uncommon. In A. L. Strauss (Ed.), *Chronic illness and the quality of life* (pp. 89–98). St. Louis: C. V. Mosby.

**Ben-Sira, Z.** (1976). The function of the professional's affective behavior in client satisfaction: A revised approach to social interaction theory. *Journal of Health and Social Behavior, 17,* 3–11.

**Ben-Sira, Z.** (1980). Affective and instrumental components of the physician-patient relationship: An additional dimension of interaction theory. *Journal of Health and Social Behavior, 21,* 170–180.

**Ben-Sira, Z.** (1985). Primary medical care and coping with stress and disease: The inclination of primary care practitioners to demonstrate affective behavior. *Social Science and Medicine, 21,* 485-498.

**Benson, H.** (1974). Your innate asset for combatting stress. *Harvard Business Review, 52,* 49–60.

**Benson, H., Beary, J. F., & Carol, M. P.** (1974). The relaxation response. *Psychiatry, 37,* 37–46.

**Benson, R. C.** (Ed.). (1984). *Current obstetrical and gynecologic diagnosis and treatment* (5th ed.). Los Altos, CA: Lange Medical Publications.

**Berger, K., & Bostwick, J., III.** (1984). *A woman's decision: Breast care, treatment, and reconstruction.* New York: Ballantine.

**Berkman, L. F., & Syme, S. L.** (1979). Social networks, host resistance, and mortality: A nine-year followup of Alameda County residents. *American Journal of Epidemiology, 109,* 186–204.

**Berkowitz, L.** (1980). *A survey of social psychology* (2nd ed.). New York: Holt, Rinehart & Winston.

**Bernarde, M. A., & Mayerson, E. W.** (1978). Physician-patient negotiation. *Journal of the American Medical Association, 239*(14), 1413–1415.

**Bernstein, L., & Bernstein, R. S.** (1980). *Interviewing: A guide for health professionals* (3rd ed.). New York: Appleton-Century-Crofts.

**Bernstein, N. R.** (1976). *Emotional care of the facially burned and disfigured.* Boston: Little, Brown.

**Bertman, S., & Krant, M. J.** (1977). To know of suffering and the teaching of empathy. *Social Science and Medicine, 11,* 639–644.

**Best, J. A., Thomson, S. J., Santi, S. M., Smith, E. A., & Brown, K. S.** (1968). Preventing cigarette smoking among school children. In L. Breslow, J. E. Fielding, & L. B. Lave (Eds.), *Annual review of public health* (Vol. 9). Palo Alto, CA: Annual Reviews.

**Bibace, R., & Walsh, M. E.** (1979). Developmental stages in children's conceptions of illness. In G. C. Stone, F. Cohen, & N. E. Adler (Eds.), *Health psychology—a handbook* (pp. 285–301). San Francisco: Jossey-Bass.

**Bibace, R., & Walsh, M. E.** (1980). Development of children's concepts of illness. *Pediatrics, 66,* 912–917.

**Billings, A. G., & Moos, R. H.** (1981). The role of coping responses and social resources in attenuating the stress of life events. *Journal of Behavioral Medicine, 4,* 139–158.

**Blachly, P. H., Disher, W., & Roduner, G.** (1968, December). Suicide by physicians. *Bulletin of Suicidology,* pp. 1–18.

**Blair, S. N., Kohl, H. W., III, Paffenbarger, R. S., Jr., Clark, D. G., Cooper, K. H., & Gibbons, L. W.** (1989). Physical fitness and all-cause mortality: A prospective study of healthy men and women. *Journal of the*

*American Medical Association, 262*(17), 2395–2436.

Blanchard, E. B. (1987). Long-term effects of behavioral treatment of chronic headache. *Behavior Therapy, 18,* 375–385.

Blanchard, E. B., & Andrasik, F. (1985). *Management of chronic headaches: A psychological approach.* New York: Pergamon Press.

Blanchard, E. B., Andrasik, F., Applebaum, K. A., Evans, D. D., Myers, P., & Barron, K. D. (1986). Three studies of the psychologic changes in chronic headache patients associated with biofeedback and relaxation therapies. *Psychosomatic Medicine, 48,* 73–83.

Blanchard, E. B., Andrasik, F. A., Guarnieri, P., Neff, D. F. & Radichoc, L. D. (1987). Two-, three-, and four-year follow-up on the self-regulatory treatment of chronic headache. *Journal of Consulting and Clinical Psychology, 55*(2), 257–259.

Blanchard, E. B., & Epstein, L. H., (1977). The clinical usefulness of biofeedback. In M. Hersen, R. M. Eisler, & P. M. Miller (Eds.), *Progress in behavior modification* (vol. 4). New York: Academic Press.

Blondis, M. N., & Jackson, B. E. (1977). *Nonverbal communication with patients.* New York: Wiley.

Bloom, S. W. (1963). *The doctor and his patient: A sociological interpretation.* New York: Russell Sage Foundation.

Blum, R. H. (1960). *The management of the doctor-patient relationship.* New York: McGraw-Hill.

Blumenthal, J. A., & McCubbin, J. A. (1987). Physical exercise as stress management. In A. Baum & J. E. Singer (Eds.), *Handbook of psychology and health* (vol. 5). Hillsdale, NJ: Erlbaum.

Bok, S. (1978). *Lying: Moral choice in public and private life.* New York: Random House.

Boone, D. R., & Hartman, B. H. (1972). The benevolent over-reaction. A well-intentioned but malignant influence on the handicapped child. *Clinical Pediatrics, 11,* 268–271.

Booth-Kewley, S., & Friedman, H. S. (1987). Psychological predictors of heart disease: A quantitative review. *Psychological Bulletin, 101*(3), 343–362.

Borysenko, J. (1984). Stress, coping, and the immune system. In J. D. Matarazzo, S. M. Weiss, J. A. Herd, N. E. Miller, & S. M. Weiss (Eds.), *Behavioral health: A handbook of health enhancement and disease prevention.* New York: Wiley.

Borysenko, M., & Borysenko, J. (1982). Stress, behavior, and immunity: Animal models and mediating mechanisms. *General Hospital Psychiatry, 4,* 59–67.

Bowlby, J. (1961). Childhood mourning and its implications for psychiatry. *American Journal of Psychiatry, 118,* 481–498.

Branden, N. (1969). *The psychology of self-esteem* (chap. 7). Los Angeles: Nash.

Branden, N. (1971). *The disowned self.* Los Angeles: Nash.

Branden, N. (1983). *Honoring the self.* Los Angeles: Jeremy P. Tarcher.

Bregman, D. J., & Langmuir, A. D. (1990). Farr's law applied to AIDS projections. *Journal of the American Medical Association, 263,* 1522–1525.

Brenner, M. H. (1976). *Estimating the social costs of national economic policy: Implications for mental and physical health, and criminal violence* (Report prepared for the Joint Economic Committee of Congress). Washington, DC: U.S. Government Printing Office.

Brent, R. L., & Brent, L. H. (1978). Medicine: An excuse from living. *Resident and Staff Physician, 24*(24), 61–65.

Breslow, L., & Buell, P. (1960). Mortality from coronary heart disease and physical activity of work in California. *Journal of Chronic Diseases, 11,* 615–626.

Brim, O. G., & Wheeler, S. (1966). *Socialization after childhood: Two essays.* New York: Wiley.

Brodland, G. A., & Andreasen, N. J. C. (1974). Adjustment problems of the family of the burned patient. *Social Casework, 55,* 13–18.

Brody, E. M. (1985). Patient care as a normative family stress. *Gerontologist, 25,* 19–29.

Brook, R. H., Kamberg, C. J., Mayer-Oakes, A., Beers, M. H., Raube, K., & Steiner, A. (1989). Appropriateness of acute medical care for the elderly. R-3717-AARP/HF/RWJ/RC. Santa Monica, CA: RAND.

**Brooks-Gunn, J., Boyer, C. B., & Hein, K.** (1988). Preventing HIV infection and AIDS in children and adolescents. *American Psychologist, 43,* 958–964.

**Brown, G. W.** (1974). Meaning, measurement, and stress of life events. In B. S. Dohrenwend & B. P. Dohrenwend (Eds.), *Stressful life events: Their nature and effects* (pp. 217–244). New York: Wiley.

**Brown, J. T., & Stoudemier, G. A.** (1983). Normal and pathological grief. *Journal of the American Medical Association, 250,* 378–382.

**Brown, R. S., Ramirez, D. E., & Taub, J. M.** (1978). The prescription of exercise for depression. *The Physician and Sports Medicine, 6,* 34–45.

**Brownell, K. D.** (1986). Public health approaches to obesity and its management. *Annual Review of Public Health, 7,* 521–533.

**Brownell, K. D., Marlatt, G. A., Lichtenstein, E., & Wilson, G. T.** (1986). Understanding and preventing relapse. *American Psychologist, 41,* 765–782.

**Brownell, K. D., & Stunkard, A. J.** (1980). Exercise in the development and treatment of obesity. In A. J. Stunkard (Ed.), *Obesity.* Philadelphia: Saunders.

**Buchsbaum, D. G.** (1986). Reassurance reconsidered. *Social Science and Medicine, 23*(4), 423–427.

**Buck, R.** (1988). *Human motivation and emotion* (2nd ed.). New York: Wiley.

**Bulman, J. R., & Wortman, C. B.** (1977). Attributions of blame and coping in the "real world": Severe accident victims react to their lot. *Journal of Personality, 35,* 351–363.

**Bunch, J., Barraclough, B., Nelson, B., & Sainsbury, P.** (1971). Suicide following death of parents. *Social Psychiatry, 6,* 193–199.

**Bush, C., Ditto, B., & Feuerstein, M.** (1985). A controlled evaluation of paraspinal EMG biofeedback in the treatment of chronic low back pain. *Health Psychology, 4,* 307–321.

**Bush, J. P.** (1987). Pain in children: A review of the literature from a developmental perspective. *Psychology and Health, 1,* 215–236.

**Bush, J. P., Melamed, B. G., Sheras, P. L., & Greenbaum, P. E.** (1986). Mother-child patterns of coping with anticipatory medical stress. *Health Psychology, 5,* 137–157.

**Butler, R. N., & Lewis, M. I.** (1977). *Aging and mental health* (2nd ed.). St. Louis: C. V. Mosby.

**Butt, H. R.** (1977). A method for better physician-patient communication. *Annals of Internal Medicine, 86,* 478–480.

**Cady, L. D., Gertler, M. M., Gotsch, L. D., & Woodbury, M. A.** (1961). The factor structure concerned with coronary artery disease. *Behavioral Science, 6,* 37–41.

**Cain, A., & Fast, I.** (1972). The legacy of suicide: Observations on the pathogenic impact of suicide upon marital partners. In A. Cain (Ed.), *Survivors of suicide.* Springfield, IL: Charles C Thomas.

**Cain, A., Fast, I., & Erickson, M.** (1964). Childrens' disturbed reactions to the death of a sibling. *American Journal of Orthopsychiatry, 34,* 741–752.

**Califano, J. A., Jr.** (1979a). *Healthy people: Background papers.* Washington, DC: U.S. Government Printing Office.

**Califano, J. A., Jr.** (1979b). *Healthy people: The surgeon general's report on health promotion and disease prevention.* Washington, DC: U.S. Government Printing Office.

**Campbell, B. J.** (1987). Safety belt injury reduction related to crash severity and front seat position. *Journal of Trauma, 27,* 733–739.

**Cannell, C. F., Oksenberg, L., & Converse, J. M.** (1977). Striving for response accuracy: Experiments in new interviewing techniques. *Journal of Marketing Research, 14,* 306–315.

**Cannon, W. B.** (1932). *The wisdom of the body.* New York: Norton.

**Cannon, W. B.** (1957). "Voodoo" death. *Psychosomatic Medicine, 19,* 182–190.

**Caplan, R.** (1979). Patient, provider, and organization: Hypothesized determinants of adherence. In S. J. Cohen (Ed.), *New directions in patient compliance.* Lexington, MA: Heath.

**Carey, R. M., Reid, R. A., Ayers, C. R., Lynch, S. S., McLain, W. L., III, & Vaughan, E. D., Jr.** (1976). The Charlottesville Blood Pressure Survey: Value of repeated blood pressure measurements. *Journal of the American Medical Association, 236,* 847–851.

Cartwright, L. K. (1977). Personality changes in a sample of young woman physicians. *Journal of Medical Education, 52,* 467–474.

Cartwright, L. K. (1978). Career satisfaction and role harmony in a sample of young woman physicians. *Journal of Vocational Behavior, 12,* 184–196.

Cartwright, L. K. (1979). Sources and effects of stress in health careers. In G. C. Stone, F. Cohen, & N. E. Adler (Eds.), *Health psychology.* San Francisco: Jossey-Bass.

Caspi, A., Bolger, N., & Eckenrode, J. (1987). Linking person and context in the daily stress process. *Journal of Personality and Social Psychology, 52*(1), 184–195.

Cassata, D. M. (1978). Health communication theory and research: An overview of the communication specialist interface. In D. Nimmo (Ed.), *Communication yearbook II,* Austin, TX: International Communication Association.

Cassell, E. J. (1985a). *Talking with patients.* Vol. 1, *The theory of doctor-patient communication.* Cambridge: MIT Press.

Cassell, E. J. (1985b). *Talking with patients.* Vol. 2, *Clinical technique.* Cambridge: MIT Press.

Cassileth, B. R. (Ed.). (1979) *The cancer patient: Social and medical aspects of care.* Philadelphia: Lea & Febiger.

Cassileth, B. R., Lusk, E. J., Miller, D. S., Brown, L. L., & Miller, C. (1985). Psychosocial correlates of survival in advanced malignant disease? *New England Journal of Medicine, 312*(24), 1551–1555.

Cassileth, B. R., Lusk, E. J., Strouse, T. B., Miller, D. S., Brown, L. L., & Cross, P. A. (1985). A psychological analysis of cancer patients and their next-of-kin. *Cancer, 55,* 72–76.

Cates, W. (1987). Epidemiology and control of sexually transmitted diseases: Strategic evolution. *Infectious Disease Clinics of North America, 1,* 1–23.

Centers for Disease Control. (1988). Quarterly report to the Domestic Policy Council on the prevalence and rate of spread of HIV and AIDS. *Mortality and Morbidity Weekly Report, 37,* 551–559.

Centers for Disease Control. (1988 update). AIDS and human immunodeficiency virus infection in the United States. *Mortality and Morbidity Weekly, 38*(Suppl. S-4), 1–38.

Centers for Disease Control. (1990, July). *HIV/AIDS Surveillance Report,* pp. 1–18.

Chambers, C. D., & Griffey, M. S. (1975). Use of legal substances within the general population: The sex and age variable. *Addictive Diseases: An International Journal, 2,* 7–19.

Chapman, C. R. (1984). New directions in the understanding and management of pain. *Social Science and Medicine, 19,* 1261–1277.

Chapman, C. R., Casey, K. L., Dubner, R., Foley, K. M., Gracely, R. H., & Reading, A. E. (1985). Pain measurement: An overview. *Pain, 22,* 1–31.

Chassin, L., Corty, E., Presson, C. C., Olshavsky, R. W., Bensenberg, M., & Sherman, S. J. (1981). Predicting adolescents' intentions to smoke cigarettes. *Journal of Health and Social Behavior, 22,* 445–455.

Chekryn, J. (1984). Cancer recurrence: Personal meaning, communication, and marital adjustment. *Cancer Nursing, 7,* 491–498.

Chesney, M. A., Frautschi, N. M., & Rosenman, R. H. (1985). Modifying Type A behavior. In J. C. Rosen & L. J. Solomon (Eds.), *Prevention in health psychology.* Hanover, NH: University Press of New England.

Chesney, M. A., & Rosenman, R. H. (1985). *Anger and hostility in cardiovascular and behavioral disorders.* New York: Hemisphere.

Chesney, M. A., & Shelton, J. L. (1976). A comparison of muscle relaxation and electromyogram biofeedback treatment for muscle contraction headache. *Journal of Behavior Therapy and Experimental Psychiatry, 7,* 221–225.

Chrisman, N. J. (1977). The health seeking process: An approach to the natural history of illness. *Culture, Medicine and Psychiatry, 1,* 351–377.

Christophersen, E. R. (1989). Injury control. *American Psychologist, 44,* 237–241

Christy, N. P. (1979). English is our second language. *New England Journal of Medicine, 300*(17), 979–981.

Ciccone, D. A., & Grzesiak, R. C. (1984). Cognitive dimensions of chronic pain. *Social Science and Medicine, 19*(2), 1339–1345.

**Citron, M. L., Johnston-Early, A., Boyer, M., Krasnow, S. H., Hood, M., & Cohen, M. H.** (1986). Patient-controlled analgesia for severe cancer pain. *Archives of Internal Medicine, 146,* 734–736.

**Clarke, T. A., Maniscalco, W. M., Taylor-Brown, S., Roghmann, K. J., Shapiro, D. L., & Hannon-Johnson, C.** (1984). Job satisfaction and stress among neonatologists. *Pediatrics, 74*(1), 52–57.

**Clayton, P. J.** (1974). Mortality and morbidity in the first year of widowhood. *Archives of General Psychiatry, 30,* 747–750.

**Clayton, P. J.** (1979). The sequelae and nonsequelae of conjugal bereavement. *American Journal of Psychiatry, 136,* 1530–1543.

**Coates, T. J.** (1984). Insomnia: Managing emotions to improve sleep. In C. Van Dyke, L. Temoshok, & L. S. Zegans (Eds.), *Emotions in health and illness: Applications to clinical practice* (pp. 135–149). New York: Grune & Stratton.

**Cobb, B.** (1954). Why do people detour to quacks? *Psychiatric Bulletin, 3,* 66–69.

**Cobb, S.** (1976). Social support as a moderator of life stress. *Psychosomatic Medicine, 38,* 300–314.

**Cobb, S., & Rose, R. M.** (1973). Hypertension, peptic ulcer, and diabetes in air traffic controllers. *Journal of the American Medical Association, 224,* 489–492.

**Cody, J., & Robinson, A.** (1977). The effect of low-cost maintenance medication on the rehospitalization of schizophrenic outpatients. *American Journal of Psychiatry, 134,* 73–76.

**Coggan, P. G., Macdonald, S. C., Camacho, Z., Carline, J., & Taylor, T.** (1985). An analysis of the magnitude of clinical reasoning deficiencies in one class. *Journal of Medical Education, 60,* 293–301.

**Cohen, F., & Lazarus, R. S.** (1979). Coping with the stress of illness. In G. C. Stone, F. Cohen, & N. E. Adler (Eds.), *Health psychology—a handbook* (pp. 217–254). San Francisco: Jossey-Bass.

**Cohen, F., & Lazarus, R. S.** (1983). Coping and adaptation in health and illness. In D. Mechanic (Ed.), *Handbook of health, health care, and the health professions.* New York: Free Press.

**Cohen, S., & McKay, G.** (1983). Social support, stress, and the buffering hypothesis: A theoretical analysis. In A. Baum, S. E. Taylor, & J. Singer (Eds.), *Handbook of psychology and health* (Vol. 4). Hillsdale, NJ: Erlbaum.

**Cohen, S., & Wills, T. A.** (1985). Stress, social support, and the buffering hypothesis. *Psychological Bulletin, 98,* 310–357.

**Conway, T. L., Vickers, R. R., Ward, H. W., & Rahe, R. H.** (1981). Occupational stress and variation in cigarette, coffee and alcohol consumption. *Journal of Health and Social Behavior, 22,* 155–165.

**Cook, T., & Flay, B.** (1978). The temporal persistence of experimentally induced attitude change: An evaluative review. In L. Berkowitz (Ed.), *Advances in experimental social psychology* (Vol. 11). New York: Academic Press.

**Coombs, R. H., & Hovanessian, H. C.** (1988). Stress in the role constellation of female resident physicians. *Journal of the American Medical Women's Association, 43*(1), 21–27.

**Cormier, L. S., Cormier, W. H., & Weisser, R. J.** (1984). *Interviewing and helping skills for health professionals.* Belmont, CA: Wadsworth.

**Cottington, E. M., & House, J. S.** (1987). Occupational stress and health: A multivariate relationship. In A. Baum & J. E. Singer (Eds.), *Handbook of psychology and health* (vol. 5). Hillsdale, NJ: Erlbaum.

**Cottington, E. M., Matthews, K. A., Talbott, E., & Kuller, L. H.** (1986). Occupational stress, suppressed anger, and hypertension. *Psychosomatic Medicine, 48,* 249–260.

**Cousins, N.** (1976, December 23). Anatomy of an illness (as perceived by the patient). *New England Journal of Medicine, 295,* 1458–1463.

**Cousins, N.** (1979). *Anatomy of an illness.* New York: Norton.

**Cousins, N.** (1981a). Internship: Preparation or hazing? *Journal of the American Medical Association, 245*(4), 377.

**Cousins, N.** (1981b). Norman Cousins responds. *Journal of the American Medical Association, 246,* 2144.

Cousins, N. (1983). *The healing heart: Antidotes to panic and helplessness.* New York: Norton.

Cousins, N. (1985). How patients appraise physicians. *New England Journal of Medicine, 313,* 1422–1424.

Coyne, J. C.. Aldwin, C., & Lazarus, R. S. (1981). Depression and coping in stressful episodes. *Journal of Abnormal Psychology, 90*(5), 439–447.

Coyne, J. C., & Holroyd, K. (1982). Stress, coping, and illness: A transactional perspective. In T. Millon, C. Green, & R. Meagher (Eds.), *Handbook of clinical health psychology.* New York: Plenum.

Craun, A. M., & Deffenbacher, J. L. (1987). The effects of information, behavioral rehearsal, and prompting on breast self-exams. *Journal of Behavioral Medicine, 10,* 351–365.

Croog, S. H., & Fitzgerald, E. F. (1978). Subjective stress and serious illness of a spouse: Wives of heart patients. *Journal of Health and Social Behavior, 19,* 166–178.

Croog, S. H., & Levine, S. (1973). After the heart attack: Social aspects of rehabilitation. *Medical Insights, 5,* 10.

Curbow, B., Somerfield, M., Legro, M., & Sonnega, J. (1990). Self-concept and cancer in adults: Theoretical and methodological issues. *Social Science and Medicine, 31*(2), 115–128.

Dackman, L. (1987, September). Sex and the single-breasted woman. *Vogue,* pp. 420–436.

Dahlberg, C. C., & Jaffe, J. (1977). *Stroke: A doctor's personal story of his recovery.* New York: Norton.

Dahlquist, L. M., Gil, K. M., Armstrong, F. D., DeLawyer, D. D., Greene, P., & Wuori, D. (1986). Preparing children for medical examinations: The importance of previous medical experience. *Health Psychology, 5,* 249–259.

Dattore, P. J., Shontz, F. C., & Coyne, L. (1980). Premorbid personality differentiation of cancer and noncancer groups: A test of the hypothesis of cancer proneness. *Journal of Consulting and Clinical Psychology, 48*(3), 388–394.

Davidson, R. J., & Schwartz, G. E. (1976). Psychobiology of relaxation and related states. A multiprocess theory. In D. Mostofsky (Ed.), *Behavior modification and control of physiologic activity.* Englewood Cliffs, NJ: Prentice-Hall.

Davis, F. (1960). Uncertainty in medical prognosis: Clinical and functional. *American Journal of Sociology, 66,* 41–47.

Davis, M. (1973). *Living with multiple sclerosis.* Springfield, IL: Charles C Thomas.

Davis, M. S. (1966). Variations in patients' compliance with doctors' orders: Analysis of congruence between survey responses and results of empirical investigations. *Journal of Medical Education, 41,* 1037–1048.

Davis, M. S. (1971). Variations in patients' compliance with doctors' orders. Medical practice and doctor-patient interaction. *Psychiatry in Medicine, 2,* 31–54.

Dawber, T. R. (1980). *The Framingham Study: The epidemiology of atherosclerotic disease.* Cambridge: Harvard University Press.

deCharms, P. (1968). *Personal causation: The internal affective determinants of behavior.* New York: Academic Press.

DeLongis, A., Coyne, J. C., Dakof, G., Folkman, S., & Lazarus, R. S. (1982). Relationship of daily hassles, uplifts, and major life events to health status. *Health Psychology, 1,* 119–136.

Derogatis, L., Abeloff, M., & Melasaratos, N. (1979). Psychological coping mechanisms and survival time in metastatic breast cancer. *Journal of the American Medical Association, 242,* 1504–1508.

Derogatis, L., & Spencer, M. S. (1982). *The Brief Symptom Inventory (BSI) administration, scoring, and procedures manual I.* Baltimore: Clinical Psychometric Research.

Des Jarlais, D. C., & Friedman, S. R. (1988). The psychology of preventing AIDS among intravenous drug users: A social learning conceptualization. *American Psychologist, 43,* 865–870.

Diamond, E. L. (1982). The role of anger and hostility in essential hypertension and coronary heart disease. *Psychological Bulletin, 92,* 410–433.

Diamond, E. L., Massey, K. L., & Covey, D. (1989). Symptom awareness and blood glucose estimation in diabetic adults. *Health Psychology, 8,* 15–26.

**Diller, L.** (1976). A model of cognitive retraining in rehabilitation. *Journal of Clinical Psychology, 29,* 74–79.

**DiMatteo, M. R.** (1979). A social-psychological analysis of physician-patient rapport: Toward a science of the art of medicine. *Journal of Social Issues, 35,* 12–33.

**DiMatteo, M. R.** (1985). Physician-patient communication: Promoting a positive health care setting. In J. C. Rosen & L. J. Solomon (Eds.), *Prevention in health psychology.* Hanover, NH: University Press of New England.

**DiMatteo, M. R., & DiNicola, D. D.** (1981). Sources of assessment of physician performance: A study of comparative reliability and patterns of intercorrelation. *Medical Care, 19,* 829–842.

**DiMatteo, M. R., & DiNicola, D. D.** (1982). *Achieving patient compliance: The psychology of the medical practitioner's role.* Elmsford, NY: Pergamon Press.

**DiMatteo, M. R., & Friedman, H. S.** (1982). *Social psychology and medicine.* Cambridge, MA: Oelgeschlager, Gunn & Hain.

**DiMatteo, M. R., & Hays, R.** (1980). The significance of patients' perceptions of physician conduct: A study of patient satisfaction in a family practice center. *Journal of Community Health, 6*(1), 18–34.

**DiMatteo, M. R., & Hays, R.** (1981). Social support and serious illness. In B. H. Gottlieb (Ed.), *Social networks and social support* (pp. 117–148). Beverly Hills: Sage.

**DiMatteo, M. R., Hays, R., & Prince, L. M.** (1986). Relationship of physicians' nonverbal communication skill to patient satisfaction, appointment noncompliance, and physician workload. *Health Psychology, 5*(6), 581–594.

**DiMatteo, M. R., Linn, L. S., Chang, B. L., & Cope, D. W.** (1985). Affect and neutrality in physician behavior. *Journal of Behavioral Medicine, 8*(4), 397–409.

**DiMatteo, M. R., Prince, L. M., & Taranta, A.** (1979). Patients' perceptions of physician behavior: Determinants of patient commitment to the therapeutic relationship. *Journal of Community Health, 4,* 280–290.

**DiMatteo, M. R., & Taranta, A.** (1979). Nonverbal communication and physician-patient rapport: An empirical study. *Professional Psychology, 10*(4), 540–547.

**DiMatteo, M. R., Taranta, A., Friedman, H. S., & Prince, L. M.** (1980). Predicting patient satisfaction from physicians' nonverbal communication skills. *Medical Care, 18,* 376–387.

**Dimsdale, J. E., Alpert, B. S., & Schneiderman, N.** (1986). Exercise as a modulator of cardiovascular reactivity. In K. A. Matthews, S. M. Weiss, T. Detre, T. M. Dembroski, B. Falkner, S. B. Manuck, & R. B. Williams (Eds.), *Handbook of stress, reactivity, and cardiovascular disease.* New York: Wiley.

**Dishman, R. K.** (1982). Compliance/adherence in health-related exercise. *Health Psychology, 1,* 237–267.

***Dorland's Illustrated Medical Dictionary*** (24th ed.). (1965). Philadelphia: Saunders.

**Doyle, Sir A. C.** (1984). *The illustrated Sherlock Holmes treasury.* New York: Avenel Books.

**Doyle, B. J., & Ware, J. E.** (1977). Physician conduct and other factors that affect consumer satisfaction with medical care. *Journal of Medical Education, 52,* 793–801.

**Drotar, D.** (1981). Psychological perspectives in chronic childhood illness. *Journal of Pediatric Psychology, 6,* 211–228.

**Dubos, R.** (1959). *Mirage of health.* New York: Harper & Row.

**Duffy, J. C.** (1970). *Emotional issues in the lives of physicians.* Springfield, IL: Charles C Thomas.

**Dunbar, F.** (1943). *Psychosomatic diagnosis.* New York: Paul B. Hoeber.

**Dunham, C. S.** (1978). Social-sexual relationships. In R. M. Goldenson, J. R. Dunham, & C. S. Dunham (Eds.), *Disability and rehabilitation handbook* (pp. 28–35). NY: McGraw-Hill.

**Dunkel-Schetter, C.** (1984). Social support in cancer: Findings based on patient interviews and their implications. *Journal of Social Issues, 40,* 77–98.

**Dunkel-Schetter, C., & Wortman, C.** (1982). The interactional dynamics of cancer: Problems in social relationships and their impact on the patient. In H. S. Friedman

& M. R. DiMatteo (Eds.), *Interpersonal Issues in Health Care*. New York: Academic Press.

Eckhardt, M. J., Harford, T. C., Kaelber, C. T., Parker, E. S., Rosenthal, L. S., Ryback, R. S., Salmoiraghi, G. C., Vanderveen, E., & Warren, K. R. (1981). Health hazards associated with alcohol consumption. *Journal of the American Medical Association, 246*, 648–666.

Eddy, D. M. (1982). Probabilistic reasoning in clinical medicine: Problems and opportunities. In D. Kahneman and A. Tversky (Eds.), *Judgment under uncertainty: Heuristics and biases*, (pp. 249–267). Cambridge: Cambridge University Press.

Edelwich, J., & Brodsky, A. (1980). *Burnout: Stages of disillusionment in the helping professions*. New York: Human Sciences Press.

Edwards, M. T., & Zimet, C. N. (1976). Problems and concerns among medical students—1975. *Journal of Medical Education, 51*, 619–625.

Egbert, L. D., Battit, G. E., Turndorf, H., & Beecher, H. K. (1963). Value of preoperative visit by anesthetist: Study of doctor-patient rapport. *Journal of the American Medical Association, 185*, 553–555.

Egbert, L. D., Battit, G. E., Welch, C. E., & Bartlett, M. K. (1964). Reduction of postoperative pain by encouragement and instruction of patients: A study of doctor-patient rapport. *New England Journal of Medicine, 270*(16), 825–827.

Eisenberg, C. (1989). Sounding board: Medicine is no longer a man's profession or When the men's club goes coed it's time to change the regs. *New England Journal of Medicine, 321*, 1542–1544.

Eisenberg, J. M. (1979). Sociological influences on decision-making by clinicians. *Annals of Internal Medicine, 90*, 957–964.

Eisenberg, L. (1977). The search for care. *Daedalus, 106*, 235–246.

Eisenthal, S., Emery, R., Lazare, A., & Udin, H. (1979). Adherence and the negotiated approach to patienthood. *Archives of General Psychiatry, 36*, 393–398.

Eiser, J. R., & van der Plight, J. (1986). Smoking cessation and smokers' perception of their addiction. *Journal of Social and Clinical Psychology, 4*, 60–70.

Ekman, P., & Friesen, W. V. (1974). Detecting deception from the body or face. *Journal of Personality and Social Psychology, 29*, 288–298.

Elias, W. S., & Murphy, R. J. (1986). The case for health promotion programs containing health care costs: A review of the literature. *American Journal of Occupational Therapy, 40*(11), 759–763.

Elizur, E., & Kaffman, M. (1982). Children's bereavement reactions following death of the father: II. *Journal of the American Academy of Child Psychiatry, 21*, 474–480.

Ellis, A. (1962). *Reason and emotion in psychotherapy*. New York: Lyle Stuart.

Ellis, A. (1977). The basic clinical theory of rational-emotive therapy. In A. Ellis & R. Grieger (Eds.), *Handbook of rational-emotive therapy*. New York: Springer.

Ellsworth, P. (1975). Direct gaze as a social stimulus: The example of aggression. In P. Pliner, L. Krames, & T. Alloway (Eds.), *Nonverbal communication of aggression*. New York: Plenum.

Ellsworth, P., Friedman, H., Perlick, D., & Hoyt, M. (1978). Some effects of gaze on subjects motivated to seek or to avoid social comparison. *Journal of Experimental Social Psychology, 14*, 69–87.

Elstein, A. S. (1976). Clinical judgment: Psychological research and medical practice. *Science, 194*, 696–700.

Enelow, A. J., & Swisher, S. N. (1972). *Interviewing and patient care*. London: Oxford University Press.

Engel, G. L. (1971). Sudden and rapid death during psychological stress: Folklore or folk wisdom? *Annals of Internal Medicine, 74*, 771–782.

Engel, G. L. (1977). The need for a new medical model: The challenge for biomedicine. *Science, 196*, 129–136.

Engel, G. L. (1980). The clinical application of the biopsychosocial model. *American Journal of Psychiatry, 137*, 535–544.

Engel, G. L., Reichsman, R., & Segal, H. L. (1956). A study of an infant with a gastric fistula: I. Behavior of total hydrochloric acid secretion. *Psychosomatic Medicine, 18*, 374–398.

**English, E. H., & Baker, T. B.** (1983). Relaxation training and cardiovascular response to experimental stressors. *Health Psychology, 2*, 239–259.

**Epstein, L. H., Miller, G. J., Stitt, F. W., & Morris, J. N.** (1976). Vigorous exercise in leisure time, coronary risk factors, and resting electrocardiogram in middle-aged civil servants. *British Heart Journal, 38*, 403.

**Epstein, L. H.** (1984). The direct effects of compliance on health outcome. *Health Psychology, 3*(4), 385–393.

**Epstein, L. H., & Clauss, P. A.** (1982). A behavioral medicine perspective on adherence to long-term medical regimens. *Journal of Consulting and Clinical Psychology, 50*, 950–971.

**Epstein, L. H., & Wing, R. R.** (1980). Behavioral approaches to exercise habits and athletic performance. In J. M. Ferguson & C. B. Taylor (Eds.), *The comprehensive handbook of behavioral medicine. Vol. 1, Systems interventions*, pp. 125–137. New York: S. P. Medical & Scientific Books.

**Epstein, L. H., Wing, R. R., Valoski, A., & DeVos, D.** (1988). Long-term relationship between weight and aerobic fitness change in children. *Health Psychology, 7*, 47–53.

**Eraker, S. A., Kirscht, J. P., & Becker, M. H.** (1984). Understanding and improving patient compliance. *Annals of Internal Medicine, 100*, 258–268.

**Eraker, S. A., & Politser, P.** (1982). How decisions are reached: Physician and patient. *Annals of Internal Medicine, 97*, 262–268.

**Erdelyi, M. H.** (1985). *Psychoanalysis: Freud's cognitive psychology.* New York: W. H. Freeman.

**Eriksen, M. P., Le Maistre, C. A., & Newell, G. R.** (1988). Health hazards of passive smoking. In L. Breslow, J. E. Fielding, & L. B. Lave (Eds.), *Annual review of public health* (Vol. 9). Palo Alto, CA: Annual Reviews.

**Erikson, E. H.** (1963). *Childhood and society* (2nd ed). New York: Norton, 1963.

**Eron, C.** (1988). Fat chance: Predicting breast cancer's course. *Science News, 134*, 100.

**Evans, E.** (1926). *A psychological study of cancer.* New York: Dodd, Mead.

**Evans, R. I.** (1985). Psychologists in health promotion research: General concerns and adolescent smoking prevention. In J. C. Rosen & L. J. Solomon (Eds.), *Prevention in Health Psychology* (pp. 18–33). Hanover, NH: University Press of New England.

**Evans, R. I., Smith, C. K., & Raines, B. E.** (1984). Deterring cigarette smoking in adolescents: A psychosocial-behavioral analysis of an intervention strategy. In A. Baum, S. E. Taylor, & J. E. Singer (Eds.), *Handbook of psychology and health. Vol. 4, Social psychological aspects of health.* Hillsdale, NJ: Erlbaum.

**Everson, R. B., & Fraumeni, J. F.** (1975). Mortality among medical students and young physicians. *Journal of Medical Education, 50*, 809–811.

**Fagerhaugh, S. Y.** (1973). Getting around with emphysema. *American Journal of Nursing, 73*, 94–99.

**Falck, H. S.** (1987). Social and psychological care before and during hospitalization. *Social Science and Medicine, 25*, 711–720.

**Feldenkreis, M.** (1981). *The elusive obvious.* Cupertino, CA: Meta Publications.

**Feller, B. A.** (1979). *Characteristics of general internists and the content of care of their patients* (HRA-79-652). Washington, DC: U.S. Department of Health, Education, and Welfare.

**Fernandez, E.** (1986). A classification system of cognitive coping strategies for pain. *Pain, 26*, 141–151.

**Feuerstein, M., Papciak, A. S., & Hoon, P. E.** (1987). Biobehavioral mechanisms of chronic low back pain. *Clinical Psychology Review, 7*, 243–273.

**Fine, C.** (1981). *Married to medicine: An intimate portrait of doctors' wives.* New York: Atheneum.

**Fischbach, R. L., Sionelo-Bayog, A., Needle, A., & DelBanco, T. L.** (1980). The patient and practitioner as co-authors of the medical record. *Patient Counseling and Health Education, 1*, 1–5.

**Fischer, R.** (1976). I can't remember what I said last night, but it must have been good. *Psychology Today, 10*, 68–72.

Fischer, R., & Landon, G. (1972). On the arousal state- dependent recall of "subconscious" experience: Stateboundness. *British Journal of Psychiatry, 120,* 159–172.

Fischer, S., & Cleveland, S. E. (1958). *Body image and personality.* Princeton, NJ: Van Nostrand.

Fishbein, M. (1980). A theory of reasoned action: Some applications and implications. In M. M. Page (Ed.), *1979 Nebraska Symposium on Motivation.* Lincoln: University of Nebraska Press.

Fishbein, M., and Ajzen, I. (1975). *Belief, attitude, intention, and behavior: An introduction to theory and research,* Reading, MA: Addison-Wesley.

Fisher, E. B., & Rost, K. (1986). Smoking cessation: A practical guide for the physician. *Clinics in Chest Medicine,* 7(4), 551–565.

Fisher, S. (1986). *In the patient's best interest: Women and the politics of medical decisions* (pp. 29–58). New Brunswick: Rutgers University Press.

Fleming, I., Baum, A., Davidson, L. M., Rectanus, E., & McArdle, S. (1987). Chronic stress as a factor in physiologic reactivity to challenge. *Health Psychology,* 6, 221–237.

Fleming, R., Baum, A., Gisriel, M. M., & Gatchel, R. J. (1982). Mediating influences of social support on stress at Three Mile Island. *Journal of Human Stress,* 8, 14–22.

Foley, K. M. (1985). The medical treatment of cancer pain. *New England Journal of Medicine, 313,* 84–95.

Folkman, S., & Lazarus, R. S. (1980). An analysis of coping in a middle-aged community sample. *Journal of Health and Social Behavior, 21,* 219–239.

Follette, W., & Cummings, N. A. (1967). Psychiatric services and medical utilization in a prepaid health plan setting. *Medical Care,* 5, 25–35.

Fordyce, W. E. (1976). *Behavioral methods for chronic pain and illness.* St. Louis: C. V. Mosby.

Fordyce, W. E. (1985). Back pain, compensation, and public policy. In J. C. Rosen & L. J. Solomon (Eds). *Prevention in health psychology* (pp. 390–400). Hanover, NH: University Press of New England.

Fordyce, W. E. (1988). Pain and suffering: A reappraisal. *American Psychologist, 43,* 276–283.

Fordyce, W. E., & Steger, J. C. (1979). Behavioral management of chronic pain. In O. F. Pomerleau & J. P. Brady (Eds.), *Behavioral medicine: Theory and practice.* Baltimore: Williams & Wilkins.

Fox, R. C. (1959). *Experiment perilous.* Philadelphia: University of Pennsylvania Press.

Fox, R. C., & Swazey, J. P. (1974). *The courage to fail: A social view of organ transplants and dialysis.* Chicago: University of Chicago Press.

Frame, P. S. (1986). A critical review of adult health maintenance. Part 3: Prevention of cancer. *Journal of Family Practice,* 22(6), 511–520.

Frank, A. F., & Gunderson, J. G. (1990). The role of the therapeutic alliance in the treatment of schizophrenia. *Archives of General Psychiatry,* 47, 228–236.

Frankenhaeuser, M. (1975). Sympathetic-adrenomedullary activity, behavior, and the psychosocial environment. In P. H. Venables and M. J. Christie (Eds.), *Research in psychophysiology.* New York: Wiley.

Frankenhaeuser, M. (1986). A psychobiological framework for research on human stress and coping. In M. H. Appley & R. Trumbull (Eds.), *Dynamics of stress: Physiological, psychological, and social perspectives.* New York: Plenum.

Franks, P., Culpepper, L., & Dickinson, J. (1982). Psychosocial bias in the diagnosis of obesity. *Journal of Family Practice,* 14, 745–750.

Freemon, B., Negrete, V. F., Davis, M., & Korsch, B. M. (1971). Gaps in doctor-patient communication: Doctor-patient interaction analysis. *Pediatric Research,* 5, 298–311.

Freidson, E. (1970). *Profession of medicine.* NY: Dodd, Mead.

Freud, S. (1924). The dynamics of transference. In *Collected papers* (Vol. 2). London: Institute of Psychoanalysis and Hogarth Press.

Fried, M. (1982). Endemic stress: The psychology of resignation and the politics of scarcity. *American Journal of Orthopsychiatry, 52*, 4–19.

Friedman, H. S. (1979). Nonverbal communication between patients and medical practitioners. *Journal of Social Issues, 35*, 82–99.

Friedman, H. S. (1982). Nonverbal communication in medical interaction. In H. S. Friedman & M. R. DiMatteo (Eds.), *Interpersonal issues in health care.* New York: Academic Press.

Friedman, H. S., & Booth-Kewley, S. (1987). The "disease-prone personality": A meta-analytic view of the construct. *American Psychologist, 42*(6), 539–555.

Friedman, H. S., & Booth-Kewley, S. (1988). Validity of the Type A construct: A reprise. *Psychological Bulletin, 104*(3), 381–384.

Friedman, H. S., Hall, J. A., & Harris, M. J. (1985). Type A behavior, nonverbal expressive style, and health. *Journal of Personality and Social Psychology, 48*, 1299–1315.

Friedman, H. S., Harris, M. J., & Hall, J. A., (1984). Nonverbal expression of emotion: Healthy charisma or cornary-prone behavior? In C. Van Dyke, L. Temoshok, & L. S. Zegans (Eds.), *Emotions in health and illness: Applications to clinical practice* (pp. 151–165). San Diego: Grune & Stratton.

Friedman, M., & Powell, L. H. (1984). The diagnosis and quantitative assessment of Type A behavior: Introduction and description of the videotaped structured interview. *Integrative Psychiatry, 2*, 123–129.

Friedman, M., & Rosenman, R. H. (1974). *Type A behavior and your heart.* New York: Knopf.

Friedman, M., & Ulmer, D. (1984). *Treating Type A behavior and your heart.* New York: Knopf.

Furman, E. (1974). *A child's parent dies.* New Haven: Yale University Press.

Gail, M. H., & Brookmeyer, R. (1990). Projecting the incidence of AIDS. *Journal of the American Medical Association, 263*(11), 1538.

Gal, R., & Lazarus, R. S. (1975). The role of activity in anticipating and confronting stressful situations. *Journal of Human Stress, 1*, 4–20.

Gapen, P. (1980). Stress: Medical school's per- ilous rites of passage. *New Physician, 29*, 18–22.

Garrity, T. F. (1975). Morbidity, mortality, and rehabilitation. In W. D. Gentry and R. B. Williams, Jr. (Eds.), *Psychological aspects of myocardial infraction and coronary care.* St. Louis: C. V. Mosby.

Garrity, T. F. (1981). Medical compliance and the clinician-patient relationship: A review. *Social Science and Medicine, 15*, 215–222.

Garrity, T. F., & Marx, M. B. (1979). Critical life events and coronary disease. In W. D. Gentry & R. B. Williams (Eds.), *Psychological aspects of myocardial infarction and coronary care* (2nd ed.). St. Louis: C. V. Mosby.

Geisel, T. S. (1976). *Dr. Seuss's Sleep Book.* New York: Random House. (Originally published 1962.)

Gelfand, D. M. (1978). Social withdrawal and negative emotional states: Behavior therapy. In B. B. Wolman, J. Egan, & A. O. Ross (Eds.), *Handbook of treatment of mental disorders in childhood and adolescence.* Englewood Cliffs, NJ: Prentice-Hall.

Gelfand, D. M., Gelfand, S., & Rardin, M. W. (1965). Some personality factors associated with placebo responsivity. *Psychological Reports, 17*, 555–562.

Gentry, W. D. (1979). Preadmission behavior. In W. D. Gentry & R. B. Williams (Eds.), *Psychological aspects of myocardial infarction and coronary care* (2nd ed.), pp. 67–77. St. Louis: C. V. Mosby.

Gentry, W. D., & Williams, R. B. (Eds.). (1979). *Psychological aspects of myocardial infarction and coronary care* (2nd ed.). St. Louis: C. V. Mosby.

Gerber, L. A. (1983). Married to their careers: Career and family dilemmas in doctors' lives. New York: Tavistock.

Gerhardt, U. (1990). Patient careers in end-stage renal failure. *Social Science and Medicine, 30*, 1211–1224.

Gillum, R. F., Manning, F., Margolis, S. R., Fabsitz, R. R., & Brasch, R. C. (1976). Delay in the prehospital phase of acute myocardial infarction. *Archives of Internal Medicine, 136*, 649–654.

Glass, D. C. (1977). *Behavior patterns, stress, and coronary disease.* Hillsdale, NJ: Erlbaum.

Glass, D. C., & Singer, J. E. (1972). *Urban stress.* New York: Academic Press.

Glasser, P., & Glasser, L. (Eds.). (1969). *Families in crisis.* New York: Harper & Row.

Glueckauf, R. L., & Quittner, A. L. (1984). Facing physical disability as a young adult: Psychological issues and approaches. In M. G. Eisenberg, L. C. Sutkin, & M. A. Jansen (Eds.), *Chronic illness and disability through the life span: Effects on self and family* (pp. 167–183). New York: Springer.

Godwin, G. (1982). *A mother and two daughters* (pp. 11–22). New York: Avon.

Goffman, E. (1963). *Stigma.* Englewood Cliffs, NJ: Prentice-Hall.

Goldenson, R. M. (1978a). Dimensions of the field. In R. M. Goldenson, J. R. Dunham, & C. S. Dunham (Eds.), *Disability and rehabilitation handbook* (pp. 3–11). New York: McGraw-Hill.

Goldenson, R. M. (1978b). Independent living: Ways and means. In R. M. Goldenson, J. R. Dunham, & C. S. Dunham (Eds.), *Disability and rehabilitation handbook* (pp. 36–52). New York: McGraw-Hill.

Goldenson, R. M., Dunham, J. R., & Dunham, C. S. (Eds.), (1978). *Disability and rehabilitation handbook.* New York: McGraw-Hill.

Goldstein, A. P. (1980). Relationship-enhancement methods. In F. H. Kanfer & A. P. Goldstein (Eds.), *Helping people change* (2nd ed.) (pp. 18–57). New York: Pergamon Press.

Goldstein, A. P., & Kanfer, F. H. (Eds.). (1979). *Maximizing treatment gains: Transfer enhancement in psychotherapy.* New York: Academic Press.

Goldstein, M. J. (1973). Individual differences in response to stress. *American Journal of Community Psychology, 1,* 113–137.

Goldwater, B. C., & Collis, M. L. (1985). Psychologic effects of cardiovascular conditioning: A controlled experiment. *Psychosomatic Medicine, 47,* 174–181.

Goodwin, J. S., Goodwin, J. M., & Vogel, A. V. (1979). Knowledge and use of placebos by house officers and nurses. *Annals of Internal Medicine, 91,* 106–110.

Gordon, T., & Doyle, J. T. (1987). Drinking and mortality: The Albany Study. *American Journal of Epidemiology, 125,* 263–270.

Gordon, T., & Kannel, W. B. (1984). Drinking and mortality: The Framingham Study. *American Journal of Epidemiology, 120,* 97–107.

Gorer, G. (1965). *Death, grief, and mourning.* New York: Doubleday.

Gotay, C. C. (1984). The experience of cancer during early and advanced stages: The views of patients and their mates. *Social Science and Medicine, 18,* 605–613.

Graham, D. T. (1972). Psychosomatic medicine. In N. S. Greenfield & R. A. Sternbach (Eds.), *Handbook of psychophysiology.* New York: Holt, Rinehart & Winston.

Gray, P. G., & Cartwright, A. (1953, December 19). Choosing and changing doctors. *Lancet,* 1308.

Grundy, S. M. (1986). Cholesterol and coronary heart disease: A new era. *Journal of the American Medical Association, 256,* 2849–2858.

Gulledge, A. D. (1979). Psychological aftermaths of myocardial infarction. In W. D. Gentry & R. B. Williams (Eds.), *Psychological aspects of myocardial infarction and coronary care* (2nd ed.) (pp. 113–130). St. Louis: C. V. Mosby.

Guyton, A. C. (1985). *Anatomy and physiology.* Philadelphia: Saunders.

Hackett, G. F., & Horan, J. J. (1978). Focused smoking: An equivocally safe alternative to rapid smoking. *Journal of Drug Education, 8,* 261–265.

Hackett, T. P., & Cassem, N. H. (1969). Factors contributing to delay in responding to the signs and symptoms of acute myocardial infarction. *American Journal of Cardiology, 24,* 651.

Haight, W. L., Black, J. E., & DiMatteo, M. R. (1985). Young children's understanding of the social roles of physician and patient. *Journal of Pediatric Psychology, 10*(1), 31–43.

Hall, J. A., Roter, D. L., & Katz, N. R. (1988). Meta-analysis of correlates of provider behavior in medical encounters. *Medical Care, 26*(6), 1–19.

Hall, J. A., Roter, D. L., & Rand, C. S. (1981). Communication of affect between patient and physician. *Journal of Health and Social Behavior, 22,* 18–30.

Hall, R. G., Sachs, D. P., Hall, S. M., & Benowitz, N. L. (1984). Two-year efficacy and safety of rapid smoking therapy in patients with cardiac and pulmonary disease. *Journal of Consulting and Clinical Psychology, 52*(4), 574–581.

**Hamberger, K., & Lohr, J.** (1984). *Stress and stress management: Research and applications.* New York: Springer.

**Hamburg, D. A., Hamburg, B., & DeGoza, S.** (1953). Adaptive problems and mechanisms in severely burned patients. *Psychiatry, 16,* 1–20.

**Hamilton, H. K., & Rose, M. B.** (Ed.). (1982). *Professional guide to diseases.* Springhouse, PA: Springhouse.

**Harburg, E., Erfurt, J. C., Hauenstein, L. S., Chape, C., Schull, W. J., & Schork, M. A.** (1973). Socio-ecological stress, suppressed hostility, skin color, and black-white male blood pressure: Detroit. *Psychosomatic Medicine, 35,* 276–296.

**Hardison, J. E.** (1986). The house officer's changing world. *New England Journal of Medicine, 314*(26), 1713–1715.

**Hare, B. D., & Milano, R. A.** (1985). Chronic pain: Perspectives on physical assessment and treatment. *Annals of Behavioral Medicine, 7*(3), 6–10.

**Harper, F. D.** (1978). Outcomes of jogging: Implication for counseling. *Personnel and Guidance Journal, 57,* 74–78.

**Harrigan, J., Oxman, T., & Rosenthal, R.** (1985). Rapport expressed through nonverbal behavior. *Journal of Nonverbal Behavior, 9,* 95–110.

**Harris, L., & Associates** (1984). *Healthy lifestyles/Unhealthy lifestyles: A national research report of behavior, knowledge, motivation, and opinions concerning individual health practices.* Garland, NY: Garland.

**Harris, M. B.** (1981). Runner's perceptions of the benefits of running. *Perceptual and Motor Skills, 52,* 153–154.

**Harrison, R. F.** (1986). The use of non-essential drugs, alcohol, and cigarettes during pregnancy. *Irish Medical Journal, 79*(12), 338–341.

**Haskell, W. L., Camargo, C., Jr., Williams, P. R., Vranizan, K. M., Krauss, R. M., Lindgren, F. T., & Wood, P. D.** (1984). The effect of cessation and resumption of moderate alchol intake on serum high-density lipoprotein subfractions. *New England Journal of Medicine, 310,* 805–810.

**Haskell, W. L., Montoye, H. J., & Orenstein, D.** (1985). Physical activity and exercise to achieve health related physical fitness components. *Public Health Reports, 100,* 202–212.

**Haug, M., & Lavin, B.** (1983). *Consumerism in medicine: Challenging physician authority.* Beverly Hills: Sage.

**Hawkins, M. R., Vichick, D. A., Silsby, H. D., Kruzich, D. J., & Butler, R.** (1985). Sleep and nutritional deprivation and performance of house officers. *Journal of Medical Education, 60,* 530–535.

**Hay, D., & Oken, D.** (1972). The psychological stresses of intensive care unit nursing. *Psychosomatic Medicine, 34,* 109–118.

**Haynes, R. B.** (1979a). Determinants of compliance: The disease and the mechanics of treatment. In R. B. Haynes, D. W. Taylor, & D. L. Sackett (Eds.), *Compliance in health care* (pp. 49–62). Baltimore: Johns Hopkins University Press.

**Haynes, R. B.** (1979b). Strategies to improve compliance with referrals, appointments, and prescribed medical regimens. In R. B. Haynes, D. W. Taylor, & D. L. Sackett (Eds.), *Compliance in health care* (pp. 121–143). Baltimore: Johns Hopkins University Press.

**Haynes, R. B., Taylor, D. W., & Sackett, D. L.** (Eds.). (1979). *Compliance in health care.* Baltimore: Johns Hopkins University Press.

**Haynes, S. G., Levine, S., Scotch, N., Feinleib, M., & Kannel, W. B.** (1978). The relationship of psychosocial factors to coronary heart disease in the Framingham Study: I. Methods and risk factors. *American Journal of Epidemiology, 107,* 362–383.

**Hays, R. D., Stacy, A. W., & DiMatteo, M. R.** (1984). Covariation among health related behaviors. *Addictive Behaviors, 9,* 315–318.

**Heinrich, R. L., Cohen, M. J., Naliboff, B. D., Collins, G. A., & Bonnebakker, A. D.** (1985). Comparing physical and behavior therapy for chronic low back pain on physical abilities, psychological distress, and patients' perceptions. *Journal of Behavioral Medicine, 8,* 61–78.

**Hellerstein, D.** (1986). *Battles of life and death.* Boston: Houghton Mifflin.

**Helsing, K. J., Szklo, M., & Comstock, G. W.** (1981). Factors associated with mortality after widowhood. *American Journal of Public Health, 71,* 802–809.

**Hendrick, C., Wells, K. S., & Faletti, M. V.** (1982). Social and emotional effects of geographical relocation on elderly retirees. *Journal of Personality and Social Psychology, 41,* 951–962.

**Henley, N. M.** (1977). *Body politics.* Englewood Cliffs, NJ: Prentice-Hall.

**Herman, M.** (1972). The poor: Their medical needs and the health services available to them. *Annals of the American Academy of Political and Social Sciences, 399,* 12–21.

**Heron, E.** (1987). *Intensive care: The story of a nurse.* New York: Ballantine.

**Herzberger, S. D., & Potts, D. A.** (1982). Interpersonal relations during the childbearing years. In H. S. Friedman & M. R. DiMatteo (Eds.), *Interpersonal issues in health care* (pp. 101–117). New York: Academic Press.

**Heszen-Klemes I.** (1987). Patients' noncompliance and how doctors manage this. *Social Science and Medicine, 24,* 409–416.

**Hewitt, J. P.** (1979). *Self and society: A symbolic interactionist social psychology* (2nd ed.). Boston: Allyn & Bacon.

**Hilgard, E. R.** (1968). *The experience of hypnosis.* New York: Harcourt, Brace & World.

**Hilgard, E. R.** (1969). Pain as a puzzle for psychology and physiology. *American Psychologist, 24,* 103–113.

**Hilgard, E. R.** (1978). Hypnosis and pain. In R. A. Sternbach (Ed.). *The psychology of pain.* New York: Raven Press.

**Hilgard, E. R., & Hilgard, J. R.** (1975). *Hypnosis in the relief of pain.* Los Altos, CA: Kaufman.

**Hingson, R., Scotch, N. A., Sorenson, J., & Swazey, J. P.** (1981). *In sickness and in health: Social dimensions of medical care.* St. Louis: C. V. Mosby.

**Hinton, J.** (1977). Bearing cancer. In R. H. Moos (Ed.). *Coping with physical illness* (pp. 59–72). New York: Plenum.

**Hippocrates.** (4th century B.C./1923 translation). Vol. 2, *On decorum and the physician* (W. H. S. Jones, Trans.). London: Heinemann.

**Holahan, C. K., Holahan, C. J., & Belk, S. S.** (1984). Adjustment in aging: The roles of life stress, hassles, and self-efficacy. *Health Psychology, 3,* 315–328.

**Holmes, T. H., & Masuda, M.** (1974). Life change and illness susceptibility. In B. S. Dohrenwend & B. P. Dohrenwend (Eds.), *Stressful life events: Their nature and effects* (pp. 45–72). New York: Wiley.

**Holmes, T. H., & Rahe, R. H.** (1967). The Social Readjustment Rating Scale. *Journal of Psychosomatic Research, 11,* 213–218.

**Holroyd, K. A., Andrasik, F., & Westbrook, T.** (1977). Cognitive control of tension headache. *Cognitive Therapy and Research, 1,* 121–133.

**House, J. S.** (1981). *Work stress and social support.* Reading, MA: Addison-Wesley.

**House, J. S., Robbins, C., & Metzner, H. L.** (1982). The association of social relationships and activities with mortality: Prospective evidence from the Tecumseh Community Health Study. *American Journal of Epidemiology, 116,* 123–140.

**Hovland, C. I.** (1959). Reconciling conflicting results derived from experimental and survey studies of attitude change. *American Psychologist, 14,* 8–17.

**Hovland, C. I., Janis, I. L., & Kelley, H. H.** (1953). *Communication and persuasion.* New Haven: Yale University Press.

**Howard, J.** (1978). Patient-centric technologies: A case for "soft science." In Gallagher, E. B. (Ed.), *The doctor-patient relationship in the changing health scene* (NIH No. 78–183) (pp. 347–361). Washington, DC: U.S. Department of Health, Education, and Welfare.

**Hughes, J. R.** (1984). Psychological effects of habitual aerobic exercise: a critical review. *Preventive Medicine, 13,* 66–78.

**Hulka, B. S., Zyzanski, S. J., Cassel, J. C., & Thompson, S. J.** (1970). Scale for the measurement of attitudes toward physicians and primary medical care. *Medical Care, 8*(5), 429–435.

**Hull, J. G.** (1981). A self-awarness model of the cause and effects of alcohol consumption. *Journal of Abnormal Psychology, 90,* 586–600.

**Hunt, W. A., Barnett, L. W., & Branch, L. G.** (1971). Relapse rates in addiction programs. *Journal of Clinical Psychology, 27,* 455–456.

**Hunter, R. C. A., Lohrenz, J. G., & Schwartzman, A. E.** (1964). Nosophobia and hypochondriasis in medical students. *Journal of Nervous and Mental Disease, 139,* 147–152.

**Hurtado, A., Greenlick, M., & Columbo, T.** (1973). Determinants of medical care utilization: Failure to keep appointments. *Medical Care, 11,* 189–198.

**Ice, R.** (1985). Long term compliance. *Physical Therapy, 65* (12), 1832–1839.

**Imboden, J. B., Canter, A., & Cluff, E.** (1961). Convalescence from influenza: A study of the psychological and clinical determinants. *Archives of Internal Medicine, 108,* 393–399.

**Ingelfinger, F. J.** (1978). Medicine: Meritorious or meritricious. *Science, 200,* 942–946.

**Ireys, H. T., & Burr, C. K.** (1984). Apart and a part: Family issues for young adults with chronic illness and disability. In M. G. Eisenberg, L. C. Sutkin, & M. A. Jansen (Eds.), *Chronic illness and disability through the life span: Effects on self and family* (pp. 184–206). New York: Springer.

**Isselbacher, K. J., Adams, R. D., Braunwald, E., Petersdorf, R. G., & Wilson, J. D.** (1980). *Harrison's principles of internal medicine* (9th ed.). New York: McGraw-Hill.

**Izard, C. E.** (1977). *Human emotions.* New York: Plenum.

**James, G. D., Yee, L. S., Harshfield, G. A., Blank, S. G., & Pickering, T. G.** (1986). The influence of happiness, anger, and anxiety on the blood-pressure of borderline hypertensives. *Psychosomatic Medicine, 48,* 502–508.

**Janet, P.** (1929). *The major symptoms of hysteria: Fifteen lectures given in the medical school of Harvard University.* New York: Hafner.

**Janis, I. L.** (1958). *Psychological stress.* New York: Wiley.

**Janz, N. K., & Becker, M. H.** (1984). The health belief model: A decade later. *Health Education Quarterly 11*(1), 1–47.

**Jarvinen, K. A.** (1955). Can ward rounds be a danger to patients with myocardial infarction? *British Medical Journal, 1,* 318–320.

**Jay, S., Litt, I. F., & Durant, R. H.** (1984). Compliance with therapeutic regimens. *Journal of Adolescent Health Care, 5*(2), 124–136.

**Jemmott, J. B., & Locke, S. E.** (1984). Psychosocial factors, immunological mediation, and human susceptibility to infectious diseases: How much do we know? *Psychological Bulletin, 95,* 78-108.

**Jenkins, C. D., Zyzanski, S. J., & Rosenman, R. H.** (1979). *Jenkins Activity Survey.* Cleveland: Psychological Corporation.

**Jennings, G., Nelson, L., Nestel, P., Esler, M., Korner, P., Burton, D., & Bazelmans, J.** (1986). The effects of changes in physical activity on major cardiovascular risk factors, hemodynamics, sympathetic function, and glucose utilization in man: A controlled study of four levels of activity. *Circulation, 73,* 30–40.

**Johnson, D. W.** (1972). *Reaching out: Interpersonal effectiveness and self-actualization.* Englewood Cliffs, NJ: Prentice-Hall.

**Johnson, D. W.** (1980). Attitude modification methods. In F. H. Kanfer & A. P. Goldstein (Eds.), *Helping people change* (2nd ed.) (pp. 58–96). New York: Pergamon Press.

**Johnson, D. W., & Matross, R. P.** (1975). Attitude modification methods. In F. H. Kanfer & A. P. Goldstein (Eds.), *Helping people change* (1st ed.) (pp. 51–88). New York: Pergamon Press.

**Johnson, J. E.** (1975). Stress reduction through sensation information. In I. G. Sarason & D. C. Spielberger (Eds.), *Stress and anxiety* (Vol. 2). Washington, DC: Hemisphere.

**Johnson, J. E., & Leventhal, H.** (1974). Effects of accurate expectations and behavioral instructions on reactions during a noxious medical examination. *Journal of Personality and Social Psychology, 29,* 710–718.

**Johnson, J. H.** (1986). *Life events as stressors in childhood and adolescence.* Newbury Park, CA: Sage.

**Johnson, J. H., Sarason, I. G., & Siegel, J. M.** (1979). Arousal seeking as a moderator of life stress. *Perceptual and Motor Skills, 49,* 665–666.

**Johnson, S. M., Kurtz, M. E., Tomlinson, T., &**

**Howe, K. R.** (1986). Students' stereotypes of patients as barriers to clinical decision-making. *Journal of Medical Education, 61*, 727–735.

**Jones, J. W.** (1981). Diagnosing and treating staff burnout among health professionals. In J. W. Jones (Ed.), *The burnout syndrome.* Park Ridge, IL: London House Management Press.

**Jones, P. K., Jones, S. L., & Katz, J.** (1987). Improving compliance for asthmatic patients visiting the emergency department using a health belief model intervention. *Journal of Asthma, 24*(4), 199–206.

**Kalisch, B. J.** (1971). Strategies for developing nurse empathy. *Nursing Outlook, 19*, 714–718.

**Kamerow, D., Pincus, H. A., & MacDonald, D. I.** (1986). Alcohol abuse, other drug abuse, and mental disorders in medical practice. *Journal of the American Medical Association, 255*, 2054–2057.

**Kane, R. L., & Deuschle, K. W.** (1967). Problems in doctor-patient communications. *Medical Care, 5*(4), 260–271.

**Kanfer, F. H., & Phillips, J. S.** (1970). *Learning foundations of behavior therapy.* New York: Wiley.

**Kanner, A. D., Coyne, J. C., Schaefer, C., & Lazarus, R. S.** (1981). Comparison of two models of stress measurement: Daily hassles and uplifts versus major life events. *Journal of Behavioral Medicine, 4*, 1–39.

**Kanner, R.** (1986). Pain management. *Journal of the American Medical Association, 256*, 2110–2114.

**Kanouse, D. E., Berry, S. H., Hayes-Roth, B., Rogers, W. H., & Winkler, J. D.** (1981). *Informing patients about drugs: Summary report on alternative designs for prescription drug leaflets* (R-2800-FDA). Santa Monica: RAND.

**Kaplan, B. H., Cassel, J. C., & Gore, S.** (1977). Social support and health. *Medical Care, 15* (Suppl. 1), 47–58.

**Karoly, P.** (1980). Operant methods. In F. H. Kanfer & A. P. Goldstein (Eds.), *Helping people change* (2nd ed.). New York: Pergamon Press.

**Karoly, P.** (1985). The assessment of pain: Concepts and procedures. In P. Karoly (Ed.), *Measurement strategies in health psychology.* New York: Wiley.

**Kasl, S. V.** (1975). Issues in patient adherence to health care regimens. *Journal of Human Stress, 1*, 5–17.

**Kasl, S. V.** (1980). Cardiovascular risk education in a community setting: Some comments. *Journal of Consulting and Clinical Psychology, 48*, 143–149.

**Kasl, S. V., & Cobb, S.** (1966). Health behavior, illness behavior, and sick role behavior. I. Health and illness behavior. *Archives of Environmental Health, 12*, 246–266.

**Kasteler, J., Kane, R. L., Olsen, D. M., & Thetford, C.** (1976). Issues underlying prevalence of "doctor-shopping" behavior. *Journal of Health and Social Behavior, 17*, 328–337.

**Kastenbaum, R.** (1977). Death and development through the lifespan. In H. Feifel (Ed.), *New meanings of death.* New York: McGraw-Hill.

**Kastenbaum, R., & Aisenberg, R. B.** (1972). *The psychology of death.* NY: Springer.

**Kastenbaum, R. J.** (1977). *Death, society, and human experience.* St. Louis: C. V. Mosby.

**Katon, W.** (1982). Depression: Somatic symptoms and medical disorders in primary care. *Comprehensive Psychiatry, 23*, 274–287.

**Katz, J. L., Weiner, H., Gallagher, T. F., and Hellman, L.** (1970). Stress, distress, and ego defenses: Psychoendocrine response to impending breast tumor biopsy. *Archives of General Psychiatry, 23*, 131–142.

**Katz, R. C., & Zlutnick, S.** (1975). *Behavior therapy and health care: Principles and applications.* New York: Pergamon Press.

**Kaufman-Cartwright, L.** (1972). Conscious factors entering into decisions of women to study medicine. *Journal of Social Issues, 28*, 201–215.

**Keesling, B., & Friedman, H. S.** (1987). Psychosocial factors in sunbathing and sunscreen use. *Health Psychology, 6*(5), 477–493.

**Kegeles, S. S.** (1963). Why people seek dental care: A test of a conceptual formulation. *Journal of Health and Human Behavior, 4*, 166–173.

**Kegeles, S. S.** (1985). Education for breast self-examination: Why, who, what, and how? *Preventive Medicine, 14,* 702–720.

**Kellner, R.** (1965). Neurosis in general practice. *British Journal of Clinical Practice, 19,* 681–682.

**Kellner, R.** (1986). *Somatization and hypochondriasis.* New York: Praeger.

**Kelly, M. P.** (1986). The subjective experience of chronic disease: Some implications for the management of ulcerative colitis. *Journal of Chronic Disease, 39*(8), 653–666.

**Kiecolt-Glaser, J. K., Fisher, L. D., Ogrocki, P., Stout, J. C., Speicher, C. E., & Glaser, R.** (1987). Marital quality, marital disruption, and immune function. *Psychosomatic Medicine, 49,* 13–34.

**Kiecolt-Glaser, J. K., Garner, W., Speicher, C., Penn, G. M., Holliday, J., & Glaser, R.** (1984). Psychosocial modifiers of immunocompetence in medical students. *Psychosomatic Medicine, 46,* 7–14.

**Kiecolt-Glaser, J. K., & Glaser R.** (1986). Psychological influences on immunity. *Psychosomatics, 27,* 621–624.

**Kiecolt-Glaser, J. K., Stephens, R. E., Lipetz, P. D., Speicher, C. E., & Glaser, R.** (1985). Distress and DNA repair in human lymphocytes. *Journal of Behavioral Medicine, 8,* 311–320.

**Kiesler, C. A.** (1971). *The psychology of commitment.* New York: Academic Press.

**Kiesler, C. A., & Sakamura, J. A.** (1966). A test of a model for commitment and dissonance. *Journal of Personality and Social Psychology, 3,* 349–353.

**Kimball, C. P.** (1977). Psychological responses to the experience of open heart surgery. In R. H. Moos (Ed.). *Coping with physical illness* (pp. 113–133). New York: Plenum.

**Klapper, J. T.** (1960). *The effects of mass communication.* Glencoe, IL: Free Press.

**Klass, P.** (1987a). *A not entirely benign procedure: Four years as a medical student.* New York: Putnam.

**Klass, P.** (1987b). Sick jokes. *Discover, 8*(11), 30–35.

**Kleck, R.** (1968). Physical stigma and nonverbal cues emitted in face-to-face interaction. *Human Relations, 21,* 119–128.

**Klein, R. F., Dean, A., & Bogdonoff, M. D.** (1967). The impact of illness upon the spouse. *Journal of Chronic Diseases, 20,* 241–248.

**Kleinke, C. L., & Spangler, A. S.** (1988). Psychometric analysis of the audiovisual taxonomy for assessing pain behavior in chronic back-pain patients. *Journal of Behavioral Medicine, 11,* 83–94.

**Kleinman, A.** (1988). *The illness narratives: Suffering, healing, and the human condition.* New York: Basic Books.

**Knowles, J. H.** (1977). The responsibility of the individual. *Daedalus, 106,* 57-80.

**Kobasa, S. C.** (1979). Stressful life events, personality and health: An inquiry into hardiness. *Journal of Personality and Social Psychology, 37,* 1–11.

**Kobasa, S. C.** (1982). The hardy personality: Toward a social psychology of stress and health. In G. S. Sanders & J. Suls (Eds.), *Social psychology of health and illness* (pp. 3–32). Hillsdale, NJ: Erlbaum.

**Kobasa, S. C., Maddi, S. R., & Kahn, S.** (1982). Hardiness and health: A prospective study. *Journal of Personality and Social Psychology, 42,* 168–177.

**Kobasa, S. C., Maddi, S. R., & Puccetti, M. C.** (1982). Personality and exercise as buffers in the stress-illness relationship. *Journal of Behavioral Medicine, 5,* 391–403.

**Kobasa, S. C., Maddi, S. R., Puccetti, M. C., & Zola, I.** (1985). Effectiveness of hardiness, exercise, and social support as resources against illness. *Journal of Psychosomatic Research, 29*(5), 525–533.

**Kobasa, S. C., & Puccetti, M. C.** (1983). Personality and social resources in stress resistance. *Journal of Personality and Social Psychology, 45*(4), 839–850.

**Koocher, G. P.** (1985). Promoting coping with illness in childhood. In J. C. Rosen & L. J. Solomon (Eds.), *Prevention in health psychology* (pp. 311–327). Hanover, NH: University Press of New England.

**Koos, E.** (1954). *The health of Regionville.* New York: Columbia University Press.

**Koplan, J. P., Capersen, C. J., & Powell, K. E.** (1989). Physical activity, physical fitness, and health: Time to act. *Journal of the American Medical Association, 262*(17), 2437.

**Korsch, B. M., Gozzi, E. K., & Francis, V.** (1968). Gaps in doctor-patient communication. I. Doctor-patient interaction and patient satisfaction. *Pediatrics, 42,* 855–871.

Korsch, B. M., & Negrete, V. F. (1972). Doctor-patient communication. *Scientific American, 227,* 66–74.

Kosa, J., & Robertson, L. (1975). The social aspects of health and illness. In J. Kosa & I. Zola (Eds.), *Poverty and health: A sociological analysis.* Cambridge: Harvard University Press, 1975.

Kottke, T. E., Battista, R. N., DeFriese, G. H., & Brekke, M. L. (1988). Attributes of successful smoking cessation interventions in medical practice. *Journal of the American Medical Association, 259*(19), 2883–2889.

Krakowski, A. J. (1982). Stress and the practice of medicine: II. Stressors, stresses, and strains. *Psychotherapy and Psychosomatics, 38,* 11–23.

Kramer, M. (1974). *Reality shock: Why nurses leave nursing.* St. Louis: C. V. Mosby.

Kramer, R. F. (1987). Living with childhood cancer: Impact on the healthy siblings. In T. Krulik, B. Holaday, & I. M. Martinson (Eds.), *The child and family facing life-threatening illness* (pp. 258–272). New York: Lippincott.

Krantz, D. S., Baum, A., & Singer, J. E. (Eds). (1983). *Handbook of psychology and health.* Vol. 3, *Cardiovascular disorders and behavior.* Hillsdale, NJ: Erlbaum.

Krantz, D. S., Baum, A., & Wideman, M. V. (1980). Assessment of preferences for self-treatment and information in health care. *Journal of Personality and Social Psychology, 39,* 977–990.

Krantz, D. S., & Deckel, A. W. (1983). Coping with coronary heart disease and stroke. In T. G. Burish & L. A. Bradley (Eds.), *Coping with chronic disease: Research and applications.* New York: Academic Press.

Kraus, A. S., & Lilienfeld, A. M. (1959). Some epidemiological aspects of the high mortality rate in the young widowed group. *Journal of Chronic Diseases, 10,* 207–217.

Kronfol, Z., Silva, J., Greden, J., Dembinski, S., Gardner, R., & Carroll, B. (1983). Impaired lymphocyte function in depressive illness. *Life Sciences, 33,* 241–247.

Krulik, T. (1987). Loneliness and social isolation in school-age children with chronic life-threatening illness. In T. Krulik, B. Holaday, & I. M. Martinson. *The child and family facing life-threatening illness* (pp. 133–161). New York: Lippincott.

Kübler-Ross, E. (1969). *On death and dying.* New York: Macmillan.

Lachman, M. E. (1986). Personal control in later life: Stability, change and cognitive correlates. In M. M. Baltes, & P. B. Baltes (Eds.), *The psychology of control and aging* (pp. 207–236). Hillsdale, NJ: Erlbaum.

La Crosse, M. B. (1975) Nonverbal behavior and perceived counselor attractiveness and persuasiveness. *Journal of Counseling Psychology, 22,* 563–566.

Langer, E. J., Janis, I. L., & Wolfer, J. A. (1975). Reduction of psychological stress in surgical patients. *Journal of Experimental Social Psychology, 11,* 155–165.

Langer, E. J., & Rodin, J. (1976). The effects of choice and enhanced personal responsibility for the aged: A field experiment in an institutional setting. *Journal of Personality and Social Psychology, 34,* 191–198.

Larsen, K. M., & Smith, C. K. (1981). Assessment of nonverbal communication in the patient-physician interview. *Journal of Family Practice, 12*(3), 481–488.

Larson, E. B., & Bruce, R. A. (1987). Health benefits of exercise in an aging society. *Archives of Internal Medicine, 147,* 353–356.

Larson, R., & Sutker, S. (1966). Value differences and value consensus by socioeconomic levels. *Social Forces, 44,* 563–569.

Lau, R. R., Hartman, K. A., & Ware, J. E., Jr. (1986). Health as a value: Methodological and theoretical considerations. *Health Psychology, 5*(1), 25–43.

Lau, R. R., & Hartman, K. A. (1983). Common-sense representations of common illness. *Health Psychology, 2,* 167–185.

Lauer, M., Mulhern, R., Wallskog, J., & Camitta, B. (1983). A comparison study of parental adaptation following a child's death at home or in the hospital. *Pediatrics, 71,* 101–111.

Lavee, Y., McCubbin, H. I., & Patterson, J. M. (1985). The Double ABCX Model of family stress and adaptation: An empirical test by analysis of structural equations with latent variables. *Journal of Marriage and Family, 47,* 811–825.

**Lavey, R. S., & Taylor, C. B.** (1985). The nature of relaxation therapy. In S. R. Burchfield (Ed.), *Stress: Psychological and physiological interactions.* Washington, DC: Hemisphere.

**Lazare, A., Eisenthal, S., Frank, A., & Stoeckle, J.** (1978). Studies on a negotiated approach to patienthood. In E. B. Gallagher (Ed.), *The doctor-patient relationship in the changing health scene* (NIH No. 78–183), pp. 119–139. Washington, DC: U.S. Department of Health, Education, and Welfare.

**Lazarus, R. S.** (1980). The stress and coping paradigm. In C. Eisdorfer, D. Cohen, & A. Kleinman (Eds.), *Conceptual models for psychopathology.* New York: Spectrum.

**Lazarus, R. S.** (1984a). On the primacy of cognition. *American Psychologist, 39*(2), 124–129.

**Lazarus, R. S.** (1984b). Puzzles in the study of daily hassles. *Journal of Behavioral Medicine, 7,* 375–389.

**Lazarus, R. S.** (1985). The trivialization of distress. In J. C. Rosen & L. J. Solomon (Eds.), *Prevention in health psychology* (pp. 279–298). Hanover, NH: University Press of New England.

**Lazarus, R. S., & Cohen, J. B.** (1977). Environmental stress. In I. Altman & J. E. Wohlwill (Eds.), *Human behavior and the environment* (Vol. 2). New York: Plenum.

**Lazarus, R. S., & Folkman, S.** (1984). *Stress, appraisal, and coping.* New York: Springer.

**Lazarus, R. S., & Launier, R.** (1978). Stress-related transactions between person and environment. In L. A. Pervin & M. Lewis (Eds.), *Internal and external determinants of behavior.* New York: Plenum.

**Lazarus, R. S., Opton, E. M., Jr., Nomikos, M. S., & Rankin, N. O.** (1965). The principle of short-circuiting of threat: Further evidence. *Journal of Personality, 33,* 622–635.

**Leach, C. S., & Rambaut, P. C.** (1974). Biochemical responses of the Skylab crewmen. *Proceedings of the Skylab Life Sciences Symposium, 2,* 427–454.

**Lederer, H.** (1952). How the sick view their world. *Journal of Social Issues, 8,* 4–16.

**Leigh, H., & Reiser, M. F.** (1980). *The patient: Biological, psychological, and social dimensions of medical practice.* New York: Plenum.

**Lemp, G. F., Payne, S. F., Rutherford, G. W., Hessol, N. A., Winkelstein, W., Jr., Wiley, J. A., Moss, A. R., Chaisson, R. E., Chen, R. T., Feigal, D., Jr., Thomas, P. A., & Werdegar, D.** (1990). Projections of AIDS morbidity and mortality in San Francisco. *Journal of the American Medical Association, 263*(11), 1497–1501.

**Leon, A. S., & Blackburn, H.** (1977). The relationship of physical activity to coronary heart disease and life expectancy. *Annals of the New York Academy of Sciences, 301,* 561–578.

**Lerner, M. J.** (1980). *The belief in a just world: A fundamental delusion.* New York: Plenum.

**Le Shan, L. L., & Worthington, R. E.** (1956). Personality as a factor in the pathogenesis of cancer: A review of the literature. *British Journal of Medical Psychology, 29,* 49–56.

**Leventhal, H., & Cleary, P. D.** (1980). The smoking problem: A review of the research and theory in behavioral risk modification. *Psychological Bulletin, 88,* 370-405.

**Leventhal, H., Nerenz, D. R., & Strauss, A.** (1980). Self-regulation and the mechanisms for symptom appraisal. In D. Mechanic (Ed.), *Psychosocial epidemiology.* New York: Watson.

**Leventhal, H., & Nerenz, D. R.** (1982). A model for stress research and some implications for the control of stress disorders. In D. Meichenbaum & M. Jaremko (Eds.), *Stress prevention and management: A cognitive behavioral approach.* New York: Plenum.

**Levi, L.** (1965). The urinary output of adrenalin and noradrenalin during pleasant and unpleasant emotional stress. *Psychosomatic Medicine, 27,* 80–85.

**Levinson, W., Tolle, S. W., and Lewis, C.** (1989). Women in academic medicine. *New England Journal of Medicine, 231*(22), 1511–1517.

**Levy, S. M.** (1985a). *Behavior and cancer.* San Francisco: Jossey-Bass.

**Levy, S. M.** (1985b). Emotional response to disease and its treatment. In J. C. Rosen &

L. J. Solomon (Eds.), *Prevention in health psychology* (pp. 299–310). Hanover, NH: University Press of New England.

Lewis, F. M. (1986). The impact of cancer on the family: A critical analysis of the research literature. *Patient Education and Counseling, 8*, 269–289.

Lewis, F. M., Woods, N. F., Hough, E. E., & Bensley, L. S. (1989). The family's functioning with chronic illness in the mother: The spouse's perspective. *Social Science and Medicine, 29*(11), 1261–1269.

Ley, P., & Spelman, M. S. (1965). Communication in an outpatient setting. *British Journal of Social and Clinical Psychology, 4*, 114–116.

Lichtenstein, E. (1982). The smoking problem: A behavioral perspective. *Journal of Consulting and Clinical Psychology, 50*, 804–819.

Lichtman, R. R. (1982). *Close relationships after breast cancer.* Unpublished doctoral dissertation, University of California, Los Angeles.

Lieberman, M. A. (1979). *Self-help groups for coping with crisis: Origins, members, processes, and impact.* San Francisco: Jossey-Bass.

Lieberman, M. A. (1982). The effects of social supports on responses to stress. In L. Goldberger & L. Breznitz (Eds.), *Handbook of stress.* New York: Free Press.

Lief, H. I., & Fox, R. C. (1963). Training for "detached concern" in medical students. In H. I. Lief, V. P. Lief, & N. L. Lief (Eds.), *The psychological basis of medical practice* (pp. 12–35). New York: Harper & Row, Hoeber Medical Books.

Like, R., & Zyzanski, S. J. (1987). Patient satisfaction with the clinical encounter: Social psychological determinants. *Social Science and Medicine, 24*, 351–357.

Lindeman, C. (1984). Nursing and health education. In J. D. Matarazzo, S. Weiss, J. A. Herd, N. E. Miller, & S. M. Weiss (Eds.), *Behavioral health* (pp. 1214–1217). New York: Wiley.

Lindemann, E. (1944). The symptomatology and management of acute grief. *American Journal of Psychiatry, 101*, 141–148.

Lindheim, R., & Syme, S. L. (1983). Environ-ments, people, and health. *Annual Review of Public Health, 4*, 335–359.

Linn, B. S., & Zeppa, R. (1984). Stress in junior medical students: Relationship to personality and performance. *Journal of Medical Education, 59*, 7–12.

Linn, L. S., & DiMatteo, M. R. (1983). Humor and other communication preferences in physician-patient encounters. *Medical Care, 21*(12), 1223–1231.

Linn, L. S., Yager, J., Cope, D. W., & Leake, B. (1985). Health status, job satisfaction, job stress, and life satisfaction among academic and clinical faculty. *Journal of the American Medical Association, 254*(19), 2775–2782.

Linn, L. S., Yager, J., Cope, D. W., & Leake, B. (1986). Factors associated with life satisfaction among practicing internists. *Medical Care, 24*(9), 830–837.

Lloyd, C., & Gartrell, N. K. (1983). A further assessment of medical school stress. *Journal of Medical Education, 58*, 964–967.

Loan, W. B., & Morrison, J. D. (1967). The incidence and severity of postoperative pain. *British Journal of Anaesthesia, 39*, 695–698.

Long, B. C. (1984). Aerobic conditioning and stress inoculation: A comparison of stress-management interventions. *Cognitive Therapy and Research, 8*, 517–541.

Long, L., Paradise, L. V., & Long, T. J. (1981). *Questioning: Skills for the helping process.* Pacific Grove, CA: Brooks/Cole.

Lorber, J. (1975). Good patients and problem patients: Conformity and deviance in a general hospital. *Journal of Health and Social Behavior, 16*, 213–225.

Lown, B. (1983). Introduction. In N. Cousins, *The healing heart: Antidotes to panic and helplessness.* New York: Norton.

Lundberg, U., & Frankenhaeuser, M. (1976). Adjustment to noise stress. *In Reports from the Department of Psychology.* Stockholm: University of Stockholm.

Lurie, N., Rank, B., Parenti, C., Woolley, T., & Snoke, W. (1989). How do house officers spend their nights? A time study of internal medicine staff on call. *New England Journal of Medicine, 320*(25), 1673–1677.

Lykken, D. T. (1987). Psychophysiology. In R. J.

Corsini (Ed.), *Concise encyclopedia of psychology*. New York: Wiley.

**Lynch, J. J., Thomas, S. A., Mills, M. E., Malinow, K., & Katcher, A. H.** (1974). The effects of human contact on cardiac arrhythmia in coronary care patients. *Journal of Nervous and Mental Disease, 158*, 88–99.

**MacMahon, S., Cutler, J., & Brittain, E.** (1987). Obesity and hypertension: Epidemiological and clinical issues. *European Heart Journal* (Suppl. B), *8*, 57–70.

**Mages, N. L., & Mendelsohn, G. A.** (1979). Effects of cancer on patients' lives: A personological approach. In G. C. Stone, F. Cohen, & N. E. Adler (Eds.), *Health psychology: a handbook* (pp. 255–284). San Francisco: Jossey-Bass.

**Magnus, R., Matroos, A., & Strackee, J.** (1979). Walking, cycling, gardening with or without seasonal interruption in relation to acute coronary events. *American Journal of Epidemiology, 110*, 724–773.

**Maheux, B., Dufort, F., & Béland, F.** (1988). Professional and sociopolitical attitudes of medical students: Gender differences reconsidered. *Journal of the American Medical Women's Association, 43*, 73–76.

**Maheux, B., Dufort, F., Béland, F., Jacques, A., & Lévesque, A.** (1990). Female medical practitioners: More preventive and patient-oriented. *Medical Care, 28*(1), 87–92.

**Mahoney, M. J.** (1977). Personal science: A cognitive learning therapy. In A. Ellis & R. Grieger (Eds.), *Handbook of rational emotive therapy*. New York: Springer.

**Mahoney, M. J., & Thoreson, C. E.** (1974). *Self-control: Power to the person*. Pacific Grove, CA: Brooks/Cole.

**Maier, S. F., & Seligman, M. E. P.** (1976). Learned helplessness: Theory and evidence. *Journal of Experimental Psychology: General, 105*, 3–46.

**Marlatt, G. A.** (1982). Relapse prevention: A self-control program for the treatment of addictive behaviors. In R. B. Stuart (Ed.), *Adherence, compliance, and generalization in behavioral medicine*. New York: Brunner/Mazel.

**Marlatt, G. A., & Gordon, J. R.** (1980). Determinants of relapse: Implications for the maintenance of behavioral change. In P. O.

Davidson & S. M. Davidson (Eds.), *Behavioral medicine: Changing health lifestyles* (pp. 410–452). Elmsford, NY: Pergamon Press.

**Marlatt, G. A., & Rohsenow, D. J.** (1980). Cognitive processes in alcohol use: Expectancy and the balanced placebo design. In N. Mello (Ed.), *Advances in substance abuse: Behavioral and biological research*. Greenwich, CT: JAI Press.

**Marquis, K. H.** (1970). Effects of social reinforcement on health reporting in the household interview. *Sociometry. 33*, 203–215.

**Marsland, D. W., Wood, M. B., & Mayo, F.** (1976). The databank for patient care, curriculum and research in family practice: 526,196 patient problems. *Journal of Family Practice, 3*, 25–28.

**Maslach, C.** (1976). Burned-out. *Human Behavior, 5*(9), 16–22.

**Maslach, C.** (1982). *Burnout: The cost of caring*. Englewood Cliffs, NJ: Prentice-Hall.

**Maslach, C., & Jackson, S. E.** (1982). Burnout in health professions: A social psychological analysis. In G. S. Sanders & J. Suls (Eds.), *Social psychology of health and illness*. Hillsdale, NJ: Erlbaum.

**Mason, J. W.** (1975). A historical view of the stress field. *Journal of Human Stress, 1*, 22–36.

**Matthews, D., & Hingson, R.** (1977). Improving patient compliance: A guide for physicians. *Medical Clinics of North America, 61*, 879–889.

**Matthews, J. J.** (1983). The communication process in clinical settings. *Social Science and Medicine, 17*, 1371–1378.

**Mattsson, A.** (1977). Long term physical illness in childhood: A challenge to psychosocial adaptation. In R. H. Moos (Ed.), *Coping with physical illness* (pp. 183–199). New York: Plenum.

**Mawardi, B. H.** (1979). Satisfactions, dissatisfactions, and causes of stress in medical practice. *Journal of the American Medical Association, 241*(14), 1483–1485.

**May, H. J., & Revicki, D. A.** (1985). Professional stress among family physicians. *Journal of Family Practice, 20*(2), 165–171.

**Mayerson, E. W.** (1976). *Putting the ill at ease*. New York: Harper & Row.

**Mayou, R.** (1973). Chest pain in the cardiac clinic. *Journal of Psychosomatic Research, 17,* 353–357.

**McAuliffe, W. E., Rohman, M., Santangelo, S., Feldman, B., Magnuson, E., Sobol, A., & Weissman, J.** (1986). Psychoactive drug use among practicing physicians and medical students. *New England Journal of Medicine, 315*(13), 805–810.

**McCann, I. L., & Holmes, D. S.** (1984). Influence of aerobic exercise on depression. *Journal of Personality and Social Psychology, 46,* 1142–1147.

**McCrady, B. S.** (1988). Alcoholism. In E. A. Blechman & K. D. Brownell (Eds.), *Handbook of behavioral medicine for women.* New York: Pergamon.

**McCubbin, H. I., Joy, C. B., Cauble, A. E., Comeau, J. K., Patterson, J. M., & Needle, R. H.** (1980). Family stress and coping: A decade review. *Journal of Marriage and Family, 42,* 125–141.

**McCue, J. D.** (1982). The effects of stress on physicians and their medical practice. *New England Journal of Medicine, 306,* 458–463.

**McCue, J. D.** (1985). The distress of internship: Cause and prevention. *New England Journal of Medicine, 312*(7), 449–452.

**McGuire, W. J.** (1969). The nature of attitudes and attitude change. In G. Lindzey & E. Aronson (Eds.), *Handbook of social psychology* (Vol. 3) (pp. 136–314). Reading, MA: Addison-Wesley.

**McNeil, B. J., Stephen, G., Pauker, M. D., Sox, H. C., Jr., & Tversky, A.** (1982). Special articles on the elicitation of preferences for alternative therapies. *New England Journal of Medicine, 306*(21), 1259–1262.

**Meares, A.** (1957). *The medical interview: A study of clinically significant interpersonal reactions.* Springfield, IL: Charles C Thomas.

**Mechanic, D.** (1964). The influences of mothers on their children's health attitudes and behavior. *Journal of Pediatrics, 33,* 444–453.

**Mechanic, D.** (1968). *Medical sociology: A selective view.* New York: Free Press.

**Mechanic, D.** (1972). Social psychologic factors affecting the presentation of bodily complaints. *New England Journal of Medicine, 286*(21), 1132–1139.

**Mechanic, D.** (1978a). Effects of psychological distress on perceptions of physical health and use of medical psychiatric facilities. *Journal of Human Stress, 4,* 26–32.

**Mechanic, D.** (1978b). *Medical sociology* (2nd ed.). New York: Free Press.

**Mechanic, D.** (1979). The stability of health and illness behavior: Results from a 16-year follow-up. *American Journal of Public Health, 69,* 1142–1145.

**Mechanic, D., & Volkart, E. H.** (1961). Stress, illness behavior, and the sick role. *American Sociological Review, 26,* 51–58.

**Mehrabian, A.** (1972). *Nonverbal communication.* Chicago: Aldine-Atherton.

**Meichenbaum, D. H.** (1975). A self-instructional approach to stress management: A proposal for stress inoculation training. In C. D. Spielberger & I. Sarason (Eds.), *Stress and anxiety* (Vol. 2). New York: Wiley.

**Meichenbaum, D. H.** (1977). *Cognitive behavior modification.* Morristown, NJ: General Learning Press.

**Meichenbaum, D. H.** (1985). *Stress inoculation training.* New York: Pergamon Press.

**Meichenbaum, D. H., & Cameron, R.** (1983). Stress inoculation training: Toward a general paradigm for training coping skills. In D. Meichembaum & M. E. Jaremko (Eds.), *Stress reduction and prevention.* New York: Plenum.

**Meichenbaum, D. H., & Genest, M.** (1980). Cognitive behavior modification: An integration of cognitive and behavioral methods. In F. H. Kanfer & A. P. Goldstein (Eds.), *Helping people change* (2nd ed.) (pp. 390–422). New York: Pergamon Press.

**Melzack, R.** (1973). *The puzzle of pain.* New York: Basic Books.

**Melzack, R.** (Ed.) (1983). *Pain measurement and assessment.* New York: Raven Press.

**Melzack, R., & Torgerson, W. S.** (1971). On the language of pain. *Anesthesiology, 34,* 50–59.

**Melzack, R., & Wall, P. D.** (1965). Pain mechanisms: A theory. *Science, 150,* 971–979.

**Melzack, R., & Wall, P. D.** (1970). Psychophysiology of pain. *International Anesthesiology Clinics, 8,* 3–34.

**Melzack, R., & Wall, P. D.** (1982). *The challenge of pain.* New York: Basic Books.

Menkes, M. S., Comstock, G. W., Vuilleumier, J. P., Helsing, K. J., Rider, A. A., & Brookmeyer, R. (1986). Serum beta-carotene, vitamins A and E, selenium, and the risk of lung cancer. *New England Journal of Medicine, 315*(20), 1250–1254.

Meyer, D., Leventhal, H., & Gutman, M. (1985). Commonsense models of illness: The example of hypertension. *Health Psychology, 4,* 115–135.

Meyerowitz, B. E. (1983). Postmastectomy coping strategies and quality of life. *Health Psychology, 2,* 117–132.

Miller, S. M., & Mangan, C. E. (1983). Interacting effects of information and coping style in adapting to gynecologic stress: Should the doctor tell all? *Journal of Personality and Social Psychology, 45,* 223–236.

Milmoe, S., Rosenthal, R., Blane, H. T., Chafetz, M. L., & Wolf, I. (1967). The doctor's voice: Postdictor of successful referral of alcoholic patients. *Journal of Abnormal Psychology, 72,* 78–84.

Minuchin, S. (1974). *Families and family therapy.* Cambridge: Harvard University Press.

Minuchin, S., Rosman, B. L., & Baker, L. (1978). *Psychosomatic families.* Cambridge, MA: Harvard University Press.

Mitchell, D. K. (1979). Vocational rehabilitation and the coronary patient. In W. D. Gentry & R. B. Williams (Eds.), *Psychological aspects of myocardial infarction and coronary care* (2nd ed.) (pp. 131–146). St. Louis: C. V. Mosby.

Mizrahi, T. (1984). Managing medical mistakes: Ideology, insularity and accountability among internists-in-training. *Social Science and Medicine, 19,* 135–146.

Modlin, H. C., & Montes, A. (1964). Narcotics addiction in physicians. *American Journal of Psychiatry, 121,* 358-369.

Moertel, C. G., Fleming, T. R., Creagan, E. T., Rubin, J., O'Connell, M. J., & Ames, M. M. (1985). High-dose vitamin C versus placebo in the treatment of patients with advanced cancer who have had no prior chemotherapy: A randomized double-blind comparison. *New England Journal of Medicine, 312,* 137–141.

Moertel, C. G., Rubin, J., Sarna, G., Young, C., Jones, S., & Fleming, T. (1981). A Phase II trial of amygdalin (Laetrile) in the treatment of human cancer. *Proceedings of the American Association for Cancer Research, 22,* 383.

Montagu, A. (1978). *Touching.* New York: Harper & Row.

Montgomery, R. J. V., Gonyea, J. G., & Hooyman, N. R. (1985). Caregiving and the experience of subjective and objective burden. *Family Relations, 34,* 19–26.

Moos, R. H. (Ed.). (1977). *Coping with physical illness.* New York: Plenum.

Moos, R. H., & Finney, J. W. (1983). The expanding scope of alcoholism treatment evaluation. *American Psychologist, 38,* 1036–1044.

Moos, R. H., & Tsu, V. D. (1977a). The crisis of physical illness: An overview. In R. H. Moos (Ed.), *Coping with physical illness* (pp. 3–21). New York: Plenum.

Moos, R. H., & Tsu, V. D. (1977b). Overview and perspective. In R. H. Moos (Ed.), *Coping with physical illness.* New York: Plenum.

Morgan, M., Curran, J. W., & Berkelman, R. L. (1990). The future course of AIDS in the United States. *Journal of the American Medical Association, 263*(11), 1539–1540.

Moses, R., & Cividali, M. (1966). Differential levels of awareness of illness: Their relation to some salient features in cancer patients. *Annals of the New York Academy of Sciences, 125,* 984–994.

Moss, A. J., & Goldstein, S. (1970). The prehospital phase of acute myocardial infarction, *Circulation, 41,* 737–742.

Mountcastle, V. B. (1974). Pain and temperature sensibilities. In V. B. Mountcastle (Ed.), *Medical physiology* (13th ed.). St. Louis: C. V. Mosby.

Mountcastle, V. B. (1980). *Medical physiology* (14th ed.). St. Louis: C. V. Mosby.

Mullan, F. (1983). *Vital signs: A young doctor's struggle with cancer.* New York: Farrar, Straus, Giroux.

Multiple Risk Factor Intervention Trial Research Group. (1982). Multiple Risk Factor Intervention Trial: Risk factor changes and mortality results. *Journal of the American Medical Association, 248,* 1465–1477.

Murphy, J. M., Nadelson, C. C., & Notman, M. T. (1984). Factors influencing first-year medical students' perceptions of stress. *Journal of Human Stress, 10,* 165–173.

Murray, D. M., Davis-Hearn, M., Goldman, A. I., Pirie, P., & Leupker, R. V. (1988). Four- and five-year follow-up results from four seventh-grade smoking prevention strategies. *Journal of Behavioral Medicine, 11*, 395–405.

Nader, P. R. (1985). Improving the practice of pediatric patient education: A synthesis and selective review. *Preventive Medicine, 14*, 688–701.

Nagy, M. (1948). The child's theories concerning death. *Journal of Genetic Psychology, 73*, 3–27.

Nathanson, C. (1977). Sex, illness, and medical care. *Social Science and Medicine, 11*, 13–15.

National Cancer Institute. (1980). *Breast cancer: A measure of progress in public understanding* (U.S. Department of Health and Human Services/National Institutes of Health Publication No. 81-2291). Washington, DC: U.S. Government Printing Office.

National Institute of Alcoholism and Alcohol Abuse (NIAAA). (1981). *First statistical compendium on alcohol and health.* (U.S. Department of Health and Human Services Publication No. 81-115). Washington, DC: U.S. Government Printing Office.

National Institute of Health. (1989). *How to help your patients stop smoking. A National Cancer Institute manual for physicians* (National Institutes of Health Publication No. 89-3064). Bethesda, MD: U.S. Department of Health and Human Services.

Nelson, G. E. (1984). *Biological principles with human perspectives* (2nd ed.). New York: Wiley.

Nemiah, J. C. (1961). *Foundations of psychopathology.* New York: Oxford University Press.

Nemiah, J. C. (1975). Denial revisited: Reflections on psychosomatic theory. *Psychotherapy and Psychosomatics, 26*, 140–147.

Nerenz, D. R., & Leventhal, H. (1983). Self-regulation theory in chronic illness. In T. G. Burish & L. A. Bradley (Eds.), *Coping with chronic disease: Research and applications.* New York: Academic Press.

Newman, R. I., & Seres, J. (1986). The interdisciplinary pain center: An approach to the management of chronic pain. In A. D. Holzman & D. C. Turk (Eds.), *Pain manage-ment: A handbook of psychological treatment approaches.* New York: Pergamon Press.

Newsom, J. A. (1977). Help for the alcoholic physician in California. *Alcoholism: Clinical and experimental research, 1*(2), 135–137.

Northouse, P. G., & Northouse, L. L. (1985). *Health communication: A handbook for health professionals.* Englewood Cliffs, NJ: Prentice-Hall.

Ogden-Niemeyer, L., & Jacobs, K. (1989). *Work-hardening: State of the art.* Thorofare, NJ: Slack.

Olin, H. S., & Hackett, T. P. (1964). The denial of chest pain in 32 patients with acute myocardial infarction. *Journal of the American Medical Association, 190*, 977–981.

Orne, M. T. (1974). Pain suppression by hypnosis and related phenomena. In J. J. Bonica (Ed.), *Advances in neurology: International symposium on pain.* New York: Raven Press.

Orne, M. T. (1989). On the construct of hypnosis: How its definition affects research and its clinical application. In G. D. Burrows & L. Dennerstein (Eds.), *Handbook of hypnosis and psychosomatic medicine.* Amsterdam: Elsevier.

Orsay, A. M., Turnbull, T. L., Dunne, M., Barrett, J. A., Langenberg, P., & Orsay, C. P. (1988). Prospective study of the effects of safety belts on morbidity and health care costs in motor vehicle accidents. *Journal of the American Medical Association, 260*, 3598–3603.

Osler, Sir William. (1899). Lecture to medical students. *Albany Medical Annals, 20*, 307.

Osler, Sir William. (1904). The master word in medicine. In *Aequanimitas, with other addresses to medical students, nurses, and practitioners of medicine* (pp. 369–371). Philadelphia: Blakiston.

Osterweis, M., Solomon, F., & Green, M. (Eds.). (1984). *Bereavement: Reactions, consequences, and care.* Washington, DC: National Academy of Sciences Press.

Oxford, J., Oppenheimer, E., & Edwards, G. (1976). Abstinence or control: The outcome for excessive drinkers two years after consultation. *Behavior Research and Therapy, 14*, 409–418.

Pace, J. B. (1977). Psychophysiology of pain: Diagnostic and therapeutic implications. *Journal of Family Practice, 5*(2), 533–557.

Paffenbarger, R. S., Wing, A. L., & Hyde, R. T. (1978). Physical activity as an index of heart risk in college alumni. *American Journal of Epidemiology, 108,* 161–175.

Paffenbarger, R. S., & Hale, W. E. (1975). Work activity and coronary heart mortality. *New England Journal of Medicine, 292,* 545–550.

Parkes, C. M. (1964). Effects of bereavement on physical and mental health: A study of the medical records of widows. *British Medical Journal, 2,* 274–279.

Parkes, C. M. (1970). The first year of bereavement. *Psychiatry, 33,* 422–467.

Parkes, C. M. (1972). *Bereavement: Studies of grief in adult life.* London: Tavistock.

Parkes, C. M., & Brown, R. (1972) Health after bereavement: A controlled study of young Boston widows and widowers. *Psychosomatic Medicine, 34,* 449–461.

Parkes, C. M., & Weiss, R. S. (1983). *Recovery from bereavement.* New York: Basic Books.

Parkes, K. R. (1982). Occupational stress among student nurses: A natural experiment. *Journal of Applied Psychology, 67*(6), 784–796.

Parkes, K. R. (1985). Stressful episodes reported by first year student nurses: A descriptive account. *Social Science and Medicine, 20*(9), 945–953.

Parkes, K. R. (1986). Coping in stressful episodes: The role of individual differences, environmental factors, and situational characteristics. *Journal of Personality and Social Psychology. 51*(6), 1277–1292.

Parsons, T. (1951). *The social system* (pp. 428–479). Glencoe, IL: Free Press.

Parsons, T. (1958). Definitions of health and illness in the light of American values and social structure. In E. G. Jaco (Ed.), *Patients, physicians, and illness* (pp. 165–187). New York: Free Press.

Parsons, T. (1975). The sick role and the role of the physician reconsidered. *Millbank Memorial Fund Quarterly, 53,* 257–278.

Patterson, B. H., & Block, G. (1988). Food choices and the cancer guidelines. *American Journal of Public Health, 78,* 282–286.

Pauker, S. G., & Kassirer, J. P. (1987). Medical progress decision analysis. *New England Journal of Medicine, 316*(5), 250–257.

Pavlov, I. P. (1927). *Conditioned reflexes.* New York: Dover.

Pearlin, L. I., & Lieberman, M. (1979). Social sources of distress. In R. Simms (Ed.), *Research in community health,* Greenwich, CT: Jai Press.

Pearlin, L. I., & Schooler, C. (1978). The structure of coping. *Journal of Health and Social Behavior, 19,* 2–21.

Pearlman, R. A., & Uhlmann, R. F. (1988). Quality of life in chronic diseases: Perceptions of elderly patients. *Journal of Gerontology, 43*(2), 25–30.

Pelletier, K. (1977). *Mind as healer; mind as slayer.* New York: Dell.

Pennebaker, J. W. (1982). *The psychology of physical complaints.* New York: Springer-Verlag.

Pennebaker, J. W. (1983) Accuracy of symptom perception. In A. Baum, S. E. Taylor, & J. Singer (Eds.), *Handbook of psychology and health* (Vol. 4). Hillsdale, NJ: Erlbaum.

Pennebaker, J. W., Burnam, M. A., Schaeffer, M. A., & Harper, D. C. (1977). Lack of control as a determinant of perceived physical symptoms. *Journal of Personality and Social Psychology, 35,* 167–174.

Perrine, M. W., Waller, J. A., & Harris, L. S. (1971). *Alcohol and highway safety: Behavioral and medical aspects* (U.S. Department of Transportation Report No. HS-800 600). Washington, DC: National Highway Traffic Safety Administration.

Peters, L. C., & Esses, L. M. (1985). Family environment as perceived by children with a chronically ill parent. *Journal of Chronic Diseases, 38,* 301–308.

Peterson, C., & Seligman, M. E. P. (1984). Causal explanations as a risk factor for depression: Theory and evidence. *Psychological Review, 91,* 347–374.

Peterson, C., & Seligman, M. E. P. (1987). Explanatory style and illness. *Journal of Personality, 55,* 237–265.

Peterson, C., Seligman, M. E. P., & Vaillant, G. E. (1988). Pessimistic explanatory style as a risk factor for physical illness: A thirty-five-year longitudinal study. *Journal of Personality and Social Psychology, 55*(1), 23–27.

**Pfeiffer, R. J.** (1983). Early-adult development in the medical student. *Mayo Clinic Proceedings, 58,* 127–134.

**Pinkerton, S. S., Hughes, H., & Wenrich, W. W.** (1982). *Behavioral medicine: Clinical applications.* New York: Wiley Interscience.

**Pinkston, M., & Linsk, N. L.** (1984). *Care of the elderly: A family approach.* New York: Pergamon Press.

**Pitts, F. N., Schuller, A. B., Rich, C. L., & Pitts, A. F.** (1979). Suicide among U.S. Women Physicians, 1967–1972. *American Journal of Psychiatry, 136,* 694–696.

**Pollock, G. H.** (1970). Anniversary reactions, trauma, and mourning. *Psychoanalytic Quarterly, 34,* 347–371.

**Pollock, G. H.** (1982). The mourning-liberation process and creativity: The case of Kathe Kollwitz. *Annual of Psychoanalysis, 10,* 333–354.

**Pomeroy, W. B.** (1972). *Dr. Kinsey and the Institute for Sex Research.* New York: Harper & Row.

**Porter, J., & Jick, H.** (1980). Addiction rate in patients treated with narcotics. *New England Journal of Medicine, 302,* 123.

**Powell, K. E., Thompson, P. D., Caspersen, C. J., & Kendrick, J. S.** (1987). Physical activity and the incidence of coronary heart disease. In L. Breslow, J. E. Fielding, & L. B. Lave (Eds.), *Annual review of public health* (Vol. 8). Palo Alto, CA: Annual Reviews.

**Pratt, C. C., Schmall, V. L., Wright, S., & Cleland, M.** (1985). Burden and coping strategies of caregivers to Alzheimer's patients. *Family Relations, 34,* 27–33.

**Pratt, L.** (1976). *Family structure and effective health behavior: The energized family.* Boston: Houghton Mifflin.

**Pratt, L., Seligmann, A., & Reader, G.** (1957). Physicians' views on the level of medical information among patients. *American Journal of Public Health, 47,* 1277–1283.

**Pratt, O. E.** (1982). Alcohol and the developing fetus. *British Medical Bulletin, 38,* 48–52.

**Putnam, S. M., Stiles, W. B., Jacob, M. C., & James, S. A.** (1985). Patient exposition and physician explanation in initial medical interviews and outcomes of clinic visits. *Medical Care, 23*(1), 74–83.

**Quick, J. C., & Quick, J. D.** (1984). *Organiza-tional stress and preventive management.* New York: McGraw-Hill.

**Rahe, R. H., Mahan, J. L., & Arthur, R. J.** (1970). Prediction of near-future health change from subjects' preceding life changes. *Journal of Psychosomatic Research, 14,* 401–406.

**Raphael, B.** (1983). *The anatomy of bereavement.* New York: Basic Books.

**Reidenberg, M. M., & Lowenthal, D. T.** (1968). Adverse non-drug reactions. *New England Journal of Medicine, 279,* 678–679.

**Reuben, D. B.** (1985). Depressive symptoms in medical house officers. *Archives of Internal Medicine, 145,* 286–288.

**Reuben, D. B., & Noble, S.** (1990). House officer responses to impaired physicians. *Journal of the American Medical Association, 263*(7), 958–960.

**Reuler, J. B., Girard, D. E., & Nardone, D. A.** (1980). The chronic pain syndrome: Misconceptions and management. *Annals of Internal Medicine, 93,* 588–596.

**Revenson, T. A.** (1986). Debunking the myth of loneliness in late life. In E. Seidman & J. Rappaport (Eds.), *Redefining social problems* (pp. 115–135). New York: Plenum.

**Revicki, D. A.** (1989). Health-related quality of life in the evaluation of medical therapy for chronic illness. *Journal of Family Practice, 29*(4), 377–380.

**Richards, J. S., Nepomuceno, C., Riles, M., & Suer, Z.** (1982). Assessing pain behavior: The UAB Pain Behavior Scale. *Pain, 14,* 393–398.

**Richardson, S. A., Goodman, N., Hastorf, A. H., & Dornbusch, S. M.** (1961). Cultural uniformity in reaction to physical disabilities. *American Sociological Review, 26,* 241–247.

**Richman, J. A., & Flaherty, J. A.** (1990). Gender differences in medical student distress: Contributions of prior socialization and current role-related stress. *Social Science and Medicine, 30*(7), 777–787.

**Richter, C. P.** (1957). On the phenomenon of sudden death in animals and man. *Psychosomatic Medicine, 19,* 191–198.

**Riessman, C. K.** (1990). Strategic uses of narrative in the presentation of self and illness: A research note. *Social Science and Medicine, 30,* 1195–1200.

**Riggio, R. E., & Friedman, H. S.** (1983). Individual differences and cues to deception. *Journal of Personality and Social Psychology, 45,* 899–915.

**Rimm, D. C., & Masters, J. C.** (1974). *Behavior therapy: Techniques and empirical findings.* New York: Academic Press.

**Rimm, D. C., & Masters, J. C.** (1979). *Behavior therapy: Techniques and empirical findings* (2nd ed.). New York: McGraw-Hill.

**Roberts, A. H.** (1986). The operant approach to the management of pain and excess disability. In A. D. Holzman & D. C. Turk (Eds.), *Pain management: A handbook of psychological treatment approaches.* New York: Pergamon Press.

**Roberts, M. C.** (1986). *Pediatric psychology: Psychological interventions and strategies for pediatric problems.* New York: Pergamon Press.

**Robin, E. D.** (1984). *Matters of life and death: Risks versus benefits of medical care.* New York: W. H. Freeman.

**Robins, L. S., and Wolf, F. M.** (1988). Confrontation and politeness strategies in physician-patient interactions. *Social Science and Medicine, 27,* 217–221.

**Robinson, D.** (1971). *The process of becoming ill.* London: Routledge & Kegan Paul.

**Robinson, D.** (1973, July 15). Ten noted doctors answer ten tough questions. *Parade.*

**Robinson, I.** (1990). Personal narratives, social careers, and medical courses: Analyzing life trajectories in autobiographies of people with multiple sclerosis. *Social Science and Medicine, 30,* 1170–1186.

**Robinson, V. M.** (1977). *Humor and the health professions.* Thorofare, NJ: Slack.

**Rochlin, G.** (1965). *Griefs and discontents.* Boston: Little, Brown.

**Rodin, J.** (1986). Aging and health: Effects of the sense of control. *Science, 233,* 1271–1276.

**Rodin, J., & Langer, E. J.** (1977). Long-term effects of a control-relevant intervention with the institutionalized aged. *Journal of Personality and Social Psychology, 35,* 897–902.

**Rogers, C. R.** (1951). *Client-centered therapy.* Boston: Houghton Mifflin.

**Rogers, C. R.** (1957). The necessary and sufficient conditions of therapeutic personality change. *Journal of Consulting Psychology, 21,* 95–103.

**Roglieri, J. L.** (1980). *Odds on your life: How to make informed decisions about the health factors you control.* New York: Seaview Books.

**Rokeach, M.** (1973). *The nature of human values.* New York: Free Press.

**Ronis, D. L., Harel, Y.** (1989). Health benefits and breast examination behaviors: Analyses of linear structural relations. *Psychology and Health, 3,* 259–285.

**Rose, K. D., & Rosow, I.** (1973). Physicians who kill themselves. *Archives of General Psychiatry, 29,* 800–805.

**Rose, R. J., & Chesney, M. A.** (1986). Cardiovascular stress reactivity: A behavior-genetic perspective. *Behavior Therapy, 17,* 314–323.

**Rose, R. M.** (1980). Endocrine responses to stressful psychological events. *Psychiatric Clinics of North America, 3,* 251–276.

**Rosenberg, D. A., & Silver, H. K.** (1984). Medical student abuse: An unnecessary and preventable cause of stress. *Journal of the American Medical Association, 251*(6), 739–741.

**Rosenberg, M. J., & Hovland, C. I.** (1960). Cognitive, affective, and behavioral components of attitudes. In C. I. Hovland & M. J. Rosenberg (Eds.), *Attitude organization and change.* New Haven: Yale University Press.

**Rosenman, R. H.** (1978). The interview method of assessment of the coronary-prone behavior pattern. In T. M. Dembroski, S. Weiss, J. Shields, S. G. Haynes, & M. Feinleib (Eds.), *Coronary-prone behavior* (pp. 55–69). New York: Springer-Verlag.

**Rosenman, R. H., Swan, G. E., & Carmelli, D.** (1988). Definition, assessment, and evolution of the Type A behavior pattern. In B. K. Houston & C. R. Snyder (Eds.), *Type A behavior pattern: Research, theory, and intervention.* New York: Wiley.

**Rosenstock, I. M.** (1966). Why people use health services. *Millbank Memorial Fund Quarterly, 44,* 94–127.

**Rosenstock, I. M.** (1974). Historical origins of the health belief model. *Health Education Monographs, 2,* 328–335.

**Rosenstock, I. M.** (1985). Understanding and enhancing patient compliance with diabetic regimens. *Diabetes Care, 8*(6), 610–616.

**Rosenstock, I. M.** (1988). Enhancing patient compliance with health recommendations. *Journal of Pediatric Health Care, 2*(2), 67–72.

**Rosenstock, I. M., & Kirscht, J. P.** (1979). Why people seek health care. In G. C. Stone, F. Cohen, & N. E. Adler (Eds.), *Health psychology.* (pp. 161–188). San Francisco: Jossey-Bass.

**Rosenthal, R.** (1969). Interpersonal expectations: Effects of the experimenter's hypothesis. In R. Rosenthal & R. L. Rosnow (Eds.), *Artifact in behavioral research.* (pp. 181–277). New York: Academic Press.

**Rosenthal, R.** (1984). *Meta-analytic procedures for social research.* Beverly Hills: Sage.

**Rosenthal, R., Hall, J. A., DiMatteo, M. R., Rogers, P. L., & Archer, D.** (1979). *Sensitivity to nonverbal communication: The PONS test.* Baltimore, MD: Johns Hopkins University Press.

**Rosenthal, T.** (1970). *How could I not be among you?* Berkeley, CA: Benchmark Films.

**Roskies, E., Spevack, M., Surkis, A., Cohen, C., & Gilman, S.** (1978). Changing the coronary-prone (Type A) behavior pattern in a nonclinical population. *Journal of Behavioral Medicine, 1,* 201–216.

**Ross, C. E., & Mirowsky, J.** (1979). A comparison of life-event-weighing schemes: Change, undesirability, and effect-proportional indices. *Journal of Health and Social Behavior, 20,* 166–177.

**Ross, M.** (1971). Suicide among physicians. *Psychiatry in Medicine, 2,* 189–198.

**Roter, D. L.** (1984). Patient question asking in physician-patient interaction. *Health Psychology, 3*(5), 395–410.

**Roth, D. L., & Holmes, D. S.** (1985). Influences of physical fitness in determining the impact of stressful life events on physical and psychological health. *Psychosomatic Medicine, 47,* 164–173.

**Roth, J. A.** (1972). The necessity and control of hospitalization. *Social Science and Medicine, 6,* 426–446.

**Rundall, T. G., & Wheeler, J. R. C.** (1979). The effect of income on use of preventive care: An evaluation of alternative explanations. *Journal of Health and Social Behavior, 20,* 397–406.

**Russell, P. O., & Epstein, L. H.** (1988). Smoking. In E. A. Blechman & K. D. Brownell (Eds.), *Handbook of behavioral medicine for women.* New York: Pergamon.

**Rustad, L. C.** (1984). Family adjustment to chronic illness and disability in mid-life. In M. G. Eisenberg, L. C. Sutkin, & M. A. Jansen (Eds.), *Chronic illness and disability through the life span: Effects on self and family.* (pp. 222–242). New York: Springer.

**Rutter, M.** (1966). *Children of sick parents: An environmental and psychiatric study* (Maudsley Monographs, No. 16). London: Oxford University Press.

**Ryan, W.** (1971). *Blaming the victim.* New York: Random House.

**Safer, M. A., Tharps, Q. J., Jackson, T. C., & Leventhal, H.** (1979). Determinants of three stages of delay in seeking care at a medical care clinic. *Medical Care, 17,* 11–29.

**Safran, C.** (1977). I don't intend to die this year. In Moos, R. H. (Ed.), *Coping with physical illness.* (pp. 403–411). New York: Plenum.

**Samora, J., Saunders, L., & Larson, R. F.** (1961). Medical vocabulary knowledge among hospital patients. *Journal of Health and Human Behavior, 2,* 83–89.

**Saunders, C. E.** (1987). Patient compliance in filling prescriptions after discharge from the emergency department. *American Journal of Emergency Medicine, 5*(4), 283–286.

**Sawyer, T.** (1966). Measurement and prediction: Clinical and statistical. *Psychological Bulletin, 66,* 178–200.

**Scalzi, C. C., & Dracup, K.** (1979). Sexual counseling of cardiac patients. In W. D. Gentry & R. B. Williams (Eds.), *Psychological aspects of myocardial infarction and coronary care* (2nd ed.) (pp. 162–171). St. Louis: C. V. Mosby.

**Schachter, S.** (1980). Urinary pH and the psychology of nicotine addiction. In P. O. Davidson & S. M. Davidson (Eds.), *Behavioral medicine: Changing health lifestyles.* New York: Brunner/Mazel.

**Schachter, S.** (1982). Recidivism and self-cure

of smoking and obesity. *American Psychologist, 37,* 436–444.

**Schaeffer, C., Coyne, J. C., & Lazarus, R. S.** (1981). The health-related functions of social support. *Journal of Behavioral Medicine, 4,* 381–406.

**Scheier, M. F., & Carver, C. S.** (1987). Dispositional optimism and physical well being: The influence of generalized outcome expectancies on health. *Journal of Personality, 55,* 169–210.

**Scherwitz, L., Berton, K., & Leventhal, H.** (1978). Type A behavior, self-involvement, and cardiovascular response. *Psychosomatic Medicine, 40,* 593–609.

**Scherwitz, L., Graham, L. E., II, & Ornish, D.** (1985). Self-involvement and the risk factors for coronary heart disease. *Advances: Journal of the Institute for the Advancement of Health, 2*(2), 6–18.

**Schienle, D. R., & Eiler, J. M.** (1984). Clinical intervention with older adults. In M. G. Eisenberg, L. C. Sutkin, & M. A. Jansen (Eds.), *Chronic illness and disability through the life span: Effects on self and family* (pp. 245–268). New York: Springer.

**Schiffman, H. R.** (1976). *Sensation and perception: An integrated approach.* New York: Wiley.

**Schmale, A. J., Jr.** (1958). The relation of separation and depression to disease. *Psychosomatic Medicine, 20,* 259–277.

**Schneider, J. W., & Conrad, P.** (1980). In the closet with illness: Epilepsy, stigma potential, and information control. *Social Problems, 28,* 32–44.

**Schulman, B. A.** (1979). Active patient orientation and outcomes in hypertensive treatment: Application of a socio-organizational perspective. *Medical Care, 17*(3), 267–280.

**Schulz, R.** (1976). Effects of control and predictability on the physical and psychological well-being of the institutionalized aged. *Journal of Personality and Social Psychology, 33,* 563–573.

**Schwab, J. J., & Hameling, J.** (1968). Body image and medical illness. *Psychosomatic Medicine, 30,* 51–71.

**Schwenk, T. L., & Hughes, C. C.** (1983). The family as patient in family medicine.

Rhetoric or reality? *Social Science and Medicine, 17,* 1–16.

**Seeman, M., & Evans, J. W.** (1961a). Stratification and hospital care. Part 1: The performance of the medical intern. *American Sociological Review, 26,* 67–80.

**Seeman, M., & Evans, J. W.** (1961b). Stratification and hospital care. Part 2: The objective criterion of performance. *American Sociological Review, 26,* 193–204.

**Segall, A., & Roberts, L. W.** (1980). A comparative analysis of physician estimates and levels of medical knowledge among patients. *Sociology of Health and Illness, 2*(3), 317–334.

**Seligman, M. E. P.** (1975). *Helplessness: On depression, development and death.* San Francisco: W. H. Freeman.

**Selye, H.** (1956). *The stress of life* (rev. ed.). New York: McGraw-Hill.

**Shapiro, A.** (1960). A contribution to a history of the placebo effect. *Behavioral Science, 5,* 109–135.

**Shapiro, A. P., Schwartz, G. E., Ferguson, D. C. E., Redmond, D. P., & Weiss, S. M.** (1977). Behavioral methods in the treatment of hypertension: A review of their clinical status. *Annals of Internal Medicine, 86,* 626–636.

**Shapiro, D., & Goldstein, I. B.** (1982). Biobehavioral perspectives on hypertension. *Journal of Consulting and Clinical Psychology, 50,* 841–858.

**Shapiro, D. H.** (1985). Meditation and behavioral medicine: Application of a self-regulation strategy to the clinical management of stress. In S. R. Burchfield (Ed.), *Stress: Psychological and physiological interactions:* Washington, DC: Hemisphere.

**Shapiro, J.** (1986). Assessment of family coping with illness. *Psychosomatics, 27*(4), 262–271.

**Shattuck, F. C.** (1907). The science and art of medicine in some of their aspects. *Boston Medical and Surgical Journal, 157,* 63–67.

**Sheehan, K. H., Sheehan, D. V., White, K., Leibowitz, A., Baldwin, D. C.** (1990). A pilot study of medical student 'abuse': Student perceptions of mistreatment and misconduct in medical school. *Journal of the American Medical Association, 263*(4), 533–537.

Shekelle, R. B., Gayle, M., Ostfeld, A. M., & Paul, O. (1983). Hostility, risk of coronary heart disease, and mortality. *Psychosomatic Medicine, 45,* 109–114.

Shepherd, D. M., & Barraclough, B. M. (1976). The aftermath of parental suicide for children. *British Journal of Psychiatry, 129,* 267–276.

Sher, K. J., & Levenson, R. W. (1982). Risk for alcoholism and individual differences in the stress-response-dampening effect of alcohol. *Journal of Abnormal Psychology, 91,* 350–367.

Shiffman, S. (1982). Relapse following smoking cessation: A situational analysis. *Journal of Consulting and Clinical Psychology, 50,* 71–86.

Shlain, L. (1979). Cancer is not a four-letter word. In C. A. Garfield, (Ed.), *Stress and survival: The emotional realities of life-threatening illness.* St. Louis: C. V. Mosby.

Shneidman, E. (1981). *Suicide thoughts and reflections, 1960–1980.* New York: Human Sciences Press.

Shneidman, E. (1985). *Definition of suicide.* New York: Wiley.

Shore, B. E., & Franks, P. (1986). Physician satisfaction with patient encounters. *Medical Care, 24*(7), 580–589.

Shubin, S. (1978). The professional hazard you face in nursing. *Nursing, 78*(8), 22–27.

Shumaker, S. A., & Grunberg, N. E. (Eds.). (1986). Proceedings of the National Working Conference on Smoking Relapse. [Special issue]. *Health Psychology, 5*(Suppl.), 1–99.

Shuy, R. W. (1976). The medical interview: Problems in communication. *Primary Care, 3,* 365–386.

Silver, H. K. (1982). Medical students and medical school. *Journal of the American Medical Association, 247*(3), 309–310.

Silver, H. K., & Glicken, A. D. (1990). Medical student abuse: Incidence, severity and significance. *Journal of the American Medical Association, 263*(4), 527–533.

Simon, A. B., Alonzo, A. A., & Feinleib, M. (1974). Patient response to acute episodes of coronary heart disease. *Archives of Internal Medicine, 133,* 824–828.

Simon, A. B., Feinleib, M., & Thompson, H. K. (1972). Components of delay in the prehospital phase of acute myocardial infarction. *American Journal of Cardiology, 30,* 476.

Simonton, C., Matthews-Simonton, S., & Creighton, J. (1978). *Getting well again: A step-by-step self-help guide to overcoming cancer for patients and their families.* New York: St. Martin's Press.

Singer, J. E., Lundberg, U., & Frankenhaeuser, M. (1978). Stress on the train: A study of urban commuting. In A. Baum, J. E. Singer, & S. Valins (Eds.), *Advances in environmental psychology* (vol. 1.) Hillsdale, NJ: Erlbaum.

Skinner, B. F. (1938). *The behaviors of organisms: An experimental analysis.* New York: Appleton-Century-Crofts.

Skinner, K. (1979). Burnout: Is nursing dangerous to your health? *Journal of Nursing Care, 12,* 8–30.

Smith, D. L. (1989). Compliance packaging: A patient education tool. *American Pharmacy, 29*(2), 42–53.

Smith, J. W., Denny, W. F., & Witzke, D. B. (1986). Emotional impairment in internal medicine house staff: Results of a national survey. *Journal of the American Medical Association, 255,* 1155–1158.

Smith-Hanen, S. (1977). Effects of nonverbal behaviors on judged levels of counselor warmth and empathy. *Journal of Counseling Psychology, 24,* 87–91.

Snyder, S. H. (1977). Opiate receptors and internal opiates. *Scientific American, 236,* 44–56.

Sonstroem, R. J. (1984). Exercise and self-esteem. *Exercise and Sports Science Review, 12,* 123–155.

Spaide, R. (1983). Patientspeak. *New Physician, 5,* 5–6.

Speedling, E. J., & Rose, D. N. (1985). Building an effective doctor-patient relationship participation. *Social Science and Medicine, 21,* 115-120.

Speisman, J., Lazarus, R. S., Mordkoff, A., & Davidson, L. (1964). Experimental reduction of stress based on ego defense theory. *Journal of Abnormal and Social Psychology, 68,* 367–380.

Spiegel, D. A., Smolen, R. C., & Hopfensperger, K. A. (1986). Medical student stress and clerkship performance. *Journal of Medical Education, 61,* 929–931.

Spiegel, D. A., Smolen, R. C., & Jonas, C. K. (1986). An examination of the relationships among interpersonal stress, morale and academic performance in male and female medical students. *Social Science and Medicine, 23*(11), 1157–1161.

Spiegel, P., & Machotka, P. (1974). *Messages of the body.* New York: Free Press.

Spinetta, J. J., & Maloney, L. J. (1987). Death anxiety in the outpatient leukemic child. In T. Krulik, B. Holaday, & I. M. Martinson. *The child and family facing life-threatening illness* (pp. 126–132). New York: Lippincott.

Squier, R. W. (1990). A model of empathic understanding and adherence to treatment regimens in practitioner-patient relationships. *Social Science and Medicine, 30*(3), 325–339.

Stall, R. D., Coates. T. J., & Hoff, C. (1988). Behavioral risk reduction for HIV infection among gay and bisexual men: A review of results from the United States. *American Psychologist, 43,* 878–885.

Stang, D. J., & Wrightsman, L. S. (1981). *Dictionary of social behavior and social research methods.* Pacific Grove, CA: Brooks/Cole.

Starfield, B., Steinwachs D., Morris, I., Bause, G., Siebert, S., & Westin, C. (1979). Patient-doctor agreement about problems needing follow-up visit. *Journal of the American Medical Association, 242,* 344–346.

Starfield, B., Wray, C., Hess, K., Gross, R., Birk, P. S., & D'Lugoff, B. C. (1981). The influence of patient-practitioner agreement on outcome of care. *American Journal of Public Health, 71,* 127–131.

Steele, T. E., Finkelstein, S. H., & Finkelstein, F. O. (1976). Hemodialysis patients and spouses: Marital discord, sexual problems, and depression. *Journal of Nervous and Mental Diseases, 162,* 225–237.

Stein, L. I., Watts, D. T., & Howell, T. (1990). The doctor-nurse game revisited. *New England Journal of Medicine, 322*(8), 546–549.

Stephens, T. (1988). Physical activity and mental health in the United States and Canada: Evidence from four population surveys. *Preventive Medicine, 17,* 35–47.

Stephens, T., Jacobs, D. R., Jr., & White, C. C. (1985). A descriptive epidemiology of leisure time physical activity. *Public Health Reports, 100,* 147–158.

Sternbach, R. A. (1968). *Pain, a psychophysiological analysis.* New York: Academic Press.

Sternbach, R. A. (1974). *Pain patients: Traits and treatments.* New York: Academic Press.

Sternbach, R. A., & Tursky, B. (1965). Ethnic differences among housewives in psychophysical and skin potential responses to electric shock. *Psychophysiology, 1,* 241–246.

Stetz, K., Lewis, F. M., & Primomo, J. (1986). Family coping strategies and chronic illness in the mother. *Family Relations, 35,* 515–522.

Stiles, W. B., Putnam, S. M., & Jacob, M. C. (1982). Verbal exchange structure of initial medical interviews. *Health Psychology, 1*(4), 315–336.

Stiles, W. B., Putnam, S. M., Wolf, M. H., & James, S. A. (1979). Interaction exchange structure and patient satisfaction with medical interviews. *Medical Care, 17,* 667–681.

Stoeckle, J. D., Zola, I. K., & Davidson, G. E. (1964). The quality and significance of psychological distress in medical patients. *Journal of Chronic Diseases, 17,* 959–970.

Stone, G. C. (1979). Patient compliance and the role of the expert. *Journal of Social Issues, 35,* 34–59.

Stone, R., Cafferata, G. L., & Sangl, J. (1987). Caregiving of the frail elderly: A national profile. *Gerontologist, 27,* 616–629.

Stotland, E. (1987). Stress. In R. Corsini (Ed.), *Concise encyclopedia of psychology.* New York: Wiley.

Strauss, A. L., & Glaser, B. G. (1975). *Chronic illness and the quality of life.* St. Louis: C. V. Mosby.

Straw, M. K. (1983). Coping with obesity. In T. G. Burish and L. A. Bradley (Eds.), *Coping with chronic disease: Research and application.* New York: Academic Press.

Stringham, J., Riley, J. H., & Ross, A. (1982). Silent birth: Mourning a stillborn baby. *Social Work, 27,* 322–327.

Stuart, R. B., & Davis, B. (1972). *Slim chance in a fat world: Behavioral control of obesity.* Champaign, IL: Research Press.

Stuart, R. B., & Guire, K. (1978). Some correlates of the maintenance of weight loss through behavior modification. *International Journal of Obesity, 2*, 225–235.

Stunkard, A. J. (1979). Behavioral medicine and beyond: The example of obesity. In O. F. Pomerleau & J. P. Brady (Eds.), *Behavioral medicine: Theory and practice.* Baltimore: Williams & Wilkins.

Suls, J. (1982). Social support, interpersonal relations, and health: Benefits and liabilities. In G. S. Sanders & J. Suls (Eds.), *Social psychology of health and illness.* Hillsdale, NJ: Erlbaum.

Surgeon General. *Healthy People: The Surgeon General's Report on Health Promotion and Disease Prevention* (1979). Washington, DC: U.S. Department of Health, Education, and Welfare, Public Health Services, Office of Assistant Secretary of Health and the Surgeon General.

Surgeon General's Report. (1964). *Smoking and Health* (Public Health Services Publication No. 1103). Washington, DC: U.S. Department of Health, Education, and Welfare.

Sutton, S. R., & Eiser, J. R. (1990). The decision to wear a seat belt: The role of cognitive factors, fear, and prior behaviour. *Psychology and Health, 4*, 111–123.

Sutton, S., & Hallett, R. (1988). Understanding the effects of fear-arousing communications: The role of cognitive factors and the amount of fear aroused. *Journal of Behavioral Medicine, 11*, 353–360.

Svarstad, B. (1976). Physician-patient communication and patient conformity with medical advice. In D. Mechanic (Ed.), *The growth of bureaucratic medicine* (pp. 220–238). New York: Wiley.

Sweeting, H. N., & Gilhooly, M. L. M. (1990). Anticipatory grief: A review. *Social Science and Medicine, 30*, 1073–1080.

Szasz, T. S., & Hollender, M. H. (1956). A contribution to the philosophy of medicine. The basic models of the doctor-patient relationship. *Archives of Internal Medicine, 97*, 585–592.

Taylor, S. E. (1982). Hospital patient behavior: Reactance, helplessness, or control? In H. S. Friedman & M. R. DiMatteo (Eds.), *Interpersonal issues in health care* (pp. 201–231). New York: Academic Press.

Taylor, S. E., Lichtman, R. R., & Wood, J. V. (1984). Attributions, beliefs about control, and adjustment to breast cancer. *Journal of Personality and Social Psychology, 46*, 489–502.

Taylor, S. E., Lichtman, R. R., Wood, J. V., Bluming, A. Z., Dosik, G. M., & Leibowitz, R. L. (1985). Illness related and treatment related factors in psychological adjustment to breast cancer. *Cancer, 55,*(10), 2506–2513.

Tempelaar, R., DeHaes, J. C., De Ruiter, J. H., Bakker, D., Van Den Heuvel, W. J. A., & Van Nieuwenhuijzen, M. G. (1989). The social experiences of cancer patients under treatment: A comparative study. *Social Science and Medicine, 29*(5), 635–642.

Tennent, J. (1734). *Every man his own doctor: or the poor planter's physician.* Printing office of Colonial Williamsburg, Virginia, 1734. Rare book collection, University of Texas Medical Branch, Galveston.

Tharp, G. D., & Schegelmilch, R. P. (1977). Personality characteristics of trained versus nontrained individuals. *Medicine and Science in Sports, 9*, 55.

Theorell, T. (1974). Life events before and after the onset of a premature myocardial infarction. In B. S. Dohrenwend & B. P. Dohrenwend (Eds.), *Stressful life events: Their nature and effects.* New York: Wiley.

Theorell, T., & Rahe, R. H. (1975). Life change events, ballistocardiography, and coronary death. *Journal of Human Stress, 1*, 18–24.

Thomas, L. (1979). *The medusa and the snail.* New York: Viking.

Thompson, S. C. (1981). Will it hurt less if I can control it? A complex answer to a simple question. *Psychological Bulletin, 90*, 89–101.

Thoreson, C. E., & Mahoney, M. J. (1974). *Behavioral self-control.* New York: Holt, Rinehart & Winston.

Thorne, S. (1985). The family cancer experience. *Cancer Nursing, 8*, 285–291.

Tokarz, J. P., Bremer, W., & Peters, K. (1979). *Beyond survival.* Chicago, IL: American Medical Association.

Torrens, P. R. (1978). *The American health care system.* St. Louis: C. V. Mosby.

Triandis, H. C. (1977). *Interpersonal behavior.* Pacific Grove, CA: Brooks/Cole.

Trostle, J. A. (1988). Medical compliance as an ideology. *Social Science and Medicine, 27,* 1299–1308.

Trotta, P. (1980). Breast self-examination: Factors influencing compliance. *Oncology Nursing Forum, 7,* 13–17.

Trumbull, R., & Appley, M. H. (1986). A conceptual model for examination of stress dynamics. In M. H. Appley & R. Trumbull (Eds.), *Dynamics of stress: Physiological, psychological, and social perspectives.* New York: Plenum.

Tucker, L. A. (1985). Physical, psychological, social, and lifestyle differences among adolescents classified according to cigarette smoking intention status. *Journal of School Health, 55*(4), 127–131.

Turk, D. C., Litt, M. D., Salovey, P., & Walker, J. (1985). Seeking urgent pediatric treatment: Factors contributing to frequency, delay, and appropriateness. *Health Psychology, 4*(1), 43–59.

Turk, D. C., Meichenbaum, D., & Berman, W. H., (1979). Application of biofeedback for the regulation of pain: A critical review. *Psychological Bulletin, 86*(6), 1322–1338.

Turk, D. C., Meichenbaum, D., & Genest, M. (1983). *Pain and behavioral medicine: A cognitive-behavioral perspective.* New York: Guilford.

Turk, D. C., & Rudy, T. E., (1986). Assessment of cognitive factors in chronic pain: A worthwhile enterprise? *Journal of Consulting and Clinical Psychology, 54,* 760–768.

Turk, D. C., Wack, J. T., & Kerns, R. D. (1985). An empirical examination of the "pain-behavior" construct. *Journal of Behavioral Medicine, 8,* 119–130.

Tursky, B. (1976). The development of pain perception profile: A psychophysical approach. In M. Weisenberg & B. Tursky (Eds.), *Pain: New perspectives in therapy and research* (pp. 171–194). New York: Plenum.

Tursky, B., & Sternbach, R. A. (1967). Further physiological correlates of ethnic differences in response to shock. *Psychophysiology, 4,* 67–74.

Tversky, A., & Kahneman, D. (1974). Judgment under uncertainty: Heuristics and biases. *Science, 185,* 1124–1131.

Tversky, A., & Kahneman, D. (1981). The framing of decisions and the psychology of choice. *Science, 211,* 453–458.

U.S. Department of Health, Education, & Welfare & U.S. Public Health Service, Centers for Disease Control. (1964). *Smoking and health: Report of the advisory committee to the Surgeon General of the Public Health Service* (Publication No. PHS 1103.) Washington, DC: U.S. Government Printing Office.

U.S. Department of Health and Human Services. (1981). *The health consequences of smoking. The changing cigarette: A report of the Surgeon General* (Publication No. PHS 81-50156). Washington, DC: U.S. Government Printing Office.

U.S. Department of Health and Human Services. (1989). *Reducing the health consequences of smoking. 25 years of progress: A report of the Surgeon General* (Publication No. PHS 89-8411). Rockville, MD: Department of Health and Human Services.

U.S. Office on Smoking and Health. (1979). *Smoking and health: A report of the Surgeon General* (U.S. Department of Health, Education, and Welfare Publication No. 79-50066). Washington, DC: U.S. Government Printing Office.

U.S. Preventive Services Task Force. (1989). *Guide to Clinical Preventive Services.* Baltimore: Williams & Wilkins.

U.S. Public Health Service. (1971, January). *Chronic conditions and limitations of activity and mobility: July 1965–June 1967* (No. 1000, Series 10-61). Washington, DC: U.S. Department of Health, Education, and Welfare, Public Health Service, Mental Health Administration.

Uhlenberg, P., & Cooney, T. M. (1990). Male and female physicians: Family and career comparisons. *Social Science and Medicine, 30*(3), 373–378.

Vaccarino, J. M. (1977). Malpractice: The problem in perspective. *Journal of the American Medical Association, 238,* 861–863.

Vaillant, G. E., Sobowale, N. C., & McArthur, C. (1972). Some psychologic vulnerabilities of physicians. *New England Journal of Medicine, 287,* 372–375.

Valdiserri, R. O., Tama, G. M., & Ho, M. (1988). A survey of AIDS patients regarding their

References 465

experiences with physicians. *Journal of Medical Education, 63,* 726–728.

**Valko, R. J., & Clayton, P. J.** (1975). Depression in the internship. *Diseases of the Nervous System, 36,* 26–29.

**Van Komen, R. W., & Redd, W. H.** (1985). Personality factors associated with anticipatory nausea and vomiting in patients receiving cancer chemotherapy. *Health Psychology, 4,* 189–202.

**Vertinsky, P., & Auman, J. T.** (1988). Elderly women's barriers to exercise, Part I: Perceived risks. *Health Values, 12,* 13–19.

**Videka-Sherman, L.** (1982). Coping with the death of a child: A study over time. *American Journal of Orthopsychiatry, 52,* 688–698.

**Viorst, J.** (1986). *Necessary losses.* New York: Simon & Schuster.

**Voytovich, A. E., Rippey, R. M., & Suffredini, A.** (1985). Premature conclusions in diagnostic reasoning. *Journal of Medical Education, 60,* 302–307.

**Wachter, R. M., Cooke, M., Hopewell, P. C., & Luce, J. M.** (1988). Attitudes of medical residents regarding intensive care for patients with the acquired immunodeficiency syndrome. *Archives of Internal Medicine, 148,* 149–152.

**Wadden, T. A., Stunkard, A. J., & Brownell, K. D.** (1983). Very low calorie diets: Their efficacy, safety, and future. *Annals of Internal Medicine, 99,* 675–684.

**Waitzkin, H.** (1984). Doctor-patient communication: Clinical implications of social scientific research. *Journal of the American Medical Association, 252,* 2441–2446.

**Waitzkin, H.** (1985). Information giving in medical care. *Journal of Health and Social Behavior, 26*(2), 81–101.

**Waitzkin, H., & Stoeckle, J. D.** (1972). The communication of information about illness: Clinical, sociological, and methodological considerations. *Advances in Psychosomatic Medicine, 8,* 180–215.

**Waitzkin, H., & Stoeckle, J. D.** (1976). Information control and the micropolitics of health care: Summary of an ongoing research project. *Social Science and Medicine, 10,* 263–276.

**Wallston, K. A., & Wallston, B. S.** (1983). Who is responsible for your health? The construct of health locus of control. In G. Saunders & J. Suls (Eds.), *Social psychology of health and illness.* Hillsdale, NJ: Erlbaum.

**Wanburg, K. W., & Horn, J. L.** (1983). Assessment of alcohol use with multidimensional concepts and measures. *American Psychologist, 38,* 1055–1069.

**Warburg, M. M., Cleary, P. D., Rohman, M., Barnes, H. N., Aronson, M., & Delbanco, T. L.** (1987). Residents' attitudes, knowledge, and behavior regarding diagnosis and treatment of alcoholism. *Journal of Medical Education, 62,* 497–503.

**Ware, J. E., Jr., & Young, J.** (1979). Issues in the conceptualization and measurement of value placed on health. In S. J. Mushkin & D. W. Dunlop (Eds.), *Health: What is it worth?* (pp. 141–166). New York: Pergamon Press.

**Ware, J. E., Jr., Davies-Avery, A., & Stewart, A. L.** (1978). The measurement and meaning of patient satisfaction. *Health and Medical Care Services Review, 1,* 1–15.

**Wartman, S. A., Morlock, L. L., Malitz, F. E., & Palm, E. A.** (1983). Patient understanding and satisfaction as predictors of compliance. *Medical Care, 21,* 886–891.

**Wasserman, R. C., Innui, T. S., Barriatua, R. D., Carter, W. B., & Lippincott, P.** (1984). Pediatric clinicians' support for parents makes a difference: An outcome-based analysis of clinician-parent interaction. *Pediatrics, 74,* 1047–1053.

**Watzlawick, P., Beavin, J. H., & Jackson, D. D.** (1967). *Pragmatics of human communication.* New York: Norton.

**Watzlawick, P., & Weakland, J. H.** (Eds). (1977). *The interactional view: Studies at the Mental Research Institute, 1965–1974.* New York: Norton.

**Weakland, J. H.** (1976). Communication theory and clinical change. In P. J. Guerin, Jr. (Ed.), *Family therapy and practice.* New York: Garden Press.

**Webb, E. J., Campbell, D. T., Schwartz, R. D., Sechrest, L., & Grove, J. B.** (1981). *Nonreactive measures in the social sciences.* Boston: Houghton Mifflin.

**Webb, W. B.** (Ed.). (1982). *Biological rhythms, sleep, and performance.* New York: Wiley.

**Weed, L. L.** (1967). Medical records that guide

and teach. *New England Journal of Medicine, 278,* 593–652.

Weidner, G., Friend, R., Ficarrotto, T. J., & Mendell, N. R. (1989). Hostility and cardiovascular reactivity to stress in women and men. *Psychosomatic Medicine, 51,* 36–45.

Weidner, G., Sexton, G., McLellarn, R., Connor, S. L., & Matarazzo, J. D. (1987). The role of the Type A behavior and hostility in an elevation of plasma lipids in adult women and men. *Psychosomatic Medicine, 49,* 450–457.

Weinberger, M., Hiner, S. L., & Tierney, W. M. (1987). In support of hassles as a measure of stress in predicting health outcomes. *Journal of Behavioral Medicine, 10,* 19–31.

Weiner, C. (1975). The burden of rheumatoid arthritis: Tolerating the uncertainty. *Social Science and Medicine, 9,* 97–104.

Weinstein, H. M. (1983). A committee on well-being of medical students and house staff. *Journal of Medical Education, 58,* 373–381.

Weinstein, N. D. (1982). Unrealistic optimism about susceptibility to health problems. *Journal of Behavioral Medicine, 5,* 441–460.

Weisenberg, M. (1977). Pain and pain control. *Psychological Bulletin, 84,* 1008–1044.

Weisman, C. S., & Teitelbaum, M. A. (1985). Physician gender and the physician-patient relationship: Recent evidence and relevant questions. *Social Science and Medicine, 20*(11), 1119–1127.

Weiss, J. M. (1984). Behavioral and psychological influences on gastrointestinal pathology: Experimental techniques and findings. In W. D. Gentry (Ed.), *Handbook of behavioral medicine.* New York: Guilford.

Wellisch, D. K., Fawzy, F. I., Landsverk, J., Pasnau, R. O., & Wolcott, D. L. (1983). Evaluation of psychosocial problems of the home-bound cancer patient: The relationship of disease and the sociodemographic variables of patients to family problems. *Journal of Psychosocial Oncology, 1,* 1–15.

Wertlieb, D., Hauser, S. T., & Jacobson, A. M. (1986). Adaptation to diabetes: Behavior symptoms and family context. *Journal of Pediatric Psychology, 11*(4), 463–479.

West, C. (1983). "Ask me no questions . . .": An analysis of queries and replies in physician-patient dialogues. In S. Fisher & A. D. Todd (Eds.), *The social organization of doctor-patient communication* (pp. 75–106). Washington, DC: Center for Applied Linguistics.

West, C. (1984). *Routine complications: Troubles with talk between doctors and patients.* Bloomington: Indiana University Press.

Wheaton, B. (1983). Stress, personal coping resources, and psychiatric symptoms: An investigation of interactive models. *Journal of Health and Social Behavior, 24,* 208–229.

White, K. L., Williams, T. F., & Greenberg, B. G. (1961). The ecology of medical care. *New England Journal of Medicine, 265,* 885–892.

Whyte, L. L. (1960). *The unconscious before Freud.* New York: Basic Books.

Wickersham, B. A. (1984). The exercise program. In G. K. Riggs & E. P. Gall (Eds.), *Rheumatic diseases: Rehabilitation and management.* Boston: Butterworth.

Wideman, M. V., & Singer, J. E. (1984). The role of psychological mechanisms in preparation for childbirth. *American Psychologist, 39*(12), 1357–1371.

Williams, A. W., Ware, J. E., Jr., & Donald, C. A. (1981). A model of mental health, life events, and social supports applicable to general populations. *Journal of Health and Social Behavior, 22,* 324–336.

Williams, R. B., Haney, T. L., Lee, K. L., Kong, Y. H., Blumenthal, J. A., & Whalen, R. F. (1980). Type A behavior, hostility, and coronary atherosclerosis. *Psychosomatic Medicine, 42,* 539–549.

Wills, T. A. (1978). Perceptions of clients by professional helpers. *Psychological Bulletin, 85*(5), 968–1000.

Wills, T. A. (1984). Supportive functions of interpersonal relationships. In S. Cohen & L. Syme (Eds.), *Social support and health.* New York: Academic Press.

Wilson, G. T. (1980). Cognitive factors in lifestyle changes. A social learning perspective. In P. O. Davidson & S. M. Davidson (Eds.), *Behavioral medicine: Changing health lifestyles.* New York: Brunner/Mazel.

Wilson-Pessano, S. R., & McNabb, W. L. (1985). The role of patient education in the management of childhood asthma. *Preventive Medicine, 14,* 670–687.

Wing, R. R., Nowalk, M. P., & Guare, J. C. (1988). Diabetes mellitus. In E. A. Blechman & K. D. Brownell (Eds.), *Handbook of behavioral medicine for women.* New York: Pergamon.

Winters, R. (1985). Behavioral approaches to pain. In N. Schneiderman & J. T. Tapp (Eds.), *Behavioral medicine: The biopsychosocial approach.* Hillsdale, NJ: Erlbaum.

Wishnie, H. A., Hackett, T. P., & Cassem, N. H. (1977). Psychological hazards of convalescence following myocardial infarction. In R. H. Moos (Ed.), *Coping with physical illness* (pp. 103–112). New York: Plenum.

Wolf, S., & Wolff, H. G. (1947). *Human gastric function* (2nd ed.). New York: Oxford University Press.

Wolpe, J. (1958). *Psychotherapy by reciprocal inhibition.* Stanford: Stanford University Press.

Wolpe, J. (1973). *The practice of behavior therapy* (2nd ed.). Elmsford, New York: Pergamon.

Woods, S. M., Natterson, J., & Silverman, J. (1966). Medical students' disease: Hypochondriasis in medical education. *Journal of Medical Education, 41,* 785–790.

World Health Organization. (1946). *Official Record,* Vol. 2, p. 100.

Wortman, C. B. (1984). Social support and the cancer patient. *Cancer 53*(Suppl.)(10), 2339–2360.

Wortman, C. B., & Dunkel-Schetter, C. (1979). Interpersonal relationships and cancer: A theoretical analysis. *Journal of Social Issues, 35,* 120–155.

Wortman, C. B., & Dunkel-Schetter, C. (1987). Conceptual and methodological issues in the study of social support. In A. Baum & J. E. Singer (Eds.), *Handbook of psychology and health* (vol. 5). Hillsdale, NJ: Erlbaum.

Yates, A. J., & Thain, J. (1985). Self-efficacy as a predictor of relapse following voluntary cessation of smoking. *Addictive Behaviors, 10,* 291–298.

Yeater, R. A., & Ullrich, I. H. (1985). The role of physical activity in disease prevention and treatment. *West Virginia Medical Journal, 81*(2), 35–39.

Young, C. G., & Barger, J. D. (1975). *Learning medical terminology step by step.* St. Louis: C. V. Mosby.

Zajonc, R. B. (1968). Attitudinal effects of mere exposure. *Journal of Personality and Social Psychology* (Monograph suppl.), *9*(2), 1–27.

Zarit, S. H., & Zarit, J. M. (1984). Psychological approaches to families of the elderly. In M. G. Eisenberg, L. C. Sutkin, & M. A. Jansen (Eds.). *Chronic illness and disability through the life span: Effects on self and family* (pp. 269–288). New York: Springer.

Zarski, J. J. (1984). Hassles and health: A replication. *Health Psychology, 3,* 243–251.

Zborowski, M. (1952). Cultural components in responses to pain. *Journal of Social Issues, 8,* 16–30.

Zborowski, M. (1969). *People in pain.* San Francisco: Jossey-Bass.

Ziegler, J. L., Kansas, N., Strull, W. M., & Bennet, N. E. (1984). A stress discussion group for medical interns. *Journal of Medical Education, 59,* 205–207.

Zifferblatt, S. M. (1975). Increasing patient compliance through the applied analysis of behavior. *Preventive Medicine, 4,* 173–182.

Zilbergeld, B. (1979). Sex and serious illness. In C. A. Garfield (Ed.), *Stress and survival: The emotional realities of life-threatening illness.* St. Louis: C. V. Mosby.

Zimbardo, P. G., Ebbesen, E. B., & Maslach, C. (1977). *Influencing attitudes and changing behavior* (2nd ed.). Reading, MA: Addison-Wesley.

Zisook, S., Devand, R. A., & Click, M. A. (1982). Measuring symptoms of grief and bereavement. *American Journal of Psychiatry, 139,* 1590–1593.

Zola, I. K. (1958). Definitions of health and illness in the light of American values and social structure. In E. G. Jaco (Ed.), *Patients, physicians, and illness* (pp. 165–187). New York: Free Press.

Zola, I. K. (1973). Pathways to the doctor—from person to patient. *Social Science and Medicine, 7,* 677–689.

Zonderman, A. B., Costa, P. T., & McCrae, R. R. (1989). Depression as a risk for cancer morbidity and mortality in a nationally representative sample. *Journal of the American Medical Association, 262*(9), 1191–1195.

# Author Index*

*First authors only

# Subject Index